EQUITY AND LAW

The fusion of law and equity in common law systems was a crucial moment in the development of modern law. Common law and equity were historically the two principal sources of rules and remedies in the judge-made law of England, and this bifurcated system travelled to other countries whose legal systems were derived from the English legal system. The division of law and equity – their fission – was a pivotal legal development and is a feature of most common law systems. The fusion of the common law and equity has brought about major structural, institutional and juridical changes within the common law tradition. In this volume, leading scholars undertake historical, comparative, doctrinal and theoretical analysis that aims to shed light on the ways in which law and equity have fused, and the ways in which they have remained distinct even in a 'post-fusion' world.

John C. P. Goldberg is the Carter Professor of General Jurisprudence at the Harvard Law School in Harvard University.

Henry E. Smith is the Fessenden Professor of Law and Director of the Project on the Foundations of Private Law at the Harvard Law School in Harvard University.

P. G. Turner is a University Senior Lecturer and a Fellow of St Catharine's College in the University of Cambridge.

Equity and Law

FUSION AND FISSION

Edited by

JOHN C. P. GOLDBERG
Harvard Law School

HENRY E. SMITH
Harvard Law School

P. G. TURNER
University of Cambridge

CAMBRIDGE
UNIVERSITY PRESS

CAMBRIDGE
UNIVERSITY PRESS

University Printing House, Cambridge CB2 8BS, United Kingdom

One Liberty Plaza, 20th Floor, New York, NY 10006, USA

477 Williamstown Road, Port Melbourne, VIC 3207, Australia

314–321, 3rd Floor, Plot 3, Splendor Forum, Jasola District Centre, New Delhi – 110025, India

79 Anson Road, #06-04/06, Singapore 079906

Cambridge University Press is part of the University of Cambridge.

It furthers the University's mission by disseminating knowledge in the pursuit of
education, learning, and research at the highest international levels of excellence.

www.cambridge.org
Information on this title: www.cambridge.org/9781108421317
DOI: 10.1017/9781108367820

© Cambridge University Press 2019

First published 2019

Printed and bound in Great Britain by Clays Ltd, Elcograf S.p.A.

A catalogue record for this publication is available from the British Library.

Library of Congress Cataloging-in-Publication Data
NAMES: Goldberg, John C. P., 1961-, editor. | Smith, Henry E., editor. |
    Turner, P. G. (Peter G.), editor.
TITLE: Equity and law : fusion and fission / Edited by John C. P. Goldberg, Harvard Law School,
    Massachusetts, Henry E Smith, Harvard Law School, Massachusetts, Peter G Turner,
    University of Cambridge.
DESCRIPTION: New York, NY : Cambridge University Press, 2019. | Includes bibliographical
    references and index.
IDENTIFIERS: LCCN 2019004231 | ISBN 9781108421317 (hardback : alk. paper) |
    ISBN 9781108431750 (pbk. : alk. paper)
SUBJECTS: LCSH: Equity. | Equity pleading and procedure.
CLASSIFICATION: LCC K247 .E64 2019 | DDC 346/.004–dc23
LC record available at https://lccn.loc.gov/2019004231

ISBN 978-1-108-42131-7 Hardback

Contents

Contents   vii

Figures

Figures

Table

Table

Contributors

Samuel L. Bray is a Professor of the University of Notre Dame Law School.

Daniel J. Carr is a Senior Lecturer in Private Law of the Edinburgh Law School in the University of Edinburgh.

Kellen Funk is an Associate Professor of the Columbia Law School of Columbia University in the city of New York.

Philip Girard is a Professor of the Osgoode Hall Law School in York University, Toronto.

John C. P. Goldberg is the Carter Professor of General Jurisprudence at Harvard Law School in Harvard University.

Matthew Harding is a Professor of the Law School of the University of Melbourne.

Dennis Klinck is a Professor Emeritus of the Faculty of Law of McGill University.

Ben Kremer is a Barrister of the State of New South Wales who practises in Sydney.

Mark Leeming is a Judge of Appeal of the Supreme Court of New South Wales and the Challis Lecturer in Equity in the University of Sydney.

Michael Lobban is a Professor of Legal History of the Department of Law of the London School of Economics.

James McComish is a Barrister of the State of Victoria who practises in Melbourne and is a Fellow of the Law School of the University of Melbourne.

Ben McFarlane is a Professor of Law of the Faculty of Laws of University College, London.

Patricia I. McMahon is a Lawyer of the Province of Ontario who practises in Toronto.

Emily Sherwin is the Frank B. Ingersoll Professor of Law at Cornell Law School in Cornell University.

Henry E. Smith is the Fessenden Professor of Law and the Director of the Project on the Foundations of Private Law at Harvard Law School in Harvard University.

P. G. Turner is a University Senior Lecturer and a Fellow of St Catharine's College in the University of Cambridge.

Stephen Waddams is a University Professor and the Goodman/Schipper Professor of the Faculty of Law of the University of Toronto.

Acknowledgements

Ten of the seventeen chapters of this book began life as papers prepared for a seminar held in St Catharine's College, Cambridge, in 2016; the other seven were specially commissioned afterwards. The seminar was hosted jointly by the Project on the Foundations of Private Law, which operates from the Harvard Law School, and the Centre for Private Law in the University of Cambridge. The editors are grateful for the financial support provided by the Project and the Centre, as well as the various forms of support provided by St Catharine's College and by the University of Cambridge through the Faculty of Law and a grant from the Cambridge Humanities Research Grant Scheme.

Ms Kim Hughes commissioned the book, and was succeeded in that role by Mr Tom Randall as the manuscript advanced. They judiciously accommodated and guided the editors, who express their thanks. The assistance of Ms Trina Malone in the checking of references in many chapters, and applying the house style, was substantial and is gratefully acknowledged.

Abbreviations

Printed law reports and legal periodicals, other than those referred to in this list, are cited according to the usual legal conventions. The abbreviations will be found in D. Raistrick, *Index to Legal Citations and Abbreviations*, 4th edn (London: Sweet & Maxwell, 2013).

Ashburner, *Principles of Equity*, 2nd edn	W. W. Ashburner, *Principles of Equity*, 2nd edn, D. Browne (ed.) (London: Butterworth, 1933)
Baker, *I.E.L.H.*, 4th edn	J. H. Baker, *An Introduction to English Legal History*, 4th edn (London: Butterworths, 2002)
Baker, 'The Common Lawyers and the Chancery: 1616'	J. Baker, 'The Common Lawyers: 1616', in *Collected Papers on English Legal History* (Cambridge University Press, 2013), vol. I, ch. 28
Baker and Milsom	J. Baker, *Baker and Milsom: Sources of English Legal History*, 2nd edn (Oxford University Press, 2010)
Bankton, *Institute*	Lord Bankton (A. McDouall), *An Institute of the Laws of Scotland* (Edinburgh: Kincaid and Donaldson, 1751)
B.L.	British Library
B.L. MS Add. 25199	Reports of Thomas Sterrell
B.L. MS Add. 32527	Abstracts of law cases by Roger North
Burrows, 'We Do This at Common Law'	A. Burrows, 'We Do This at Common Law but That in Equity' (2002) 22 O.J.L.S. 1
C.6	P.R.O., Chancery, pleadings, Collins series

C.9	P.R.O., Chancery, pleadings, Reynardson series
C.10	P.R.O., Chancery, pleadings, Whittington series
C.22	P.R.O., Chancery, country depositions
C.33	P.R.O., Chancery, decree and order books
ch.	chapter
C.J.	Chief Justice
C.J.C.P.	Chief Justice of the Common Pleas
C.J.K.B.	Chief Justice of the King's Bench
C.O.201	P.R.O., Colonial Office, New South Wales original correspondence
col.	column
C.P.	Court of Common Pleas
(E. [year])	(Easter Term [year])
E.126	P.R.O., Exchequer, king's remembrancer, entry book of decrees
E.H.R.	English Historical Review
Equity and Administration	P. G. Turner (ed.), *Equity and Administration* (Cambridge University Press, 2016)
f.	folio
Feldman and Smith, 'Behavioral Equity'	Y. Feldman and H. E. Smith, 'Behavioral Equity' (2014) 170 J. Inst'l & Theoretical Econ. 137
Finch, 'Manual' and 'Prolegomena'	H. Finch (Lord Nottingham), *Lord Nottingham's 'Manual of Chancery Practice' and 'Prolegomena of Chancery and Equity'*, ed. by D. E. C. Yale (Cambridge University Press, 1965)
First Report Chancery Commissioners	United Kingdom, Chancery Commissioners, *First Report of Her Majesty's Commissioners Appointed to Inquire into the Process, Practice, and System of Pleading in the Court of Chancery, &c.* (London: H.M.S.O., 1852)
First Report Common Law Commissioners	United Kingdom, Common Law Commissioners, *First Report from the Commissioners for Inquiring into the Process, Practice, and System of Pleading in the Superior Courts of Common Law* (London: Eyre and Spottiswoode, 1851)

First Report Judicature Commissioners	United Kingdom, Judicature Commission, *First Report into the Operation and Constitutions of High Court of Chancery, Superior Courts of Common Law, Central Criminal Court, High Court of Admiralty, and Other Courts in England and into the Operation and Effect of Present Separation and Division of Jurisdiction between Courts* (London: H.M.S.O., 1868–69)
Funk, 'Equity without Chancery'	K. Funk, 'Equity without Chancery: The Fusion of Law and Equity in the Field Code of Civil Procedure, New York 1846–76' (2015) 36 J.L.H. 152
Getzler, 'Patterns of Fusion'	J. S. Getzler, 'Patterns of Fusion', in P. Birks (ed.), *The Classification of Obligations* (Oxford: Clarendon Press, 1997), ch. 7
Goff and Jones: Unjust Enrichment, 9th edn	C. Mitchell, P. Mitchell and S. Watterson (eds), *Goff and Jones: The Law of Unjust Enrichment*, 9th edn (London: Sweet & Maxwell, 2016)
(H. [year])	(Hilary Term [year])
H.C. Deb.	United Kingdom, House of Commons' Debates
H.C. Jour.	United Kingdom, House of Commons Journal
H.C.P.P.	United Kingdom, House of Commons Parliamentary Papers
H.L. Deb.	United Kingdom, House of Lords' Debates
H.L. Jour.	United Kingdom, House of Lords Journal
H.L.S.P.	United Kingdom, House of Lords Sessional Papers
Ibbetson, *Historical Introduction*	D. Ibbetson, *A Historical Introduction to the Law of Obligations* (Oxford: Clarendon Press, 1999)
Ibbetson, 'A House Built on Sand'	D. Ibbetson, 'A House Built on Sand: Equity in Early Modern English Law', in E. Koops and W. J. Zwalve (eds), *Law & Equity: Approaches in Roman Law and Common Law* (Leiden: Martinus Nijhoff, 2014), ch. 3
Ibbetson, 'The Earl of Oxford's Case'	D. Ibbetson, 'The Earl of Oxford's Case (1615)', in Charles Mitchell and Paul Mitchell (eds),

Meagher, Gummow and Lehane, 1st edn	R. P. Meagher, W. M. C. Gummow and J. R. F. Lehane, *Equity: Doctrines and Remedies*, 1st edn (Sydney: Butterworths, 1975)
Meagher, Gummow and Lehane, 5th edn	J. D. Heydon, M. J. Leeming and P. G. Turner, *Meagher, Gummow and Lehane's Equity: Doctrines and Remedies*, 5th edn (Sydney: LexisNexis, 2015)
(M. [year])	(Michaelmas Term [year])
Milsom, *Historical Foundations*, 2nd edn	S. F. C. Milsom, *Historical Foundations of the Common Law*, 2nd edn (Butterworths: London, 1981)
M.R.	Master of the Rolls
MS	manuscript
M.T.	Middle Temple Library, London
M.T. MS 2C	Reports of Sir George Treby
n.	note
O.D.N.B.	*Oxford Dictionary of National Biography* (2004)
O.H.L.E., vol. VI	J. Baker, *The Oxford History of the Laws of England Volume VI 1483 – 1558* (Oxford University Press, 2003)
O.H.L.E., vol. XI	W. Cornish, J. S. Anderson, R. Cocks, M. Lobban, P. Polden and K Smith, *The Oxford History of the Laws of England: vol. XI: The Legal System, 1820–1914* (Oxford University Press, 2010)
O.J.L.S.	*Oxford Journal of Legal Studies*
pl.	placitum (case-number within a term)
Polden, 'Mingling the Waters'	P. Polden, 'Mingling the Waters: Personalities, Politics and the Making of the Supreme Court of Judicature' [2002] C.L.J. 575
Plucknett and Barton, *Doctor and Student*	T. F. T. Plucknett and J. L. Barton (eds), *St German's Doctor and Student* (London: Selden Society, 1974), vol. 91
P.R.O.	Public Record Office, Kew, Surrey
R.S.C.	Rules of the Supreme Court of Judicature
Second Report Common Law Commissioners	United Kingdom, Common Law Commissioners, *Second Report of her Majesty's Commissioners for Inquiring into the Process, Practice and System of Pleading in the Superior Courts of Common Law* (London: H.M.S.O., 1853)

Simpson, *History of Contract*	A. W. B. Simpson, *A History of the Common Law of Contract: The Rise of the Action of Assumpsit* (Oxford: Clarendon Press, 1975; repr. 1987)
Simpson, 'Penal Bond'	A. W. B. Simpson, 'The Penal Bond with Conditional Defeasance' (1966) 82 L.Q.R. 392
Smith, 'Fusing the Equitable Function'	H. E. Smith, 'Fusing the Equitable Function in Private Law', in K. Barker, K. Fairweather and R. Grantham (eds), *Private Law in the 21st Century* (Oxford: Hart, 2017), ch. 9
S.S.	Selden Society (annual volumes, 1887–)
Stair, *Institutions*	Viscount Stair (J. Dalrymple), *The Institutions of the Law of Scotland*, 2nd edn (Edinburgh: printed by heir of A. Anderson, 1693)
Subrin, 'How Equity Conquered Common Law'	S. N. Subrin, 'How Equity Conquered Common Law: The Federal Rules of Civil Procedure in Historical Perspective' (1987) 135 U. Pa L. Rev. 909
(T. [year])	(Trinity Term [year])
Third Report Chancery Commissioners	United Kingdom, Chancery Commission, *Third Report of Her Majesty's Commissioners appointed to inquire into the Process, Practice and System of Pleading in the Court of Chancery* (London: H.M.S.O., 1856)
Third Report Common Law Commissioners	United Kingdom, Common Law Commissioners, *Third Report of the Commissioners Appointed to Inquire into the Process, Practice, and System of Pleading in the Superior Courts of Law at Westminster* (London: H.M.S.O., 1860)
V.P.R.S. 31	Public Record Office Victoria, equity case files
V.P.R.S. 282	Public Record Office Victoria, equity case files, ecclesiastical jurisdiction
V.P.R.S. 1697	Public Record Office Victoria, equity suit books
V.P.R.S. 5507	Public Record Office Victoria, judge's note book series, Mr Justice Molesworth
Worthington, *Equity*, 2nd edn	S. Worthington, *Equity*, 2nd edn (Oxford: Clarendon, 2006)
Y.B.	Year Book

Table of Cases

Statutes

RULES AND STATUTORY INSTRUMENTS

Western Australia

CANADA

Federal

British Columbia

Newfoundland

Acts

1

Fusion and Theories of Equity in Common Law Systems

P. G. TURNER[*]

INTRODUCTION

The following essays address the idea that moved major law reform beginning two centuries ago and in most jurisdictions ending by 1940:[1] that of the 'fusion' of the common law and equity. Under the names of 'fusion', 'merger' or 'union', similar moves were made in several common law jurisdictions to assimilate the courts and procedures of equity with the courts and procedures of the common law. Past complications and problems were to make way for rational simplicity. Separate law and equity courts with distinct procedural rules were brought under one roof, where law and equity would be administered concurrently under uniform procedures. Single courts with distinct law and equity sides operating under different procedures were likewise simplified. These reforms inaugurated the form of superior court now typical in common law jurisdictions.

The reforms also had a side-effect. Fusion became the portal to discussions of equity's very nature and its place in common law systems. To decide how modern judicatures ought to be structured and administered, the reformers and all interested others had pursued large questions: the nature of the laws and courts then operating and, therein, the nature of equity, the source of courts' equity powers and the bearing of equity on common law. Fusion became a byword for matters beyond the reform of courts and their processes that the reforming statutes then made. Once the institutions and their administration had been reformed, fusion was no longer a prospect: it had succeeded, even if that success was understood differently between the United

---

[*] Dr Jamie Glister, Dr Lorenzo Maniscalco, Dr Rose Melikan, Professor Richard Nolan, Professor Henry Smith and Dr Andreas Televantos generously discussed this chapter with the author, saving him from numerous errors and infelicities.

[1] Contrast Law Reform (Law and Equity) Act 1972 (N.S.W.), s. 5.

States and Commonwealth jurisdictions.[2] But afterwards, fusion would still be associated with the larger questions the reformers had discussed, which had troubled lawyers for centuries. Discourse on fusion slid into theorising on equity. Discourse on equity theories slid into discussions of fusion. To enquire into fusion was to enquire into the relationship of equity doctrines to doctrines of common law, and so into the nature and place of equity in common law systems. This intellectual inheritance shapes the modern lawyer's mind today.

Measured by how seldom a judge must decide a point about fusion, questions about fusion and equity's place in common law systems might seem unimportant. But there is more to consider. In unsettled times, legal systems receive scrutiny – and historically, equity and the common law, and the courts, judges and officials administering them, have received such scrutiny. Thus, the reformers' studies of equity in the nineteenth century were done amidst reforms spurred by the French Revolution and the upheavals and progress of industrialisation. Earlier, theories of equity, *epieikeia*, conscience and courts of equity were scrutinised in seventeenth-century England around civil war, revolution and the threat of absolute monarchical power. Similar enquiries were stimulated earlier still, in Tudor England, by the Protestant Reformation and the break with Rome. And the scrutiny of equity courts and the equity jurisdiction amidst the famous crisis of 1616 between Coke C.J. and Lord Ellesmere L.C. is notable.[3] The questions about equity raised at such moments are basic and weighty even in settled times, whatever the statistics on how often fusion is currently a ground of judicial decisions. Similarly, theories of equity and fusion are of practical importance, which such raw statistics cannot show.

As fusion and theories of equity are paired together in the traditions of most common law jurisdictions, readers will find them paired together throughout this book. In presenting this collection of essays, the editors mainly wish to show how one might gain a perspective on both fusion and equity that will enable the modern lawyer to pursue, if not to reach, answers to basic questions. What is equity's place in a modern common law system? Is equity's purpose, as a distinct ingredient of common law systems, spent? Should equity be distributed through the law? If equity should remain a distinct ingredient, in what form? History, doctrine and theory all speak to these enquiries. Studies of the institutional accommodation (or not) of equity in specific jurisdictions,

---

[2] See Bray, Chapter 2; Funk, Chapter 3; and Lobban, Chapter 4.
[3] C. M. Gray, 'The Boundaries of the Equitable Function' (1976) 20 A.J.L.H. 192; Baker, 'The Common Lawyers and the Chancery: 1616'; Knafla, *Law and Politics*, ch. 7, and this chapter, text to nn. 13–28.

studies of doctrines where law and equity are rivals, and studies of equity using one theoretical approach or another: all these mark points in the wide perspective this book is intended to open on fusion and equity's place in common law systems.

The contributors stress one or the other of those twin topics according to how each perceives it best to show something true about fusion or equity. This chapter looks at equity and fusion from a greater distance. Depictions of modern equity and deliberations over fusion seldom acknowledge that the place of equity in common law systems is constitutional in character, both in positive law and in the jurisprudence of common law systems. The chapter will outline how equity acquired this position, and then recall great failed theories of equity and suggest what a theory of equity today might include. The final portion of the chapter shows the practical significance of how modern equity is understood, particularly as influenced by theories of equity and how discussions of fusion are framed. Through a study of the theory that equity is common law travelling by another name, it will be shown that a fusion of substantive common law and equity is unappealing for reasons which – contrary to what is sometimes thought – do not depend on unsubstantiated anti-fusion dogma.

CONSCIENCE AND EQUITY IN THE CONSTITUTION

All legal systems seem to employ moral equity.[4] Many also employ the variety of equity called *epieikeia*, after Aristotle's exposition.[5] Both those recurring forms of equity are given a place by modern common law systems. In most common law jurisdictions,[6] the specialised equity traceable to the equitable jurisdiction of the traditional role of Lord Chancellor,[7] and the Court of Chancery as abolished in England in 1875, holds a place for those and other senses of equity. It is convenient to call this specialised equity 'Chancery equity'.

In England and most jurisdictions based on English law, the position of Chancery equity is constitutional owing to its place in the judicature and its dependence on the crown or state. The early stages in which equity gained this position are unclear. As departments of state, the medieval Chancery and Exchequer depended on royal power, like the *curia regis* and its progeny, the

---

[4] R. A. Newman, *Equity in the World's Legal Systems* (Brussels: Bruylant, 1973).
[5] Aristotle, *Nicomachean Ethics*, trans. by C. D. C. Reeve (Indianapolis, IN: Hackett Publishing, 2014), ¶ 1137a–1138a.
[6] India is the major exception.   [7] Preceding the Constitutional Reform Act 2005 (U.K.).

Courts of Common Pleas and King's Bench.[8] However, the work in what
became Chancery's equity side[9] soon differed from elsewhere. Adjudication
and process were conciliar in being delegated from the king's council[10] and
standing outside the common law writ system and applied to complaints
informally narrated in English bills unlimited by formulaic Latin or French.
Until 1534 the resulting judgment was unrecorded[11] because '[e]ach case had
to be decided solely on its own merits; the Chancellors simply must not
remember their former decisions'.[12] If there was Chancery law, it was 'not
the law of the land'.[13]

The status of the Chancery and its decisions changed in the early modern
period, by which time Chancery business had considerably grown.[14] The
common law was weakened by the quantities of litigation occurring in
prerogative courts without regular legal safeguards. Although efforts were
made during the tenures of Sir Thomas More,[15] Sir Nicholas Bacon[16] and
Sir Thomas Egerton (later Lord Ellesmere and Viscount Brackley)[17] to regu-
larise the Chancery's proceedings, litigation in the Chancery was part of the
cause.[18] In one effort to halt the slide, the common law judges decided in
1597 that judgments of the king's common law courts could not be re-
examined by the Chancery after judgment.[19] According to Sir Edward Coke,
they also decided that re-examination was prohibited by the Acts of

---

[8]   Baker, *I.E.L.H.*, 4[th]edn, 12, 98–99.
[9]   On its 'Latin side', the Chancery issued writs: A.D. Hargreaves, 'Equity and the Latin Side of
      the Chancery' (1952) 68 L.Q.R. 481.
[10] J. F. Baldwin, 'The King's Council and the Chancery' (two parts) (1910) 14 Am. Hist. Rev. 496
      and 744.
[11] J. H. Baker, 'English Law and the Renaissance', in J. H. Baker (ed.), *The Reports of Sir John
      Spelman* (London: Selden Society, 1978) (94 S.S.), vol. II, 39. See S. E. Thorne, 'Courts of
      Record and Sir Edward Coke' (1937–8) 2 U.T.L.J. 24, 47–49.
[12] F. Metzger, 'The Last Phase of the Medieval Chancery', in A. Harding (ed.), *Law-Making and
      Law-Makers in British History* (London: Royal Historical Society, 1980), 87. The Chancery
      decree rolls begin in 1534, the Chancery decree and order books in 1544.
[13] Anon., Reading on Magna Carta c. 29, prob. Lincoln's Inn, *c.* 1491/1508 in J. Baker (ed.),
      Selected Readings and Commentaries on Magna Carta 1400–1604 (London: Selden Society,
      2015) (132 S.S.), 252; also the reading attr. W. Fletewood (*c.* 1558), ibid., 372–73; but contrast Sir
      Edward Coke's 1604 memorandum on c. 29: ibid., 396 (Chancery proceedings within jurisdic-
      tion are justifiable by the law of the land).
[14] J. A. Guy, 'Introduction', in J. A. Guy (ed.), *Christopher St German on Chancery and Statute*
      (London: Selden Society, 1985), 64–68; P. Tucker, 'The Early History of the Court of
      Chancery: A Comparative Study' (2000) 115 E.H.R. 791.
[15] L.C. 1529–32.   [16] L.K. 1558–79.   [17] M.R. 1594–96, L.K. 1596–1603, L.C. 1603–16.
[18] Knafla, *Law and Politics*, ch. 7.
[19] *Throckmorton v. Finch* (1597) B.L. MS Harley 6686A f.224, printed in J. Baker, *The Reinvention
      of Magna Carta 1216–1616* (Cambridge University Press, 2017), 287.

praemunire 27 Edw. III st. 1 c. 1 (1353) and 4 Hen. IV c. 23 (1403), which provided penalties for suing after judgment at law.[20] Lord Keeper Egerton made no immediate protest. But in 1606, as Lord Ellesmere L.C., he refused to follow the judges' 1597 ruling. The political and legal status of the Chancery – and therefore the common law – would be formally unsettled for the next decade.

The political settlement of 1616 was announced in lawyers' words that established the constitutional position of the Chancery and its law. Ellesmere had studied the major statutes touching the Chancery. Those, he said,[21] legitimated the Chancery jurisdiction; and the Acts of *praemunire* went solely against interference from the papal courts at Rome. Ellesmere briefed the king's advisors to that effect and they assented.[22] In his judgment in the *Earl of Oxford's Case*,[23] Ellesmere successfully claimed royal authority for the Chancellor, influenced by relatively new ideas of sovereignty.[24] He considered the Chancellor the keeper of the king's conscience – an idea not seen in Christopher St German's writings of the 1530s, nor other known sources of early Tudor England[25] – and claimed the Chancellor's authority in the Chancery – and the king's authority in matters of equity and conscience – was absolute.[26] James I vindicated Ellesmere's account, ultimately by decree.[27] Ellesmere's theory of the Chancery's authority became law. Orders of the Chancery became dominant over judgments of the common law courts.

---

[20] Ibid., ff. 223v. –224r.; Baker, *Reinvention*, 287. St German had thought so: Plucknett and Barton, *Doctor and Student*, 106–9 (even-numbered pages in the first dialogue give the Latin, odd-numbered pages the English translation and later inclusions not written in Latin; the second dialogue was originally printed in English).

[21] Lord Ellesmere, 'A Breviate or Direccion for the Kinges Learned Councell Collected by the Lord Chaunccellor Ellesmere, *Mense Septembris* 1615. *Anno Jacobi Regis*', in Knafla, *Law and Politics*, 319–36 (analysed at 164–67, 174–75). Coke's corresponding interpretations are discussed: J. P. Dawson, 'Coke and Ellesmere Disinterred: The Attack on the Chancery in 1616' (1941) 36 Ill. L. Rev. 127.

[22] Knafla, ibid., 175–76.

[23] (1615) 1 Ch. Rep. 1. The judgment may have been a tract: Ibbetson, 'The Earl of Oxford's Case'.

[24] Knafla, *Law and Politics*, 72–73; I. Williams, 'Developing a Prerogative Theory for the Authority of the Chancery: The French Connection', in M. Godfrey (ed.), *Law and Authority in British Legal History*, 1200–1900 (Cambridge University Press, 2016).

[25] Baker, *Reinvention*, 411 n. 6; Williams, ibid., 51–52.

[26] *Earl of Oxford's Case* (1615) 1 Ch. Rep. 1, 14–15. By 'absolute', he may merely have meant that the power was exercisable free of a specific procedure or rules, in contradistinction to an 'ordinary' power subject to such procedure or rules: Williams, 'Developing a Prerogative Theory', 36–37; Baker, *Reinvention*, 413 (Coke's drawing of the distinction).

[27] See James I, 'A Speach in the Starre-Chamber, *The xx. of Jvne. Anno* 1616', in J. P. Sommerville (ed.), *King James VI and I: Political Writings* (Cambridge University Press, 1994), 204–28 and the decree printed in Cary 133–35.

1616 formally settled the Chancery's place in the judicature, but the stability of the settlement took the efforts of subsequent presidents of the Chancery.[28] Sir Francis Bacon,[29] Bishop Williams,[30] Sir Thomas Coventry,[31] Sir Edward Hyde[32] and Sir Heneage Finch[33] all cultivated good relations with the common law courts by ensuring not to subvert common law.[34] Corrupt officers and abuses of procedure still soured litigants' encounters in Chancery, though such problems were not Chancery specialisms. Parliament knew these shortcomings when it considered proposals to abolish the Chancery under Cromwell in 1653[35] and at the Glorious Revolution. But Parliament considered that Chancery equity could not be done without.[36]

Finch, later Lord Nottingham,[37] worked prodigiously in the later seventeenth century to bring Chancery practice and laws into the form ordained in 1616. He established new doctrines while following his forebears' doctrines on the place of Chancery in the judicature. He wrote: 'all men agree, that the King is the fountain of justice and mercy, of law and equity'.[38] Afterwards 'justice and equity ... were ... settled in courts, as God, who is the fountain of light, did settle it in the sun and moon'.[39] Drawing on opinions of the judges early that century, Nottingham said equity was 'opposite to regular law', 'in a manner an arbitrary disposition' emanating from 'a special trust committed to the King'[40] in 'a fundamental constitution' of the state.[41] This was maintained as good constitutional theory and doctrine in England,[42] colonial North

---

[28] See D. E. C. Yale, 'Introduction', in Finch, *'Manual' and 'Prolegomena'*, 69–74; Macnair, 'Imitations of Equitable Relief'. For prohibitions against equity courts after 1616, see Gray, 'Boundaries of the Equitable Function'.

[29] L.K. 1617–18; L.C. 1618–21 (Lord Verulam 1618, Viscount St Albans 1621). [30] L.K. 1621–25.

[31] L.K. 1625–40 (Lord Coventry 1628).

[32] L.C. 1658–67 (Lord Hyde 1660, Earl of Clarendon 1661).

[33] L.K. 1673–75, L.C. 1675–81. See n. 37 in this chapter.

[34] See Yale, 'Introduction', 69–74; Baker, 'The Common Lawyers and the Chancery: 1616', 507–10.

[35] J. Parkes, *A History of the Court of Chancery* (London: Longman et al., 1828), 148–58.

[36] H. S. Holdsworth, *A History of English Law*, 7th edn (London: Methuen, 1956), vol. 1, 463–65; Yale, 'Introduction', 73. The same was true of Cromwell, whose short-lived Chancery Ordinance left the court in place: Chancery Regulation Ordinance 1654 (Eng.), in C. H. Firth and R. S. Rait (eds), *Acts and Ordinances of the Interregnum, 1642–1660* (London: H.M.S.O., 1911), vol. 2, 958. See [B. Whitelocke], *Memorials of the English Affairs* (London: Ponder, 1682), 601–08; Parkes, *A History of the Court of Chancery*, 167–72.

[37] Lord Finch 1674, Earl of Nottingham 1681. [38] Finch, *'Manual' and 'Prolegomena'*, 191.

[39] Ibid., 190. [40] Ibid., 189.

[41] Ibid., 192. These passages elaborate Hobart's report of *Martin* v. *Marshal* (1615) Hob. 63, where opinions of Popham C.J.K.B. (d. 1607), Anderson C.J.C.P. (d. 1605), Gawdy C.J.C.P. (d. 1605) and Walmsley J. (d. 1612) were canvassed.

[42] *R.* v. *Hare and Mann* (1719) 1 Str. 146, 158–59.

America[43] and Australia[44] and, afterwards, the United States[45] and Canada.[46] It required adaptation to the republican constitution of the United States,[47] in which a sovereign's conscience – let alone a king's prerogative – is alien. Indeed, it must now be untenable to consider the modern equity jurisdiction to be a prerogative power anywhere.[48]

Otherwise equity's constitutional aspects continue. The decree of James I effectively became parliamentary legislation in England in 1875, and is so in England and former colonies today.[49] The distinctness of equity and its primacy over the common law in England was acknowledged in American colonies before the Declaration of Independence in 1776. Unless ordinary colonial courts were invested with equitable jurisdiction, the jurisdiction was typically exercisable only by a colonial governor alone or in council.[50] If the governor or colonial council or assembly were not invested with equity jurisdiction, then it was exercisable only by the king in council at London.[51] The doctrine of primacy also carried into the new American republic and through the reform era. For all the distaste that the reformer David Dudley Field felt for equity,[52] his legacy – the Field Code of Civil Procedure and its progeny, including the federal Rules of Civil Procedure of 1938[53] – depended on equity continuing and taking primacy over the common law in New York

---

[43] *Simpson v. Smyth* (1847) 1 E. & A. 172, 194; *A.-G. (Upper Canada) v. Grasett* (1860) 8 Gr. 130, 155.

[44] *R. v. Bank of Victoria (in liq.)* (1895) 1 Arg. L.R. 1, 4.

[45] *McCartee v. Orphan Asylum,* 9 Cow. 437, 471, 481–83 (1827) (Court for the Correction of Errors of New York); *Fontain v. Ravenel,* 17 How. (58 U.S.) 369, 385 (1854) (subject to the American authorities, n. 48).

[46] *Re Bulger* (1911) 21 Man. R. 702, 705; *Aherne v. Chang* (2011) 106 O.R. (3d) 297, [16]; 2011 ONSC 2067.

[47] *Fontain v. Ravenel,* 17 How. (58 U.S.) 369, 385 (1854).

[48] In England, see *R. (Miller) v. Secretary of State for Exiting the European Union* [2018] A.C. 61, [45]; [2017] UKSC 5. In the United States, see e.g., *The Will of Sarah Zane* printed as *The Opinion of the Circuit Court of the United States in and for the Eastern District of Pennsylvania on the Will of Sarah Zane* (Philadelphia, PA: Kite, 1834), 19, 33–34, 59, 62, 65, 70; *Late Corp. of the Church of Jesus Christ of Latter-Day Saints v. United States,* 136 U.S. 1, 56–59 (1890).

[49] Senior Courts Act 1981 (U.K.) s. 49, re-enacting Judicature Act 1873 s. 25(11). Equivalent provisions are found on the statute-books of Commonwealth common law jurisdictions generally.

[50] W. Smith, *The History of the Province of New-York,* 2nd edn (Philadelphia, PA: Carey, 1792), 45, 112–13, 122, 130, 148–49, 166–67, 183, 188–89, 191, 253, 268–71, 274–76; D. Ramsay, *Ramsay's History of South Carolina* (Newberry, SC: Duffie, 1858), vol. II, 72; A. Laussat, *An Essay on Equity in Pennsylvania* (Philadelphia, PA: Desilver, 1826), 17–31. In Upper Canada, see Girard, Chapter 5.

[51] A. M. Schlesinger, 'Colonial Appeals to the Privy Council' (two parts) (1913) 28 P.S.Q. 279 and 432.

[52] See text to nn. 83–85.

[53] These replaced the Federal Equity Rules and the Conformity Act, 28 U.S.C. 724 [1934].

state, where Field's work was concentrated, and in the federal courts. The established principle of judicature that, when a new remedy enters the common law, the equitable jurisdiction to grant relief in the same type of case is undiminished also emerged from these various developments.[54] And in different ways, written constitutions such as those of the United States[55] and the Commonwealth of Australia[56] constitutionalise equity afresh and confirm equity's status in the common law inheritance from which those new world polities were made.

What cannot yet be assessed is how far the laws and institutions of Courts of Chancery might have helped form the ideas that shape the modern democratic state.[57] If the contribution was minimal, it seems curious that Chancery equity was retained through the trouble in early modern England over the uncertain reach of Chancery jurisdiction, the corruption of its officers and the expense of Chancery litigation. Chancery equity was found indispensable, once divorced from sovereign absolutism. The Court of Chancery was one of the developing institutions of state, and Chancery equity and the common law were part of the developing system of government. These institutions and systems formed a basis for government in British colonies and, under the further influence of the Enlightenment, were adjusted to new life after American independence and, later again, when modern representative democracy was born in common law jurisdictions.[58] Also notable was the culture of equity and conscience in law and society in the early modern period,[59] particularly the 'atmosphere of trust' which Maitland still saw surrounding the societies, corporations and of course private and public express trusts in the twentieth century.[60] The culture of responsibility generated in that

---

[54] E.g., *Kemp* v. *Pryor* (1802) 7 Ves. Jun. 237, 249–50; *Greenshields* v. *Barnhart* (1851) C.R. 2 A.C. 91, 185 (aff'd *sub. nom. Barnhart* v. *Greenshields* (1853) 9 Moo. P.C. 18).

[55] United States Constitution, Art. III §2 and Seventh Amendment (1791).

[56] Commonwealth Constitution, s. 75(v); see *Plaintiff S157/2002* v. *Commonwealth* (2003) 211 C.L.R. 476, [5]–[6]; [2003] HCA 2.

[57] For a preliminary hint: Metzger, 'The Last Phase of the Medieval Chancery', 82.

[58] Parkes, *A History of the Court of Chancery*, 148–58; Publius [A. Hamilton], *Federalist, on the New Constitution, Written in the Year 1788* (Hallowell, ME: Glazier, Masters & Smith, 1837), No. 81, 377–79 and No. 83, 393, 396; Rules of the Supreme Court, 2 Dall. 411, 413–14 (1792): 'The Court Considers the practice of the courts of King's Bench and Chancery in England, as affording outlines for the practice of this court'.

[59] D. R. Klinck, *Conscience, Equity and the Court of Chancery in Early Modern England* (Ashgate: Farnham, 2010); M. Fortier, *The Culture of Equity in Early Modern England* (London: Routledge, 2016); M. Fortier, *The Culture of Equity in Restoration and Eighteenth-Century Britain and America* (London: Routledge, 2016).

[60] F. W. Maitland, 'Trust and Corporation', in D. Runciman and M. Ryan (eds), *F. W. Maitland: State, Trust and Corporation* (Cambridge University Press, [1904] 2003), 126–27.

atmosphere has direct lines to the legal and political responsibilities of those who now govern local authorities and, through modern administrative law,[61] those who now govern the state. The common law receives credit for its contribution towards the development of modern law and government. It would be odd if that credit went alone to courts of common law defined in opposition to equity courts, and to the common law defined to exclude equity.

GREAT FAILED THEORIES

Scrutiny led lawyers to formulate theories of the Court of Chancery and adjudication on its equity side from the sixteenth century onwards to grasp at questions of Chancery's origins, authority and especially its review of common law judgments. Lawyers today typically reach fundamental questions about equity through discussion of fusion, but certain past theories of the Chancery and its equity have left impressions even if no single theory of equity has come down to lawyers today. The lack of a perfect theory of equity is sometimes counted against Chancery equity and, indeed, given as a reason to abandon equity as it is currently known.[62] What should one take from the failure of great equity theories? Four will be mentioned.

Lawyers long studied the theory of St German, who wrote in the 1530s.[63] He wrote the first theory of English equity, thereby connecting equity with conscience-based adjudication by the Court of Chancery. St German rooted equity in concepts familiar among medieval theologians. At base was *synderesis*, 'that rational faculty which compels our assent to self-evident propositions, [and] shows us that good is to be done and evil eschewed'.[64] Conscience was the derivation from that general rule of rules of conduct applicable in particular situations.[65] If the particular derived rules diverged from a human law – say, a law concerning deeds – the Court of Chancery might find cause to do equity, relieving from the human rule to meet the exigencies of the case.[66]

---

[61] W. Gummow, 'Equity in the Modern Administrative State', in *Equity and Administration*, ch. 16. See also B. Hilton, *A Mad, Bad, and Dangerous People? England 1783–1846* (Oxford: Clarendon, 2006), 169–70.

[62] J. Beatson, *The Use and Abuse of Unjust Enrichment* (Oxford: Clarendon, 1991), ch. 9; P. Birks, 'Equity in the Modern Law: An Exercise in Taxonomy' (1996) 26 U.W.A.L. Rev. 1, 22–25; Worthington, *Equity*, 2nd edn.

[63] Vinogradoff, 'Reason and Conscience in Sixteenth-century Jurisprudence', 373–74; L. A. Knafla, 'Conscience in the English Common Law Tradition' (1976) 26 U.T.L.J. 1, 8.

[64] Plucknett and Barton, 'Introduction', xxvi.

[65] Ibid., xxvi–xxvii; N. Doe, *Fundamental Authority in Late Medieval English Law* (Cambridge University Press, 1990), 133.

[66] Ibid.; Baker, 'English Law and the Renaissance', 37–39.

Conscience was not arbitrary. Moreover, St German thought that the common law largely squared with conscience. He took the example of the obligor on a bond. Where an obligor was sued after having paid the sum due without obtaining a deed of acquittance, the obligee could still recover at law. In Chancery the obligor could be relieved of paying twice – which, a modern lawyer might assume, was because Chancery proceeded according to conscience while the common law did not. However, following the medieval common lawyers, St German thought it contrary to conscience *and* to common law that the obligor should pay twice. It was not common law that the obligor ought to pay the money again; 'that law were both against reason and conscience'. Rather, the obligor must pay twice because 'a general ground' of English law was that 'great inconvenience' and 'hurt' would come of allowing the obligor to avoid an obligation through pleading payment 'by a bare word'.[67] This accorded with conscience except where the obligor was neither careless nor defaulted, in which case the obligor might be helped in Chancery. St German's innovation was to call 'equity' the relief the Chancery awarded from such general rules where, by its informal procedures, conscience was found to lie outside the general rule.

St German's theory contained other influential ideas. Because the common law could be consistent with conscience, the Court of Chancery need not always intervene.[68] And some matters were non-justiciable by Chancery and any court, since they were properly matter for a person's private conscience.[69] St German considered the Chancery's jurisdiction special, even if Chancery principles made it a court of constant resort from sealed instruments, the denial of uses and the like. Had all lawyers understood Chancery equity as special, many complaints about the overlapping jurisdictions of Chancery and other courts in the seventeenth century would have been prevented.[70] The concurrent jurisdiction of law and equity courts was too large to pretend that disputes in that terrain did not attract two systems of law relating to the one subject, in courts of law and courts of equity.[71]

---

[67] Plucknett and Barton, *Doctor and Student*, 77, 79 (first dialogue, orthography modernised). This discussion continues at 189–90 (second dialogue); in the anonymous *Replication of a Serjeant at the Laws of England*, printed in Guy (ed.), *Christopher St German on Chancery and Statute*, 99–101; and in St German's reply in A *Little Treatise Concerning Writs of Subpoena*.

[68] Especially *Doctor and Student*, 120–31.

[69] Ibid., 113; Finch, *'Manual' and 'Prolegomena'*, 194.

[70] See James I, 'A Speach in the Starre-Chamber', 213. See also Knafla, *Law and Politics*, 108–09, 120–22.

[71] See Gray, 'Boundaries of the Equitable Function'.

The fundamentals of modern equity were shaped more by St German than any single other lawyer. But his theory fails as a universal theory of Chancery equity. For instance, while the basic harmony which lawyers can perceive in the relations between law and equity today was perceived by St German in his own time, the explanation of that harmony in terms of conscience went quiet as English minds became persuaded that laws were human laws.[72]

A type of prerogative theory of the equity of the Chancery was advanced by Lord Ellesmere in the 1610s, as noted previously. The prerogative belonged to the king. Although features of Ellesmere's general account remain tenable, his prerogative theory specifically is faulty. As mentioned earlier, while the Chancellor's office as keeper of the king's conscience[73] became good constitutional theory in common law realms, a republic has no king with a conscience to be kept; the royal prerogatives cannot explain Chancery equity today even in constitutional monarchies.[74] The central plank of Ellesmere's theory is now missing in the United States and Commonwealth jurisdictions. A prerogative theory also fails as an account of Chancery equity from the beginnings of the court up to 1616. The Chancery's authority always drew from the king's duty to do justice among subjects, but the idea that the Chancery's judicial authority came directly from the king's prerogative only became current once Bodin's theory of sovereignty became current in the English constitution, late in Elizabeth's reign.[75]

Parts of Lord Nottingham's Restoration-era theory of equity were noticed earlier. Nottingham supposed that English equity began with the king, as the fountain of justice, administering equity according (it seems) to natural equity.[76] Equity stood outside the law; the king's power was to supply 'or correct the rigour of positive law'.[77] However, equity could not arbitrarily dispose of the legal system and laws. While equity stood outside law, through 'discretion'– i.e., prudence – equity 'entertains some form, which it may justly leave in special cases'.[78] And, as the king's power was to correct the rigour of positive law, Nottingham said it became 'a maxim in our books that the Chancery can only relieve in such cases where the party hath no remedy at

---

[72] Plucknett and Barton, 'Introduction', xxvii–xxix; T. S. Haskett, 'The Medieval English Court of Chancery' (1996) 14 L.H.R 245, 271–73.

[73] M. S. Bilder, *The Transatlantic Constitution: Colonial Legal Culture and the Empire* (Cambridge, MA: Harvard University Press, 2004), 78–83.

[74] N. 48.

[75] Williams, 'Developing a Prerogative Theory', 42–48. See Knafla, *Law and Politics*, 49, 68–69, 72–73.

[76] Finch, 'Manual' and 'Prolegomena', 190–91.

[77] Ibid., 193–94, citing Year Book and other sources.   [78] Ibid., 189.

the Common Law'.[79] That incapacity was again born of prudence not constitutional incapacity.

Accounts of modern equity still show the influence of these ideas.[80] However, Nottingham's account also fails on its own terms. Whereas Nottingham
considered equity the opposite of law and outside it, medieval and early
modern lawyers did not think Chancery law and common law were opposed.[81]
To them, the Chancery *fulfilled* the common law when it corrected the
'mechanical failures' of common law procedures and methods of proof.[82]

David Dudley Field, the New York reformer, held a procedural theory of
Chancery equity. Procedural theories maintain that Chancery equity consists
of distinct procedures and proofs without distinct substantive principles, doctrines and remedies. Field's variant ran through the Field Code of civil
procedure.[83] The Code was supposed to merge (or fuse or unite) law and
equity in New York, and was adopted in many states. The Federal Rules of
Civil Procedure 1938 followed the model, raising Field's equity theory onto
the federal plane.[84] Field thought that legal and equitable rules could be
distinguished only if legal rules were cognizable in courts of law while
equitable rules were cognizable in courts of equity, and different procedures
applied in each court. The differences 'disappear the moment the two courts
and the two modes of procedure are blended'.[85] However, just as a procedural
theory of the common law or statute would fail, so do procedural theories of
equity. They are incomplete. Once everything has been said about procedure,
the substance – here, equity – remains unexplained.

Formally, these great theories have failed. Yet they have profoundly influenced legal understanding. Lawyers have found them persuasive and useful. If
lacking a perfect modern theory can be counted against Chancery equity,
then St German's, Ellesmere's, Nottingham's and Field's theories should have
been inept and worthless. But it does not follow that a perfect theory should
not be pursued. Indeed, is it not drastic to abandon a subject to fate merely
because the best theories prove imperfect? Milsom thought the Chancellor's
equitable jurisdiction 'probably the most important and certainly the most

---

[79] Ibid., 193–94.
[80] R. *Griggs Group Ltd* v. *Evans* [2005] Ch. 153, [39]; [2004] EWHC 1088 (Ch); *Akers* v. *Samba Financial Group* [2017] A.C. 424, [24]; [2017] UKSC 6.
[81] E.g., Plucknett and Barton, *Doctor and Student*, 76–79.
[82] See Milsom, *Historical Foundations*, 2nd edn, 82–86, 91–92; Baker, 'English Law and the Renaissance', 37–39.
[83] 1848 N.Y. Laws c. 379.   [84] See Funk, Chapter 3.
[85] D. D. Field, 'Law and Equity', in A. P. Sprague (ed.), *Speeches, Arguments, and Miscellaneous Papers of David Dudley Field* (New York, NY: Appleton, 1884), 579.

astonishing of English contributions to legal thought':[86] reason enough to suppose that casually discarding Chancery equity would be unwise. The discarding would seem capricious. No one would seriously suggest that such other social creations as representative government, parliament or the common law should be abandoned because no perfect theory explains them. However, the flaws of past theories suggest what one might expect of a modern theory of equity in common law systems.

EXPECTATIONS OF THEORY

It should be expected that a theory of modern equity will be composite. This expectation is not currently the norm. People normally suppose a sound theory of equity must be unitary: that a theory must reveal all Chancery equity to have a single source of legal authority (e.g., the prerogative, *epieikeia*[87]) or to be manifested in one form (e.g., orders commanding the defendant personally).[88] Other people require that Chancery equity have a single object (e.g., moral equity, simple fairness).[89] Some people suppose Chancery equity must be united by the character of its rules (e.g., opposition to legal rules, flexibility).[90] Such accounts suppose that a theory of equity can be valid only if its explanation of equity is single and simple. But legal institutions rarely have a single root of authority unless deliberately created by statute or instrument of state. None of the royal courts was. Institutions that come into being unplanned, and then grow organically, have no single simple plan.[91] No wonder the courts of Chancery and common law had no single object, or rules of a single character. A unitary theory of modern equity is inapt. A composite theory, according to which two or more ideas may be necessary to explain aspects of Chancery equity, is essential.

Any thorough account of equity will focus on individual doctrines, entitlements and remedies within equitable jurisdiction. A further expectation, with

---

[86] Milsom, *Historical Foundations*, 82.

[87] Text to nn. 73–75; Ibbetson, 'A House Built on Sand'.

[88] S. A. Smith, 'Form and Substance in Equitable Remedies', in A. Robertson and M. Tilbury (eds), *Divergences in Private Law* (Oxford: Hart, 2015), ch. 16.

[89] *Murad v Al-Saraj* [2005] W.T.L.R. 1573, [80]–[83]; [2005] EWCA Civ 959.

[90] Worthington, *Equity*, 2nd edn, ch. 10; also M. Macnair, 'Equity and Conscience' (2007) 27 O.J.L.S. 659, 680–81 (truth-discovery).

[91] Such developments are pejoratively called 'accidental': *Vidal-Hall* v. *Google Inc.* [2016] Q.B. 1003, [48]; [2015] EWCA Civ 311; Worthington, *Equity*, 2nd edn, 20; L. Smith, 'Common Law and Equity in R3RUE' (2011) 68 Wash. & Lee L. Rev. 1185, 1187. Contrast Getzler, 'Patterns of Fusion', 176.

two parts, occurs on this level. First, although analysis shows a plurality of specific objectives among the doctrines of Chancery equity, the objectives are similar enough that they cluster together. For instance, the specific objectives of achieving *restitutio in integrum* between transaction parties, declaring an appointment outside of power void, and restraining a registered holder of land from allowing buildings to become dilapidated, are distinct. But where each is pursued to remedy an express trustee's misconduct, these specifics manifest one general objective: to constrain a holder of legal title – the trustee – to act according to the trustee's obligations of conscience under the trust instrument, legislation and general law. Distinct specific objectives thus cluster together. Likewise, the particular ends of correcting a mis-recorded agreement by rectification, of permitting a mortgagor to redeem upon late payment and of ordering specific performance are different. But they group together around their larger objective of giving effect to the parties' substantial intentions rather than the mere form.

Secondly, the similarities within these groups can be expected to exceed the similarities between those groups and groups found by analysing common law doctrines, entitlements and remedies similarly. Most equitable doctrines and remedies operate via principles, whereas most of the civil (and criminal) common law operates via rules. Most legal disputes addressed by the common law are suitably expressed in rules and remedies set in advance, whereas various doctrines and remedies of Chancery equity address disputes that can be sensibly resolved only by *ex post* adjudication within principles and practices expressed relatively loosely in advance. To argue that a perceived similarity between one rule of equity and one rule of common law proves that the whole body of common law and the whole body of Chancery equity display no meaningful differences[92] is to make an error of scale. It also ignores the close group similarities among equitable doctrines – and their distinctness from groups of common law rules.

Any theory should acknowledge that Chancery equity since the seventeenth century has included 'technical equity'. When the cases use those[93] or cognate words,[94] what do they mean? It would be wrong to suppose that technical equity consists of rules of Chancery equity of fixed arbitrary positions, spouting

---

[92] Worthington, *Equity*, 2nd edn, ch. 10 makes a series of such comparisons. Also, Beatson, *The Use and Abuse of Unjust Enrichment*, ch. 9.

[93] *Foster* v. *Blackstone* (1833) 1 My. & K. 297, 305; *The 'Victoria'* (1859) Sw. 408, 409; *Maddison* v. *Alderson* (1883) 8 App. Cas. 467, 489; *Re Diplock* [1947] Ch. 716, 764, 777; *Fibrosa Spolka Akcyjna* v. *Fairbairn Lawson Combe Barbour* [1943] A.C. 42, 64.

[94] *Gee* v. *Pritchard* (1818) 2 Swan. 402, 414.

injustice and capriciousness. When pieces of Chancery equity are called technical, that is to distinguish them from moral equity and simple fairness. The latter operate outside law and contradict it. Technical equity stands within law, yet avoids empty formalism by having the open texture, discretionariness and concern with legal disputes suited to *ex post* adjudication that much of Chancery equity has.

A theory of modern equity should allow for positivism.[95] Together with the application of doctrines of precedent to Chancery equity, positivism has produced the idea that Chancery equity is common law by another name – a kind of monism discussed later.[96] It has also nourished dualist ideas (by which a rift separates common law from Chancery equity[97]) and captious rhetoric[98] and reductionism in depictions of modern equity.[99] A full understanding must await historical work on the inception of positivism and precedent in Chancery courts[100] (though a brief acquaintance reveals the problems here). The need to allow for positivism and its monist and dualist children in an account of modern equity is apparent already.

Finally, an explanation of conscience should be expected of a modern equity theory. It is easy – Milsom wondered whether too easy[101] – to assume that early Chancellors directly applied theological notions because they were ecclesiastics. Before St German's writings gained influence, the Chancery was called a court, not of equity, but of conscience. We do not know how far the Chancellors proceeded on theological notions of conscience, nor what

---

[95] Milsom, *Historical Foundations*, 2nd edn, 88–91.

[96] Field, 'Law and Equity', 577 (law-equity distinction 'little more than a play on words'), 580, 582 (analogy of imaginary system of men's common law courts and women's equity courts); Birks, 'Equity in the Modern Law', 16–17 (using equitable vocabulary is playing with words); Burrows, 'We Do This at Common Law', 1, 2, 5, 7, 9, 12, 15–16 ('equity' and 'law' mere 'historical labels').

[97] Anon., *Replication of a Serjeant at the Laws of England*, 100–01; *Prolegomena*, 189; R. Atkyns, *An Enquiry into the Jurisdiction of the Chancery in Causes of Equity* (London: [s.n.] 1695), 15–16; [Anon.], *The Present State of the Practice and Practisers of the Law* (London [n.d., c. 1750], printed for the author), 46; Parkes, *A History of the Court of Chancery*, 399; Worthington, *Equity*, 2nd edn, xiii ('This book . . . is an argument against dualism'); contrast at 12 n. 4 ('sharp opposition' between law and equity is a 'myth'). See D. E. C. Yale, 'St German's Little Treatise Concerning Writs of Subpoena' (1975) 10 Ir. Jur. 324, 330.

[98] N. 96.

[99] Worthington, *Equity*, 2nd edn, 3–7 (analogy of imaginary kindergarten games played by 'red' rules or 'blue' rules with 'red' and 'blue' umpires). This adapts the analogy of J. Getzler, 'Patterns of Fusion', in P. Birks, *The Classification of Obligations* (Oxford: Clarendon, 1997), 157 (analogy of imaginary system of mathematics using red numbers and blue numbers).

[100] See W. H. D. Winder, 'Precedent in Equity' (1941) 57 L.Q.R. 245.

[101] Milsom, *Historical Foundations*, 2nd edn, 89–90.

conceptions of conscience were most important in Chancery adjudication.[102] However, notions of conscience in Chancery since Lord Nottingham have been avowedly civic and secular, and distinct from the thin notion that conscience equals any belief held with conviction.[103] Potentially, the required account of conscience will be special to law and have legal, more than moral-philosophical, qualities in comparison with accounts of conscience in Chancery equity in earlier periods.[104]

What more might be demanded of an account of Chancery equity need not be considered here. A satisfactory account will dissatisfy those who demand single simple explanations of phenomena. But a composite theory will be truer and useful for longer. Consider Lord Ellesmere's theory in the *Earl of Oxford's Case*,[105] conveniently summarised by Professor Ibbetson:

> The Chancery is always open, and not bound by the law terms, the periods in which [c]ommon law business could be done. Equity is always ready to render every man his due. It is impossible to frame a general law to apply properly to all particular acts. The function of the Chancellor is to correct consciences for frauds, breaches of trust, wrongs and oppression. He should soften the rigour of the law. Equity and [law] work together to achieve justice. Equity can be done at [c]ommon law as well as in the Chancery, provided that there is a [c]ommon law process available to fit the circumstances.[106]

Apart from the flaw already discussed,[107] this can be considered 'little more than a collection of standard points which could be said to justify equitable intervention, and in particular the intervention of the Chancery': hardly a theory at all.[108] Or it can be considered a composite theory conceived with a skill – and Ellesmere's political moderateness and variety of experience[109] – that has ensured lawyers ever since have found utility and enduring truth in it.

---

[102] See J. Martínez-Torrón, *Anglo-American Law and Canon Law* (Berlin: Dunker and Humblot, 1998), ch. 4; Klinck, *Conscience, Equity and the Court of Chancery*, ch. 1; R. Hedlund, 'The Theological Foundations of Equity's Conscience' (2015) 4 O.J.L.R. 119.

[103] Klinck, *Conscience, Equity and the Court of Chancery*, chs 8–9.

[104] See n. 63; D. E. C. Yale, 'Introduction', in E. Hake, *Epieikeia: A Dialogue on Equity in Three Parts*, ed. by D. E. C. Yale (Yale University Press: London, 1953), xiii–xxv; Fortier, *The Culture of Equity in Restoration and Eighteenth-Century Britain and America*.

[105] (1615) 1 Ch. Rep. 1, 6–11.   [106] Ibbetson, 'A House Built on Sand', 74–75 (citations omitted).

[107] Nn. 73–75.   [108] Ibbetson, 'A House Built on Sand', 75.

[109] Knafla, *Law and Politics*, 60, 164–67, 174–75, 181; Fortier, *Culture of Equity*, 4–8; contrast Ibbetson, 'A House Built on Sand', 74–76.

PRACTICALITY AND THEORY

To show that theories of equity influence how lawyers approach the formulation and answering of everyday questions in legal disputes, attention will now be given to a form of the monist theory mentioned earlier in the chapter, that Chancery equity is common law under another name. A theory can influence a lawyer's thought whether the theory is consciously or unconsciously adopted. Illustrations from the equitable doctrine of relief from forfeiture, and the field of restitution for unjust enrichment, will be used to show that the monist theory tends towards a substantive fusion of equity and the common law from which impractical results and unwanted complexity follow. Any lawyer minded to view legal rules and the legal system prudently would consider substantive fusion undesirable, given this inherent tendency of monist theories of equity.

Cause of Action, Form of Action

The form of monism in question assimilates equitable claims to claims arising at common law. The hidden cause of this assimilation in England arises from the procedural reforms of 1875. Administrative fusion was then effected: the former courts of Chancery, Queen's Bench, Common Pleas, Exchequer, Admiralty, Probate, Divorce and Matrimonial Causes were abolished and succeeded by a court bearing an American name, the new Supreme Court of Judicature.[110] Procedural fusion also occurred: the procedures of the old courts, particularly the distinct procedures of the common law and equity courts, were replaced by new uniform procedures.

The theory that equity is common law by another name has found a footing in lawyers' understanding of the central concept of the uniform procedure: the cause of action. The Judicature system made a uniform requirement that all pleadings henceforth disclose a cause of action. Immediately before the Judicature Acts commenced on 1 November 1875, common law and equitable pleadings differed radically. Equity pleadings had been by bill and informal, always in English.[111] Bills must disclose *an equity* to relief. Common law pleadings were required to show *a cause of action* and were long written in Latin and spoken in law French. Because this common law pleading requirement was formal,

---

[110] Judicature Act 1873 (U.K.), ss. 3, 16, 24–25. See P. M. Hamlin and C. E. Baker, *Supreme Court of Judicature of the Province of New York, 1691–1704* (New York, NY: New-York Historical Society, 1959), vol. I, 54–57.

[111] Text after n. 9.

causes of action became differentiated into various rather fixed formulae which, since medieval times, 'were ... seen as defining the rights and remedies recognised by the common law, and thus as fixing the common law within an immutable formulary framework'.[112] The writs on which these forms of action were inscribed were abolished in 1832 and 1833. Most of the forms of action were abolished in 1852, with the rest seen off by the Judicature Acts.[113]

Although the old writs were largely replaced with a uniform initiating process for common law claims in 1832 and 1833, the uniformity established by the Judicature Acts is the more important here. A new procedure fusing elements of the old common law and equitable procedures was established. Under the Judicature procedure *all* civil cases, no matter the claim, were to begin by action[114] upon a writ of summons[115] adapted from the Chancery subpoena.[116] A statement of the nature of the claim made or of the relief or remedy required in the action must be endorsed on that writ.[117] Precision was not essential,[118] provided the writ disclose a cause of action.[119] The cause of action, an old common law idea, was injected with equitable liberality for the new system.

Because the new procedure was uniform it had to do work that the old common law cause of action had never done. Unless claims in equity, admiralty, probate and so forth were to be reshaped as common law claims, 'cause of action' in the new system required an extended meaning. It acquired this, applying to common law, equitable and other grounds of complaint.[120] Decisions after 1875 held that doctrines of law and equity were unaltered by this procedural change.[121] As to the old jurisdictions, the new cause of action was neutral: it is 'simply a factual situation the existence of which entitles one person to obtain from the court a remedy against another person'.[122]

---

[112] Baker, *I.E.L.H.*, 4th edn, 56.

[113] Common Law Procedure Act 1852 (U.K.), 15 & 16 Vict. c. 16, s. 41.

[114] Judicature Rules O. 1, r. 1.

[115] Judicature Rules O. 2, r. 1. See now the claim form which in England replaced the statement of claim in 1999: C.P.R. 1998 Pt 7 rr. 7.2, 7.4, Pt 16 r. 16.2.

[116] Baker, *I.E.L.H.*, 4th edn, 68.

[117] Judicature Rules O. 2, r. 1; Forms, App. (A), Part I Nos 1, 2, 4 (writs), Part II (indorsements). Sutton likened the statement of claim to the old common law bill: Sutton, *Personal Actions at Common Law*, 37.

[118] Judicature Rules O. 3, r. 2.

[119] Judicature Rules O. 28, rr. 1–2; Forms, App. (C), No. 28 (demurrer).

[120] A commentator said that 'action ... to say the least, is an awkward form' of name: W. D. Griffith, *The Supreme Court of Judicature Acts 1873 & 1875* (London: Stevens and Haynes, 1875), 127.

[121] *Salt* v. *Cooper* (1880) 16 Ch.D. 544, 549; *Joseph* v. *Lyons* (1884) 15 Q.B.D. 280, 285–86, 287. See *Kendall* v. *Hamilton* (1879) L.R. 4 App. Cas. 504, 516, 521, 534, 545.

The assimilation of equitable to common law claims nevertheless occurs. If equity were common law by another name, this might be unobjectionable. It would effect no legal change. But it effects legal change and makes problems. Often the assimilation is unconscious. Once an equitable obligation is recognised as founding a *cause* of action, the lawyer's mind tends to concentrate on the forms of action in the *ostensurus quare* writs which were remedied by damages, and the modern actions formerly sued through those writs. The conclusion then easily reached is that damages must be available for breach of equitable obligations.[123] Another tendency is to press equitable claims into the mould of common law claims. Equitable claims become assimilated to the narrower sense of cause of action abandoned or modified in 1875. Justice according to equitable principles is hampered.[124]

It is important to be clear as to the level on which these occurrences happen.

Common Law and Equitable Claims Compared

Consider some features of common law causes of action.

First, common law causes of action tend to be formulary even in a procedurally fused system. The more formulaic the action, the more the elements of common law causes of action can be stated in terms of specific facts. If a given fact exists, then that finding satisfies the first element of the cause of action. The pleading and proof in a case afterwards proceed to the second fact and element of the claim, thence to the third fact and element, and so forth. The facts that will satisfy each element are determined in advance.

Secondly, because each required fact and element is typically specific (not general), each element is satisfied independently of the preceding element and the next. The elements are mutually independent.

Thirdly, the elements of a cause of action generally form a single chain. Only that chain leads to success on the given cause of action.

---

[122] *Letang* v. *Cooper* [1965] 1 Q.B. 232, 242–43.

[123] P. G. Turner, 'Rudiments of the Equitable Remedy of Compensation for Breach of Confidence', in S. Degeling and J. N. E. Varuhas (eds), *Equitable Compensation and Disgorgement* (Oxford: Hart, 2017), 241–44.

[124] The process would also move in the opposite direction: the judge-made common law would be assimilated in parts to equity, reducing the clarity and efficiency typical of common law rules. See Publius [A. Hamilton], *Federalist*, No. 83, 395–96; Goldberg and Smith, Chapter 13; and A. Burrows, *The Law of Restitution*, 3rd edn (Oxford University Press, 2011), 132 (tracing rules).

Proof of a different chain leads to failure or, at best, the establishment of a different cause of action.

These features have outlasted the procedural system that generated them. Common law pleading had the end and object of producing an issue for decision by a jury. Pleading consisted of sequential moves, likened by *Bracton* to chess.[125] And each stage was defined to produce a question suitable for jury decision in an affirmative or a negative.[126] Thus, a claimant in trespass who demonstrates that the defendant entered upon certain land then needs to establish that he or she (the claimant) had the immediate right to the possession of that land. After establishing the defendant's entry, will the next element require the claimant to prove, say, the manner in which the defendant entered upon the land? It will not. Is proof of entry followed by fixed alternative elements that must be satisfied next? It is not. Nor is the next element a matter of judicial evaluation of how a loose principle applies in the circumstances of the case. Common law causes of action displaying these features are abundant.

Few equitable claims have the properties just described,[127] largely because equitable claims arise from the application of equitable principles rather than rules and because equity supplements rather than copies the common law.[128]

First, when claims depend on equitable principles they generally require proof of one or more states of affairs, not a series of simple facts. These states of affairs are found through evaluative conclusions of fact reached by equity judges in the peculiar circumstances of the case.

Secondly, whereas the pleading and proof of common law claims tends to proceed from one discrete element to the next, the elements of equitable claims often overlap. On common law claims the analysis always moves forwards; on equitable claims it can be necessary at the same time to consider the element next before or next after. To that extent, the elements are interdependent and overlap.

Thirdly, because equitable claims tend to require that some principle be infringed or engaged, the ways of proving that requirement are undefined and in principle unlimited. These features are recognisable in the informal fact-pleading that was always allowed in the Court of Chancery by proceedings on

---

[125] Baker, *I.E.L.H.*, 4th edn, 77.

[126] See Sutton, *Personal Actions at Common Law*, ch. 5; Baker, *I.E.L.H.*, 4th edn, 76–78.

[127] *The 'Juliana'* (1822) 2 Dods. 504, 521. On the unsuitability of classic equity matters to jury decision, see *Jenyns v. Public Curator (Q.)* (1953) 90 C.L.R. 113, 118–19.

[128] E.g., *James v. London and South Western Railway Co.* (1872) L.R. 7 Ex. 187, 195 (the Court of Chancery had no original jurisdiction to entertain a suit in respect of a personal injury).

bills, in judges' refusal to attempt to define such notions as equitable fraud[129] or what will show that relief at law is inadequate[130] and elsewhere.[131]

Other differences, too, are important. Common law relief is normally as of right, while equitable relief is not. This means that common law relief, fixed in form and extent, is meant to satisfy a pre-existing right. But equitable relief must often be worked out after the event: it may depend on a claimant's active involvement (e.g., by making elections) and that of the judge (e.g., by identifying the available forms of relief and deciding any terms on which those might be offered).[132] Common law questions and equity questions differ – without opposition to one another. Tightening the elements of many equitable claims to make them like common law claims will constrain a court to ignore many facts on which the application of equitable principles depends.

Relief from Forfeiture

A case of relief from forfeiture illustrates that artificial and harsh results tend to follow such tightening. *Çukurova Finance International Ltd* v. *Alfa Telecom Turkey Ltd*[133] was a novel application for relief. The plaintiff provided shares as collateral to secure the repayment of a loan, and sought equitable relief from their forfeiture after default. The forfeiture of the collateral was by 'appropriation', a statutory process by which the collateral vested absolutely in the creditor through the creditor's act – satisfying and extinguishing the secured obligation.

How might a court of equitable jurisdiction decide such a novel point?[134] According to conventional understanding, a claimant seeking relief from a forfeiture would look to established categories for means of relief from the consequences of his or her default. Classic situations are where a landlord determines a term by re-entry upon a tenant's default in payment of rent, or a contractual right to redeem is determined automatically under the terms of a mortgage instrument because a mortgagor defaults in repayment of a secured loan. Those alternative elements of a cause of action for relief from forfeiture

---

[129] *Allcard* v. *Skinner* (1887) 36 Ch. D. 145, 183; *National Westminster Bank plc* v. *Morgan* [1985] A.C. 686, 705; *Cavell U.S.A. Inc.* v. *Seaton Insurance Co.* [2009] 2 C.L.C. 991, [15]–[16], [29]; [2009] EWCA Civ 1363.

[130] *Loan Investment Corp. of Australasia* v. *Bonner* [1970] N.Z.L.R. 724, 741–42 (P.C.); *A.-G.* v. *Blake* [2001] 1 A.C. 268, 285.

[131] Also *Hospital Products Ltd* v. *United States Surgical Corp.* (1984) 156 C.L.R. 41, 68, 69–72, 102, 141–42.

[132] See R. Zakrzewski, *Remedies Reclassified* (Oxford University Press, 2005), ch. 6, 214–17.

[133] [2016] A.C. 923; [2013] UKPC2; [2013] UKPC 20; [2013] UKPC 25.

[134] For suggested guidelines, see *Meridien Airlie Beach Pty Ltd (in liq.)* v. *Karamist Pty Ltd* [2015] QCA 192, [58]–[60]; *Meagher, Gummow and Lehane*, 5th edn [18–270].

are determinate. Next the claimant must establish a ground for relief. Though relatively determinate,[135] this requirement is not exhaustively defined[136] and can be satisfied by several alternatives: that the forfeiture of collateral was intended merely to secure performance of covenants, or resulted from fraud practised by the defendant on the claimant, or resulted from accident that is the fault of neither party (and which conscience forbids the defendant to enjoy), or occurred through the claimant's mistake.[137] Once such a ground is established, the claimant must show that he or she can compensate the defendant. Payment of principal, interest and costs may suffice. Should compensation be possible, the court will consider the proper form of relief. The relief is not limited to financial loss. Specific relief can issue. The relevant evidence is correspondingly wide. Next, the claimant must be ready, willing and able to make the required compensation and resume the performance of his or her side of the relationship. Relief is not a strict right. Courts typically offer relief conditional on the claimant's undertaking to resume to perform his or her side of the bargain, providing the required compensation, and doing any other acts the court may require. Although the conditions on relief cannot be arbitrarily chosen, predicting them exactly is often impossible: they depend on the facts of the case.

In Çukurova, relief from forfeiture would have been suitable – on the ground that the forfeiture was merely to bolster the security for repayment – and conditions requiring the claimant to be ready, willing and able to repay the amount of principal due, plus interest at the applicable contract rate and costs, were suitable.[138] Relief from a statutory 'appropriation' was novel. But, applying classic Chancery equity, the Privy Council straightforwardly found the claimant entitled to claim relief from the forfeiture.[139] They refused to hold that the grounds of relief are confined to fixed categories of case. Since the case was within the principle that forfeiture should be available where the purpose of a forfeiture is merely to secure a collateral obligation, the novelty was no bar. Nor did it matter that the forfeiture related to personal property (company shares),

---

[135] Meagher, Gummow and Lehane, 5th edn, [18–250]–[18–280]. Although it misreads the speech of Lord Wilberforce in Shiloh Spinners Ltd v. Harding to say that the claimant must at this stage show that the forfeiture is 'unconscionable', such a reading would accentuate the difference between an equitable cause of action for relief from forfeiture and common law causes of action.

[136] Hannam v. South London Waterworks Co. (1816) 2 Mer. 61, 67.

[137] Shiloh Spinners Ltd v. Harding [1973] A.C. 691, 722–23.   [138] Ibid., 722.

[139] Çukurova Finance International Ltd v. Alfa Telecom Turkey Ltd (No. 3) [2016] A.C. 923.

even though land was supposedly once considered the only subject matter of this relief.[140]

However, the discussion in the case tried to squeeze a classic equitable claim – a modern-day *cause* of action – into a mould shaped to common law *forms* of action. The discussion assumed that the form of relief must be predetermined rather than decided in light of the facts of the case; that a court merely declares what equitable rules had predetermined; and that the relief was virtually a right. As understood by Lords Mance, Kerr and Clarke JJ.S.C., the claimant's submissions required the court to treat 'the contractual obligation to repay the debt with default interest *either* as running continuously despite the satisfaction of the debt . . . *or* as reviving retrospectively at some point during the process of affording relief'.[141] The former analysis, which deemed the form of relief fully predetermined, was rejected because it supposed the discharged debt 'continue[d] to run in a parallel equitable world despite its discharge'.[142] However, their Lordships rejected it, not because it wrongly supposed the form of relief was predetermined, but because the debt was absolutely discharged. They merely qualified the alternative analysis of retrospective reviver where 'strong countervailing considerations of equity' required departure from that ordinary predetermined position.[143] Lord Neuberger P.S.C. and Lord Sumption J.S.C. suggested that that exception concealed a wide judicial discretion,[144] but accepted the majority's premise: the substance of equitable relief from forfeiture is largely fixed, and the parties' entitlements and the relief available to them are predetermined. Equity only supplied a fiction that the parties' common law contract continued.

Fusion through the assimilation of equity to common law is often assumed to be costless for the common law and common law systems. The cost to equity is written off because equity is considered strongly dualist or as truly being common law under a different name. *Çukurova* suggests that the assimilation of equitable relief from forfeiture to common law ideas is costly – for the legal system, the common law specifically and for Chancery equity because the latter too has distinct properties and functions.

Çukurova complicates the common law of contracts. The assimilation adds to the common law a type of ghostly contract which somehow subsists after discharge according to common law rules. This constructive contract

---

[140] Ibid., [92]–[94].
[141] *Çukurova Finance International Ltd v. Alfa Telecom Turkey Ltd (No. 4)* [2016] A.C. 923, [11] (emphasis original).
[142] Ibid., [12].   [143] Ibid., [13].   [144] Ibid., [111]–[119], [180].

harbours uncertainty. For, in the exceptional cases allowed by Lords Mance, Kerr and Clarke JJ.S.C., the terms of the constructive contract cannot be known in advance. They thought the terms of the constructive contract would in those cases come from inanimate 'equity' rather than the voluntary acts of the parties or the judges, exercising an acknowledged discretion.

The cost to Chancery equity is unfairly to mystify it. The openly acknowledged judicial power to offer conditional equitable relief is anxiously subsumed into the idea of the constructive contract. Another cost is to alter Chancery equity's character and lessen its usefulness. The power to grant conditional relief has deliberately been undefined in traditional equity because definition would destroy it. Its object of ensuring reciprocal justice has been openly announced, the better to keep it under watch. The maxim 'those who seek equity must do equity' has applied, pointing to the technical equity that constrains judges to identify conditions 'which the known principles of a court of equity may make it proper to give'.[145] A crucial limit on equity's intervention in forfeiture cases is also overlooked. Unlike under a constructive contract, a party who seeks equitable relief is not forced to accept any conditions on which it is offered. The party can refuse the relief, in which case the parties' relations will be worked out under applicable common law and statute. When a party accepts a court's conditional offer of equitable relief from forfeiture, the contract henceforth governing the parties' relations *inter se* arises from an instrument into which the claimant voluntarily enters. Admittedly, the defendant is ordered to execute the instrument, but only where the court is satisfied that the relief will place the defendant and the claimant in the positions they would have occupied had the default and the forfeiture never taken place. *Çukurova* instead posits that the contract and its history are rewritten, and that the rewriting is done by the agency of 'equity' and imposed on the parties, willing or unwilling.

These doctrines and their corollaries would not appeal to the lawyer who inclines to prudence in the servicing of legal rules.

Cause of Action for Restitution

Knowingly or unknowingly, writers of legal literature can assimilate equity to law, remoulding modern equitable *causes* of action to resemble old *forms* of action. In England, writing on restitution seeks to assimilate

---

[145] *Colvin v. Hartwell* (1837) 5 Cl. & F. 484, 522–23; *Langman v. Handover* (1929) 43 C.L.R. 334, 348, 351.

'restitutionary' claims to an idealised common law cause of action with four elements: 'Was the defendant enriched? If so, Was he enriched at the plaintiff's expense? If so, Was there any factor calling for restitution? If so, Was there any reason why restitution should none the less be withheld?'[146] Though offered to re-organise existing legal decisions rather than to change the law,[147] such re-organising changes the law. Writers commit to bring equitable grounds of recovery within the four-question formula,[148] ensuring each element of the formula is articulated as simply and clearly as possible.[149] Principles are disfavoured as uncertain. Crystalline rules are prized. The gist of these exhortations is that equitable complaints should have the properties of common law claims, as described.[150] The open-textured interdependent elements characteristic of many equitable grounds of complaint should be replaced by independent elements tested by bright-line rules.[151] Relief should follow as of right. Relief should be predetermined, never worked out after the event in the knowledge of all that occurred. Matter not meeting these criteria – such as equitable relief on terms – is moved to the margins[152] or dropped.[153]

These imperatives proceed from monism: all private law rules should have the same qualities; Chancery equity is common law under alias. Ironically, while restitution literature prizes simplicity, the law becomes more complex when equitable principles are assimilated to the supposed common law restitution framework. The work of one indeterminate principle can be done only by larger numbers of simple clear rules, thus changing the law. Thus, in equity a party desiring rescission of a contract for undue influence must

---

[146] P. Birks, *An Introduction to the Law of Restitution* (Oxford University Press, 1990 reprint), 7, adopted undiluted in *Banque Financière de la Cité* v. *Parc (Battersea) Ltd* [1999] 1 A.C. 221, 227, 234.

[147] Birks, *Introduction*, 1; A. Burrows, *The Law of Restitution*, 3rd edn (Oxford University Press, 2011), 4. Contrast A. Burrows, *A Restatement of the English Law of Unjust Enrichment* (Oxford University Press, 2012), x (seeking 'the best interpretation of the present law. In some limited circumstances, this may clash with existing precedents') and see the comments on Birks's purpose in G. Virgo, *The Principles of the Law of Restitution*, 3rd edn (Oxford University Press, 2015), v–vi.

[148] Birks, *Introduction*, 39; Burrows, *The Law of Restitution*, 3rd edn, 25–26, 120–21.

[149] Birks, *Introduction*, chs 1–2, 74, 91, 102; Burrows, *The Law of Restitution*, 3rd edn, 15–16.

[150] Text to nn. 124–27.

[151] E.g., the novel distinction between tracing and claiming: P. Birks, 'The Necessity of a Unitary Law of Tracing', in R. Cranston (ed.), *Making Commercial Law: Essays in Honour of Roy Goode* (Oxford: Clarendon, 1997), 242, 243; L. Smith, *The Law of Tracing* (Oxford University Press, 1997), 6–24; *Foskett* v. *McKeown* [2001] 1 A.C. 102, 113, 128 (*obiter dicta*).

[152] Burrows, *The Law of Restitution*, 3rd edn, 20, 572; C. Mitchell and S. Watterson, *Subrogation: Law and Practice* (Oxford University Press, 2007), [7.120].

[153] Smith, *The Law of Tracing*.

generally prove the contract and entry into the contract under another's
undue influence, and – since those who seek equity must do equity – be
ready and willing to make whatever restitution is needed to return the defendant to its prior position. Each element is essential, and the elements are
interrelated: a claimant who (for example) will not or cannot return goods
received under the contract cannot obtain rescission, even if all other requirements are satisfied.[154] In contrast, English restitution writing generally considers the claimant automatically entitled to restitution of any sum paid, once
the contract and undue influence are shown. The claimant is freed of the
requirement to do equity when seeking it. Instead the defendant is given a
defence that the claimant cannot make 'counter-restitution'.[155] Counter-
restitution is defined without the open texture of traditional equitable consideration of whether restitution is possible. It is narrowed to the value of any
enrichment obtained by the claimant at the defendant's expense,[156] and the
impossibility of making counter-restitution is rejected[157] – contrary to judicial
decisions reflecting equitable practice.[158] Where ordinary equitable principles
require the matter to be evaluated by a human in the office of a judge,
counter-restitution is supposed to be mechanical. Undue influence thus loses
some of its open texture.

The effect on equitable personal liability for knowing receipt of trust property has been similar. On conventional equitable principles, a person who
receives trust property knowing that it derives from a breach of trust becomes
personally liable for receiving the property to his or her own use, since
the circumstances make the recipient an accounting party who, as such, is
liable to account as if an express trustee.[159] Liability for the value of the
property received is but one aspect of a general liability to account. Others
are the third party's liability to return the asset *in specie*, if possible, and a
potential liability to account for profits in the alternative to making restitution
of the property's value plus interest. When this cause of action is analysed

---

[154] D. O'Sullivan, S. Elliott and R. Zakrzewski, *The Law of Rescission*, 2nd edn (Oxford University Press, 2014), [15.44]–[15.60].

[155] Burrows, *The Law of Restitution*, 3rd edn, 187, 569–70 ('probably best regarded as a defence'; defined as requiring that the defendant have a counterclaim for the claimant's unjust enrich-ment at the defendant's expense; may be a 'general law ... set-off defence'); *Goff and Jones: Unjust Enrichment*, 9th edn, [31-02]–[31-05].

[156] Ibid., 570, 572.

[157] Ibid., 571–72; *Goff and Jones: Unjust Enrichment*, 9th edn, [31-02]–[31-05].

[158] *Hanson v. Keating* (1844) 4 Hare 1, 4–5. See O'Sullivan, Elliott and Zakrzewski, *The Law of Rescission*, 2nd edn, [15.47]–[15.49], [15.60].

[159] *Williams v. Central Bank of Nigeria* [2014] A.C. 1189, [9]; [2014] UKSC 10.

within the four-part restitutionary formula,[160] the receipt of property stands on its own as a liability arising strictly regardless of knowledge;[161] and the accounting liability is ignored,[162] even though it is the orthodox basis of liability and guides the decision of other questions: what elections the claimant has, whether personal or proprietary relief is available, and whether the liability among defendant assistants, recipients and express trustees is joint and several or several only.[163]

The potential effects of assimilating equitable claims to common law ideas (constrained by the old forms of action) are also evident from developments that may simply be mentioned: specifically, the notion that equitable relief via subrogation,[164] and tracing into 'negative assets'[165] should exist in respect of transfers of value as such – divorced from actual payment.[166] The countermeasures recently taken by the U.K. Supreme Court and the Privy Council in common law[167] and equitable[168] claims suggest that the prudent lawyer invoked earlier may also be persuaded that these effects of assimilating equity to the common law should not be wished for.

CONCLUSION

The most important aspect of fusion happened in the past in most common law jurisdictions possessing a living equity tradition. The results of the nineteenth-century legal reforms were to fuse the administration of common law and equity to allow them to be administered concurrently in a court under a uniform procedure and, in England, to abolish the old royal courts and

---

[160] E.g., Birks, *Introduction*, 394–95, 439–47; Lord Nicholls, 'Knowing Receipt: The Need for a New Landmark', in W. R. Cornish, R. Nolan, J. O'Sullivan and G. Virgo (eds), *Restitution: Past, Present and Future* (Oxford: Hart, 1998), ch. 15.

[161] Nicholls, 'Knowing Receipt: The Need for a New Landmark'.

[162] Birks, *Introduction*, 80–82.

[163] See e.g., *Eaves* v. *Hickson* (1861) 30 Beav. 136, 141–42; *Ultraframe (U.K.) Ltd* v. *Fielding* [2005] EWHC 1638 (Ch), [1600]–[1601]; *Williams* v. *Central Bank of Nigeria* [2015] A.C. 1189, [9].

[164] *Menelaou* v. *Bank of Cyprus plc* [2016] A.C. 176; [2015] UKSC 66.

[165] Ibid., 84, 96. As a 'negative' asset must be a 'quasi-asset', it is noticeable that Birks did not disapprove of this term as he did of 'quasi-contract', 'constructive trust', 'quasi-assignment' and others: at 22.

[166] See *Akita Holdings Ltd* v. *A.-G. (Turks and Caicos)* [2017] A.C. 590, [6]–[12]; [2017] UKPC 7 and Birks, *Introduction*, 7, 13 (money had and received).

[167] *International Trust Companies* v. *Revenue and Customs Commissioners* [2018] A.C. 275, [41]; [2017] UKSC 29.

[168] *D.D. Growth Premium 2X Fund* v. *R.M.F. Market Neutral Strategies (Master) Ltd* [2018] Bus L.R. 1595, [58]; [2017] UKPC 36 (knowing receipt of 'trust' property); *Swynson Ltd* v. *Lowick Rose L.L.P.* [2018] A.C. 313; [2017] UKSC 32 (equitable subrogation).

replace them with a new single Supreme Court of Judicature. The practical separation of the old courts, and the procedural pitfalls litigants encountered in their various systems, ceased as the source of injustice and inconvenience they had been. But the basic questions that the minds of the day had considered with regard to equity in a system of laws were carried forth. The relations of substantive common law and substantive equity were to continue as before, with equity prevailing at points where it and the common law truly conflicted. Thus, discussion of fusion (or merger or union) became paired with the question of how to account for equity in common law jurisdictions. Discussion of either soon leads to discussion of the other. The help lawyers have sought in physical metaphors in which law–equity relations are imagined in the terms of division,[169] seams in fabric[170] and watery streams[171] has proved limiting.[172] The reforms of the courts, court procedures and legal adminis-tration under the banner of fusion concerned more than equity and the common law: they concerned all sources of law and all the distinct courts that had administered them, as well as their various procedures. The larger questions about equity in modern common law systems can only be asked – and answers attempted – if those questions are first put in a wide perspective.

If all that points to questions beyond the scope of this book, it also says that fusion and equity theory concern issues that will not disappear. They are matters of perennial interest and significance. The surest guide for a lawyer who seeks to address the basic questions posed by fusion and the presence of Chancery equity in modern common law systems will be an attitude of insisting on an account of equity to which all the evidence lends itself, and no other. The essays in this book are offered to that end.

---

[169] *O'Neill* v. *Philips* [1999] 1 W.L.R. 1092, 1101.

[170] *A.I.B. Group (U.K.) Ltd* v. *Mark Redler & Co. Solicitors* [2015] A.C. 1503, [1]; [2014] UKSC 58.

[171] Ashburner, *Principles of Equity*, 2nd edn, 18; *United Scientific Holdings Ltd* v. *Burnley Borough Council* [1978] A.C. 904, 924–25.

[172] See *Felton* v. *Mulligan* (1971) 124 C.L.R. 367, 392.

PART I

Legal Systems and Legal Institutions

2

Equity

Notes on the American Reception

SAMUEL L. BRAY[*]

INTRODUCTION

The Earl of Oxford's Case[1] famously presents equity as a solution to the problem of exceptional cases. In an exceptional case, equity offers a moral reading of the law. In this moral reading – this appeal to *Conscience* – the chancellor could make a 'nice adjustment' to keep clever people from circumventing the law, from exploiting its inevitable gaps and ambiguities.[2] Below the surface, *The Earl of Oxford's Case* also shows another distinguishing trait of equity. Equity was willing to tell people what to do. The intricate history of this seventeenth-century case does not need to be recounted here,[3] but it should be noted that the defendants in equity, the master and bursar of Magdalene College, Cambridge, spent five weeks imprisoned in the Fleet for their refusal to submit to Chancery's jurisdiction.[4]

---

[*] I am grateful for comments from Will Baude, Nathan Chapman, Dennis Klimchuk, Andrew Kull, Mark Leeming, Paul Miller, Irit Samet, Henry Smith, David Waddilove and Stephen Yelderman, as well as the participants in a workshop at the University of Arizona. This chapter is dedicated to Andrew Kull, recalling with affection our many conversations about equity at the Crown and Anchor.

[1] *Earl of Oxford's Case* (1615) 1 Ch. Rep. 1, 6. For legal and political context, see Baker, 'The Common Lawyers and the Chancery: 1616'; for discussion, Ibbetson, 'A House Built on Sand'. Ibbetson's analysis is outstanding, but I find his conclusion unduly pessimistic. Where he sees incoherence, I see a demonstration that English equity developed within a place and time to serve particular needs instead of being deduced from abstract principles.

[2] The language of 'nice adjustment' comes from US Supreme Court cases such as *Weinberger v. Romero-Barcelo*, 456 U.S. 305, 312 (1982) and *Hecht Co v. Bowles*, 321 U.S. 321, 329 (1944). An analogous phrase in *The Earl of Oxford's Case* is 'proportionable Satisfaction'.

[3] See Ibbetson, 'The Earl of Oxford's Case'.

[4] Ibid., 19–20. See *Chadwick v. Janecka*, 312 F.3d 597 (3d Cir. 2002) (defendant imprisoned for contempt for eight years and counting).

In the centuries since *The Earl of Oxford's Case*, equity has been received in the United States. That reception is the topic of this chapter. 'Reception' is used not only in the technical sense of adoption of a body of law as binding but also in a looser sense: how has equity made its way in the United States? Particular attention is given to two ideas from equity: first, a small-scale moral reading of the law, analysed under the rubric of 'nice adjustment', and second a willingness of courts to give direct orders to private parties and government officials, analysed under the rubric of 'judicial command'. These two ideas have common premises and are subject to common criticisms. But their reception in the United States has been strikingly different. Nice adjustment has faded, while judicial command has been embraced with enthusiasm.

IDEA ONE: NICE ADJUSTMENT

In the *Nicomachean Ethics*, Aristotle famously describes 'the equitable' as a kind of justice: 'a correction of law where it is defective owing to its universality'.[5] The equitable is not an everyday justice, but is something exceptional and extraordinary. It responds, in the form of a 'correction', to a defect in the ordinary law. As other scholars have noted, Aristotle had a conception of equity that was not limited to the unanticipated, exceptional case.[6] Nevertheless, the point here is not about Aristotle's precise meaning as much as about how Aristotle has been understood by common lawyers – not Aristotle's equity, one might say, but Aristotelian equity.[7]

Now, once the problem of unanticipated circumstances is recognised what is a legal system to do about it? Several responses are possible. One is the rapid updating of the law. The legislature might be always in session, waiting expectantly for each new circumstance to emerge so the laws could be revised. Or the task might fall to courts, with judicial interpretation stretching the text to cover the new circumstance, and judicial recognition of new extensions of principles in new cases. Or stability and clarity might be prized above all else,

---

[5] Aristotle, *Nicomachean Ethics*, in *The Complete Works of Aristotle*, ed. by J. Barnes, trans. by W. D. Rosee, rev. by J. O. Urmson (Princeton University Press, 1984), bk V, ch. 10, 1795–96. See W. F. R. Hardie, *Aristotle's Ethical Theory*, 2nd edn (Oxford: Clarendon, 1980), 209–10; A. Beever, 'Aristotle on Equity, Law, and Justice' (2004) 10 Leg. Theory 33.

[6] See D. Klimchuk, 'Aristotle at the Foundations of the Law of Equity', in D. Klimchuk, I. Samet and H. E. Smith (eds), *Philosophical Foundations of the Law of Equity* (Oxford University Press, forthcoming).

[7] See Plucknett and Barton, *Doctor and Student*, 97. Roman and biblical sources are also important in the intellectual history of equity: M. Fortier, *The Culture of Equity in Restoration and Eighteenth-Century Britain and American* (Ashgate: Farnham, 2015), 6–7, 8–9.

with no concession made to the unanticipated circumstance. In principle, English equity offered a way to mitigate the danger that unscrupulous persons would take advantage of unanticipated circumstances. The law remained in place – the 'Law is the Law'[8] – but equity sidled up to the person trying to get around the law, trying to exploit the unanticipated circumstance, tapped his or her shoulder and said 'Don't you dare'. To the exploiter, what equity showed was rigour; to the one who would have suffered, it was mercy.[9]

In short, the English solution was a two-system model, with the common law system operating until a question needed to be routed over to the equity system, *without the results in the equity system immediately updating the law system*.[10] 'Immediately' is an important word. Over time, as the Chancellor saw a number of similar cases and resolved them the same way, one could identify the equitable rule.[11] In this sense, a predictable equity would in effect update the law (in a broad sense, comprehending both common law and equity). But equity's distinct operation – with separate institutions, personnel and principles, all self-consciously extraordinary – meant that there was something short of full consolidation. Equity might write in a law book, but as Maitland saw, what equity wrote was a 'gloss'.[12] Equity was the common law's marginalia.[13]

This is not the place for a thorough evaluation of the two-system model, but a comment on its basic rationality is needed for later discussion. A legal system cannot achieve substantial justice, and also be intelligible to the citizens who must live within its rules, if it *always* favours substance over form. Nor can a legal system achieve substantial justice, and also be worthy of praise from citizens, if it *always* favours form over substance. There must be some mixing

---

[8] W. H. Auden, 'Law, Like Love'. So Coke C.J.: 'It is better, saith the law, to suffer a mischief [i.e., an injustice] that is peculiar to one, than an inconvenience [i.e., a change in rule] that may prejudice many': 1 Inst. 97b; see *Waberly* v. *Cockeral* (1542) 1 Dyer 51.

[9] See Feldman and Smith, 'Behavioral Equity'. The four responses to an unanticipated circumstance mentioned in the text are in essence (a) legislation, (b) fiction, (c) do nothing and (d) equity. See H. S. Maine, *Ancient Law* (London: Murray, 1861), 25.

[10] See Smith, 'Fusing the Equitable Function'. Yet the equity system did eventually update the common law system. Sometimes it did so in points of detail (especially in the concurrent jurisdiction) and sometimes it did so by filling a large gap left by the law system (especially in the exclusive jurisdiction). See P. B. Miller, 'Equity as Supplemental Law', in Klimchuk, Samet and Smith, *Philosophical Foundations of the Law of Equity*.

[11] See W. H. D. Winder, 'Precedent in Equity' (1941) 57 L.Q.R. 245.

[12] Maitland, *Equity*, 18–19.

[13] This metaphor is consistent with Paul Miller's point that 'remedial equity might be an important driver of supplemental equity': Miller, 'Equity as Supplemental Law'. It is well-known that marginalia may, through the copying and recopying of manuscripts, move into the text itself.

or oscillating to achieve the cluster of goods that come from the law (including retribution for wrongs, clarity about legal consequences, freedom for individual action and the expression of a society's morality). In the two-system model of common law and equity, one system offered an initial resolution that would suffice for the vast majority of cases, while the other offered the potential for a different resolution of a few cases, a resolution that favoured substance over form. Although unplanned, the two systems were a clever response to the enduring need to join form and substance in the resolution of disputes.

One last point should be noted about the difference between English equity and Aristotelian equity. In Aristotelian equity the defect of the law does not arise from its insufficient correspondence with justice or prudence as such. Aristotelian equity is stepping into the shoes of the lawmaker and doing what he would have done. It is inhabiting the perspective of the actual lawmaker, but with knowledge of the unexpected case that has now arisen, not a better, higher, truer, wiser lawmaker.[14] By contrast, the English Chancellor was not appealing to the unimproved views of the legislature or the common law judges. He was explicitly appealing to moral considerations, to 'Conscience'.

Yet there were two significant limits on this invocation of conscience. First, it was not to be the idiosyncratic conscience of the Chancellor, but rather the king's conscience, the conscience of the realm, the public conscience, the conscience of a good Christian.[15] Second, the appeal to conscience was not a way of bending the arc of the law's development. Rather, it was case-specific, often small-bore, a nice adjustment to keep the law from bearing down too heavily on this particular plaintiff or defendant.[16]

IDEA TWO: JUDICIAL COMMAND

Another distinctive characteristic of equity was that judges would tell people what to do[17] – *exactly* what to do, on pain of imprisonment for contempt.

---

[14] This distinction between 'the actual lawmaker' and 'a better, higher, truer, wiser lawmaker' can be criticised as failing to take into account Aristotle's treatment of the equitable as a kind of justice: Klimchuk, 'Aristotle at the Foundations'. See R. A. Shiner, 'Aristotle's Theory of Equity' (1994) 27 Loyola LA L. Rev. 1245, 1259.

[15] E.g., Finch, 'Manual' and 'Prolegomena', 200 ('[T]he Lord Chancellor must order his conscience after the rules and grounds of the laws of this realm'). See further R. Hedlund, 'The Theological Foundations of Equity's Conscience' (2015) 4 O.J.L.R. 119; I. Samet, 'What Conscience Can Do for Equity' (2012) 3 Jurisprudence 13.

[16] E.g., *Marine Insurance Co.* v. *Hodgson*, 7 Cranch (11 U.S.) 332 (1813) (Marshall C.J.).

[17] For this point and its crisp formulation, I thank Andrew Kull.

It might seem obvious that a judge would issue personal commands, but at law it was not so. When awarding damages, whether in seventeenth-century London or twenty-first-century New London, Connecticut, it would not be the practice of a judge to order a defendant to pay them upon pain of contempt. Rather, the judge would say what must be done. The defendant might choose to pay up, willingly so to speak. Or, choosing not to, the defendant might find his property attached or his wages garnished (in US terminology). But the personal participation of the defendant was not required. Law made something happen, but it did not compel the defendant to do the work with his own hands.[18]

Equity was different. Its concept was that it would constrain, compel and even reform the corrupt conscience of the defendant. It had no problem telling people what to do. This difference can be clearly seen in the remedies awarded by the Chancellor, such as the injunction and accounting for profits. It can be seen in the *in personam* characteristic of equitable decrees. It can be seen in the enforcement of those decrees with contempt.

THE COMMON PREMISES AND CRITICISMS OF THESE IDEAS

There is much that unites nice adjustment and judicial command. In both, equity is seen as a response to the common law's defects. For nice adjustment, the defect is in the application of a crisply stated legal rule to a case where the rule produces a perverse result. For judicial command, the defect is in the manifestly superior efficiency that could be attained by controlling the defendant's behaviour, either with prohibitions or prescriptions. Both corrections of the law are presented as if they were not changes to the law itself: instead of amending the law, equity supplements it.[19]

Moreover, with both ideas equity is enmeshed to a significant degree in the factual particularity of cases. Nice adjustment is not presented as a change in the law's principles, but as one-off (or two-off, or three-off) correction of its application. If that correction were sustained through a series of cases, however, it would become a new principle of equity (and thus a principle of the

[18] It is true that courts of law would sometimes direct action, as with the prerogative writs. The acts required, however, were typically 'narrow and discrete, rather than open-ended and indeterminate' as is possible with equitable remedies: S. L. Bray, 'The System of Equitable Remedies' (2016) 63 UCLA L. Rev. 530, 559.

[19] One could say the chancellors amended the law in the way chancellors do, that is, as if supplementing it or controlling its use. Compare *James B. Beam Distilling Co.* v. *Georgia*, 501 U.S. 529, 549 (1991) (Scalia J. concurring in the judgment) (noting that judges make law, but 'they make it *as judges make it*, which is to say *as though* they were "finding" it').

'law', to use the term in a broader sense encompassing both equity and the common law). Judicial command requires a consideration of what is possible, and at what cost, for the person being given the command. It also requires the court to consider its own ability to oversee obedience, to ensure the success of the command. Thus the wisdom and even plausibility of a judicial command depend on the judge's view of the future. That is not true of damages, for example, where the impecuniosity of the defendant is not a standard consideration.

The factual particularity of both ideas – nice adjustment and judicial command – pushes equity towards a broad range of choice across a distribution of cases. The familiar term for this range of choice is *discretion*. Even in the United States, where knowledge of equity has faded, lawyers still know of the remark made by the most learned man in seventeenth-century England about 'the chancellor's foot'.[20] Yet equity is not unique in relying on discretionary standards; there are many parts of the law that include discretion for the judge or for the jury. Something else motivates the jeremiads about equitable discretion.

Here it is crucial to observe the sequence of arguments. The sequence is not from 'equity has discretion' to 'equity is dangerous'. Rather, the prior premise is 'equity corrects the law', and it is that power to correct the law that becomes dangerous when allied with discretion. One could hypothetically posit equity as having *less* discretion than law, and the danger from equity's discretion would remain: as long as equity can correct the law and there is discretion in equity, then someone – the chancellor – has a discretionary power to correct the law. That is the source of the hopes and fears about equity.

EQUITY IN THE UNITED STATES

Equity was controversial at the founding of the United States.[21] The US Constitution, as proposed to the People for ratification, granted to the federal

[20] E.g., *United States* v. *Russell*, 411 U.S. 423, 435 (1973) ('[T]he defense of entrapment ... was not intended to give the federal judiciary a "chancellor's foot" veto over law enforcement practices of which it did not approve'.); J. C. Yoo, 'Who Measures the Chancellor's Foot? The Inherent Remedial Authority of the Federal Courts' (1996) 84 Cal. L. Rev. 1121. On Selden's remark and references to it in Canada, see D. R. Klinck and L. Mirella, 'Tracing the Imprint of the Chancellor's Foot in Contemporary Canadian Judicial Discourse' (1998) 13 Can. J.L. & Soc'y 63.

[21] This was understandable given the experience of equity in the American colonies: S. N. Katz, 'The Politics of Law in Colonial America: Controversies over Chancery Courts and Equity Law

judiciary the power to decide 'all Cases, in Law and Equity'. But critics argued that equity would be unusually dangerous in the new nation. One pamphleteer, writing under the name 'Federal Farmer', called it 'a very dangerous thing to vest in the same judge power to decide on the law, and also general powers in equity; for if the law restrain him, he is only to step into his shoes of equity, and give what judgment his reason or opinion may dictate'.[22] A leading supporter of the proposed Constitution, Alexander Hamilton, emphasised the value of equity as a separate mode of adjudication. For him, 'The great and primary use of a court of equity is to give relief *in extraordinary cases*, which are exceptions to general rules. To unite the jurisdiction of such cases with the ordinary jurisdiction must have a tendency to unsettle the general rules and to subject every case that arises to a *special* determination'.[23] Hamilton argued that giving the federal courts distinct legal and equitable jurisdictions would secure the benefits of equity for exceptional or complex cases without sacrificing the complementary benefits of 'general rules' and 'trials by jury'.[24]

The dispute over whether the federal courts could have equitable powers was decided by the ratification of the US Constitution.[25] Then, after ratification, the first Congress gave the federal courts jurisdiction over 'all suits … in equity'.[26] That grant of jurisdiction remains, and it is the basis today for equitable decisions and remedies in the federal courts. The Supreme Court has often reiterated that 'the "jurisdiction" … conferred' by this statute 'is an authority to administer in equity suits the principles of the system of judicial remedies which had been devised and was being administered by the English Court of Chancery at the time of the separation of the two countries'.[27]

in the Eighteenth Century', in D. Fleming and B. Bailyn (eds), *Law in American History* (Cambridge, MA: Harvard University Press, 1971), vol. 5, 257, 257–84. On the reception of equity in English colonies, see B. H. McPherson, 'How Equity Reached the Colonies' (2005) 5 Q.U.T.L.J. 108.

[22] 'Federal Farmer No. 3' (10 October 1787), in H. J. Storing (ed.), *The Complete Anti-Federalist* (Chicago: University of Chicago Press, 1981), vol. 2, 244. Federal Farmer added another concern: 'we have no precedents in this country, as yet, to regulate the divisions in equity as in Great Britain; equity, therefore, in the supreme court for many years will be mere discretion': ibid.

[23] A. Hamilton, 'The Federalist No. 83', in J. E. Cooke (ed.), *The Federalist* (Middletown, CT: Wesleyan University Press, 1961), 569.

[24] Ibid.   [25] US Constitution, Art. III.   [26] Judiciary Act 1789, § 11, 1 Stat. 78.

[27] *Grupo Mexicano de Desarrollo S.A. v. Alliance Bond Fund Inc.*, 527 U.S. 308, 318 (1999); see also *Gordon v. Washington*, 295 U.S. 30, 36 (1935); *Robinson v. Campbell*, 3 Wheat. (16 U.S.) 212, 221–23 (1818); P. T. Gillen, 'Preliminary Injunctive Relief against Governmental Defendants: Trustworthy Shield or Sword of Damocles?' (2016) 8 Drexel L. Rev. 269, 284–87. Justice

It is true that there has been a partial fusion of law and equity. In most of the states, there either were no separate equity courts or they have been fully merged with the law courts.[28] Until 1938 each federal court had a law 'side' and an equity 'side', but with the coming of the Federal Rules of Civil Procedure, the two sides were merged. Legal and equitable procedures were combined.

Nevertheless, it is easy to overstate the legal effect of these kinds of partial merger. The adoption of the Federal Rules of Civil Procedure had no effect on the equitable jurisdiction of the federal courts.[29] Moreover, US courts, both federal and state, continue to make sharp distinctions between legal and equitable remedies.[30] Legal claims and equitable claims are distinguished for the Seventh Amendment civil jury trial right,[31] and for equitable defences such as laches.[32] And when American courts perceive a question to be equitable, they continue to look for guidance to Story, Pomeroy and other American treatises on equity.[33] Thus, despite the merger of institutions and procedures, looking strictly at legal authority, one would be tempted to conclude that the state of equity is strong in the United States.

A quite different prospect appears if one looks at the law schools, the nurseries of the profession. Equity has not been offered as a course in most American law schools since the 1960s. The basic terminology and conceptual content of equity are unfamiliar to generations of students.[34] Decades ago Zechariah Chafee, Jr, observed that much of the content of equity was being

---

Story made the same point about Article III of the US Constitution: J. Story, *Commentaries on Equity Jurisprudence* (Boston: Hilliard, Gray & Co., 1836), vol. 1, 64–65.

[28] Bray, 'System of Equitable Remedies', 538. For an exemplary particular study, see Funk, 'Equity without Chancery'. Generally, see Getzler, 'Patterns of Fusion'.

[29] *Stainback v. Mo Hock Ke Lok Po*, 336 U.S. 368, 383 n. 26 (1949): 'Notwithstanding the fusion of law and equity by the Rules of Civil Procedure, the substantive principles of Courts of Chancery remain unaffected.'

[30] See Bray, 'System of Equitable Remedies'; S. L. Bray, 'The Supreme Court and the New Equity' (2015) 68 Vand. L. Rev. 997. More sceptically, see D. Laycock, *The Death of the Irreparable Injury Rule* (Oxford University Press, 1991).

[31] E.g., *City of Monterey v. Del Monte Dunes at Monterey Ltd*, 526 U.S. 687, 707–11 (1999).

[32] E.g., *S.C.A. Hygiene Products Aktiebolag v. First Quality Baby Products L.L.C.*, 137 S.Ct. 954 (2017); *Petrella v. Metro-Goldwyn-Mayer Inc.*, 572 U.S. 663 (2014).

[33] See Bray, 'The Supreme Court and the New Equity', 1014–15. On the thought of Kent and Story, see Kessler, *Inventing American Exceptionalism*; on that of Pomeroy, see D. M. Rabban, *Law's History: American Legal Thought and the Transatlantic Turn to History* (Cambridge University Press, 2013), 32–35.

[34] As one court asked rhetorically and discouragingly, 'How many law students have a basic understanding of the genesis and nature of courts of equity?': *Federal Housing Finance Agency v. Nomura Holding America Inc.*, 873 F.3d 85, 157 n. 53 (2d Cir. 2017).

parcelled up among other fields,[35] and the trend has continued: trust and confidence to fiduciary law and tort law, undue influence to contract, the equity of redemption to secured transactions, personal incapacity to family law, class actions and equitable discovery to civil procedure, constructive trust to restitution, injunctions to remedies. If all of these adverse possessions were allowed, how much would be left?

Yet neither of these perspectives takes in the whole. The course of equity in the United States is varied. Some of the equitable inheritance has fallen into desuetude, while some has been developed with almost manic enthusiasm. One has only to contrast equity's ideas of nice adjustment and judicial command.

On the one hand, American lawyers and judges have almost entirely lost the sense of equity as an alternative and exceptional mode of decision-making. A striking example of this, for which I am indebted to Andrew Kull, is *In re Motors Liquidation Co.*[36] The case was provoked by the bankruptcy of General Motors, and it involved perhaps the single most costly mistake ever made by a paralegal. General Motors was paying off a loan from a syndicate of lenders represented by J. P. Morgan, and the security interests for the loan were being terminated. In listing the security interests to be terminated, a paralegal mistakenly included the security interest for an entirely unrelated loan from another syndicate of lenders, also represented by J. P. Morgan, also made to General Motors – a loan for $1.5 billion. None of the lawyers who reviewed the documents caught the mistake. Then, once General Motors went bankrupt, the mistakenly terminated security interest was enormously significant: with respect to that $1.5 billion, would the lenders be secured or unsecured creditors? What is relevant here is the ground that J. P. Morgan decided to stand on. Its lawyers – some of the most elite lawyers in the United States – argued that J. P. Morgan had not 'authorised' the filing of the mistaken termination statement by outside counsel. The argument went nowhere, as it deserved. What is striking is that none of the elite lawyers representing J. P. Morgan invoked equity and its concern for substance rather than form.[37] Nor did the Second Circuit Court of Appeals. Nor did the Delaware Supreme Court, when a question about 'authorisation' was certified

---

35 Z. Chafee, Jr, *Cases on Equitable Remedies* (Cambridge, MA: priv. pub., 1938), v: 'Equity in American law schools seems to be suffering the fate of the Austrian Empire. One part after another has been split off to take on an independent existence.'

36 *In re Motors Liquidation Co.*, 777 F.3d 100 (2d Cir. 2015).

37 The Uniform Commercial Code indicates that its provisions are to be supplemented by 'the principles of law and equity': § 1-103(b); see also ibid. at § 9-328 cmt 8.

to it.[38] A few unwitting keystrokes wiped out the security interest for a $1.5 billion loan, and some of the leading lawyers and judges in the United States decided the question strictly with respect to form. Among the possible equitable responses that were neglected were reformation or rectification (of the termination statement) or cancellation (of the termination). But whether the lawyers' choice was due to ignorance of equity or to their calculated assessment of what would persuade a judge in the United States today, the effect is the same: the disappearance of classic equitable arguments.

On the other hand, American lawyers and judges have embraced with general enthusiasm the idea of judicial command.[39] Over the last century, Americans have come to expect that judges will have the last word in great public controversies, that what judges say will be obeyed by all parties, and that judges may legitimately prescribe in the minutest detail how states and cities and private businesses should operate. Those who lose in the rough and tumble of politics now routinely seek another decision from the courts, and when the courts render that decision, most elected officials will voice their criticisms only *sotto voce*.[40]

It is easy to miss this point if one is distracted by the debate over what is called a 'structural injunction'. This is an American innovation by which a court in effect takes over the management of a school district, a prison or a hospital. The conventional narrative in US legal scholarship is about a rise and fall, with the rise of the structural injunction in the 1960s and early 1970s and its slow fade ever since.[41] Yet structural injunctions, which are anomalous in the history of equity, are only the most extreme example of the idea of

[38] The Delaware judges were certainly familiar with equity: the Chief Justice writing the opinion was a former Chancellor of the state's Court of Chancery, and a Vice Chancellor was sitting by designation. Yet they batted away the idea of an equitable exception: *Official Committee of Unsecured Creditors of Motors Liquidation Co.* v. *J.P. Morgan Chase Bank N.A.*, 103 A.3d 1010, 1010 n.21 (Del. 2014).

[39] There have always been dissenters. Justice Brandeis, describing the 'storms of protest' against labour injunctions, cited five different law review articles with the title 'Government by Injunction': *Truax* v. *Corrigan*, 257 U.S. 312, 367 n. 34 (1921) (Brandeis J., dissenting).

[40] The current president of the United States is considered remarkable for his criticism of the judiciary, but questions of finesse aside, what makes his criticisms stand out is a marked decline in public officials criticising judicial decisions. For most of US history, there was not an easy equation of judicial opinions with 'the law of the land': L. Kramer, *The People Themselves: Popular Constitutionalism and Judicial Review* (Oxford University Press, 2005).

[41] The literature on structural injunctions is voluminous. Places to begin are O. M. Fiss, *The Civil Rights Injunction* (Bloomington, IN: Indiana University Press, 1978); G. L. McDowell, *Equity and the Constitution: The Supreme Court, Equitable Relief, and Public Policy* (University of Chicago Press, 1982).

judicial command. Even when courts do not issue structural injunctions, the depth and breadth of their commands is astonishing.

One need only look to the lawsuits against the federal government late in the Obama administration and early in the Trump administration.[42] In case after case, states and private parties who lost in the political branches sought injunctions that would block the enforcement of a federal regulation or order. In case after case – having carefully selected a friendly trial court and friendly reviewing court – the litigants won. In case after case, the court enjoined the federal government from enforcing the regulation or order against anyone, not just against the plaintiffs. Within living memory it would have been unthinkable for a single district judge, deciding a single case, to command the entire federal government not to do something.[43] Now it is routine.

EXPLAINING THE DIVERGENCE

The reasons are complex for why these two ideas have had such different careers in the United States. In this country, there has been a general deterioration of equity, in part due to a loss of the conditions under which equity could be trusted to correct the law and in part due to a loss of knowledge in the legal profession. That deterioration is sufficient to explain the neglect of nice adjustment. But, for America's enthusiastic embrace of judicial command the explanation lies elsewhere: in changing conceptions of the judiciary's role and in the disrepute of other branches of the federal government.

The place to begin is the decline of equity more generally in the United States. Equity has always had its critics, but they never succeeded in killing it. It was too useful. But the critics were, in one sense, right. A discretionary power to correct the law *is* dangerous. What the early and middle modern critics missed, however, were the conditions that made it tolerable for this power to exist.

One was the distinctiveness of equity – a different court, a different terminology, a different set of powers and constraints and at times a different bar. That distinctiveness let equity have an appearance of being compartmentalised; what happened in equity stayed in equity. That was not wholly true,

---

[42] See S. L. Bray, 'Multiple Chancellors: Reforming the National Injunction' (2017) 131 Harv. L. Rev. 417; M. T. Morley, 'De Facto Class Actions? Plaintiff- and Defendant-Oriented Injunctions in Voting Rights, Election Law, and Other Constitutional Cases' (2016) 39 Harv J.L. & Pub. Pol'y 487; Z. Siddique, 'Nationwide Injunctions' (2017) 117 Colum. L. Rev. 2095.

[43] Bray, 'Multiple Chancellors', 428–37.

because equity and law would freely borrow good ideas from each other.[44] But though it was permeable, there was a barrier; equity was distinct even if the distinction was not as absolute as it was professed to be.[45] It was easier to accept 'nice adjustment' so long as we understood it was special.

Another condition was the numerous doctrines announcing what equity would not do. Equity will not protect personal rights that do not touch rights of property.[46] Equity will not protect political rights.[47] Equity will not remove a public officer.[48] Equity will not enjoin a crime.[49] Equity will not enjoin a criminal prosecution.[50] And so on. With these 'equity will not' doctrines, equity embraced a rhetoric of humility as well as a rhetoric of righteousness.

Under these conditions of compartmentalisation and constraint it was easier to trust equity to correct the law. These conditions let equity be the anti-formalist element in a formalist system, a 'safety valve' that released the pressure on what would otherwise have been brittle and rigid.[51] In this way, we can see that equity can support and add resilience to a larger legal system; the relationship of equity and the rule of law need not be hostile as is sometimes assumed.

But in the United States these conditions have disappeared. As noted previously, there has been a general merger of legal and equitable institutions and procedure. There is diminished use of equitable terminology in areas of substantive law. Influential scholars have explicitly rejected the idea that equitable jurisdiction is in any way extraordinary.[52] The idea that law could

---

[44] See Simpson, *History of Contract*, 280 ('[T]hough the doctrinal proposition is that equity follows the law, historically the tendency has frequently been the reverse.'). For a twenty-first-century American lawyer the temptation is to call the compartmentalisation of equity a 'fiction', though this is an instance of using a hammer because one lacks a plenitude of tools.

[45] See J. P. Dawson, 'Coke and Ellesmere Disinterred: The Attack on the Chancery in 1616' (1941) 36 Ill. L. Rev. 127, 148 (noting the 'bipartition' in arguments made by lawyers when they were in Chancery and at law in the late sixteenth century).

[46] *Angelus v. Sullivan*, 246 F. 54, 64 (2d Cir. 1917). See *Weinberger v. Romero-Barcelo*, 456 U.S. 305, 312 (1982).

[47] E.g., *Rockefeller v. Hogue*, 246 Ark. 712, 721–24 (1969) (Fogelman J. concurring); see also H. L. McClintock, *Handbook of the Principles of Equity*, 2nd edn (St Paul, MN: West, 1948), 451.

[48] *In re Sawyer*, 124 U.S. 200, 210 (1888). See *Hynes v. Grimes Packing Co.*, 337 U.S. 86, 98–99 (1949).

[49] E.g., *A.-G. v. Utica Insurance Co.*, 2 Johns. Ch. 370, 378 (N.Y. Ch. 1817). For discussion of the limits on injunctions against crimes and criminal prosecutions in one American jurisdiction (Arkansas), see H. W. Brill, 'Equity and the Criminal Law' 2000 Ark. L. Notes 1.

[50] E.g., *Paulk v. City of Sycamore*, 104 Ga. 24 (1898).

[51] This metaphor is from H. E. Smith, 'Why Fiduciary Law Is Equitable', in A. S. Gold and P. B. Miller (eds), *Philosophical Foundations of Fiduciary Law* (Oxford University Press, 2014), ch. 13

[52] Laycock, 'Triumph of Equity'.

be 'found' was also widely scorned;[53] the spirit of *Erie*[54] is inhospitable for equity. Also striking has been the steady disappearance of the stated constraints on what equity would do. Again scholars cheered the erosion of equity's levees.[55] Given the disappearance of the conditions that made it possible to trust equity to correct the law, it is reasonable to ask whether this function of equity can even be legitimate in a constitutional system that distinguishes the legislative power from the judicial.

Another part of the story is sociological: it is about the loss of knowledge in the profession. In 1938, the Federal Rules of Civil Procedure merged the legal and equitable procedures used in federal courts,[56] and that procedural merger seems to have contributed to equity's decline as a separate subject of professional concern. 'The merger of law and equity practice led the profession, after about a generation, to the practical conclusion that equitable doctrine could be ignored.'[57] Meanwhile, in law schools, the Equity course disappeared from the curriculum, with only parts of it being incorporated into the new Remedies course.[58]

These points explain the decline of nice adjustment, but they do not explain the superabundance of judicial command. What has accompanied the rise and rise of the judicial command idea is a change in what courts are expected to do. The traditional understanding in the United States is that courts decide cases between litigants.[59] According to this understanding, judges might issue commands to those litigants (including injunctions), but they were constrained by doctrines and habits of reticence, as described earlier, and their commands were directed only to the relationship of the parties.[60] Much of the black letter law is still consistent with the traditional conception of the courts. The rival conception, beginning in the middle of the twentieth century, casts the courts not primarily as case-deciders but as

[53] See generally S. E. Sachs, 'Finding Law' (2019) 107 Cal. L. Rev. 527.
[54] *Erie Railroad Co.* v. *Tompkins*, 204 U.S. 64 (1938).
[55] E.g., R. Pound, 'Equitable Relief against Defamation and Injuries to Personality' (1916) 29 Harv. L. Rev. 640, 641.
[56] The conventional view is that the Rules chose equity over the common law: S. N. Subrin, 'How Equity Conquered Common Law: The Federal Rules of Civil Procedure in Historical Perspective' (1987) 135 U. Pa L. Rev. 909. With respect to discovery, however, the better view is that the Rules combined the powers of the common law and of equity without sufficient attention to the limits in either system: McMahon, Chapter 12.
[57] A. Kull, 'The Simplification of Private Law' (2001) 51 J. Leg. Educ. 284, 290.
[58] D. Laycock, 'How Remedies Became a Field: A History' (2008) 27 Rev. Litig. 161.
[59] A. de Tocqueville, *Democracy in America*, tr. H. Reeve (London: Saunders & Otley, 1835), vol. 1, 135–44; *Frothingham* v. *Mellon*, 262 U.S. 447, 488–89 (1923).
[60] J. Harrison, 'Severability, Remedies, and Constitutional Adjudication' (2014) 83 Geo. Wash. L. Rev. 56, 85.

law-declarers and even law-makers.[61] Courts that subscribe to this newer conception will be more willing to see themselves as resolving great national questions, they will be quicker on the trigger with issuing commands and they will be more likely to issue broad commands – such as a single district court's national injunction.

In addition, with respect to the commands of the federal courts, it must be admitted that the other branches of the national government do not elicit the respect they used to. One American political scientist, Keith Whittington, wrote a review of a book about constitutional deliberation in Congress, a review to which he gave the title 'James Madison Has Left the Building'.[62] That could be said of more than one building on Pennsylvania Avenue. If the legislative and executive branches were able to inspire respect from American citizens and to articulate with vigour the powers and constraints of the US Constitution – the Constitution that the People themselves adopted – then perhaps there would be some moderation of judicial command. Until then, judges are able to fill the void.[63]

THE FUTURE AND THE PAST

What lies ahead for equity in the United States is not easy to predict. As the American baseball player Yogi Berra said, 'It's tough to make predictions, especially about the future.' Nor is it easy to say what lessons should be drawn from the American experience with equity. One way to join prediction of the future with assessment of the past is to ask which of our existing beliefs about law should be revised in light of the American experience of equity. Here are several possibilities:

1. Professional knowledge matters more than we thought, and what the law says matters less than we thought.[64] There have been huge changes in the American *practice* with respect to these two ideas from equity, even though there has been essentially no change in relevant legal authority.

---

[61] H. P. Monaghan, 'Constitutional Adjudication: The Who and When' (1973) 82 Yale L.J. 1363, 1365–71.
[62] K. E. Whittington, 'James Madison Has Left the Building' (2005) 72 U. Chi. L. Rev. 1137, 1139.
[63] Whether they in fact do so depends on the relationship between judges and administrative agencies.
[64] A. W. B. Simpson, 'The Common Law and Legal Theory', in A. W. B. Simpson (ed.), *Oxford Essays in Jurisprudence, 2nd Series* (Oxford: Clarendon, 1973); J. H. Baker, *The Law's Two Bodies* (Oxford University Press, 2001).

2. Professional knowledge is more fragile than we thought, and more dependent than we thought on what is taught by the law schools and other institutions that transmit legal knowledge.

3. There was once a vigorous argument among legal writers about whether equity needed to be special in order to be useful. On one side, some argued that getting rid of equity's sense of separateness would bring its demise. On the other side, some said that was ridiculous: equity could offer its gifts to the legal system without being considered something special or distinctive. Now we know who was right. Step by step, the decline of equity's distinctiveness coincided with a decline in the knowledge and appreciation of equity.

Relatedly, there may be an implication regarding the efforts to pare equity down to its unique essentials.[65] If equity is to make a differentiated contribution to the law, it might need a certain scale, along with ample markers of distinctiveness. Perhaps it is only a larger, woollier equity that can fend off the predators.

What lies ahead, and what lessons should be learned from what lies behind, depend on the knowledge of equity among future generations of American lawyers. If that knowledge continues to decay, then by the end of this century in the United States an analysis of equity may seem as quaint as an analysis of mortmain. But if the knowledge of equity grows, that knowledge can be used: all of the legal authorities that make equity relevant are still there, waiting to be picked up by an enterprising lawyer.

---

[65] E.g., Burrows, 'We Do This at Common Law'. See K. H. York, Book Review (1974) 7 Loy. LA L. Rev. 394, 395–96, 400–1, speaking of equity's 'undistributable core'.

3

The Union of Law and Equity

The United States, 1800–1938

KELLEN FUNK

INTRODUCTION

Writing to the *Albany Law Review* in 1878, the renowned trial lawyer, codifier and New York law reformer David Dudley Field succinctly if unwittingly highlighted the ambiguities of law and equity in the United States. 'Fusion of law and equity is an expression common in England, though little used in this country', he explained. 'We express the same general idea by the phrase, union of legal and equitable remedies.'[1] Indeed, American commentators since the time of Joseph Story (an Associate Justice of the United States Supreme Court and professor of law at Harvard) had discussed the union of law and equity in ways resonant of the more famous Union formed by America's federated constitutional system. By vesting legal and equitable jurisdiction in the same judges, the federal courts of the United States had proven that an institutional union of law and equity was workable; but like the States in the Union, federal law and equity remained jurisdictionally and operationally distinct. The same federal judge could sit 'at law' or 'in equity', but not at the same time, and a case framed in the wrong posture or set on the wrong calendar would be dismissed with costs.[2] Yet while the Constitution's 'more perfect Union' may have left its component States distinct and intact, fusionists like Field insisted that 'the perfect union of law and equity' required, 'to express differently the same idea[,] ... the complete obliteration of every distinction between them'.[3]

---

[1] D. D. Field, 'Law and Equity', in A. P. Sprague (ed.), *Speeches, Arguments, and Miscellaneous Papers of David Dudley Field* (New York, NY: Appleton & Co., 1884), vol. 1, 578.
[2] See J. Story, *Commentaries on Equity Jurisprudence, as Administered in England and America* (Boston, MA: Hilliard, Gray & Co., 1838), vol. 1, 35.
[3] Field, 'Law and Equity', 578.

Field made his proposal sensible to practitioners by subtly shifting his terms: from 'fusion of law and equity' to 'union of legal and equitable *remedies*'. To Field and other American fusionists, there was no difference between the two expressions. Law and equity were perceived to be simply two sets of remedies, with no natural or necessary relationship between remedies and substantive rules or doctrines. The relationship between rights and remedies, the modes of reasoning about rights and the mechanisms for vindicating rights between the two systems were seen to be, if not already the same, at least amenable to assimilation: legal doctrine (one need not say whether it was legal or equitable) offered substantive *rules*, while a trans-substantive *procedure* navigated the practitioner to an open menu of remedies. Convinced of this view, fusionists appeared perplexed by their adversaries' contention that law and equity were traditions in which rights, remedies and the processes that linked them were complexly interwoven and might inhere – to use a ubiquitous phrase from this era – in 'the nature of things'.[4]

This chapter sketches a history of the American debates and tensions over the fusion of law and equity during the critical era from the drafting of Field's Code of Procedure in New York (mandated by the state's 1846 constitution) to the promulgation of the Federal Rules of Civil Procedure in 1938. Depending on the year, the United States comprised some forty distinct jurisdictions, each of which came up with different institutional arrangements of law and equity. Scholarship to date has largely ignored the history of fusion in the states after the colonial era and paid scant more attention to the topic at the federal level. A single chapter can provide only a cursory treatment of these many topics. While gesturing to developments in several jurisdictions, this essay focuses on lawyers' debates of fusion in mid-nineteenth century New York and the operation of New York's fusion in actual practice in the 1870s. I conclude that Field's view of fusion has become the dominant one in America, and his aim to replace the distinction between law and equity with a distinction between 'substance' and 'procedure' has been largely successful – in theory. In practice, the distinct traditions of law and equity continue to meaningfully structure day-to-day legal reasoning about remedies, not just in the special case of the right to jury trial, but in myriad other ways.

---

[4] On this oppositional view to fusion, see S. Warren, *A Popular and Practical Introduction to Law Studies* (New York, NY: Appleton & Co., 1846), 197–99.

CHAPTERS OF ERIE: A CASE OF LAW AND EQUITY

The most famous photographic image of Field is Matthew Brady's, made
around the time of Field's *Albany Law Journal* essay, which depicts the future
president of the American Bar Association as a dignified and elderly statesman
of the bar.[5] At exactly the same time, quite a different image of Field was in
circulation. The political cartoonist Thomas Nast despised Field. Throughout
the 1870s, Nast depicted Field binding Justice in procedural red tape or
standing guard as a lion over his clients' wealth. In Nast's final illustration of
Field in early 1878, the Devil himself visits the brooding lawyer's office,
seeking to retain Field's famous services.[6] Nast saw Field not as a tireless
reformer and codifier but rather as the chief lieutenant of a legal corps who
exploited technicalities to exonerate and protect the corrupt leaders of an
especially corrupt age. Field first earned the disdain of Nast and other Republican municipal reformers in the late 1860s when he and his partner Thomas
Shearman became lead counsel to the notorious robber barons Jim Fisk and
Jay Gould.[7]

After the Civil War, American railroads became massive financial assets,
offering their owners and managers abundant opportunities for profit and
plunder. Although Fisk and Gould liked to call their acquisitions 'raids', they
excelled in forming teams of attorneys who kept their investments within legal
bounds – stopping just short of fraud while clandestinely buying up shares or
the power to vote their proxies, and seeing their allies become court-appointed
'receivers' over rail lines mired in bankruptcy or litigation. With Field's help,
Fisk and Gould wrested control of the Erie Railroad from Cornelius Vanderbilt in what Charles Francis Adams dubbed the 'Erie War' in 1868.[8]

---

[5] Available at Library of Congress Prints and Photographs Division, LC-DIG-cwpbh-05048,
     www.loc.gov/pictures/item/brh2003002394/PP/.
[6] For a presentation and description of Nast's cartoons of Field, see R. L. Lerner, 'Thomas Nast's
     Crusading Legal Cartoons' (2011) Green Bag Almanac 59.
[7] On Field's corporate clients and career, see D. Van Ee, 'David Dudley Field and the
     Reconstruction of the Law' (Ph.D. Dissertation, Johns Hopkins University, 1974).
[8] C. F. Adams and H. Adams, *Chapters of Erie and Other Essays* (Boston, MA: Osgood and Co.,
     1871); G. Martin, *Causes and Conflicts: The Centennial History of the Association of the Bar of
     New York* (New York, NY: Fordham University Press, 1997), 3–15. On the securitisation and
     personal profits in nineteenth-century railroad ownership and management, see R. White,
     Railroaded: The Transcontinentals and the Making of Modern America (New York, NY: Norton
     & Co., 2011). On the Erie War, see J. S. Gordon, *The Scarlet Woman of Wall Street: Jay Gould,
     Jim Fisk, Cornelius Vanderbilt, the Erie Railroad Wars, and the Birth of Wall Street* (New York,
     NY: Weidenfeld & Nicolson, 1988).

Of particular interest to Adams was 'an Erie raid' which unfolded after Vanderbilt had withdrawn. Seeking access to Pennsylvania's coal mines, Fisk and Gould commenced their distinctive style of raid against the Albany and Susquehanna Railroad, a 150-mile spur through western New York. Its president, Joseph Ramsey, proved more recalcitrant than Vanderbilt and, with headquarters in Albany, had no lack of skilful legal counsel. Each side continually checked the other over the summer. As Fisk and Gould's Erie party bought up stock, Ramsey's Albany party diluted it with stock offerings to their allies (including the rising banker J. P. Morgan). Field and Shearman then secured decrees from a New York City judge enjoining both the issuance of new stock and the voting of recently transferred stock. Ramsey's lawyers secured a decree from an Albany judge enjoining the enforcement of the New York City injunction. Months of injunctions and counter-injunctions followed until the New York City judge granted Shearman's request to declare the Albany and Susquehanna in receivership: the entire line and all its assets were transferred to two temporary receivers pending the next corporate election (one of the receivers was Fisk himself). But the court in Albany decreed its own receivership in favour of Ramsey and managed to issue process one hour earlier than New York City. The injunctive decrees continued, as did new receiverships – this time as stock was seized from its purchasers and transferred to referees. The largest stock receivership went to one of Field's law clerks.[9]

The manoeuvring came to a head at the annual corporate election in Albany on 7 September 1869. Per the bylaws, shareholder voting could not begin until noon and the poll had to remain open one hour. Field and Shearman waited literally until the eleventh hour to spring their trap. Their reliable New York City judge had ordered the arrest of Ramsey and the other officers as an 'attachment' proceeding to a civil case (filed in the name of the corporation, against its officers, for the misappropriation of corporate records). At 11:45 a.m., Shearman proceeded to the officers' boardroom with the sheriff while Field transferred the Erie party's proxies to a band of fifty Irish 'roughs' brought to town (and plied with drink) for the occasion, and together they proceeded to the meeting room for the vote. The Erie-favoured directors won overwhelmingly.[10]

9 Adams and Adams, *Chapters of Erie*, 135–91; Lerner, 'Thomas Nast's Crusading Legal Cartoons', 65–68.
10 Adams and Adams, *Chapters of Erie*, 174–81; G. T. Curtis, *An Inquiry into the Albany & Susquehanna Railroad Litigations of 1869 and Mr David Dudley Field's Connection Therewith* (New York, NY: Appleton & Co., 1871); A. Stickney, 'The Truth of a "Great Lawsuit"' (1872) 14 Galaxy 576.

The tale was all that a muckraker could want, and Adams relished telling it; but how to explain it? Here in a land of liberty, fresh from a war of emancipation – 'this, be it remembered, was ... in New York, and not in Constantinople', Adams drolly reminded his readers – judges of the lowest trial courts were issuing secret decrees of imprisonment, seizing and redistributing property – entire railroads even – and enjoining the enforcement of one another's decrees.[11] And so far as lawyers then and later could determine, none of it ran afoul of the state's Code of Procedure drafted decades earlier by Field. The problem as Adams saw it thus arose from the law – particularly Field's Code – under which 'local judges ... are clothed with certain ... powers in actions commenced before them, which run throughout the State'.[12] Adams relished the irony that the name of these 'certain powers' that prospered injustice was *equity*.[13] Like Field himself, equitable jurisprudence in the nineteenth century could at times appear stately and dignified, and at other times as the diabolic assistant of the robber barons.

THEN AND NOW: THE PROBLEM OF DEFINING *EQUITY*

Historians of nineteenth-century American law have been hasty in their treatment of equity. Ignoring the cautious arguments of colonial legal historians that 'Americans objected to chancery courts rather than to equity law', some scholars have assumed that the post-Revolution disappearance of chancery courts meant that in America, equity was disfavoured, discarded and 'moribund' until coming to life again at the end of the century.[14] Influential jurisdictions like Massachusetts and Pennsylvania largely did without courts of chancery, it is noted, while New York and Virginia abolished theirs around mid-century, and new states in the West never created them. Not until late in the century did federal judges seem to rediscover the equitable injunction, which they deployed against striking labourers.

---

[11] Adams and Adams, *Chapter of Erie*, 175.   [12] Ibid., 22.   [13] Ibid., 23.
[14] S. N. Katz, 'The Politics of Law in Colonial America: Controversies over Chancery Courts and Equity Law in the Eighteenth Century', in D. Fleming and B. Bailyn (eds), *Perspectives in American History* (Boston, MA: Little, Brown and Co., 1971), vol. 5, 257–84, 265; see also D. J. Hulsebosch, *Constituting Empire: New York and the Transformation of Constitutionalism in the Atlantic World, 1664–1830* (Chapel Hill, NC: University of North Carolina Press, 2008), 60. For the 'moribund' view of equity, see P. C. Hoffer, *The Law's Conscience: Equitable Constitutionalism in America* (Chapel Hill, NC: University of North Carolina Press, 1990), 147; S. N. Subrin, 'David Dudley Field and the Field Code: A Historical Analysis of an Earlier Procedural Vision' (1988) 6 L. & Hist. Rev. 311.

The problem is that many of these accounts tend to reduce the sprawling and sophisticated system of chancery to a small subset of its functions and then eulogise the demise of American 'equity'. Thus Roscoe Pound and his admirers Charles Clark and Edson Sunderland (the main drafters of the 1938 Federal Rules of Civil Procedure), interested as they were in judicial discretion and pre-trial investigation powers, thought they were reviving a long-dormant equity in their reforms.[15] More recently, scholars have made 'inquisitorial' devices like written, juryless process an essential feature of equity, while some have emphasised equity's flexible moral maxims over the 'rigid' decrees of legislatures or common law courts.[16] In this respect, modern commentary differs little from that of the nineteenth century. What counts as equity in the United States has often been in the eye of the beholder. One aim of this chapter is to trace the diverse array of ideas among American lawyers and jurists of what equity was, and how equity might be united with law.

For many ordinary lawyers, the description of equity as a set of procedures, remedies and precedents probably summed up their views on the system. The workaday practitioner understood from experience which remedies could be pleaded at law and which required him to don the title of 'solicitor' and file in chancery.[17] However, an impressive number of lawyers – especially among those who would become America's leading corporate counsel – devoted significant effort to think philosophically and systematically about their dual system of jurisprudence. For the most part, they never published their conclusions in books or pamphlets and rarely did their views on jurisprudential abstractions enter their courtroom arguments. They did, however, speak up at the numerous constitutional conventions held around mid-century and in legislative reports each time the Code was introduced or revised in a jurisdiction.

One of the earliest and most influential of these occasions, New York's 1846 constitutional convention, featured the arguments and themes that

---

[15] See Subrin, 'How Equity Conquered Common Law'; Hoffer, The Law's Conscience, 91.

[16] A. D. Kessler, 'Our Inquisitorial Tradition: Equity Procedure, Due Process, and the Search for an Alternative to the Adversarial' (2005) 90 Cornell L. Rev. 1181; M. J. Horwitz, The Transformation of American Law: 1780–1860 (Cambridge, MA: Harvard University Press, 1979), 266.

[17] The leading treatises on equity practice in pre-Code New York include J. W. Moulton, The Chancery Practice of the State of New York (New York, NY: Halsted, 1829–32), 2 vols; J. Parkes, The Statutes and Orders of the Court of Chancery and the State Law of Real Property of the State of New York (London: Maxwell and Stevens, 1830); D. Graham, A Treatise on the Organization and Jurisdiction of the Courts of Law and Equity in the State of New York (New York, NY: Halsted & Voorhies, 1839); O. L. Barbour, A Treatise on the Practice of the Court of Chancery (Albany, NY: Gould and Gould, 1844).

would be debated across the country. Through the month of August 1846, twenty of the state's leading attorneys spoke one after the other, each describing in detail an ideal judicial system and the role of law and equity within that system. Attention then shifted westward, as Iowa, Indiana, Ohio and Kentucky became early adopters of the Field Code – the latter two nevertheless maintaining the law–equity divide.[18]

Legal history was a favourite starting point among the lawyers debating law and equity, and practitioners showed an impressive facility with the history of Greek, Roman and English law. Most agreed on the general outlines of this history, though they disputed the lesson it presented. Many accounts began with Aristotle's distinction between Law, which was necessarily universal in its nature, and Επιεικέια, 'a correction of law, where by reason of its universality, it is deficient'.[19] Roman praetors were said to have introduced laws of Æquitas 'for the sake of helping out, supplementing, and correcting the Civil Law'.[20] As for the English tradition, the story ran that after the writs had become fixed in number and form (around the common law forms of action), the Chancellor began making new writs returnable to his own court, establishing jurisdiction over extraordinary remedies. As the early Chancellors were high church officials holding the title 'keeper of the king's conscience', their jurisprudence emphasised their ability to rule according to discretion to do justice between the parties when the law by its ordinary processes and general rules was deficient. During the reign of Elizabeth I, it was settled that chancery could enjoin the enforcement of a common law judgment, but chancery would not interfere where common law could adequately provide for a case.[21]

As New Yorkers looked around America, they noted that states without courts of chancery – the favoured examples were Massachusetts and Pennsylvania – either incorporated or mimicked equity jurisprudence and

---

[18] See S. Croswell and R. Sutton (eds), *Debates and Proceedings in the New-York State Convention* (Albany, NY: Argus, 1846); W. G. Bishop and W. H. Attree (eds), *Report of the Debates and Proceedings of the Convention for the Revision of the Constitution of the State of New York* (Albany, NY: Evening Atlas, 1846); *Report of the Commissioners Appointed to Prepare a Code of Practice for the Commonwealth of Kentucky* (Frankfurt, KY: Hodges, 1850) [hereinafter 1850 Kentucky Code Report]; *Revision of 1860 Containing All the Statutes of a General Nature of the State of Iowa* (Des Moines, IA: John Teesdale, 1860) [hereinafter 1860 Iowa Code Report]; H. Fowler and A. H. Brown (eds), *Report of the Debates and Proceedings of the Convention for the Revision of the Constitution of the State of Indiana* (Indianapolis, IN: Brown, 1850).

[19] A. Laussat, *An Essay on Equity in Pennsylvania* (Philadelphia, PA: Desilver, 1826), 17.

[20] W. Whewell, *The Elements of Morality, Including Polity* (London: Parker, 1845), 329.

[21] 1860 Iowa Code Report, 440–43; Whewell, *Elements of Morality*, 330–32; Laussat, *Essay on Equity*, 13–17; Bishop and Attree, *Report of the Debates*, 600–2 (Nicoll). For a twenty-first century account of seventeenth-century equity, see Ibbetson, 'The Earl of Oxford's Case'.

devices over time. Pennsylvania may not have had a court of chancery, but from the colonial period onward it maintained an Orphans' Court in which equity powers and procedures pertaining to guardianship were administered. Unwilling to grant judges the power to imprison for civil contempt, state lawmakers approximated chancery's injunctive powers to compel specific performance with conditional judgments: juries returned catastrophically high damages awards but execution was conditioned on the defendant's failure to perform what the court determined – following equity jurisprudence – he or she should do.[22]

THE NATURE OF THINGS: SEPARATIST VISIONS OF LAW AND EQUITY

From this history, the opponents of fusion – call them 'separatists' for ease – worked out a taxonomy of law that to the New York lawyer George Simmons proved that the 'division of remedies into legal and equitable, is founded on a natural distinction, and that it is impracticable to blend them under a common code of procedure, or to administer them by the machinery of courts similarly organized'.[23] In Simmons's taxonomy, capital-e Equity was synonymous with justice itself. It encompassed all of morality, from the 'voluntary' precepts of religion to obligations 'established by the State. This [latter] part is the law', Simmons explained. 'It is not *made*, but *discovered*, and it is reared to perfection only by much observation and reflection.'[24] Written law was thus equity calcified, a subset of justice whose principles had been articulated by judges and legislators. But even the best of human wisdom was fallible and incomplete; its expressions of justice aimed at universality but were insufficiently nuanced and failed to account for all the accidents and contingencies of life. A third subset of equity, then (in addition to morality and positive law) was the technical, little-e equity administered in chancery, the discretionary search for as-yet unexpressed or half-expressed principles of justice that could correct the occasional mishaps caused by human pretensions to universalise short-sighted legal principles. By reserving discretion for these extraordinary cases, the rule of law was maintained without granting too much arbitrary

---

[22] See Laussat, *An Essay on Equity*, 56–57, 105–8. The Orphans' Court took written proofs, relied on bench trial, and could decree injunctions and imprisonment for contempt. On equity in Massachusetts, see P. M. Johnson, *No Adequate Remedy at Law: Equity in Massachusetts 1692-1877*, Yale Law School Student Legal History Papers, Paper 2 (2012), available at http://digitalcommons.law.yale.edu/student_legal_history_papers/2.

[23] Bishop and Attree, *Report of the Debates*, 664.

[24] Ibid., 667 (emphasis original). See also J. T. Humphry, 'Lecture at the Incorporated Law Society' (1856) 51 Leg. Obs. 67.

power to the courts. As Simmons concluded, human wisdom could 'only divide the great mass of such cases into classes of actions, to be followed by the ordinary courts, and then constitute an extraordinary tribunal to take charge of the residue, and nothing but the residue, that its *action* may be at least so far limited by reason of its jurisdiction being so far confined'.[25]

The fusionists' mistake, according to New York City lawyer Lorenzo Shepard, was their belief that all wrongs could be 'reduced to the same class, and be comprehensible in the same general remedies'.[26] Abstracting a menu of remedies and making them available for all cases ignored how 'wrongs are infinitely diversified in their natures and infinitely diversified in their remedies'.[27] The best that lawmakers wishing to spread the one rule of law over the many exigencies of life could hope to achieve was to classify similar enough injuries under particular remedies (the forms of action), yet leave enough room for discretion when those classifications failed (equity). Abolishing these classifications would empower judges to grant injunctions, one of the most powerful and closely guarded tools of equity in every case: a danger Shepard was particularly keen to avert. Without the traditional confines created by the jurisdictional distinction between law and equity, the only alternatives Shepard saw were for courts to arrogate the injunctive power – an act of tyranny – or for the legislature to enumerate every possible case in which the device would be permitted – a hopelessly tedious task that would inevitably remain incomplete.[28]

These remarks on the infinite diversity of wrongs and the difficult classifications of law show that what was at stake for the separatists was the fundamental legitimacy of the legal order. Equity and the rule of law required that like cases should be treated alike, but even this principle involved a manifest legal fiction, for no two cases in human experience were completely alike. It was the artifice of the lawmaker to discern commonalities between cases and invest them with legal significance, usually by applying a particular remedy to a certain set of common harms.[29] Abolishing the classification and making all remedies available to every case would not 'simplify' procedure, but make it enormously more unwieldy, one lawyer concluded, 'as each case would rest upon its own particular circumstances and [become] its own form'.[30] Every case, that is, would become an equity case, but separatists argued that it was

---

[25] Bishop and Attree, *Report of the Debates*, 666. See also Humphry, 'Lecture', 68–69; Whewell, *Elements of Morality*, 316–27.
[26] Bishop and Attree, *Report of the Debates*, 622.   [27] Ibid., 624.   [28] Ibid., 621.
[29] For a succinct contemporary discussion on this point, see B. Tucker, *Principles of Pleading* (Boston, MA: Little, Brown, 1846), 1–4.
[30] Bishop and Attree, *Report of the Debates*, 591 (Marvin).

'dangerous to convert [New York's] standing army of judges into so many chancellors, with all the arbitrary power of that court'.[31] Equitable discretion was tolerable only because there were so many definite categories of legal cases to which it could not apply, Simmons argued:

Cases cognizable in the law courts are limited and prescribed by law; that is to say, injuries to be redressed there, are by law defined and enumerated, in order to prevent the capricious and arbitrary action of the court, and to make those remedies easy, clear, and free from uncertainty. Injuries to be redressed in equity courts are undefined, unclassed, non-enumerated.[32]

It had taken centuries to enumerate the categories of remedies that worked for the run of cases and excluded equitable discretion. 'To unite law and equity would be to retrograde for three centuries', a colleague of Simmons's warned.[33]

'Retrograde' was usually hurled at the separatists, but lawyers like Simmons and Shepard insisted they were at the leading edge of legal modernisation. Like craftsmen seeking to return to feudal labour practices, it was the fusionists who, Shepard argued, were 'at variance with a principle that has done more for the development of human industry, both physical and mental, than any other. I allude to the division of labor – This has been the great cause of perfection in every art'.[34] The division of labour, the infallible principle of economic modernisation, ensured that 'the tendency of society is to separate the courts of law and equity, and so to secure more expert and competent judges, more prompt and perfect remedies', developments Simmons perceived in all modernising jurisdictions.[35]

Behind these arguments frequently lay the suspicion that the jury posed a problem for the fusionists. Separatists lauded the value of the common law jury – so long as it was confined to actions at common law – but, said Shepard, 'it may be accounted among our misfortunes that [there] are causes to which it cannot be applied'.[36] The fusionists thus faced a dilemma: to truly achieve fusion, they would either have to abandon the jury – an important safeguard of democratic liberty, at least within its sphere – or make all cases triable by jury, reducing New York's sophisticated business law to amateurism. Separatists recognised that in many instances equity's supposedly extraordinary

---

[31] Ibid., 491 (Simmons).   [32] Ibid., 665.
[33] Croswell and Sutton, *Debates and Proceedings*, 446 (Marvin).
[34] Bishop and Attree, *Report of the Debates*, 622.
[35] Ibid., 663. See also ibid., 572 (Jordan). Similar arguments were deployed in England, as discussed by Lobban, Chapter 4.
[36] Ibid., 621. See also Croswell and Sutton, *Debates and Proceedings*, 446–49 (Jordan).

intervention had become routine and bound to precedent as tightly as any common law form of action, but this did not mean the court could be abolished and its cases transferred to law. It was rather an indication of how successfully the division of labour and the absence of the jury had fitted New York law for modern commerce. 'The exceeding complication of many subjects of equity jurisdiction, though it may be regretted', Shepard reasoned, 'is one of the necessary incidents to high civilization – to extended commerce, and to the vast and involved circle of the transactions of men'.[37]

The danger of chancery's arbitrary discretion convinced the separatists that the distinction of law and equity was a 'difference resting not solely in the will of the Legislature – nor in any great degree dependent on or controlled by it, but existing in the unalterable nature of things themselves', according to Shepard.[38] If they did not convince any fusionists with this ontological claim, they did at least win over a few lawyers with the argument that, at the very least, fusion could not be accomplished merely through the abstraction of procedure from substance, with only the former undergoing reformation. As Simmons argued, 'the very *forms* of proceedings stick so close to the *substance* – the practice of courts is so adhesive to their doctrines – that I am afraid' fusion would prove impracticable if it were attempted.[39] Sympathetic fusionists agreed that fusion could be achieved only gradually and would involve many substantive changes. Merely redrafting the rules of pleading and expanding available remedies would not result in fusion, for 'the present modes are incorporated and interwoven with all our habits of business, and I may say, almost with all our legal notions and ideas', one fusionist conceded.[40] To these lawyers, traditional practices ran deep through the legal order and would not disappear within a generation – and certainly not within a single legislative session.

A PLAY UPON WORDS: FUSIONIST VIEWS ON LAW AND EQUITY

To committed fusionists, the history of legal development in England and America proved only that the distinction between law and equity 'has no foundation in the nature of things', as Field put it.[41] 'Its existence is accidental,

---

[37] Bishop and Attree, *Report of the Debates*, 621. See also 1850 Kentucky Code Report, vi.

[38] Bishop and Attree, *Report of the Debates*, 621 (Shepard); see also ibid., 590 (Stetson) ('The forms of practice he believed were not the result of arbitrary rules, but existed in reasons behind the causes themselves. An uniformity of practice might be effected, but he did not believe that the distinction in the various actions at law and equity could be abolished').

[39] Ibid., 664 (emphasis original).   [40] Ibid., 575 (Kirkland); see also at 639–41 (Harris).

[41] [D. D. Field], 'The Convention', *New York Evening Post*, 13 August 1846.

and continues till now only because we have been the slaves of habit.'[42] Unlike his more moderate colleagues, Field was confident these old habits of thought could be transformed if lawyers better understood that names like 'equity' and legal forms of action were not 'real existences' but 'rather ancient formulas, scholastic in their structure and origin, whose vitality has long since departed'.[43]

This strong form of nominalism commonly appeared in fusionist arguments. After the delegates agreed to create 'one supreme court, having general jurisdiction in law and equity', the New York City corporate attorney Charles O'Conor regretted that the phrase 'law and equity' entered the constitution, fearing that 'as long as we spoke of law and equity as distinct things in our constitution ... the legislature would not feel at liberty to unite and blend them into one'.[44] Arphaxad Loomis, a future co-drafter of the Field Code, agreed. 'Law and equity' seemed to have talismanic power to his colleagues, but 'the difference was more in words than in reality ... There might as well be any other hieroglyphical symbol by which to proceed as to retain those under which the practice was now conducted'.[45]

To support their point, the fusionists spent entire days at the convention arguing that equity had lost its distinct emphases on discretionary justice and had become indistinguishable from law in its precedent-bound jurisprudence. The separatists' fears about arbitrary discretion dated back to the early seventeenth century, when John Selden famously joked that equitable 'conscience' could be as variable as the size of 'a Chancellor's foot'.[46] But, O'Conor argued, after two centuries of building precedents:

> there was not at present any such thing recognized in jurisprudence, as the will or arbitrement of a good and conscientious man finding some measure of justice between neighbors, which the law did not define and declare. It was the law of the land, and not the conscience of the chancellor, by which the right of the citizen must be determined ... The maxim that our rights were to be measured by the length of the chancellor's foot was exploded long ago.[47]

---

[42] Ibid.   [43] Ibid.

[44] Croswell and Sutton, *Debates and Proceedings*, 440. See also 1860 Iowa Code Report, 440 ('soon they came to confound *names* with *things*').

[45] Bishop and Attree, *Report of the Debates*, 590.

[46] F. Pollock (ed.), *Table Talk of John Selden* (London: Quaritch, 1927), 43.

[47] Croswell and Sutton, *Debates and Proceedings*, 443. See also Bishop and Attree, *Report of the Debates*, 601 (Nicoll); ibid., 576 (Kirkland), 638 (Loomis). On the regularisation of equity in the late seventeenth century, see D. R. Klinck, 'Lord Nottingham's "Certain Measures"' (2010) 28 L. & Hist. Rev. 711.

Fusionists declared that equity's 'extraordinary' jurisdiction and its power to 'supply the deficiencies' of the law were likewise empty phrases. The elderly Jacksonian lawyer Michael Hoffman insisted that 'for more than a hundred years no court of equity has claimed or exercised the power to modify or soften the rigor of the law – or grant relief on mere grounds of moral right, or conscience, that was not given it by fixed rules of law'.[48] On this point, the fusionists boasted the support of so eminent a jurist as William Blackstone, who had written that both systems 'are now equally artificial systems, founded on the same principles of justice and positive law; but varied by different usages in the forms and modes of their proceedings'.[49]

Blackstone's distinction between principles of justice and modes of proceeding inspired the fusionists to argue that 'procedural' fusion could be accomplished without disturbing the 'substantive' law. 'The difference between law and equity, and the only difference', O'Conor claimed, 'was in the form of pleading and the remedies'.[50] Again and again, delegates drew contrasts between 'form', 'mode', 'proceedings' on the one hand and 'substance' on the other. 'The difference between "law" and "equity" is a difference in the *remedies*, and *substantially* in nothing more', one fusionist concluded.[51]

Concerning those remedies, equity judges could decree money damages as at common law but also administer a variety of other injunctive and declarative remedies backed by their power to hold parties in contempt. No case in equity required pleading the forms of action; rather, bills in chancery consisted of (often quite detailed) factual statements, usually verified under oath.[52] Fusionists commonly understood, then, that uniting law and equity basically involved extending equitable procedure – perhaps with some alterations to diminish verbose pleadings – to all cases. O'Conor's 'view was that the forms of pleading used in chancery, reduced and cut down to the extent they might be, were the true forms by which civil justice might be administered in all cases, in one court, and by a uniform mode of practice'.[53] That was because equity had 'literally no form about it. The party stated his case, and asked the relief he desired, and the court, if he proved his case, gave him that relief.'[54]

---

[48] Bishop and Attree, *Report of the Debates*, 679.
[49] Ibid.; see W. Blackstone, *Commentaries on the Laws of England* (Oxford: Clarendon, 1768), vol. 3, 434, discussed by Sherwin, Chapter 15.
[50] Croswell and Sutton, *Debates and Proceedings*, 443; see also ibid., 464 (Nicoll).
[51] Bishop and Attree, *Report of the Debates*, 576 (Kirkland).
[52] See Barbour, *Practice of the Court of Chancery*, vol. 1, 115–19.
[53] Bishop and Attree, *Report of the Debates*, 562.   [54] Ibid. See also ibid., 648 (Morris).

This view of equity's straightforward proceedings provided the fusionists with a rebuttal to the separationist argument that law and equity improved the law through a division of labour. As in any trade, the division of labour spurred progress only when it created *efficiency*, a term that became a favourite among the fusionists. But when two courts performed similar functions, and when the same case often had to seek remedies in both courts, law and equity were not sharpening expertise but creating needless redundancies. 'Why may not the judge have the power to administer to the party, what in his case the law determines to be a proper and necessary remedy?', asked Hoffman.[55] 'Why should he be obliged, if he wants one remedy, to go to one court, and if he wants another to go into another?'[56]

Enough lawyers wished to see jury trial preserved that fusionists adjusted their plans to accommodate a possible expansion of jury trial into formerly equitable proceedings, generally optimistic that the factual complexities of equity were perhaps no worse than certain cases at common law. Even if equity proved too complicated for jury trial, Hoffman argued it might have a salutary effect on equitable jurisprudence if judges and lawyers had to make equitable jurisprudence clear enough that it could be presented to a jury in the course of a few hours.[57]

In all these points, Field was the consummate fusionist. Perhaps no other exceeded Field's legal nominalism and legislative positivism. To Field, the supposed distinctions of equity were 'little more than a play upon words'[58]; 'law and equity ought to mean precisely the same thing'.[59] In the past century, 'it would not at any time have been thought proper or safe for the Courts to disregard an established precedent', and 'in almost every instance where an improvement has been made in the laws, it has come from the Legislature'.[60] The only reason New York had separate court systems, 'if reason it may be called', was purely historical',[61] which was to say, accidental. As positive law kept the courts distinct, so positive law could unite them and eliminate the distinction forever.[62]

---

55 Ibid., 676.
56 Ibid.; see also 1860 Iowa Code Report, 444. On efficiency, see especially Bishop and Attree, *Report of the Debates*, 643–46 (Harris); D. D. Field et al., *First Report of the Commission on Practice and Pleadings* (New York, NY: Van Benthuysen, 1848); *Opinions of Lord Brougham, on Politics, Theology, Law* (Paris: Baudry's European Library, 1841), 227.
57 Bishop and Attree, *Report of the Debates*, 678; see also at 600–1 (Nicoll), 616 (Brown).
58 Field, 'Law and Equity', 577.
59 D. D. Field, 'Legal System of New York', in *Speeches*, vol. 1, 340.
60 D. D. Field and A. Bradford, *The Civil Code of New York Reported Complete* (Albany, NY: Weed, Parsons & Co., 1865), xxvii.
61 Field, 'Law and Equity', 580.   62 Field, 'Legal System of New York'.

Field insisted that the distinction 'grows out of legal procedure; it does not spring from distinct, inseparable rights; it does not inhere in the nature of things'.[63] The only difference between law and equity were the remedies each court could decree; there was no such thing as a *legal right* distinct from an *equitable right*. Lawyers commonly spoke that way, 'but only because there are legal remedies and equitable remedies. Once abolish the distinction between the latter, and the distinction between the former perishes with it.'[64] By defining rights as 'substantial' and remedies as 'procedural', Field thought he saw a way through the legitimacy problems raised by the separatists. The latter worried that in a fused system every case would become a long recitation of facts. Unmoored from the precedents that defined which facts legally triggered a cabined set of remedies, judges could rule arbitrarily. But Field argued that the rule of law was secured not by stringently defining *remedies* and their availability, but by positively defining *rights*. The written law enumerated the rights of social actors. When those rights were violated, pleading need only show the fact of violation without contorting itself to fit a particular remedy. Instead of cabined remedies, positivism protected against judicial arbitrariness. If no positive right had been violated, a judge had no discretion to grant a remedy; if a right had been violated, then *any* remedy that vindicated the right would be appropriate. Field was not particularly concerned that judges would decree the 'wrong' remedy. Professional experience would guide lawyers and judges towards appropriate remedies, and the appellate process would correct any windfall awards.[65]

After New York abolished its court of chancery, Field and two other commissioners crafted his Code to provide 'a uniform course of proceeding, in all cases, legal and equitable'.[66] Acting on his belief that fusion was a problem only of procedure, Field sought to solve it in the Code of Procedure. 'The distinction between actions at law and suits in equity, and the forms of all such actions and suits heretofore existing, are abolished', an opening section read.[67] Complaints had to contain 'a statement of the facts constituting the cause of action' and a demand for relief, but no matter what remedy a plaintiff requested, the court could grant 'any relief consistent with the case'.[68] Judges were empowered to order sheriffs to arrest defendants, seize their property, or,

---

[63] Ibid., 340.   [64] Field, 'Law and Equity', 579.

[65] Field et al., *First Report of the Commission on Practice*, 74–75. Lobban, Chapter 4, records Lord Cairns representing one of the three schools of thought on English fusion along these lines.

[66] D. D. Field, *What Shall Be Done with the Practice of the Courts: Shall It Be Wholly Reformed?* (New York, NY: Voorhies, 1847), 7.

[67] 1848 N.Y. Laws c. 379, § 62.   [68] Ibid., §§ 120, 231.

if it appeared the plaintiff might suffer irreparable injury, enjoin a defendant's actions.[69] As New York now had only one court of general jurisdiction, these powers were conferred on the thirty-three district court judges across the state. (Twenty years later those judges would use nearly every remedy Field provided in the Albany and Susquehanna litigation.)

Most other states that adopted the Code likewise abolished their separate chancery courts (or started out with the Code and thus never established such courts). Overall, the commissioners insisted that 'the basis' for code procedure 'was substantially that upon which courts of equity were originally founded'.[70] Like chancery, the code required straightforward, factual pleadings, allowed liberal powers of joinder and amendment and made the jury waivable in all cases. (Constitutional strictures kept the commission from dispensing with the jury entirely.) All equitable remedies, including injunctions, contempt and processes for accounting, partitioning, receiving and disposing of property continued under the expansive provision for 'any relief consistent with the case made by the complaint'.[71] Until the legislature enacted a substantive civil code, judges were to look to legal and equitable precedents (though without regard to the division) to determine whether a complaint made out an appropriate 'cause of action' by stating facts showing the violation of the plaintiff's rights.[72]

As this volume shows, the fusion of law and equity was a common project across the common law world in the nineteenth century. In general, one might say that Americans sought to accomplish *fusion* largely through equity's *diffusion*.[73] Under the Field Code, every judge, in effect, became a chancellor. Even jurisdictions that did not adopt the Field reforms vested equity powers in many more judges than England's lone Chancellor (before 1813) and Vice-Chancellors (after 1841).[74] Most southern states employed two to four

[69] Ibid., tit. 7.

[70] *Second Report of the Commissioners of Practice and Pleadings* (New York, NY: Weed, Parsons and Co., 1849), 7.

[71] 1849 N.Y. Laws c. 438, § 275.

[72] 1848 N.Y. Laws c. 379, § 231; *Final Report of the Commissioners on Practice and Pleadings*, in *Documents of the Assembly of New York*, 73rd Sess., No. 16 (New York, NY: Weed, Parsons & Co., 1850), vol. 2, 314, § 751 [hereinafter Field Code Final Report].

[73] For greater detail, see Funk, 'Equity without Chancery'. That article joins a growing literature showing how much procedural fusion had been accomplished in America and England before the celebrated dates of fusion in the Field Code 1848 and the Judicature Acts 1873–75: see Kessler, *Inventing American Exceptionalism*, ch. 3; McMahon, 'Field, Fusion and the 1850s'.

[74] Until 1813, the Master of the Rolls could sit in place of the English Chancellor, but both could not sit concurrently. England added a Vice-Chancellor to the Chancery bench in 1813, and two more in 1841: Lobban, 'Preparing for Fusion', 393.

chancellors early on, before granting equity jurisdiction to county or district courts in the 1820s and 1830s. Federal district judges received a uniform equity code from the Supreme Court in 1822. Most code jurisdictions and an increasing number of reform states allowed the joinder of legal and equitable claims and encouraged the use of equitable practices – temporary injunctions and bench trial – in all litigation.[75]

The enduring importance of equity within the American system is thus only surprising because historical scholarship has for so long repeated a narrative about the demise of equity. In the experience of lawyers in virtually every American jurisdiction – as Field's Erie Wars illustrate in part – equity grew more diffuse, sophisticated and powerful across the century. To be sure, not every practice of the old English Court of Chancery persisted in America. In time, for instance, most jurisdictions moved away from chancery's require-ment to reduce all proofs to written statements, preferring to take witness examinations orally in court (although even this would become a distinction without a difference with the rise of courtroom stenography). Some experi-mented with making equity cases triable by jury. But no jurisdiction made jury trial compulsory, and the tendency over the course of the century was in the opposite direction: more cases were tried by the bench as the jury became waivable.[76]

Despite the scandals of the Erie War, most lawyers and reformers over time did not find the extension of equity's powers to more judges, or its novel applications for railroad corporations, problematic. Even Adams's commen-tary treated Erie as the exception that proved the rule. The equitable powers of

---

[75] See C. M. Hepburn, *The Historical Development of Code Pleading in America and England* (Cincinnati, OH: Anderson & Co., 1897); K. Collins, "'A Considerable Surgical Operation": Article III, Equity, and Judge-Made Law in the Federal Courts' (2010) 60 Duke L.J. 249; Laussat, *Essay on Equity*, 153–57.

[76] On written proof in New York, see Kessler, 'Our Inquisitorial Tradition', 1224–38; but see 1850 Kentucky Code Report, vi (preserving 'the advantage of having the evidence in writing'). England too moved away from written proceedings, in part prompted by Field's advocacy: McMahon, 'Field, Fusion and the 1850s', 424–62. On the decline of jury trial after waiver, see R. L. Lerner, 'The Failure of Originalism in Preserving Constitutional Rights to Civil Jury Trial' (2014) 22 Wm & Mary Bill of Rights J. 811. Much of the confusion over the persistence of equity has developed from Realist historiography. The code abolished bills of discovery, while the Realists valued discovery for pre-trial investigation: Subrin, 'David Dudley Field and the Field Code', 332–33; Hoffer, *The Law's Conscience*, 91. I have argued elsewhere that the Code's abolition of certain processes for discovery was not a repudiation of equity and that the Realists were not *reviving* the traditions of equity in their own reforms, but rather *innovating*: Funk, 'Equity without Chancery'; see also S. N. Subrin, 'Fishing Expeditions Allowed: The Historical Background of the 1938 Federal Discovery Rules' (1998) 39 Boston Coll. L. Rev. 691.

trial judges were not as much of a problem as the fact that these judges did not 'co-ordinate' and use 'the delicate powers of equity with a careful regard to private rights and the dignity of the law'.[77] The Code's fusion required 'a high average of learning, dignity, and personal character in the occupants of the bench', which those who ruled in the Erie litigation did not possess.[78] Adams's ultimate complaint, then, was not with the Code's fusion but with New York's elective judiciary. The New York bar largely shared Adams's assessment. The judges who had been most liberal with the injunctive power were eventually impeached on corruption charges, but the bar did not censure any Erie War attorneys or recommend changes to the Code. The problem, ruled the Association of the Bar of the City of New York, had been the judges.[79]

THE DIFFUSION OF EQUITY AND THE LIMITATIONS OF FUSION

Then as now, judges also received blame for halting the progress of fusion. In the early years of the Code, Field and other fusionists dashed off pamphlets and law review articles criticising judicial decisions that distinguished between law and equity or forced 'common law' litigants to follow the old forms of action. One New York judge said he could not understand how 'forms of pleading' could be 'abolished', so he concluded that in the Code, 'the principles of pleading are left untouched'.[80] Among New York's eminent jurists, Alexander Smith Johnson received the praise of fusionists for disregarding the distinction and allowing non-traditional joinders and remedies. Henry Selden on the Court of Appeals received their condemnation. It was 'plain', Selden wrote, that the state constitution's grant of jurisdiction 'in "law and equity", has not only recognized the distinction between them, but placed that distinction beyond the power of the legislature to abolish'.[81] Lawrence Friedman has written of these judges that 'it was as if upper courts tried, not cases, but printed formulae, and tried them according to warped and unreal distinctions'.[82]

---

[77] Adams and Adams, *Chapters of Erie*, 23.   [78] Ibid.
[79] See *Charges of the Bar Association of New York Against Hon. George G. Barnard and Hon. Albert Cardozo and Hon. John H. McCunn* (New York, NY: Polhemus, 1872); Martin, *Causes and Conflicts*, 87–103; Lerner, 'Thomas Nast's Crusading Legal Cartoons', 76–78.
[80] [D. D. Field], *The Administration of the Code* (New York, NY: Voorhies, 1852), 16 (quoting *Dollner v. Gibson*, 3 Code Reporter 153 [1850]).
[81] *Reubens v. Joel*, 13 N.Y. 488, 497 (1859).
[82] L. M. Friedman, *A History of American Law*, 2nd edn (New York, NY: Simon & Schuster, 1985), 400. See C. E. Clark, 'The Union of Law and Equity' (1925) 25 Colum. L. Rev. 1, 4.

64 *Kellen Funk*

These criticisms tend to overlook how extensively Code legislation guided separatist jurisprudence. Throughout the Code, rights to certain remedies and modes of proceeding depended on the form of the complaint. Defendants could not be arrested in contract claims. Actions seeking the recovery of real property or money damages received different procedures in regard to timing, summons and default mode of trial (jury) from 'all other cases';[83] a distinction between legal and equitable traditions in all but name. The final draft of the Code which became popular in other states admitted it was 'following the beaten track already enlightened by the judicial consideration to which the code has been subjected' and included 'special proceedings' for actions regarding mortgages, corporations and legacies, among others, while nevertheless insisting that the general sections of the Code were in their 'nature adapted to almost every case requiring the interposition of judicial authority'.[84]

After judges and treatise writers reasoned that these rules preserved a distinction between law and equity and bound certain remedies to the form of the pleadings, Field retorted with a hypothetical: imagine there used to be separate courts for men and women, with different proceedings. Those who could not see that the Code accomplished fusion were arguing in effect that there was something 'in the nature of things' which prevented a fusion of men and women's proceedings using 'uniform pleadings, a uniform manner of taking testimony, trial by jury in every case in which a man was the suitor, and the reëxamination of a verdict only after the manner practiced in men's courts'.[85] The analogy may have been apt but was not very instructive, as even the language of this hypothetical formula preserved the old conceptual distinctions on which separatists relied.

Rather than distinguish between cases for money damages and 'all other cases', the Code states of Kentucky, Iowa, Oregon, Tennessee and Arkansas explicitly preserved the distinction between law and equity. Because these states – like most others – scheduled different court sessions for jury trial and for bench trial, they referred cases to either the 'law' or 'equity' calendar and forbad the joinder of legal and equitable claims. Even New York continued the latter practice, while judges spoke in their decisions of sitting 'in equity' or 'at law'. 'They tend to keep up a distinction that no longer exists', Field

---

[83] 1848 N.Y. Laws c. 379, §§ 154, § 203; Field Code Final Report, 227–33, 318–19.
[84] Field Code Final Report, 378, note to tit. 11.
[85] Field, 'Law and Equity', 582. See H. Whittaker, *Practice and Pleading Under the Code, Original and Amended, With Appendix of Forms*, 2nd edn (New York, NY: Jenkins, 1854), vol. 1, 56 ('Although ... the preamble [of the Code] seems to contemplate the abolition of all distinction between legal and equitable remedies also, that abolition is, to some extent, and must always continue to be, impracticable').

lamented of his home state in 1878, 'and go far to confuse and mislead'.[86] Thus, as the Erie Wars drew to a close and the federal struggle to control labour commenced, the 'revival' of equity was of no surprise to American lawyers who had seen the same sophisticated equitable remedies, procedures and precedents survive and prosper during their lifetimes. What did surprise the fusionists was the relentless distinction judges and lawyers continued to draw between these practices and those of 'the law'.

THE TRIUMPH OF A TRADITION IN ERIE'S LAST CHAPTER

Field and Shearman's deployment of equity in what could have been the culminating battle of the Erie War had been nearly flawless. Through their strategic combination of injunctions, receiverships and arrests for attachment, they cobbled together a shareholder majority at their 7 September 1869 meeting during the arrest of their Albany rivals. But whether through lack of nerve or simple miscalculation, the Erie party's sheriff did not remove President Ramsey from the building but merely detained him in the boardroom. It took Ramsey only half an hour to draw up the proper bond paperwork and pay bail – $25,000 a piece for him and his favoured directors. (Ramsey's 'arrest' in the same room in which J. P. Morgan was currently sitting helped his cause.) The liberated directors then held their own meeting within the bylaws' conditions and elected their slate of directors before one o'clock. After all the *ex parte* injunctions and receiverships, an actual trial would finally determine who controlled the Albany and Susquehanna.[87]

At the conclusion of the trial the next January, Judge Darwin Smith of Rochester employed yet another power of equity to cut through the knot of injunctions, receiverships and attachments: the power to declare acts of fraud void. He found that from the beginning, the Erie party had been acting under a fraudulent conspiracy. The initial injunction had been decreed in a 'suit instituted for [a] fraudulent purpose'[88] and all the receiverships of track and stocks had been procured 'in aid of ... fraudulent purposes'.[89] Thus, 'in equity' these acts were void, the votes of Erie-received stock were void, and the Ramsey directors were duly elected and rightfully in possession of the

---

[86] Field, 'Law and Equity', 583. These states mimicked the federal arrangement, which preserved a distinction between law and equity within a tribunal that had jurisdiction over both, a similar situation as described for New South Wales by Leeming, Chapter 6.

[87] See Adams and Adams, *Chapters of Erie*, 181–85.

[88] *People of New York v. Albany & Susquehanna Railroad Co.*, 7 Abbr.Pr.N.S. 265, 291 (S.C. N.Y. 1869).

[89] Ibid., 297.

railroad. 'As the case was on the equity side of the court', Charles Francis Adams commented approvingly, 'there was no intervention of a jury, no chance of an inability to agree on a verdict'.[90] The mess that equitable remedies had created, equitable precepts had cleaned up. The Albany party swept the field.

As Erie's lead counsel, Field appealed Judge Smith's decision, and the absence of a jury became the basis for his remarkable appeal. The foundation of Field's argument was the 1860 case *Hartt* v. *Harvey*.[91] Fusionists usually did not regard *Hartt* as important enough to include on their lists of offensive cases, but its reasoning followed Selden's insistence on the natural distinction between law and equity: 'Although the distinction between actions at law and in equity is abolished', its key section read, 'yet the inherent distinction between legal and equitable jurisdiction and relief exists, and it is not in the power of constitutions or legal enactments, to abolish it'.[92] The decision claimed that even the Code recognised this truth 'in prescribing different modes of trial for the two classes of action'.[93] Accordingly, the *Hartt* court held that in a suit to remove a corporate officer on the basis of fraudulent voting, equitable remedies were inappropriate, and the plaintiff should have sought a common law writ of *quo warranto*. Well before its abolition, the New York Court of Chancery had strongly established the precedent that chancellors would not become involved too deeply with corporate elections. So long as duly installed inspectors collected and counted the votes, equity would not allow the losers to re-run an election through litigation. Common law courts could remove officers who lacked a proper basis for holding office, but the *quo warranto* writ carried the procedural requirements that the 'people of New York' be joined as litigants (effectively a public interest requirement) and the claim of official authority be subjected to jury trial. After a contested election, the plaintiff in *Hartt* sought to remove two directors without joinder of the people or jury trial, so the court dismissed the complaint.

As much as *Hartt* must have offended Field's vision of reform, the precedent was invaluable to his appeal. 'As a court of equity', Field argued, Judge Smith's court 'could not entertain jurisdiction ... respecting the title to the office of directors'.[94] It was a settled principle that 'equity cannot interfere in the government of corporations', and if 'the action was one in the nature of *quo warranto*', the 'defendants had the right of trial by jury'.[95] Justice Johnson – the same who was lauded by fusionists for his sympathetic

---

[90] Ibid., 188.   [91] 32 N.Y. 55 (1860).   [92] Ibid., 66.   [93] Ibid.
[94] *People* v. *Albany & Susquehanna Railroad Co.*, 57 N.Y. 161, 164 (1874).   [95] Ibid.

views – approved Field's arguments. 'Elections to office' were never 'matters of equitable consideration. They depended only on legal inquiries and legal principles',[96] Johnson ruled. That the case was 'eminently proper for jury trial is obvious',[97] and thus the court vacated the more important judgments of Judge Smith and ordered a new trial.

One could, of course, treat these cases only as an instance of Field's professional lawyering, his ability to set aside personal philosophies of law in order to use every precedent that advantaged his clients.[98] Field may have been able to satisfy himself that *Hartt's* flawed substantive reasoning could be separated from the useful procedural rule that it provided, but the *Hartt* line of cases tended to belie the fusionists' claims that there were no 'substantial' distinctions of law and equity that would be affected by a merger of the courts. So much of New York's corporation jurisprudence had arisen out of church disputes that its chancery court had long established precedents that it would not invade corporate ballot boxes and remove officers. (The disputed election in *Hartt* itself was in a church, not a business enterprise.[99]) By sending corporate litigants to seek their remedy at law, the chancellors created a rule that was indistinguishably substantive *and* procedural to preserve the legitimacy of their functions. Equitable discretion was too invasive for corporate elections, but a jury drawn from the community – in a case with a sufficiently high public interest – might arrive at a remedy that was both just and socially approvable. In Field's ideal jurisprudence, either the Erie party or the Albany party had the right to corporate office, and a judge sitting without a jury could vindicate that right (precisely as happened when Judge Smith ruled against Field). His appeal, however, drew on the logic that procedure itself created rights – the right to a jury trial, to corporate office, to vindication of the public's interest – but as they had for centuries, those rights depended upon which remedy a litigant sought.

---

[96] Ibid., 171–72.
[97] Ibid., 176. The Albany party successfully outmanoeuvred Fisk and Gould once again, by leasing the road while the appeal was pending to the Delaware & Raritan Canal Company, a corporation with sufficient wealth and legal counsel to withstand further litigation by the Erie party. Field's successful appeal vacated punitive damages that Judge Smith had assessed on Fisk in Gould. Contented with that outcome, they turned their attention to other ventures: Adams and Adams, *Chapters of Erie*, 190–91.
[98] See M. Schudson, 'Public, Private, and Professional Lives: The Correspondence of David Dudley Field and Samuel Bowles' (1977) 21 A.J.L.H. 194.
[99] On New York chancery's reluctance to enter into church disputes, see *Robertson v. Bullions*, 11 N.Y. 243 (1854).

CONCLUSION

Although the project to fuse law and equity and sunder rights from remedies remained incomplete, its attempt in the Field Code powerfully influenced the development of American law. When the Massachusetts native Walter Ashburner produced his *Principles of Equity* in 1902, he insisted that 'the two streams of jurisdiction, though they run in the same channel, run side by side and do not mingle their waters'.[100] Ashburner's views were influential around the world, especially in Australia, where jurists insisted Americans were pursuing a 'fusion fallacy'.[101] Ashburner had little influence in his native country, however. In America, trans-substantive procedure became the dominant paradigm; even as academic lawyers wrangled over the legitimacy of the theory, they tended to brush off seemingly law- or equity-specific procedures as anomalies. Such a posture goes back to the early days of the Field Code. The persistence of special proceedings for the vindication of certain rights may have annoyed Field and contradicted his ultimate goals, but it represented a remarkable reversal of Sir Henry Maine's famous aphorism: after the Field Code, action-specific procedures had the look of being gradually secreted in the interstices of a substantive law of rights.[102]

As diffuse as equity became, several jurisdictions remained committedly opposed to fusion. Illinois, Delaware and New Jersey maintained separate courts of chancery and left common law procedures relatively unaltered until the mid-twentieth century. By the late 1870s, fusionists liked to joke that Illinois and New Jersey were 'the Yellowstone Park of common law pleading'.[103] The jest shows how pervasive the fusionists' views became and how closely linked they were to a modernisation thesis: the distinction of law and equity and the preservation of the forms of action were obsolete patches of wilderness in the modern world of corporate capitalism. Without the persistence of these state governments, their practices were doomed to extinction.

Yet these states *were* persistent, and their persistence troubles the fusionist modernisation narrative. Despite their 'retrograde' procedures, Illinois and New Jersey prospered commercially. That the leading edge of corporate and finance capitalism – futures trading in Illinois, general incorporation in New

---

[100] W. Ashburner, *Principles of Equity* (London: Butterworth, 1902), 18.
[101] *Meagher, Gummow and Lehane*, 1st edn [220]–[222]. See M. Tilbury, 'Fallacy or Furphy?: Fusion in a Judicature World' (2003) 26 U.N.S.W.L.J. 357.
[102] Contrast H. S. Maine, *On Early Law and Custom* (London: Murray, 1890), 389.
[103] See Anon., 'Current Topics' (1885) 32 Alb. L.J. 161; C. E. Clark, 'The New Illinois Civil Practice Act' (1933) 1 U. Chi. L. Rev. 209.

Jersey – could originate and flourish in these Yellowstone Parks indicated that modern capitalism might find sufficient 'certainty' and 'efficiency' in the forms of action as it could under fact pleading. The elite lawyer Charles O'Conor (Field's chief opponent in the Erie Wars) admitted as much in the 1846 convention. Although O'Conor favoured fusion and codification at the time, he conceded that the forms of action and the law–equity distinction were 'tolerably understood by the profession generally', who could use the devices 'to bring in such a verdict as worked out the ends of justice'.[104] In the 1870s, O'Conor abandoned the drive towards fusion, while his erstwhile allies grew frustrated with half-reformed jurisdictions.

As the first generation of American fusionists passed, Charles E. Clark became the standard bearer for the next. As dean of the Yale Law School, Clark joined in mocking unreformed Illinois lawyers and was pleased to see the state finally adopt several Field reforms in 1933. Using Field's arguments and even his very words, Clark insisted that nothing made the 'old distinctions ... inherent in the nature of things'.[105] In fact, 'it is unfortunate to continue to speak of law and equity', as, to their dismay, the fusionists found that by debating the distinction between law and equity, their very words were keeping the distinction alive.[106] As a key drafter of the 1938 Federal Rules of Civil Procedure, Clark sought to solve the same problem as Field. The opening provision accordingly declared 'there is one form of action – the civil action' and Clark's note explained that 'reference to actions at law or suits in equity ... should now be treated as referring to the civil action prescribed in these rules'.[107] On the whole, the project has been counted successful, and leading casebooks assert that the Field Code and the Federal Rules 'merged law and equity'. Nevertheless, American jurisprudence continues to rely on the traditional categories to determine whether certain rights or remedies are available to litigants, such as the Seventh Amendment right to a civil jury trial or the application of laches in the absence of a statute of limitations.[108] Over one hundred and seventy years after Field insisted, with sound historicist reasoning, that the distinction between law and equity 'does not inhere in the nature of things',[109] their union in America remains contested and elusive.

---

[104] Croswell and Sutton, *Debates and Proceedings*, 441.
[105] Clark, 'The Union of Law and Equity', 7.   [106] Ibid., 5.
[107] U.S. Federal Rule of Civil Procedure 1, comment 1b (1938).
[108] D. Crump et al., *Cases and Materials on Civil Procedure* (2012), 258–59; J. Oldham, *Trial by Jury: The Seventh Amendment and Anglo-American Special Juries* (New York University Press, 2006), 5–24; S. L. Bray, 'A Little Bit of Laches Goes a Long Way: Notes on *Petrella v. Metro-Goldwyn-Mayer, Inc.*' (2014) 67 Vanderbilt L. Rev. En Banc 1.
[109] Field, 'Legal System of New York', 340.

4

What Did the Makers of the Judicature Acts Understand by 'Fusion'?

MICHAEL LOBBAN

By the middle of 1851, the 'fusion of law and equity' had become 'the slang of the day'.[1] In part inspired by the recent reforms in New York piloted by David Dudley Field, the reformist Law Amendment Society resolved in May that all justice could be administered in one tribunal under one procedural code and that, in cases of conflict, rules of equity should prevail over rules of law.[2] Nearly a quarter of a century later the Supreme Court of Judicature Act 1873 (U.K.) passed,[3] and paved the way for the creation of a single High Court unifying the existing superior courts in one body, which would operate according to a single set of Rules and in which equity was to prevail. The Chancery and common law courts were now fused into one; but whether this constituted a fusion of law and equity has remained a contested issue ever since.

In what follows, we will explore what reformers understood by 'fusion' in this era of reform, in order to understand what they thought the Judicature Act was meant to achieve. In some respects, the fusion of the judicatures was a natural outcome of half a century's agitation by reformist lawyers, often crossing party lines, to modernise England's archaic judicial system.[4] At the same time, by the 1870s the common law and Chancery bars had become quite distinct, with practitioners having a strong sense of the distinct nature of their courts. Although in the eighteenth century practitioners could find work on both sides of Westminster Hall, by the early nineteenth century the bar had

---

[1] Anon., 'The Lord Chancellor, The Law Reformers, and The Profession' (1851) 42 Leg. Ob. 229, 230.
[2] 'Society for Promoting the Amendment of the Law' (1851) 17 L.T. 119, 119.
[3] 36 & 37 Vict. c. 66.
[4] For a view of law reform in the mid-nineteenth century, see M. Lobban, 'Henry Brougham and Law Reform' (2000) 115 E.H.R. 1184.

become increasingly specialised.[5] The abolition of the equity jurisdiction of the Court of Exchequer in 1841 further reduced the opportunities for practice across jurisdictions, and by the middle of the century equity leaders were confining their practice to one of the Chancery courts. While common law men prided themselves on their forensic skills of testing truth through cross examination, the Chancery bar took the view that its paper proceedings were generally more complex.[6] The common law court was an unfamiliar environment for many Chancery men, akin to stepping into a different world. Being about to appear in a copyright case in the Common Pleas, in November 1860 one member of the Chancery bar even felt it necessary to write formally to the Chief Justice, Sir William Erle, to ask whether there was any objection to his 'wearing a moustache which he is desirous of continuing during the winter months'.[7]

As shall be seen, during the debates over fusion both Chancery lawyers and common law men worried about whether the reform might undermine distinctive, valuable features of their system. However, the divergent views over reform did not merely reflect the rival views of different practitioners. Law reformers themselves had different views of the nature of the problem to be solved. Some took the view that the distinction between law and equity was simply a product of a historical development during which the procedure of the common law courts had become ossified, and needed to be supplemented by a more modern and rational court. According to this view, both equity and common law courts applied systems of positive rules, though equity's were more appropriate to modern needs. Once the common law's artificial forms and procedures were done away with, the argument went, a harmonious system would ensue naturally.[8] Others took the view that law and equity were distinct in their very nature. Not only did they deal with different kinds of

---

[5]　O.H.L.E., vol. XI, 1050–51.
[6]　See Sir Edward Sugden's comments in Report of the Select Committee on Official Salaries, H.C.P.P. 1850 (611), XV. 179, 218, q. 2144.
[7]　Letter from Coryton to Sir William Erle (13 November 1860), Bodleian Library, MS Don. c. 71, 91.
[8]　See, for example, [T. H. Farrer], 'The Severance of Law and Equity' (1848) 8 L. Rev. & Q.J. Brit. & Foreign Juris. 62, which reviews C. F. Trower, *The Anomalous Condition of English Jurisprudence*, 1st edn (London: Hatchard & Son, 1848). See also the report of the Law Amendment Society's Special Committee on Law and Equity Procedure (Anon., 'Progress of Union of Law and Equity' (1851) 14 L. Rev. & Q.J. Brit. & Foreign Juris. 143, 152–66) and R. Bethell, 'Inaugural Address', in *Papers Read before the Juridical Society 1855–58* (London: Stevens, Stevens and Norton, 1858), 1–6 and his response to David Dudley Field in Anon., 'Proceedings of Law Societies: Society for Promoting the Amendment of the Law' (1851) 16 L.T. 352, 353 and his observations reported in Anon., 'Proceedings of Law Societies: Juridical Society' (1858) 32 L.T. 140.

rights – seen particularly in the distinction between legal and equitable property – but the very mentality of equity was distinct. Whereas the common law refined all its issues for determination by a jury, equity probed and directed the conscience of multiple parties in a way which could not be done by a jury, but needed the discretionary powers of a judge, exercised in accordance with the maxims of equity. For such reformers, there were limits to how far their procedures could be fused, since the matters dealt with by Chancery judges would need the kind of machinery which had developed in their courts. A third view was held by those who felt that law and equity could be fused into one system, but that it would not occur naturally. Since the rules of law and equity were distinct and often in conflict, any complete fusion would require a codification of the relevant rules.

EARLY DEBATES OVER FUSION

In the first half of the nineteenth century, calls for fusion were rare. Although Jeremy Bentham proposed a new code which would see no distinction between law and equity, his *pannomion* project was not taken up by reformers.[9] It was not until the late 1840s that works such as Charles Francis Trower's *Anomalous Condition of English Jurisprudence* helped put fusion back onto the agenda. Trower called for 'a fusion of the principles on which Legislation is to proceed'; and argued that since equity was based on a set of principles more suited to modern society, the legal ones should be merged into the equitable.[10] He also spent much time exposing the inefficiency and expense of sending parties to different courts and arguing for a simple uniform mode of procedure. This was a topic which was to take up most of the attention of reformers in the early 1850s.[11] The call for fusion continued to be made by reformers attached to the Law Amendment Society throughout this decade. In his first speech as Solicitor General, in February 1853, Richard Bethell told the Commons that in spite of the 'large portion' of Chancery reform effected in

---

[9] One of his admirers, A. J. Johnes, did propose a union of the two jurisdictions in *Suggestions for a Reform of the Court of Chancery, by a Union of the Jurisdictions of Equity and Law with a Plan of a New Tribunal for Cases of Lunacy* (London: Saunders and Benning, 1834). Johnes later wrote a letter: 'On the Union of Law and Equity in relation to the County Courts' (1852) 15 L. Rev. & Q.J. Brit. & Foreign Juris. 313.

[10] Trower, *The Anomalous Condition of English Jurisprudence*, 73. This work may have been the first to use the word 'fusion' in England in relation to this topic. See also C. F. Trower, 'On the Union of Law and Equity' (1851) 15 L. Rev. & Q.J. Brit. & Foreign Juris. 107, 119.

[11] See Special Committee on Law and Equity Procedure, 'Second Report' (1851) 14 L. Rev. & Q.J. Brit. & Foreign Juris. 231; Anon., 'Fusion of Law and Equity' (1852) 16 L. Rev. & Q.J. Brit. & Foreign Juris. 184, 185.

the previous year much remained to be done, and declared that he would himself 'never be content' without 'the consolidation of jurisdiction, and the administration of equity and common law from the same bench'.[12] Five years later, he argued that it should not be implemented gradually, but immediately and completely.[13] His fellow reformers also looked forward to greater fusion. 'The fusion of law and equity was certain to come in time', G. W. Hastings declared in 1859, 'and a uniform code of procedure would follow, of course'.[14]

But many in the profession were more cautious. Responding to Bethell, the *Law Times* observed that it did not yet 'understand what precisely are the changes desired, or even what are the precise things objected to'.[15] When reformers called for fusion, did they mean the fusion of legal and equitable rights, or of procedures or of judicatures? This journal not only felt that different legal and equitable rights could not be fused but also doubted whether the distinct procedures could be fused. As to the fusion of jurisdiction, it noted that the recent trend had been for greater specialisation of courts – such as the separation of bankruptcy from the Chancery. Bethell's projected fusion was if anything 'a policy contrary to the advance of civilisation'.[16] There was nothing illogical in one court determining that a trustee had property in certain assets (as when a trustee was sued in ejectment) and another court determining that the *cestui que trust* should have the benefit of it. Even in a fused court, these questions would need to be dealt with separately. Given the ever-expanding nature of judicial business, the *Law Times* was unconvinced by the project to give all courts complete jurisdiction.[17] Other voices were more progressive, but urged caution. The Metropolitan and Provincial Law Association argued that gradual reform was to be preferred to 'sudden and sweeping change' and supported measures which allowed the court before which a case was brought to determine the entire matter.[18] The *Solicitors' Journal* was also keen on proceeding cautiously.[19] It pointed out that New York's famous reforms had resulted in a large amount of litigation on technical points – often to resolve the question of which

---

[12] H.C. Deb., 14 February 1853, vol. 124, col. 96.

[13] Anon., 'Proceedings of Law Societies: Juridical Society' (1858) 32 L.T. 140. See also Anon., 'Juridical Society' (1858) 3 Sol. Jo. 33, 33, where he urged 'the consolidation of the principles of both law and equity'.

[14] Anon., 'Societies and Institutions: The Travers Lectures' (1859) 3 Sol. Jo. 536.

[15] Anon., 'The Fusion of Law and Equity' (1859) 32 L.T. 170, 170.   [16] Ibid., 171.

[17] Ibid., 170–71.

[18] Anon., 'Metropolitan and Provincial Law Association' (1858) 2 Sol. Jo. 977, 978.

[19] Anon., 'The Chancery Amendment Bill' (1858) 2 Sol. Jo. 518, 518.

cases should go to a jury – and the lesson to be drawn from America was to avoid hasty fusion.[20]

The 1850s saw a number of steps taken by the legislature, on the recommendations of royal commissions appointed to reform the practice and procedure of the Chancery and the common law courts, to confer powers on each of the courts to deal completely with any case which commenced in them. The commissioners were cautious on the question of fusion. In its first report of 1852, the Chancery Commission admitted that it was often difficult to ascertain 'on which side of the boundary line between Law and Equity a particular case may range itself'.[21] However, the commissioners were wary of the proposal to remove the distinction between law and equity, taking the view that any such step 'must be accompanied by a revision of the whole body of our Laws'.[22] They also felt that the distinct subject matter which went to equity would always need a distinct procedure, even if there were to be a single court.[23] They consequently recommended the more modest approach of conferring the jurisdiction exercised by the Chancery on the common law courts, and vice versa, to allow them to 'administer complete justice'. The commissioners postponed discussion of the issue to their third report in 1856 (in part to see the effects of the Common Law Procedure Acts and the Chancery Amendment Acts). This report again reflected their cautious approach, with their main recommendations being to give the Chancery the power to award damages and to hear oral evidence. Any eventual fusion would arrive by slow steps.[24] The common law commissioners similarly felt that a 'consolidation of all the elements of a complete remedy in the same court is obviously desirable' in cases where the two sets of courts 'operate upon the same subject matter in different ways', or applied different forms of remedy.[25] Both courts were accordingly given some of the powers of the other court, notably in the Common Law Procedure Act of 1854 and Cairns's Act of 1858.[26]

However, the piecemeal approach to assimilating the procedures of the courts proved both difficult and controversial. Neither the common law nor

---

[20] Anon., 'The Experience of New York' (1859) 3 Sol. Jo. 182, 182.

[21] *First Report Chancery Commissioners*, 2.   [22] Ibid., 2.

[23] These objections made them doubt the very project of fusion, for 'If the distinction in the procedure be preserved, the union of Equity and Common Law Courts would seem to effect a change more nominal than real': ibid., 3.

[24] This attitude can be seen in Edwin Field's evidence, in which he argued that the first steps towards fusion were to be found in the assimilation of procedure: *Third Report Chancery Commissioners*, 54.

[25] *Second Report Common Law Commissioners*, 39.

[26] For more detail, see Lobban, 'Preparing for Fusion', 565.

the equity judges showed great enthusiasm for using the powers newly conferred on them. By 1858, it was already evident that the common law judges were taking a restrictive view of their power to hear equitable pleas.[27] In this context, two attempts were made to confer greater powers on the common law courts, in areas where they had concurrent jurisdiction with equity. In 1858, Sir William Atherton introduced a bill to amend the 1854 Common Law Procedure Act to 'remove doubts' about the common law courts' equitable power. The bill aimed to give them the same power regarding specific performance and injunctions as the Chancery held and to empower them to 'give the same Relief, absolute, conditional, or other, in Actions of Ejectment and all other Actions' as the Chancery could give. They were to have the same power to enforce their decrees as the Chancery; and the common law Masters were to have the same powers as the Chief Clerks in Chancery to deal with any matter referred to them.[28]

The bill caused some alarm among those – like the *Solicitors' Journal* – who regarded it not as a cautious step towards reducing the cost and inconvenience to litigators, but as a danger to the substantive law. In the view of this journal, the common law's technical system of pleading prevented it from being able to apply the 'larger and more liberal doctrines of courts of equity';[29] for while it was able to deal with simple facts giving rise to defined rights, it was unable to determine whether certain dealings were consistent with good faith or whether a court should exercise a discretionary power. Before common lawyers could begin to deal with equitable principles, their system of pleading would need to be changed. In its view, a simple edict that a common law court would have the powers of a court of equity would mean either that 'the jurisdiction will be tacitly dropped, or the whole equity system will be corrupted by being thrown bodily into the hands of courts and officers utterly unprepared' for this business.[30] It was particularly incredulous at the proposal that the common law courts be empowered to make orders restraining a party from setting up a legal title in cases of ejectment, directing the real title to be tried, as would be done in Chancery. 'It is intelligible that a court which recognises trusts should restrain the setting up in another court which refuses to acknowledge equitable states of a title not equitable good', it commented:

---

[27] E.g., *Mines Royal Society* v. *Magnay* (1854) 10 Ex. 489, 493.

[28] Common Law Procedure Act Amendment Bill, *H.C.P.P.* 1857–58 (85), I. 419, 420–21, cll. 3, 5.

[29] Anon., 'Competition of Law and Equity' (1858) 2 Sol. Jo. 597, 597, invoking J. Story, *Commentaries on Equity Pleadings* (London: Maxwell, 1838), 2.

[30] Anon., 'Competition of Law and Equity' (1858) 2 Sol. Jo. 597, 597.

'But what can surpass the absurdity of a Court issuing an injunction against the production of particular evidence before itself?'[31]

Atherton's bill stalled, but the nature of the common law's powers to deal with matters of equity returned to parliament in 1860 in the wake of the third report of the common law commissioners. This report again disavowed any intention to deal with anything which was part of Chancery's exclusive jurisdiction; but reiterated the view that one court should be able to deal fully with each case before it. The commissioners regretted that the Common Law Procedure Act of 1854 had been too cautious, in not giving the courts the power to issue decrees of specific performance or to issue injunctions to prevent potential infringements of rights. They also wanted to extend the common law's powers to hear equitable pleas, so that the court would hear such pleas even where the conditional relief would be given in equity. They proposed that parties who could have raised equitable defences in a common law case should be prevented from going to equity after the case had commenced; for they were particularly concerned by the continued resort to equity to stop proceedings at law.[32] Only if the common law declared that it was unable to do justice should the case be allowed to go to equity. Less controversially, they proposed giving common law courts the power to relieve against forfeiture for non-payment of rent.

The commissioners' aim was not a fusion of the courts: rather, they claimed they had devised an 'effectual mode of putting an end to the contest between Courts of Common Law and Chancery by so distributing their jurisdiction as to render their interference with one another impossible'.[33] It would abolish the distinction 'between Common Law and Chancery Law' in those areas where the common law courts had jurisdiction – though it would not interfere in Chancery's own area. It would allow each court to confine its operation to the subject matters peculiar to each. There could be no conflict of jurisdiction since 'each court will be armed in itself with exclusive jurisdiction over the subject matter within its cognizance'.[34] However, the bill which embodied their ideas greatly alarmed the Master of the Rolls (Romilly) and the three Vice-Chancellors (Kindersley, Stuart and Wood), who realised that there was more at stake than simply giving the common lawyers the auxiliary powers of equity.[35] They were concerned that under this proposal, a plaintiff would be

---

[31] Ibid., 598.

[32] See *Prothero* v. *Phelps* (1855) 7 De G.M. & G. 722; *Wild* v. *Hillas* (1858) 28 L.J. Ch. 170; *Kingsford* v. *Swinford* (1859) 4 Drew. 705; *Gompertz* v. *Pooley* (1859) 4 Drew. 448.

[33] *Third Report Common Law Commissioners*, 14.   [34] Ibid.

[35] One of the problems for suitors identified by the common law commissioners was that cases at common law could be 'stayed by injunction, upon the ground that there was something in the

able to deprive a defendant of the benefit of having his equitable pleas considered by the judges most competent to deal with them, by taking the case to common law. Just as the *Solicitors' Journal* had in 1858, so the equity judges focused on the fact that the common law courts' procedures and structures were not competent to deal with the kinds of issues which went to equity. This had substantive ramifications: 'As long as the distinction exists between legal and equitable interests', they argued, 'so long will two different courses of procedure be required'.[36] They also predicted that confusion would ensue, as courts of common law and equity would come to different conclusions on the same questions if these powers were conceded. They ended their letter by stating, 'We think no attempt should be made to alter our tribunals until a careful revision has been made of our whole law'.[37]

The common law judges responded by arguing that the changes proposed were much more modest than the equity men seemed to fear. The key question was the common law's inability to hear equitable pleas where the equity was 'conditional on something to be done *in futuro*, or on a contingency'.[38] The common law was unable to deal with such cases, since it had no power over a defendant who failed to perform the condition, having barred the plaintiff's claim. By conferring a power on the common law judges to enforce the condition, the impediment to their entertaining equitable pleas would be removed. The commissioners downplayed the threat to equity. To begin with, they noted that there was no intention to allow the common law courts to consider questions of equitable title to property.[39] They agreed that where the common law's machinery was inadequate, it could not deal with questions of equity. However, they argued that – apart from cases involving property, which were omitted from the bill – there were few cases where equitable rights could not be determined without multiple parties having to be brought before the courts, as the equity judges seemed to fear. They also seemed to concede that the principles of equity required specialist learning, but argued that the cases which would go to common law courts would only involve the simpler questions of equity.[40] The commissioners accepted that bringing law and equity into unison would be better done by substantive law reform rather than

---

proceedings contrary to the law administered in the Court of Chancery, technically called Equity': ibid., 8.
[36] Anon., 'Observations on the Law and Equity Bill' (1860) 4 Sol. Jo. 408, 409.   [37] Ibid.
[38] Anon., 'Law and Equity Bill: Memorial of the Common Law Commissioners Respecting this Bill' (1860) 4 Sol. Jo. 639, 639.
[39] Anon., 'Law and Equity Bill: Memorial of the Common Law Commissioners Respecting this Bill' (1860) 4 Sol. Jo. 657, 662.
[40] Ibid., 663.

through 'a fusion of jurisdiction and procedure'; but they argued that such an approach would be to postpone reform indefinitely – to the 'Greek Kalends'.[41]

Despite the apparently unambitious claims of the commissioners, much of the legal press was ambivalent about the reform. The *Law Times* defended the modern principle of the division of labour, which left specialist questions in the hands of experts, though it also felt that common law judges should be given the power to deal fully with the cases which came before them.[42] The *Solicitors' Journal*'s main concern was not that the principle of fusion was wrong, but that the bill would 'destroy the larger and more comprehensive system' by transferring equitable cases to the common law, 'whose technical forms are utterly incapable of giving free play to equitable principles'.[43] The best way to obtain fusion was to give both sets of courts concurrent powers and give them time to accommodate their practice to their new duties, until it was seen on which foundation a single court of universal jurisdiction could be set up. The idea that there should continue to be separate courts – given the distinct nature of the cases which came before them – but with concurrent powers was attractive to other lawyers as well.[44]

The bill, sponsored by Lord Campbell, ran into trouble. In parliament, Lord St Leonards jumped to the defence of the equity side. While equity men had to know the rules of common law, since equity followed law, equity was 'utterly unimportant' for the common lawyer. Yet this bill (he argued) proposed 'to transfer a great mass of equity business to the common law Courts'.[45] Even that great old champion of reform Lord Brougham argued that 'there could not be a greater mistake than to suppose that a general fusion, as it was called, of law and equity was possible in this country'.[46] In the end, a much more modest bill passed, giving the common law courts power to relieve in cases involving the forfeiture of leases, but leaving the wider question of fusion for the future.

Despite the Law Amendment Society's great push for fusion in 1851, the debate over the next decade concentrated largely on the more modest proposals of reforming the procedures and powers of the courts in order to allow complete justice to be done in one court, in cases where there was concurrent jurisdiction but alternative remedies. The equity judges in particular remained sceptical over whether law and equity could be fused; certainly,

[41] Ibid., 664.
[42] Anon., 'The Equity Judges on the Law and Equity Bill' (1860) 35 L.T. 38; Anon., 'The Fusion' (1860) 35 L.T. 157.
[43] Anon., 'The Fusion of Law and Equity' (1860) 4 Sol. Jo. 552, 552.
[44] See A. H. Houston, *The Fusion of Law and Equity* (London: Sweet, 1867).
[45] H.L. Deb., 22 June 1860, vol. 159, col. 839.   [46] Ibid., col. 840.

they did not feel that there could be a fusion of law and equity without first seeing a reform of the procedures of the common law and a careful consolidation of the rules. At the same time, how far each court could be given the powers of the other without treading on to its proper territory remained controversial.

HATHERLEY'S JUDICATURE BILL

In the late 1860s, reformers began to realise that the approach hitherto followed was unworkable. Litigants still had to deal with a multiplicity of courts, for the Chancery was still issuing injunctions to restrain cases at common law, even where an equitable defence might be pleaded there. Parties still ran the risk of being told by the House of Lords that cases taken to a court of equity should have been brought in a common law court, only to find that the statute of limitations barred their common law action. Addressing the Metropolitan and Provincial Law Association in 1865, H. J. Francis said, 'I have known the ablest counsel at the two bars to meet in consultation and with blank looks declare they did not know whether law or equity should be applied to.'[47] However, there remained divergent views of what fusion meant. While some took the view that the need for any division of business would disappear once 'the present artificial distinction between suits in equity and actions at law' was abolished,[48] others continued to argue that the business of the equity side would still be distinct.[49] Others still felt that there could be no assimilation of the courts without prior legislative preparation in the form of a code of laws.[50]

In was in this context of debate that a Judicature Commission was appointed in September 1867 to inquire 'into the operation and effect of the present separation and division of jurisdictions' and to consider 'uniting and consolidating' them.[51] The appointment of this commission followed a speech in the Commons in February 1867 by Sir Roundell Palmer, which called attention to the problems caused both by the exclusive jurisdiction enjoyed by a number of different courts, and by the problematic system of appeals. Its

[47] Anon., 'Societies and Institutions: Metropolitan Provincial Law Association: Some Remarks on the Fusion of Law and Equity' (1866) 10 Sol. Jo. 206, 207.

[48] Anon., 'Suggestions Addressed to the Judicature Commission' (1868) 12 Sol. Jo. 631, 632.

[49] See Houston, *The Fusion of Law and Equity*, and Anon., 'The Judicature Commission' (1868) 12 Sol. Jo. 621, 622.

[50] Anon., 'Societies and Institutions: Articled Clerks' Society: Codification' (1867) 11 Sol. Jo. 1041, 1041, reporting a lecture on codification by E. Charles to the Articled Clerks' Society.

[51] *First Report Judicature Commissioners*, 4.

remit was consequently wider than the consolidation of law and equity, a topic which had not occupied much of Palmer's time in his speech.[52] The Commission issued its first report in March 1869. Its main concern was with the problems faced by suitors who still had to use multiple courts, despite the recent reforms. The commissioners illustrated the continuing problems caused by the existence of two courts by alluding to the litigation arising from the failure of Overend Gurney and Co., in which the liability of the same set of London Stock Exchange jobbers had to be determined by both the Exchequer Chamber and the Chancery Court of Appeal.[53] The commissioners were critical of a system whereby defendants were 'exposed to the risk of conflicting decisions' from 'Courts operating under different forms of procedure, and being controlled by different Courts of Appeal'.[54] They perceived a particular problem arising from complex company failures: in such cases, the liability of directors had 'frequently been brought into question in both jurisdictions and sometimes with opposite results'.[55] This convinced them that a tribunal was needed with 'full power of dealing with all the complicated rights and obligations springing out of such transactions', whether legal or equitable.[56] The commissioners also noted the 'strange working of a system of separate jurisdictions' in the county courts, which had a jurisdiction in common law, equity and chancery matters; but which dealt with them through distinct procedures and sent appeals to different courts.[57] The solution to the problem was not to be found in any further 'transfer or blending of jurisdiction between the Courts'[58]: there had to be a single court.

What kind of fusion did this entail? The commissioners did not elaborate in detail on the kind of fusion they had in mind. On the one hand, the report's proposals relating to the structure of the new court suggested that the reform they had in mind was more one of procedure than substance, aimed at making life easier for the litigant rather than transforming the law. The report thus proposed that there be separate divisions, based on the existing courts, with different classes of business going to the different divisions.[59] On the other

---

[52] Palmer had, however, defended the notion of an appeal court composed of lawyers with different specialisms: at this level 'a fusion of the two would be an absolutely good thing in itself': H.C. Deb., 22 February 1867, vol. 185, col. 849. Palmer's views were enthusiastically endorsed by *The Times*, which argued that 'a great deal would be gained by requiring every Judge to transact every kind of business': 'The Speech of Roundell Palmer', *The Times*, 25 February 1867, 8.

[53] *Coles v. Bristowe* (1868) L.R. 4 Ch. App. 3; *Grissell v. Bristowe* (1868) L.R. 4 C.P. 36.

[54] *First Report Judicature Commissioners*, 7.   [55] Ibid.   [56] Ibid.   [57] Ibid., 8.

[58] Ibid., 9.

[59] Ibid., 10. See also Anon., 'The Report of the Judicature Commission – No. I' (1869) 13 Sol. Jo. 489, which stressed the need for distinct procedures.

hand, the commissioners' allusions to the Overend Gurney cases – and the rival approaches to misrepresentation developing in courts of law and equity – suggest that they sought a court which in which a unified set of substantive rules would emerge.

Less than a year after the report, Lord Hatherley announced to the Lords his plans to introduce legislation based on the recommendations of the Judicature Commission. It had become clear that 'the only plan is to intrust to one Court jurisdiction over the whole subject-matter of any cause'.[60] However, while deprecating the existence of separate courts, Hatherley argued that the new court 'should have the power of dividing itself into separate divisions' in order that business could be assigned 'to that Court which shall seem most appropriate for it'.[61] This meant that 'you will still have a Court of Chancery, or a Court equivalent to the Court of Chancery – for, as to names, there is no great magic in them'.[62] The bill duly divided the High Court into five divisions which were named after the courts they were to replace, though the judges were given unlimited power to transfer proceedings from one divisional court to another.[63]

Hatherley did not lay very firm foundations for his measure. To begin with, he failed to consult the judges beyond sending them copies of the bill, resting content that their views had been sufficiently represented by the members of the Judicature Commission.[64] Moreover, the bill was very short on detail about how fusion was to be effected. Although the Lord Chancellor told the Lords that the procedure of the different divisions was to be assimilated 'so far as is possible', he left the details to be worked out by rules. Nor did the bill say anything regarding the relation between law and equity, leaving it entirely open as to which was to prevail in case of conflict. The maintenance of separate divisions and the absence of provisions relating to the substantive law suggested that the aim of the bill was largely procedural, designed primarily to solve the practical problem faced by litigants of needing to use different courts.

Hatherley's initial bill was amended in April to address two areas of concern. First, there was concern among many Lords with the proposal to leave it to the judges to frame the Rules of Court. Lord Westbury objected that if the

---

[60] H.L. Deb., 18 February 1870, vol. 199, col. 510.   [61] Ibid., col. 513.   [62] Ibid., col. 514.
[63] High Court of Justice Bill, H.L.S.P. 1870 (32), IV.463.
[64] The *Law Magazine* criticised the Lord Chancellor for introducing the bill before the Judicature Commission had finished its work, and for giving only a skeleton procedure bill: Anon., 'The Lord Chancellor's Judicature Bills' (1870) 29 Law Mag. 152, 153.

full implementation of the scheme had to await the agreement of the common law and equity judges on a set of rules, it could take forty years.[65] In response, Hatherley proposed to give the crown power to issue rules by Order in Council on the advice of the Privy Council. Secondly, the amended bill included a provision determining how conflicts between law and equity were to be resolved. An initial amendment was proposed in committee by Lord Penzance, to declare that 'The existing distinction between the principles upon which justice is administered in courts of law and the courts of equity is hereby abolished'. The principles acted on in equity were to 'be deemed part of the common law' and where common law principles conflicted with them, they were to be held 'restrained, modified, or wholly superseded' to the extent of such conflict. The proposed clause also provided that it was not to be construed to 'impair, alter, qualify, or in any way vary the rights of property' and that 'the relations hitherto recognized under the names of legal and equitable estate' should remain in full force.[66] The version which eventually found its way into the bill printed in early April was more modest, declaring that any jurisdiction hitherto exercised by the Chancery or Admiralty (otherwise than by statute) was to be declared part of the common law and to modify the common law to the extent to which it differed from it.[67] This formulation worried Lord Westbury,[68] who proposed a different formulation which was incorporated into the bill at the end of May: equity 'shall henceforth be blended and united with the common law of England' and 'control and modify the defects thereof', with the effect that 'equity and common law, so united as aforesaid, may be administered in all the aforesaid courts without difference or distinction'.[69]

Even as amended, the bill was vague on the nature of the fusion, though it was clear that the shape of court would echo the existing division of common law and Chancery business. But did it entail fusion? It became evident over the summer of 1870 that there was a great deal of disagreement over what fusion entailed. Three approaches may be discerned. First, some took the view that there could never be a fusion of law and equity. Sir Richard Malins V.-C. said that any attempt to fuse law and equity would be as futile as any attempt to fuse the army and navy: one could no sooner imagine equity administered by a common law court than a warship sailing over land.[70] This was also the view

---

[65] H.L. Deb., 18 March 1870, vol. 200, col. 176.   [66] H.L.S.P. 1870 (32a) IV.479.
[67] H.L.S.P. 1870 (72) IV.483.   [68] H.L. Deb., 29 April 1870, vol. 200, cols 2049–50.
[69] H.L.S.P. 1870 (72d) IV.507, 1870 (120) IV.513. It also provided that every right or defence available in equity should be available in any division of the High Court.
[70] Anon., 'The Abortive Law Reforms' (1870) 15 Sol. Jo. 67, 68.

taken by Lord St Leonards, who reiterated the opposition to fusion he had raised in 1860.[71] Even some supporters of the bill, such as Lord Penzance, felt that law and equity were essentially distinct. He rejoiced:

> that this Bill provides for the re-distribution of business, by which the class of business which flows into the Common Law Courts shall find its way to the common law division, and the class of business which flows into the Courts of Equity shall find its way to the equity division of the Court.[72]

At the other end of the reformist spectrum, a second view was put forward which held that fusion was desirable, but that it could not be effected by the simple creation of a unified code of procedure. This was the position taken by Lord Romilly, who argued that substantive questions would need to be addressed. He gave as an illustration the rival views of courts of law and equity on estates for life without impeachment of waste. At common law, the tenant of such an estate was not liable for waste, yet in equity he could be restrained from making an inequitable use of his legal right. If the courts were to be fused, there would have to be one rule laid down: and it would be necessary to define exactly what was meant by 'an estate for life without impeachment of waste'.[73]

A third intermediate view suggested that once a common court operating on a common procedure was set up, then substantive fusion would follow naturally. Some, such as Lord Cairns, argued that the difference between the systems was one of procedure rather than principle,[74] which meant that once procedure was reformed, fusion would follow. Others agreed that fusion could occur once a common procedure was created, but argued that there were distinctions of principle which could only be removed by careful distribution of the judicial personnel. As Lord Westbury pointed out, 'the jurisdiction and principles of the one set of Courts are almost *terra incognita* to the practitioners in the other'.[75] Complete fusion would require time, as equity lawyers educated the common lawyers in their principles.

A number of commentators in the press agreed that a full consolidation of the courts and their procedure would result in substantive fusion.

---

[71] Lord St Leonards, *Observations on Transfer of Land Bill and other Law Bills in Parliament* (London: Murray, 1870), 50–65, 112–20. See also *The Times*, 10 May 1870, 4.

[72] H.L. Deb., 18 March 1870, vol. 200, col. 185. See also his views in H.L. Deb., 29 April 1870, vol. 200, col. 2051, where he argued that '[s]o long as the substance and subject-matter of cases remain different, so long will one form of procedure be proper for one form of case, and a different form for another'.

[73] H.L. Deb., 29 April 1870, vol. 200, col. 2039.   [74] Ibid., col. 2041.

[75] H.L. Deb., 18 February 1870, vol. 199, col. 523.

The *Saturday Review* was critical of Lord Penzance's approach, taking his description of the reform to mean that the new court would be designed in such a way to empower the common law judges to cast off anything which savoured of equity, and to allow the equity side to transfer anything which savoured of law: '[t]he bandying of suitors from Court to Court will continue as now, but the operation will be a little more conveniently performed'.[76] In this journal's view, it was fatal to any scheme of fusion to keep the judges grouped in their divisions. Commenting on Lord Cairns's position, the *Law Times* agreed that there was no fundamental distinction between matters of law and equity. In its view, the only equitable matter the common law courts could not deal with was the discretionary trust, and this was only because it lacked the requisite administrative machinery. Unlike the *Saturday Review*, however, this journal supported the division of the court, observing that:

> though a common law Judge may exercise the equitable or other peculiar jurisdiction in easy cases, there will often be others which it will be more safe and more proper to refer to the division more versed in such matters.[77]

The measure's chances of passing were fatally undermined by the intervention of the Lord Chief Justice, Cockburn, who in May 1870 published a pamphlet, *Our Judicial System*.[78] Cockburn's most pressing objections were not to the fusion of law and equity, for he admitted that distinction between them was an anomaly which needed to be removed and agreed that where they differed, law should follow equity.[79] His main objections were to Hatherley's proposal to give the Privy Council the power to make the rules, which was widely seen as an unconstitutional assumption of powers by the executive; and to the merger of the Queen's Bench's non-civil law jurisdiction (in respect of crime and the prerogative writs) into the High Court.[80] Paradoxically, he favoured the substantive fusion of law and equity much more than the union of criminal, public and civil law judicatures. However, he raised some telling questions about the nature of the proposed fusion of law and equity. He pointed out that it was entirely unclear from the bill whether it was intended to substitute equity for law where the two were in conflict, or whether the common law was to apply equitable principles to common law rights. Cockburn accepted that there was no reason why the common law should not recognise trusts or the married woman's separate property; there was no reason for different rules relating to the priority of creditors; nor any reason for formal

---

[76] Anon., 'The Chancellor's Law Reforms' (1870) 29 Sat. Rev. 400, 401.
[77] Anon., 'The Debate on the Judicature Bills' (1870) 49 L.T. 2, 3.
[78] (London: Ridgway, 1870).   [79] Ibid., 4–5.   [80] Ibid., 43.

deeds to be recognised at common law which were denied in equity. But like Westbury and Romilly, he argued that these were major questions which could not be settled by rules, but needed 'a careful collation of the two systems with a view to the blending of the two into something more complete and perfect than either'.[81] Soon after the publication of his pamphlet, Cockburn and the other common law judges also responded formally to the bill by sending series of resolutions to the Lord Chancellor which largely reiterated Cockburn's position.[82]

Three different reactions to Cockburn's objections and the consequent failure of the bill can be identified, which echo the three positions already outlined. The first came from the *Solicitors' Journal*, which took a very conservative view of the aims of the bill. According to this journal, the bill was not intended to expand equity so that it would be applied to every case at common law. It simply sought to enact that every right existing at law or in equity should be enforceable in every court and that 'whenever the doctrines of law and equity are conflicted, the latter must prevail'.[83] This was a modest view of the changes envisaged: since, under the old divided system, the equitable rule would always prevail – albeit at some cost to the parties – this only ensured that the same result would obtain within one unified court. G. W. Hastings similarly told the Law Amendment Society that the bill did not change the law, but only the procedure.[84]

The second came from the *Saturday Review*, which feared the very kind of watering down of an ambitious reform which the Lord Chief Justice's pamphlet seemed to herald. This journal was convinced that the new system should be based on equitable procedure and be administered by men who understood equity, the system most adapted to the needs of modern life. It was particularly concerned by Cockburn's view that one could simply leave it to the common lawyers to administer equity in 'Common Law Courts absolutely untouched with their old privileges and their old traditions'.[85] Left in the hands of the common law judges, equity would soon become unrecognisable. It was better to wait for a proper reform, it concluded, than to fail. As this journal saw it, equity was not simply a set of rules which common law judges

---

[81] Ibid., 27.

[82] Thus, they resolved that a 'careful collation of the Common Law and Equity Law' was needed, or at least the framing by parliament of clear principles on this issue. Willes J. (who did not attend the meeting) issued his own response. See Anon., 'The High Court of Justice Bill and the Appellate Jurisdiction Bill', *The Times*, 23 May 1870, 13.

[83] Anon., 'The Lord Chief Justice on the Judicature Bills' (1870) 14 Sol. Jo. 567, 567.

[84] Anon., 'Law Societies: Law Amendment Society' (1870) 49 L.T. 18, 18.

[85] Anon., 'The Fight for the Legal Championship' (1870) 29 Sat. Rev. 629, 630.

could administer in their own courts: the tribunals which administered equity
had to be 'informed with the spirit of Equity'.[86] This meant that they would
have to sit side-by-side with the Chancery men: '[t]he fusion of Law and
Equity is a practical impossibility without the fusion of the Courts'.[87]

The third reaction came from Romilly and Lush, who were asked for their
observations on the bills after their failure. Like Cockburn, they argued that
much more attention needed to be paid to the substantive detail.[88] Romilly
was particularly concerned by Westbury's provision that equity should be
blended with and control the common law, and that every right and defence
recognised in equity should be recognised in the High Court. He envisaged
'an enormous amount of litigation'[89] resulting from these changes, particularly
from the rule that in cases of clash, equity was to prevail. According to the bill,
where equity would relieve against them, the rules of common law were put
an end to: 'But in putting an end to these rights Equity is shaken to her very
foundations, which all rest upon those very rights'.[90] Romilly explained that
'[t]he system of Equity is not a distinct system of law, but a personal interference with persons having legal rights, preventing them from making an unfair
use of them'.[91] If the legal rights underpinning both systems were considered
to be repealed, that might generate much confusion.[92] For Romilly, 'a fusion
of law and equity can only be accomplished, as it has been in India, by
framing and passing a new code'.[93] 'The vice of the measure', Lush noted,
'consists in its dealing with the "fusion" as a matter of jurisdiction, instead of a
matter of substantive law; thus making it the law of the Court, instead of the
law of the land'.[94] He anticipated a dual system in future, where the law
administered in the inferior courts would be different from that applied in the
superior courts. Like Romilly, Lush argued that fusion had to be effected 'by
way of substantive enactment' declaring what the law in each case should be.

---

[86] Anon., 'The Judges and the Chancellor' (1870) 29 Sat. Rev. 696, 697.   [87] Ibid.
[88] 'Copy of the Observations of the Lord Chief Justice, the Master of the Rolls, and Mr Justice
Lush on the High Court of Justice Bill and the Supreme Court of Appeal Bill', H.L.S.P. 1872
(57) XVIII.93.
[89] Ibid., 13.   [90] Ibid.   [91] Ibid.
[92] Ibid. Romilly asked (ibid.) whether the legal estate of the mortgagee would be considered
repealed: if the relevant section of the bill were regarded as 'a new Statute of uses', it would
seem 'rather a considerable change in the law to be effected by a side wind, and will impose
prodigious legislative duties on the 19 judges'. He added, 'It was established in *Kellock's case*
[(1868) L.R. 3 Ch. App. 769], that a secured creditor having acquired at law an absolute right to
a pledge, that right would not be interfered with in Equity till he had received the whole
amount due to him, and that accordingly he could prove against a company in liquidation for
the whole sum due, but if the legal right to both the pledge and the debt be destroyed . . . how
can that case be supported?'
[93] Ibid.   [94] Ibid., 13–14.

The general enactment in the bill – that equity should be blended with common law 'and control and modify the same' – would only cause confusion and litigation.[95]

In light of the experience of Hatherley's bill, the prospects for fusion did not look optimistic in the early 1870s. When Vernon Harcourt sought to put reform back on the agenda in July 1872, the Solicitor General, Sir George Jessel, poured cold water on the idea, reminding the house of the 'universal disapprobation' given to the previous bill by the superior court judges.[96] Two months later, the Attorney General, Sir John Coleridge, addressed the Social Science Association on the topic of law reform, defending a piecemeal approach to reform. Although he argued that it was barbaric and inconvenient to have two rival sets of courts, he added that law and equity were distinct by their nature and that the procedures used in each were adapted to their distinct nature. This did not make him hostile to fusion, but made him observe that the best way to obtain fusion would be through a code: 'Fusing law and equity by an enactment in terms that they shall be fused, and that whenever they conflict, equity shall prevail, appears to me ... an utterly impracticable and slovenly way of dealing with the question.'[97] Short of such fusion he advocated giving each court the powers of the other, in effect the policy of the previous decade.

SELBORNE'S JUDICATURE BILL

Reform of the Superior Courts returned to the political agenda with the appointment of Roundell Palmer as Lord Chancellor (with the title of Lord Selborne) in October 1872. Unlike his predecessor, Selborne took care to consult the judges before introducing his bill. Cockburn and Romilly continued to argue for a more substantive fusion. Cockburn wished to see the distinction between law and equity removed:

> for ever – even to the very name of Equity – by Equity being converted into Law – instead of the distinction being retained and the remedy for the short-comings of the Law – as distinguished from Equity – being sought in the fusion, not of the substantive law, but of jurisdiction.[98]

[95] Ibid.
[96] H.C. Deb., 26 July 1872, vol. 212, cols 1920 and 1933. See also Sir John Coleridge A.-G.'s response at cols 1943–44.
[97] Anon., 'The Attorney General's Address on Law Reform' (1872) 1 Law Mag. 795, 800.
[98] Selborne MSS 1865, f. 215 (7 February 1873).

Romilly reiterated his desire to have a reform after the Indian model: every court should deal with the same matter, with cases commenced by simple plaints being heard by single judges. He also wanted business to be assigned to different courts alphabetically, so that it would be dealt with in different courts by rotation. 'The subdivision and conflict of law has arisen principally from the division and substitution of different sorts of business amongst different courts', he added, 'and will arise again if not prevented.'[99]

Selborne's bill aimed to overcome some of the objections raised by the lawyers in 1870, both in setting out rules of procedure in a schedule (which the judges were empowered to modify) and in preserving the old judicial titles. It provided that law and equity were to be 'concurrently' administered in the High Court and Court of Appeal. It stipulated that the court should give any plaintiff or defendant the same equitable rights or relief which would have been available in Chancery. The courts were to take note of all equitable estates, titles and rights, just as the Chancery would; and subject to the provisions giving effect to equitable rights, the courts 'shall recognise and give effect to all legal claims and demands, and all estates, titles, rights, duties, obligations, and liabilities existing by the Common Law'.[100] This overcame Romilly's objections to the previous bill, that the triumph of equity would kill law. However, like Hatherley's bill, Selborne's provided for divisions of the High Court reflecting the old pre-fusion courts.

It did not seek to codify law and equity, but it did set out ten areas where common law rules conflicted with equity and specified the solution. While it went into greater detail than Hatherley's bill in dealing with potential conflicts, the limited number addressed suggested that there was no perception in the government's mind that there was a general clash of doctrines which needed radical reconciliation, in the way Cockburn and Romilly thought. The initial bill did not include a general clause providing that in case of conflict or variance between rules of law and equity, the latter should prevail, though such a clause was introduced at the report stage.[101] Among the ten

---

[99] He also proposed that every three or five years, a committee of the judges should harmonise the decisions of different Courts of Appeal 'and make rules for the guidance of the Judges in future; after which previous decisions should not be cited. In this way you would gradually form one complete and consistent code': Letter from Romilly to Selborne (undated), Selborne MS 1865, ff. 233–35. See also Romilly's views expressed in H.L. Deb., 11 March 1873, vol. 214, col. 1723.
[100] *H.L.S.P.* 1873 (14) VII, s. 25.
[101] Cockburn had suggested to Selborne the inclusion of such a clause: Selborne MS 1865, ff. 215–16.

specific provisions, one provision was to solve the problem relating to conflicting rules on waste which Romilly had raised in 1870.[102] Other provisions related to conflicts in the way the courts dealt with the custody of children and time clauses in contracts. The bill also initially included a clause relating to conflicting approaches to misrepresentation. The proposed section 26(8) read:

> In any suit or proceeding for damages or other relief on the ground of any untrue representation of fact, by reason of which any loss is alleged to have been sustained, it shall not be necessary to prove knowledge of the untruth of such representation by the person who made the same, if such person knew that information was being sought thereon by the person to whom the representation was made in any matter concerning his interest.

If this is an example of an attempt by Selborne to devise a rule which would fuse conflicting approaches in law and equity, it soon ran into trouble from a judge who felt it made an undesirable substantive change to the law. Lord Justice Mellish – a common lawyer who had been appointed a Chancery appeal judge – set out his objections to the Lord Chancellor. These included the objection that the clause would abolish 'the distinction which now prevails in Courts of Common Law between representations and warranties in the sales of personal chattels':

> At present the rule of law well known to every broker, who draws up written contracts, is that whatever representations may have been made respecting the chattels during the negociation of the bargain by the seller, he will not be bound to make them good, unless they are introduced into the contract as warranties, or unless the seller was guilty of fraud in making the representations. I think this rule of law ought not to be altered, first because it enables the parties to talk to each other freely during the negociation, secondly because if the parties intend that the seller should be liable in all events to make good his representations, there is a stipulation which is part of the contract, and ought to be inserted in the contract, and thirdly if the parties do not so intend, it is unjust to put a purchaser who has purchased goods at a lower price because he has got no warranty in the same position as if he had got a warranty.[103]

---

[102] W. F. Finlason argued that the provision had been inserted to pacify Romilly, and he argued that it was unnecessary: W. F. Finlason, *An Exposition of Our Judicial System and Civil Procedure as Reconstructed under the Judicature Acts* (London: Longmans, Green & Co., 1877), 125.

[103] Selborne MS 1865, ff. 228–30.

Although when Selborne brought the bill, he announced that it would 'adopt the equitable rule as to liability for misrepresentation',[104] the clause was dropped during the passage of the bill.

When the bill was first printed, it got mixed reactions.[105] The *Solicitors' Journal* (whose articles on fusion were written by Arthur Wilson[106]) anticipated that the immediate effects of the measure would be slight, 'the apparent object being, not to revolutionise – nay, scarcely even to reform – our judicature, but rather to supply it with the power of gradually effecting the needful reforms'.[107] While there would be a preponderance of common lawyers in the new court, the journal was confident that the Court of Appeal could ensure the purity of equity jurisprudence.[108] Commenting (anonymously) on the bill in the *Saturday Review*, G. W. Hemming (an equity man) described the fusion as nominal: for the allocation of business between divisions mimicking the existing courts was to 'exclude all real union'.[109] 'What is the use of saying that each Court shall have universal jurisdiction if rules are framed for distributing the business in precisely the same grooves which it has hitherto followed?'[110] He argued that the 1873 bill reflected Penzance's view – that it was impossible to fuse the two. Hemming felt that the 'hard, coarse doctrines of the Law must be merged and swallowed up in the higher, broader, and more refined principles of Equity'.[111] This could only be done by abandoning the idea that the names, constitution and personnel of the old courts should be maintained: there had to be equity judges sitting in each of the courts.

When the bill came on for a second reading in the Lords, Lord Hatherley explained what he understood fusion to mean. It did not mean any abolition of the distinction between law and equity: '[t]here must be distinctions between legal and beneficial ownerships'.[112] The aim of the bill was the more modest one of allowing one court to have charge of any case brought before it from start to end. Some lords objected that the bill would simply preserve the old separate structures, with law and equity flowing in different channels. Selborne's response was to argue that parliament had to move 'by practical

---

[104] H.L. Deb., 13 February 1873, vol. 214, col. 340.
[105] Anon., 'Societies and Institutions: Law Amendment Society: The Judicial System' (1873) 17 Sol. Jo. 388, 389.
[106] They were reprinted as A. Wilson, *Equity and the Judicature Bill* (London: King & Co., 1873).
[107] Anon., 'Societies and Institutions: Law Amendment Society: The Judicial System' (1873) 17 Sol. Jo. 388, 389.
[108] Anon., 'The Projected Law Reform' (1873) 17 Sol. Jo. 361, 361.
[109] Anon., 'The Lord Chancellor's Bill' (1873) 35 Sat. Rev. 232, 233.   [110] Ibid.   [111] Ibid.
[112] H.L. Deb., 11 March 1873, vol. 214, col. 1717.

steps and degrees ... Time and experience were requisite to bring to perfection the union of law and equity'.[113] There was no intention merely to reproduce the old separate courts: the divisions were created for 'the more convenient dispatch of business only'.[114] The plan was not that all equitable questions should go to the Chancery Division, though he expected that the destination of the business would be to a 'great extent determined by the nature of the business and the experience acquired by the different Judges in administering that particular class of business'.[115] In the early stages of the reform at least, Selborne argued, it was better to classify the business according to its subject matter.[116]

Selborne's explanation seemed to suggest that the government had in mind a natural convergence of law and equity, which would follow a union of courts and procedures. However, this fuelled the fears of equity barristers that the preponderance of common law judges in the new court could result (as Hemming put it) in 'the deterioration of Equity jurisprudence'.[117] With seventeen common law judges and only four equity ones it would take two generations for the common law's numerical preponderance to be overcome, by which time the principles of equity jurisprudence would have been fatally damaged.[118] Hemming urged that equity jurisprudence rested on the court of Chancery and was preserved by its power to issue injunctions to prevent parties going to common law: this injunctive power (removed by the bill) needed to be maintained until the full fusion had been effected.[119] In a series of articles over the summer, he reiterated his objections to the Chancery side being 'crippled' by having its authority limited, while equity jurisprudence was confined to inexperienced hands in other divisions. Hemming protested against what he perceived to be the 'degradation' of the Chancery Division into a largely administrative tribunal and argued that each of the Vice-Chancellors courts should form the basis of a new division, since they were as much distinct courts as the common law ones.[120] While Hemming disowned any suggestion that he simply wanted to maintain the old separation,

[113] Ibid., 1731.   [114] Ibid., 1733.   [115] Ibid., 1734.
[116] 'He could not but think that under the Bill there would be abundant opportunity for administering equity in all the Divisions of the Court, while at the same time care was taken to adhere to the natural principles of classification, such as experience indicated as the most convenient to adopt in the first instance': ibid., cols 1734–35.
[117] Anon., 'The Chancellor's Defence of his Bill' (1873) 35 Sat. Rev. 332, 332.   [118] Ibid., 333.
[119] Ibid., 332.
[120] Anon., 'The Judicature Bill' (1873) 35 Sat. Rev. 436; Anon., 'The Judicature Bill' (1873) 35 Sat. Rev. 705.

he was ambivalent about a form of fusion which he feared would undermine the specialist knowledge of equity.[121]

The wider equity bar was also alarmed. Both the silks and the juniors addressed letters to the Lord Chancellor and the members of the Lords' select committee on the bill, expressing concern that the paramount powers of the Court of Chancery were lost under the bill. Like Hemming, they worried that the Lord Chancellor would not be part of this division and that much of its time would be taken up with administrative business. Rather than promoting fusion, the bill would endanger equity jurisprudence.[122] Lord Cairns shared the equity lawyers' concern that the Lord Chancellor was not a member of the High Court, telling the Lords that the effect of the bill would be to reduce the number of primary equity judges. Since its aim was to bring about fusion, it was of the greatest importance that the Chancery court should not be weakened 'either numerically or morally'.[123] He argued that just as a fusion of gold and silver with 15 parts silver and 4 parts gold would create an alloy which would be more silver than gold, so a fusion of 15 parts common law and 4 parts equity would result in the preponderance of the common law.

A number of common lawyers responded sceptically to the equity lawyers' arguments. The *Law Magazine* was sceptical about the entire measure, seeking to rebut the notion that the common law was mere chicanery while equity was pure morality and to reject a reform they saw as subordinating the common law to equity. It was perfectly natural that the common law 'should be made to absorb in a more complete matter Equity principles ... but that Equity the accessory should supplant Common Law the principal is not so'.[124] In the view of this journal, all that was needed was an extension of the principles behind the Common Law Procedure Act of 1854. Other periodicals also took the common lawyers' side, albeit with greater enthusiasm for the measure. The *Law Times* was ready to concede that there should be an equity judge in each division, but was of the view that there was 'nothing mysterious or occult about equity jurisprudence'.[125] Nor did the *Solicitors' Journal* see equity as forming the larger part of modern jurisprudence: indeed, it commented that the notion that common law be merged into equity was akin to a

---

[121] His writings were gathered in G. W. Hemming, *Thoughts on the Fusion of Law and Equity, suggested by the Lord Chancellor's Bill* (London: MacMillan, 1873). See also G. W. Hemming, 'Equity, Law and Justice', *The Times*, 15 May 1873, 12, in answer to W. Forsyth, 'Law, Equity and Justice', *The Times*, 12 May 1873, 13.

[122] The letters were published in 'The Judicature Bill' (1873) 17 Sol. Jo. 521, 521–23.

[123] H.L. Deb. 1 May 1873, vol. 215, col. 1265. See also Selborne MS 1865, f. 270 (18 April 1873).

[124] Anon., 'Ought the Judicature Bill to Pass?' (1873) 2 Law Mag. 534, 539.

[125] Anon., 'The Law and the Lawyers' (1873) 55 L.T. 92.

proposal to merge Great Britain into Berwick-upon-Tweed, adding 'Equity, great as is its importance, and beneficial as is its influence, is, when compared with the Common Law, extremely limited in its range."[126] The *Solicitors' Journal* agreed with Hemming that both legal and equitable forms of property would continue to exist after fusion, and that every court would have to recognise every kind of property. However, the only difficulty common lawyers would encounter would be in areas where legal and equitable doctrines were inconsistent (as in mortgages, fraud or undue influence). Since equity was not 'an aroma, nor a mystic tradition' but a body of positive law, it could be learned and applied by common lawyers.[127] They might occasionally make mistakes when applying the rules of equity, but that was the price which had to be paid for fusion.[128]

At the same time, the *Solicitors' Journal* was sceptical about plans to spread the equity judges across all the divisions, preferring to maintain a degree of specialisation. There was a natural division of labour, it argued, and it was 'impossible to suppose that Common Law Judges could manage the administrative business of the Court of Chancery, or work out a complicated suit with anything like the efficiency of Equity Judges'.[129] A similar view was put forward by William Forsyth. In Forsyth's view, the equity lawyers' opinions about the distinct nature of their jurisprudence were exaggerated.[130] At the same time, he argued that no one in their right mind would think of abolishing trusts and that it made sense to maintain a division of labour when it came to dealing with a subject as 'artificial and complicated' as trusts, even though every court should recognise all legal and equitable rights.[131]

Selborne's response to the criticisms about the staffing of the divisions was not to increase the number of equity judges – which the Treasury would not allow – but to accept Cairns's proposal that the Lord Chancellor should be head of the Chancery Division (though it was not expected that he would sit often in that court).[132] For further reassurance, when the bill went to the Commons, Sir John Coleridge reassured the equity men that the common law divisions should be strengthened from the outset with judges trained in equity.[133] This was not to be written into the legislation, but implemented

---

[126] Anon., 'Mr Hemming on Fusion' (1873) 17 Sol. Jo. 496, 497.

[127] Anon., 'Fusion' (1873) 17 Sol. Jo. 513, 514.

[128] Ibid. See Anon., 'Fusion' (1873) 17 Sol. Jo. 549, 552.

[129] Anon., 'Fusion' (1873) 17 Sol. Jo. 529, 530, answering a restatement of the equity bar's position by A. E. Miller Q.C., 'General Correspondence: Fusion' (1873) 17 Sol. Jo. 532.

[130] 'Law, Equity and Justice', *The Times*, 12 May 1873, 13.   [131] Ibid.

[132] See Anon., 'The Last Stage of the Judicature Bill in The Lords' (1873) 55 L.T. 21, 21.

[133] Anon., 'The Judicature Bill' (1873) 35 Sat. Rev. 770, 771.

informally. In fact, by the time the bill reached the Commons it was becoming increasingly clear that the ambitions of this bill – which preserved the old divisions with their distinct personnel, and which retained a preponderance of common law judges – were modest indeed. The spokesman for the equity men in the Commons, Osborne Morgan, feared that the bill would only effect a paper fusion. It was not enough to enact that in cases of conflict, equity would prevail: it would be impossible effectually to fuse Law and Equity 'until all the Courts were provided with the same machinery'.[134] Vernon Harcourt also complained that the bill 'perpetuated and stereotyped the distinctions in the existing system' through the different divisions.[135] Harcourt wanted the old titles of the chiefs of the courts to be removed, so that the divisions would not reflect a law/equity distinction. Other members agreed that the bill kept everything 'in the old groove'.[136]

Responding to these criticisms, the law officers offered conflicting visions. Sir George Jessel, the Solicitor General, told the Commons that the Chancery Division was meant to be transitional rather than permanent, and that no additional staff were needed. In his view, as each side became acquainted with the other's doctrines so fusion would be effected.[137] Jessel's vision thus suggested an unproblematic fusion following naturally from the union of the present judicatures, somewhat like the view expressed by Cairns in 1870. Coleridge, speaking after him, took a different view: 'Law and Equity were two things inherently distinct, and the distinction was not capable of being destroyed by Act of Parliament.'[138] The aim of the bill was the rather more modest one of ensuring that parties were not sent from one court to another for a remedy. As he put it, 'the object was not that Law and Equity should be fused, but that they should be concurrently administered'.[139]

CONCLUSIONS

The Judicature Act created a single High Court, in which cases would be commenced in the same way in each division and in which each division had power to administer complete justice. There was a division of labour, and the Chancery Division was given a distinct administrative machinery, adapted to dealing with the complicated questions arising from the execution of trusts and the distribution of estates. In the early years of the court, efforts were made

---

[134] H.C. Deb., 9 June 1873, vol. 216, col. 666.
[135] H.C. Deb., 30 June 1873, vol. 216, cols 1574–75.   [136] Ibid., col. 1591 (C. E. Lewis).
[137] Ibid., cols 1587–89.   [138] Ibid., col. 1601.
[139] Ibid. See his comments in H.C. Deb., 9 June 1873, vol. 216, col. 644.

to 'mingle the waters' by placing equity men in the common law side and vice versa. This reflected the ambition of men like Cairns and Jessel that once the judicatures were united and a common procedure created, there might be a gradual assimilation of common law and equity into one fused body of doctrine, as judges from one side imbibed the approach of the other and applied it to their developing law.

Certainly, the Judicature Act created conditions in which such an assimilation could occur. Once common law courts were free to use affidavit evidence and equity courts to use oral evidence when most appropriate, and once the civil jury had begun to decline (particularly after 1883), the structural and procedural distinctions which once hindered complete fusion began to be eroded. Nonetheless this was a slow process, which made it hard to think across categories: judges developing the law of negligence were still thinking of formulations to put to juries, which judges dealing with breaches of trust were not. Moreover, the very nature of the 1873 reform created obstacles to such a fusion. The administrative machinery of the Chancery Division made it distinct.[140] Section 25(11) may have enacted that in case of any conflict, the equitable rule was to prevail: but its position at the end of a series of enumerated clashes indicated that it was designed to cover the kind of clear conflicts already enumerated, rather than heralding a rethinking of common law principles on equitable lines. The limits on fusion were perhaps best illustrated by the excision of the proposed rule on misrepresentation: and in 1889, in *Derry* v. *Peek*,[141] the House of Lords confirmed that a common law view would continue to be applied in cases where damages were sought even though an equitable view was available where rescission was sought. Despite the calls for a more thoroughgoing reform by men like Romilly, there was to be no wider rethinking of the law and equity division. Equity's traditionally exclusive jurisdiction – trusts – was to remain a distinctly 'equitable' matter.

Furthermore, as Patrick Polden has shown, within a decade of the legislation, 'the divisions of the High Court were staffed entirely from their respective bars', and for the most part 'it was the common lawyers who went circuit as of old'.[142] Even two decades after fusion, in 1896, one common law barrister

---

[140] As Arthur Underhill put it, 'No fusion of Law and Equity can make the same procedure applicable to the decision of an action for goods sold and delivered, and the administration of the property of a deceased millionaire': A. Underhill, *A Practical and Concise Manual of the Procedure of the Chancery Division of the High Court of Justice Both in Actions and Matters* (London: Butterworths, 1881), vii–viii.

[141] (1889) 14 App. Cas. 337.   [142] Polden, 'Mingling the Waters', 611.

could write of the Chancery men that 'they are a thing apart from the Common Law Bar, a society within themselves'.[143] If the procedures had been put in place for a natural convergence of the cultures of both bars, the force of habit and professional self-interest could also put a brake on how far there would be a complete fusion.

[143] Quoted in *O.H.L.E.*, vol. XI, 1052.

5

At the Crossroads of Fusion

British North America/Canada, 1750–2000

PHILIP GIRARD

Recent scholarship on 'fusion' has shown that while the topic animated reformers in a variety of common law jurisdictions, the contours of these reform campaigns were shaped by local needs and circumstances in different ways. The goal of this chapter is to bring the British North American/Canadian experience into conversation with the existing literature. While most jurisdictions eventually got to the same place at least with regard to procedural fusion, the chronology and circumstances of these developments, and their eventual impact on the substantive law, varied considerably. Fusion in British North America is not a single story, but a set of stories, just as developments in the United States cannot be reduced to an account of the 'fusion' effected by New York State's Code of Civil Procedure of 1848 – the Field Code[1] – although it provides a useful organising principle. The transplantation of the doctrines of equity and courts of Chancery to British North America was a far from uniform process, containing some rather unusual features. These colonial stories also reveal that Britain was prepared to acquiesce in, and even encourage, novel visions of the interaction between law and equity that were in advance of what occurred at home.

THE GROWTH OF BRITISH NORTH AMERICA

The colonisation of the parts of British North America that did not join in the American Revolution was a long and slow process. Outside Quebec, which is not part of our story, the English Canadian colonies did not really achieve demographic take-off until the early nineteenth century in spite of a British presence in Newfoundland dating back to the early seventeenth century and

---

[1] 1848 N.Y. Laws c. 379, as to which see McMahon, 'Field, Fusion and the 1850s' and Funk, Chapter 3.

in Rupert's Land to 1670, when that vast territory was granted to the Hudson Bay Company by royal charter. Both of these were commercial territories rather than colonies of settlement, with Newfoundland not being endowed with a Supreme Court until 1792 or even a year-round governor until 1818. Rupert's Land was subject to Company rule until 1869 when it was sold to the recently created (1867) Dominion of Canada, which later incorporated the territory into the provinces of Manitoba (1870), Saskatchewan and Alberta (both 1905). Peninsular Nova Scotia was ceded to Britain by France in 1713 at the end of Queen Anne's War but there was virtually no British population aside from a small garrison at Annapolis Royal, and no attempt to impose English civil law on the resident Acadians and Mi'kmaq.

The founding of Halifax in 1749 was the turning point; with it, in short order the whole panoply of English law came to Nova Scotia: counties, sheriffs, juries, lawyers, freeholders and a Supreme Court with a royally appointed chief justice (1754), a pattern replicated at the founding of each of the later colonies. The deportation of the Acadians in 1755 opened up their rich lands to immigrants from the New England colonies. In the Treaty of Paris the formerly French Île St-Jean was ceded to Britain, then erected as a separate colony, later named Prince Edward Island, in 1769. The influx of thousands of Loyalists following the American Revolution led to a more radical redrawing of the map of British North America. New Brunswick and Cape Breton Island were separated from Nova Scotia in 1784 and erected as separate colonies meant as havens for Loyalists (Cape Breton would be re-annexed to Nova Scotia in 1820). And a new colony of Upper Canada was created in 1791 out of the immense province of Quebec (then renamed Lower Canada) in order to satisfy Loyalists who did not wish to live under the civil law and seigneurial tenure prevailing in that colony. With its large and fertile territory bounded by the Great Lakes, Upper Canada would become the demographic anchor of English-speaking British North America as British immigrants poured in after the close of the Napoleonic wars. The American Civil War and the desire of British North Americans to expand into the West north of the 49th parallel nudged the four colonies of Nova Scotia, New Brunswick, Ontario and Quebec (the former Upper and Lower Canada) into Confederation in 1867; Prince Edward Island would join in 1873, Newfoundland only in 1949. British Columbia, where settlement only began in earnest in the 1850s, joined the new Dominion of Canada in 1871 on the promise of a transcontinental railway, completed in 1885. The much later dates of settlement in western Canada mean that the issue of fusion was essentially settled by the time their judicial structures were organised; hence the focus in this chapter on the situation from Ontario east.

EQUITY IN THE ATLANTIC PROVINCES

In the Maritime Provinces of Nova Scotia, Prince Edward Island and New Brunswick, equity was administered in theory by the governor, pursuant to the old colonial device that his custody of the great seal of the province gave him the authority to act as chancellor. In practice, however, one or more judges of the Supreme Court of the colony usually 'advised' the governor when he dealt with such cases. In small colonies where the population size could not justify a separate court, this course had much to recommend it. It meant, however, that there was already a kind of fusion of personnel. In practice, the same judges administered both law and equity, albeit not in the same court. Nor were these judges necessarily expert in equity; indeed, some of them were lay judges until the late eighteenth century. By the 1820s and 1830s, the case load of the Supreme Courts in Nova Scotia and New Brunswick had grown to such an extent that it was thought best to separate the equity business and transfer it to a distinct court. There was also a sense that it was incongruous for the two bodies of doctrine to be administered by the same judges, when the two systems were supposed to be based 'upon principles, and ... administered in modes, widely differing from each other'.[2] Thus both provinces created distinct equity courts staffed by a Master of the Rolls, in 1826 and 1838, respectively. Colonial leaders could feel gratified that they were emulating the English model in doing so. While justifiable administratively, however, the creation of generously salaried positions in a court dealing mainly with the foreclosure of mortgages made the new judges an easy target for those seeking political reform in the colonies in the form of responsible government, as will be seen in this chapter. The new positions would last barely a generation.[3]

Newfoundland presented a different challenge. Throughout the seventeenth and eighteenth centuries the imperial government had cast the island in the role of a seasonal fishing station, discouraged settlement and tried to avoid creating any kind of governmental infrastructure. The 'Governor as Chancellor' model would not work when the governor was only present for

---

[2] Message from Sir John Harvey, Lieutenant-Governor of New Brunswick to the House of Assembly (18 January 1838), read in the House of Assembly and in the Legislative Council on 22 January 1838: New Brunswick, House of Assembly, *Journal of the House of Assembly of the Province of New Brunswick* (Fredericton: Queen's Printer, 1838), 72; New Brunswick, Legislative Council, *Journal of the Legislative Council of the Province of New Brunswick* (Fredericton: Queen's Printer, 1838), 283.

[3] See generally P. Girard, 'History and Development of Equity', in F. Woodman and M. Gillen (eds), *Trusts: A Contextual Approach*, 3rd edn (Toronto: Emond, 2015), ch. 3; D. G. Bell, 'Maritime Legal Institutions under the *Ancien Régime*, 1710–1850' (1995) 23 Man. L.J. 103.

the fishing season, as he was until 1818. Well before then the imperial government had finally relented and created a single-judge Supreme Court of Newfoundland by statute in 1792.[4] It did not make any reference to equity, but the court, especially under Chief Justice Francis Forbes (1816–22), seems to have administered both law and equity without undue trouble, allowing, for example, specific performance of contracts.[5] And in spite of the peculiar state of land titles in Newfoundland, based on actual possession and a form of customary tenure, rather than estates flowing from Crown grants, the court seems to have had no trouble recognising mortgages and the equity of redemption.[6]

In 1824 the imperial Parliament passed a Judicature Act[7] for Newfoundland (the island would not get its own legislature until 1832), authorising the Crown in effect to re-found the Supreme Court of Newfoundland via a royal charter of justice,[8] expanding it to three judges,[9] directing it to go on circuit[10] and vesting it with the same jurisdiction as 'his Majesty's Courts of King's Bench, Common Pleas, Exchequer and High Court of Chancery'.[11] A later attorney-general of Newfoundland, E. M. Archibald, opined that there was not:

> in Her Majesty's dominions, any single court of judicature invested with such extensive powers as the supreme court of Newfoundland, within the limits of its jurisdiction. It resembles and almost equals the *Aula Regia*, from which all the courts in the text were carved out.[12]

---

[4] Judicature Act 1792 (U.K.), 32 Geo. III c. 46, s. 1.   [5] *Freeman v. Kenny* (1817) 1 Nfld R. 3.

[6] *Trustees of Graham Little v. Dullahanty* (1818) 1 Nfld R. 131; B. Kercher and J. Young, 'Formal and Informal Law in Two New Lands: Land Law in Newfoundland and New South Wales under Francis Forbes', in C. English (ed.), *Essays in the History of Canadian Law: Two Islands: Newfoundland and Prince Edward Island* (University of Toronto Press, 2005), vol. IX, ch. 6; T. Johnson, 'Defining Property for Inheritance: The Chattels Real Act of 1834', in English (ed.), *Essays in the History of Canadian Law*, ch. 7. Chief Justice Forbes observed colourfully that 'possession peaceably acquired, and use had in the fishery, are the best title-deeds which can be produced in Newfoundland': *R. v. Row* (1818) 1 Nfld R. 144, 146.

[7] Judicature Act 1824 (U.K.), 5 Geo. IV c. 67.   [8] Ibid., s. 1.   [9] Ibid., s. 2.

[10] Ibid., ss. 7–9, 22.

[11] Ibid., s. 1. The Act's provisions were brought into effect by the Royal Charter of Justice of 1825, effective 2 January 1826. On the background to the passage of the Act, see C. English, 'From Fishing Schooner to Colony: The Legal Development of Newfoundland, 1791–1832', in L. A. Knafla and S. W. S. Binnie (eds), *Law, Society and the State: Essays in Modern Legal History* (University of Toronto Press, 1995), 86–92.

[12] E. M. Archibald, *Digest of the Laws of Newfoundland: Comprehending the Judicature Act and Royal Charter* (St John's: Winton, 1847), 45.

In spite of this institutional fusion, the rules framed by the judges of the court in 1825[13] refer in passing to the 'equity side'[14] of the court, suggesting that the fluidity of the Forbes period was already fading. New rules promulgated in 1834 for the equity side of the court more or less followed English Chancery procedure of the day. Much of the fact-finding was to be done by masters of the court, who could examine witnesses on interrogatories or viva voce at their discretion. Indeed, the increase in equity business by the 1840s suggested to the attorney general that the best recourse would be 'the establishment of a separate tribunal, to be presided over by one judge, ... [to] provide for the hearing and determining of all matters in equity'.[15] Archibald, himself a Nova Scotian lawyer transplanted to Newfoundland in the 1830s, undoubtedly knew that events had proceeded this way in Nova Scotia and New Brunswick, but his advice was not followed in the island province. Newfoundland was in advance of those two provinces, however, in administering equity along with law when the Supreme Court went on circuit.

EQUITY IN UPPER CANADA

Upper Canada had the most peculiar history of all where equity was concerned. Its 1792 reception statute declared the English laws as of 15 October of that year to provide the rule for decision in all legal controversies 'relative to property and civil rights'.[16] Equity was not expressly mentioned, nor was it mentioned in the 1794 Act establishing the province's superior court; it became the accepted view that it had not been received into the colony. It may be that the reception statute's omission to mention equity was intended implicitly to exclude equity and thus to preclude the lieutenant-governor from administering it as he did in the Maritime Provinces. At any rate, he did not do so. While the common law courts were sometimes able to stretch the law to mimic equitable doctrine, at other times they made clear that specific performance was not available, nor the enforcement of trusts, nor the supervision of the guardians of infants. Occasional legislative intervention to validate a particular trust or remedy a particular injustice was not a satisfactory long-term solution to these important gaps in the law.[17]

---

[13] General Rules and Orders of the Supreme Court of Newfoundland 1825, reprinted in R. A. Tucker, Select Cases of Newfoundland 1817-1828 (Toronto: Carswell, 1979), 575–90.
[14] General Rules and Orders of the Supreme Court of Newfoundland 1825, r. 9.
[15] Archibald, Digest of the Laws of Newfoundland, 49.
[16] An Act Introducing English Civil Law into Upper Canada 1792 (S.U.C.), 32 Geo. III c. 1, s. 3.
[17] E. Brown, 'Equitable Jurisdiction and the Court of Chancery in Upper Canada' (1983) 21 Osgoode Hall L.J. 275, 279–86.

When the lack of a tribunal to dispense equity began to be agitated seriously in the 1820s, the governor sought the advice of the imperial government as to how to rectify the situation. He was advised by the colonial secretary that a separate court was not required: a judge of the King's Bench could perform the required duties under the title of Master of the Rolls or Vice-Chancellor.[18] Later in 1827 the English law officers of the Crown were of the same view, suggesting that:

> whether instead of erecting a distinct & independent Tribunal, it might not be expedient to invest the existing Common Law Court with so much of an equitable jurisdiction as upon due consideration may be thought useful or necessary to the Province, & ... that this jurisdiction might be exercised as in the Court of Exchequer in England, in the same Tribunal, & by the Same Judges who administer the Common Law.[19]

Ironically, just as the Maritime Provinces were adopting separate Chancery courts because they thought they should follow the course of the mother country, Britain was telling the Upper Canadian authorities the opposite, that they should vest both law and equity jurisdiction in the common law judges, as indeed had been done in Newfoundland.

By the 1830s the issue of a Chancery court became caught up with that of providing relief to mortgagors. The Assembly passed two statutes in 1834 recognising the equity of redemption, but limiting its assertion to a period of twenty years after the mortgagee took possession of the land, or provided a written acknowledgement of the mortgagor's title. Without a Court of Chancery, however, this reform benefited mortgagors but left mortgagees without the means of obtaining a decree of foreclosure. This gap was remedied three years later with the creation of a distinct Court of Chancery, in which was vested most of the jurisdiction of the English High Court of Chancery. For various reasons the province did not take the easy way out suggested by the English law officers of the Crown, but decided to follow the two-track model used in England.[20] The imperial government obliged in turn by naming an English equity lawyer, Robert Sympson Jameson, to the post of Vice-Chancellor (and

---

[18] J. Weaver, 'While Equity Slumbered: Creditor Advantage, a Capitalist Land Market, and Upper Canada's Missing Court' (1990) 28 Osgoode Hall L.J. 871, 883.

[19] Letter from W. Huskisson, Colonial Secretary, to Sir Peregrine Maitland, Lieutenant-Governor (25 November 1827), printed in A. Doughty and N. Story (eds), *Documents Relating to the Constitutional History of Canada 1819–1828* (Ottawa: King's Printer, 1935), 370.

[20] These developments are reviewed in Weaver, 'While Equity Slumbered'.

sole judge) in the new Court of Chancery.[21] In one important respect the Act innovated on the English model. Section 5 of the Act of 1837 directed that all evidence provided by witnesses should be given viva voce before the Master or the Vice-Chancellor, and be subject to examination by counsel before them, unless specially ordered by the Vice-Chancellor or by agreement of the parties.[22] While this was a decade earlier than the Field Code, it appears that New York Chancery had already begun to move towards oral examination of witnesses before the enactment of the code, which essentially ratified the practice.[23] It is not yet known whether this practice directly influenced the Upper Canadian legislators in 1837.

Thus, as of 1850 in British North America law and equity were administered by the same court in Newfoundland, and had been administered by the same judges, if not in the same court, prior to the 1820s in the Maritimes, while equity was not administered at all in Upper Canada until the creation of a stand-alone Court of Chancery in 1837. Far from slavishly following the English model, the British North American colonies had adopted a variety of approaches to the difficult question of how to administer both bodies of law within their systems of judicature. The imperial authorities seemed to accept and even encourage this diversity, pointing to the equity side of the Court of Exchequer as a possible model for Upper Canada, even if that option was not followed in the end.

THE IMPACT OF POLITICAL REFORM ON THE
FUSION–FISSION DEBATE

The 1830s saw the beginning of the campaign for what was called responsible government in British North America. What the reformers hoped to achieve was cabinet government, where the party with a majority in the popular branch of the legislature would form the government and the governor or lieutenant-governor would be obliged to assent to any legislation passed by both houses. While the governor would remain a formal link with the Crown and the imperial government, he would now be harnessed to the local government rather than be an agent for the implementation of imperial designs. The rebellions in Upper and Lower Canada in 1837–38 hastened this

---

[21] Jameson had served as Chief Justice of Dominica for some years but detested the plantation culture of the West Indies and lobbied strongly for a transfer to another colony.

[22] An Act to Establish a Court of Chancery in this Province 1837 (S.U.C.), 7 Wm IV c. 2, s. 5. As to Nova Scotia on this point, see the citation at n. 31.

[23] See McMahon, Chapter 12, and Kessler, *Inventing American Exceptionalism*.

process, which was achieved by the late 1840s.[24] The 1850s were characterised by legislation of a more populist character than had been the norm, and by a turn to American as well as English models of legislation.

THE MARITIME PROVINCES

As noted earlier, the separate Chancery courts in Nova Scotia and New Brunswick proved to be an irresistible target for reformers anxious to tear down symbols of the *ancien regime*. Reform campaign propaganda tended to parrot the English critique of Chancery even if it was not always applicable in British North America. Complaints about expense had some justification, given the relatively high fee scales in Chancery, which were in turn based on the extensive written pleadings required. As Nova Scotia treatise writer Beamish Murdoch lamented in 1833:

> Any one who will deliberately read through the long, unmeaning, but expensive forms of bills and answers in Chancery, and the absurd and unnecessary processes of contempt ... must be blinded by a reverence for antiquity, if he does not think them unreasonable.[25]

Complaints about delay, however, were mostly not accurate. The British North American courts of Chancery did not have the high case load or constant arrears of the English parent, nor did they have the bankruptcy jurisdiction that contributed so significantly to its backlog. During the busiest period of its existence, 1814–28, forty-six cases per year were commenced on average in the Nova Scotia Court of Chancery, declining to thirty-seven cases per year during the court's final two decades. The court sat once a week year round, which was enough to keep up with its work. The time taken to proceed from bill of complaint to decree was seldom more than a year, and delays were usually attributable to the parties rather than the court process itself.

---

[24] The distinct colonies of Upper Canada and Lower Canada were joined in the United Province of Canada from 1841 to 1867, during which time there was a sole legislature for the hybrid jurisdiction, which nonetheless enacted separate legislation for the legal systems of what were now known as Canada West (the former Upper Canada) and Canada East (the former Lower Canada), similar to the way in which the United Kingdom Parliament legislated separately for Scotland and England after 1707. Only with the separation of the Province of Canada into two distinct provinces in 1867 did the current province of Ontario take that name. In order to simplify matters I have used the term 'Upper Canada' throughout, except for a brief excursus into the twentieth century when I use the term 'Ontario'.

[25] B. Murdoch, *Epitome of the Laws of Nova-Scotia* (Halifax: Howe, 1833), vol. 4, 49.

If anything, complaints might have been made about foreclosure proceedings in particular being too expeditious rather than too dilatory.[26] In both provinces the Chancery courts were abolished in the mid-1850s[27] and equity jurisdiction given to the Supreme Court of the province.[28] In New Brunswick the complaints about the court were less partisan and more of a constitutional nature. A commission appointed by the legislature in 1852 to undertake a general statutory revision concluded that it was inappropriate that the Master of the Rolls alone should have the power to deprive citizens of their property, from whom there was an appeal only to the lieutenant-governor as Chancellor, and thence to the Privy Council. Striking a rather modern note, the commission observed in its second report that 'conscience', the central idea of equitable doctrine, 'must afford a pretty extensive latitude of interpretation'.[29] In other words, reasonable people could differ on such matters and it was better to have the viewpoints of a number of judges rather than just one. The incumbent Master of the Rolls was moved to the Supreme Court, but any single judge could hear an equitable matter, with an appeal to the entire bench of five judges, as was the norm in common law adjudication. If the legislation anticipated the English Judicature Acts by twenty years in this regard, in other respects it was conservative, mostly adopting English Chancery practice as it existed at this date, including the Court of Chancery Procedure Act of 1852.[30]

Nova Scotia also abolished its Court of Chancery and transferred all equity jurisdiction to the Supreme Court, but the existing Master of the Rolls, a conspicuous high Tory, was pensioned off rather than given a seat on the Supreme Court. Unfortunately, this was cutting off one's nose to spite one's face, as it deprived the court of the equity expertise of the incumbent. The Nova Scotia reform was more ambitious in directing that the existing process

[26] J. Cruikshank, 'The Chancery Court of Nova Scotia: Jurisdiction and Procedure 1751–1855' (1992) 1 Dalhousie J. Legal Stud. 27.

[27] An Act Relating to the Administration of Justice in Equity 1854 (S.N.B.), 17 Vict. c. 18, s. 1; Chancery Abolition Act 1855 (S. N. S.), 18 Vict. c. 23, s. 3.

[28] An Act Relating to the Administration of Justice in Equity 1854 (S.N.B.), 17 Vict. c. 18, ss. 1, 4; Chancery Abolition Act 1855 (S.N.S.), 18 Vict. c. 23, s. 1. See P. Girard, 'Married Women's Property, Chancery Abolition and Insolvency Law: Law Reform in Nova Scotia, 1820-1867', in P. Girard and J. Phillips (eds), Essays in the History of Canadian Law, Volume III: Nova Scotia (University of Toronto Press, 1990), 106–13. See now Judicature Act R.S.N.B. 1973 c. J-2, s. 26; Judicature Act R.S.N.S. c. 240 1989, s. 41.

[29] New Brunswick, Law Commissioners, Second Report of the Law Commissioners (1854), in New Brunswick, The Public Statutes of New Brunswick Passed in the Year 1854 (Fredericton: Queen's Printer, 1854), vol. 2, viii.

[30] 15 & 16 Vict. c. 86 (U.K.).

of the Supreme Court be used for all matters formerly cognisable in Chancery, which were to be:

commenced in the same manner as personal actions by writ of summons, in which the cause of action, and the relief or remedy sought by the plaintiff, shall be briefly and clearly stated, and it shall not be necessary that the same should be set forth in any technical or formal language or manner.[31]

The answer of the defendant was likewise to be 'briefly and distinctly stated, and there shall be no further pleading after the defence, unless by the special leave of the court'.[32] Attorney General William Young described his bill in private correspondence as 'a new and pretty bold experiment ... the fruit of a good deal of thought and labour'.[33] In introducing it he stated that he had tried to adapt the best features of the New York and Ohio versions of the Field Code as well as the English Act of 1852. One advantage of the new system was a decentralisation of the administration of justice. Chancery courts did not go on circuit, and all their business had at some point to be routed through the provincial capital even if the initial stages could be handled by local masters in Chancery. After fusion of the courts, the Supreme Court circuits brought justice to the litigants rather than the other way round.

Abolition was somewhat easier to contemplate in the Maritimes than in the mother country, for a number of reasons. The English Court of Chancery had an extensive jurisdiction intertwined in complex ways with the common law courts; it had a small army of officials and clerks who had to be compensated for the abolition of their posts; and it employed a fair-sized Chancery bar that was somewhat apprehensive about far-reaching changes to its home jurisdiction. The Nova Scotia Court of Chancery had none of these characteristics. Its jurisdiction was very largely mortgage foreclosure, making up 68 per cent of the court's caseload before 1821, rising to 79 per cent in the period from 1822–33.[34] A mini-fusion statute of 1833 prohibited the issuing of injunctions to halt common law process, directed partnership accounts to the Supreme Court and permitted witnesses in Chancery suits to be examined viva voce 'when and as the said Court shall think proper',[35] though it did not ban the use of interrogatories. The only official who had to be pensioned off was the registrar, at £100 a year; it appears that the masters in Chancery, who were

---

[31] Chancery Abolition Act 1855 (S. N. S.), 18 Vict. c. 23, s. 4.   [32] Ibid., s. 5.
[33] Letter from William Young to E. B. Chandler (24 February 1855), held in New Brunswick Museum, E. B. Chandler Papers 566, box 2, file 3–133.
[34] Cruikshank, 'The Chancery Court of Nova Scotia', 31–32.
[35] An Act for Amending the Practice of the Court of Chancery, and Diminishing the Expences Thereof 1833 (S.N.S.), 3 Wm IV c. 52, s. 12.

remunerated solely by fees, were not considered to have a compensable interest. And finally, the Chancery bar was of necessity small and not particularly influential.

UPPER CANADA

The same anti-Chancery sentiment evident in the Maritimes also appeared in Upper Canada as part of the campaign for responsible government, but the outcome was different. Attempts to abolish the court and transfer its jurisdiction to the courts of common law were made in 1845, 1846, 1850, 1851 and 1853, with the 1851 attempt being only narrowly defeated.[36] The difference in Upper Canada was the emergence of strong and credible voices advocating a broader reform of all the courts, including Chancery, rather than abolition of the latter. Chancery lawyer William Hume Blake outlined these arguments in an 1845 pamphlet,[37] and was able to implement his proposals as Solicitor General in the first governmental session after the achievement of responsible government. To populist demands for fewer lawyers, conciliation courts without legally trained judges and cheaper access to justice, Blake responded determinedly with a prescription for more judges;[38] advocacy exclusively by professionally skilled lawyers;[39] appointment of the judges from those skilled ranks;[40] and complete judicial independence from the executive.[41] Arguing that appeals to the lieutenant-governor in council and the Privy Council were not desirable in the first case[42] and not practical in the second,[43] he successfully advocated for the creation of a true appellate jurisdiction in the province[44] along with an expansion of the Chancery Court[45] and remunerating its officers by salary rather than fees.[46]

Blake's Administration of Justice Acts accomplished a major reform of the courts with effect from 1 January 1850.[47] They expanded the Chancery Court

[36] J. D. Blackwell, 'William Hume Blake and the Judicature Acts of 1849: The Process of Legal Reform at Mid-Century in Upper Canada', in D. H. Flaherty (ed.), *Essays in the History of Canadian Law* (Toronto: Osgoode Society, 1981), vol. I, 151, 162–63; Brown, 'Equitable Jurisdiction and the Court of Chancery in Upper Canada', 294–97.
[37] W. H. Blake, *A Letter to the Hon. Robert Baldwin upon the Administration of Justice in Western Canada* (Toronto: Brown, 1845).
[38] Ibid., 21–23, 25–27.   [39] Ibid., 34–36.   [40] Ibid., 25.   [41] Ibid., 14–19.
[42] Ibid., 11–12.   [43] Ibid., 12, 14, 18.   [44] Ibid., 12–19, 26–27.   [45] Ibid., 21–23, 25–27.
[46] Ibid., 32. See Blackwell, 'William Hume Blake and the Judicature Acts of 1849', 146–51.
[47] Administration of Justice Act 1849 (S.P.C.), 12 Vict. c. 63, s. 50; Administration of Justice (Chancery) Act 1849 (S.P.C.), 12 Vict. c. 64, s. 16. As to court officers' remuneration, see Administration of Justice (Chancery) Act 1849 (S.P.C.), 12 Vict. c. 64, ss. 12–14. In 1857 it was enacted that the masters in the 'outer counties' should be remunerated entirely by fees and

from one to three judges,[48] reorganised the common law courts into two three-judge courts[49] and created a distinct court of appeal, initially called the Court of Error and Appeal.[50] This shake-up of the courts would have responded to some of the concerns expressed in New Brunswick about the concentration of equitable jurisdiction in the hands of a single judge. It also meant that at the appellate level, common law judges were frequently called upon to decide on points of equity and vice versa.[51] Occasionally, the three Chancery judges found themselves in a minority vis-à-vis the common law judges, but this was exceptional. As the court's historian has observed, the infrequency of decisions dividing strictly on law–equity lines 'must have helped break down the barriers that had previously been fiercely maintained between equity and common law'.[52]

The expansion of the Court of Chancery required the appointment of two new judges. Both positions went to respected equity lawyers: James Christie Palmer Esten, who had been born in Bermuda and trained at the Inns of Court before immigrating to Canada, and John Godfrey Spragge, who had been the court's registrar since its foundation in 1837. The incumbent Vice-Chancellor, Robert Sympson Jameson, was the last English official imported into the colony, and he soon retired, to be replaced by William Hume Blake himself as Chancellor. This was a very strong bench, and the Court of Chancery continued to benefit from the presence of skilled equity judges for a long time thereafter. While there is no detailed study of the court's jurisprudence, which runs to many thousands of pages in *Grant's Chancery Reports* from 1850 to 1882, it is clear that the judges looked to both English and American case law in seeking guidance with regard to the issues that came before them, and that they tried to reconcile loyalty to English authority with developing a law suitable for local conditions. As Chancellor Spragge observed in 1873, after quoting James Kent and various American authorities in support of his expansive interpretation of the circumstances under which trustees could claim remuneration, 'I do not, of course, quote the opinions and decisions of American Judges as *authority*; but I refer to them as the opinions of Jurists of high legal reputation, and as such entitled to respectful consideration at our hands'.[53]

were not obliged to account to the Crown for them: Proceedings of Court of Chancery Act 1857 (S.P.C.), 20 Vict. c. 56, s. 16. Masters in the inner counties, closest to Toronto, remained salaried.

48 Administration of Justice (Chancery) Act 1849 (S.P.C.), 12 Vict. c. 64, ss. 1–2.
49 Administration of Justice Act 1849 (S.P.C.), 12 Vict. c. 63, ss. 1–3.
50 Ibid., ss. 37–40. A quorum of the Court was specified as seven in 1857 (Act Respecting the Court of Error and Appeal (S.P.C.), 20 Vict c. 5, s. 4), reduced to six in 1869 (Act Respecting the Court of Error and Appeal (S.P.C.), 31 & 32 Vict. c. 24, s. 6).
51 C. Moore, *The Court of Appeal for Ontario: Defining the Right of Appeal in Canada, 1792–2013* (University of Toronto Press, 2014), 37.
52 Ibid., 38.   53 *Deedes v. Graham* (1873) 20 Gr. 258, 270 (emphasis original).

Blake's reforms were continued after he ascended to the bench. Authority over some equitable matters was given to the county court judges in 1853, and these were to be decided in a summary way unless either party requested a jury or the judge so directed.[54] The Chancery Court itself was obliged to go on circuit as of 1857,[55] thus following in the footsteps of the Maritime Provinces where abolition had led to the Supreme Court taking the equity show on the road during its own circuits.[56] This created the need for a familiarity with equitable principles in a broader segment of the bar. In 1860 an observer noted that:

> Chancery business is not now, as formerly, confined to a few offices in Toronto. Many country practitioners, who a few years ago would have entered the regions of equity with great distrust, have now undertaken, to some extent at least, the conduct of Chancery suits.[57]

Local authors were not slow to fill the rising demand for information and guidance on equity law and procedure.[58]

While complaints continued about delays and backlogs in the masters' offices, some Upper Canadian lawyers were not above patting themselves on the back that they had achieved reforms that were still elusive in England. In 1859 the *Upper Canada Law Journal* reproduced a paper[59] presented to the National Association for the Promotion of Social Science at Liverpool in October 1858 recommending the local administration of equity as a panacea. The editor boasted that:

> It is not a little singular that in many law reforms we have taken the lead of the mother country ... We are beginning to feel our strength, and to acquire the confidence of manhood. We are not trammelled by the ruin and decay of expiring customs, and their handiwork, obsolete statutes.[60]

Nonetheless, in spite of the various colonial innovations catalogued here, all Canadian provinces and the Dominion of Newfoundland repealed their own legislation and adopted the English Judicature Acts of 1873–75, mostly in the

---

54 County Courts Equity Extension Act 1853 (S.P.C.), 11 Vict. c. 119, ss. 1–2, 8.
55 Proceedings of Court of Chancery Act 1857 (S.P.C.), s. 6.
56 An Act Relating to the Administration of Justice in Equity 1854 (S.N.B.), 17 Vict. c. 18, s. 6.
57 T. W. Taylor, *Orders of the Court of Chancery for Upper Canada, with Notes* (Toronto: Rowsell, 1860), iii.
58 In addition to Taylor, see, for example, R. Snelling and F. T. Jones, *The General Orders, and Statutes, Relating to the Practice, Pleading, and Jurisdiction of the Court of Chancery for Upper Canada* (Toronto: Rowsell, 1863); C. W. Cooper, *Digest of Reports of Cases Decided in the Court of Chancery, in the Court of Error & Appeal, on Appeal from the Court of Chancery, and in Chancery Chambers* (Toronto: Blackburn, 1868–73), 2 vols.
59 J. Smale, 'Local Equity Jurisdiction' (1859) 5 Upp. Can. L.J. 219.
60 Anon., 'Local Equity Jurisdiction' (1859) 5 Upp. Can. L.J. 218, 219.

Philip Girard

1880s.[61] This form of self-inflicted legal colonialism was increasingly common in the fin-de-siècle, as British legal literature became widely available in Canada and more frequent appeals to the Judicial Committee of the Privy Council enhanced an already strong loyalty to English legal culture. In the mid-nineteenth century British parliamentarians had sometimes sought out information on colonial innovations when reforming their own law, as in the case of married women's property. But by the end of the nineteenth century, as with the Judicature Acts, Canadian legislatures were repealing their own earlier statutes and adopting the new married women's property Acts being enacted in England.[62] The constant refrain in provincial legislatures was that local legislation should mirror the English as much as possible because then Canadians would have the benefit of English decisions interpreting the Act. Such attitudes not only demonstrated a lack of confidence in the local judiciary, but also reflected an increasingly formalist and professionalised view of law, where responsiveness to local conditions was no longer seen as a particularly desirable feature of the statute book.[63]

FUSION AND THE SUBSTANTIVE LAW: THE EXAMPLE
OF MORTGAGE REMEDIES

I turn now from the procedural aspects of fusion to its relationship with substantive law. Much of the literature on the consequences of fusion deals with contract law and corporate law. The land law has attracted less attention. In North America, where landholding was much more widespread than in Britain, land law – in particular, mortgage law – was a critical element of the legal infrastructure. Foreclosure proceedings were, as we have seen, a significant element of Chancery courts' caseloads in the nineteenth century.

The traditional tenderness of Chancery courts towards holders of the equity of redemption in England was, in general, not replicated in North America, subject to an exception in Ontario and possibly British Columbia.[64] Prior to the American Revolution, many of the Thirteen Colonies plus Nova Scotia

---

61 Newfoundland: Judicature Act 1889 (S.N.), 52 Vict. c. 29; Nova Scotia: Judicature Act 1884 (S.N.S.), 47 Vict. c. 25; New Brunswick: Judicature Act 1909 (S.N.B.), c. 5; Ontario: Judicature Act 1881 (S.O.), 44 Vict. c. 5; North West Territories: Judicature Ordinance 1886 (N.W.T.), 49 Vict. no. 2; British Columbia: Judicature Act 1879 (S.B.C.), 42 Vict. c. 12.
62 C. B. Backhouse, 'Married Women's Property Law in Nineteenth-Century Canada' (1988) 6 L.H.R. 211, 212, 231–32, 241.
63 G. B. Baker, 'The Reconstitution of Upper Canadian Legal Thought in the Late-Victorian Empire' (1985) 3 L.H.R. 219, 266–85, 286–87.
64 On the English experience, see R. Warrington and D. Sugarman, 'Land Law, Citizenship, and the Invention of "Englishness": The Strange World of the Equity of Redemption', in J. Brewer and S. Staves (eds), *Early Modern Conceptions of Property* (London: Routledge, 1995), ch. 6.

adopted an approach to foreclosure and mortgage redemption somewhat different from England. The device used was foreclosure and sale under judicial authority. With this type of proceeding, once the amount owing was settled, the property was offered for public sale at an auction conducted under the authority of either a master in Chancery or the county sheriff. The sale extinguished the equity of redemption of the mortgagor, and conveyed full legal and equitable title to the purchaser. The master or sheriff did the accounting and if the sale produced a surplus, it was given back to the mortgagor. If it produced a deficiency, the mortgagee could still sue the mortgagor for it. Sometimes foreclosure and sale was mandated by statute but usually it was simply adopted by Chancery courts on their own initiative, supposedly because it was considered more favourable to mortgagors than English foreclosure (which was known as 'strict foreclosure' in North America). It was also the usual mode of foreclosure used in Ireland.[65]

In the early years of settlement, when land values were rising rapidly, this process probably did produce fair results for both mortgagor and mortgagee. However, one American innovation changed the landscape considerably. Neither in Ireland, where foreclosure and sale existed, nor in England, where public sale was authorised by court (as it was after 1852), could the mortgagee bid at the sale. In America, the mortgagee could. Where the mortgagee bid, this typically discouraged bidding by others, depressing sale prices. Sales at undervalue became common by the early nineteenth century, yet the courts considered the public sale to have established conclusively the market value of the property at the time. Even if it could be shown that the mortgagee, having purchased at the sale, then resold soon afterwards at a much higher price, courts declared this to be irrelevant. Having 'purchased' the equity of redemption, the mortgagee could do with it as he or she chose, and any surplus realised on a resale did not have to be accounted for at the behest of the mortgagor. Moreover, if the mortgagee had not recovered the full amount of the mortgage debt, he or she could still sue to recover a deficiency from the mortgagor. While English foreclosure law imposed a choice, commonly phrased as 'the money or the mud', American law, including that of Nova Scotia, allowed a mortgagee to have both under some circumstances. Finally, it will be obvious from the preceding that the public sale, even if to the mortgagee, was regarded as precluding any reopening of the foreclosure. These innovations were all well established by the 1830s in the United States. As one scholar has noted, they 'represented substantial concessions to the

[65] H. W. Seton, *Forms of Decrees in Equity* (London: Saunders and Benning, 1830), 172, 174; W. R. Fisher, *The Law of Mortgage* (London: Butterworths, 1856), § 277. On US practice, see J. Kent, *Commentaries on American Law* (New York, NY: Halsted, 1830), vol. 4, 173–75; on Nova Scotia, Murdoch, *Epitome of the Laws of Nova-Scotia*, vol. 2, 115–19.

mortgagee: they made his remedies much more potent'.[66] He went on to observe that in spite of some statutory changes introduced to simplify the procedure, as of 1943, foreclosure and sale 'continue[d] to be comparatively costly and complicated'.[67]

Concerns about sales at undervalue led to the adoption of statutory redemption periods in some states in the 1820s and 1830s. At first dealing only with sales of land on execution, they were extended later to foreclosure sales, and typically specified periods between six months and two years within which the debtor could redeem. New York adopted such a law after the crash of 1837[68] but then repealed it in 1838.[69] The New York version of the Field Code did not contain any mandatory provision on this point, noting that:

> [u]ntil otherwise provided by the legislature, the existing provisions of law relating to executions, and their incidents, including the sale and redemption of property, the powers and rights of officers, their duties thereon, and the proceedings to enforce those duties and the liability of their sureties, shall apply to the executions prescribed by this chapter.[70]

In other words, the Field Code was very much a status quo document with regard to mortgage law, in effect upholding the advantaged position of the mortgagee. And the statutory redemption periods adopted in some Field Code states did not really provide much protection for mortgagors, especially when courts in some states and legislatures in others allowed for such rights to be waived by the mortgagor.[71]

The Nova Scotia Court of Chancery had practised the English form of foreclosure for the first thirty years or so of its existence, then abruptly adopted foreclosure and sale in the early 1780s and never again permitted strict foreclosure.[72] As this change coincided with the influx of the Loyalists, whose arrival put considerable pressure on land values, it may be that the change was initially adopted as a means of protecting mortgagors by allowing them to recoup sudden increases in land value in the case of sales to third parties, windfalls that would otherwise be allocated to mortgagees under strict foreclosure. But if this was the initial motivation, when land prices stabilised or declined the same problems with foreclosure and sale began to appear as had manifested in the United States. Mortgagees were allowed to bid at the sale from at least 1790 but whether this practice resulted from a conscious adoption of US practice or from independent decision is not known. Just as the Field Code had remained

---

[66] R. H. Skilton, 'Developments in Mortgage Law and Practice' (1943) 17 Temp. U.L.Q. 315, 320.
[67] Ibid., 320.   [68] 1837 N.Y. Laws c. 410, § 1 (1 year).   [69] 1838 N.Y. Laws c. 266, § 9.
[70] 1848 N.Y. c.379, § 246.   [71] Skilton, 'Developments in Mortgage Law and Practice', 330.
[72] P. Girard, 'Land Law, Liberalism, and the Agrarian Ideal: British North America, 1750–1920', in J. McLaren, A. R. Buck and N. E. Wright (eds), *Despotic Dominion: Property Rights in British Settler Societies* (Vancouver: University of British Columbia Press, 2004), 131–35.

neutral on the subject of the respective rights of mortgagors and mortgagees, so the Nova Scotia legislation abolishing the Court of Chancery in 1855 was careful to preserve the status quo, stating that '[i]t shall be competent for a mortgagor to bring suit for the redemption of his mortgage, and for a mortgagee to bring suit for the foreclosure thereof, on the same principles as now obtain in the court of chancery'.[73] Possibly the ability of the court to conduct foreclosure proceedings while on circuit may have reduced costs associated with foreclosures, but this was at best an indirect effect of the legislation.

The ability of the mortgagee to purchase at the judicial sale was questioned only once in Nova Scotia, in an 1883 case where a mortgagee-purchaser was suing the mortgagor for a deficiency judgment after having resold the property. The Supreme Court in banco upheld the mortgagee's action, observing that Nova Scotia law had diverged from English law in this respect, and citing Joseph Story and James Kent as upholding the mortgagee's right to sue for a deficiency in such cases.[74] One judge, however, concurred in the result but expressed doubt (unsupported by any citation of authority) as to the legality of the mortgagee bidding at such sales. The legislature quickly responded with a statute declaring that '[o]n sale of mortgaged premises under foreclosure and sale, it is hereby declared and enacted that it has been and shall be lawful for the mortgagee to purchase'.[75]

The mortgage law of Nova Scotia and New York, and the results produced by it, remained remarkably similar to each other over the following century and more, in spite of the many economic, social and constitutional differences that one might catalogue between the two jurisdictions. This point was brought home by two empirical studies of mortgage foreclosure and sale, conducted independently in the two jurisdictions in the late twentieth century. In the New York study, Professor Steven Wechsler of Syracuse University College of Law examined all 118 mortgage foreclosure actions begun in 1979 in Onondaga County, New York, that culminated in a confirmed foreclosure sale.[76] In the Nova Scotian study, the author of this chapter studied 331 foreclosure files opened in the Halifax County Sheriff's Office between 1 January 1994 and 30 June 1996, which resulted in a foreclosure sale.[77] A comparison of the results of the two studies is as follows:[78]

---

[73] Chancery Abolition Act 1855 (S.N.S.), 18 Vict. c. 23, s. 12.
[74] *Kenny v. Chisholm* (1883) 19 N.S.R. 497, 500–1.
[75] An Act to Confirm Sales of Land under Order of Supreme or Equity Courts 1885 (S.N.S.), 48 Vict. c. 31, s. 3.
[76] S. Wechsler, 'Through the Looking Glass: Foreclosure by Sale as *De Facto* Strict Foreclosure – An Empirical Study of Mortgage Foreclosure and Subsequent Resale' (1985) 70 Cornell L. Rev. 850.
[77] The research was conducted for the Law Reform Commission of Nova Scotia in connection with its study of mortgage law: *Discussion Paper: Mortgage Foreclose and Sale* (1997); *Final Report: Mortgage Foreclosure and Sale* (1998).
[78] See Wechsler, 'Through the Looking Glass', 875–78, 880.

TABLE 5.1 *Mortgage foreclosures in late twentieth-century Nova Scotia and New York State*

	Nova Scotia	New York State
Property purchased by mortgagee	77%	77%
Property purchased by third party	23%	23%
Surplus produced on sale to mortgagee	1.4%	0.8%
Surplus produced on sale to third party	60%	54%
Deficiency results from sale	87%	80%
Deficiency judgment sought	25%	?
Mortgagee profits from resale[79]	?	48.6%

In both jurisdictions, the impressive-sounding process of judicial sale had in fact degenerated into what Professor Wechsler said was often 'a meaningless ceremony whereby the mortgagee exchanges the property for the debt, then retains any surplus generated through a profitable resale, takes any loss on an unprofitable disposal of the property, or if the property is not resold, absorbs the deficiency owed by the mortgagor'.[80] The author's own research revealed that most of the time, the sheriff's sale in Nova Scotia was conducted in a basement room of the courthouse after minimal advertising in local newspapers, and attended only by the sheriff and the bank's representative. Both Professor Wechsler and the Nova Scotia Law Reform Commission concluded that the current practice of foreclosure and sale was not achieving its objectives and stood in urgent need of reform. As far as the author can tell, neither New York nor Nova Scotia has implemented any reforms to its law in the ensuing decades.

Upper Canada, by contrast, stayed within the English tradition, permitting strict foreclosure after the Court of Chancery was created in 1837, but following the trend to include private powers of sale in mortgage documents. The Short Forms of Mortgage Act of 1864[81] directed that the words 'Provided, that the said mortgagee on default of payment for [blank] months, may on [blank] notice enter on and lease or sell the said lands'[82] gave the mortgagee the power to sell 'by public auction or private contract, or partly by public

---

[79] Price data on resales in Nova Scotia were not publicly available at the time the research was conducted.
[80] Wechsler, 'Through the Looking Glass', 884.   [81] (S.U.C.) 1864, c. 31.
[82] Sch. 2, par. 3, col. 1, form 14.

auction and partly by private contract, as to him shall seem meet',[83] and should not be liable for any loss arising therefrom 'unless the same shall happen by reason of his wilful neglect or default'.[84] The courts showed themselves willing to police the conduct of such sales; indeed, more willing than the English courts in some instances, as the Ontario courts for some time interpreted the 'wilful neglect or default' standard as more akin to a straight negligence standard than the more elevated standard required to set aside a sale as articulated in English cases such as *Kennedy v. De Trafford*.[85] Ironically, the very absence of equity in early Upper Canada had permitted it to start afresh with mortgage law in the 1830s, at a time when the reform movement was identified with the interests of mortgagors. This balance of power led to a decision to follow the more mortgagor-identified trend of English law, rather than utilise the distinctive device of foreclosure and sale that had emerged elsewhere in North America.

In both England and Ontario, a straight negligence standard increasingly won out after the mid-twentieth century. In Ontario today, mortgage sales must be conducted using real estate agents in a manner as close as possible to the ordinary sale of residential or commercial property, as the case may be, on pain of being set aside. Current scholarly opinion in Canada is of the view that only in Ontario and British Columbia have the courts articulated and enforced a standard of conduct in mortgage sales that provides adequate safeguards for the mortgagor.[86]

CONCLUSION

What does this review of the Canadian experience have to add to the debate about the fusion of law and equity? Two main conclusions may be hazarded. The first is that there were many fusions because the starting points for the fusion debate were so various. The colonial experience in pre-revolutionary America and pre-Confederation Canada with what was supposed to be one of the most distinctive and indispensable aspects of the administration of justice under the common law was in fact extremely varied. Upper Canada got along without equity for nearly fifty years, Pennsylvania for much longer, while in Newfoundland law and equity were comfortably dispensed by the same court from an early date. The late arrival of a Court of Chancery in Upper Canada probably saved it when the peak agitation for Chancery abolition arose barely

---

[83] Ibid.   [84] Ibid.   [85] [1896] 1 Ch. 762.
[86] J. T. Robertson, 'The Problem of Price Adequacy in Foreclosure Sales' (1987) 66 Can. Bar Rev. 671, 678, 726.

a decade after the court had been established. The argument that one should attempt to reform such a recently arrived institution before throwing it out had some common sense appeal, and was made at the time.[87] The Maritime Provinces, meanwhile, had had ample opportunity to become disillusioned with their Chancery courts over the lengthy period of their existence, especially in Nova Scotia, where a Chancery court in some form had existed for over a century by the early 1850s.

The second conclusion has to do with the impact of fusion on the substantive law. English scholars have advanced opposing views, some suggesting that the common law judges swallowed equity whole in the wake of the Judicature Acts, others that it retained a certain autonomy.[88] British North America provides support for both views but also suggests a third: that in the area of mortgage law at least, the relationship between law and equity was already fixed due to local conditions, such that it retained a relative autonomy from the debates over fusion. In both Nova Scotia and New York equity was sufficiently malleable in the eighteenth century that the traditional English approach to the mortgage relationship could be upended, with the mortgagee gaining the upper hand. In part, this simply reflected the very different position of land in North America compared to England: land as a fungible commodity rather than land as the foundation of family honour, identity and power. This view of the mortgage relationship was well entrenched by the time the debate over fusion began in the nineteenth century, leading to a kind of path dependency whereby long-established procedures seemed beyond challenge. But the existing law also served the interests of those possessing capital, such that there was no strong push to alter mortgage law. Occasional populist measures in New York to redress the balance between lenders and borrowers fizzled out or were relatively ineffective, as noted earlier.

By the mid-nineteenth century, the underlying power dynamics of the system for raising credit on land in North America had shifted decisively towards the suppliers of credit (if indeed they had ever favoured borrowers), such that reformers did not wish to rock the boat. One of the few jurisdictions not to follow this trajectory was Upper Canada; the late creation of a Court of Chancery, staffed with an imported English judge familiar with English equity, insulated it from the North American mainstream on this point, and meant that mortgage law evolved more in line with English norms.

---

[87] Brown, 'Equitable Jurisdiction and the Court of Chancery in Upper Canada', 297.
[88] E.g., W. R. Cornish and G. de N. Clark, *Law and Society in England, 1750–1950* (London: Sweet & Maxwell, 1989), 220–23; M. Lobban, 'Nineteenth-Century Frauds in Company Formation: *Derry* v. *Peek* in Context' (1996) 112 L.Q.R. 287.

On the whole, however, mortgage law was something of an exception to the general pattern of law–equity interaction in North America. The colonial period in the former United States and in British North America witnessed a wide variety of approaches to the difficult question of how to accommodate the peculiar relationship between law and equity in a frontier setting. Over time, with the growth of the local bar, the expansion of legal publishing and growing connections in the transatlantic legal world, there was a certain convergence in approaches to the institutional accommodation of the law–equity binary. In British North America, domestic approaches to fusion were eventually abandoned in favour of the model sanctioned by the Judicature Acts 1873–75, which in turn were largely influenced by the Field Code reforms. Mortgage law, except in Ontario, remained something of a holdout to this pattern of convergence, but it reminds us that questions of power cannot be excluded from any consideration of the fusion debate over the *longue durée*.

6

Fusion–Fission–Fusion

Pre-Judicature Equity Jurisdiction in New South Wales, 1824–1972

MARK LEEMING [*]

INTRODUCTION

Here is a vivid account of the pre-Judicature Act system which prevailed in New South Wales at the end of the nineteenth century and its origins:

> To the litigant who sought damages before an Equity Judge, a grant of Probate before a Divorce Judge or an injunction before a Common Law Judge, there could be no remedy. He had come to the wrong Court, so it was said. He might well have enquired on what historical basis he could thus be denied justice. It cannot be questioned that the Court required specialization to function properly and that a case obviously falling within one jurisdiction ought not to be heard by a Judge sitting in another jurisdiction. Yet from this the fallacious extension was made that a Judge sitting in one jurisdiction could not in any circumstances hear a case which ought to have originated in another jurisdiction.[1]

The words are those of the distinguished Australian legal historian J. M. Bennett. There is no doubt that the jurisdictions at common law and in equity came to be treated in many respects as if they were separate courts, despite the failure of sustained efforts to create a separate equity court; despite it being clear that there was a single Supreme Court of New South Wales with full jurisdiction at common law and in equity; and despite efforts by its first Chief Justice, Sir Francis Forbes, in the opposite direction. But was that a 'fallacious extension'?[2] If that conclusion is to be drawn, it requires a careful assessment of incremental developments throughout the nineteenth

[*] I am indebted to Ms Kate Lindeman and to the staff of the Joint Law Courts Library, Sydney, especially Ms Larissa Reid, for assistance with the historical materials on which this chapter is based.
[1] J. M. Bennett, 'The Separation of Jurisdiction in the Supreme Court of New South Wales, 1824–1900', LL.M. thesis, University of Sydney (1963), 179.
[2] Ibid.

century – some of which were directed to separating common law from equity, but others to assimilating the two jurisdictions.

The historical position in New South Wales may be of some wider importance. Judicial and academic scholarship from New South Wales has been prominent in the efflorescence of equity in the decades since Bennett wrote the passage at the beginning of this chapter. For example, the term 'fusion fallacy' was created in the first edition of *Equity: Doctrines and Remedies*,[3] written in the early 1970s by three young practitioners in Sydney, all of whom became distinguished Australian judges.[4] Moreover, the idea – now widely accepted throughout the British Commonwealth[5] – that the Judicature legislation effected an administrative but not substantive fusion is associated with much academic and judicial contributions from New South Wales.

The principal purpose of this chapter is to explain how the fission of jurisdiction, effected during the nineteenth century but whose influence extends well into the twenty-first century, came about. Much of the material on which the chapter is based is unpublished.[6] The chapter also offers an assessment of the influence of the pre-Judicature system in New South Wales – the only such system in mainland Australia after 1883 – in the wider Anglo-Australian legal system. Before addressing either of those matters, something should be said immediately of the English Judicature legislation and its context.

THE JUDICATURE LEGISLATION AND ITS CONTEXT

The English Judicature legislation can be poorly understood, and for a number of reasons. It may be helpful to bear in mind the following basal notions.

---

[3] Meagher, Gummow and Lehane, 1st edn, [220]–[222].
[4] Meagher became President of the N.S.W. Bar Association and a Judge of Appeal of the Supreme Court of New South Wales (1989–2004); Gummow became in turn a Judge of the Federal Court of Australia (1986–95), a Justice of the High Court of Australia (1995–2012), and a Non-Permanent Judge of the Hong Kong Court of Final Appeal (2013–); Lehane became a judge of the Federal Court of Australia (1995–2001). See further the text to n. 143.
[5] See generally, S. Degeling and J. Edelman (eds), *Equity in Commercial Law* (Sydney: Lawbook Co., 2005).
[6] In addition to Bennett's thesis referred to at n. 1, I am especially indebted to J. M. Bennett, 'Equity Law in Colonial New South Wales: 1788–1902', Research Project 59/20(c), University of Sydney (1962) (kindly made available by the author); J. P. Bryson, 'Rules of Court in the Time of Chief Justice Francis Forbes', unpublished paper (2 March 2013), available: www .forbessociety.org.au/wordpress/wp-content/uploads/2013/03/NSW-Rules-of-Court-1823-1839.doc; and J. E. Rogers, 'Legal Argument and the Separateness of Equity in New South Wales, 1824-1900', LL.B Thesis, Macquarie University (2002), available: www.researchonline.mq.edu .au/vital/access/manager/Repository/mq:44076.

First, by the 'Judicature legislation' is meant the Supreme Court of Judicature Act 1873,[7] and more particularly, the provisions which abolished many of the separate superior courts of law replacing them with the High Court of Justice with a complete jurisdiction at common law and in equity (and other discrete areas of law including admiralty) and a single procedure, subject to appeal to the newly created Court of Appeal.[8] It may be contrasted with the more substantial reforms associated with the Field Codes in the United States in the 1840s.[9]

Secondly, the Judicature legislation was not just about equity. The Judicature legislation changed a small number of conflicting rules: for example, by permitting the Court of Admiralty's 'half-damages under the both-to-blame rule'[10] in collision cases to prevail over the common law's complete defence of contributory negligence.[11] This had nothing to do with equity at all, but was made necessary when a single court was to determine all collision cases. The Judicature legislation also introduced a small number of significant innovations (for example, by authorising a general mode for the assignment at law of choses in action),[12] while confirming some long-established rules (for example, that a trustee could not plead a limitation statute).[13]

Thirdly, it is at least arguable that the most important practical change was procedural – the assimilation of very different procedural rules between the common law and chancery courts.[14] Prior to 1 November 1875, every aspect of procedure was different. Before 1854, discovery could only be obtained in

---

7 36 & 37 Vict. c. 66 (U.K.), as amended by the Supreme Court of Judicature (1873) Amendment Act 1875 (U.K.), 38 & 39 Vict. c. 77.

8 For details, see P. Polden, 'The Judicature Acts', in *O.H.L.E.*, vol. XI, 757–84.

9 See McMahon, 'Field, Fusion and the 1850s' and Lobban, Chapter 4.

10 See G. Bruce and C. F. Jemmett, *A Treatise on the Jurisdiction and Practice of the English Courts in Admiralty Actions and Appeals* (London: Maxwell and Son, 1886), 85–87.

11 Judicature Act 1873 (U.K.), s. 25(9).

12 Modelled on 1867 and 1868 provisions permitting assignment of insurance policies: see *Lloyd v. Fleming* (1872) L.R. 7 Q.B. 299. For the other innovations, see M. Leeming, 'Equity, the Judicature Acts and Restitution' (2011) 5 J. Eq. 199, 211–12.

13 Judicature Act 1873 (U.K.), s. 25(2). See J. Brunyate, *Limitation of Actions in Equity* (London: Stevens and Sons, 1932), 56 and M. Leeming, '"Not Slavishly nor Always" – Equity and Limitation States', in P. Davies, S. Douglas and J. Goudkamp (eds), *Defences in Equity* (Oxford: Hart, 2018), ch. 14.

14 There is a measure of simplification in this. The superior courts at common law had, until 1832, all themselves employed different originating process. The uniformity of Process Act 1832 (U.K.), 2 Wm IV c. 39 replaced those various processes with a single writ on which the form of action was required to be stated. It was said at the time that this was 'to put to an end the *perplexity* and frequent errors occasioned by the great *variety* of process antecedently in use': see J. Chitty, *The Practice of the Law in All Its Departments* (London: Sweet & Maxwell, 1836), vol. 3, 59 (emphasis in original).

equity (necessitating the filing of a separate bill), and even after a power was conferred on common law courts in 1854, evidence suggests it was not used to its fullest extent.[15] The mode of trial (with a jury at common law) was different, while appeals were much more widely available in equity. As the Judicature Commission said in 1869:

> [T]he forms of pleadings are different, the modes of trial and of taking evidence are different, the nomenclature is different, the same instrument being called by a different name in different Courts; almost every step in the cause is different.[16]

Fourthly, there was nothing radically new about the central tenet of fusion – namely, vesting both common law and equitable jurisdiction in the same court. It had long been the case that the same appellate courts (the Judicial Committees of the House of Lords and the Privy Council respectively) heard and determined appeals from common law and equitable jurisdictions,[17] while the Court of Exchequer had possessed a full equitable jurisdiction, concurrent with that of the Court of Chancery, until abolished in 1841.[18]

Fifthly, there was no obstacle to the introduction of English statutory reforms in the Australian colonies. English statute law was received in the Australian colonies no later than 1836,[19] and thereafter colonial Attorneys-General attended to the legislation passed at Westminster with a view to advising what ought to be enacted by the colonial legislatures.[20] Thus it was that most of the mid- and late nineteenth-century procedural reforms (notably,

---

[15] See Polden, 'Mingling the Waters', 580; see McMahon, Chapter 12.

[16] *First Report Judicature Commissioners*, 10.

[17] Not to mention Scottish appeals in the case of the House of Lords, and the 'bewildering variety' of appeals in the case of the Privy Council: see D. Swinfen, *Imperial Appeal: The Debate on the Appeal to the Privy Council 1833–1986* (Manchester University Press, 1987), 5.

[18] Administration of Justice Act 1841 (U.K.), 5 Vict. c. 5, s. 1. See the text to n. 32.

[19] For details, see M. Leeming, *Resolving Conflicts of Laws* (Sydney: Federation Press, 2011), 36–37.

[20] Sir Roger Therry, who had been Attorney General of New South Wales twenty years earlier, wrote in 1863:

> 'A part of the duty of the Attorney-General (or at least it was so during my tenure of that office) is to attend to the Acts of each session of the British Parliament, and apprise the local Government of such measures as might advantageously be adopted and declared to extend to New South Wales.'
>
> (R. Therry, *Reminiscences of Thirty Years' Residence in New South Wales and Victoria*, 2nd edn (London: Low, Son and Co., 1863), 316.)

Sir John Rolt's[21] and Lord Cairns' Act[22]) were more or less promptly enacted in the Australian colonies,[23] including in New South Wales, as were some of the substantive rules.[24]

One might think, then, that replacing the separate courts by a single High Court of Justice would be more easily and less controversially achieved in the Australian colonies. And so it was in the younger colonies of Queensland, South Australia, Victoria and Western Australia where local equivalents of the English legislation of 1873 and 1875 were rapidly enacted.[25]

Why was it different in the case of the Supreme Court of New South Wales, one of the oldest continually existing superior courts in the common law world, which at all times has enjoyed full common law and equitable jurisdiction?

EQUITY JURISDICTION IN NEW SOUTH WALES

One remarkable aspect of the Judicature legislation in New South Wales is that it was necessary at all. From 1824, there was a single Supreme Court with plenary jurisdiction at common law and in equity. Yet, as Bennett observed,[26] that did not stand in the way of the introduction and assimilation of the very features of the English legal system – the separation of common law and equitable jurisdictions – which were done away with by the Judicature legislation. It is that process of fission, creating separate common law and equity jurisdictions within the same court, which gives rise to the title of this chapter. This section describes how it occurred.

The section proceeds chronologically. It addresses the creation of the modern Supreme Court in 1824, the early period from 1824–38, 1838–41 (a tumultuous period), the period 1841–80 leading up to the enactment of the Equity Act 1880[27] and its interpretation, and the position in the mid-twentieth century, before the Judicature legislation commenced in 1972.

---

[21] Chancery Regulation Act 1862 (U.K.), 25 & 26 Vict. c. 42, s. 1, itself an elaboration of the Court of Chancery Procedure Act 1852 (U.K.), 15 & 16 Vict. c. 86, s. 62 (which had been enacted as section 49 of the Equity Practice Act 1853 (N.S.W.), 17 Vict. no. 7).

[22] Chancery Amendment Act 1858 (U.K.), 21 & 22 Vict. c. 27.

[23] For example, in South Australia: Equity Act 1867 (S.A.), 30 Vict. no. 20, s. 141 (enacting Lord Cairns' Act), ss. 142–43 (enacting Sir John Rolt's Act). See the text to nn. 100 and 101.

[24] For example, the assignment at law of choses in action was authorised by Supreme Court Act 1878 (S.A.), 41 & 42 Vict. no. 116, s. 6(6) and Conveyancing Act 1919 (N.S.W.), s. 12.

[25] Judicature Act 1876 (Qld), 40 Vict. no. 6; Supreme Court Act 1878 (S.A.); Judicature Act 1883 (Vic.), 47 Vict. no. 761; Supreme Court Act 1880 (W.A.), 44 Vict. no. 10.

[26] N. 1.   [27] 44 Vict. no. 18 (N.S.W.).

The Creation of the Supreme Court of New South Wales

The First Charter of Justice (in fact, letters patent of 2 April 1787) envisaged a civil court, presided over by the Judge-Advocate who sat with two 'fit and proper persons' taken from the limited free population, from which an appeal lay to the Governor. A new civil court, confusingly known as the Supreme Court, was established in 1814 pursuant to the Second Charter of Justice (letters patent of 4 February 1814). Reforms suggested by Commissioner Bigge led to the enactment of the New South Wales Act 1823,[28] authorising the issue of Letters Patent on 13 October 1823 establishing the Supreme Court of New South Wales[29] which exists to this day almost two centuries later.

Anticipating the Judicature legislation by precisely five decades, a wide civil jurisdiction at common law and in equity was conferred on the Supreme Court of New South Wales over all matters excluding matrimonial causes.[30] The New South Wales Act provided (section 2) that the Supreme Court was to be a court of record with a complete common law jurisdiction defined by reference to the superior courts of law at Westminster, and (section 9) that the court should be a Court of Equity with all the power and authority of the Lord High Chancellor.

That Act made it clear beyond argument that equity was received in the colony.[31] And it could not have been plainer that here was created a superior court with full jurisdiction at common law and in equity. A contemporary example of such a court was the Court of Exchequer. Until 1841, that Court had a full equitable jurisdiction,[32] and in fact the preferred court for some ancillary

---

[28]   4 Geo. IV c. 96 (U.K.).

[29]   The same letters patent established the Supreme Court of Van Diemen's Land.

[30]   By conscious design of the Colonial Office, there was no provision in the colony for relief in failed marriages, short of a private Act of Parliament, until 1873: see J. M. Bennett, *Sir Frederick Darley: Sixth Chief Justice of New South Wales: 1886–1910* (Sydney: Federation Press, 2016), 41–42, and the Matrimonial Causes Act 1873 (N.S.W.), 36 Vict. no. 9.

[31]   Contrast B. H. McPherson, 'How Equity Reached the Colonies', in M. Cope (ed.), *Interpreting Principles of Equity: The W.A. Lee Lectures 2000–2013* (Sydney: Federation Press, 2014), 94 (pointing out that, absent statute, various difficulties accompanied the conclusion that equity was received in a colony).

[32]   See H. Horwitz, *Exchequer Equity Records and Proceedings, 1649–1841* (London: Public Record Office, 2001); D. B. Fowler, *The Practice of the Court of Exchequer: Upon Proceedings in Equity*, 2nd edn (London: Butterworth, 1817), 2 vols. Volume 1 of the work commences, at page 1, as follows: 'The Court of Exchequer at Westminster, with respect to its equitable jurisdiction, is a supreme, independent, Court of Equity, possessing a concurrent jurisdiction with the Court of Chancery, in all matters which are the subject of relief, and discovery, in that court'.

procedures,[33] such as discovery,[34] and whose common injunction was 'universally understood, in the profession, to be more beneficially comprehensive than that which issues from the Court of Chancery'.[35] Accordingly, there was never a need to abolish existing courts and to create a single new court of common law and equitable jurisdiction; that existed from the beginning. What was ultimately necessary was legislation to override the lack of jurisdiction, initially merely perceived, later enshrined in law, limiting the common law side of the Court from hearing and determining equitable claims and vice versa.

The Period from 1824 to 1838

The first Chief Justice, Sir Francis Forbes, is widely and rightly known for simplifying the procedure in the Supreme Court in the young colony. He had not been burdened by a junior's practice at the Bar, with its inevitable focus upon procedure. As John Bryson has pointed out, Forbes C.J. took considerable steps to simplify and assimilate equitable procedure in what was, in the 1820s and 1830s, a very minor part of the jurisdiction of the Supreme Court.[36] This was a reaction, in part, to unduly complex procedures introduced by Barron Field, which Forbes said the public 'might be excused for believing, were not so operative in facilitating the ends of justice, as in filling the pockets of the practitioners'.[37] The steps were lauded contemporaneously.[38] Forbes's rules of 1825 were said to have 'anticipated the legislation of modern times, by

---

[33] Leeming, 'Equity, the Judicature Acts and Restitution', 201–2.

[34] M. Leeming, [s.n.] (Commentary on 'Seeking Documentary Evidence in Transnational Litigation: Problems and Pitfalls'), in K. E. Lindgren and N. Perram (eds), *International Commercial Law, Litigation and Arbitration* (Sydney: Ross Parsons Centre of Commercial, Corporate and Taxation Law, 2011), 90.

[35] *Rolfe v. Burke* (1827) 1 Y. & J. 404, 405 (Knight *arguendo*). See H. Horwitz, 'Chancery's "Younger Sister": The Court of Exchequer and Its Equity Jurisdiction, 1649–1841' (1999) 72 Hist. Res. 160, 175.

[36] For example, permitting witnesses to be examined *viva voce*, something which did not at that time occur in England: see Bryson, 'Rules of Court in the Time of Chief Justice Francis Forbes'.

[37] Letters, Catton Papers, Australian Joint Copying Project, Reel M791, quoted in note 3 to the Practice Note [1824] NSWSupC 23 (originally printed in 'Supreme Court', *The Australian*, 16 December 1824, 3); see also J. Bennett, *A History of the Supreme Court of New South Wales* (Sydney: Law Book Co., 1974), 62–64; C. H. Currey, *Sir Francis Forbes: The First Chief Justice of New South Wales* (Sydney: Angus and Robertson, 1968), 109–10.

[38] See the editorial in *The Australian*, 7 October 1826, 3, summarised in S. Dorsett, 'Procedural Innovation: The First Supreme Court Rules of New South Wales and New Zealand' (2011) 35 Aust. Bar Rev. 128, 135.

simplifying pleadings and dispensing with the costly course of procedure then prevalent in the Courts of Westminster'.[39]

Thus it may said, at a high level, that it was only after Forbes C.J.'s departure that steps were taken to bring about a jurisdictional separation between common law and equity within the same court. The actual position is more nuanced.

In the first months of his tenure, Forbes C.J. preserved the procedure which had evolved under the Second Charter. However, he intimated in court on 13 December 1824 that he had received instructions that 'on the equity, as well as the plea side of the Court, the practice should be assimilated to that of England, after the end of the present Term'.[40] That reflected advance notice of the Order in Council conferring rule-making power upon Forbes C.J. And that in itself was an innovation, which had been sought by the reform movement in England and America; New South Wales was the first colony in which such a grant was made.[41] However, the power was qualified by the requirement that:

> such Rules and Orders ... shall be consistent with, and similar to, the Law and Practice of His Majesty's Supreme Courts at Westminster, so far as the Condition and Circumstances of the said Colony will admit.[42]

Even in January 1825, the separate jurisdictions of the Supreme Court were reflected in the rules. Rule 2 was that:

> the Proceedings of the said Supreme Court, within its several and respective Jurisdictions as aforesaid, be commenced and continued in a distinct and separate Form.

The reference to the same court having 'several and respective Jurisdictions' was a natural consequence of a rule-making power which required assimilation to English practice where there were separate courts. Hence rule 1 of the

---

[39] Therry, *Reminiscences of Thirty Years' Residence*, 335.
[40] 'Supreme Court', *The Australian*, 16 December 1824, 3.
[41] See Dorsett, 'Procedural Innovation', 131.
[42] New South Wales, Supreme Court, Rules of the Supreme Court, 22 June 1825, Preamble. The rules were printed in the *Sydney Gazette and New South Wales Advertiser*, 23 June 1825, 1. Forbes had been pressing for a resolution of the problem of the lack of Rules and the absence of any power to make them. He had advised that it would be better if the power were delegated to himself, the Chief Justice, subject to the power of revocation in London: 'pray do not fetter us too much, for be assured we can do the thing better here, than it can be done at home – you cannot command our local knowledge and experience, without which it will be next to impossible to legislate beneficially': Letter from Forbes to Wilmot Horton (14 August 1824), quoted by Dorsett, 'Procedural Innovation', 130.

rules made on 22 June 1825, described in Charles Clark's influential practice
book as perhaps the most important,[43] confirmed that the 'rules and orders,
forms and manner of practice and proceeding' in, relevantly, the High Court
of Chancery shall 'be adopted and followed' so far as the circumstances and
condition of the colony shall require and admit.[44] That was reflected in
judgments. As Forbes C.J. put it:

> The general rules of the Equity courts of England were in force here so far as
> they were applicable to the state of the Colony and its juridical
> establishment.[45]

The rule that proceedings in the court's 'several and respective Jurisdictions'
be kept distinct was continued as rule 2 of the 1831 rules and rule 14 of the 1834
rules. This had substantive, rather than merely procedural, consequences. In
an action in ejectment to recover possession of land in Burwood in 1832,
Forbes C.J., Stephen and Dowling JJ. said, anticipating the future separation
of jurisdiction, that the matter 'must be determined strictly according to the
rules of law, and we are precluded in the present mode of proceeding from
any equitable considerations'.[46]

1838–1841: John Walpole Willis and the Primary Judge in Equity

The period from 1838 to 1841 was immensely important in leading to the
fission of common law and equitable jurisdiction. The catalyst for change was
a new judge, Justice John Walpole Willis.

Unlike his judicial brethren, Willis J. had practised extensively in equity at
the English Bar. He was of considerable ability, and had published three
books on equity.[47] It was not surprising that he would take the lead in equity

---

[43] C. Clark, *A Summary of Colonial Law, the Practice of the Court of Appeals from the Planta-*
tions, and of the Laws and Their Administration in All the Colonies &c. (London: Maxwell and
Stephens, 1834), 613.

[44] Ibid.   [45] *Lord v. Dickson* [No. 1] (1828) N.S.W. Sel. Cas. (Dowling) 487.

[46] *Doe d. Harris v. Riley* (1832) 78 Dowl. Proc. Sup. Ct. 61, 67; *Sydney Herald*, 18 October 1832.
See Rogers, 'Legal Argument and the Separateness of Equity', 27. Other examples are given in
Dorsett, 'Procedural Innovation', 146.

[47] J. W. Willis, *A Digest of Rules and Practice as to Interrogatories for the Examination of*
Witnesses &c. (London: Pheney, 1816); J. W. Willis, *Pleadings in Equity Illustrative of Lord*
Redesdale's Treatise on the Pleadings in Suits in Chancery, by English Bill (London: Pheney,
1820); J. W. Willis, *A Practical Treatise on the Duties and Responsibilities of Trustees* (London:
Pheney, 1827).

business. With his arrival in February 1838, there seems to have commenced a process of specialisation. The Governor wrote in an official despatch that 'Mr Justice Willis, having been in England at the Chancery Bar, has almost invariably up to the present time heard singly all cases in Equity.'[48]

It is necessary, in order to understand the legislative separation of jurisdiction which took place in 1840, to say something about the character of Willis J. He has been said to be 'as troublesome a judge as could be imagined'.[49] He had been expelled from Charterhouse, his marriage to a daughter of the Earl of Strathmore had been ended by Act of Parliament in 1833, and he had been appointed to the King's Bench in Upper Canada through the influence of his then father-in-law – but 'amoved' two years later under the Colonial Leave of Absence Act 1782[50] following several disputes after his proposal to establish a separate chancery court was rejected. The Privy Council affirmed the amotion, but the order was later set aside.[51] Willis then served as Vice-President of the Court of Civil and Criminal Justice of British Guiana, before being appointed to the Supreme Court of New South Wales.

General rules in equity were drafted by the newly arrived Willis J. in 1838. Consistently with the terms of the rule-making power, they commenced with the command that the rules and orders in Chancery be followed so far as local circumstances would admit.[52] Rule 5 provided for injunctions to stay proceedings at law, and rule 22 authorised petitions for rehearing before all the judges 'as prescribed by the English Rules of Practice for a petition of re-hearing by the Lord Chancellor of England, of a case previously heard and decided by the Master of the Rolls or Vice Chancellor in that Kingdom'. Thus, from the beginning (filing originating process) until the end (appeals) the rules replicated the procedure in England, even though at all times the plaintiff was litigating in the Supreme Court of New South Wales.

---

[48] Despatch from Sir George Gipps to Lord Russell (1 January 1841), located in F. Watson (ed.), *Historical Records of Australia: Series I: Governors' Despatches to and from England: Volume XXI: October 1840 to March 1842* (Sydney: Library Committee of the Commonwealth, 1924), 156.

[49] J. M. Bennett, *Sir James Dowling: Second Chief Justice of New South Wales: 1837–1844* (Sydney: Federation Press, 2001), 111. See also J. V. Barry, 'John Walpole Willis (1793–1877)', in D. Pike, *Australian Dictionary of Biography: Volume 2: 1788–1850* (Melbourne University Press, 1967), 602–4; J. McLaren, *Dewigged, Bothered, and Bewildered: British Colonial Judges on Trial, 1800–1900* (University of Toronto Press, 2011), 74–87.

[50] 22 Geo. III c. 75 (U.K.) (Burke's Act).

[51] See McLaren, *Dewigged, Bothered, and Bewildered*, 171. For a more sympathetic account, see J. Phillips, 'Judicial Independence in British North America, 1825–67; Constitutional Principles, Colonial Finances, and the Perils of Democracy' (2016) 34 L.H.R. 689, 694 ff.

[52] See *Government Gazette*, 18 May 1838, 8–11.

Just as he had in Canada, so too in New South Wales, Willis J. advocated the creation of a separate court, with himself at its head, as Chief Baron.[53] That was rejected by the other judges and the governor, but led to the insertion of section 20 in the Administration of Justice Act 1840,[54] which was the first legislative fission of the jurisdiction of the Supreme Court of New South Wales:

> [I]t shall be lawful for the Governor of New South Wales for the time being to nominate and appoint from time to time either the Chief Justice or if he shall decline such appointment then one of the Puisne Judges to sit and hear and determine without the assistance of the other Judges or either of them all causes and matters at any time depending in the said Supreme Court in Equity and coming on to be heard and decided at Sydney and every decree or order of such Chief Justice or of the Judge so appointed shall in any such cause or matter (unless appealed from in the manner hereinafter provided) be as valid effectual and binding to all intents and purposes as if such decree or order had been pronounced and made by the full Court.

Deficiencies in the drafting of section 20 soon became manifest. In the following year, the Advancement of Justice Act 1841[55] authorised judges other than the judge appointed to sit in Equity, in cases of his absence or illness, to 'sit alone and hear and determine all causes and matters in Equity in like manner',[56] and altered the appeal structure so that appeals were heard by the three judges in Sydney (including the judge at first instance).[57]

The legislation 'made for the first time in the Colony's legal history a division in the function of the Court',[58] resulting in one judge of the Supreme Court, the Primary Judge in Equity, being at first exclusively, and then primarily, responsible for hearing and determining all proceedings of a particular subject matter otherwise within the jurisdiction of the Supreme Court.[59] Further, those proceedings were governed by different procedural rules,[60] not least as to pleadings and mode of trial. The judge's orders and decrees were deemed to be those of the Full Court.

This was the first legislative formalisation of a split in the court's jurisdiction. Litigation of a particular subject matter would not merely be governed by

---

53 'Your Lordship will see that His Honor was desirous that a Judge should be appointed exclusively for Equity business, to whom he proposed to give the Title of Chief Baron': Gipps to Russell (1 January 1841), 156.
54 4 Vict. No. 22 (N.S.W.).   55 5 Vict. no. 9 (N.S.W.).   56 Ibid., s. 12.   57 Ibid., s. 13.
58 Bennett, 'Equity Law in Colonial New South Wales', 43.
59 See the citations at nn. 54 and 55.
60 Made under Administration of Justice Act 1840 Act (N.S.W.), s. 23.

different procedural rules. It would from 1840 ordinarily be determined by a particular judge, whose decision would have a different status.

Although drafted with Willis J. in mind, Dowling C.J. claimed the position of Primary Judge in Equity following a series of slights between the men.[61] Willis J. was relocated to Port Phillip (now, Melbourne) apparently at his own request.[62] From there, he also protested against changes to the Equity rules, including the innovation established by Forbes C.J. that witnesses in an Equity suit give evidence *viva voce*, and many other matters.[63] Governor Gipps amoved him by order dated 17 June 1843.[64]

Justice Willis's legacy included not merely the office of Primary Judge in Equity, whose jurisdiction and decisions were different from those of other members of the Court. In addition, and presumably with the intention of confining Willis J.'s activities to the Port Phillip District, the Administration of Justice Act 1841 contained provisions vesting exclusive *geographic* jurisdiction in different judges of the court. Section 1 conferred exclusive common law and equitable jurisdiction on the Resident Judge over 'persons residing and property situate within Port Phillip', with the Judges of the Supreme Court at Sydney having exclusive jurisdiction over persons residing and property situate elsewhere in the colony. Section 4 created a concurrent jurisdiction in criminal and civil cases within 25 miles of the border. Those distinctions

---

[61] 'It is due to the Chief Justice to say that I believe he had not originally any intention of claiming the office, and that he has now done so, in consequence of what he considers the injurious statements of his want of ability to discharge the duties of it, which have been made by Mr Justice Willis': Gipps to Russell (1 January 1841), 164. The disagreements between Dowling and Willis are described in detail by Bennett, *Sir James Dowling*, 114–31 and McLaren, *Dewigged, Bothered, and Bewildered*, 173–75, the latter describing (at 174) what seemed to be 'a calculated campaign to undermine Dowling's position'. A more sympathetic account is given in M. Bonnell, *I Like a Clamour: John Walpole Willis, Colonial Judge, Reconsidered* (Sydney: Federation Press, 2017), ch. 18. The starting point was the claim (tersely rejected by the Colonial Office) that Dowling C.J.'s commission was forfeited by his acting as a judge of the Admiralty Court, followed up by the claim that an assignment of convicts to Dowling contravened an Order in Council prohibiting judges from owning slaves.

[62] 'It is due to Mr Justice Willis however to add that he has not only acquiesced in this arrangement, but that he himself proposed it': Gipps to Russell (1 January 1841), 165.

[63] See Bennett, 'Equity Law in Colonial New South Wales', 101; Bonnell, *I Like a Clamour*, chs 19–20; and, generally, McLaren, *Dewigged, Bothered, and Bewildered*.

[64] Once again, without notice to him, leading to another appeal to the Privy Council, which declared that he was entitled to notice, although there had been cause for his amoval: *Willis v. Gipps* (1846) 5 Moo. P.C. 379. He was not reinstated to any judicial office. He was described by the clerk in the Colonial Office responsible for New South Wales as 'one of the weakest men I ever knew ... He has within my knowledge been ruined three or four times over by sheer vanity and an absurd self-importance': C.O.201/306, f. 446r., cited by Bennett, *Sir James Dowling*, 128.

disappeared after the colony of Victoria was carved out of New South Wales in 1851, although until then, the *exclusive* jurisdiction went beyond even the concurrent equitable jurisdiction then exercised by the palatine courts.[65] However, the recurring theme – that different judges exercised different jurisdictions within the same court – may be seen as a further example of the process whereby at the same time as English courts were being unified, their New South Wales counterpart was being divided.

1841–80: Separate Jurisdictions at Law and in Equity

In England, the middle decades of the nineteenth century amounted to a period of almost continual reform, leading to substantial improvements in common law and chancery procedure.[66] The caricature described by Dickens in *Bleak House* was perceived even at the time to depict a system that no longer prevailed.[67] However, in New South Wales the Equity registry and the Primary Judge in Equity nearly ground to a halt.

For one thing, there seems not to have been much work. Dowling said at the time that 'the amount of [equity business] pending was very small compared with other branches of jurisdiction'.[68] The rules made on 28 October 1844 stated that the Primary Judge would sit in Equity on every Saturday during term, save on the last Saturday, and every Tuesday during the vacation. One judge sitting one day a week suggests that significantly less than

---

[65] Notably, the Court of Chancery of Lancaster and the Court of Chancery of the County Palatine of Durham, which had a concurrent jurisdiction with the court of Chancery, confined to persons residing within its geographical limits. See Lord Simonds (gen. ed.), *Halsbury's Laws of England*, 3rd edn (London: Butterworths, 1954), vol. 9, [1080]–[1094] and P. Polden, 'Local Courts', in *O.H.L.E.*, vol. XI, 872–75.

[66] See Lobban, 'Preparing for Fusion'; Polden, 'The Judicature Acts', in *O.H.L.E.*, vol. XI; Polden, 'Mingling the Waters'; McMahon, 'Field, Fusion and the 1850s', 424–62; Leeming, 'Equity, the Judicature Acts and Restitution'; M. J. Leeming, 'Five Judicature Fallacies', in J. T. Gleeson, R. C. A. Higgins and J. A. Watson (eds), *Historical Foundations of Australian Law* (Sydney: Federation Press, 2014), vol. 1, 169, 171–77.

[67] See for example, 'The Court of Chancery As it Is', in (1857) 8 Chambers's Journal of Popular Literature, Science and Arts 16:

   The Court of Chancery has been thoroughly reformed. The changes began in 1850; and in 1852 an entire revolution was effected in its mode of procedure. ... Works like Mr Dickens's *Bleak House* still continue to gain credence, although written long ago, and before Chancery reform began.

[68] Letter from Dowling to Willis (1 December 1840), C.O.201/306, f. 375, cited by Bennett, *Sir James Dowling*, 125. The best way of confirming this proposition (something which I have not undertaken) would be to review Dowling's note books, which are retained in the State Records.

10 per cent of judicial resources were devoted to Equity. That is consistent with the provision made for appeals to be set down for the Friday and Saturday in the week preceding each term (that is, all appeals could be dealt with in two days).

A snapshot of practice may be obtained from Alfred Stephen's *Introduction to the Practice of the Supreme Court of New South Wales*, published in 1843.[69] The author, who was well placed to do so, described the nature of the 1840 and 1841 Acts as a *delegation* of jurisdiction, rather than a transfer:

> [W]ith respect to the Equity jurisdiction, ... neither is this, strictly speaking, transferred from [the Judges]. It is delegated only. The Primary Judge decides, without the assistance of his Colleagues; but his Decrees have effect, as the Decrees of the Court. The consideration is important; because the question respecting the Appeal, whether it be or not in the nature of a *Rehearing*, mainly depends on it.[70]

That reflected what the Full Court had said in *McLaughlin v. Little*:[71]

> [H]ere, though the practice has been for the Primary Judge, alone, to sign the decrees and orders made by him, the Court is one and the same. There is no new Court created, nor is the one Court divided. Neither (as in [57 Geo. III c. 18 (1817),[72] s. 2], giving jurisdiction to one Baron of the Exchequer only) is there any provision vesting the *entire Equity jurisdiction of the Court in the one Judge*. That jurisdiction remains, it would seem, where the statute placed it. ... The Decrees of the single Judge, however, have no force given to them *as his*. The provision is so worded, apparently, as to admit of the inference, that he acts as representing the Court.[73]

That reasoning did not prevent the establishment of a body of law holding that there were separate jurisdictions at law and in equity. Bennett states that:

> With a large recruitment to the colonial legal profession of practitioners accustomed to the strict Common Law/Chancery division in England, the Colony's 'equity division' came to be regarded, without justification in terms of history or practice, as equivalent to the Chancellor's Court.[74]

---

[69] A. Stephen, *Introduction to the Practice of the Supreme Court of New South Wales* (Sydney: Welch, 1843). The work is of 364 pages with a 50-page appendix. The copy in the Joint Law Courts Library in Sydney includes typeset pages which date from 1845 or 1846.

[70] Ibid., 281.

[71] Seemingly reported only in the *Sydney Morning Herald*, 7 February 1845, 2; the extract in the text is reproduced in Stephen's volume in the Joint Law Courts Library.

[72] Court of Exchequer (England) Act 1817 (U.K.).

[73] *Sydney Morning Herald*, 7 February 1845, 2 (emphasis original).

[74] Bennett, *Sir Frederick Darley*, 59.

Typical of the mid-nineteenth century approach was the Full Court's decision in *Bank of Australasia* v. *Murray*.[75] The Full Court (Stephen C.J., Dickinson and Therry JJ.) dismissed an appeal from Therry J., the Primary Judge in Equity. The Court said, of the defendant to the suit in equity:

> He might, therefore, have been sued at law; and we can perceive no reason why he should not have been. So, if he be still liable, he is liable at law; and the resort to a Court of Equity was unnecessary.[76]

Similarly, in *Thompson* v. *Thompson*[77] in 1863, an equitable replication was struck out. Wise J. said:

> there are limits to equitable replications. [The claimant] may have a right to redress in a Court of Equity; but I am of opinion that the facts spread out on these pleadings, afford no ground of action in a Court of Law; and we cannot enforce mere equitable grounds of action. [78]

The decision turned on the Common Law Procedure Act 1857 (20 Vict. no. 31) (N.S.W.), section 50, which authorised equitable replications mirroring the English Common Law Procedure Act 1854,[79] but only where they would be a complete answer to the common law claim. Thereafter, from 1857 until 1958, in circumstances where an absolute verdict in favour of the party asserting the equitable plea or replication would be impossible (say, because equitable relief would only be available on terms), it remained necessary to seek a common injunction just as it had in England between 1854 and 1875.[80]

The Enactment of the Equity Act 1880

From around the middle of the nineteenth century, Equity litigation declined. A number of causes appear to have contributed to this. Undoubtedly, one was the procedural technicality and complexity and accompanying expense and delay. Another was the perception that Equity business always came last. Sir Alfred Stephen described equity as 'an unfavoured child – kicked, it might be said, from one room to another until it ran the risk of being utterly neglected'.[81] A recurring theme in the evidence given to a Select Committee in 1857, including by judges and practitioners, was the delays and inefficiencies in the Primary Judge's time being absorbed by other work – so

---

[75] (1850) 1 Legge 612.   [76] Ibid., 614. The Court went further, and regarded it as bad in equity.
[77] (1863) 2 S.C.R. (L.) 242.   [78] Ibid., 251–52.   [79] 17 & 18 Vict. c. 125, s. 85 (U.K.).
[80] See *Meagher, Gummow and Lehane*, 5th edn [1–315].
[81] *Sydney Morning Herald*, 27 August 1857, 3, quoted in Bennett, *A History of the Supreme Court of New South Wales*, 98.

much so that all members of the Supreme Court urged the creation of a separate Equity court, in a separate building, so that 'it would be impossible for Counsel to run from one to the other'.[82]

Sir Alfred Stephen accepted that a separate court would form 'an additional difficulty in the way of a future amalgamation of [the] two branches', and was firmly opposed to such a step: 'I do not believe that a complete amalgamation of the two jurisdictions ever *will* take place; and I am one of those who think that it never *can*'.[83]

A third contributing cause may simply have been personalities. The appointment of Justice John Fletcher Hargrave (perhaps best known as the father of the aeronautical pioneer Lawrence) as Primary Judge in Equity in 1865 was controversial. His swearing in was boycotted by the local Bar and, remarkably, led to the resignation of the Attorney General (J. B. Darvall) and his return to England.[84] Hargrave J. served as Primary Judge in Equity from 1865 until he retired in 1881, and it was during his tenure of office that proceedings were said to have ground to a halt. Certainly, Sir Alfred Stephen had a very poor opinion of him, comparing him to Willis.[85]

In the late 1860s, there was awareness of overseas developments, and a move for law reform. On 30 June 1869 a barrister, T. J. Fisher,[86] urged in the *Sydney Morning Herald* a fusion of the systems of law and equity, citing developments in the United States, Canada and India and the recommendations of the English Judicature Commission: 'The distinction between actions at law and suits in equity should be abolished, and there should be but one form of action for the enforcement or protection of private rights, or the redress or prevention of private wrongs'.[87] In July 1870, the Law Reform Commission was

---

[82] New South Wales, Legislative Council, *Report of the Select Committee of the Legislative Council on the Business of the Supreme Court* (1857), 1–17 (minutes of evidence taken 21, 22, 28 October 1857).

[83] Ibid., 4 (21 October 1857), qq. 47 and 48.

[84] See H.T.E. Holt, *A Court Rises: The Lives and Times of the Judges of the District Court of New South Wales (1859–1959)* (Sydney: Law Foundation of N.S.W., 1976), 43.

[85] See 'A Trio of Judges', (1894), available: Stephen papers, Law Courts Library, Sydney; see also K. Mason, 'The Office of Solicitor General for New South Wales' (Autumn 1988) Bar News: J. N.S.W. Bar Ass. 22, 24, who described him as habitually deciding against women suitors, apparently due to an 'inability to forgive his wife for having committed him to a lunatic asylum in the mid 1850s'. Perhaps there is an element of over-reaction. Griffith C.J. regarded him as a distinguished equity lawyer: *Loxton v. Moir* (1914) 18 C.L.R. 360, 369, and see Holt, *A Court Rises*, 45–46.

[86] See J. M. Bennett, *Sir Alfred Stephen: Third Chief Justice of New South Wales: 1844–1873* (Sydney: Federation Press, 2009), 364.

[87] 'Heads of Colonial Law Reform', *Sydney Morning Herald*, 30 June 1869, 5. Details from Fisher followed in the next month: 'Colonial Law Reform – No. 1', *Sydney Morning Herald*, 9 July

established by letters patent. It comprised five distinguished lawyers under the
chairmanship of Stephen C.J. One of its purposes was to propose amendments
with a view 'to the removal of the inconveniences arising from the separation
of jurisdictions at Law and in Equity'.[88]

Although the Equity Act 1880 was often described as 'Darley's Equity Act', it
was in fact a draft proposed by William Owen, a leading equity junior who
supplied it to the Law Reform Commission in 1870. The bill was twice
unsuccessfully introduced in 1870. It was enacted in substantially the same
form a decade later, the position before the Primary Judge in Equity having
deteriorated. Owen gave evidence in 1880 to a Select Committee of the
Legislative Assembly that the Equity jurisdiction was 'ruinous to suitors and
not in accord with the judicial progress of the age'.[89]

At the same time, Sir Alfred Stephen was a frequent correspondent of David
Dudley Field.[90] Australian readers were kept well informed of English legislative developments. The *Sydney Morning Herald* of Saturday 10 May
1873 reported that:

> Lord Selborne's Judicature Bill was read a second time on Tuesday, amid a
> perfect chorus of approval from all the legal personages in the House. Lord
> Hatherley concurred with Lord Selborne from beginning to end; Lord
> Chelmsford regarded the bill as a great and comprehensive measure; and
> Lord Romilly held it to be the first which had promised to be really
> effective.[91]

It is impossible to determine why it was decided to enact Owen's draft bill,
rather than to follow the more extensive reforms enacted at Westminster.[92]
One influence must have been the attitude of Sir Alfred Stephen. The former
Chief Justice (then aged 77) spoke in the Legislative Council against adopting
the English legislation. He considered that 'a litigant should be able to get

1869, 3 (citing in detail the Field Code reforms of New York); 'Colonial Law Reform – No. 2',
Sydney Morning Herald, 14 July 1869, 3.
[88] See J. M. Bennett, 'Historical Trends in Australian Law Reform' (1969) 9 U.W.A. L. Rev. 211,
213.
[89] See M. Rutledge, 'Owen, Sir William (1834–1912)' (1988) 11 Aust. Dict. Biog. 113, 114.
[90] Bennett, *Sir Alfred Stephen*, 370.
[91] 'The Judicature Bill', *Sydney Morning Herald*, 10 May 1873, 5.
[92] Bennett wrote:

> Where in the 1830's complete reliance was placed on English precedent, it is found that
> by the 1880's colonial lawyers were disinclined to follow slavishly the extensive reforms of
> the English courts. It may never be known with certainty whether that disinclination was
> bred of sloth or of individualism.
>
> (Bennett, 'Equity Law in Colonial New South Wales', 51.)

equity in a Court of law, and the redress of law in a Court of Equity', but consistently with his evidence in 1857 he regarded the merging of historically separate English courts as 'a great bungle'.[93]

THE OPERATION OF THE EQUITY ACT 1880

The 1880 legislation was a success on many measures. The decade was one of sustained economic growth and foreign investment. It is unsurprising that litigation in the Supreme Court of New South Wales expanded, but what is dramatic is the extent to which Equity litigation flourished. A crude measure may be seen in the series of New South Wales Reports which commenced in 1880: volumes 1 and 2 had 362 and 407 pages devoted to cases at law, and only 85 and 82 pages on cases in Equity. A decade later, volumes 11 and 12 in 1890 and 1891 had 489 and 337 pages on cases at law, and 335 and 329 pages on cases in Equity, many with a distinctly commercial flavour. A less subjective approach may be seen from the relative growth in filings after 1881.[94]

That success is partly attributable to two distinguished Equity judges: Sir William Manning and William Owen. On the resignation of Owen C.J. in Eq. in 1896,[95] it was said that he had 'raised this Court to an eminence it had never before attained'.[96]

The Equity Act 1880 repeated the power to appoint one of the judges the 'Primary Judge in Equity' in order 'to exercise the jurisdiction of the said Court in Equity',[97] and then defined the 'Court' for the purposes of the Act 'to mean the Court holden before the Judge so appointed'.[98] However, it also included provisions based on the mid-nineteenth-century reforms, including, in sections 4 and 32, equivalents to Sir John Rolt's Act of 1862 (permitting the determination of legal titles and rights) and Lord Cairns' Act of 1858

---

[93] New South Wales, Legislative Council, Parl. Deb., 4 December 1879, vol. 1, 474. See also the text to n. 82.

[94] See T. A. Coghlan, *N.S.W. Statistical Register 1890 and Previous Years* (Sydney: Acting Government Printer, 1891), table 33, 302, which shows enormous increases, and increases disproportionately larger than increases at common law, in originating processes and final decrees. For the years from 1876 until 1890, the register showed:

Petitions: 21, 48, 72, 65, 53, 33, 50, 41, 91, 69, 78, 87, 102, 131, 136.
Claims: 0, 0, 0, 0, 35, 87, 106, 153, 166, 162, 184, 218, 234, 218, 224 (a streamlined process was introduced in 1880).
Decrees and orders: 152, 102, 115, 153, 166, 93, 96, 210, 289, 295, 294, 298, 441, 525, 644.

[95] His obituarist stated that the move was to avoid criticism of sons practising in jurisdictions where their fathers presided: *Truth*, 24 November 1912, 8.

[96] See Memoranda (1896) 17 N.S.W.R. ix.   [97] 44 Vict. no. 18 (N.S.W.), s. 1.   [98] Ibid., s. 3.

(authorising an order for damages in addition to or in lieu of an injunction or specific performance).

Three things may be seen in this legislation. The first to note is that the premise of section 4 was that there was an inhibition upon making findings of legal title in 'any suit or proceeding in Equity'. To that extent, the section amounts to a legislative entrenchment of the limitations which had been held to attach to the separate Equity court identified in sections 1, 2 and 3.

The second is that nowhere in the Equity Act 1880 was there a provision analogous to the Judicature provisions enacted in 1873, vesting all jurisdiction in a single court. That reflects in part the fact that although enacted in 1880, it had been drafted ten years earlier. It may also reflect the scepticism of the now retired Stephen C.J., who still sat in the Legislative Council.

The third is that section 4 might be construed, if read literally, to prevent a suitor being struck out for commencing in the wrong jurisdiction. After some initial uncertainty,[99] a line of authority quickly established the contrary. The leading decision was *Horsley* v. *Ramsay*.[100] Owen C.J. in Eq. held:

> This section of the Act, which was passed after the *Judicature Act* in England, was certainly intended by the draftsman (for I drew the section myself), and presumably was intended by the Legislature, to give to the Court of Equity as wide and complete jurisdiction in all matters that came before it as the Court of Chancery had under the *Judicature Act*. The subsequent sections, 32 to 37, of the *Equity Act* are taken from the English Act, 21 and 22 Vic. c. 27 (known as *Cairns's Act*). Section 32 empowers the Court to grant damages in all cases in which the Court has jurisdiction to entertain an application for an injunction against a breach of contract or against the commission or continuance of any wrongful act, or for specific performance of any contract, either in addition to or in substitution for such injunction or specific performance. I think that section 4 must be read in connection with section 32. The latter section only gives the Court a limited power to grant damages. If this Court,

---

[99] J. Parkinson, *The Equity Practice Procedure Act 1880* (Sydney: Government Printer, 1880) contributed to this. The preface stated:

> The old practice has been universally condemned and reformed years ago in England. The system established by this new Act will do much to assimilate the practice and procedure on the Equity side of the Supreme Court to that on the Common Law side. This alone is a beneficial reform, it being difficult to see any good reason for having two entirely different systems of procedure in two branches or divisions of the one Supreme Court. The Act goes far towards effecting a fusion of Law and Equity.

[100] (1888) 10 N.S.W.R. Eq. 41.

under section 4, had power to entertain suits in respect of breaches of contract in the same way as Courts of common law, it would have been unnecessary to have conferred the power under section 32. But as those powers are expressly given, and only to a limited extent, I think the Court's jurisdiction as to damages must be measured by the limits under section 32, and not by the plenary powers under section 4.[101]

The same views were repeated in *Fell v. N.S.W. Shale and Oil Company*[102] and *Want v. Moss*,[103] and in other cases.[104] Consequently, the distinguished authors of the 1902 *Practice in Equity*[105] wrote:

Decisions upon this section have imposed a limitation upon the apparent generality of its closing words. The section does not make the Court a Court of law, but only empowers the Court to decide common law questions incidentally arising in an equity suit. The plaintiff must establish some recognised equitable ground for coming to the Court, and then all questions, whether legal or equitable, arising in the suit can be determined[106]

Thus, if a suit were commenced in Equity, it was necessary for a plaintiff to 'shew some equitable grounds for coming to this Court'. Conversely, as A. H. Simpson J. said in *Merrick v. Ridge*:[107]

[I]f a plaintiff's suit is really a common law action disguised in the form of an equity suit, I am bound to give effect to the objection that he has not come to the proper Court for his relief.[108]

This chapter does not chart the course of the ensuing decisions of the High Court, which ultimately accepted what had been established by the Supreme Court as to the separate jurisdictions at law and in equity.[109] At one time, it seemed that the High Court would dispel the fission which had developed between the Common Law and Equitable jurisdictions of the Supreme Court, but that did not occur.

---

[101] Ibid., 45–46.   [102] (1889) 6 W.N. (N.S.W.) 51, 52.   [103] (1891) 12 N.S.W.R. Eq. 101, 108.
[104] See *Cameron v. Cameron* (1891) 12 N.S.W.R. Eq. 135, 141 (point not affected by the appeal: at 142–43); *Ricketson v. Smith* (1895) 16 N.S.W.R. Eq. 221, 226; *Crampton v. Foster* (1897) 18 N.S.W.R. Eq. 136, 138–39.
[105] G. E. Rich, A. Newham and J. M. Harvey, *The Practice in Equity* (Sydney: Law Book Co., 1902). Rich later became a High Court judge; Harvey later became Chief Judge in Equity.
[106] Ibid., 7.   [107] (1897) 18 N.S.W.L.R. Eq 29.
[108] Ibid., 30. See also *Burnham v. Carroll Musgrave Theatres Ltd* (1926) 26 S.R. (N.S.W.) 372, 374.
[109] See *McLaughlin v. Fosbery* (1904) 1 C.L.R. 546; *Maiden v. Maiden* (1909) 7 C.L.R. 727; *Schnelle v. Dent* (1925) 35 C.L.R. 494; *David Jones Ltd v. Leventhal* (1927) 40 C.L.R. 357.

The Position by the Middle of the Twentieth Century

By the middle of the twentieth century, the long serving Chief Justice, Sir Frederick Jordan, could write: 'it is still of common occurrence for a Judge of the Supreme Court sitting in the exercise of its equitable jurisdiction to have occasion to grant an injunction restraining a party from proceeding at *nisi prius* before another Judge of the same Court'.[110] The same Chief Justice had, in *Coroneo v. Australian Provincial Assurance Association Ltd*,[111] dismissed a mortgagor's complaint against the exercise of his mortgagee's power of sale at a gross undervalue because it had been brought at Common Law. Conversely, in *Hawdon v. Khan*,[112] Street C.J. in Eq. said that a statement of claim seeking injunctions against the repeated trespass on land the plaintiff claimed to own was in substance 'an action of ejectment triable, not on this side of the Court, but in its Common Law jurisdiction', and upheld the defendant's demurrer.[113]

One of the last legislative reforms prior to the adoption of the Judicature system occurred in 1957, when provision was made for orders that 'the action be transferred into the jurisdiction of the Court in equity', and, conversely, for an order that a suit or proceeding in equity be transferred into the Common Law jurisdiction of the Supreme Court if it appeared that there was 'no jurisdiction' in Equity to deal with its subject matter.[114] This legislation had as its premise that there were separate jurisdictions between which a matter could be transferred. It is inconsistent with anything other than a fission of jurisdiction.

There was also a *physical* fission between common law and equity, just as Stephen C.J. had hoped in 1857, and as there had been before 1883 in England. The three judges who sat in Equity were located, from 1963, in the top three floors of Mena House on 225 Macquarie

---

[110] F. Jordan, *Chapters on Equity in New South Wales*, 6th edn by F. C. Stephen (University of Sydney Law School, 1947), 10. See, for example, *In re Graham's Estate* (1901) 1 S.R. (N.S.W.) Eq. 69; *High v. Bengal Brass Company and Bank of New South Wales* (1921) 38 W.N. (N.S.W.) 65.

[111] (1935) 35 S.R. (N.S.W.) 391.   [112] (1920) 37 W.N. (N.S.W.) 131.

[113] Ibid., 133. See also *King v. Poggioli* (1923) 32 C.L.R. 222, where a vendor who had sought specific performance in equity instead of damages for breach of contract recovered nothing, especially at 247 (Starke J.): 'But the *Judicature Act* has not been adopted in New South Wales, and this case must be resolved on the law as it is settled under *Cairns' Act*. We must therefore, in my opinion, first decide whether the plaintiff in this suit was entitled to a decree for specific performance. If he was, damages might properly be awarded for the loss occasioned by the delay in giving possession. If he was not, then damages cannot, as I understand the law in force in New South Wales, be awarded in this suit, whatever the position is at law.'

[114] Equity Act 1901 (N.S.W.), s. 8A, as inserted by the Supreme Court Procedure Act 1957 (N.S.W.), s. 5(2)(b).

Street, Sydney.[115] By 1974, when Street C.J. in Eq. resigned his office and Bowen C.J. in Eq. was appointed, there were four judges sitting in equity (the other three being Helsham, Mahoney and Holland JJ.).[116] Holland J. had chambers in the Old Mint Building.[117]

The New South Wales Legislature ultimately enacted the remaining provisions of the nineteenth century Judicature legislation in the 1970s. The Supreme Court Act 1970 (N.S.W.)[118] repealed the Common Law Procedure Act 1899 (N.S.W.) and the Equity Act 1901 (N.S.W.), and it became possible, for the first time, for there to be a single practice book for the procedure of the court. In particular, section 64 of the Supreme Court Act enacted section 25 (11) of the Judicature Act 1873, but was repealed prior to its commencing,[119] no differently from parts of the 1873 Act. It was replaced by section 5 of the Law Reform (Law and Equity) Act 1972 (N.S.W.), in order to avoid its being given a narrow construction by reason of its legislative context.[120]

CONSEQUENCES OF THE DELAYED ENACTMENT OF JUDICATURE LEGISLATION IN NEW SOUTH WALES

One obvious consequence of the delayed enactment of the Judicature legislation in New South Wales was critical comment from appellate courts having to deal with what had become quite an unfamiliar legal system. Foremost of these was Higgins J., an early Justice of the High Court. In *Perpetual Trustee Co. Ltd v. Orr*,[121] Higgins J. said:

I may be permitted to add that, in my opinion, fully one half of the time and labour which this case has involved could, in all probability, have been saved

---

[115] See Anon., 'Mena House Courts' (1963) 6 N.S.W. Bar Gaz. 11, 11.

[116] See New South Wales, Supreme Court, 'Report by the Chief Justice on Business of the Supreme Court', (1974), 37, held in the Joint Law Courts Library, Sydney.

[117] See New South Wales, Supreme Court, 'Report by Chief Justice on Business of the Supreme Court for General Meeting of the Supreme Court Judges' (20 November 1972), 11, held in the Law Courts Library, Sydney. Part of the Mint Building had been used by courts since 1817: see C. Currey, *The Brothers Bent* (Sydney University Press, 1968), 71–74.

[118] Section 5, Sch. 1.

[119] The Supreme Court Act 1970 (N.S.W.) was originally proclaimed to commence on 1 January 1972, but this was later postponed to 1 July 1972.

[120] The Law Reform Commission observed that 'it may perhaps be open to argument that section 64 is confined to the rules to be applied in the determination of proceedings in the Supreme Court. Such an argument might be founded on the context provided by the Supreme Court Act generally': New South Wales, Law Reform Commission, *Report of the Law Reform Commission Law and Equity*, Report No. 13 (1971), [8].

[121] (1907) 4 C.L.R. 1395.

to the Court and to counsel if, as under the English Judicature Acts, the same Court could deal freely with equitable and legal rights, so as to do justice once and for all between the parties litigating.[122]

Other judges expressed similar concerns.[123] Putting to one side those superficial comments, which seem to amount to expressions of irritation falling short of any substantive effect, strong arguments may be made for more significant consequences of the delayed introduction of Judicature legislation.

One commentator who is well-placed to express a view is Paul Finn. He wrote:

> This almost century long New South Welsh exceptionalism had profound effects. It produced generations of practising lawyers, judges and educators who were masters of equity jurisprudence. I mention only Sir Frederick Jordan, Sir Frank Kitto, Sir Kenneth Jacobs, Sir Anthony Mason and Sir William Deane. The legacy of this in turn was that Australia alone of the Commonwealth countries was to have some number of large, well-known textbooks devoted to equity, or to specific aspects of it (to the exclusion of trusts and property law).[124]

Much could be written of the profound effects to which Finn referred. I shall identify four.

First, one consequence of the continuation of nineteenth-century common law pleading was that New South Wales law and, indirectly, the common law of Australia was resistant to innovations based upon the abandonment of common law pleading. An example may be seen in the law of trespass to the person. It seems clear that it was the abandonment of common law pleading that led the English courts to alter the substantive law of trespass to the person. Following *Fowler* v. *Lanning*[125] and *Letang* v. *Cooper*,[126] it seems that a plaintiff who is struck by the negligent act of a defendant has a cause of action only in negligence, and must prove both breach of duty and damage. Both Diplock J.[127] and Lord Denning M.R.[128] justified a substantive change to the law of trespass in part by reason of the change in

---

[122] Ibid., 1410. See also *Maiden* v. *Maiden* (1909) 7 C.L.R. 727, 743 and *Davis* v. *Hueber* (1923) 31 C.L.R. 583, 597.

[123] See *Turner* v. *New South Wales Mont De Piete Deposit & Investment Co. Ltd* (1910) 10 C.L.R. 539, 542–43, 549, 554; *Loxton* v. *Moir* (1914) 18 C.L.R. 360, 370, 377. Contrast Rich J. (who had had extensive personal experience with the New South Wales regime) in *David Jones Ltd* v. *Leventhal* (1927) 40 C.L.R. 357, 384.

[124] P. Finn, 'Common Law Divergences' (2013) 37 M.U.L.R. 509, 516.   [125] [1959] 1 Q.B. 426.

[126] [1965] 1 Q.B. 232.   [127] *Fowler* v. *Lanning* [1959] 1 Q.B. 426, 434–35, 440–41.

[128] *Letang* v. *Cooper* [1965] 1 Q.B. 232, 238–40.

the rules of pleading.[129] However, in Australia it remains clear law that it was sufficient for a plaintiff to prove that the defendant had struck directly, with a blow or missile, and that a defendant has a valid answer if he or she can prove that the blow was unintentional or negligent.[130]

Secondly, the separation of common law and equitable jurisdictions created an environment where the conflation of substantive doctrine was impeded. For example, a mortgagor's complaint that a mortgagee's power of sale was reckless or negligent was demurrable if brought as an action at common law.[131] Such an environment was ill-disposed to the innovations illustrated by *Cuckmere Brick Co. Ltd* v. *Mutual Finance Ltd*.[132] It has been left to legislation to heighten the standards to which a mortgagee is required to adhere.[133]

Thirdly, and related to the foregoing, concerns as to some of the most prominent innovations consequential upon the adoption of the Judicature legislation led to the writing of *Equity: Doctrines and Remedies* and the coining of the 'fusion fallacy' to describe and condemn a reasoning process to the effect that because the same court now had jurisdiction to determine both common law and equitable claims and to give common law or equitable remedies, there had been a substantive change in the law.[134] Those authors were critical, for example, of (a) the reliance on equity decisions in *Hedley Byrne & Co. Ltd* v. *Heller & Partners Ltd*[135] to sustain an action in negligence for damages for pure economic loss, (b) the reliance on common law decisions in *Cuckmere Brick Co. Ltd* v. *Mutual Finance Ltd*[136] to alter the law governing the exercise of a mortgagee's power of sale, and (c) statements in

---

[129] The justification was criticised by J. Jolowicz, 'Forms of Action – Causes of Action – Trespass and Negligence' [1964] C.L.J 200.

[130] See *McHale* v. *Watson* (1966) 115 C.L.R. 199; *Stingel* v. *Clark* (2006) 226 C.L.R. 442, [47]; [2006] HCA 37; *Croucher* v. *Cachia* (2016) 95 N.S.W.L.R. 117, [23]–[26]; [2016] NSWCA 132, quoting (at [23]) Jacobs J.A.'s words, in *Timmins* v. *Oliver* (unreported, New South Wales Court of Appeal, 12 October 1972), three months after the commencement of the judicature legislation in New South Wales:

> Nothing more has ever been required in an action based on trespass than an allegation of the battery and it is too late in the day to change this now. . . . Can we as the curtain falls for the last time on declarations in trespass which have held the stage for centuries say that the play has all this time been played wrongly and according to a bad script? I think not.

[131] See especially, *Coroneo* v. *Australian Provincial Assurance Association Ltd* (1935) 35 S.R. (N.S.W.) 391.   [132] [1971] Ch. 949.

[133] Conveyancing Act 1919 (N.S.W.), s. 111A.

[134] *Meagher, Gummow and Lehane*, 1st edn, [220]–[257].   [135] [1964] A.C. 465.

[136] [1971] Ch. 949.

Seager v. *Copydex (No. 1)*[137] supporting the availability of damages for breach of an equitable obligation of confidence.[138] The consequences of that book were considerable:

> *Equity: Doctrines and [R]emedies* did as much as any book could do to guide judicial legislators towards legitimacy in the process of judicial legislation. Not the least of its achievements in the age of fusion was its explanation of the true character of 'fusion' and its exposure of fallacies on that subject.[139]

Those criticisms, principally of decisions of the English Court of Appeal, which were highly persuasive but which did not bind Australian courts,[140] encouraged independence of thinking and discipline in the development of the law.

In the longer term, the book influenced Australian law schools. As Dyson Heydon has put it:

> [The work] arrested the decay of equity in university law schools. These grew rapidly in number and in population from the late 1960s on throughout the country. In the law schools there was massive pressure to reduce or keep compulsory courses to a minimum in order to accommodate a greater number of optional courses conforming to contemporary *quarante-huitard* tastes. Equity was a prime candidate for jettison or dismemberment. In places where equity was compulsory, *Equity: Doctrines and [R]emedies* caused it to remain compulsory; in places where it was optional, its status did not decline further. To some extent the subject was restored as a field of wide interest among academic lawyers, this being assisted by the writings of P.D. Finn, particularly *Fiduciary Obligations* (1977).[141]

The result in the twenty-first century is a legal environment in New South Wales where the teaching and practice of equity flourishes. Within the universities, as indicated in the passage reproduced earlier, in 1992 the Law Admissions Consultative Committee identified eleven areas, equity being one, whose study was mandatory in order to obtain admission as a legal practitioner. That list now has statutory force.[142] Most law schools at Australian universities accordingly teach equity as a compulsory undergraduate course. Within legal practice, two superficial measures of the vibrancy of equity may be noted. The first is that the database maintained by the New South Wales

---

[137] [1967] R.P.C. 349.   [138] *Meagher, Gummow and Lehane*, 1st edn, [229]–[231].
[139] J. D. Heydon, 'The Role of the Equity Bar in the Judicature Era' (Winter 2002) Bar News: J. N.S.W. Bar Ass. 53, 55.
[140] See, for example, *Sharah* v. *Healey* [1982] 2 N.S.W.L.R. 223, 227–28.
[141] Heydon, 'The Role of the Equity Bar in the Judicature Era', 55.
[142] See now the Legal Profession Uniform Admission Rules 2015 (N.S.W.), Sch. 1, para. 7.

Bar Association lists 569 barristers who claim to practise in 'Equity', from a total of 2,506.[143] The second is that a great deal of commercial litigation in Australia takes place in the 'Commercial List' within the Equity Division of the Supreme Court of New South Wales.

Many other forces have been at work. However, the matters outlined in this section are at least indirect consequences of the delayed enactment of the Judicature legislation in New South Wales.

CONCLUSIONS

The principal question addressed by this chapter is how, within New South Wales, there was a fission of jurisdiction in the nineteenth century in contrast with the fusion elsewhere in the world. Like most historical developments, it was the product of a series of small steps, the significance of many of which would not have been apparent at the time. With the utmost respect to Dr Bennett, it simplifies matters to conclude that it was a fallacious extension. To answer the question why those steps came about would be to undertake a large and uncertain endeavour. A large element of the answer would be the growth in scale of litigation, coinciding with the economic development of the colony. Another aspect of the answer may lie in the influx of lawyers who had trained and practised in pre-Judicature courts in England and Ireland. But it would also appear that part of the answer to the question of why the New South Wales fission of jurisdiction came about turns on completely serendipitous considerations: the particular problems associated with Justice Willis between 1839 and 1841, and the happenstance that a law reform commission had produced an alternative draft bill in 1870.

---

[143] See the New South Wales Bar website: http://archive.nswbar.asn.au/findabarrister/ (accessed 16 November 2018).

7

Fusion without Fission

Equity and the Judicature Acts in Colonial Victoria

JAMES MCCOMISH

INTRODUCTION

Unlike in England and various other territories, no Australian jurisdiction – not even New South Wales – ever had a separate court of equity.[1] Nonetheless, the relative importance of equity within the system of colonial law, and the relative harmony with which law and equity were administered, varied markedly over time and between places, both outside and within colonial Australia. The first Chief Justice of New South Wales, Francis Forbes (1784–1841), famously remarked that 'in an early stage of society there is comparatively but little occasion for resorting to a Court of Equity'.[2] By contrast, the early history of the Colony of Victoria – and its predecessor, the Port Phillip District of New South Wales – shows a remarkable interest in equity on the part of judges, practitioners and litigants alike.

This chapter is a contribution to the growing literature on law, equity and procedural reform in the nineteenth-century common law world;[3] but it is also a contribution to a wider historiographical debate. The approach taken in this chapter is familiar in many historical contexts, emphasising 'processes rather

---

[1] Separate equity courts existed at some time in Ireland and various North American territories including Nova Scotia, New Brunswick, Upper Canada (Ontario), New York, Virginia, Maryland and Delaware. Of these, only Delaware still retains a separate equity court.

[2] Letter from Francis Forbes to Governor Darling (15 December 1827), quoted in J. M. Bennett, *Sir Francis Forbes: First Chief Justice of New South Wales, 1823–1837* (Sydney: Federation Press, 2001), 106.

[3] E.g., M. L. Smith, 'The Early Years of Equity in the Supreme Court of New South Wales' (1998) 72 A.L.J. 799; G. Taylor, 'South Australia's Judicature Act Reforms of 1853: The First Attempt to Fuse Law and Equity in the British Empire' (2001) 22 J.L.H. 55; Lobban, 'Preparing for Fusion', 389; S. Dorsett, 'Reforming Equity: New Zealand 1843–56' (2013) 34 J.L.H. 285; Funk, 'Equity without Chancery'; McMahon, 'Field, Fusion and the 1850s'.

than structure' and looking to 'the ways in which government actually worked', not simply the formal structure of legal institutions.[4]

In nineteenth-century Victoria, as in other times and places, the law as experienced in real life was not always commensurate with the law on the books. Many contemporaries considered themselves to live in a 'fused' system well before the Judicature Act 1883 (Vic.). Thanks to the unusual diligence and longevity of one man – Justice Robert Molesworth – the 'unfused' pre-Judicature administration of law and equity in Victoria was perceived by many as more efficient and harmonious than the post-Judicature system prevailing after his retirement. Local perceptions contrasted dramatically with those elsewhere in the Empire.[5]

The Victorian experience sheds light on wider themes in legal history and in doctrinal thought about fission and fusion. First, it highlights the way that equity – conspicuously more so than common law – was affected by the varying personalities and working habits of its judges and practitioners. Second, it shows the importance of viewing substance and procedure in combination, rather than as independent domains. Third, it demonstrates the persistent salience to equity of administrative processes, and not simply processes of decision-making. Finally, it emphasises that the comparative experience of English and colonial law — and their interrelationship — may be more complicated than is sometimes supposed.

EQUITY AND VICTORIAN JUDGES, 1841–56

In 1834, the first permanent British settlement in what is now the State of Victoria was established at Portland. The town that became Melbourne was established in 1835, and in the following year the Port Phillip District was proclaimed as a separate administrative division of the colony of New South Wales.

In the earliest days of the new settlement — as in the earliest days of Sydney — there were few trained lawyers. Captain William Lonsdale (1799–1864) was appointed as the first resident magistrate in 1836. According to one early observer, the colonist John Pascoe Fawkner:

---

[4] P. Williams, *The Tudor Regime* (Oxford: Clarendon, 1979), vii. Williams makes a pointed contrast with the institutional focus and historiographical style of G. R. Elton, particularly his *The Tudor Revolution in Government: Administrative Changes in the Reign of Henry VIII* (Cambridge University Press, 1953).

[5] See Girard, Chapter 5 and Leeming, Chapter 6.

and a butcher named M'Nall were allowed to act as advocates before the Police Magistrate; and considering the surroundings of the place, it was no misnomer to put them down as bush lawyers, for they were literally so. M'Nall kept a large butcher's shop ... in Collins Street; and here he followed his dual calling, but the people preferred his mutton to his law, and affected his sirloins more than his equity.[6]

Knowledge of equity within the District increased markedly with the appointment of John Walpole Willis (1793–1877) as the first Resident Judge in 1841.[7] Willis had been a noted equity specialist in London, and wrote such works as *A Digest of the Rules and Practice as to Interrogatories for the Examination of Witnesses* (1816),[8] *Pleadings in the Courts of Equity and Common Law with Precedents* (1820)[9] and *A Practical Treatise on the Duties and Responsibilities of Trustees* (1827).[10] He held judicial office in Canada and British Guiana before appointment to the Supreme Court of New South Wales in 1838.

In Port Phillip, Willis was appointed under the Administration of Justice Act 1840 (N.S.W.), which authorised the Governor of New South Wales to 'appoint from time to time one of the Judges of the said Court not being the Chief Justice to reside in the said District of Port Phillip'.[11] That Act also provided for the designation of a primary judge in equity, sitting in Sydney, to 'hear and determine without the assistance of the other Judges or either of them all causes and matters at any time depending in the said Supreme Court in Equity'.[12] By force of the Advancement of Justice Act 1841 (N.S.W.), equity appeals were to be 'heard and decided before and by the three Judges at Sydney'.[13]

Unfortunately, Willis was as much noted for his irascible and disputatious temperament as for his equity knowledge. More than once Willis's self-regard as an equity specialist led to an unseemly disagreement. While Willis sat as a

---

[6]   Garryowen, [E. Finn], *The Chronicles of Early Melbourne, 1835 to 1852: Historical, Anecdotal and Personal* (Melbourne: Fergusson and Mitchell, 1888), 36. 'Bush lawyer' is an Australian and New Zealand colloquialism for a layperson with pretensions to legal knowledge and, often, a disputatious temperament. On 'the bush' as a landscape and as a theme in Australian cultural history, see D. Watson, *The Bush: Travels in the Heart of Australia* (Melbourne: Hamish Hamilton, 2014).

[7]   B. A. Keon-Cohen, 'John Walpole Willis: First Resident Judge in Victoria' (1972) 8 M.U.L.R. 703; H. F. Behan, *Mr Justice J.W. Willis: With Particular Reference to His Period as First Resident Judge in Port Phillip, 1841–1843* (Glen Iris: Behan, 1979).

[8]   (London: Pheney, 1816).   [9]   (London: Pheney, 1820).

[10] (London: Pheney, Sweet, Steven & Sons, 1827); Behan, 'John Walpole Willis', 5. Pheney was a law publisher of less enduring distinction than his contemporaries Sweet, Maxwell and Butterworth.

[11] 4 Vict. c. 22 (N.S.W.), s. 4.   [12] Ibid., s. 20.   [13] 5 Vict. c. 9 (N.S.W.), s. 13.

FIGURE 7.1 W. F. E. Liardet, *The Opening of the Supreme Court* (State Library of Victoria)

judge of the Court of King's Bench of Upper Canada, the failure of the colonial government to create a separate court of equity to which he could be appointed led to much animus on his part.[14] Likewise, in New South Wales, Willis resented being overlooked as the first primary judge in equity in favour of the Chief Justice, Sir James Dowling (1787–1844).[15]

Justice Willis's time in Melbourne was no more pacific than any of his previous judicial appointments. He oversaw the opening of the Supreme Court of New South Wales for the District of Port Phillip in 1841, but he soon came into sharp conflict with leading residents, the legal profession and the colonial government (Figure 7.1).

Willis's conduct was so unbecoming that he was removed from office in 1843.[16] His successor, William Jeffcott (1800–55), was described in the Melbourne press as 'bland in his manner, of first-rate talents, and about forty years

[14] Behan, 'John Walpole Willis', 11–13. After Willis's departure, a separate Court of Chancery was created in Upper Canada in 1837, and fused into a Supreme Court of Judicature in 1881: see Girard, Chapter 5, and E. Brown, 'Equitable Jurisdiction and the Court of Chancery in Upper Canada' (1983) 21 Osgoode Hall L.J. 275, 277–78.

[15] On Willis in New South Wales, see J. M. Bennett, *A History of the Supreme Court of New South Wales* (Sydney: Law Book Co., 1974), 95–98.

[16] Behan, 'John Walpole Willis', 281–82, 292.

of age'; high praise indeed, in comparison with Willis.[17] An observer recorded:

> He was good-tempered, firm, impartial, and methodical. He presided on Mondays in Common Law, Tuesdays in Equity, Fridays in Insolvency ... He was a vast improvement upon the gentleman he succeeded, and the Court business was no longer a series of gratuitous farces for public amusement.[18]

While Justice Jeffcott was on the bench, John Willis successfully appealed his dismissal to the Privy Council.[19] Jeffcott was sufficiently scrupulous to resign before the result of the appeal was known, lest his own appointment be held invalid.

Jeffcott's successor as resident judge was Roger Therry (1800–74). In his lively memoirs, Therry remarked of Willis that:

> [i]f he had retained office in Sydney, and confined his attention as Equity Judge to the business transacted there – the unexciting nature of Equity proceedings – his acquaintance with its practice and principles, and a quickness of parts which he possessed, would have rendered him a very useful judge in the exercise of the equitable jurisdiction of the Court.[20]

Unfortunately, the 'excited ... state' of Melbourne in the early 1840s, beset as it was by economic downturn and '[n]umerous insolvencies – many of them very fraudulent ones', was hardly conducive to a personality as combustible as Willis's.[21]

Therry arrived in 1845 during a continued economic downturn. Melbourne was a poor and undeveloped place. While Therry could enjoy the bucolic pleasures of 'a pleasant walk through green paddocks to the Court-house' from his house, cultural stimulation in the small town was limited to 'a small third-rate theatre open twice a week'.[22] After a year Therry returned to Sydney.

Therry's successor as Resident Judge was Justice William a'Beckett (1806–69), then sitting as the Primary Judge in Equity in Sydney.[23] Therry took over a'Beckett's position as Primary Judge in Sydney. Archibald Michie – then a Sydney barrister – perceived a'Beckett to have 'suffered in his official

---

[17] Quoted in J. L. Forde, *The Story of the Bar of Victoria: From Its Foundation to the Amalgamation of the Two Branches of the Legal Profession, 1839–1891. Historical. Personal. Humorous* (Melbourne: Whitcombe and Tombs, c.1893), 83.

[18] Garryowen, *The Chronicles of Early Melbourne*, 83.   [19] Behan, 'John Walpole Willis', 292.

[20] R. Therry, *Reminiscences of Thirty Years' Residence in New South Wales and Victoria*, 2nd edn (London: Low, Son and Co., 1863), 342.

[21] Ibid..   [22] Ibid., 356.

[23] Bennett, *A History of the Supreme Court of New South Wales*, 97; J. M. Bennett, *Sir William a'Beckett: First Chief Justice of Victoria 1852–1857* (Sydney: Federation Press, 2001), 18.

removal from Sydney' to the 'dismallest and most desolate hole a civilized and social being could be buried alive in'.[24] Little could a'Beckett have known how soon things would change.

A'Beckett's skill in equity was noted during his time on the bench in New South Wales. His colleague, Alfred Stephen, noted:

> The Equity business ... now demands, more than ever, the most able and efficient superintendence. It is right to say that Mr a'Beckett's great knowledge and experience as an Equity lawyer, increased during the term of his judicial service by most unwearied and industrious study, cannot in this Colony be equalled.[25]

Soon enough, a'Beckett's talents would adorn a new colony: the last Resident Judge of the Port Phillip District became the first Chief Justice of the Supreme Court of Victoria. Of his time in Victoria, it was said that a'Beckett was 'a sound lawyer who [was] equally at home with the principles of equity or the technicalities of common law pleading and who, whatever his subject, [wrote] clearly and with distinction'.[26]

While the Australian Constitutions Act 1850 (U.K.) creating the new colony of Victoria provided that a Court of Judicature for the colony might be established by letters patent, the Supreme Court of Victoria was actually established by local statute in 1852.[27] The Supreme Court was established as a court of record[28] and invested separately with common law,[29] equitable[30] and ecclesiastical jurisdiction,[31] and a right of appeal to the Privy Council.[32] A Master in Equity was created.[33] The Court's equitable jurisdiction was the same as that 'possessed by the Lord High Chancellor of England in the exercise of similar jurisdiction within the Realm of England'.[34]

The discovery of gold in 1851 changed everything. What had been an unattractive backwater suddenly became a place of great opportunity – especially

---

[24] A. Michie, *Readings in Melbourne: With an Essay on the Resources and Prospects of Victoria, for the Emigrant and Uneasy Classes* (London: Low et al., 1879), 3, cited in Bennett, *Sir William a'Beckett*, 20–21 and in Forde, *The Story of the Bar of Victoria*, 105. Archibald Michie himself later moved to Victoria, where he became a member of the Legislative Assembly and the colony's first Q.C.: Forde at 105; H. L. Hall, 'Michie, Sir Archibald (1813–1899)' (1974) 5 *Aust. Dict. Biog.* 246, 247, available: http://adb.anu.edu.au/biography/michie-sir-archibald-4196.

[25] Letter from Alfred Stephen to George Gipps (6 October 1845), quoted in Bennett, *Sir William a'Beckett*, 18.

[26] E. G. Coppel, 'The First Chief Justice of Victoria' (1953) 27 A.L.J. 209, 215.

[27] Supreme Court (Administration) Act 1852 (Vic.), 15 Vict. c. 10.   [28] Ibid., s. 9.

[29] Ibid., s. 10.   [30] Ibid., s. 14.   [31] Ibid., s. 15.   [32] Ibid., s. 33.   [33] Ibid., s. 7.

[34] Ibid., s. 14.

FIGURE 7.2 Mr Justice Molesworth, Alfred Martin Ebsworth, Melbourne (State Library of Victoria)

for those lacking opportunities at home in England or Ireland.[35] In 1856 the former Resident Judge, Roger Therry, who had spent such a dismal time in Melbourne, revisited the now-booming colony:

> [I]n size, in wealth, in numbers, in varied social enjoyments, the humble town which I had quitted in 1846 had been transformed in 1856 into a splendid city, and presented such a transition from poverty to splendour, as no city in the ancient or modern world had heretofore exhibited in a corresponding period.[36]

Also in 1856, the Victorian Parliament amended the Act constituting the Supreme Court to provide for the appointment of additional judges,[37] and the designation of a judge in equity.[38] The Act provided for the determinations of the judge in equity sitting alone to be 'as valid effectual and binding as if made by any two or more of such Judges sitting in the said Court in *Banco*'.[39]

SIR ROBERT MOLESWORTH – PRIMARY JUDGE IN EQUITY, 1856–86

The first judge appointed under the newly amended Act was Robert Molesworth (1806–90). He was appointed to the Supreme Court in 1856 and sat as the Primary Judge in Equity for nearly thirty years until his retirement in 1886 (Figure 7.2).

[35] Forde, *The Story of the Bar of Victoria*, 112–13.
[36] Therry, *Reminiscences of Thirty Years' Residence*, 357.
[37] Administration of Justice Amendment Act 1856 (Vic.), 19 Vict. c. 13, s. 1.   [38] Ibid., s. 4.
[39] Ibid., s. 4.

Justice Molesworth was born in Ireland and educated at Trinity College, Dublin, before being called to the Irish bar in 1828.[40] He emigrated to Australia in 1852. Before his appointment to the bench, he was successively a barrister at the Victorian Bar, Acting Chief Justice for a term during the illness of William a'Beckett, and Solicitor General. A later Victorian judge wrote of him that, in his thirty years as judge in equity, 'he established a great reputation for learning, industry, courtesy, and expedition – qualities not always combined in one judge'.[41] His judicial endeavours went beyond equitable work: his greatest endeavour outside that field was his establishment of mining law in Victoria. No less a figure than Sir Samuel Griffith considered it to be 'a well-known fact that the mining law of Australia was practically made by the decisions of Mr Justice Molesworth and the Supreme Court of Victoria'.[42]

Justice Molesworth's judicial achievements are startling in light of his unhappy personal life. Upon the passage of the Divorce and Matrimonial Causes Act 1861 (Vic.), Justice Molesworth became one of the first petitioners for divorce in the colony. Thereafter, he ceased to sit on purely matrimonial causes. However, he continued to deal, with remarkable sensitivity and open-mindedness, with cases involving marital elements that came before him in equity.[43]

SIR ROBERT MOLESWORTH'S JUDICIAL STYLE

Robert Molesworth dominated equity in Victoria for three decades. The story of equity in Victoria in the mid-to-late 1800s is the story of his equity. When appointed a judge, Molesworth joined a group of judges whom Parkinson characterises as having a 'strong sense of civic duty', 'a common understanding of Victoria's governmental system based on personal experience' and an 'entrenched ... conservative judicial and social outlook'.[44]

---

[40] Molesworth, like Redmond Barry, was an Irish Anglican, but something of his tolerance when religious questions arose in court can be gauged from *Re Pennington* (1875) 1 V.L.R. (E.) 97.

[41] Mr Justice Sholl, 'Administration of Justice in Victoria: The State and its Lawyers: 118 Years in Retrospect' (1955–57) 7 Res. Jud. 33, 36.

[42] *Theodore v. Theodore* (1897) 8 Q.L.J. 76, 78. Griffith was Premier and then Chief Justice of Queensland, a framer of the Australian Constitution and first Chief Justice of the High Court of Australia.

[43] An extraordinary example is *Bishop v. Smith* (1875) 1 V.L.R. (E.) 313, in which the judge's sympathy for the wronged wife is evident.

[44] C. Parkinson, *Sir William Stawell and the Victorian Constitution* (Melbourne: Australian Scholarly Publishing, 2004), 55.

An 1863 probate dispute gives a flavour of Molesworth's legal conservatism and the kind of work then coming before the court. The question was whether a given document could be proved as a will, the signature of the testator being upside down and on the back of the page:

> My dear Ned, – I am in a state of dying. All I wish for is that all expenses be paid out of the moneys I have in the bank, and the remainder is all to come to you.
>
> Signed in the presence of
>
> Dr L Reynard   &   William Read, miner,
> his mate.

Justice Molesworth considered that the Wills Amendment Act 1852 (Vic.)[45] 'has given a considerable laxity and indulgence to the manner in which the signatures of testators may be affixed', but that '[w]ith all the latitude of the words of the Act I do not think this case comes within any of them'.[46] The Full Court allowed would-be executor's appeal. The judgment was given by Chief Justice Stawell. There being no suspicion about the circumstances in which the signature was obtained, 'the mere circumstance of its being upside down does not, in our opinion, decide the question'.[47] Probate was granted, and a small contribution to the history of Australian 'mateship' was made.[48]

Justice Molesworth had little time for the ignorant or ill-advised, and took seriously what he considered his duty to exercise impartial justice. In responding to an application for enlargement of an order *nisi*, where he considered the defendant 'an ignorant person who [would] suffer injustice if [the] application [were] not granted', he stated:

> I am quite aware that ignorant persons do suffer under the law from their ignorance occasionally; but I cannot administer one sort of law for one class of persons and another sort of law for another class.[49]

There were, however, limits to his punctiliousness and deference to English modes of practice. In one case, an objection was taken to a bill on the basis that it listed the defendants by initial rather than full first name, which had been a ground for demurrer in England:

[45] 18 Vict. c. 19, adopting the Wills Amendment Act 1852 (U.K.), 15 & 16 Vict. c. 24.
[46] *In the goods of G. Campbell* (1863) 2 W. & W. (I.E. & M.) 119, 120–21.   [47] Ibid., 122.
[48] On 'mateship' and solidarity in Australia of the gold rush era, see R. B. Ward, *The Australian Legend*, 2nd edn (Melbourne: Oxford University Press, 2003), ch. 5.
[49] *Re M'Manomonie* (1864) 1 W.W. & a'B. (I.E. & M.) 53, 55.

The objection was frequently presented in pleadings in the mother country. It has never been raised in pleadings here, and I am not disposed to give it validity by allowing it on the present demurrer.[50]

Most importantly, Justice Molesworth emphasised what would now be seen as judicial virtues of speed and cost-effectiveness. The need for expeditious and efficient administration was a consistent theme. In a suit necessitated by the 'sulky obstructiveness' of an overseas trustee, he unhesitatingly ordered: '[w]hen practical inconvenience such as this arises it is high time that the Court should interfere and take care that it shall not be prolonged'.[51] The judge also had a horror of the uncertainty caused by delay.[52] A case in which argument had 'extended over three days' was exceptional enough to warrant mention.[53] Even in a case raising a troublesome point – as did *Evans* v. *Guthridge*,[54] in which the judge 'hesitated over a little',[55] and *Jordan* v. *Walker*,[56] in which he 'considered the case a good deal before giving [his] decision'[57] – the judgment was unlikely to be reserved long. By the standards of nineteenth-century English Chancery, a 'hesitation' of only nine days and a 'good deal' of consideration lasting only a month showed celerity.

What Justice Molesworth demanded of litigants, he demanded of himself. The law reports give some insight into his astonishing diligence and productivity – which was probably aided by his practice of not adjourning for lunch.[58] Of the matters reported in Wyatt, Webb and a'Beckett's Reports in 1864, Chief Justice Stawell gave judgment in forty-five, Justice Barry in fifteen and Justice Williams in twelve. Eighteen reported cases were decided *per curiam*. By contrast, Justice Molesworth gave judgment in no fewer than sixty-seven reported matters – an extraordinary achievement when he must have been preoccupied by his very public divorce. Sir Arthur Dean – himself a noted equity judge – rightly remarked in 1968 that it 'seems incredible ... that so much work was disposed of and disposed of so well'.[59]

---

[50] A.-G. v. *Gee* (1863) 2 W. & W. (E.) 122, 132.
[51] *Knox* v. *Postlethwaite* (1864) 1 W.W. & a'B. (E.) 62, 65.
[52] *Re M'Manomonie* (1864) 1 W.W. & a'B. (I.E. & M.) 53, 54.
[53] *Evans* v. *Guthridge* (1863) 2 W. & W. (E.) 83, 89.   [54] (1863) 2 W. & W. (E.) 2.
[55] Ibid., 36 (judgment reserved from 10 to 19 March 1863).   [56] (1885) 11 V.L.R. 346.
[57] Ibid., 354 (judgment reserved from 30 June to 30 July 1885).
[58] Sholl, 'Administration of Justice in Victoria', 36.
[59] A. Dean, *A Multitude of Counsellors: A History of the Bar of Victoria* (Melbourne: Bar Council of Victoria, 1968), 47.

EQUITY PRACTICE IN VICTORIA

What was equity practice like in nineteenth-century Victoria? Except John Willis,[60] judges in Australia and New Zealand almost never referred to the absence of separate equity courts.[61] The institutional structure of the courts was less important than the substantive content of the law they administered, in which the distinction between law and equity was preserved.

Still, the existence of the separate Court of Chancery in England cast a long shadow. The absence of local models meant that early practitioners in Australia made do with English precedents which referred to Chancery. The earliest Victorian equity bills of the 1840s were large parchment documents headed 'In the Supreme Court of New South Wales for the District of Port Phillip, In Chancery'.[62] An early writ of *dedimus potestatem* referred to a plaintiff who 'hath lately exhibited a Bill of Complaint before us in our Court of Chancery for the District of Port Phillip in our Colony of New South Wales'.[63] Later documents referred more consistently to proceedings 'In Equity'.[64]

Distance from 'home' led to an ambiguous relationship with English practice, which was not treated with the deference one might perhaps have supposed. In *Walker* v. *Webb*,[65] an early case about constructive trusts, Justice a'Beckett remarked that:

> in a colony like this, it is inevitable that contracts and dealings will take place,
> for which no analogy can be found at home. In such cases, whilst we look for
> our guidance to English law, it is better to risk the misapplication of one of its
> principles, than of rejecting it altogether.[66]

Differences in procedure were stark. Before the establishment of Victoria as a separate colony, a'Beckett pointed to 'the distinction between the rule of [the Supreme Court], and the courts at Westminster'.[67] In another case, he denied a parallel between an appeal from a judge sitting in Port Phillip to the Full

---

[60] Willis wished to be the 'Chief Baron in Equity' of a separate court of equity in New South Wales: Smith, 'The Early Years of Equity in the Supreme Court of New South Wales', 802; Bennett, *A History of the Supreme Court of New South Wales*, 95.

[61] One rare exception is *King* v. *Johnston* (1859) 3 N.Z. Jur. (N.S.) 94.

[62] *Davidson* v. *Walker* (1845) V.P.R.S. 31/P0001/1.

[63] *Highett* v. *Willis* (1845) V.P.R.S. 31/P0001/3.

[64] Wills and probate disputes were equivalently referred to as being 'In the Supreme Court's Ecclesiastical Jurisdiction': *Re George Brooks* (1841) V.P.R.S. 282/P0000/1. The court continued to have an 'ecclesiastical' jurisdiction until it became 'probate': Administration Act 1872 (Vic.), 36 Vict. c. 427, s. 3.

[65] (1845) 1 Legge 253.   [66] Ibid., 264; compare Anon., 'The Last Page' (1992) 66 A.L.J. 872.

[67] *Stainforth* v. *Duff* (1846) A'Beckett's Res. Judg. 5, 7.

Court in Sydney and an appeal either from the Master of the Rolls to the Lord Chancellor or from the Lord Chancellor to the House of Lords:

> I consider it quite open to me to determine what the practice on the point now contested ought to be, without any reference to the English Rules; and as no decision has been given on the point, nor indeed required in this Court, it is right that I should endeavour to frame such a precedent as will most easily and conveniently carry out the directions of the appellate Court.[68]

The establishment of the Supreme Court of the new colony of Victoria in 1852 consolidated earlier practice, but it was soon found desirable to revise the Rules. By the Rules of 1854,[69] it was hoped that 'simplicity attended with expedition and unburthened with expense, will characterize proceedings at Law; and in Equity, similar results will follow from a like pervading influence'.[70] The letter from the Acting Chief Justice accompanying the Rules when they were tabled in Parliament stated that they were framed on six principles:

1. The establishment of a uniform system of process and pleading in the Court, in every branch of its jurisdiction.

2. The total abolition of fictions, and fictitious or unnecessary proceedings.

3. The diminution of those numerous dilatory steps in the progress of a Suit and of the performance of acts of a purely formal nature productive only of expense to the Suitor.

4. The classification of Actions into two forms only; the simplification of the mode of stating on the record the complaint, defence, and judgment of the Court, and the prevention in some measure of the unjust postponement of the fair demands of creditors, by rendering it necessary to verify certain pleas by affidavit.

5. The rendering more easy and less expensive the mode of proof of documentary, and the admission of secondary evidence.

6. And especially the adoption of a new Form of Action, instead of the fictitious process in Ejectment, and a complete alteration of proceedings in Equity, and the substitution of a system different, on the one hand, from the voluminous, tedious, and ruinous process which formerly oppressed the suitor; and on the other, from the summary and

---

[68] *Marquis of Ailsa v. Watson* (1846) A'Beckett's Res. Judg. 63, 65.

[69] Supreme Court Rules 1854 (Vic.), ch. V, r. 6.

[70] Letter from Sir Redmond Barry to the Colonial Secretary (John Foster) (30 November 1853), printed in Victoria, Parliament, *Supreme Court Rules*, PP. No. A 46 (1853–54), 4.

informal expedient by Rule nisi, which has been found to be in many instances unsatisfactory.[71]

The contrast with multifarious and unreformed contemporary English procedure was pointed:

> The Judges trust that by discouraging special Demurrers, Verbal Distinctions, and Technical objections, and the judicious exercise of large powers of amendment of formal mistakes, or omissions, much benefit will accrue to the Suitor; and that the reproach, arising from an affection for overstrained precision, and subtlety in non-essential particulars which has rested heretofore on the administration of the Law in the Superior Courts in England, may not be applicable to its administration in the Supreme Court of the Colony of Victoria.[72]

The letter overstated the harmony and simplicity that the rules brought to equity practice. Equity practice was, literally, contained in the same Rules as common law practice. But chapter V of those Rules adopted the practice of the English Court of Chancery 'so far as the circumstances and condition of the Colony shall require and admit' or as otherwise provided by local rules and legislation.[73] Evidence in equity proceedings was not confined to affidavits or interrogatories, but could be taken by viva voce examination and cross-examination on oath before the judge.[74]

The English Trustee Act 1850 (U.K.)[75] and Trustee Act 1852 (U.K.)[76] were applied in Victoria by force of the Trustee Act 1856 (Vic.). Rather than enact the full text of the English statutes, the Victorian Act simply declared that they were 'adopted and directed to be applied', with appropriate changes such as replacing 'Lord Chancellor' with 'Supreme Court of Victoria in its equitable jurisdiction'. Later, the English Chancery Procedure Act 1852 and Common Law Procedure Act 1854 were substantially adopted by the Equity Practice Statute 1865 (Vic.) and Common Law Procedure Statute 1865 (Vic.).

Professional opinion in Victoria was aware of English and American procedural reforms, including the Field Code of New York. Books on those topics were held in the earliest collections of the Supreme Court Library in Melbourne, which, while naturally weighting towards English materials, contained a large collection of American reports, statutes and treatises.[77]

---

[71] Ibid., 3–4.   [72] Ibid., 4.   [73] Supreme Court Rules 1854 (Vic.), ch. V, r. 6.
[74] Ibid., ch. VI, r. 15.   [75] 13 & 14 Vict. c. 60.   [76] 15 & 16 Vict. c. 55.
[77] See *Catalogue of the Library of the Supreme Court of Victoria, 1861* (Melbourne: Lucas, 1861). Gold Rush money, and Redmond Barry's bibliophilia, allowed for the acquisition of works including H. Denio and W. Tracy, *Revised Statutes of the State of New-York* (New York, NY: Gould, Banks & Co., 1852), H. Whittaker, *Practice and Pleading in Actions in the Courts of*

Consistently with the judge's letter accompanying the 1854 Rules, there was a local tendency to overstate how far administrative fusion had already been attained.[78] Nonetheless, the perception behind that sentiment is readily explained.

First, even judges who primarily sat in equity were nonetheless familiar with common law procedure, and were obliged to preside over jury trials and hear their share of common law matters. The small size of nineteenth-century colonial Supreme Court benches meant that to confine 'the work of a single judge to equity matters would have been considered a misallocation of judicial resources'.[79] Justice Molesworth was, for example, the trial judge in the noteworthy homicide case of *R* v. *Melville*.[80] The Court Book of his associate contains the full repertory of procedure for criminal trials: swearing in the jury, challenges, reading the charge, arraignment and oaths for various kinds of witnesses, including a special form of 'Chinese Oath': 'If I A B do not tell the truth, the whole truth or if I tell anything but the truth at this trial, may the Great God extinguish my soul hereafter as I now extinguish this light.'[81]

Secondly, there was little risk of inconsistency or bifurcation in the administration of law and equity, especially while the court comprised one judge. Plaintiffs never needed to shuttle between different courts. A word from the bench could often indicate the likely result of any action commenced with the 'wrong' procedure. The 1846 case of *Martin & Anor, Trustees of Hodge* v. *Jamieson*[82] concerned an alleged breach of trust arising out of a commercial contract relating to a theatre. Justice a'Beckett dismissed the plaintiff's bill as improperly brought and observed that common law litigation was likely to be equally unavailing:

> [I]t may make the plaintiffs' pause, before proceeding to further litigation, if I observe, that there is to say the least very strong evidence, on the testimony before me, to satisfy a jury that Hodge had waived all his interest in the

---

Record in the State of New York, under the Code of Procedure, 2nd edn (New York, NY: Whittaker, 1854), J. Story, *Commentaries on Equity Jurisprudence, as Administered in England and America*, 6th edn (Boston, MA: Little, Brown and Co., 1853).

[78] See, for example, (1856) Vict. L.T. 193.

[79] M. W. Bryan and V. J. Vann, *Equity and Trusts in Australia* (Cambridge University Press, 2012), 11.

[80] Bennett, *Sir William a'Beckett*, 84–85. The case turned on whether the prisoner was in lawful custody when he killed a man while attempting to escape. As trial judge, Molesworth reserved the question for the Full Court, which found on technical grounds that the prisoner was not in lawful custody, and therefore that the killing was not murder.

[81] Court Book of Associate to Justice Molesworth, V.P.R.S. 5507/P0000h, 8. On Molesworth sitting in criminal proceedings, see Forde, *The Story of the Bar of Victoria*, 291.

[82] (1846) A'Beckett's Res. Judg. 57.

theatre, very soon after its erection, if not by express agreement, at least by his conduct.[83]

In view of such a warning, common law proceedings were unlikely to have been instituted.

Thirdly, once the Supreme Court expanded beyond a single judge, appeals from the judge sitting in equity were likely to be heard by a Full Court lacking an equity specialist or in which an equity specialist was a minority of one. For most of Justice Molesworth's time in office, the Full Court usually comprised Chief Justice Stawell and Justices Barry and Williams,[84] none of whom had any noteworthy experience in equity. Given the relative youth at which each of these men was appointed to the bench, the composition of the Supreme Court remained constant between 1857 and 1872.[85] A second judge with an equity background was not appointed until 1881, when Edward Holroyd joined the bench.

Something of the atmosphere of equity practice in Victoria is captured in an 1881 illustration of the proceedings in the celebrated Lamont will case (Figure 7.3).[86]

George Lamont was a wealthy Scotsman who came to know a certain Mrs Maria Teresa Jackson. She was the leader of a circle that regularly discussed 'God, His providence, and the beauties of nature; sometimes spiritualism, mesmerism, animal magnetism, electro-biology, re-incarnation, &c.'.[87] She denied being a 'spiritualist medium'; Justice Molesworth described her as appearing to be 'a woman of high powers in conversation and declamation, and to have become a kind of priestess in this society'.[88] Lamont's will was said to have been procured by her undue influence, and various fanciful allegations were made about her supposedly mesmeric powers of mind control.

Justice Molesworth rejected these allegations in a judgment that gives a flavour of his sceptical disposition:

> [N]obody seems to have imagined [Mrs Jackson had] any such influence as would make the subject of it go to a solicitor to instruct him to prepare a will and to execute, all appearing to him in the ordinary course of free discretion. ... People used to believe in magic. I find no case in which it was sought to set aside a will or other instrument as procured by magic.[89]

[83] Ibid., 63. This case did indeed concern the 'small third-rate theatre' so despised by Roger Therry.
[84] Parkinson, *Sir William Stawell and the Victorian Constitution*, 56.   [85] Ibid., 55.
[86] *In the Will of George Lamont* (1881) 7 V.L.R. (I.P. & M.) 86.   [87] Ibid., 94.   [88] Ibid.
[89] Ibid., 99.

THE LAMONT WILL CASE IN THE EQUITY COURT

FIGURE 7.3 The Lamont Will case in the equity court, *Illustrated Australian News*, 1881 (State Library of Victoria)

As can be seen from the illustration, the affidavit evidence in the case was 'very voluminous',[90] but parties in probate and equity proceedings in Victoria also had the option of calling viva voce evidence from at least 1854.[91] In New South Wales, in contrast, the old methods of taking written evidence persisted much longer.[92]

Compared with the negative stereotype of Dickensian Chancery in England – and indeed New South Wales[93] – judicial delay in equity work does not seem to have been a great problem in pre-Judicature Act Victoria. In 1860, a question was asked in Parliament about delays in reserved judgments: the response listed all judgments in the period 1851–1860 which had been reserved for more than three months.[94] There were forty-nine such cases at law and only sixteen in equity (there having been 1,072 equity bills filed in that

[90] Ibid., 87.
[91] *Viva voce* evidence had been allowed in equity suits since at least the Supreme Court Rules 1854 (Vic.). On evidence *per testes* in probate cases, see *Re Pyke* (1861) 1 W. & W. (I.E. & M.) 20.
[92] Bennett, *A History of the Supreme Court of New South Wales*, 100–1.   [93] Ibid., 94–101.
[94] Supreme Court of Victoria, *Reserved Judgments*, PP. No. A 55 (1860). By modern standards, it is itself remarkable that a delay of three months was thought to warrant mention in Parliament.

92   MELBOURNE PUNCH.   [Oct. 23, 1856.

THE SUPREME COURT SITTING IN EQUITY.
(A VERY IMPORTANT CASE ON.)

FIGURE 7.4 The Supreme Court sitting in equity, *Melbourne Punch*, 1856 (National Library of Australia)

period). Of those sixteen, the longest delay was twenty-three months; the average delay was nine months.

Perhaps it is telling that in 1856 *Melbourne Punch* satirised the equity court as being boring, not scandalous. The Lamont will case was a rare example of popular journalistic interest in equity work (Figure 7.4).

VOLUME OF EQUITY WORK IN VICTORIA, 1854–70

Some sense of the volume of equity work in Victoria can be found in the Equity Suit Books which survive for the period from 1841 to 1870. These show the number of new equity bills filed each year, and the relief claimed.[95] In Figures 7.5–7.13, the relevant date is the year in which the bill was first filed: a long-running suit might well traverse more than one year, but then as now most litigation was resolved without lengthy proceedings.

The resident judges in the Port Phillip District saw a modest amount of equity work, albeit no more than sixteen new bills a year. In 1841, the first year

[95] V.P.R.S. 1697/P/0000/000001; V.P.R.S. 1697/P/0000/000002; V.P.R.S. 1697/P/0000/000003.

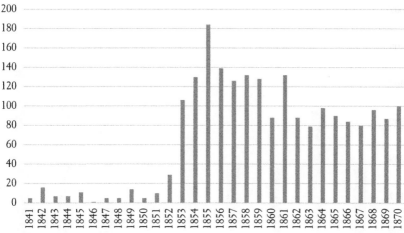

FIGURE 7.5 Equity bills filed by year, 1841–70

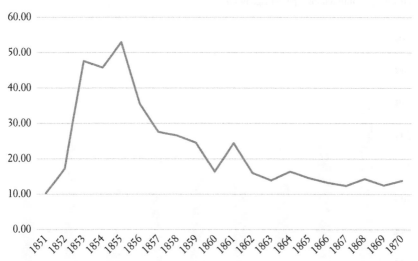

FIGURE 7.6 Equity suits per 100,000 persons, 1851–70

of the Supreme Court, five equity bills were filed, representing just under half a suit per 1,000 people.[96]

To put these figures in context, in the Supreme Court of Tasmania's first year (1824), eleven equity suits and 360 common law actions were

[96] In 1841 the population of the Port Phillip District in 1841 was 11,738 and five equity bills were filed.

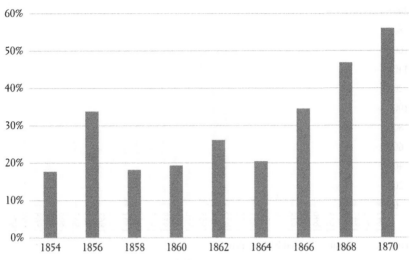

FIGURE 7.7 Injunctions – percentage of bills

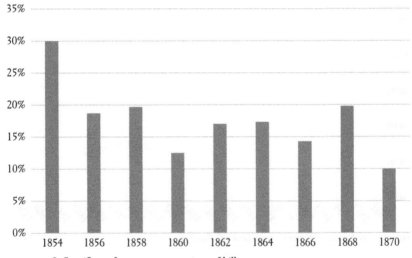

FIGURE 7.8 Specific performance – percentage of bills

commenced; but no equity suit was actually decided until 1835.[97] That represented just over one equity suit per 1,000 of the free population of

---

[97] R. Ely (ed.), *Carrel Inglis Clark: The Supreme Court of Tasmania, Its First Century 1824–1924* (Hobart: University of Tasmania Law Press, 1995), 13. Interlocutory decrees were, however, pronounced before 1835. On the equitable jurisdiction of the Supreme Court, see also A. C. Castles, *Lawless Harvests or God Save the Judges: Van Diemen's Land 1803–55, A Legal History* (Melbourne: Australian Scholarly Publishing, 2007), 114.

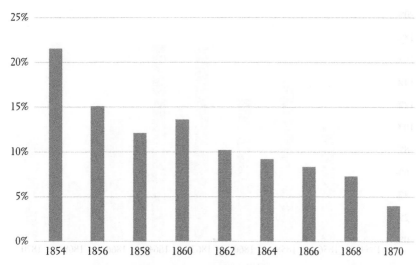

FIGURE 7.9 Partnership proceedings – percentage of bills

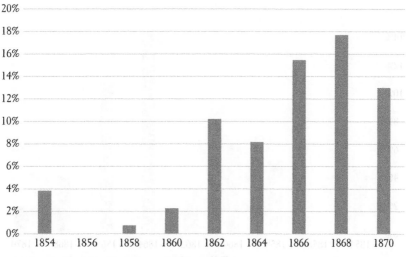

FIGURE 7.10 Administration suits – percentage of bills

Tasmania.[98] In New Zealand, it seems there were only six cases decided in the Supreme Court's equitable jurisdiction between 1843 and 1856.[99] In New South Wales, Roger Therry remarked that, on his arrival in 1829, equity work

[98] Ely (ed.), *Carrel Inglis Clark*, 13.
[99] Dorsett, 'Reforming Equity: New Zealand 1843–56', 302, n. 88.

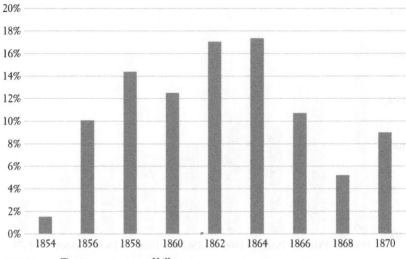

FIGURE 7.11 Trusts – percentage of bills

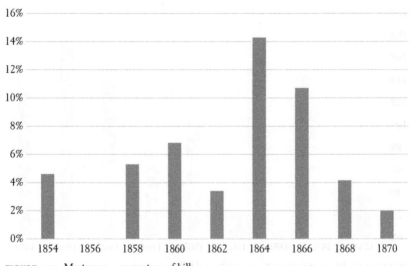

FIGURE 7.12 Mortgages – percentage of bills

was so sparse that 'half a dozen days in the course of a year would dispose of' it all.[100] By mid-century, the number of equity suits in New South Wales had increased, but was smaller than that in Victoria. In 1853, there were nearly

---

[100] Anon., 'Supreme Court', *Sydney Morning Herald*, 27 August 1857, 3, quoted in Bennett, *Sir Francis Forbes*, 106.

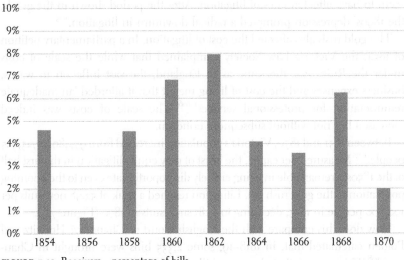

FIGURE 7.13 Receivers – percentage of bills

100 suits in New South Wales; and in the three years to 1856 there were nearly 350 suits.[101]

With the establishment of the Victorian Supreme Court in 1852 there was a remarkable increase in the number of new equity bills, rising from twenty-nine in 1852 to a peak of 184 in 1855 – the year before Robert Molesworth was appointed as the fourth Supreme Court judge and the Primary Judge in equity.[102] Thereafter, the pressure of work declined to, on average, 100 new bills per year from 1857 to 1870.

The spike in new suits in the first half of the 1850s coincides neatly with the discovery of gold at Clunes in 1851 and the ensuing gold rush, which tailed off by the early 1860s.[103] Within the period shown by the graph, later economic and political factors, such as the political and fiscal crisis of 1864–66,[104] do not

[101] Bennett, A History of the Supreme Court of New South Wales, 98.
[102] The smaller gold rush and commercial boom in New South Wales had similarly come to 'place abnormal pressure on the equity jurisdiction': Bennett, A History of the Supreme Court of New South Wales, 99.
[103] G. Blainey, The Rush that Never Ended: A History of Australian Mining (Melbourne University Press, 1963), 60.
[104] Z. Cowen, 'A Century of Constitutional Development in Victoria, 1856–1956', in Z. Cowen, Sir John Latham and Other Papers (Melbourne: Oxford University Press, 1965), 107, 138–41; Dean, A Multitude of Counsellors, 50–53.

seem to have affected rates of litigation. After the period shown in the graph, the 1890s' depression prompted a radical downturn in litigation.[105]

The gold rush also affected the cost of litigation. In a parliamentary petition of 1854, the Victoria Law Society complained that while the scale of costs under the Rules was the same as in England, the vast inflation in wages, business expenses and the cost of living meant that it afforded 'an inadequate remuneration for professional services'.[106] The scale of costs was indeed increased but not without subsequent criticism.

Between 1851 and 1870, Victoria's population increased from 97,489 to 723,925 people.[107] Measured per capita, the burst of new equity litigation in the first half of the 1850s is remarkable in being entirely disproportionate even to the booming population of the gold rush era. Litigation reached a peak of 52.98 new suits per 100,000 people in 1855, declining to 13.81 such suits in 1870 (Figure 7.6).

How does this compare with the English Court of Chancery? Horwitz and Polden calculated that, in 1818–19, some 2,335 bills were brought in Chancery.[108] This suggests that about 21.2 bills were brought per 100,000 persons.[109] For the later period 1871 to 1876, the average 'total proceedings' in a given year was 4,633 (or around 22.1 proceedings per 100,000 persons).[110] 'Total proceedings' is not quite the same as new bills, so one would expect the latter figure in fact to be somewhat lower. The impression created by the English figures highlights the gold rush boom of equity litigation in Victoria, and the subsequent settling to a stable rate that was somewhat lower than at 'home'.

TYPES OF EQUITY WORK IN VICTORIA, 1854–70

From 1854, it is possible to determine – at least generally – the relief sought in each bill from the Equity Suit Books. More than one kind of relief was claimed in most equity suits, and the total number of suits varied from year to year. Thus,

[105] Dean, *A Multitude of Counsellors*, 118.
[106] D. Ogilvy, R. Macfarland and F. M. P. Brookfield, *Supreme Court Rules: Petition to the Honourable the Legislative Council of the Colony of Victoria in Council Assembled*, PP. No. E 21 (1854), 1.
[107] Australian Bureau of Statistics, '3105.0.65.001: Australian Historical Population Statistics, 2014: Population Size and Growth' (18 September 2014).
[108] H. Horwitz and P. Polden, 'Continuity or Change in the Court of Chancery in the Seventeenth and Eighteenth Centuries?' (1996) 35 J. Br. Stud. 24, 30.
[109] The population was about 11 million: E. A. Wrigley and R. S. Schofield, *The Population History of England, 1541–1871: A Reconstruction* (Cambridge University Press, 1989), 595.
[110] P. Polden, 'The Chancery Division', in *O.H.L.E.*, vol. XI, 834. The population was about 21 million: Wrigley and Schofield, *The Population History of England*, 595.

the figures that follow refer to the *percentage* of all suits in which a given kind of relief was claimed. For example, a bill seeking an account and an injunction will appear in the tables for both 'Account' and 'Injunction'.

The Suit Books reveal a different picture of equity litigation from what one might gain looking solely at the law reports.[111] 'Remedial' suits for specific performance and the like were rarely worth reporting, yet made up a substantial proportion of the Supreme Court's incoming work.

The relative importance of some forms of relief clearly changed over time. For example, broadly speaking the proportion of suits in which an injunction was sought rose from 17.7 per cent (twenty-three bills) in 1854, when records commenced, to 56 per cent (fifty-six bills) in 1870 (Figure 7.11). This mirrors the increase in the percentage of suits in which an injunction was the sole relief claimed from 3.8 per cent (five bills) in 1854 to 13 per cent (thirteen bills) in 1870.[112] The Suit Books do not allow us readily to distinguish between common and special injunctions. Some entries specify that a bill sought an 'injunction against suit at law', but most state only that an 'injunction' was sought. Whether common or special, it is unclear why there should have been such an increase in the demand for injunctions over time.

By contrast, the proportion of suits concerning specific performance tended to fall somewhat, from 30 per cent (thirty-nine bills) in 1854 to 10 per cent (ten bills) in 1870.

The social and economic reasons for the steep decline in partnership proceedings is obvious. Proceedings encompassing relief specifically identified as being in relation to a partnership fell from 21.5 per cent of all proceedings (twenty-eight bills) in 1854 to 4 per cent (four bills) in 1870 (Figure 7.9).

Partnerships were of decreasing significance in commercial life, and partnership proceedings declined accordingly. The Companies Statute 1864 (Vic.) revolutionised the structure of business in the colony. The shift towards corporate forms was largely driven by the change from alluvial to deep-cut gold mining, which by nature was more capital-intensive.[113] Later local innovations included the creation of 'No Liability' companies by the Mining

---

[111] See in the case of litigation in England: Horwitz and Polden, 'Continuity or Change in the Court of Chancery in the Seventeenth and Eighteenth Centuries?', 35, table 6; P. Polden 'The Court of Chancery', in *O.H.L.E.*, vol. XI, 652; Polden, 'The Chancery Division', 835.

[112] The low point for suits in which an injunction was the sole relief sought was 1862 (1.1 per cent; 1 suit), and the high point 1868 (18.8 per cent; 18 suits).

[113] P. Lipton, 'A History of Company Law in Colonial Australia: Economic Development and Legal Evolution' (2007) 31 M.U.L.R. 805; G. Blainey, *A History of Victoria*, 2nd edn (Cambridge University Press, 2013), 61–62; Blainey, *The Rush that Never Ended*, ch. 6.

Companies Act 1871 (Vic.) and proprietary companies by the Companies Act 1896 (Vic.).

As one might expect, the companies involved in equity litigation were almost exclusively gold mining companies. Indeed, the uncertainty of gold mining led to the development of one novel feature of equity practice in Victoria, namely the order for 'inspection of mine'. Bills for this order began to appear from 1867: they amounted to 11.5 per cent of bills in 1868 (eleven bills) and 5 per cent in 1870 (five bills).[114]

Another marker of changing social and economic circumstances in Victoria was the proportion of administration suits and bills concerning trusts or mortgages. Plainly, in the colony's early days there were few deceased estates or trusts in need of administration. It is no surprise to see the proportion of such suits increasing over the century.

By contrast, there was a less consistent trend in the proportion of non-administration suits concerning trusts (such as suits for a declaration that property was held on trust and suits under the Trustee Act 1856 (Vic.)) and in the proportion of mortgage-related proceedings (such as suits for foreclosure and redemption, and suits for the taking of accounts in relation to a mortgage).

Trust-related proceedings varied over time, reaching a peak of 17.3 per cent of proceedings (seventeen bills) in 1864 (Figure 7.11). Most express trusts cases appear to have concerned private trusts: charitable trusts seem to have come before the court so infrequently that in 1882 – after some twenty-six years on the bench – Justice Molesworth was able to remark that '[t]his subject is new to me'.[115]

1864 also saw the peak of mortgage-related proceedings: 14.3 per cent of proceedings (fourteen bills) (Figure 7.12). This peak may be related to the decline of the immediate gold rush land boom: between 1856 and 1865, the output of gold almost halved.[116]

Bills seeking the appointment of receivers also varied markedly with no evident chronological pattern. There was a peak of 8 per cent (seven bills) in 1862, and a low of 0.7 per cent (one bill) in 1856 (Figure 7.13).

Proceedings for other types of relief were much rarer. The sampled years saw only two bills for discovery and one bill for revivor.[117]

---

[114] The order was that the defendant 'permit some proper person' on behalf of the plaintiff to 'enter, inspect and examine the shaft and drives' of the defendant's mine: see, for example, A.-G. v. *Gee* (1863) 2 W. & W. (E.) 122, 125.

[115] *Wilson* v. A.-G. (1882) 8 V.L.R. (E.) 215, 226.

[116] Blainey, A *History of Victoria*, 62; Blainey, *The Rush that Never Ended*, 60.

[117] The need for revivor in cases of marriage or death, however, was abolished: Supreme Court Rules 1854 (Vic.), ch. V, r. 13.

The very different economic and social structure of Victoria – as well as a much simpler system of land ownership, even before the introduction of Torrens title in 1862[118] – makes it likely that less time was spent dealing with the complications of land ownership and the administration of difficult trusts and estates than was the case at 'home'.

INTRODUCING THE JUDICATURE ACT

At the dawn of the 1880s, the state of equity in Victoria appeared stable. The same Primary Judge had been in office for twenty-four years. Owing to his labours there appear to have been no prominent complaints from the public or the profession about delay, cost or disharmony in the administration of law and equity. Nonetheless, in September 1880 a Royal Commission into the functioning of the Supreme Court – under the presidency of the Chief Justice, Sir William Stawell – recommended that the English Judicature Acts be adopted 'so far as they are suitable'.[119]

The Commission believed there was 'no doubt that the procedure under them [would] effect a great improvement'.[120] Yet the Commission was deeply conscious of the different circumstances in Victoria and England, particularly the existence in England of the separate superior courts to be consolidated into the Supreme Court of Judicature.[121] By contrast, the absence of such difficulties in Victoria meant that it was inappropriate to adopt the divisional system in England whereby the old courts, 'although consolidated, should retain their distinctive titles, and could constitute so many Divisions of the High Court of Justice'.[122]

In the absence of separate courts to be merged, what was the point of administrative fusion? The Commission reported:

> The disadvantages of the separate systems of Law and Equity at present prevailing here, and the evils arising from this mode of administration, can be remedied only by fusing the Equity and Common Law Jurisdictions of the Supreme Court, and providing for the concurrent administration of Law and Equity by the Court or any Judge thereof ... The Court will possess the power to recognize all equitable rights incidentally appearing in any action,

---

[118] Real Property Act 1862 (Vic.), 25 Vict. c. 140; compare the Real Property Act 1858 (S.A.), 22 Vict. c. 16.

[119] Victoria, Royal Commission Appointed to Inquire into the Operation and Effect of the Present Constitution of the Supreme Court of the Colony of Victoria, *Report of the Royal Commission*, Report No. 28 (1880), 5.

[120] Ibid.   [121] Ibid.   [122] Ibid.

and to apply all appropriate remedies, and dispose of all the matters in controversy between the parties, so that multiplicity of legal proceedings concerning any of such matters may be avoided.[123]

Quite what those disadvantages and evils were is not spelled out in the report, save for the reference to multiplicity of legal proceedings.

The report of the Royal Commission did not bear fruit immediately. The Judicature Act was passed in 1883 and gained force in July 1884. The text of the Act and the Rules in its schedule were taken fairly directly from their English progenitors, though the judges were given the power to amend the Rules or enact new ones.

Almost immediately, the Victorian Judicature Act aroused complaints about expense and delay in litigation that were generated – rather than remedied – by the Act. In equity suits, the problem seemed to be delay and the inefficient use of judicial resources; in common law cases, the problem was excessive costs generated by a new and unnecessarily complex procedure. Before the Act came into force, *Melbourne Punch* accurately forecast that it would not reduce the cost of litigation. It was probably unfair, if unsurprising, for *Punch* to single out the cupidity of the legal profession as the likely reason for the failure of the Act; but it was correct to characterise the Act (depicted in the rolls of paper at the bottom of the illustration) as a 'pleading reform' and a 'costs reform'.

Section 54 of the Judicature Act obliged the judges of the Supreme Court to report on 'any defects which may appear to exist in the system of procedure or the administration of the law'. In 1886 – coincidentally, the year of Justice Molesworth's retirement – they reported that the concurrent administration of law and equity was a 'real and an enduring improvement upon the twofold system which it [had] superseded'.[124] However, in practice the Rules had in some instances imposed 'unnecessary expenses upon suitors', and encouraged 'numerous technical and frivolous and always costly objections on points of pleading and procedure' in part generated by the 'frequent obscurity' of the drafting.[125] Their Honours therefore proposed that the Rules be 'thoroughly revised and re-cast'.[126]

Those concerns were eventually acted upon, and the judges set about drafting new rules under the direction of Chief Justice Higinbotham and Justices Williams and Holroyd. The practising profession was not consulted.

[123] Ibid., 7.
[124] Victoria, Council of Judges, *Report of the Council of Judges under Section 54 of 'The Judicature Act 1883'*, Report No. 51 (1886), 3.
[125] Ibid., 4.   [126] Ibid.

THE NEW JUDICATURE ACT.

The Public.—"COME, I SAY, I'M TO HAVE A LITTLE BIT OF THE OYSTER NOW, JUST FOR A CHANGE."

Barrister.—"So YOU SHALL, BUT IT WON'T BE FOR LONG. ME AND MY SOLICITOR FRIEND HERE WILL SOON FIND A WAY OF HAVING THE WHOLE OYSTER AGAIN AND PRESENTING YOU, AS USUAL, WITH THE SHELLS."

FIGURE 7.14 'The New Judicature Act', *Melbourne Punch*, 1884 (National Library of Australia)

Such was the trepidation and ill will that the Rules eventually laid before Parliament in December 1890 were annulled.[127]

Concern about cost and delay in litigation, the debacle of the annulled rules, the ineffective attempt to amalgamate the solicitors' and barristers' branches of the profession in the Legal Profession Practice Act 1891 (Vic.) and lingering dissatisfaction with the Judicature Act led to the appointment of a Royal Commission chaired by Henry Bourne Higgins to investigate 'the means of avoiding unnecessary delay and expense, and of making

---

[127] Dean, *A Multitude of Counsellors*, 115.

improvements in the administration of the justice and in the working of the law'.[128] Higgins was a noted equity practitioner[129] later celebrated for his understanding of the social context of law in the field of industrial relations.

Higgins's Commission reported in 1899 and was more realistic than many subsequent law reform bodies about what could actually – or desirably – be achieved:

> [L]itigation, even if expensive, is much cheaper than the private warfare for which it is a substitute. There must be delay, there must be expense; and the function of any system of procedure is to reduce both to the minimum of what is necessary. Each party to a dispute endeavours to obstruct the other as far as he can. In the tug and strain of the contest advantage is taken of every device which the system of procedure allows, abuses of the procedure become apparent from time to time, and perpetual vigilance is necessary on the part of those responsible for any system of procedure to see what provisions therein lead to miscarriage of justice, unnecessary expense, or unnecessary delay.[130]

The Commission viewed complaints about the Judicature Act system in essentially socio-legal terms:

> [M]uch allowance must be made for the inevitable predilections of lawyers, the whole of whose training and practice were under a different system. The attitude of many of the older lawyers with regard to the Judicature Act may be compared with that of the late Lord Wensleydale, formerly Baron Parke, towards the Common Law Procedure Statute. Baron Parke's disgust at the procedure introduced by that Statute was so great as to induce him to resign his seat in the Court of Exchequer; and now we find gentlemen trained under the Common Law Procedure Statute regarding it as creating a perfect system and condemning the innovations of the Judicature Act.[131]

Aside from the 'intrinsic merits' of that system, the Commission considered that there were three practical reasons not to go back.[132] First, books on the former system were, by that time, 'long out of use and probably to a considerable extent out of print'; second, a 'new school of practitioners [had] arisen familiar only with the judicature system'; and third, there was a benefit in

---

[128] Victoria, Royal Commission for Inquiring as to the Means of Avoiding Unnecessary Delay and Expense, and of Making Improvements in the Administration of Justice and in the Working of the Law, *Report of Royal Commission*, Report No. 15 (1899).

[129] J. Rickard, *H. B. Higgins: The Rebel as Judge* (North Sydney: Allen & Unwin, 1984), 56–57.

[130] Royal Commission for Inquiring as to the Means of Avoiding Unnecessary Delay and Expense, *Report of Royal Commission*, v.

[131] Ibid., vii–viii.   [132] Ibid., viii.

retaining a system as near as possible to England, to have the benefit of English decision-making.[133]

What of the disallowed rules? The Commission saw a lack of consultation with the profession as the largest ground for complaint, particularly regarding costs and 'the friction and inconvenience in litigation which certain regulations create'.[134] In fact, the standard Judicature scale of costs in Victoria was substantially higher than the contemporary English scale because of the higher cost of labour.[135] A writ of summons cost 12s. in Victoria but only 6s. 8d. in England; a subpoena cost 8s. in Victoria but 6s. 8d. in England.[136] The Commission concluded that labour costs were 'not so much higher in Victoria as to justify such a difference', and recommended a commensurate reduction.[137]

The unnecessary complexity of Judicature pleading was noted. Especially in common law suits, 'the practice [had] degenerated until the paragraphs [were] often of great length and many issues [were] raised which [were] never intended to be seriously contested'.[138] This was particularly notorious in the case of simple common law matters, which used to be much more straightforward. The Commission therefore recommended that pleadings not be necessary in such cases, but that they should be preserved for equitable claims, which often required 'the history of successive transactions has to be set forth with, usually, the substantial effect of a series of instruments, in a manner which is unknown in the so-called common law actions'.[139]

So far as equity practice was concerned, the main theme of the evidence given to the Commission was how successful the administration of equity had been in the time of Justice Molesworth. The noted equity barrister Samuel St John Topp remarked:

> The equity cases are a particular branch of law in which a particular class of advocates plead, and a particular class of judges are trained, such as Mr Justice Holroyd and Mr Justice a'Beckett. The common law judges make no secret that they do not understand anything about it, and without reflecting on the judges, it is apparent that a judge trained all his life in common law cannot understand equity practice and pleading principles as well as a judge trained in equity; we have common law judges who say every day that they do not understand it. I should like to revert to the old practice of putting one judge aside to sit constantly in equity and take equity and originating summonses, just as the late Sir Robert Molesworth did.[140]

[133] Ibid.   [134] Ibid., vi.   [135] Ibid., xii.   [136] Ibid.   [137] Ibid.   [138] Ibid., xxi

[139] Ibid., xxiii.   [140] Ibid., 199.

What had gone wrong? Topp's view was that things had worked well when Justice Molesworth had 'sat entirely in the Equity Court' and then, after the Judicature Act 'continued to take all the equity cases' until his retirement, when Justice Webb took over. However, in 1890 Chief Justice Higinbotham:

> announced that for the future there would be no distinction between equity and common law cases, so you had two or three lists; that prevented advocates versed in equity appearing in equity cases, and the equity cases were tried before a judge who had never argued an equity case in his life. That went on for some time; then the present Chief Justice Madden … announced that for the future equity would be separated from the common law cases and put in two lists, and that was done for some time and worked very well, but now we have reverted back, without any announcement from the bench, to the old system.[141]

The next Chief Justice, Sir John Madden, recalled that '[w]hen Mr Justice Molesworth sat there was only one equity judge on the bench; the other judges knew nothing whatever of equity'.[142] After Molesworth's retirement, it was hard to find as enthusiastic a taker of the court's equity work:

> Mr Justice Holroyd and Mr Justice a'Beckett, who are the equity judges *par excellence*, do not like it, for the obvious reason that it is much heavier work than the common law work is, but they do it nevertheless with perfect willingness.[143]

It was especially difficult to convince anyone to sit in equity permanently or on a regular rotation, because such a judge 'would have to bear the most burthensome work always, and … would say he ought not to be bound to the drudgery of the whole business'.[144] Chief Justice Madden considered that while the concurrent administration of law and equity was a good idea, so far as pleading was concerned 'the judicature system could only be set right by being abolished'.[145]

Justice Thomas a'Beckett – one of the two judges trained in equity – was more enthusiastic about the Judicature system, and considered that 'it would be a complete retrograde step that could scarcely be tolerated to revert to a system condemned by experience'.[146]

By contrast, Justice Hartley Williams – a common law judge – was nostalgic for the old system of pleading: 'I approve of it infinitely more than I do of the present system. I would like to do away with pleadings altogether if I could,

---

[141] Ibid., 200.   [142] Ibid., 338.   [143] Ibid.   [144] Ibid.   [145] Ibid., 342.   [146] Ibid., 350.

though I was brought up as a pleader.'[147] It was no use 'tinkering with the present system of judicature at all; the only thing [was] to make a radical and sweeping change'.[148] Justice Hood was of the same view, thinking the Judicature rules a 'mistake' and 'founded on a wrong principle'.[149]

Justice Hodges was more equable. He did not recommend a wholesale repeal of the Judicature Act, which he saw as 'a return to the old equity pleadings which had existed in the early times, say, in Judge Molesworth's time'.[150] On being asked whether it was beneficial to have a single procedure at law and in equity, he replied:

> That has always been the only element in favour of the Judicature Act, that it made one procedure in courts of law and courts of equity, though I am inclined to think it is a mistake, and that there should be two kinds of procedure for the two different classes of cases[151]

Justice Holroyd – the other equity judge – felt that the Judicature system 'would work much better if it were liked better by the members of the profession; I think both common law lawyers and equity lawyers dislike it equally'.[152] Ostensibly, he opposed having a separate equity list on point of principle:

> [I]f you do have such a distinction you will never have the fusion of law and equity that was contemplated by the Act. It was distinctly intended when the first Judicature Act was passed in England that every judge should deal with every part of the law.[153]

His real motivation – as the opinion of Chief Justice Madden hinted – was a more personal dislike of being singled out for equity work:

> For many years I have always had the equity list put against me and my brother a'Beckett, if possible. I am not so good natured as my brother a'Beckett, and I fought against it – I do not like it at all; I was not appointed as an equity judge.[154]

The Commission ultimately recommended the preservation of the Judicature system, but had 'no hesitation' in recommending that there be a separate equity list.[155] The concurrent administration of law and equity was a good thing, but Victoria had

> gone too far in treating an equitable cause as not being radically different from a common law cause. This radical distinction was expressly recognised

---

[147] Ibid., 361.   [148] Ibid., 362.   [149] Ibid., 377.   [150] Ibid., 385.   [151] Ibid., 393.
[152] Ibid., 400.   [153] Ibid.   [154] Ibid., 401.   [155] Ibid., xxxi.

in the English Act, which assigned each class of causes to a separate division of the court.[156]

The Commission perceived that '[i]n spite of the efforts of the late Chief Justice to disregard the distinction' by assigning equity work 'indiscriminately to common law and equity judges', it was undoubtedly in the public interest 'that an equity judge should take equity causes, as Mr Justice Molesworth took equitable causes with such marked success for so many years'.[157]

What of the Rules disallowed in 1890? It took until 1906 for the first locally drafted Judicature rules to be made, twenty-three years after the enactment of the Judicature system in Victoria and twenty years after Robert Molesworth's retirement.[158]

FUSION AND FISSION

In the nineteenth century, it was thought that there was excessive compartmentalisation when the Supreme Court of Victoria sat in two divisions: at law and in equity. In 2019, the court sits in six divisions and thirty-one lists.[159] Perceptions about the value of specialisation can change over time.

The example of the nineteenth-century Supreme Court of Victoria points to four wider themes in the debate about fusion and fission. First, the law on the books is often less important to the practical administration of justice than the skill and diligence of the people administering it. For the thirty years of Robert Molesworth's judgeship, there seems to have been a more harmonious administration of law and equity in Victoria than in the twenty years following the enactment of the Judicature Act. As the contrasting examples of Lord Eldon and Robert Molesworth show, both before and after the Judicature Act the practice of equity was more susceptible to the varying personalities and working habits of its judges and practitioners than was the practice of law. The persistence of separate spheres of professional activity – including distinct 'common law' and 'equity' professional styles – highlights the naïveté of thinking – as, for a time, did Victorian judges – that procedural fusion would automatically result in a new generation of omnicompetent judges and lawyers, equally at ease in equity as at law.

Second, the Victorian experience highlights the importance of the way substance and procedure are intertwined in any legal system. Ultimately, the

---

[156] Ibid.   [157] Ibid.   [158] Dean, *A Multitude of Counsellors*, 116.
[159] Court of Appeal; Criminal Division; Common Law Division (twelve specialist lists, including 'Trusts, Equity and Probate'); Commercial Court (eleven named lists, seven specialist lists); Costs Court; Practice Court.

absence of a separate equity court in Victoria was less significant than the persistence of non-jury procedure and the administrative convenience of grouping certain types of legal problems together, largely because they involve questions which are 'evaluative rather than binary'.[160] Conversely, the greatly increased difficulty of managing *common law* cases under the post-Judicature procedure – despite the substantive common law being unchanged – illustrates the importance at law of obtaining quick answers to yes/no questions.

Third, one sees very clearly in Victoria the persistent salience, in equity, of administrative processes; not simply processes of decision-making. Administrative processes such as the ability to take accounts – and the presence of officers to undertake that task – almost never led to reported decisions, yet the existence of such administrative machinery had important substantive effects. For example, one distinctive feature of the 'immediate duty'[161] between trustee and beneficiary is the necessity of the particular institutional apparatus that supports the duty. In particular, the continued ability of courts exercising equitable jurisdiction literally to hold trustees and other fiduciaries to account tends to highlight the difficulty and inappropriateness of assimilating that institutional structure to a common law model confined to the award of damages after breach. As John Goldberg and Henry Smith emphasise in Chapter 13, even in a fused system, liability for equitable wrongdoing is not commensurate with – and is not remedied in the same way as – liability for common law torts.

Finally, the example of Victoria serves to indicate that the comparative experience of law in England and Australia may be more complicated than is sometimes supposed. English solutions no doubt responded to English problems, but at least some Australian writers are too quick to assume that the persistence of the separate administration of law and equity in Australia was a cringing or atavistic retention of 'English' norms that inhibited the development of 'Australian' law. For Kercher, the presence of an 'equity side' in the colonial Supreme Courts 'could not be justified by reference to administrative convenience', and was 'a system with little rational basis'.[162] Castles criticised 'the strong attachment of the members of the Supreme Court [of New South Wales] and others to the almost slavish adoption of many English-based practices in the life of the colony'.[163] Similarly, for Crawford and Opeskin,

---

[160] *Wu* v. *Ling* [2016] NSWCA 322, [7] (Leeming J.A.); compare *Jenyns* v. *Public Curator (Qld)* (1953) 90 C.L.R. 113, 118–19.

[161] See McFarlane, Chapter 14.

[162] B. Kercher, *An Unruly Child: A History of Law in Australia* (St Leonards: Allen & Unwin, 1995), 97.

[163] A. C. Castles, *An Australian Legal History* (Sydney: Law Book Co., 1982), 197.

practitioners in Australia 'were so attached to English models' that they treated their courts as 'notionally divided into a court of law and a court of equity, with appropriate remedies available only when the judge was wearing the appropriate "hat"'.[164] On this telling, the reception of English law 'was not merely assumed but clung to, as a mark of Englishness in a strange land', such that:

> common law and equity were also administered separately, as nearly as possible in the English mode, despite being vested in the same Supreme Court. By such imitation, the professional lawyers managed to avoid the Judicature Act system until its adoption in England in 1875 – and in New South Wales, for a century beyond that.[165]

Each of these accounts should be rejected. Quite aside from their anachronistic nationalism, they ignore the lived experience of the law. In Victoria, where that experience was shaped so deeply by Sir Robert Molesworth over so many years, it was by no means clear that the Judicature system was much of an improvement on what had gone before. Where there had been no fission, fusion may well have been a solution in search of a problem.

---

[164] J. Crawford and B. Opeskin, *Australian Courts of Law*, 4th edn (Melbourne: Oxford University Press, 2004), 135.
[165] Ibid., 17 (emphasis original).

8

Are Equity and Law in Scotland Fused, Separate or Intertwined?

DANIEL J. CARR

INTRODUCTION

'It is of less moment what the law of England is on this head, for we follow the civil law, and the distinction between law and equity introduces an element perplexing to us, but I imagine the principle to be the same'.[1]

'Equity' is a controversial word for some in Scottish legal circles; certainly it is a difficult word. The difficulty flows from a perennial problem faced by equity in many places: the elusiveness of a comprehensive definition which satisfies formalist or positivist sensibilities. Complicating the situation is the classification of Scotland as a mixed[2] legal system, one substantially influenced by both the civilian and common law traditions.[3] The composition of that mixture of the civil and common law is dynamic, and probably can never be captured or determined at one moment or continually. From all this emerges the Scottish conception of equity. Both the civilian and common law traditions have understandings of equity. Arguably, the core substance of equity in the two traditions is similar, or at least was at one time,[4] but how equity was institutionally imposed or done was very different. The institutional understandings of equity in common law and civilian jurisdictions have diverged. The historic institutional separation of equity from common law in the common law

---

[1] *Pirie* v. *Pirie* (1873) 11 M. 941, 949.
[2] The term 'mixed' is itself complex. For criticism, see S. Thomson, 'Mixed Jurisdiction and the Scottish Legal Tradition: Reconsidering the Concept of Mixture' (2014) 7 J. Civ. L. Stud. 51.
[3] Other notable mixed legal systems are Israel, South Africa, Sri Lanka and Louisiana. See e.g., V. V. Palmer, M. Y. Mattar and A. Koppel (eds), *Mixed Legal Systems, East and West* (Farnham: Ashgate, 2015); V. V. Palmer, *Mixed Jurisdictions Worldwide: The Third Legal Family*, 2nd edn (Cambridge University Press, 2012).
[4] See Milsom, *Historical Foundations*, 2nd edn, 82–86.

tradition is unknown in the modern[5] civilian tradition. In turn, the idea of a
separate equity jurisdiction has had little influence on the Scottish legal
system, but some.

The close political and economic ties between Scotland and England since
the Union of 1707 have meant that English law has been a substantial influence upon Scottish law.[6] With that influence came doctrinal rules and
structures which have not always been easy to integrate within the existing
body of Scottish law. Particular difficulty has been caused by chancery
jurisprudence, most specifically in relation to property law and trusts law.
Scotland's law of property is traditionally understood to be based on a civilian
model,[7] and so the idea of divided ownership is a difficult one to project across
a system where the orthodox characterisation of ownership is of singular
indivisible *dominium*.[8] The traditional explanation of the English trust in
terms of distinct legal and beneficial ownership has caused some anxiety.[9]
The concept of something like equitable ownership, which emerged in
relation to trusts, has been applied[10] – for a time[11] – in other contexts such
as the transfer of land. Furthermore, especially in recent years, the apparent
emergence of other English Chancery-inspired legal institutions – such as the
constructive trust, and the doctrines of knowing receipt and dishonest assistance – has also been the subject of critical comment.[12]

In this chapter I trace the development of Scottish ideas of equity which
were heavily associated with, and in many cases synonymous with, natural law
and associated schools of thought. The natural law heritage proceeded upon
the basis of a theoretical dualism, but the two forms of law were administered

5 On the possible analogy with the praetorian jurisdiction, see W. W. Buckland, *Equity in Roman Law* (London: University of London Press, 1911), 1–8.
6 The common law tradition is relatively under-theorised: see M. C. Meston, W. D. H. Sellar and Lord Cooper, *The Scottish Legal Tradition*, new edn (Edinburgh: Saltire Society, 1991), 29–30 and 65–75. Under the dominant influence of English law in the last 100–150 years, there was no need to justify a common law tradition, whereas the fading civilian tradition's subtlety arguably required justification in the present age.
7 This approach is recent. Regarding its effect on ownership, see K. G. C. Reid, *The Abolition of Feudal Tenure in Scotland* ([s.l.]: LexisNexis UK, 2003), [1.27].
8 N. MacCormick, *Institutions of Law: An Essay in Legal Theory* (Oxford University Press, 2007), 149; P. Birks 'The Roman Law Concept of Dominium and the Idea of Absolute Ownership' [1985] Acta Jur. 1.
9 D. J. Carr, *Ideas of Equity* (Edinburgh: Avizandum, 2017), ch. 4.
10 *Sharp v. Thomson* 1997 S.C. (H.L.) 66. See Scottish Law Commission, *Report on Sharp v Thomson*, Report No. 208 (2007), 44 ff.
11 *Burnett's Trustee v. Grainger* 2000 S.L.T. (Sh. Ct.) 116, 124; 2004 S.C. (H.L.) 19; [2004] UKHL 8. See G. Gretton, 'Equitable Ownership in Scots Law' (2001) 5 Edin. L.R. 73, 80.
12 See N. R. Whitty, 'The "No Profit from Another's Fraud" Rule and the "Knowing Receipt" Muddle' (2013) 17 Edin. L.R. 37. See Carr, *Ideas of Equity*, ch. 5.

together in the same courts from the early modern period onwards. Later, a different dualism emerged which was more akin to that of English law in its terminology and theory, but which remained unitary in applying within the same courts. These two forms of dualism endured in legal thinking amongst judges and jurists. The result has been a rich though unsettled mixture of approaches to equity in general, which can be exemplified by examining discrete areas of private law to show how different understandings or ideas of equity have generated different results in the doctrinal law, and what implications those have had on the general development of equity in Scotland. The conclusion is that equity might be best described as being intertwined with strict law in Scotland.

HISTORY OF INTERTWINEMENT

Intellectually Separate?

Equity in Early Modern Scots Law

Medieval and early modern Scottish lawyers are familiar with contemporary Western European understandings of the concepts of equity and justice, often discussed alongside utility, as developed from the classical works of Greek and Roman antiquity.[13] In the period of the *jus commune* the Scottish lawyers' views are likely to have been the same as those of continental European jurists.[14] The different approach to equity taken in England flowed from jurisdictional differences, particularly the administration of equity in the separate Court of Chancery. In Scotland such separateness as there was did not result in an institutional separation of courts dealing with law and equity. Yet, while there was no court specifically and separately concerned with equity, there was certainly something called equity. Beyond the medieval and early modern period, the early development of the Institutional system is where reasoned discussions of equity were written down and promulgated for the first time. These written accounts of judges and jurists constitute formal sources of authority, and the earlier texts are clear examples of natural lawyers' works. One of the best known of those lawyers was James Dalrymple, Viscount Stair (1619–95), the Lord President of the Court of Session. Stair's *Institutions*

---

[13] See e.g., D. H. van Zyl, *Justice and Equity in Greek and Roman Legal Thought* (Pretoria: Academica, 1991); D. H. van Zyl, *Justice and Equity in Cicero* (Pretoria: Academica, 1991).
[14] Scots sought continental university education until the 'ancient' Scottish universities were founded: D. E. R. Watt, *A Bibliographical Dictionary of Scottish Graduates to A.D. 1410* (Oxford University Press, 1977).

of the Law of Scotland is an institutional work which follows an essentially, though somewhat altered, Romanist structure and title. Stair's approach to equity is to equate it with natural law.[15] Indeed, he is careful to note that equity does not merely ameliorate positive law; rather, it fills gaps in the law as well as suffusing the whole law:

> [F]or though mens Laws be profitable and necessar for the most part; yet being the Inventions of frail men, there occurs many *casus incogitati* wherein they serve not; But Equity takes place, and the Limitations and Fallancies, Extentions and Ampliations of Humane Laws are brought from Equity, and though Equity be taken sometimes for the moderation of the extremity of Humane Laws; yet it doth truly comprehend the whole Law of the Rational Nature, otherwise it could not possibly give remeid to the rigour, and extremity of positive Law in all Cases.[16]

Ironically, while the civilian component of the Scottish legal system is sometimes seen as a reason for downplaying equity, or at least a particular understanding of equity, the predominant view has been that civil law rules 'are only received according to their Equity and Expediency, *Secundum bonum & æquum*'.[17]

Kames's Evolutionary Dualism

Following Stair's natural law account, the next historical writer to discuss equity in Scotland at any length[18] was Henry Home, Lord Kames (1696–1782), who wrote a monograph entitled *Principles of Equity*. Kames's view of equity was of a system that allowed for the dynamic updating of the law to enable it to evolve and reflect societal change:

> In England, where the courts of equity and common law are distinct, the boundary betwixt equity and common law, where the legislature doth not interpose, will remain always the same. But in Scotland, and other countries where equity and common law are united in one court, the boundary varies imperceptibly. For what originally is a rule in equity, loses its character when, gathering strength by practice, it is considered as common law. Thus the *actio negotiorum gestorum*, retention, salvage, &c. are in Scotland scarce now considered as depending on principles of equity. But by the cultivation of

[15] Stair, *Institutions*, bk. I, tit. I, s. 6. Lord Bankton, an eighteenth century institutional writer, followed Stair: Bankton, *Institute*, vol. I, bk. I, tit. 1, s. 24.
[16] Stair, *Institutions*, bk. I., tit. I, s. 6.
[17] Ibid., s. 16. See further D. Hume, *Baron David Hume's Lectures 1786–1822*, ed. by G. C. H. Paton (Edinburgh: Stair Society, 1939), vol. I, 13.
[18] Other institutional writers address the matter similarly: Carr, *Ideas of Equity*, ch. 2.

society, and practice of law, nicer and nicer cases in equity being daily evolved, our notions of equity are preserved alive; and the additions made to that fund, supply what is withdrawn from it and transferred to common law.[19]

Equity, therefore, created new equitable rules which gradually hardened into common law by virtue of their usage across time.[20] Kames's approach is of particular interest because he specifically distinguishes between the common law and equity, perhaps owing to the greater legal connections between Scotland and England following the Union of 1707. Duality and separateness characterise the work: at its heart is his distinction between two kinds of law and the different considerations and values underpinning them.

The work has enjoyed an ambivalent reception.[21] There are those who consider it a work of high authority, while others consider it an idiosyncrasy.[22] Many deny that it has full institutional status, and hence is not an authoritative source of law. What may be stated with certainty is that despite Kames's dual approach there was no move towards separate courts to administer equity and common law – and Kames himself did not argue for such separate courts. The duality of equity and common law which had commenced with Stair's classic exposition of equity (as natural law) and positive law, was subsequently developed by Kames's discussion of equity and common law. Both were characterised by duality, and both could give similar substantive results, though they rested upon different foundations. When we turn to the modern law we see that both of these conceptions of equity have left imprints still seen in the law today.

Nineteenth Century: Positivism and Judicial Attitudes

By the nineteenth century, when developments in England, the British Empire and the United States were moving towards administering equity and common law in the same courts, the discussion of equity in Scotland

[19] Lord Kames (H. Home), *Principles of Equity*, 3rd edn (Edinburgh Legal Education Trust, [1778] 2013), vol. I, 27.

[20] Carr, *Ideas of Equity*, ch. 2; D. J. Carr, 'Introduction', in Kames, *Principles of Equity*, vol. 1, xxvii ff.

[21] See Carr, 'Introduction', in Kames, *Principles of Equity*, vol. 1, xxiv, xxxiii. Walker, who accepted much of Kames's view on equity, became ambivalent in later writings: D. M. Walker, 'Equity in Scots Law', in R. A. Newman (ed.), *Equity in the World's Legal Systems* (Brussels: Bruylant, 1973), 190–91.

[22] N. R. Whitty, 'Borrowing from English Equity and Minority Shareholders' Actions', in E. Reid and D. F. Carey Miller (eds), *A Mixed Legal System in Transition: T. B. Smith and The Progress of Scots Law* (Edinburgh University Press, 2005), vol. 1, 108.

by jurists becomes muted. No doubt this had much to do with the rise of positivist formalism, and the decline of natural law, as the dominant jurisprudence of the age. Unlike the jurists, however, the courts in Scotland continued to use 'equitable' reasoning in the nineteenth century. While deploying such reasoning, they also asserted that the Court of Session had two jurisdictions 'either as a Court of law or equity'.[23]

The Court of Session was not, by this time, the final court of appeal in civil matters: the House of Lords exercised final appellate jurisdiction. Speeches in the House of Lords often proceeded on the basis that the Court of Session was a 'court of equity and law', often to demonstrate that an English Chancery rule was equally applicable to Scotland or represented by a functional equivalent.[24] On occasion, the nature of the interaction between law and equity in Scotland was considered by the House of Lords, sometimes in the context of debates in England:

> My Lords, I entirely agree with the observations which have been made as to the laxity in the Court of Session with regard to their pleadings. It has arisen, in a great measure, I take it, from their allowing relevant and irrelevant defences, and also from the mixture of law and equity, which some persons seem so anxious to introduce in this country [England]. When they do so, I hope they will be kind enough to adopt some machinery which will prevent us from falling into the errors to which that combined system has led in Scotland.[25]

The judges of the House of Lords knew that there was no separate court in Scotland which was solely concerned with equity. Nevertheless, they often reasoned from a perspective of English law,[26] and they distinguished between law and equity in Scottish cases.

---

[23] *Cassels* v. *Lamb* (1885) 12 R. 722, 770.
[24] See *Forster* v. *Paterson* (1802) 4 Pat. 295, 302 (Lord Thurlow); *Stewart* v. *Agnew* (1823) 1 Shaw 413, 432 (Lord Eldon L.C.); *Albion Fire and Life Insurance Co.* v. *Mills* (1828) 3 W. & S. 218, 232 (Lord Lyndhurst L.C.); *Ewen* v. *Ewen's Trs* (1830) 4 W. & S. 346, 357 (Lord Wynford); *Hunter* v. *Cochrane* (1831) 5 W. & S. 639, 647 (Lord Brougham L.C.); *Napier* v. *Gordon* (1831) 5 W. & S. 745, 757 (Lord Brougham L.C.); *McMillan* v. *Campbell* (1834) 7 W. & S. 441, 451 (Lord Wynford); *Breadalbane* v. *Chandos* (1836) 2 Sh. & Macl. 377, 406 (Lord Cottenham L.C. in Chancery); *National Exchange Co. of Glasgow* v. *Drew & Dick* (1855) 2 Macq. 103, 148; 9 Sc. R.R. 551, 569 (Lord St Leonards); *Morgan* v. *Morris* (1855) 2 Macq. 342, 381 (Lord St Leonards (diss.)). In the report of *National Exchange Co. of Glasgow*, Macqueen noted: 'The Equity of the Court of Session is a Prætorian or Roman Equity. The technical Equity of England is confined to England.'
[25] *National Exchange Company of Glasgow* v. *Drew & Dick* (1855) 2 Macq. 103, 135; 9 Sc. R.R. 551, 564 (Lord St Leonards). Lord Brougham interjected, 'That is quite necessary': at 135.
[26] E.g., *Galbreath* v. *Armour* (1845) 4 Bell 374, 399.

Twentieth-Century Fluctuations

Subsequent case law has not always accepted the same duality. A well-known statement of the Lord President (Clyde) in the 1930s sums up the thinking of many modern Scottish lawyers:

> Owing to its peculiar history, the law of Scotland has never known either distinction or conflict between common law and the principles of equity. It is often said, and truly said, that in the law of Scotland law is equity, and equity law; and when a Scots lawyer uses the expression common law, he uses it in contradistinction to laws made by Parliament.[27]

This passage is sometimes cited as an encapsulation of the status and form of equity in Scotland,[28] though it is less often noted that the Lord President dissented on the question of the exercise of the *nobile officium*. The opinion of the Lord Justice-Clerk (Alness), who was in the majority, is different in tenor:

> The limits of the *nobile officium* are hard to define. No judicial definition of these limits has, so far as I know, ever been attempted. I do not essay that task now. But I bear in mind that Stair said long ago, in dealing with the topic, that, 'in new cases, there is necessity of new cures, which must be supplied by the Lords, who are authorised for that effect by the institution of the College of Justice' – IV. iii. 1. Again, More, in his Notes on Stair, after quoting the passage to which I have referred, and attributing to Lord Stair the view that 'in many instances the strict rules of law should be relieved by the equitable interposition of the judge', adds: 'Amid much that is uncertain as to the exercise of the *nobile officium*, this may be laid down as a fixed principle, – that it will never be exercised except in cases of necessity, *or very strong expediency*, and where the ordinary procedure would provide no remedy'. (Quoted in footnote to Erskine, I. iii. 22.) Erskine, in the paragraph which I have cited, states that the Court, as a Court of Equity, 'may and ought to proceed by the rules of conscience in abating the rigour of the law, and in giving aid in the actions brought before them to those who can have no remedy in a court of law'.[29]

These remarks seem to assume some duality, and are more positively disposed to the exercise of the *nobile officium* of the Court of Session when necessary. This selection of passages exemplifies the contested nature of equity in

---

[27] *Gibson's Trustees* 1933 S.C. 190, 198. For a contemporaneous view, see A. C. Black, 'The Institutional Writers 1600–1826', in H. McKechnie (ed.), *Introductory Survey of the Sources and Literature of Scots Law* (Edinburgh: Stair Society, 1936), 60.

[28] E.g., Whitty, 'Borrowing from English Equity', 102.

[29] *Gibson's Trustees* 1933 S.C. 190, 205. Lord Sands (at 211) went further, comparing the Court's powers of *nobile officium* with the powers of Parliament.

Scottish law – some judges and writers reason along intellectually dualist
lines, though none would deny that both systems of law are administered by
the Court of Session.

Other writers and judges have been concerned to assert the unity of equity
and law in Scotland and, essentially, that nothing much can be gained from
erecting a chimeric border between equity and common or positive law. Take
the following passage from a recent decision of the United Kingdom Supreme
Court concerning contractual penalty clauses:

> In Scotland, the courts administer an equitable as well as a common law
> jurisdiction without having two branches of jurisdiction. There is no free-
> standing equitable jurisdiction to render unenforceable as penalties stipula-
> tions operative as a result of events which do not entail a breach of contract.
> Such an innovation would, if desirable, require legislation.[30]

It is striking that the same debates recur periodically, and start from the same
points; and in some cases they allow for the development of Scottish law,
particularly by borrowing from English equitable concepts. Equity's role as a
means of legal development increases and decreases periodically. Kames's
evolutionary approach was partially halted in the nineteenth century, though
its fate in the twentieth century is less clear. Some jurists remain sceptical
about his theory,[31] while others accept the theory's historical accuracy[32]
though they deny that equity enjoys such rigour today.[33] As mentioned earlier,
the courts have been less reticent about their equitable powers. Another
opinion from the 1930s adopted a strong version of Kames's theory as a basis
for judicial action.[34]

Institutionally Fused

Development of the Court of Session's Equitable Jurisdiction
Having discussed ideas of substantive equity, it is useful to discuss the courts
which have administered equity in Scotland over the centuries. In the early

---

[30] *Cavendish Square Holdings B.V.* v. *Makdessi* [2016] A.C. 1172, [241]; [2015] UKSC 67 (Lord
Hodge J.S.C.); see also at [42] and *Gray* v. *Braid Group (Holdings) Ltd* 2016 S.L.T. 1003; [2016]
CSIH 68.
[31] Whitty, 'Borrowing from English Equity', 105–6.
[32] D. M. Walker, 'Equity in Scots Law' 1954 66 Jur. Rev. 103; T. B. Smith, *Short Commentary on
the Law of Scotland* (Edinburgh: Green & Son, 1962), 43.
[33] J. M. Thomson, 'The Role of Equity in Scots Law', in S. Goldstein (ed.), *Equity and
Contemporary Legal Developments* (Jerusalem: Sacher Institute, 1992), 923.
[34] *Gibson's Trustees* 1933 S.C. 190, 214–15 (Lord Sands).

modern period the foundation of the Court of Session, in 1532, marked an important institutional development in the administration of justice in Scotland.[35] The Court of Session was to be a centralised court, deciding cases from across the kingdom and staffed by permanent judges with legal training (often clergy in the early years). The immediate effect of this foundation was to create a professionalised institution to administer the law away from the other organs of state – though there was often overlap of personnel, and sometimes of competence. Two organs of the state especially are relevant when considering the equitable jurisdiction of the Court of Session: the Scottish Privy Council and the Scottish Parliament. The salient point is that the various instantiations of the Parliament had judicial powers which, in turn, had potential implications for the nature and role of the early Court of Session, and its use of equity.[36]

Privy Council

The Privy Council was the 'executive' in modern political parlance, though a considerable amount of its activity also involved the exercise of what can only be described as a judicial function.[37] The judicial function was a broad one which encompassed many types of dispute.[38] An important change brought about by the foundation of the Court of Session was the steady limiting of the Privy Council's judicial functions, particularly its jurisdiction of amelioration akin to that of the Chancellor in England. Eventually, the Privy Council's jurisdiction faded, and disappeared completely shortly after the Union of Scotland and England of 1707 when, in 1708, the Council was itself abolished.

Scottish Parliament

In the seventeenth century,[39] the role of Scottish Parliament as a judicial forum re-emerged, particularly in relation to the equitable powers of the Court

---

35 Previously, the administration of justice had centred on the Crown and then the Parliament of Scotland.

36 J. H. Burton (ed.), *The Register of the Privy Council of Scotland*, Vol. I, A.D. 1545–1569 (Edinburgh: H.M. General Register House, 1877), ix; C. Innes, *Lectures on Scotch Legal Antiquities* (Edinburgh: Edmonston and Douglas, 1872), 120.

37 See P. G. B. McNeill, 'The Jurisdiction of the Scottish Privy Council, 1532–1708' (Ph.D. Thesis, University of Glasgow, 1960), available: http://theses.gla.ac.uk/3029/1/1960McNeillPhD.pdf.

38 The English Privy Council had a similar role: J. P. Dawson, 'The Privy Council and Private Law in the Tudor and Stuart Periods' (1950) 48 Mich. L. Rev. 393, 419 ff.

39 The possibility was mentioned in a case of 1532: 'Gif ony man thinkis him heavilie hurt be the Lordis of Sessioun, in pronuncing of ane decreit aganis him, he may protest for remeid of law, and appeal to the parliament': *Cunynghame* v. *Vicar of N.* (18 January 1532), printed in P. G. B.

of Session. Litigants unhappy with determinations of the Court of Session sought the assistance of the Parliament in a process akin to an appeal known as seeking 'remeid of law'.[40] Despite uncertainty and disagreement about the competence and scope of such a procedure,[41] dissatisfaction with the determinations of the Court of Session was reflected by the inclusion in the Claim of Right 1689[42] (an important Scottish constitutional document) of the provision 'That it is the right and priviledge of the subjects to protest for remeed of law to the King and Parliament against Sentences pronounced by the lords of Sessione Provydeing the samen Do not stop Execution of these sentences'. As with the Privy Council, the Union of 1707 put an end to the uncertainty concerning the judicial role of Parliament with the rapid recognition of a right to appeal to the House of Lords of the Parliament of Great Britain.[43]

Implications for the Court of Session and Scots Law

What have these institutions to do with equity and equitable rules in Scotland's Court of Session, and what relevance to today's discussions of fusion? The demise of the judicial functions of the Privy Council and the Scottish Parliament was significant. It meant that two institutions which exercised gap-filling, novel, corrective and ameliorative functions that might be called equitable ceased to exist. The Court of Session became the undisputed main Scottish institution invested with authority over matters of equity in the law as well as its ordinary jurisdiction. To say that equity and law has always been united in the Court of Session is not incorrect, but it is important to be aware that different institutions of equal or greater prestige coexisted with it and exercised equitable jurisdictions at various points in its history.

Unlike in England, where the dichotomy endured, there was no institutional separation of forums in which to vindicate positive rights or claim equitable assistance. Nevertheless, an intellectual distinction was drawn between law and equity in the way that the Court of Session was, and still is, described as a court of law and equity:

McNeill (ed.), *The Practicks of Sir James Balfour of Pittendreich* (Edinburgh: Stair Society, 1962), vol. 1, 268. See I. Campbell, 'Preface', in Scotland, Court of Session, *The Acts of Sederunt of the Lords of Council and Session* (Edinburgh: Thomson and Co., 1811), xxxi.

[40] J. D. Ford, 'Protestations to Parliament for Remeid of Law' (2009) 88 Scott. Hist. Rev. 57.

[41] Stair, *Institutions*, bk. IV., tit. I, ss. 56–60; J. D. Ford, *Law and Opinion in Scotland During the Seventeenth Century* (Oxford: Hart, 2007), 437.

[42] c. 28 (Sc.).

[43] J. D. Ford, 'The Legal Provisions in the Act of Union' [2007] C.L.J. 106; R. Stevens, *Law and Politics: The House of Lords as a Judicial Body 1800–1976* (London: Weidenfeld & Nicolson, 1978), 6 ff.

The court of session is both a court of Law and Equity in one. Thus, where the party wants relief in equity, to which at common law he might seem not intitled, this court, in virtue of this mixed jurisdiction can give it ... There are infinite other cases where the court of session give relief in equity, when, in strict law, there seems to be none.[44]

The fact that equity and law were administered in the same court, the Court of Session, has meant that some Scottish lawyers might consider that there is no such thing as equity in the Scottish legal system or, to the extent that there is such a thing as equity, it is no different from any other type of law. Such thinking might explain statements like Lord Cooper's that '[w]ith us law and equity have never been separated, and equity has tended to predominate'.[45] At first blush this appears not to distinguish between equity and strict law, and that there is simply law. As we shall see, that is probably an imprecise, or at least incomplete, characterisation of the situation. The very fact that Lord Cooper stated that equity tended to predominate suggests that he considered there to be a conceptual distinction to be drawn between law and equity. It is more likely that Lord Cooper referred to the absence of courts of law and equity, though the remark about the predominance of equity does not fit easily into that rationalisation either.

Another reason to concentrate on Cooper's view of law and equity is the school of thought, or ideology,[46] concerning Scots law with which he is associated. Scottish law has been the subject of a debate (predominantly academic, sometimes judicial) about the nature of the legal system, which sources of law constitute its hierarchy of authority, and which foreign legal systems are closest to it in comity and potential usefulness. This occurs in most legal systems. Invariably, the Scottish discussion takes on elements of national identity, particularly the extent to which Scottish law is influenced by a Romanist-civilian tradition on the one hand, and an Anglo-centric common law tradition on the other. Indeed, as a result of such debates there has been a concerted self-identification of the Scottish legal system as a mixed legal system, a legal system which blends elements of the civilian and common law traditions.[47] The treatment of equity is a fault line within this mixed system, perceptions of which oscillate between an easily managed, barely

[44] Bankton, *Institute*, vol. II, bk. IV, tit. 7, s. 23.
[45] Lord Cooper of Culross, *Selected Papers 1922–1954* (Edinburgh: Oliver and Boyd, 1957), 124.
[46] I. D. Willock, 'The Scottish Legal Heritage Revisited', in J. P. Grant (ed.), *Independence and Devolution: The Legal Implications for Scotland* (Edinburgh: Green & Son Ltd, 1976), 1–2; H. L. MacQueen, 'Two Toms and an Ideology for Scots Law: T. B. Smith and Lord Cooper of Culross', in Reid and Carey Miller (eds), *A Mixed Legal System in Transition*, vol. I, 46.
[47] See the text at nn. 2–3.

noticed, hairline fracture and a yawning chasm. It may be added that much of the most recent debate about the true nature of equity in Scotland has been largely confined to academic writings, which, as it happens, is where equity tends to be discussed in civilian systems.[48]

Distinction between Equitable Institutional Procedure and Substantive Equity?

A distinction is often drawn between the ordinary equitable jurisdiction of the Court of Session, and the extraordinary equitable jurisdiction of the Court of Session known as the *nobile officium*.[49] The *nobile officium* is a predominantly procedural manifestation of equitable thinking, though the distinction between substantive and procedural equitable concepts in Scotland, as elsewhere, is not easily drawn. A classic description of the *nobile officium* is that of Bankton:

> Besides the *officium ordinarium*, or ordinary jurisdiction which the lords of session are vested with, there is competent to them what may be termed *Officium nobile*. This *nobile officium* is founded in their being a superior court, and as such, they are intitled, in some cases, to interpose, otherwise than according to the ordinary rules or forms of law, and even contrary to the form of ordinary proceedings, when the case requires it, in order to bring out the truth, which could not otherwise be done; or to interpose in points necessary for the public good of the society; of for making justice effectual in private cases, where the ordinary forms cannot reach the end ... This is a supereminent power, founded in their high jurisdiction, in order to the discovery of truth, and cannot be said only to proceed upon their equitable powers. Equity is a favourable construction of the law, and may be prayed by either party; but no party is intitled to demand, as his right, an examination *ex officio*; he may suggest it, but he cannot ask it as a point of right.[50]

Institutionally Fused, Intellectually Separate

The previous discussion demonstrates that although contested – there are those who dispute that there is any separation between law and equity at all – there is much evidence in the authorities of an intellectual distinction being

---

[48] G. M. Razi, 'Reflections on Equity in the Civil Law Systems' (1963) 13 Am. U. L. Rev. 24, 24.
[49] S. Thomson, *The Nobile Officium* (Edinburgh: Avizandum, 2015), ch. 1.
[50] Bankton, *Institute*, vol. II, bk. IV, tit. 7, s. 24. Bankton later says that the combination of the Court of Session's ordinary and extraordinary equitable powers give it the same powers as the English Court of Chancery: vol. II, bk. IV, tit. 7, 520 's. 4' (misnumbered).

drawn between equity and strict law. That poses deeper questions about what, exactly, is meant by that distinction and how it is manifested as, say, a distinction between substantive and adjectival law. The approach to that question has implications for the role of the lower courts and areas of doctrinal law which are said to be equitable. Of course, all commentators agree that, whether there is such an intellectual separation between equity and law or not, there is a unitary court structure as there is in England. Equity and law are fused so far as the forum hearing any cases is concerned.[51]

EXAMPLES OF EQUITABLE IDEAS IN DOCTRINE

Unjustified Enrichment

Following a period of some academic neglect, the law of unjustified enrichment in Scotland was subjected to renewed scrutiny in the 1990s following the publication of two articles by Peter Birks[52] and the first monograph on restitution (as he preferred to call it) by Stewart,[53] and as a result of events in England.[54] The fruits of this period of academic and judicial activity can be fairly described as the Scottish 'enrichment revolution'.[55] It was not, however, a juridical abiogenesis. In the three leading cases of the revolution – *Morgan Guaranty Trust Co. of New York v. Lothian Regional Council*,[56] *Shilliday v. Smith*[57] and *Dollar Land (Cumbernauld) Ltd v. C.I.N. Properties Ltd*[58] – the Scottish judiciary took a creative approach to the taxonomy of the law, which, in turn, stimulated the future development of the law. But when the courts invigorated these developments, they did so using existing terminology and ideas, including referring to the role of equity and to equitable considerations. In turn, the modern taxonomy created by judicial decisions invoking

---

51   W. G. Miller, *The Data of Jurisprudence* (Edinburgh: Green & Sons, 1903), 385–86.
52   P. Birks, 'Six Questions in Search of a Subject – Unjust Enrichment in a Crisis of Identity' 1985 Jur. Rev. 227; and P. Birks, 'Restitution: A View of Scots Law' [1985] C.L.P. 57.
53   W. J. Stewart, *The Law of Restitution in Scotland* (Edinburgh: Green, 1992). See P. Birks, *An Introduction to the Law of Restitution* (Oxford: Clarendon, 1985); R. Goff and G. Jones, *The Law of Restitution*, 4th edn (London: Sweet & Maxwell, 1993); P. Birks, *Unjust Enrichment*, 2nd edn (Oxford University Press, 2005); *Goff and Jones: Unjust Enrichment*, 9th edn.
54   Particularly, *Lipkin Gorman v. Karpnale Ltd* [1991] 2 A.C. 548; *Woolwich Equitable Building Society v. Inland Revenue Commissioners* [1993] A.C. 70; *Westdeutsche Landesbank Girozentrale v. Islington London Borough Council* [1996] A.C. 669; *Kleinwort Benson v. Lincoln City Council* [1999] 2 A.C. 349.
55   N. R. Whitty, 'The Scottish Enrichment Revolution' (2001) 6 S.L.P.Q. 167.
56   1995 S.C. 151.   57   1998 S.C. 725.   58   1998 S.C. (H.L.) 90.

an equitable basis moved towards a general enrichment action, which can be
understood as a third way between the extremes of some civilian and common
law models.[59]

The maxim *nemo debet locupletari ex aliena jactura* (no man should profit
from another's loss) was invoked frequently by judges in the revolution cases, and
it has been asserted repeatedly over centuries that this keystone maxim is an
equitable one.[60] This assertion of equitable status was, it seems, not merely a
jejune observation. The picture which emerges from the decisions is that this
equitable maxim is *the* normative underpinning of enrichment law – it repre-
sents the principle from which all aspects of enrichment law ultimately draw
their justification. Of course, while cited as a fundamental rationale, it has long
been recognised that the maxim is incapable of simple and direct application in
court, for it is too broad a formulation.[61] Further, and importantly from the
perspective of equitable creativity, it is not entirely clear from the revolution cases
what role the maxim is to play in developing enrichment law in the future, that is
to say, how is it to be used to recognise new grounds of enrichment liability.

Equity has, then, by virtue of its close association with the maxim *nemo
debet locupletari ex aliena jactura*, an apparent role at a foundational level
justifying the normative force of the law itself, but it has also an unsettled role
within an applied action for enrichment. An outstanding question is whether
the test to reverse an unjustified enrichment makes equity an ingredient of the
action or of the defence; in turn, it is not certain upon whom the burdens of
proof lie.[62] Must the pursuer in an action aver that it would be equitable to
order a return of the transfer, or is the invocation of equity to be satisfied by the
defender setting up the defence that to return something would be inequitable? Furthermore, if such is the position of equity in the new order, does this
equitable test rest latently within the nominate forms of action and defences,
or is it a ground which demands the action or defence take account of equity
in such a situation as a free-standing requirement? So, for example, if I wish to
defend an action for unjustified enrichment, would my satisfaction of the
ingredients of a change of position defence be enough in itself to demonstrate
inequity, or, would I have to, or have the option to, mount my defence upon
the potentially broader ground of inequity alone? Alternatively, can it be said
that because an action for enrichment envisages a lack of legal ground, this in

---

[59] See Carr, *Ideas of Equity*, ch. 3.
[60] See, for example, *Dollar Land (Cumbernauld) Ltd* v. *C.I.N. Properties Ltd* 1998 S.C. (H.L.)
    90, 98 (Lord Hope).
[61] Hume, *Baron David Hume's Lectures 1786–1822*, vol. III, 165–68; compare *Edinburgh and
    District Tramways Ltd* v. *Courtenay* 1909 S.C. 99, 105–6.
[62] See Carr, *Ideas of Equity*, ch. 3.

itself would satisfy the requirements of equity, or would the pursuer have to make specific averments concerning the equitable merits of the situation? There are, as yet, no clear answers to these questions, and the role of equity in this context could yet be substantial or expansive.

There are suggestions that the role of equity in this context is greater than may have been previously expected, and there are at least indications that the new judicially drawn doctrinal map provides for substantial judicial discretion in the form of this equitable requirement.[63] In turn, because Scots law would at least sometimes reason that equitable rights are awarded at the discretion of the court, it might be suggested that the new explanations of the doctrine of unjustified enrichment, specifically its equitable component, must be similarly discretionary. If so, it would represent a departure from some interpretations of the old 'Three Rs' structure: especially the requirement of restitution, which envisaged strict or absolute rights that were not necessarily subject to the discretion of the court.

Scottish law approaches equity in different ways, and the operation of equity in different areas has different objectives, forms and indeed results. In relation to enrichment law, the usage of the term 'equity' is without reference to English equity or chancery jurisprudence and its technical doctrines and rules. It is a home-grown conception and application of equity, ostensibly born of Roman law in a Latinate maxim, though made relevant by its mediation through the institutional heritage of Scottish law. The natural law treatises that take equity as the ingredient which imbues the law with normative force are the true crucibles of this idea of equity.

Cicero understood *nemo debet locupletari ex aliena jactura*, which has returned to prominence in Scotland, as positive law as well as natural law.[64] The resurrection of the maxim in Scotland is consistent with these approaches; the equity of Scottish enrichment law is equity as understood across different jurisdictions of the world. It is the idea of facilitating fair and just results without descending into an unregulated morass of absolute discretion; it is also the idea of giving a judge organised and regulated discretion to achieve a broadly just result.[65] It is not the technical equity of the English chancery, nor has it been

---

[63] See, for example, *Cullen* v. *Advocate General for Scotland* 2017 S.L.T. 1, [41]–[43]; [2016] CSOH 170.

[64] See Cicero, *De Officiis*, trans. by W. Miller (London: Heinemann, 1913), 3.5.21.22. See Cicero, *De Finibus Bonorum et Malorum*, trans. by H. Rackham (London: Heinemann, 1931), 3.21.70.

[65] See G. Del Vecchio, *General Principles of Law*, trans. by F. Forte (Boston University Press, 1956), 90–91.

used to absorb English equitable rules in the area.[66] However, this is but one of the approaches to equity in Scottish law, and it is to an area with more engagement with English equity that we now turn.

Trusts

Enrichment law in Scotland has an equitable dimension which it derives from the natural law heritage of the institutional writers. Yet, as noted earlier, the approach to equity in Scots law is not uniform, and the understanding and uses to which equity is put and expressed will vary with the terrain at hand: there are different ideas of equity. A different approach to equity from that of enrichment law was taken by the historical development of the law on trusts, though it seems to have rejected such equitable reasoning recently in favour of the 'patrimonial theory'.[67] This highlights a difference between Scottish and English law approaches in this area. While it is clear that English influences were brought to bear upon the Scottish law, the importance of equity has been minimised by subsequent rationalisations.

Stair's seventeenth century concept of the infant trust institution was based upon the nominate contracts of mandate and deposit.[68] The word 'trust' may have been borrowed from England, but it seems likely that the substantive institution itself relied more upon disparate existing Scottish instruments such as the nominate contracts.[69] For most of the seventeenth century the extent of borrowing from English equity, expressly at least, appears negligible. The nominate contract analysis was adopted and continued by subsequent writers, but it came to be supplanted by the erection of a distinct legal institution known as the trust. The distinctive trust took shape in the eighteenth century, and was refined in the nineteenth and twentieth centuries. Yet, it would be

---

[66] Similarly, see *Moses* v. *Macferlan* (1760) 2 Burr. 1005, 1012; W. Swain, '*Moses* v. *Macferlan* (1760)', in C. Mitchell and P. Mitchell (eds), *Landmark Cases in the Law of Restitution* (Oxford: Hart, 2006), ch. 2.

[67] See G. L. Gretton, 'Trust and Patrimony', in H. L. MacQueen (ed.), *Scots Law into the 21st Century: Essays in Honour of W. A. Wilson* (Edinburgh: Green/Sweet & Maxwell, 1996); K. G. C. Reid, 'Patrimony not Equity: The Trust in Scotland', in J. M. Milo and J. M. Smits (eds), *Trusts in Mixed Legal Systems* (Nijmegen: Ars Aequi Libri, 2001).

[68] Stair, *Institutions*, bk. I., tit. XII, s. 17 and bk. I., tit. XIII, s. 7. Similar things were occurring in some English writings of the time: see H. Ballow (attrib.), *A Treatise of Equity*, 2nd edn by J. Fonblanque (London: Butterworth, 1794), vol. 2, 1; W. Blackstone, *Commentaries on the Laws of England* (Oxford: Clarendon, 1768), vol. 3, 432.

[69] G. Gretton, 'Trusts', in K. Reid and R. Zimmermann (eds), *A History of Private Law in Scotland* (Oxford University Press, 2000), vol. 1, 486–91; T. B. Smith, *Studies Critical and Comparative* (Edinburgh: Green, 1962), 200–7.

wrong to say that the trust in Scotland developed purely by absorbing large swathes of English Chancery jurisprudence. The Scottish trust of the eighteenth century appears to have developed as a result of soft, almost functionalist, influence from England: it was becoming more commonly employed, possibly by analogy with England, but there is less evidence that the legal mechanisms constituting and regulating the trust instrument itself were being directly inspired by English law authorities and thinking.

Examination of the nineteenth-century approach to the trust demonstrates the increasing influence of English jurisprudence. By the same token, the distinctive character of the Scottish trust continues. It becomes more common to see references to English works on trust law, but the references to English authority often show that a similar result might be reached in Scotland in a different way. There is evidence that Scottish law continued with a contractual approach, though at times it seems to have moved away from the nominate contract approach to a general contractual theory or briefly flirted with the possibility of juristic personality.[70]

Problematic interactions between this native contractual theory, on the one hand, and understandings based upon English Chancery authority and ideas, on the other, began to emerge. The idea of an Anglo-centric dual ownership began to creep into the Scottish legal consciousness. A contributing factor was, no doubt, that Scottish law has a concept of equity: potential difficulty arose when that became a lightning rod through which alien conceptualisations of property from English equity were grounded within the apparently civilian Scottish property law.

In the twentieth century judges and lawyers appear to have perceived these different influences and property concepts as problematic and begun asserting the distinctive nature of Scottish trust law.[71] Judicial marks were set down at the highest level, though the content and doctrinal underpinning of the Scottish trust remained elusive. English equity authority continued to be freely cited. The modern patrimonial theory of trust law, developed by Gretton and Reid,[72] is now increasingly accepted as authoritative.[73] This theory, which draws heavily upon comparative civilian writings, conceives a trustee to have two separate patrimonies: the private and the trust patrimony. One of the apparent objectives of the patrimonial theory is to detach the

---

[70] See Carr, *Ideas of Equity*, ch. 4.

[71] *Camille & Henry Dreyfus Foundation* v. *Inland Revenue Commissioners* [1956] A.C. 39, 47–48 (Lord Normand); *Allan's Trustees* v. *Lord Advocate* 1971 S.C. (H.L.) 45, 53 (Lord Reid); this element of Lord Reid's speech was adopted in *Burnett's Trustees* v. *Grainger* 2004 S.C. (H.L.) 19, [44], [85]; [2004] UKHL 8.

[72] See the references in n. 67.   [73] See Carr, *Ideas of Equity*, [454]–[456].

Scottish trust from English equity jurisprudence so far as its fundamental basis
is concerned, while retaining the ability to make use of many English authorities on particular matters. The doctrinal significance of this change of
approach is the move away from theories of contract or property towards the
use of the law of persons as the organising principle. This new approach
purports to explain the trust without falling into the arms of equity, and allows
its proponents to tidy up such perceived incursions as English equitable
ownership theories had made, some of which threatened to denature the
wider system of property law.

   It is doubtful to what extent one could describe Scottish trust law as influenced by the Scottish variety of equity, yet the shared nomenclature of equity
in Scotland and England meant that aspects of English chancery equity were
being freely received at one time. The use of English reports and textbooks as
authority for a desired result entailed the proliferation of English equity
terminology. But with terminology and borrowed results often came substantive principles and instruments which apply those principles. So it was that the
Scottish trust provided passage, into the broader system of private law, for some
English rules and concepts under the seemingly shared banner of equity.[74]
These rules were in the process of being received, and were starting to exercise
substantive influence on the areas of law. The patrimonial theory's apparent
adoption would seem to restrict the role of English equity jurisprudence in
explaining the nature of the trust, without interfering with Scottish courts'
ability to adopt substantive rules of English law.

Undue Influence and Good Faith

A final example of how the place of equity in Scots law can be confused, and
provokes variable levels of borrowing from English law, can be seen in the
decision in Smith v. Bank of Scotland.[75] Shortly put, the decision concerns
'surety wives', though in Scotland they would be more accurately described as
'cautionary wives'. The facts were similar to those in Barclays Bank Plc
v. O'Brien,[76] which case could not be directly applied because Scots law did
not recognise the same equitable rules of constructive notice in the context of
undue influence. Nevertheless, as a matter of policy it was expressly stated that
the development of the English law achieved in O'Brien ought to be replicated,
somehow, in Scotland. It is perhaps telling that the House of Lords opted not to

---

[74] E.g., constructive trusts and fiduciaries duties: Carr, Ideas of Equity, chs 5 and 6.
[75] Smith v. Bank of Scotland 1997 S.C. (H.L.) 111.
[76] Barclays Bank Plc v. O'Brien [1994] 1 A.C. 180.

develop some form of Scottish equitable doctrine by analogy with English principles of equity; rather, the court decided that there was an obligation of good faith which governed the bank in the same way that constructive notice could be imputed in England. This was stark judicial legislation, though the effects of the decision have been welcomed as well as criticised.[77] An important element of the decision in *Smith* was that the House of Lords, introducing a novel rule which was designed to ameliorate recognised hardship flowing from a strict application of an existing rule, chose not to invoke equity or any form of 'equitable' reasoning in the Scottish setting.

Simple Fairness or Discretion?

Following on from the decision in *Smith* are questions concerning the proper understanding of equity in Scotland as a formal source of law. Some doubt or deny that equity is a formal source of law in Scotland at all.[78] The observations of an introductory text on jurisprudence encapsulate the basic ground of that scepticism:

> [E]quity is not a 'formal' source in the sense in which I have used that expression. It is simply a tendency to look to the spirit rather than to the letter of the law and to apply general ideas of what is fair rather than specific rules. In England it only becomes a formal source in so far as it may be embodied in a precedent or a statute[79]

Those sceptical about the nature of equity as a source of law are more likely to be sympathetic to an explanation of equity in Scotland which is closer to that of Allen:

> In many legal systems, therefore, a discretionary or moderating influence has been superadded to the rigour of formulated law. It has assumed different names at different times, but we may consider it under the general description of equity. It has exhibited itself in two principal forms: (1) a liberal and humane interpretation of law in general, so far as that is possible without actual antagonism to the law itself – this we may call *equity in general*; (2) a liberal and humane modification of the law in exceptional cases not coming within the ambit of the general rule – this we may call *particular equity*.[80]

---

77 Several cases have interpreted the decision: see S. Eden, 'Cautionary Tales – The Continued Development of *Smith* v. *Bank of Scotland*' (2003) 7 Edin. L.R. 107; S. Eden, 'More Cautionary Tales' (2004) 8 Edin. L.R. 276.

78 Whitty, 'Borrowing from English Equity', 105.

79 H. F. Jolowicz, *Lectures on Jurisprudence* (University of London Press, 1963), 262.

80 C. K. Allen, *Law in the Making*, 7th edn (Oxford: Clarendon, 1964), 385.

Discretion, fairness and a general equitable spirit are undoubtedly important components of equity as understood in Scotland. On that basis, some would prefer simply to say that, in relation to some areas of the law, the law contains scope for the exercise of judicial discretion through benign interpretation and the like in order to reach a fair result.[81] Further, it seems from the decision in *Smith* that the introduction of novel rules can be made under the broad language of good faith which, in other jurisdictions, might be a juridical concept or construct which is synonymous with concepts of fairness or equity. In that sense, one might argue that *Smith* can be understood as clear evidence that there is no intellectually separate substantive law of equity, and that the decision shows how a unified law is updated. Equally, it can be argued that the words good faith were simply a different label for the same phenomenon which can be labelled equity at other times. It is likely that Kames would have recognised such an innovation according to his developmental or evolutionary model.

CONCLUSION

Scotland has long recognised something called equity as a source of law within the legal system, though the crucial question is what exactly that means. Historically, that source of law has, in common with other jurisdictions, been considered to be intellectually distinct from strict or positive law; thus, a distinction was made between two different concepts of legal authority. Yet, Scotland differs from many other common law jurisdictions in that there was never a separate institutional apparatus of different courts to hear cases of equity.

Scotland's recognition of some distinction between law and equity, applied within a unified court structure, provides a potentially interesting comparator system for other common law jurisdictions. Scotland's long exposure to the law of England, not to mention similarly longstanding co-existence within a single sovereign state, has meant that the influence of English law upon that of Scotland has been marked. That influence has meant that many English law concepts have made their way into Scottish law, including sometimes controversial substantive rules and reasoning processes from Chancery jurisprudence. In turn, Scotland's law contains a number of different understandings of ideas of equity, some of which are more theoretically attuned to fusion or fission, respectively. Sometimes the distinction between

---

[81] See, for example, *Grahame* v. *Swan* (1882) 9 R. (H.L.) 91, 91–92; 7 App. Cas. 547, 557 (Lord Watson) and 96–97; 565 (Lord Selborne L.C.).

equity and strict law is drawn from English-inspired jurisprudence. At other times, the equitable law is rooted in deeper ideas of natural law.

In addition to these variants of equity within the substantive law, the manifestation of equity within the adjectival law and the court structure of Scotland is less often considered alongside the substantive law. It was noted earlier that a distinction is often drawn in the common law literature, particularly when discussing the Judicature Acts in England, or the Field code in the United Sates, between the fusion of substantive equity doctrines and their placement within one court system. A distinction with some similarities is drawn, in Scotland, between equity in the substantive law and equity as adjectival or procedure; as with other common law countries, that distinction can be soggy. In particular, it was noted that the Court of Session's ordinary equitable jurisdiction is sometimes contrasted with its extraordinary equitable jurisdiction, the *nobile officium*. But if Scots law is said to have equity, then it seems that it must be more than the procedural expedient of the *nobile officium*. That point is brought into sharper focus by the fact that only the Court of Session and High Court of Justiciary are said to have the inherent or super-eminent jurisdiction known as the *nobile officium*. If the sum of the equity jurisdiction in Scotland is the procedural authority of these two courts, then it follows that the lower courts such as the Sheriff court have no equitable jurisdiction, which seems incorrect. Indeed, such courts have jurisdiction to hear cases involving equitable forms of law, such as unjustified enrichment. That being so, if one accepts that the Court of Session has an ordinary equitable jurisdiction, as distinct from its extraordinary jurisdiction, then those areas of law which are amenable to that jurisdiction, and which are not subject to its privative jurisdiction,[82] are similarly equitable in other courts. In turn, it may be important when determining whether a lower court has discretion, latitude in interpretation, etc., to identify whether that area of law is equitable: once again suggesting an intellectual duality. It could be objected that this is mere labelling, but that is what a huge amount of law is about. While other terms might be used with greater precision, the term equity has a counter-advantage of greater potential content insofar as the term carries so many discrete connotations which can usefully contribute to the evolution and development of structured rules and discretion.

If, as I have suggested, there is a clear intellectual separation recognised within the authorities between two different forms of rules called equity and strict/common/positive law, then they are perhaps not as fused as some have

---

[82] An important and interesting example would be judicial review, which occupies very similar intellectual terrain to the private law 'equitable' part of the Court of Session's jurisdiction.

supposed. Indeed, it is hard to reconcile the presence of authoritative discussions of equity within the sources with an assertion that there is no intellectual separation at all. Put another way, it is hard to accept that the degree of fusion is such that there is simply only one unitary thing called 'law'. Still, it would be as difficult to argue that there is a hard separation of law of equity in Scotland that approaches fission, particularly when the historically unified court structure is taken into account. It is tentatively suggested here that it would be better to describe them as intertwined but nevertheless distinct threads of authority which contribute to the legal system.

Fusion and Fission in Doctrine and Practice

PART II

Fusion and Fission in Doctrine and Practice

9

Equity and the Common Counts

The Development of the Action for Money Had and Received

BEN KREMER

Lord Mansfield's judgment in *Moses* v. *Macferlan*[1] marks the point at which the common law acquired a coherent theoretical basis for the action for money had and received. There has long been contention over the extent to which that basis involves equity in its technical sense. To explore that subject, this chapter will consider the state of the action for money had and received leading up to the decision in *Moses*, and will then consider Mansfield's decision against it.

The debate originates from Mansfield's many somewhat ambiguous references to equity, conscience and natural justice in *Moses* and later cases. In *Moses*, he referred to the action for money had and received as '[t]his kind of equitable action, to recover back money'.[2] In *Dale* v. *Sollet*[3] he said '[t]he plaintiff can recover no more than he is in conscience and equity entitled to',[4] while in *Longchamp* v. *Kenny*[5] he said that 'the charge and defence in this kind of action, are both governed by the true equity and conscience of the case'.[6] In *Jestons* v. *Brooke*[7] he said, '[t]his is an action for money had and received; and therefore it is analogous to a bill in equity',[8] while in the abbreviated report of *Plumbe* v. *Carter*[9] he is reported to have said that the plaintiff (who sought to take 'a hard and unconscionable advantage' short of usury) 'should not be assisted in an action for money had and received, which is an equitable action, and founded in conscience under the particular circumstances of each case'.[10] In *Lindon* v. *Hooper*,[11] he described the action as 'a new experiment', where a defendant 'is liable only to refund what he has

---

[1] (1760) 2 Burr. 1005; *sub. nom. Moses* v. *Macpherlan* (1760) 1 W.Bl. 219. Burrow's report is superior; it is interesting to speculate how the law might have developed if Blackstone's report were the only one available.

[2] Ibid., 1012.   [3] (1767) 4 Burr. 2133.   [4] Ibid., 2134.   [5] (1779) 1 Dougl 137.
[6] Ibid., 138.   [7] (1778) 2 Cowp. 793.   [8] Ibid., 795.   [9] (1774) 1 Cowp. 116n.
[10] Ibid.   [11] (1776) 1 Cowp. 414.

actually received, contrary to conscience and equity'.[12] In *Sadler* v. *Evans*,[13] the Court of King's Bench, including Mansfield, said that money had and received 'is a liberal action, founded upon large principles of equity, where the defendant can not conscientiously hold the money. The defence is any equity that will rebut the action'.[14]

One view is that Mansfield imported considerations of actual (technical) equity into a common law action. In *Rogers* v. *Ingham*,[15] James L.J. said that:

> the law on the subject was exactly the same in the old Court of Chancery as in the old Courts of Common Law. There were no more equities affecting the conscience of the person receiving the money in the one Court than in the other Court, for the action for money had and received proceeded upon equitable considerations.[16]

Another view – stemming particularly from Mansfield's references in *Moses* to 'an obligation, from the ties of natural justice, to refund' and the action being 'as it were upon a contract ("quasi ex contractu", as the Roman law expresses it)' – is that he imported into the action Roman notions, or at least civilian notions of natural justice and equity, rather than true equity. In *Baylis* v. *Bishop of London*,[17] Farwell L.J. denied that equitable considerations were in play,[18] and instead took Mansfield to be drawing upon 'the jus naturale of Roman law'. A variation on that theme is that Mansfield meant equity and conscience in its loosest sense. Hanbury wrote that Mansfield 'crossed the all too narrow bridge which leads from the sound soil of implied contract to the shifting quicksands of natural equity – and equity in the mouth of a common lawyer is apt to mean equity in its ethical and somewhat nebulous sense'.[19]

Caught up in this are two related questions. Was Mansfield fusing law and equity in *Moses*? Is the action for money had and received a common law or an equitable action? The second question is not academic: statutes sometimes vest jurisdiction according to the relief sought, such that the characterisation of an action as equitable or as one at common law may mean the difference between a court having or lacking jurisdiction. An example is *Great-West Life & Annuity Ins. Co.* v. *Knudson*,[20] which will be discussed in this chapter. The classification may also affect procedure. In the United States, the Seventh Amendment preserves the right of trial by jury in 'Suits at common law, where

---

[12] Ibid., 419.   [13] (1766) 4 Burr. 1984.   [14] Ibid., 1986.   [15] (1876) 3 Ch.D. 351.
[16] Ibid., 355.   [17] [1913] 1 Ch. 127.
[18] 'It is further clear that the equity to which he was referring is not "an equity" in the sense in which it was used in the Court of Chancery': ibid., 137.
[19] H. G. Hanbury, 'The Recovery of Money' (1924) 40 L.Q.R. 31, 35.   [20] 534 U.S. 204 (2002).

the value in controversy shall exceed twenty dollars'. Given that the Seventh Amendment has not been indexed with inflation, characterisation of an action as being one 'at common law' usually determines whether a jury trial may be demanded.

Ultimately, the second question depends upon the first, which has never been conclusively answered. This chapter will attempt to show that Mansfield's new rationale for the action for money had and received did not involve the fusion of any legal doctrine, for the simple reason that there was no common law doctrine available to be fused. As is frequent in the common law, the action had developed as a grouping of cases that shared a common element (money getting into the defendant's hands which the plaintiff then claimed) but lacked any doctrinal underpinning. As a result, Mansfield needed to *create* a rationale for the action for money had and received in *Moses* because the novel and difficult facts required him to do so. Mansfield's exposition in *Moses* and later cases is inconsistent with the proposition that he drew upon, let alone fused, any propositions of substantive common law.

Although the new rationale drew very heavily on equity and equitable notions, Mansfield did not intend it to be equitable in the strict sense. Nor, despite Mansfield's references to Roman law, did he intend it to have a civilian character. Rather, the rationale was to be sui generis; Mansfield drew upon equitable substance and civilian nomenclature and pedigree to fashion a new, basal principle to rationalise an unstructured and somewhat disorganised area of the common law. This peculiar creation was one that Mansfield was well (and perhaps uniquely) placed to synthesise. The result was very much an action at common law, but one whose determinant invoked principles analogous to those found in technical equity.

It is instructive to examine what Mansfield was doing and the context in which he was acting when deciding *Moses*. For reasons of space, two important aspects of that context – Mansfield's academic background and his practice at the bar – will not be considered. It suffices to note that by the time he came to decide *Moses*, Mansfield was learned and experienced in equity, the common law, civilian law and Roman law.[21]

---

[21] J. Oldham, *The Mansfield Manuscripts* (Chapel Hill, NC: University of North Carolina Press, 1992); B. R. Kremer, 'The Action for Money Had and Received' (2001) 17 J.C.L. 93; J. Oldham, *English Common Law in the Age of Mansfield* (Chapel Hill, NC: University of North Carolina Press, 2004), ch. 1; B. R. Kremer, 'Lord Mansfield', in J. T. Gleeson, J. A. Watson and E. Peden (eds), *Historical Foundations of Australian Law* (Sydney: Federation Press, 2013), vol. 2, ch. 10.

THE ACTION FOR MONEY HAD AND RECEIVED
PRIOR TO *MOSES V. MACFERLAN*

The landscape of the common law regarding private obligations in 1760 reflected the change wrought by an interloper, the action for assumpsit. The development of assumpsit from cases of misfeasance of a promise to non-feasance of a promise, and its usurpation of debt following *Slade's Case*,[22] is well known.[23]

Of present interest is the development of indebitatus assumpsit, within which the action for money had and received arose. In a claim for indebitatus assumpsit the plaintiff's declaration stated that the consideration of the promise to pay that was sued upon was an indebtedness of the defendant to the plaintiff. Being indebted in a sum certain to the plaintiff the defendant promised to pay that sum, which promise had not been performed.[24]

Although use of the indebitatus count preceded *Slade's Case*,[25] it became widely used thereafter for a number of reasons. The removal of the need to prove a later express promise to pay[26] removed a forensic hurdle to a plaintiff. Unlike in an action for debt, a defendant in assumpsit could not 'wage his law',[27] and actually had to meet the claim on the facts through a trial by jury, rather than being able to defeat a claim in debt by the corroborating oaths of eleven compurgators.[28] Additionally, the procedure of pleading assumpsits more easily allowed a plaintiff to bring about surprise at trial, by concealing the full nature of the case that the defendant had to meet.[29] Once freed from the requirement to prove a subsequent promise to pay, indebitatus assumpsit was significantly more favourable to plaintiffs than debt. Just as water finds the

---

[22] (1594) 4 Co. Rep. 91.

[23] E.g., J. H. Baker, 'New Light on Slade's Case' (two parts) [1971] C.L.J. 51 and 213; H. K. Lücke, 'Slade's Case and the Origin of the Common Counts (Part 3)' (1966) 82 L.Q.R. 81; D. J. Ibbetson, 'Sixteenth Century Contract Law: Slade's Case in Context' (1984) 4 O.J.L.S. 295.

[24] Baker, 'New Light on Slade's Case (Part II)', 214; D. J. Ibbetson, 'Assumpsit and Debt in the Early Sixteenth Century: The Origins of the Indebitatus Count' [1982] C.L.J. 142, 142.

[25] J. B. Ames, 'The History of Assumpsit' (1888) 2 Harv. L. Rev. 1, 16.

[26] H. K. Lücke, 'Slade's Case and the Origin of the Common Counts' (1965) 81 L.Q.R. 422, 428–29; I. Jackman, *The Varieties of Restitution*, 2nd edn (Sydney: Federation Press, 2017), 25.

[27] W. Blackstone, *Commentaries on the Laws of England* (Oxford: Clarendon, 1768), vol. 3, 341–45.

[28] The contemporary perception of the benefit of a jury trial is evident from the Seventh Amendment to the United States Constitution (1791).

[29] E.g., *Rables v. Sikes* (1670) 2 Keb. 711. The eventual remedy was reform via the Hilary Term Rules of 1834: W. S. Holdsworth, 'The New Rules of Pleading of the Hilary Term, 1834' [1921] C.L.J. 261; *Young v. Queensland Trustees Ltd* (1956) 99 C.L.R. 560, 563–5; *Scott v. Davis* (2000) 204 C.L.R. 333, [181]–[183]; [2000] HCA 52.

lowest ground, artful pleaders then, as now, gravitated towards causes of action that offered forensic advantages at trial.[30]

There needed to be an underlying debt to bring an indebitatus assumpsit,[31] and a demonstration of how it had arisen. However, by the start of the seventeenth century this did not require 'any degree of specificity'.[32] The detail indispensable in a declaration for debt was not needed in a declaration for assumpsit.[33] In addition to stating the existence of the debt and its (certain) amount, the plaintiff needed only to allege the general nature of the indebtedness, and any circumstance alleged to give rise to a debt could be relied upon for an indebitatus assumpsit:[34] such as that the defendant had received money from others ('de divers psons') to the use of ('al use le pl') the plaintiff;[35] or that it arose from goods the plaintiff had sold him ('for divers wares before receiv'd'),[36] or money lent to him ('for the payment of mony lent unto him'),[37] or money paid at his request ('for certain sums of money at the instance of the defendant paid to J. Anyas for the debt of the defendant'),[38] or work done at his request ('at the . . . request of' the defendant),[39] or upon an account stated[40] or upon a combination thereof.[41] The common counts arose from the frequency of use of such words. As Mansfield was later to observe, the relative liberality allowed to a pleader was quite unlike other actions at common law. Indeed, Holt C.J. is said to have observed that the first pleader who used this method must have been a bold man.[42]

While the common counts began as a result of standardising pleadings to avoid defects that might arise from employing a novel verbal formula, in the way of the common law their use became canalised. They became true alternatives to a plain indebitatus assumpsit count, even though they remained sub-species of indebitatus assumpsit. This permitted the common counts to develop unique features and substance, and to expand beyond their original

---

[30] E.g., to invoke section 52 of the Trade Practices Act 1974 (Cth), allowing full recovery if the contravening conduct was only *a* cause of damage, where recovery in contract or tort would be unavailable or would be reducible for contributory fault: *I. & L. Securities* v. *H.T.W. Valuers (Central Qld) Pty Ltd* (2002) 210 C.L.R. 109; [2002] HCA 41.

[31] Otherwise the plaintiff must bring an action of special assumpsit.

[32] Ibbetson, *Historical Introduction*, 148. See e.g., *Bellinger* v. *Gardiner* (1614) 1 Rolle 24.

[33] Lücke, 'Slade's Case (Part 2)', 551.   [34] *Case of the Marshalsea* (1612) 10 Co. Rep. 68b, 77a.

[35] *Babington* v. *Lambert* (1616) Moo. 854.

[36] *Rock* v. *Rock* (1610) Yelv. 175 (*sub. nom. Rooke* v. *Rooke* (1610) Cro. Jac. 245).

[37] *Davenport* v. *Wood* (1616) 3 Bulst 259.   [38] *Rock* v. *Rock* (1610) Yelv. 175.

[39] *Tate* v. *Lewen* (1671) 2 Wms Saund. 372.   [40] *Sibbord* v. *Quin* (1721) 11 Mod. 344.

[41] *Rooke* v. *Rooke* (1610) Cro. Jac. 245. See Ames, 'History of Assumpsit (Part 2)' (1888) 2 Harv. L. Rev. 53, 57.

[42] Lücke, 'Slade's Case (Part 2)', 551.

bounds. Of all the common counts, this expansion was most extensive and dramatic for money had and received. The development of that action and the judgment in *Moses* can best be seen against the backdrop of perhaps the most frequently used and important of the other common counts: money paid, money lent, quantum meruit and quantum valebant.[43] The former two counts showed little in the way of expansion. The latter two showed significantly more, though neither grew anywhere near as much as the action for money had and received.

Money Paid and Money Lent

From early on, an indebitatus assumpsit lay to recover money lent and repayable upon request,[44] money that had been promised to be paid[45] and money laid out at the request of the defendant,[46] though not where a debt was claimed due on an open or running account. The proper remedy there was the action for account.[47]

Despite the commonality of the claims being for debts or their equivalent,[48] one here sees the fault lines between areas of obligations that have persisted to the present day – respectively, the action for money lent (as an alternative to debt), breach of contract (of loan), the payment of money to a third party that would unjustly enrich the defendant if not recouped and the action for account. One also sees antecedents of modern defences to recovery, and exceptions: as in more modern cases,[49] minority was a defence to an action for money lent but not where the loan was made for the purchase of necessaries.[50]

The first and third of these claims became formalised as the common counts for money lent and money paid, and remained closest to the original core of the indebitatus assumpsit as an action upon a debt. They required specific positive action by the defendant in order to lie: receipt of a loan of money *qua* loan, and a request for payment to a third party made by the

---

43   Other counts, such as for work and materials, interest or account stated, cannot be discussed here. The common counts were somewhat codified: Common Law Procedure Act 1852 (U.K.), 15 & 16 Vict. c. 76, s. 91, Sch. B.

44   *Davenport v. Wood* (1616) 3 Bulst. 259; *Luxon v. Corbin* (1684–86) 2 Show. K.B. 466.

45   *Conye v. Lawes* (1655) Sty. 472.   46   *Rock v. Rock* (1610) Yelv. 175.

47   *Willis v. Bond* (1651) Sty. 260.   48   E.g., Ames, 'The History of Assumpsit (Part I)', 2.

49   E.g., *Nash v. Inman* [1908] 2 K.B. 1; *Stocks v. Wilson* [1913] 2 K.B. 235; and legislative reforms: Minors' (Property and Contracts) Act 1970 (N.S.W.), s. 20 and Minors' Contracts Act 1987 (N.S.W.), s. 3(1).

50   *Ellis v. Ellis* (1698) Comb. 482.

defendant of the plaintiff. As a result, they were not particularly susceptible to doctrinal expansion.

The action for money lent has remained essentially within its original bounds[51] and has not attracted controversy of note, other than for its substance. It was early recognised that pleading the *request* for the loan 'was mere form and was not traversable', that liability both upon the common count and in debt itself arose instantly upon a loan of money payable on request (with attendant potential limitations problems) and that stark procedural differences arose depending on whether the defendant denied the loan or pleaded repayment.[52] Similarly, in the action for money paid at the request of another, then as now the relevant request to pay can be express or be inferred from the facts – but it must exist.[53]

Quantum Meruit and Quantum Valebant

Claims for what became formalised as the quantum meruit and quantum valebant are more interesting. The availability of indebitatus assumpsit was essential to their development: no claim in debt would lie in the absence of a fixed price (as the amount claimed would not be a sum certain); no claim in assumpsit would arise without an express promise; and no account would lie as the plaintiff and defendant were not within a category of relationship raising a duty to account.[54]

The indebitatus action for these counts originally arose from the implication by law of a true contract; the value of the contract was determined by the jury in a reasonable amount upon the evidence. In the *Six Carpenters' Case*,[55] the plaintiff failed in an action for trespass against the defendants, who had ordered and consumed but not paid for the bread and wine he had supplied. The court discussed what actions would have been open to the plaintiff:

> if I bring cloth to a tailor, to have a gown made, if the price be not agreed in certain before, how much I shall pay for the making, he shall not have an action of debt against me; which is meant of a general action of debt: but the tailor in such a case shall have a special action of debt: *scil.* that A. did put

---

[51] E.g., *Shannon v. Lee Chun* (1912) 15 C.L.R. 257.

[52] *Young v. Queensland Trustees Ltd* (1956) 99 C.L.R. 560, 566–67. A defendant who admitted a debt had the onus to prove repayment but the right to begin at the trial. Repayment was a plea in confession and avoidance.

[53] *Progressive Pod Properties Pty Ltd v. A. & M. Green Investments Pty Ltd* [2012] NSWCA 225.

[54] C. H. S. Fifoot, *History and Sources of Common Law: Tort and Contract* (London: Stevens and Sons, 1949), 360.

[55] (1610) 8 Co. Rep. 146b.

cloth to him to make a gown thereof for the said A. and that A. would pay him as much for making, and all necessaries thereto, as he should deserve, and that for making thereof, and all necessaries thereto, he deserves so much, for which he brings his action of debt: in that case, the putting of his cloth to the tailor to be made into a gown, is sufficient evidence to prove the said special contract, for the law implies it: and if the tailor over-values the making, or the necessaries to it, the jury may mitigate it, and the plaintiff shall recover so much as they shall find, and shall be barred for the residue.[56]

The basis on which the contract was implied by law was that, absent prior agreement or special circumstances, no customer of a tailor or of a public house would expect to receive the tailor's services or wine and food for free. In a public house, there was an 'implied promise' on the part of a guest 'that he will pay all duties and charges, which he caused in the house'.[57]

The early development of the action involved extending the categories of cases in which the relationship between the plaintiff and defendant allowed a contract to be implied for supply in exchange for a reasonable amount on such reasoning. Several points of interest exist.

First, during the early seventeenth century the action expanded to rest upon an implied *obligation* to pay a reasonable sum, rather than upon a true implied *contract*. This was the natural course of recognising that the claim ought not to be limited to categories in which the plaintiff performed the services in a recognised category of common callings, and should lie in respect of any services and goods supplied on request where the services or goods were clearly to be provided for remuneration.[58] As Ibbetson has recognised, this involved an almost imperceptible slide from having either an actual or implied agreement between the parties, to an implied obligation to pay – located in a fictional agreement – where no true agreement could be implied (for example, because the subject matter or key terms of such a contract were not agreed or were too uncertain).[59]

Secondly, the action became differentiated from an indebitatus assumpsit. It became a separate claim which, initially, could lie and, later, could only lie for a sum to be computed rather than a sum certain.[60] This change appears to have derived from assumpsit cases where the actual agreement was to pay a

---

[56] *Six Carpenters' Case* (1610) 8 Co. Rep. 146b, 147a, paraphrasing *Anon.* (1473) Y.B. 12 Ed. IV f. 9b.
[57] *Warbrook* v. *Griffin* (1609) 2 Brownl. 254, 255.
[58] E.g., *Young* v. *Rudd* (1695) 1 Ld Raym. 60; 5 Mod. 86; *Platt* v. *Hill* (1698) 1 Ld Raym. 381.
[59] Ibbetson, *Historical Introduction*, 270–71.
[60] See *Webber* v. *Tivill* (1669) 2 Wms Saund. 121 n. 2 (note by Williams in 1833 edition).

reasonable amount, rather than a fixed price.[61] By the mid-eighteenth century the quantum meruit had become a true alternative to indebitatus assumpsit. Plaintiffs commonly brought both claims in the alternative: an indebitatus claim for a fixed sum, and a quantum meruit for a reasonable sum to be determined by the jury.[62] By the late seventeenth century procedural differences had emerged between plain indebitatus assumpsit claims and claims for a quantum meruit, such as the effect of payment of money into court upon counts in the declaration.[63]

Third is the development of the quantum meruit claim in the context of the then-developing law of contract. A quantum meruit was, for example, held to lie where a defendant had requested work but had countermanded performance before it was complete. Although the plaintiff could not recover the complete sum promised (not having performed all of the work), the plaintiff could recover for so much of the requested work as had been performed.[64]

Fourthly, the late separation of the quantum meruit from what became known as quantum valebant is notable.[65] Originally, the indebitatus action appeared not to distinguish between whether the supply was of goods or services. Early treatises on pleading distinguished between a quantum meruit, an indebitatus assumpsit and a quantum valerent (seemingly, the more common description for a quantum valebant in the seventeenth century).[66] But it is still common to see claims in the late seventeenth and early eighteenth century for indebitatus 'for goods sold'[67] or for 'goods and services provided',[68] as well as claims for a quantum meruit for the supply of goods. Examples are claims 'upon a *quantum meruit*, for wares sold';[69] claims in both

---

[61] J. B. Ames, 'Assumpsit for Use and Occupation' (1889) 2 Harv. L. Rev. 377, 379–80.

[62] Fifoot, *History and Sources*, 361–63. The practice was not invariable. Some claims were still brought only as indebitatus assumpsit: e.g., *Hart v. Langfitt* (1702) 2 Ld Raym. 841.

[63] Payment into court entitled a regular indebitatus claim to be struck out of the declaration, but not a count of quantum meruit: *Anon.* (1686) Comb. 20; *Williams v. Cary* (1694) Comb. 264.

[64] *Howe v. Beeche* (1685) 3 Lev. 244.

[65] The quantum valebant may have emerged from the formula used in pleading a quantum meruit: see *Bowyer v. Lenthal* (1688) 3 Mod. 190, an unsuccessful case of error where the point taken by the unsuccessful defendant was that the plaintiff had used the form of words 'quantum rationabiliter *valerent*' instead of '*valebant*'. 'Rationabiliter valeret' and 'rationabilie valerent' ('reasonably worth') were words used in pleading texts beforehand (e.g., W. Brown, *Formulae benè Placitandi* (London: Place, Place and Basset, 1671), 14) and afterwards (e.g., R. Gardiner, *Instructor Clericalis*, 3rdedn (London: Bever, 1700), 169)).

[66] Gardiner, *Instructor Clericalis*, 3rd edn, 168–69.

[67] *Vanhatton v. Morse* (1702) 2 Ld Raym. 787; *Price v. Torrington* (1703) 2 Ld Raym. 873.

[68] *Case v. Barber* (1681) T. Raym. 450.

[69] *Jemy v. Norrice* (1670) 1 Mod. 295. Similarly *Boult v. Harris* (1675) 3 Keb. 469.

indebitatus assumpsit 'for goods sold and delivered by the plaintiff to the defendant'[70] and also 'upon a quantum meruit'[71]; and claims for 'a quantum meruit for goods, &c. sold and delivered'.[72] Such cases were also brought using other terminology. Usually, this was disclosed in actions in error to set aside verdicts or to arrest judgment because of a questionable choice of language.[73]

Quantum valebant (as the name of the action for the reasonable value of goods) was not clearly used in contradistinction to quantum meruit (for the reasonable value of services rendered) outside pleading books until about the middle of the eighteenth century.[74] It appears to have come into regular use following the writings of Blackstone, who styled it in the singular 'quantum valebat',[75] and Buller, who styled it in the plural 'quantum valebant'.[76]

Fifthly, the quantum meruit and quantum valebant from their inception required a request by the defendant of the plaintiff for the goods or services, regardless of the terminology. The failure to appreciate the existence of this requirement led to the ahistorical creation of 'free acceptance'. In hindsight, it can be seen that this occurred by taking the term 'unjust enrichment' as a descriptor of a principle said to have underlain the common counts; treating the term as generating liability; identifying a thought situation where someone could be thought to be 'unjustly' 'enriched'; and then asserting that that situation should generate a cause of action and sit alongside previously recognised fact situations on the basis of asserted 'coherence' or 'uniformity'. The High Court of Australia addressed this error in *Lumbers* v. *W. Cook Builders Pty Ltd (in liq.)*,[77] as Jackman has observed.[78]

---

[70] *Clapcott* v. *Davy* (1698) 1 Ld Raym. 611.

[71] *Turner* v. *Beale* (1706) 2 Ld Raym. 1262; *Mayne* v. *Harvey* (1725) 2 Ld Raym. 1383 ('in ... quantum meruit').

[72] *Winford* v. *Powell* (1712) 2 Ld Raym. 1310.

[73] A motion in arrest of judgment that the claim ought to have been 'meruerit' because 'meruit' was 'the praeterperfect tense, and denotes the time past, and consequently could be nothing' was dismissed in *Moverly* v. *Lee* (1706) 2 Ld Raym. 1223; 2 Salk. 558. See also *Clerk* v. *Udall* (1702) 2 Ld Raym. 835 ('such sums, as the plaintiff rationabiliter hebere mereretur').

[74] E.g., *Gardner* v. *Jessop* (1757) 2 Wils. K.B. 42.

[75] Blackstone, *Commentaries*, vol. 3, 16; Blackstone, *Tracts: Chiefly Relating to the Antiquities and Laws of England*, 3rd edn (Oxford: Clarendon, 1771), 84.

[76] F. Buller, *An Introduction to the Law Relative to Trials at Nisi Prius* (London: Bathurst, 1772), 126.

[77] (2008) 232 C.L.R. 635; [2008] HCA 27. Unfortunately, the High Court did not consider the thought experiment set out in F. C. Woodward, *The Law of Quasi Contracts* (Boston, MA: Little, Brown and Co., 1913), 93, which is on all fours but reaches a different result.

[78] Jackman, *Varieties of Restitution*, 2nd edn, 7.

Money Had and Received

Most interesting is the development of what eventually became the action for money had and received to the plaintiff's use. The words 'to (or for) the use of' have an ancient legal pedigree meaning 'on behalf of' or 'for the benefit of'.[79] The language of money being 'received to the use of' a plaintiff began to be used in the thirteenth century in the action for account. Where A delivered money to B for the use of C, C would have an action in account against B for that money (if A delivered goods, then C's action against B was in detinue, as title passed to C).[80]

Importantly, C's action was initially only in account and not in debt; debt only became available alongside account in the sixteenth century.[81] When, a century later, *Slade's Case* meant that assumpsit lay alongside the debt, it was possible to bring indebitatus assumpsit as an alternative to account. The procedural advantages of assumpsit over debt have been noted earlier. The advantage over account was that it avoided the slow and cumbersome dual steps needed: the action to establish liability to account, and then the action on the account. Inevitably, just as assumpsit swallowed debt, it – along with account in equity – swallowed account at common law. However, the use of the terminology and conception of the words 'to the use of', and the progression from account to debt to assumpsit which allowed the action to lie, support Ames's statement: 'the action of account is father of the count for money had and received'.[82]

From the beginning, these indebitatus assumpsit claims were brought where the plaintiff claimed sums of money in the defendant's hands that had not arrived there via loan, and they grew organically. The action lay by a payer of money against a person to whom he paid it 'to lay out to a particular use', where it had not been so applied[83]; by a payer of money against a promisor to whom he had paid it when the promisor refused to perform the services promised;[84] by a judgment creditor against a bailiff or sheriff who had received money while executing against the judgment debtor[85]; against a

---

[79] N. G. Jones, 'Uses, Trusts, and a Path to Privity' [1997] C.L.J. 175, 176.

[80] J. B. Ames, *Lectures on Legal History* (Cambridge, MA: Harvard University Press, 1913), 117–18.

[81] K. D'Anvers, *A General Abridgment of the Common Law* (London: Walthoe, 1705), vol. I, 27; Ames, *Lectures*, 118–20.

[82] Ames, *Lectures*, 121. Holdsworth agreed: J. A. Watson, *The Duty to Account* (Sydney: Federation Press, 2016), 166.

[83] *Hartup v. Wardlove* (1682) 2 Show. K.B. 301.   [84] *Holmes v. Hall* (1704) 6 Mod. 161.

[85] *Jones v. Morley* (1697) Comb. 429; *Speake v. Richards* (1683) 2 Show. K.B. 281.

stakeholder who held the stakes for a wager[86] (although not by the winner directly against the loser, which required an action on the promise itself[87]); by the owner of a house against the recipient of rents from its letting[88]; by the true holders of offices against interlopers for payments they had received[89]; and by the beneficiary of a policy of insurance for the premium paid on a void policy, even where the premium was paid by another for his benefit.[90]

By the mid- to late seventeenth century, 'the use of' had become formulaic words,[91] and pleading books described the action as indebitatus assumpsit 'for Money had and received' by the defendant.[92] Plaintiffs in their declarations, and reporters in their reports, typically used abbreviations and phrases such as 'habit. et recept.',[93] 'money received to the plaintiff's use',[94] and money 'had and received for the plaintiff's use' or 'to his use'.[95] Claims for money had and received were often pleaded in the alternative to indebitatus assumpsit and, sometimes, also money paid, money lent and account stated.[96]

When assessing how the action for money had and received stood at the time *Moses* was decided, a number of important points emerge.

First, the action for money had and received was conceptually distinct from the other common counts. There was no need for the request by the defendant, or the supply by the plaintiff pursuant to that request, that was needed for claims for money paid, quantum meruit and quantum valebant. There was no need that the money should have moved from the plaintiff, as in money paid or money lent, although that was sometimes the case. And there was no need for there to be an accounting relationship, let alone an account stated.

Secondly, the common law developed in an autochthonous form of self-organisation via the use of terminology, with an accretion of cases that shared the common element of money getting into the defendant's hands that was

---

[86] *Anon.* (1695) Holt K.B. 754; Comb. 340.

[87] *Smith* v. *Ayrey* (1704) 2 Ld Raym. 1034; contrast [*Anon.*] v. *Sterne* (1679) 2 Show. K.B. 82, where the action lay.

[88] *Asser* v. *Wilks* (1708) Holt K.B. 36; *sub. nom. Asher* v. *Wallis* (1708) 11 Mod. 146; *sub. nom. Hasser* v. *Wallis* (1708) 1 Salk. 28.

[89] *Howard* v. *Wood* (1677) 2 Show. K.B. 21; *Woodward* v. *Foxe* (1690) 3 Lev. 289.

[90] *Martin* v. *Sitwell* (1691) 1 Show. K.B. 156.

[91] *Harris* v. *Ferrand* (1655) Hardr. 36; *Bucknall* v. *Swinnock* (1669) 1 Mod. 7; *Woodward* v. *Aston* (1676) 2 Mod. 95; *Sheldon* v. *Clipsham* (1681) T. Raym. 449.

[92] R. Gardiner, *Instructor Clericalis* (London: Bever, 1693), 182–83, and, the 7th edn (London: Stephens, 1727), 429, 432. In some earlier cases the action was described interchangeably as for money 'received and had': *Webber* v. *Tivill* (1669) 2 Wms Saund. 124.

[93] *Every* v. *Carter* (1690) 2 Vent. 254; *Neath* v. *Reeves* (1693) Skin. 386.

[94] *Willet* v. *Tiddy* (1691) 12 Mod. 6; *Holmes* v. *Hall* (1704) 6 Mod. 161.

[95] *Harcourt* v. *Fox* (1693) 1 Show. K.B. 426; *Asser* v. *Wilks* (1708) Holt K.B. 36; 11 Mod. 146.

[96] *Every* v. *Carter* (1690) 2 Vent. 254.

then claimed by the plaintiff.[97] However, as the cases were reported, until shortly before *Moses* there was relatively little in the way of generalisation beyond the case at hand to assist future cases. The known illustrations are few and brief. For example, a 1684 case in King's Bench set down that 'A. promises B. that when A. receives 100l. which C. owes A. that he will pay B. 20l. [I]ndebitatus assumpsit lies not; otherwise if the money had been originally the money of B'.[98]

A decade later, in a case that today would be analysed as a total failure of consideration, the plaintiff sought to recover £9 that he had paid to the defendant bailiff 'to be excused from fines for non-appearance at Court, and from the offices of constable and scavenger'.[99] The plaintiff had been fined despite the payment. Unsurprisingly, Holt C.J. dismissed the action on the basis that, while an indebitatus would lie 'where a man is over-reach'd', upon an account, &c and pays more than is due', 'that is as far as it ought to go', and he 'would discourage such foolish bargains as this'.[100] When counsel replied that '[i]t hath been resolved, that if A pays money to B for the use of C and B fails to pay it over, either A or C may bring an indebitatus', Holt C.J. is reported to have agreed, but denied that that was the present case.[101]

In *Asher v. Wallis*,[102] in response to submissions for the plaintiff that 'there is no need of a contract to maintain an indebitatus assumpsit; for where money is over-paid, this action will lie for the surplus … If rents are received by false tokens, either account or indebitatus assumpsit lies', Holt C.J. is reported to have cited a case 'where if money be over-paid, either *debt* or *indebitatus assumpsit* lies', and said '[i]f two lay a wager, and stake down the money, the winner shall have an *indebitatus assumpsit* against him that holds the stakes, as for money received to his use'.[103]

In *Holmes v. Hall*,[104] another example of what would now be analysed as a total failure of consideration, Holt C.J. said that '[i]f A. give money to B. to pay to C. upon C.'s giving writings, &c. and C. will not do it, an *indebitatus* will lie for A. against B. for so much money received to his use', but that 'these cases of *indebitatus* for money received to use have been carried too far, and no body would more willingly check them than I would'.[105] In *Astley v. Reynolds*,[106] Page J. observed that 'where an attorney delivers a bill, and the client pays it; yet if the client was overcharged, he shall recover the

---

[97] The unusual lenience in *Palmer* v. *Stavely* (1701) 1 Ld Raym. 669; 1 Com. 116 allowed recovery on a claim pleaded as for money received by the defendant 'to the use of the defendant'.
[98] *Anon*. (1684) Skin. 196.   [99] *Anon*. (1695) Comb. 341.   [100] Ibid. See n. 115.   [101] Ibid.
[102] (1708) 11 Mod. 146.   [103] Ibid.   [104] (1704) 6 Mod. 161.
[105] *Holmes* v. *Hall* (1704) 6 Mod. 161.   [106] (1731) 2 Barn. K.B. 40.

overplus-money in an indebitatus assumpsit, though he did not apply to have the bill taxed'.[107]

As can be seen, and as Allsop C.J. has recognised,[108] the tenor of the reported cases up until the death of Sir John Holt in 1710 reflected Holt's strong desire to limit the action for money had and received.[109] It is unsurprising that the action did not expand as it otherwise might have.

The first comprehensive statement of the bounds of the action appears to have come in Exchequer in *A.-G.* v. *Perry*,[110] a case decided only a couple of decades before *Moses*. The defendant had paid duty for tobacco he had imported from Virginia. He sold the tobacco to Corbet 'for exportation to Cadiz in Spain', and loaded it onto Corbet's nominated ship, after which the Crown, on account of the goods being exported, made out two debentures to drawback (repay) the defendant the amount of duty he had paid. However, without the defendant's knowledge, Corbet instead landed the tobacco in Ireland and sold it there. The Crown, having discovered this some eight years later (well after Corbet had absconded), brought an action to recover the repaid duty from the defendant, 'for so much money received by the defendant for His late Majesty's use'. The barons held, by majority, that the landing of the goods in Ireland made the debentures 'void', and:

> That the payment of the money to the defendant by the King's officers upon this void debenture renders the defendant answerable to the King for the money by him received; for whoever receives the King's money, without warrant or lawful authority, is accountable to the King for it. . . .

> And this is not from any peculiar prerogative the Crown hath above a subject, for the case would be the same with regard to a common person; *whenever a man receives money belonging to another without any reason, authority or consideration, an action lies against the receiver as for money received to the other's use;* and this, as well where the money is received through mistake under colour, and upon an apprehension, though a mistaken apprehension of having a good authority to receive it, as where it is received by imposition, fraud or deceit in the receiver (for there is always an imposition and deceit upon him that pays, where it is paid) by colour of a void warrant or authority, although the receiver be innocent of it.[111]

The barons then referred to cases in which the action lay: by the true executor against a person appointed by the administrator of an estate who collected

[107] Ibid., 42.
[108] J. L. B. Allsop, 'Restitution: Some Historical Remarks' (2016) 90 A.L.J. 561, 567–68.
[109] *Anon.* (1695) Comb. 341; *Anon.* (1697) Comb. 447.   [110] (1734) 2 Com. 481.
[111] Ibid., 490–91 (emphasis added).

debts and effects before discovery of the deceased's will, which rendered the appointment of the administrator void[112]; by the insurer of a ship who had wrongly paid out upon mistaken news that the ship had been lost[113]; by a landlord against the recipient of rents who lacked authority to receive them[114]; and (less clearly) by a borrower to recover usurious though not legal interest.[115] These were cases which Mansfield also later rationalised, including in *Moses* itself.

Thirdly, and importantly, while the previous summaries provide some exposition of factual situations in which the action might or might not lie, none of them provides any deeper explanation. That is, none purports to expose any principle of underlying operation that provides the basis for why the action lies, or that allows its present operation to be evaluated or its future operation predicted: they show *when* but not *why*, and, importantly, do not afford criteria for identifying new fact situations in which the action will lie. Indeed, in the case of the delinquent bailiff noted earlier, Holt C.J. is not reported to have adverted to the obvious illegality, which would have been a far more principled basis for refusing relief.

In *Lamine* v. *Dorrell*,[116] although protesting about how 'these actions have crept in by degrees', Holt C.J. allowed an action for money had and received for the proceeds of debentures that the defendant had sold after wrongfully becoming administrator of an estate, saying he 'could not see how it differed from an indebitatus assumpsit for the profits of an office by a rightful officer against a wrongful, as money had and received by the wrongful officer to the use of the rightful'.[117] That statement invoked and brought the case within the usurped offices cases such as *Howard* v. *Wood*,[118] where it was argued for the plaintiff that indebitatus assumpsit lay 'because it is his money, and he has a right to it; and by construction of law the defendant received it to his use'.[119] However, the statement alone was the extent of the reasoning.

The statement in *Attorney-General* v. *Perry*[120] of *when* the action would lie is extremely close to that in *Moses* itself. Yet the barons did not expressly justify *why* it lay. The words 'without any reason, authority or consideration' are pregnant with the concepts of conscience and the right to retain that Mansfield employed. Nevertheless, they do not express its rationale, and it seems

---

[112] *Jacob* v. *Allen* (1703) 1 Salk. 27.   [113] *Martin* v. *Sitwell* (1691) 1 Show. K.B. 156.
[114] *Hasser* v. *Wallis* (1708) 1 Salk. 28.
[115] *Tomkins* v. *Bernet* (1694) 1 Salk. 22; *sub. nom. Tomkyns* v. *Barnet* (1694) Skin. 411 and *Barnet* v. *Tompkins* (1694) Holt K.B. 740.
[116] (1705) 2 Ld Raym. 1216.   [117] Ibid., 1217.   [118] (1677) 2 Show. K.B. 21.   [119] Ibid., 22.
[120] (1734) 2 Com. 481.

unlikely that one existed. There does not seem to be a trace in the reports, or in such literature as there was, before *Moses*.

Fourthly, it is notable in hindsight that a number of the earlier decisions concerning claims for money had and received were harsh, and were overruled by decisions of Mansfield's. The broad statement of Holt C.J. in *Tomkyns* v. *Barnet*[121] that the action would not lie to recover money paid on a usurious contract was not followed in *Clarke* v. *Shee*,[122] where Mansfield said in argument '[t]hat case has been denied a thousand times'.[123]

In *Dewbery* v. *Chapman*,[124] the defendant took the plaintiff's son apprentice and was paid £30 'to teach him the trade of a goldsmith, and make him free of London (the defendant himself being a foreigner)', but '[i]t was ruled by Holt, that an indebitatus lieth not, the defendant hath cheated the plaintiff of his money, and the plaintiff hath no remedy, unless by special action of the case for not making him a freeman'.[125] Considered as a case of fraud, that holding did not survive *Clarke* v. *Shee*. In *Wilkinson* v. *Kitchin*,[126] the plaintiff paid the defendant sums to bribe a grand jury to release the plaintiff from charges. The bribes were paid, and the plaintiff recovered them from the defendant. That case did not survive *Holman* v. *Johnson*.[127]

Fifthly, despite the expansion of the action to cover cases where no express or implied contract existed, one still sees numerous affirmations that the action was limited to money and money's worth.[128] From the earliest pleading books, the declaration included an allegation that the money received was legal English tender ('legalis monete Anglie'),[129] just as was required in a declaration on an account, for money paid and money lent, for a quantum meruit, for a quantum valerent or for goods sold. This was no trivial aspect, as without it the action would fail. In *Dickson* v. *Willows*,[130] the defendant took an unsuccessful objection to a pleading on the basis that it declared for nine guineas. It was disallowed on the basis that guineas were money's worth. 'Our law takes conusance of guineas, and they are current for 20s.', provided that guinea coins 'have the King's Stamp'.[131]

---

[121] Salkeld 21 says 'coram Treby', which seems erroneous: Skin. 411; Holt K.B. 740.
[122] (1774) 1 Cowp. 197; *sub. nom. Clarke* v. *Johnson* (1774) Lofft 756. Former United States President John Adams noted up that remark in his copy of Cowper's report, now held by the Boston Public Library.
[123] Ibid., 199.   [124] (1695) Comb. 341.   [125] Ibid.   [126] (1696) 1 Ld Raym. 89.
[127] (1775) 1 Cowp. 341.
[128] Satisfaction received by the defendant was money's worth: *Norris* v. *Napper* (1704) 2 Ld Raym. 1007.
[129] E.g., Brown, *Formulae benè Placitandi* (1671), 77; Gardiner, *Instructor Clericalis*, 3rd edn, 164, 166, 169, 171 (misprinted as '117').
[130] (1695) Comb. 387.   [131] Ibid., 388.

Similarly, in *Bennett v. Verdun*[132] the successful plaintiff declared that the defendant was indebted to him 'in 28*l.* of money Hispaniolae'. In moving for error, the defendant's counsel argued that the plaintiff should have failed, '[f]or the defendant cannot be indebted in foreign coin[,] no more than in hogs'.[133] The objection failed, but the court, presumably Holt C.J., made clear the necessity for money or money's worth, saying that 'a man may be indebted in hogs, &c. but in such case the action must be brought in the detinet only'.[134] The court refused error because a verdict had been obtained, but afterwards (in true common law style) arrested judgment on the basis that the plaintiff had joined in the one count monies due to himself in his personal capacity with monies due to him as an executor only.

In sum: by the time *Moses* was decided, indebitatus assumpsit – particularly money had and received – was the proper form of action for 'a mass of miscellaneous duties imposed by law"[135] which involved payment or detention of money or money's worth, but had no clear direction, and often produced unfair results.

Moses *v.* Macferlan

The legal difficulty posed by the facts in *Moses* must be understood in order to appreciate Mansfield's judgment.

Moses had originally owed Macferlan £26, which he did not pay. Macferlan sued in a collection action and the claim went to arbitration, where Moses agreed to pay Macferlan £20 and endorsed (i.e., assigned) him four 30s. promissory notes (i.e., totalling £6) made out to Moses by one Jacob. Prior to the endorsement, upon Moses protesting that he could still be liable to Macferlan on the notes,[136] Macferlan assured him 'that such his indorsement should be of no prejudice to him', and an indemnity agreement was drawn up in which it was agreed 'that Moses should not be liable to the payment of the money or any part of it; and that he should not be prejudiced, or be put to any costs, or any way suffer, by reason of such his indorsement'.[137]

---

[132] (1702) 2 Ld Raym. 841.   [133] Ibid.   [134] Ibid.
[135] Allsop, 'Restitution: Some Historical Remarks', 568.
[136] An endorser of a promissory note was liable in the event of non-payment by the drawer.
[137] (1760) 2 Burr. 1005; 1 W.Bl. 219.

Macferlan presumably could not recover from Jacob, whereupon – contrary to his assurance and the agreement – he sued Moses in the Court of Conscience[138] on a separate summons for each of the four notes. Gummow J. has observed that Moses could (and probably should) have sought an injunction against Macferlan to prevent him from continuing the action in the face of their written agreement but did not do so.[139] Instead he tried to rely upon the agreement itself at trial. The Court of Conscience refused to accept evidence of the indemnity agreement, either from the document itself or from witnesses to its execution, and found against Moses upon the bare fact of his endorsement of the notes. Although only one of the four decrees was pronounced, Moses's solicitor paid the £6 into the Court of Conscience, upon which Macferlan drew it out by order of the Commissioners.

Moses then brought proceedings in the King's Bench against Macferlan for the £6 as money had and received – thus collaterally attacking the verdict of the Court of Conscience, an inferior court of competent jurisdiction. At nisi prius, the jury delivered a verdict for Moses for the £6 subject to the opinion of the Court, reserved by Mansfield, 'whether the money could be recovered in the present form of action, or whether it must be recovered by an action brought upon the special agreement only'.[140]

Blackstone's report records that in argument Mansfield 'doubted if the action would lie, after a judgment in the Court of Conscience; but wished to extend this remedial action as far as might be: to which Dennison J. agreed'.[141] He also reported that 'Foster J. was afraid of the consequences of overhauling the judgment of a Court of competent jurisdiction',[142] while Wilmot J. was concerned about inconsistent verdicts being rendered.[143] In addition to that issue, Burrow's report also records Macferlan's counsel – in support of setting aside the verdict and entering a non-suit – objecting that indebitatus assumpsit 'will never lie, but where the debt will lie', and that debt did not lie because it only lay where there was a contract, express or implied, broken and that no such contract existed.[144]

Mansfield delivered the unanimous reserved judgment of the Court in Moses's favour. He first rejected the proposition that indebitatus assumpsit would only lie where debt would lie, observing that 'an action of assumpsit will lie in many cases where debt lies, and in many where it does not lie'.[145]

---

[138] A court of request constituted by the Small Debts, Middlesex Act 1750 (U.K.), 23 Geo. II, c. 33: see Blackstone, *Commentaries*, vol. 3, 80–82; W. H. D. Winder, 'The Courts of Requests' (1936) 52 L.Q.R. 369.

[139] W. M. C. Gummow, '*Moses* v. *Macferlan*: 250 Years On' (2010) 84 A.L.J. 756.

[140] 2 Burr. 1006.   [141] 1 W.Bl. 219, 219.   [142] Ibid., 219–20.   [143] Ibid., 220.

[144] 2 Burr. 1006.   [145] Ibid., 1008.

Next, he rejected the proposition that an assumpsit would only lie upon an express or implied contract: although it was clear that no *contract* could be presumed pursuant to which Moses was entitled to recover money obtained from him by adverse suit, nevertheless 'the law implies a debt' where 'the defendant be under an obligation, from the ties of natural justice, to refund'.[146] Crucially, Mansfield located this as follows:

> the law implies a debt, and gives this action, founded in the equity of the plaintiff's case, *as it were upon a contract* ('quasi ex contractu,' as the Roman law expresses it).

> This species of assumpsit, ('for money had and received to the plaintiff's use,') lies in numberless instances, for money the defendant has received from a third person; which he claims title to, in opposition to the plaintiff's right; and which he had, by law, authority to receive from such third person.[147]

Mansfield expanded upon this in respect of the third objection to Moses's verdict, that where 'money has been recovered by the judgment of a Court having competent jurisdiction, the matter can never be brought over again by a new action'.[148] This is important, for it really raises two issues. One is the issue of public policy in preventing inconsistent verdicts between courts and preventing collateral attacks in one court upon decisions of another court within its jurisdiction.

The second is, for present purposes, more important, though little noticed since[149]: the facts in *Moses* fell outside the previously recognised categories. Moses had paid the money not under mistake or by way of overpayment, but pursuant to decrees of a court (in one case actual, and in the remaining three, apprehended) adjudging a dispute within its jurisdiction. Although it might be possible to try to stretch the concept of duress to fit the facts, this cannot be done sensibly or in a principled manner as there was no element of duress *from Macferlan*. The source of the obligation on Moses to pay was the court's decree, and to hold that there was duress sufficient to impugn the payment in *Moses* would mean that any losing defendant could similarly claim duress over judgment sums they had to pay.

Both of these points were dealt with by Mansfield in a manner that made new law. In reasoning redolent of that commonly employed in equity, Mansfield distinguished between (on the one hand) impeaching the lower court's judgment and (on the other hand) affirming the judgment but recognising that it

---

[146] Ibid.   [147] Ibid., 1008–09 (emphasis added).   [148] Ibid., 1009.
[149] An exception is Gummow, 'Moses v. Macferlan', 757. See also S. Kiefel, 'Lessons From a "Conversation" about Restitution' (2014) 88 A.L.J. 176.

was being used to generate an inequitable outcome. Not only was the King's Bench not setting aside or reversing the judgment of the Court of Conscience (indeed, it could not do so), but 'it admits the commissioners did right'.[150] Mansfield thereby approbated the judgment but made clear that because it was obtained without taking evidence of the indemnity agreement, it was iniquitous for Macferlan to rely upon the (valid) judgment to retain the £6.

> *The ground of this action is not, 'that the judgment was wrong:'* but, 'that, (for a reason which the now plaintiff could not avail himself of against that judgment,) the defendant ought not in justice to keep the money.' ... Money may be recovered by a right and legal judgment; and *yet the iniquity of keeping that money may be manifest,* upon grounds which could not be used by way of defence against the judgment.[151]

The determinant of Moses's claim was Macferlan's inequitable use of the actions in the Court of Conscience and the Court's orders, divined against the backdrop of the indemnity agreement that Macferlan had deliberately broken and that Moses had been denied the ability to adduce. This is quintessentially equitable reasoning (inequitable or unconscientious use of a legal right), and it does not lean upon any of the existing categories in which the action for money had and received had previously been recognised to have lain, including duress.

In what followed, Mansfield set out the advantages accruing from the procedural fluidity of the action:

> One great benefit, which arises to suitors from the nature of this action, is, that the plaintiff needs not state the special circumstances from which he concludes 'that, ex aequo & bono, the money received by the defendant, ought to be deemed as belonging to him:' *he may declare generally, 'that the money was received to his use;' and make out his case, at the trial.*
>
> This is equally beneficial to the defendant. It is the most favourable way in which he can be sued: he can be liable no further than the money he has received; and against that, *may go into every equitable defence, upon the general issue; he may claim every equitable allowance; he may prove a release without pleading it; in short, he may defend himself by every thing which shews that the plaintiff, ex aequo & bono, is not intitled to the whole of his demand, or to any part of it.*[152]

Here, Mansfield for the first time provides the rationale for the action for money had and received. It depends upon the plaintiff establishing that the defendant is not – according to notions of fairness and good conscience

---

[150] 2 Burr. 1009.   [151] Ibid. (emphasis added).   [152] Ibid., 1010.

('ex aequo et bono') – entitled to keep the money received, and that the defendant can retain so much as he can establish an 'equitable allowance' (clearly, along the same notions and not technical 'equity'), release or other defence showing the plaintiff 'is not entitled to' the whole or part of the demand.

After referring to *Dutch* v. *Warren*,[153] Mansfield continued:

> The Court said, that the extending those actions *depends on the notion of fraud*. If one man takes another's money to do a thing, and refuses to do it; *it is a fraud*: and it is at the election of the party injured, either to affirm the agreement, by bringing an action for the non-performance of it; or to *disaffirm the agreement ab initio, by reason of the fraud, and bring an action for money had and received to his use*.

> The damages recovered in that case, shew the liberality with which this kind of action is considered: for though the defendant received from the plaintiff 262*l.* 10*s.* yet the difference money only, 175*l.*, was retained by him against conscience: and therefore the plaintiff, ex aequo et bono, ought to recover no more; agreeable to the rule of the Roman law – *'Quod condictio indebiti non datur ultra, quam locupletior factus est, qui accepit.'*[154]

The equitable language is unmistakeable, in particular the use of the word 'fraud' in terms that only make sense if they bear the meaning of fraud in equity. Mansfield is clearly locating the determinant of the action – the plaintiff's claim to the money and the defendant's right to retain it – in notions of good conscience drawn from the same source as Chancery. He puts this beyond doubt in the subsequent passage: '*The notion of fraud* holds much more strongly in the present case, than in that: for here it is express. The indorsement, which enabled the defendant to recover, *was got by fraud and falsehood, for one purpose, and abused to another.*'[155] In other words, conduct that would amount to fraud in equity would suffice to make a defendant's retention of money against conscience for the purposes of an action for money had and received, but not all instances of retention against good conscience need to rise to that level.

Finally, in perhaps the most widely cited passage of the judgment, Mansfield said:

> *This kind of equitable action*, to recover back money, which ought not in justice to be kept, is very beneficial, and therefore much encouraged. It lies only for money which, ex aequo et bono, the defendant ought to refund: it does not lie for money paid by the plaintiff, which is claimed of him as payable in point of honor and honesty, although it could not have been

---

[153] (1720) 1 Stra. 406.   [154] 2 Burr. 1011 (emphasis added).   [155] Ibid., 1012 (emphasis added).

recovered from him by any course of law; as in payment of a debt barred by the Statute of Limitations, or contracted during his infancy, or to the extent of principal and legal interest upon an usurious contract, or, for money fairly lost at play: because in all these cases, *the defendant may retain it with a safe conscience*, though by positive law he was barred from recovering. But it lies for money paid by mistake; or upon a consideration which happens to fail; or for money got through imposition, (express, or implied;) or extortion; or oppression; or an undue advantage taken of the plaintiff's situation, contrary to laws made for the protection of persons under those circumstances.

In one word, the gist of this kind of action is, that the defendant, upon the circumstances of the case, *is obliged by the ties of natural justice and equity* to refund the money.[156]

A number of points are evident. First, when Mansfield refers to money had and received as '[t]his *kind of* equitable action', he is not saying it *is* technical equity, but that it is *like* it. The reason is that it is rooted in the same notions of fairness, conscience, 'natural justice and equity' as are actual actions in equity. They spring from the same source, and have the same underlying notion: what is against conscience. Keener captured this elegantly when considering the defence of change of position, referring to the need not to lose sight of 'the grounds upon which a recovery is allowed – namely, that the defendant has money which in conscience he cannot keep'.[157]

Secondly, Mansfield's use of Roman law rises no higher than terminology. His use of the phrase 'ex aequo et bono' imports only its general usage of 'in fairness and good conscience': a term often employed in the context of arbitrations, and used even in the statute setting up the very Court of Conscience in which Macferlan had prevailed.[158] The phrase was known to any competent civilian, Roman or common lawyer and captures only a concept. Mansfield used it without purporting to bring in substantive aspects of civilian or Roman law.[159]

Equally, so far as Mansfield refers to the action being 'as it were upon a contract ("quasi ex contractu," as the Roman law expresses it)', he is again using the concept captured in the Roman term, but no more. He explains why

---

[156] Ibid., 1012.
[157] W. A. Keener, *A Treatise on the Law of Quasi-Contracts* (New York, NY: Baker, Voorhis and Co., 1893), 67.
[158] By 23 Geo. 2 c. 33, s. 1, the Court in Middlesex was empowered to make such orders or decrees as shall seem to a majority 'to be just and agreeable to Equity and good Conscience', but this was not technical equity: Winder, 'The Courts of Requests', 389.
[159] 'The "natural justice and equity" considerations are analogous to the considerations of "equity" or "what is good and fair" of the *condictio causa data*': J. Edelman, 'The New Doctrine of Partial Failure of Consideration' (1997) 15 Aust. Bar Rev. 229, 231.

the common law implies the debt necessary to be sued upon: because the law 'gives this action, founded in the equity of the plaintiff's case' *as if* the action were upon a contract, though it is not upon a contract. Mansfield was not the first to employ this terminology. The notion of an indebitatus obligation being 'quasi ex contractu' had been deployed, if infrequently, in judgments and recorded argument for at least a century before *Moses*.[160] However, those suggestions seem to have lain unexplored until Mansfield placed them front and centre in *Moses*.

Additionally, when referring to *Dutch* v. *Warren*, Mansfield stated that the result available in an action for money had and received was '*agreeable to* the rule of the Roman law', not that it was governed by it. Nor could it be. The Latin maxim roughly translates as 'the condictio is awarded to the extent of the defendant's enrichment'; that is, the amount that he had no right to retain.[161] So employed, it is not a generative principle.[162] The fact that the Exchequer had previously taken a similar view to Mansfield as to the bounds of the action without any reference to Roman law, but with extensive reference to English authorities as they then stood, only adds to the conclusion that Mansfield was neither motivated to import, nor did import, the substance of Roman law into English law in *Moses* v. *Macferlan*.[163]

Thirdly, Mansfield's conception of the action employs equitable notions but is not an equitable action; and it applies a concept similar to one found in civil law, but is not a civilian action. The action for money had and received could not be said to be a truly equitable action because, at the time *Moses* was decided, courts of equity did not habitually grant monetary remedies. Nor did they grant relief in all circumstances where an action for money had and received might lie. As Story observed, courts of equity asserted jurisdiction over payments made by mistake, but this arose from equity's historic concern with mistake generally, and was not limited to payments.[164] There was an incidental overlap between mistake (one instance of which was a payment

---

[160] *City of London* v. *Goree* (1676) 3 Keb. 684; *Arris* v. *Stukeley* (1677) 2 Mod. 260, 262; *Boson* v. *Sandford* (1686) Carth. 58, 62.

[161] Burrow noted (2 Burr. 1011) that Mansfield employed the wrong maxim. The defendant in *Dutch* v. *Warren* was not ordered to repay the full amount of the consideration, only the value to which the shares had dropped by the time of the suit. The jury awarded the amount recoverable using modern day breach of contact reasoning rather than the amount recoverable on a total failure of consideration (for which the action was brought).

[162] J. Story, *Commentaries on Equity Jurisprudence*, 2nd edn (Boston, MA: Little and Brown, 1839), vol. 2, 502.

[163] See P. B. H. Birks, 'English and Roman Learning in Moses v. Macferlan' (1984) C.L.P. 1.

[164] J. Story, *Commentaries on Equity Jurisprudence*, 1st edn (Boston, MA: Hilliard, Gray & Co., 1836), vol. 1, 68 and 121–29.

made pursuant to a mistake) and actions to recover payments that a defendant
had no right to retain (of which, again, one instance was a mistaken payment)
but that is no basis to equate the two.

Fourthly, Mansfield's list of situations in which the action would lie is
usefully contrasted with that in *Perry*. Mansfield lists mistake, whereas the
Court of Exchequer had perhaps limited it to 'mistake under colour, and upon
an apprehension, though a mistaken apprehension of having a good authority
to receive it' – although this included 'where it is received by imposition, fraud
or deceit in the receiver'.[165] Mansfield separates these out as imposition
(express and implied), extortion, oppression and 'undue advantage taken of
the plaintiff's situation' contrary to law (which included usury cases and cases
like *Smith* v. *Cuff*[66]), as well as failure of consideration, which covers cases
such as *Martin* v. *Sitwell*,[167] referred to in *Perry*.

It was no coincidence that Mansfield extensively referred to and relied upon
equity and equitable notions in *Moses*. The action lacked a rationale, and the
facts of the case were ones in which money had and received had never
previously been held to lie. He was consciously appropriating equitable
notions in order to fashion the determinant of a right to retain in good
conscience that he used to ground the action for money had and received,
and to explain why it should lie in this new type of case.

As I have shown elsewhere,[168] after *Moses* Mansfield consistently stated that
the determinant of the action was the defendant's right to retain the monies
received. The underlying rationale was that it was against fairness, justice and
good conscience for a defendant to keep money that he did not have a right to
retain: an almost self-evident proposition that had not – apparently – been put
as such until *Moses*. The passages from *Clarke* v. *Shee*,[169] *Dale* v. *Sollet*,[170]
Longchamp v. *Kenny*[171] and *Jestons* v. *Brooke*[172] set out at the beginning of this
chapter show this. The basal consideration – 'what an honest man ought to do,
the ties of conscience upon an upright mind'[173] – was the same. But the
determinant and procedure – not to mention the forum – were different. This
is why the action for money had and received was analogous to a bill in equity
but was not one. Indeed, as the common law developed the action for money
had and received over the next century, equity showed a marked reluctance to
exercise jurisdiction in cases of money had and received, at least where there

[165] A.-G. v. *Perry* (1734) 2 Com. 481, 491.   [166] (1817) 6 M. & S. 160.
[167] *Martin* v. *Sitwell* (1691) 1 Show. K.B. 156.
[168] Kremer, 'The Action for Money Had and Received'.   [169] (1774) 1 Cowp. 197.
[170] (1767) 4 Burr. 2133.   [171] (1779) 1 Dougl. 137.   [172] (1778) 2 Cowp. 793.
[173] *Hawkes* v. *Saunders* (1782) 1 Cowp. 289, 290 (Mansfield C.J.).

was no fiduciary relationship between the parties and 'no equity to supervene by reason of the conduct of either of the parties'.[174]

Until perhaps *Roxborough v. Rothmans of Pall Mall Australia Ltd*,[175] later courts lost sight of the originally equitable notion of conscience that underlay the action and the determinant of the right to retain that derived from it. The reasons ranged from not understanding what Mansfield had done, as in *Holt v. Markham*,[176] to fundamentally mischaracterising it, as the minority did in *Great-West Life & Annuity Ins. Co. v. Knudson*. Knudson had been injured in a car accident, and received a settlement of her tort claim in state Court. Great-West, the fiduciary of her plan, brought a federal claim purportedly under section 502(a)(3) of the federal Employee Retirement Income Security Act of 1974, which authorised a civil action in federal court 'by a participant, beneficiary, or fiduciary (A) to enjoin any act or practice which violates ... the terms of the plan, or (B) to obtain other appropriate equitable relief (i) to redress such violations or (ii) to enforce any provisions of ... the terms of the plan'. Great-West sought an injunction and declaration – sounding in money – seeking to be reimbursed, pursuant to a provision in the plan, for the medical expenses of Knudson's that it had paid that were in excess of the amount allocated to Great-West under the settlement.

The majority correctly characterised the substance of Great-West's action as seeking to compel the defendant to pay money pursuant to a contractual obligation, which it held was 'relief that was not typically available in equity' and hence not within the meaning of 'equitable relief' in the statute.[177] The federal court thus had no jurisdiction. The minority reasoned that Great-West sought 'restitution' and that 'restitution' was 'typically available in equity' (relying on Mansfield's statement in Moses that 'the gist of this kind of action is that the defendant, upon the circumstances of the case, is obliged by the ties of natural justice and equity to refund the money'). Hence, the minority concluded that Great-West's federal suit was for 'equitable relief', was within

---

[174] *Rogers v. Ingham* (1876) 3 Ch.D. 351, 356.   [175] (2001) 208 C.L.R. 516; [2001] HCA 68.
[176] [1923] 1 K.B. 504, 513 ('the whole history of this particular form of action has been what I may call a history of well-meaning sloppiness of thought'). Compare *Cantiare San Rocco S.A. v. Clyde Shipbuilding and Engineering Co. Ltd* [1924] A.C. 226, 236 (Sc.). Concerning English law, the period is capped by R. Jackson, *The History of Quasi-Contract in English Law* (Cambridge University Press, 1936).
[177] *Great-West Life & Annuity Ins. Co. v. Knudson*, 534 U.S. 204, 210 (2002). A nuanced analysis might have said that injunctions and declarations were quintessential equitable relief, but injunctions were not granted to compel the payment of money pursuant to a contractual provision creating a right of recoupment where a claim for breach of contract already existed. The equitable claim was infirm and there was truly no federal controversy: *Oneida Indian Nation v. County of Oneida*, 414 U.S. 661, 666 (1974).

the statute and should have been allowed to proceed.'[178] The minority's reasoning wrongly relies upon 'restitution' – a term not in the statutory text – as a determinant, and wrongly treats *Moses* as involving equitable relief. Apart from the minority failing to appreciate that Mansfield was sitting in the King's Bench, and not in equity, it is clear that the action could not be so described. However, the case starkly illustrates that the distinction between common law and equitable actions can be determinative of whether a case succeeds.

CONCLUSION

The rationale that Mansfield created for the action for money had and received in *Moses* involved extensive use of the same concept of conscience and unconscientiousness that was used in equitable doctrine. While Mansfield used Roman terminology and concepts in explaining and justifying this rationale, he did not include in it substantive propositions of Roman law. Although Mansfield inserted this new rationale into a common law action, he did not include in it any substantive propositions of the common law. He created the determinant of a right to retain, which exemplified the use of conscience and unconscientiousness. The decision in *Moses* is best seen as an instance of synthesis, or perhaps colonisation of the action for money had and received by a wholly new creation; it is not fusion.

---

[178] *Great-West Life & Annuity Ins. Co. v. Knudson*, 534 U.S. 204, 228–30 (2002) ('restitution was "within the recognized power and within the highest tradition of a court of equity"').

10

Mistake and Unfairness in Contract Law

STEPHEN WADDAMS

INTRODUCTION

Rules, sound in themselves, often require open-ended exceptions in practice: rules should be observed, but not when their rigid application would lead to absurdity or disaster. Examples can be found both within and outside the legal system. Rules for avoiding collisions at sea, for instance, having provided methods for establishing which vessel has the right of way, provide that the vessel having the right of way shall hold her course and speed. But the rules also include a potentially overriding escape clause to the effect that, notwithstanding the other rules, if a collision is imminent, all reasonable steps must be taken to avoid it. The 'imminent collision' rule is open-ended, because the circumstances in which collision is imminent cannot be precisely defined, and what steps are reasonable may depend in some cases on a choice of the lesser of two or more evils. In one sense, all the rules belong together and form a coherent set, but in another sense the imminent collision rule is distinct from the other rules. The other rules, including the primary rule that the vessel having the right of way shall hold her course and speed are very sound, indeed essential to safe navigation, and yet there are circumstances in which those rules can be overridden. In the context of discussions of equity, such an overriding rule has been called a 'safety valve'.[1] This is a useful metaphor in that it suggests that operation of the safety valve will be rare, and that its primary purpose is not to interfere with the running of the machinery (though that is necessarily its short-term effect when it is triggered) but, on the contrary, to preserve the machinery intact for effective long-term operation. In one

---

[1] Smith, 'Fusing the Equitable Function'; J. Fullmer, 'The Outer Limits of Equity: a Proposal for Cautious Expansion' (2016) 39 Harv. J. L. & Pub. Pol'y 557, 573, P. S. Davies, 'Rectification versus Interpretation: The Nature and Scope of the Equitable Jurisdiction' [2016] C.L.J. 62, 63, 81.

sense, the collision avoidance rule might be said to conflict with the other rules, but in another sense it serves their fundamental purpose, i.e., the avoidance of collisions. This idea underlies Maitland's bold biblical allusion to the effect that '[e]quity had come not to destroy the law, but to fulfil it'.[2]

There are elements of truth in both sides of the 'fusion/fission' debate: on the one hand, there is already a kind of fusion, since equity and law are administered by a single court which necessarily considers them in relation to each other in order to maintain coherence; on the other hand it is true to say that equity had, and continues to have, distinctive characteristics that require recognition and attention from the modern courts. The fusion/fission debate cannot be resolved purely in its own terms, but it will be suggested that the dichotomy can and should, in the context of contractual mistake and unfairness, be transcended. New perspectives on the problem, including unjust enrichment, abuse of rights and good faith, may usefully be deployed in order to support the suggestion that the function served in the past by equity could be served equally well, and in some cases more effectively, under other names, but only if a distinction is maintained between rules of general application and the concept of an open-ended power to depart from those rules for sufficient reason. The preservation in modern legal language of the name 'equity' is not strictly necessary in this context, though it may sometimes be desirable from a historical perspective; but what is essential is the preservation of the concept of a supplementary power in the court to depart from generally sound legal rules where extraordinary circumstances make such a departure necessary.

The present chapter proposes to examine these questions as they relate to the power of the courts to modify contracts on grounds related to unfairness and mistake. It will be suggested that by the eighteenth century equitable powers to modify contracts had been recognised in a wide variety of circumstances, but that these powers tended to be marginalised in the nineteenth and twentieth centuries, partly as an unintended consequence of the Judicature Acts. There are some signs in the present century of a recovery of the older powers, but trends have not been uniform.

In order to assess the powers of the modern court in these respects, it is necessary to examine the extent to which equity exercised such powers in the past. This is not purely an antiquarian enquiry, because in England all the powers of the old courts of equity were assigned to the modern court in 1875, with the express provision that, in case of conflict, equity should prevail.[3]

---

[2] Maitland, *Equity*, 17. The allusion is to Matthew, 5,17: 'Think not that I am come to destroy the law, or the prophets: I am come not to destroy, but to fulfil.'

[3] Judicature Act 1873 (U.K.), s. 25(11).

For this reason, historical enquiry is essential. But it is also difficult, because assertions about the past have very often been coloured by the speaker's or writer's view of what is desirable for the present and future. So, those favouring a strict sanctity of contracts are apt to minimise the powers of the former courts of equity, while those (like the present writer) who take a more relaxed view of sanctity of contracts tend to emphasise the breadth of those powers. Nor can there be any consensus as to historical trends. Supporters of the one opinion are apt to view some point in the eighteenth century as the high water mark of equitable powers, with the implication that the waters have since permanently retreated; supporters of the other opinion are inclined to suggest that the tide has turned, or is turning, and that older equitable powers may be recovered or extended. Since there are copious historical materials to support both views, the debate is perpetually inconclusive, with the consequence that it is impossible to formulate, even in general terms, an agreed statement of the modern law on the question. This cannot be a virtue, and suggests the need to transcend the fusion/fission debate by finding a way to describe the powers of the modern court in terms that do not compel recourse to perpetually controverted historical questions.

The proposition that contracts are binding, though a sound general rule, cannot be acceptable as absolutely stringent. Public policy is not the subject of this essay, but, in the context of the proposition that contracts are absolutely binding, it is relevant to note that a large and open-ended exception undoubtedly exists in the shape of public policy. On matters related to mistake and unfairness, relief has been given, sometimes by courts of equity and sometimes by courts of law, against forfeitures and penalties, against clauses excluding damages for breach of contract, against money-lending contracts at excessive rates of interest, against sales of reversionary interests in land at an undervalue, against mistake as to existing facts and mistake as to anticipated future facts (frustration), against unfair maritime salvage agreements, against contracts induced by undue influence and more generally against very unfair contracts.

THE EXTENT OF THE EQUITABLE POWER

The statement of Finch L.C. (later Lord Nottingham) in 1676 in *Maynard v. Moseley* that 'the Chancery mends no man's bargain'[4] has sometimes been taken at face value in order to suggest that the meaning of the phrase is that

---

[4] *Maynard* v. *Moseley* (1676) 3 Swan. 653, 655.

equity lacked power to modify contractual obligations.[5] But, when the words are read in context, and in the context of Finch's other decisions, it is clear that this cannot have been his meaning.[6] He said, in *Maynard* v. *Moseley*, that relief would have been available if the transaction had not been fully executed: 'if the defendants had been plaintiffs for the money, his Lordship would hardly have decreed for them,'[7] and in a later case he did give relief in those circumstances.[8] David Yale, in his edition of Lord Nottingham's chancery cases, discusses at some length the extent to which Nottingham was willing to grant relief against burdensome contractual obligations.[9] Yale comments that 'Lord Nottingham was not lavish in the relief he was prepared to grant,'[10] but Yale makes it clear that Nottingham recognised a power to grant relief, or perhaps a series of powers in various situations. A modern judge has said of Lord Nottingham's phrase 'in fact both the courts of equity and those of common law have for centuries intervened to mend people's bargains in all sorts of circumstances'.[11] The position appears to be that, until about the middle of the eighteenth century, the courts of equity did recognise a power both to withhold enforcement of and to set aside contracts that were grossly unfair,[12] but that they used the power sparingly. Attitudes later changed, and the prevailing spirit of the nineteenth century, both in common law and in equity, favoured predictability and certainty, even at the cost of enforcing harsh contracts. But some of the nineteenth-century judges, notably Lord Selborne and Sir George Jessel, seemed to be anxious, on the eve of the Judicature Acts, to remind their common law brethren of the breadth of

---

5   *Stockloser* v. *Johnson* [1954] 1 Q.B. 476, 495 (Romer L.J.); *Campbell Discount Co. Ltd* v. *Bridge* [1961] 1 Q.B. 445, 459 (Harman L.J.). Lord Sumption J.S.C. in *International Energy Group Ltd* v. *Zurich Insurance plc* [2016] A.C. 509, [185]; [2015] UKSC 33 said 'Equity does not mend men's bargains', adding, however, that '[i]t may intervene to avoid unconscionable bargains, or to give effect to the parties' real intentions'.

6   See S. Waddams, 'Good Faith, Good Conscience, and the Taking of Unfair Advantage,' in A. Dyson, J. Goudkamp and F. Wilmot-Smith (eds), *Defences in Contract* (Oxford: Hart, 2017), 63, 64–66.

7   *Maynard* v. *Moseley* (1676) 3 Swan. 653, 657.

8   *Skip* v. *Rich* (1679/80) 79 S.S. 805, probably the same case as reported anonymously in 2 Ch. Cas. 19.

9   D. E. C. Yale, 'Introduction', in *Lord Nottingham's Chancery Cases: Volume 1* (London: Selden Society, 1957), xciii.

10 Ibid., xciv.

11 *Multiservice Bookbinding Ltd* v. *Marden* [1979] Ch. 84, 97 (Browne-Wilkinson J.).

12 *Savile* v. *Savile* (1721) 1 P. Wms 745; *Earl of Chesterfield* v. *Janssen* (1751) 2 Ves. Sen. 125; H. Ballow (attr.), *A Treatise of Equity* (London: Brown and Shuckburgh, 1737), 11; J. J. Powell, *Essay upon the Law of Contracts and Agreements* (London: Johnson and Wieldon, 1790), vol. 2, 143; J. Story, *Commentaries on Equity Jurisprudence as Administered in England and America* (Boston, MA: Hilliard, Gray & Co., 1836), 250.

equitable powers.[13] And courts in the twenty-first century are free to depart from the rigidity of the nineteenth century and to recover, if they think proper, the flexibility of an earlier era.

FORFEITURES

The power to relieve against forfeiture was early established, and vigorously enforced, in respect of mortgages of land.[14] The modern position was extensively canvassed in the recent case of *Çukurova Finance International Ltd v. Alfa Telecom Turkey Ltd.*[15] This was not a case of inequality of bargaining power. The sums of money involved were very large, and the case was argued several times before the Judicial Committee of the Privy Council. Simplifying the facts, a loan was made of US$1.352 billion at a high interest rate, the loan being secured by shares that represented a controlling interest in a very profitable Turkish cell phone company (Turkcell). On the occurrence of certain events of default, the lender was entitled to immediate repayment of the loan, and, on default of immediate repayment, entitled to appropriate the shares. An event occurred that was found to be an 'event of default' and the lender demanded repayment, which was tendered but rejected on the ground that it was too late, the lender's real motive being not to recover the loan but to take control of the cell phone company. The borrower then paid the amount into an interest-bearing escrow account.

In the Privy Council the principal question was whether the borrower was entitled to relief from forfeiture. The court held unanimously that relief from forfeiture was available, that such relief was not confined to mortgages of land,[16] that it was available in commercial cases and that the court had power to set 'appropriate conditions'[17] in determining the precise terms of relief. The Board cited with approval a case affirming 'the breadth of the court's discretion both in granting relief and as to the terms on which to grant it'.[18] On the subsequent hearing to settle the terms of relief, the court held, by a majority,

[13] See S. Waddams, 'Equity in English Contract Law: The Impact of the Judicature Acts (1873–75)' (2012) 33 J.L.H. 185, 189–90.

[14] R. H. Coote, *A Treatise on the Law of Mortgage* (London: Butterworth and Son, 1821), 20, mentions cases from the reigns of Elizabeth I and Charles I.

[15] *Çukurova Finance International Ltd v. Alfa Telecom Turkey Ltd (Nos 3 to 5)* [2016] A.C. 923; [2013] UKPC 2; [2013] UKPC 20; [2013] UKPC 25.

[16] Cited with approval on this point in *Cavendish Square Holding B.V. v. Makdessi* [2016] A.C. 1172, [10], [17], [160]; [2015] UKSC 67.

[17] *Çukurova Finance International Ltd v. Alfa Telecom Turkey Ltd (No. 3)* [2016] A.C. 923, [126].

[18] Ibid., [123].

that, though normally a party seeking relief from forfeiture would have to comply with all the terms of the original contract, this was not an inflexible rule, and in this case, where the lender had rejected the tender of repayment, and the borrower had paid the money into an escrow account, it was appropriate to grant relief from the high interest required under the contract during the period when the escrow account had existed. An order was made permitting redemption of the shares on payment of the appropriate sum by a certain date. The lender then took steps, including obtaining an injunction in New York, designed to prevent the borrower from raising the necessary sum, the motive again being to obtain control of the cell phone company. On a further hearing, the Judicial Committee held, unanimously, that a further extension of time for repayment would be allowed.

This complex case manifests a dynamic and flexible approach to the court's equitable jurisdiction. The unanimous holding that the jurisdiction to grant relief extends beyond mortgages of land is significant,[19] as is the reaffirmation that 'the mere fact that the transaction is commercial in nature does not preclude the jurisdiction to grant relief from forfeiture, provided that the forfeiture is of possessory or proprietary rights'.[20] In the second of the three cases reported in the Law Reports, *Çukurova (No. 4)*, the majority of the Board adopted a flexible approach to setting the terms of relief, with frequent references to equity and unconscionability.[21] On the question of the need for certainty (an understandable reason for restraint in the use of judicial discretion, and a central concern of the minority in this case), the majority quoted Holmes, with approval:

> The language of judicial decision is mainly the language of logic. And the logical method and form flatter that longing for certainty and for repose which is in every human mind. But certainty generally is illusion, and repose is not the destiny of man.[22]

On the relation of equity to the powers of the modern court, the majority quoted, with approval, Lord Simon's view that 'equity has an unlimited and unfettered jurisdiction to relieve against contractual forfeitures and penalties'.[23] They approved also of what they called the 'approbatory' comment in the fourth edition of *Meagher, Gummow and Lehane* 'that what was really involved was "a return to the more remote past when equity jurisprudence had

---

[19] Ibid., [92].   [20] Ibid., [95].
[21] *Çukurova Finance International Ltd* v. *Alfa Telecom Turkey Ltd (No. 4)* [2016] A.C. 923, [13], [17], [26], [44]–[45].
[22] Ibid., [43], quoting O. W. Holmes, 'The Path of the Law' (1897) 10 Harv. L. Rev. 457, 465–66.
[23] *Shiloh Spinners Ltd* v. *Harding* [1973] A.C. 691, 726.

a dynamism lost with the attainment of the rigidity for which Lord Eldon was so praised by nineteenth century positivists"'.[24] The approving reference to dynamism is significant. This might sound like signal proof of the continuing vitality of equity, and a vindication of the thesis to this effect for which Meagher, Gummow and Lehane's treatise is well known. However, the majority of the Privy Council may have read more into the quotation from the treatise than its authors intended,[25] and there is room for some doubt as to whether the majority view in the *Çukurova* case will be followed.

The majority in *Çukurova* were themselves conscious of the need not to open too wide a door to judicial relief from disadvantageous contracts. They added that:

> [n]evertheless, the Board emphasises that it is in no way suggesting that equity recognises any general or open-ended discretion. The Board's reasoning and decision in this case are based on and confined to what it sees as an exceptional situation, in which it would, in the Board's view, be both inequitable and unconscionable to ignore the background and circum-stances of the tender[,]

further adding that '[t]he unusual facts of this case are in this respect probably unlikely to be repeated'.[26] These words indicate an understandable concern to preserve a measure of certainty and predictability. But it might be observed that these words are unlikely, in practice, to restrict greatly the future powers of the court, for in any case in which the court will be inclined to grant relief it will not be difficult to describe the circumstances as inequitable, unconscion-able or exceptional. This observation might be thought to tend to support criticism of the majority view. On the other hand, it might be argued that the approval of a general power of relief, to be used in extreme cases but that cannot be precisely defined, recognises the force of what the majority had implied in the previous paragraph, that certainty, though important, cannot be a consideration that overrides every other value in legal decision-making. Lord Neuberger of Abbotsbury P.S.C., one of the two concurring judges to give 'dissenting' reasons in *Çukurova (No. 4)*, has spoken more recently of 'the

---

[24] *Çukurova Finance International Ltd* v. *Alfa Telecom Turkey Ltd (No. 4)* [2016] A.C. 923, [43], citing Meagher, Heydon and Leeming, *Meagher, Gummow and Lehane's Equity: Doctrines and Remedies*, 4th edn (Sydney: LexisNexis, 2002), [18–20].

[25] The passage quoted is absent from the fifth edition, which contains some adverse comments on *Çukurova*: *Meagher, Gummow and Lehane*, 5th edn, [18–295], [18–305]. See also P. G. Turner, '"Mending Men's Bargains" in Equity: Mortgage Redemption and Relief against Forfeiture' (2014) 130 L.Q.R. 188, 190, criticising *Çukurova*.

[26] *Çukurova Finance International Ltd* v. *Alfa Telecom Turkey Ltd (No. 4)* [2016] A.C. 923, [44].

Stephen Waddams

familiar tension between the need for principle, clarity and certainty in the law with the *equally important* desire to achieve a fair and appropriate result in each case'.[27]

Another significant feature of the majority judgment in *Çukurova (No. 4)* is the recognition of the link between the forfeiture and the penalty cases:

> Likewise, Nicholls L.J. . . . treated forfeiture of a lease on non-payment of rent and forfeiture of a mortgage together and both as stemming from the same underlying principle as that governing penalty clauses. For centuries, he said, 'equity has given relief against such provisions by not permitting the innocent party to recover . . . more than his loss'.[28]

This comment recognises the force of the unjust enrichment perspective. The fundamental objection to strict enforcement of the contractual provisions is, both in forfeiture and in penalty cases, the undue enrichment of the claimant, who may recover far more by strict enforcement than could reasonably have been expected from the ostensible purpose of the forfeiture or penalty clauses (that is, to give security for performance of the other party's principal obligation). It is true that judgment is required to determine the ostensible purpose of the transaction, and in some cases this might present difficulties, but often it does not: the substance of an ordinary mortgage, for example, is readily perceived as a way of giving security for repayment of a loan, not as a kind of wager permitting the lender to make random and disproportionate profits from trivial defaults.

PENALTIES

Forfeiture in its various forms has obvious advantages to the secured party, and the penal bond represented an attempt to secure equivalent advantages without the immediate transfer of the property to be forfeited. A common form of the bond was a covenant to pay a fixed sum of money unless some other act was performed by a certain date. The effect was to secure the performance of the other act, which might itself be the payment of a sum of money.

The court of equity gave relief from such bonds on much the same principle as in mortgages. Where the bond was, in substance, a device to secure repayment of a loan, the legitimate interest of the lender was in

---

[27] *Bilta (U.K.) Ltd v. Nazir (No. 2)* [2016] A.C. 1, [13]; [2015] UKSC 23 (emphasis added).
[28] *Çukurova Finance International Ltd v. Alfa Telecom Turkey Ltd (No. 4)* [2016] A.C. 923, [19], quoting *Jobson v. Johnson* [1989] 1 W.L.R. 1026, 1038. In *Cavendish Square Holding B.V. v. Makdessi* [2016] A.C. 1172, however, distinctions were drawn between penalty clauses and relief against forfeiture.

repayment of the principal (together with interest and costs) and no more. Later, the common law courts set aside penalties without reference to equity, and the penal bond fell into disuse. In 1880 the law on the point, out of keeping though it was with the spirit of the nineteenth century, was explained by Bramwell L.J. (who, though not himself sympathetic, accepted that this was the law) as follows:

[T]he Court of Chancery said that a penalty to secure the payment of a sum of money or the performance of an act should not be enforced; the parties were not held to their agreement; equity in truth refused to allow to be enforced what was considered to be an unconscientious bargain.[29]

Another judge said, in 1900:

The Court of Chancery gave relief against the strictness of the common law in cases of penalty or forfeiture for non-payment of a fixed sum on a day certain, on the principle that the failure to pay principal on a certain day could be compensated sufficiently by payment of principal and interest with costs at a subsequent day.[30]

Important also was the obvious factor that a borrower in urgent need was apt to sign too readily an extravagant penal bond: the need for the funds was always immediate, and the possibility of enforcement of the bond remote.

The law relating to penalties has been recently reviewed by a seven-judge panel of the U.K. Supreme Court in *Cavendish Square Holding B.V. v. Makdessi*.[31] In one of the judgments, the law in this area was described as 'an ancient, haphazardly constructed edifice which has not weathered well'.[32] The court, however, rejected arguments for abolition of the doctrine or for confining it to consumer transactions. But the court also rejected (as decisive tests) whether the clause was a genuine pre-estimate of loss and whether the clause was designed to have a deterrent effect, preferring the more flexible tests of whether the clause was extravagant, exorbitant, disproportionate or unconscionable. This greater flexibility will enable clauses that are not unreasonable to be enforced, as in the two cases decided in *Cavendish Square* (where the clauses would have failed a strict application of the former tests based on genuine pre-estimate and deterrent effect), while maintaining judicial control over clauses that would have the effect of causing extravagant enrichment. Although the court declined directly to extend the law of penalty

[29] *Protector Endowment Loan and Annuity Co.* v *Grice* (1880) 5 Q.B.D. 592, 596.
[30] *Re Dixon* [1900] 2 Ch. 561, 576 (Rigby L.J.).   [31] [2016] A.C. 1172.
[32] Ibid., [3] (Lord Neuberger P.S.C. and Lord Sumption J.S.C., Lord Carnwath J.S.C. concurring).

clauses to cases where there was no breach of contract, as had been done in Australia,[33] the indirect effect of the case, adopting a flexible test of enforceability, seems likely to extend the power to grant relief to clauses not involving breach. A distinction based on breach or non-breach will be difficult to maintain, as the court itself appeared to recognise.[34] A clause in a banking contract providing that overdrafts were prohibited, with a penalty of $10,000 per day, would (let us assume) be considered on the *Cavendish Square* test to be exorbitant, extravagant, disproportionate and unconscionable. If that conclusion is correct, the court could hardly enforce a revised clause providing that overdrafts were *permitted* for an agreed fee of $10,000 per day, assuming that the expectation was substantially the same in both cases, that is, that the customer was expected not to overdraw. In an ordinary banking contract, both clauses would be equally objectionable in that they would, if enforced, give to the bank a disproportionate enrichment at the customer's expense.

RELATION OF JUDICIAL DEVELOPMENT TO LEGISLATION

It has frequently been suggested that reform of the law is for the legislature and that, if no legislation is applicable, the court is bound to enforce contracts without regard to considerations of unfairness. In the recent case of *Arnold v. Britton*,[35] the majority of the U.K. Supreme Court enforced a compounding escalator clause for calculating a proportionate share of maintenance expenses in long leases of holiday homes, with the consequence that amounts were payable that were wholly disproportionate in comparison with payments by the other lessees, and enormous sums (over one million pounds per year) would become payable by the end of the leases. The lessees would be bound to make these payments even if they abandoned the leases. The dissenting judge (Lord Carnwath J.S.C.) described the result as 'grotesque' and as 'commercial nonsense'.[36] The majority of the court also recognised the unreasonable and unfair nature of the result, but held that the court was powerless to prevent it: 'The present case suggests that there may be a strong case for extending . . . [statutory] provisions to cases such as the present . . . But

---

[33] *Andrews* v. *Australia and New Zealand Banking Group Ltd* (2012) 247 C.L.R. 205; [2012] HCA 30.
[34] It was said in *Cavendish Square Holding B.V.* v. *Makdessi* [2016] A.C. 1172 that the penalty rule could be avoided by careful drafting (at [14], [258]) but also that the court would look to the substance and not the form in case of a 'disguised' penalty clause (at [15], [258]). An equitable power that can be defeated by careful drafting is practically a contradiction in terms: careful drafting of a mortgage could never defeat the equity of redemption.
[35] [2015] A.C. 1619; [2015] UKSC 36.   [36] Ibid., [115], [138].

that is a policy issue for Parliament'.[37] Lord Hodge J.S.C., agreeing with the majority, said that:

> it is a highly unsatisfactory outcome for the chalet tenants who are affected ... It is not clear whether there are many long leases containing fixed service charges with escalators which are beyond the reach of statutory regulation. If there are, there may be a case for Parliament to consider extending the provisions that protect tenants against unreasonable service charges ...
> If the parties cannot agree an amendment of the leases on a fair basis, the lessees will have to seek parliamentary intervention.[38]

This (it may be respectfully suggested) seems an inadequate response. Parliamentary intervention to reverse the result of a particular case cannot normally be regarded as certain, or even probable, and the bare possibility is not an adequate reason for an unjust judicial ruling. It is surprising that the court should consider itself powerless in these circumstances to avoid an avowedly unjust result. The principle that contracts are enforceable is not written in stone, and it is not absolute; contract law, with its qualifications, equitable and legal, has been created by the courts themselves in order to do justice between the parties. *Arnold* v. *Britton* is closely analogous to the kind of case in which equity intervened: it is highly unreasonable that the lessor should profit so extravagantly at the lessees' expense from a clause ostensibly designed to bring about a fair sharing of actual expenses. I would argue that the modern court has ample power to grant relief in such a case, and that it should recognise a residual power to modify contractual provisions that have disproportionate and extravagant results, much as the court of equity has done in respect of forfeitures and penalties. Such a power might be based on the powers of the modern court as a court of equity, or, alternatively, and perhaps more persuasively in the twenty-first century, on concepts such as good faith (in an objective sense), avoidance of unjust enrichment and avoidance of abuse of rights. It is ironic that extensive statutory protection of lessees and consumers from unfair provisions of this kind should operate as a reason for denying relief in a case very closely analogous to those in which statutory protection was available, but which happened to fall through the legislative cracks, as in *Arnold* v. *Britton*.

In *Seidel* v. *Telus Communications Inc.*,[39] the Supreme Court of Canada held that an arbitration clause was not effective to exclude a class action under the British Columbia Business Practices and Consumer Protection Act, but

---

[37] Ibid., [65].   [38] Ibid., [66], [79].   [39] [2011] 1 S.C.R. 531; 2011 SCC 15.

that the clause was effective to exclude other legal actions. The reasoning of the majority included the following:

> The choice to restrict or not to restrict arbitration clauses in consumer contracts is a matter for the legislature. Absent legislative intervention, the courts will generally give effect to the terms of a commercial contract freely entered into, even a contract of adhesion, including an arbitration clause.[40]

It is true that this comment is qualified by the word 'generally', and that it does suppose a contract 'freely' entered into, but it seems to contemplate that a standard form contract, even in the consumer context, and even if very burdensome, will normally be binding. The comment on legislative intervention might be read to suggest that all contractual clauses are valid unless explicitly prohibited by legislation. An alternative, more realistic, more historical and more flexible view would be (it may be suggested) that the court may develop equitable or common law doctrines, such as unconscionability or public policy, by analogy with legislation, even though legislation in the relevant jurisdiction is not precisely applicable. It is not realistic to suppose that legislative silence on the question of arbitration clauses in consumer contracts, for example, is equivalent to a statute positively requiring enforcement of such clauses in all circumstances; nor could it be supposed that the prohibition of one kind of potentially abusive clause is equivalent to an explicit legislative command that all other imaginable clauses, however unfair, must positively be enforced. As the former Chief Justice of Canada said, extra-judicially, 'legislatures only rarely intervene to correct anomalies in the law of private obligation', and 'there is a broad sphere of private action which is untouched by [legislative] constraints and which is regulated only by the common law of tort, contract and equity. Change in this area, if it is to be made at all, must be made by the courts.'[41] In the context of equity it might be said that if the courts require legislative authority for granting relief against unfair contracts, they already have it in the form of the Judicature Act provision that the modern court must administer equity and that, in case of conflict with the common law, equity is to prevail.[42] These considerations are particularly important in jurisdictions, like those in North America, where consumer protection is weak; but they are relevant also in other jurisdictions in respect of cases that fall just outside the area of legislative protection.

[40] Ibid., [2]; see also [160].
[41] B. McLachlin, 'The Evolution of the Law of Private Obligation: The Influence of Justice La Forest', in R. Johnson and J. P. McEvoy (eds), *Gérard V. La Forest at the Supreme Court of Canada, 1985–1997* (Winnipeg: Canadian Legal History Project, 2000), 23.
[42] Judicature Act 1873 (U.K.), s. 25(11) and modern counterparts.

The phrase 'sanctity of contract', which still appears in modern judicial opinions, seems scarcely appropriate in a secular era in which practically nothing remains sacred. Let us allow that enforcement of contracts is a highly beneficial principle; it does not follow that it must outweigh every other human value and every other consideration of justice. Equity, while generally respecting contracts, nevertheless intervened in a variety of circumstances to prevent very unfair consequences. Attention to the past is important in this context, for neglect of legal history may foster a simplistic formalism, ironically more rigid than anything that the American legal realists sought to displace.[43] Practical considerations also are important: Margaret Jane Radin, in a recent book,[44] has rightly objected to a form of reasoning that leads judges to turn a blind eye to the realities of commercial practice in the computer age, where submission to standard form terms is a practical necessity. It remains true, as was said 250 years ago, that 'necessitous men are not, truly speaking, free men, but, to answer a present exigency, will submit to any terms that the crafty may impose upon them'.[45]

MISTAKE

Before the Judicature Acts, the courts of equity had an undoubted power to rescind an agreement for mistake. In *Bingham v. Bingham*,[46] an eighteenth-century case expressly approved by the House of Lords in 1867[47] where there was a mistake as to the title to land, the court said, 'though no fraud appeared, and the defendant apprehended he had a right, yet there was a plain mistake, such as the court was warranted to relieve against, and not to suffer the defendant to run away with the money in consideration of the sale of an estate, to which he had no right'.[48] The phrase 'run away with the money' plainly indicates an unjust enrichment perspective. The equitable power to

---

[43] It has been suggested in a recent article that there is a political aspect to this tendency, in that the practical effect is to enable business interests to impose terms beneficial to themselves: J. M. Feinman, 'The Duty of Good Faith: A Perspective on Contemporary Contract Law' (2015) 66 Hastings L.J. 937.

[44] M. J. Radin, *Boilerplate: The Fine Print, Vanishing Rights, and the Rule of Law* (Princeton University Press, 2013).

[45] *Vernon v. Bethell* (1762) 2 Eden 110, 113.

[46] (1748) 1 Ves. Sen. 126. G. E. Palmer, *Mistake and Unjust Enrichment* (Columbus, OH: Ohio State University Press, 1962), 100, n. 14, lists several other eighteenth- and nineteenth-century equity cases.

[47] *Cooper v. Phibbs* (1867) L.R. 2 H.L. 149, 155, 164.

[48] *Bingham v. Bingham* (1948) 1 Ves. Sen. 126, 126–27.

give relief was recognised by Story,[49] Leake[50] and Benjamin,[51] and was affirmed by the House of Lords in *Cooper v. Phibbs*,[52] where Lord Westbury said:

> at the time of the agreement … the parties dealt with one another under a mutual mistake as to their respective rights … In such a state of things there can be no doubt of the rule of a Court of equity with regard to the dealing with that agreement … [I]f parties contract under a mutual mistake and misapprehension as to their relation and respective rights, the result is, that that agreement is liable to be set aside as having proceeded upon a common mistake.[53]

Though the existence of the equitable power was not doubted, its limits were ill-defined. The power of the court to rescind a contract was, like all equitable remedies, 'discretionary' and the discretion would not be exercised in the absence of what seemed to the court to be sufficient reason. After the Judicature Acts it might have been expected that the new court, uniting as it did the powers of the courts of law and equity, with equity to prevail in case of conflict, would exercise the power of the former court of equity to rescind contracts for mistake. However, despite the Judicature Acts, there was a reluctance by English writers and judges to recognise the full breadth of the equitable power to rescind for mistake. Palmer put it this way: '[i]n modern times English judges have sometimes remembered earlier English equity, but often it seems to be either forgotten or consciously discarded'.[54] The main reason for this reluctance was probably that the limits of the equitable power had not been clearly defined,[55] and so recognition of the power, without the ability to state clear limits, appeared to jeopardise the stability and certainty of contracts, and was out of keeping with the desire prevailing in the late nineteenth century to achieve a high degree of predictability and certainty in legal rules, combined with a deep suspicion of discretion in judicial decision-making.

An important and closely related reason was that it appeared unnecessary, and therefore undesirable, to separate the concept of relief for mistake from

---

[49] Story, *Commentaries on Equity Jurisprudence*, 1st edn, vol. 1, § 134. This position was maintained in subsequent editions: see J. Story, *Commentaries on Equity Jurisprudence as Administered in England and America*, 13th edn by M. M. Bigelow (Boston, MA: Little, Brown and Co., 1886), vol. 1, § 140.

[50] S. M. Leake, *The Elements of the Law of Contracts* (London: Stevens and Sons, 1867), 178.

[51] J. P. Benjamin, *A Treatise on the Law of Sale of Personal Property*, (London: Sweet, 1868), 303.

[52] (1867) L.R. 2 H.L. 149.   [53] Ibid., 170.   [54] Palmer, *Mistake and Unjust Enrichment*, 14.

[55] See C. MacMillan, *Mistakes in Contract Law* (Oxford: Hart, 2010), 48–49.

that of contract formation: it appeared to be an attractive simplification to apply a single principle (consent) to both, and thereby to eliminate altogether the need for discussion of the old equitable jurisdiction. But looking at the question in terms of contract formation was wholly alien to the methods of thought of the old equity cases. Equity intervened in order to prevent an unconscionable result, but not because the contract was void. On the contrary, the contract was assumed to be valid at law; this was precisely why the intervention of equity was both justified and required. Here, as elsewhere, the effect of merging the equitable and legal jurisdictions was, ironically, to suppress the former equitable powers to grant relief.[56]

In English law the adoption of consent as the only relevant criterion led to the assertion in *Bell* v. *Lever Bros Ltd*[57] of what came to be perceived as a very narrow view of relief for mistake. In that case, large sums of money were paid to terminate two employment contracts that could have been terminated without any compensation had the employer known of earlier misconduct by the employees. Restitution of the money was sought by the employer and allowed by the two lower courts, but disallowed by a bare majority of the House of Lords.

The actual result in *Bell* v. *Lever Bros* might be supported on the basis that the company had taken the risk of the mistake, or that the payments were intended partly as gifts. Nevertheless, as mentioned, the case was interpreted by the English courts, and by commentators, as restricting relief for mistake to very narrow grounds. Denning L.J., in *Solle* v. *Butcher*, a case decided by the Court of Appeal in 1950,[58] accepted that *Bell* v. *Lever Bros* laid down a very narrow test *at common law*, but then sought to avoid the result by reasserting the powers of the old court of equity.[59] As the previous discussion indicates, Denning L.J. could claim considerable historical support for his view of equity, but the effect of his decision was unfortunate because, partly on account of his reputation as a bold (and, his critics would say, heretical) innovator, the decision in *Solle* v. *Butcher* was inevitably seen as barely concealed defiance of the House of Lords. *Solle* v. *Butcher*, therefore, though followed in some English and Canadian cases,[60] was often regarded with a degree of suspicion, and in *The Great Peace* the case was rejected by the

---

[56] See Waddams, 'Equity in English Contract Law', 193–96.
[57] *Bell* v. *Lever Bros Ltd* [1932] A.C. 161.   [58] *Solle* v. *Butcher* [1950] 1 K.B. 671.
[59] Ibid., 691–92.
[60] *Grist* v. *Bailey* [1967] Ch. 532, 539–40; *Toronto-Dominion Bank* v. *Fortin (No. 2)* (1978) 88 D.L.R. (3d) 232, 237.

English Court of Appeal as inconsistent with the principles of *Bell* v. *Lever Bros* Lord Phillips M.R. said:

> We are *only* concerned with the question whether relief might be given for common mistake in circumstances wider than those stipulated in *Bell* v. *Lever Bros Ltd*. But that, surely, is a question as to where the common law should draw the line; not whether, given the common law rule, it needs to be mitigated by the application of some other doctrine. The common law has drawn the line in *Bell* v. *Lever Bros Ltd*. The effect of *Solle* v. *Butcher* is not to supplement or mitigate the common law: it is to say that *Bell* v. *Lever Bros Ltd* was wrongly decided.
>
> Our conclusion is that it is impossible to reconcile *Solle* v. *Butcher* with *Bell* v. *Lever Bros Ltd* ... If coherence is to be restored to this area of our law, it can only be by declaring that there is no jurisdiction to grant rescission of a contract on the ground of common mistake where that contract is valid and enforceable on ordinary principles of contract law.[61]

It is a curious irony that the equitable jurisdiction (which was supposed to prevail after 1875) should have been suppressed by reliance on the very feature (validity of the contract at common law) that had given jurisdiction to the courts of equity in the first place. Wherever equity intervened to set aside a contract, the contract was valid at common law (otherwise equity could not have intervened).

The actual result (denial of relief) in *The Great Peace* is readily justifiable in the circumstances of that case on the ground of allocation of risk: the defendant, faced with an emergency, agreed to pay a minimum charge in exchange for guaranteed availability of the plaintiff's ship for saving life in case rescue should be needed. There was no need for the court, in enforcing the contract, to seek to reverse *Solle* v. *Butcher*. A curiosity is that Lord Phillips, who gave the leading judgment, appeared to concede that a wider ground of relief than recognised in *Bell* v. *Lever Bros* was desirable and necessary, and suggested legislative reform.[62] That the court should reject *Solle* v. *Butcher*, and at the same time call for legislative reform to reinstate it (for the legislature, if it did amend the law, would be likely in the end to give back to the courts some sort of wide equitable-like power) seems somewhat perverse. In many jurisdictions, including Canada, uniform (or indeed any) legislative reform on this issue is highly unlikely. Even in the context of English law, Lord Phillips's suggestion seems regrettable, and there is a reasonable prospect

---

[61] *Great Peace Shipping Ltd* v. *Tsavliris Salvage (International) Ltd* [2003] Q.B. 679, [156]–[157]; [2001] EWCA Civ. 1407 (emphasis original).

[62] Ibid., [161].

that the United Kingdom Supreme Court may, for this reason, eventually reject the reasoning in *The Great Peace*. Sir Guenter Treitel wrote, in his discussion of *The Great Peace*, that 'the American rules on this subject are much closer to those of English equity than to those of the English common law, and do not seem to have caused widespread inconvenience',[63] and in the following editions these words were repeated, together with the express suggestion that the House of Lords and, later, the Supreme Court might overrule the Court of Appeal on this question.[64] In *Futter* v. *Futter*,[65] the U.K. Supreme Court asserted and applied a broad equitable power to rescind a trust instrument executed under a serious mistake as to its tax consequences. The court declined to extend the reasoning in *Great Peace* but stated,[66] without further comment, that it had 'effectively overruled' *Solle* v. *Butcher*. The broad approach of the Supreme Court, however, to rescission for unconscionability[67] and its attention to 'the traditional rules of equity'[68] suggest that *The Great Peace* might well be reconsidered on an appropriate occasion. Professor Andrew Burrows, in his recent *A Restatement of the English Law of Contract*, while adopting the law as stated in *The Great Peace* in the text of the Restatement, wrote in the commentary that:

Although the Supreme Court has not had the chance to consider *The Great Peace*, and while *Solle* v. *Butcher* has its strong supporters, it seems highly unlikely that, after such a detailed review of the matter by the Court of Appeal, the equitable power to rescind for mistake will be restored. Having said that, *if* one considers that the present English law on common or unilateral mistake is too narrow, the obvious way forward would be to revisit equitable rescission.[69]

This is an interesting comment, indicating that Professor Burrows recognises that the argument in favour of an equitable power to relieve has considerable force, and that *The Great Peace* is not necessarily the last word on the question. In the present context, it is interesting to note that Burrows says that if one thinks that the power of the court is too narrow, the obvious way forward is to 'revisit equitable rescission'. It might perhaps have been more natural for

---

[63] G. Treitel, *The Law of Contract*, 11th edn (London: Sweet & Maxwell, 2003), 312.
[64] G. Treitel, *The Law of Contract*, 14th edn by E. Peel (London: Sweet & Maxwell, 2015), [8–30].
[65] [2013] 2 A.C. 108; [2013] UKSC 26.   [66] Ibid., [115].   [67] See ibid., [128].
[68] Ibid., [115].
[69] A. Burrows, *A Restatement of the English Law of Contract* (Oxford University Press, 2016), 176 (emphasis original).

Burrows to say (without reference to equity) that if one considers the power too narrow the obvious way forward would be to widen it, particularly since he is the author of a highly influential article proposing that, wherever possible, distinctions between law and equity should be eliminated.[70] It will be suggested later that it is possible for a modern court to widen its powers without directly invoking equity.

Attention to the equitable treatment of mistake before the Judicature Acts is, as we have seen, necessary for an understanding of the past, and it supports an argument in favour of recognising a flexible power in the modern court to grant relief. But, one may ask, is it desirable in the twenty-first century, or likely to be productive, to propound an argument that an equitable doctrine of mistake continues to exist, a century and a half after the Judicature Acts, parallel to, but somehow still separate from the common law? Modern courts, particularly Canadian courts, are more likely to be influenced by a simple argument that the court today has full power to do justice between the parties, and that general considerations of justice require a power to give relief in some cases from contracts entered into on the basis of fundamental mistake, in order to avoid fortuitous and unjust enrichment, where the contract does not allocate the risk of the mistake to the party who suffers by it. It is certainly open to the U.K. Supreme Court or to the Supreme Court of Canada to adopt such a view, and some lower Canadian decisions lend some support to it.[71]

MISREPRESENTATION

Whenever the making of a contract is induced by a false statement by one of the parties, a mistake occurs; on the part of both parties if the misrepresentation is innocent. An innocent misrepresentation does not necessarily justify the imposition of any obligation on the representor. If the statement in question does not meet the test of contract formation there is no ground for imposing contractual liability.[72] If the statement does not meet the test of tortious liability there is no ground for imposing liability in tort.[73] These

---

[70] Burrows, 'We do This at Common Law'.

[71] *Miller Paving Ltd* v. *B. Gottardo Construction Ltd* (2007) 86 3 O.R. (3d) 161, [26]; 2007 ONCA 422 adopting the arguments in J. D. McCamus, 'Mistaken Assumptions in Equity: Sound Doctrine or Chimera?' (2004) 40 Can. Bus. L.J. 46. Also *Stone's Jewellery Ltd* v. *Arora* (2009) 484 A.R. 286, [30]; 2009 ABQB 656.

[72] *Heilbut, Symons & Co.* v. *Buckleton* [1913] A.C. 30.

[73] *Derry* v. *Peek* (1889) 14 App. Cas. 337. Negligence, though recognised as a ground of liability for misrepresentation in *Hedley Byrne & Co.* v. *Heller & Partners Ltd* [1964] A.C. 465, required proof of fault.

propositions may be accepted, so far as they go. But it does not follow from them that an innocent misrepresentation is legally irrelevant. There is another relevant principle, namely that a misrepresentation inducing a contract, even though it does not justify the *imposition* of any obligation on the misrepresentor, affords an *excuse* from contractual obligation to the party misled and, if the contract has been executed, restitution to reverse an unjust enrichment.

The concept of misrepresentation as an excuse, recognised by equity before the Judicature Acts,[74] was powerfully reinforced by Sir George Jessel M.R. six years after the Acts came into force, in *Redgrave* v. *Hurd*:[75]

> As regards the rescission of a contract, there was no doubt a difference between the rules of Courts of Equity and the rules of Courts of Common Law – a difference which of course has now disappeared by the operation of the *Judicature Act*, which makes the rules of equity prevail. According to the decisions of the Courts of Equity it was not necessary, in order to set aside a contract obtained by material false representation, to prove that the party who obtained it knew at the time when the representation was made that it was false. It was put in two ways, either of which was sufficient. One way of putting the case was, 'A man is not to be allowed to get a benefit from a statement which he now admits to be false ... ' The other was of putting it was this: 'Even assuming that moral fraud must be shewn in order to set aside a contract, you have it where a man, having obtained a beneficial contract by a statement which he now knows to be false, insists upon keeping that contract. To do so is a moral delinquency; no man ought to seek to take advantage of his own false statements'.[76]

The phrases 'get a benefit', 'obtained a beneficial contract' and 'take advantage of' show that the avoidance of unjust enrichment, though not at that time by that name, played a prominent part in the reasoning. Jessel emphasised the contrast with the common law position, and the power of the court to 'set aside', or rescind the contract, not just to refuse specific performance. In *Heilbut, Symons & Co.* v. *Buckleton*,[77] however, the House of Lords held that a statement inducing a contract did not amount to a warranty in the absence of contractual intention, with Lord Moulton observing that 'it is ... of the greatest importance ... that this House should maintain in its full integrity the principle that a person is not liable in damages for an innocent

---

[74] See E. Fry, *A Treatise on the Specific Performance of Contracts* (London: Butterworth, 1858), 193, and the updated edition, E. Fry and W. D. Rawlins, *A Treatise on the Specific Performance of Contracts*, 2nd edn (London: Stevens and Sons, 1881), 281–82.
[75] (1881) 20 Ch.D. 1.   [76] Ibid., 12–13.
[77] *Heilbut, Symons & Co.* v. *Buckleton* [1913] A.C. 30.

misrepresentation, no matter in what way or under what form the attack is made'.[78] This assertion was taken to exclude any monetary award for innocent misrepresentation,[79] and so, until statute gave some flexibility,[80] English law found itself in the very anomalous position of allowing rescission where rescission would formerly have been given by a court of equity, but denying any remedy at all where rescission was impossible, unless the claimant could establish that the statement was fraudulent (in the common law sense of actual deceit), or that it was a contractual warranty, a concept that would have opened the door to excessive damages in some cases. Thus, the equitable power of rescission for innocent misrepresentation was accepted, but minimised by being restricted to such remedies as could have been given before 1875 by the court of equity *acting alone*. Had the courts after 1875 given attention to the reasons underlying the equitable power of rescission as explained in *Redgrave* v. *Hurd* (avoidance of unjust enrichment) they would have concluded that the new court had ample power, where actual rescission was impossible, to give a money remedy that would represent the economic equivalent of rescission – not common law damages for a contractual or tortious wrong, but an award calculated to prevent the maker of a false statement from profiting by it. The neglect of this intermediate remedy has had lasting and deleterious effects on this branch of English contract law. The complexities that have caused so much trouble to Anglo-Canadian law are neatly and compendiously resolved in a recent European document, the *Draft Common Frame of Reference*, which provides that a party may avoid a contract for mistake 'if … the other party … caused the mistake'.[81] The comment explains that the concept underlying this provision is that justice requires that a person, even if completely innocent, should not be allowed to make a profit from his or her own false statement. A money obligation may arise, not as

---

[78] Ibid., 51.

[79] Earlier cases had developed a doctrine known as liability to 'make good' a representation, but this was said to be 'imaginary' by F. Pollock, *Principles of Contract, Being A Treatise on the General Principles Concerning The Validity of Agreements in The Law of England*, 3rd edn (London: Stevens and Sons, 1881), 687, and in the fifth edition, to be 'exploded': F. Pollock, *Principles of Contract, Being A Treatise on the General Principles Concerning The Validity of Agreements in The Law of England*, 5th edn (London: Stevens and Sons, 1889), 506. The doctrine is described, and forcefully rejected, by G. Spencer Bower, *The Law of Actionable Misrepresentation* (London: Butterworth, 1911), 191–94.

[80] Misrepresentation Act 1967 (U.K.), which, however, introduced new complexities and anomalies.

[81] Study Group on a European Civil Code and the Research Group on E.C. Private Law (Acquis Group), *Principles, Definitions and Model Rules of European Private Law: Draft Common Frame of Reference (DCFR)* (Munich: Sellier, 2009), vol. II, art. II, 7:201(1)(b)(i).

damages for any kind of wrongdoing, but in order to avoid or reverse an unjust enrichment.[82] It is true that the Judicature Act does not *require* this result; but neither can the Act be supposed to preclude a development of the law along these lines.

FRUSTRATION

In considering the question of fusion or fission, it is relevant to give attention to the common law doctrine of frustration and its relation to mistake. English treatises have generally treated mistake and frustration as completely separate topics, largely because of the tendency, discussed earlier, to consider mistake as an aspect of contract formation. Frustration, on the other hand, was formulated in terms of bringing the contract to an end and appeared to be related to the idea of discharge of contractual obligations. It seemed to belong at the other end of a treatise. Yet, from the perspective of avoidance of unjust enrichment, as Palmer pointed out,[83] the problems of justice are identical whether the mistake is as to an existing fact or as to a future event. It is sometimes almost impossible to distinguish between the two kinds of mistake, as in the cases arising from the cancellation of the coronation processions for Edward VII in 1902, where some contracts to rent seats or rooms had been made before announcement of the cancellation, and others just afterwards (in ignorance of the announcement).[84] Even the leading frustration case, *Krell* v. *Henry*,[85] could plausibly be regarded as a mistake case, since probably the King (unknown to both parties) was, at the time of the contract, suffering from a physical condition (incipient appendicitis) that was certain (had the medical facts been fully known) to result in cancellation of the processions.

Frustration is a common law doctrine but, ironically, while the common law courts rejected the equitable doctrine of mistake, they adopted themselves what was a very equity-like doctrine of frustration (i.e., a power to set aside contracts in order to avoid injustice).[86] The original common law explanation that frustration depended on an implied term was abandoned in the twentieth century in favour of open recognition that the court intervened to avoid an injustice between the parties. It was accepted by Lord Phillips in *The Great*

---

[82] Ibid., art. II, 7:212.

[83] Palmer, *Mistake and Unjust Enrichment*, 36. See also: A. Swan, J. Adamski and A. Y. Na, *Canadian Contract Law*, 4th edn (Toronto: LexisNexis, 2018), 885.

[84] *Griffith* v. *Brymer* (1903) 47 Sol. Jo. 493; 19 T.L.R. 434.　　[85] [1903] 2 K.B. 740.

[86] *Multiservice Bookbinding Ltd* v. *Marden* [1979] Ch. 84, 89, Browne-Wilkinson J. mentioned frustration as an instance of the common law mending people's bargains.

Peace that the implied term explanation was inadequate both in the context of frustration and of mistake:

> What do these developments in the law of frustration have to tell us about the law of common mistake? First that the theory of the implied term is as unrealistic when considering common mistake as when considering frustration.[87]

A conceptual amalgamation of the frustration and mistake cases would have several far-reaching and, it is suggested, potentially beneficial consequences. It would make recognition of relief for mistake easier to establish and accept, since it is now recognised that relief for frustration is based on broad considerations of justice. It is true that mistake is an older juridical concept than frustration, but if they are recognised as resting on the same principles the following argument has force: if relief is available (as it is) for mistake as to future facts (i.e., frustration), it must also be available for mistake as to existing facts. Recognition of the decisive importance of risk-allocation to both mistake and frustration would benefit the analysis of both topics. The treatment of benefits conferred under the contract, and of reliance, which have been much discussed in the context of frustration, could be carried over to mistake cases, where the potential problems of restitution and reliance are closely analogous, if not identical. The rigidities incidentally imposed in respect of reliance and restitution by the Law Reform (Frustrated Contracts) Act 1943 (U.K.) could be avoided in the context of mistake, and could in turn lead to a more flexible approach to the same problems in the context of frustration in jurisdictions that have not adopted the Act. Even in jurisdictions that have adopted the Act, a more flexible approach applicable both to mistake and frustration might produce benefits in the shape of statutory interpretation on doubtful points, on questions where the statute is not precisely applicable and in suggesting possible legislative reform.

Finally, viewing the question as one of avoidance of unjust enrichment is conducive to flexibility in several respects by avoiding the all-or-nothing 'on/off' concepts implicit in former and present approaches both to mistake (contract valid or void) and frustration (contract valid or discharged). The concept of a contract that is not necessarily void, but that may be set aside by the judgment of the court for sufficient reason (i.e., one that is voidable), admits the possibility of enforcement by the mistaken party, if that party so chooses; it admits the possibility of partial relief, or relief on terms, which the court can fashion in order to meet the justice of the particular case; and it

---

[87] *Great Peace Shipping Ltd* v. *Tsavliris Salvage (International) Ltd* [2003] Q.B. 679, [73].

admits the possibility of denying or restricting relief in order to protect third parties who may have relied on the validity of the contract. These possibilities may be relevant in cases of frustration as well as in cases of mistake. A coherent approach to mistake and frustration would transcend the fusion/fission debate by recognising, in both kinds of case, a general power in the court to grant relief from strict contractual obligations insofar as necessary to prevent extreme injustice.

UNJUST ENRICHMENT

Many of the cases on mistake and unfairness, though perhaps not all,[88] can be thought of in terms of unjust enrichment. Although the origins of the law relating to unjust enrichment did not lie in the Chancery court, there are affinities between equity and unjust enrichment. Lord Mansfield said, of the action for money had and received, that it was 'a liberal action in the nature of a bill in equity'.[89] Buller J. said:

> Of late years this Court has very properly extended the action for money had and received; it is founded on principles of justice, and I do not wish to restrain it in any respect. But it must be remembered that it was extended on the principle of its being considered like a bill in equity. And therefore, in order to recover money in this form of action, the party must shew that he has equity and conscience on his side, and that he could recover it in a Court of Equity.[90]

Equitable concepts can be seen here to have influenced the common law a century before the Judicature Acts. The suggestion that the principal reason for modifying unfair contracts, and those entered into by mistake, is closely related to avoidance of unjust enrichment is one that has roots both in law and equity.

UNCONSCIONABILITY, GOOD FAITH AND ABUSE OF RIGHTS

The power of the courts of equity to grant relief against unfair contracts was often expressed by reference to the concept of conscience, and by use of the words unconscientious and unconscionable to denote transactions against which the court would grant relief. The word 'unconscionable' did not imply any wrongdoing on the part of the stronger party at the time of entering into

---

[88] One could suppose a forfeiture or penalty clause in favour of a third party.
[89] *Clarke* v. *Shee* (1774) 1 Cowp. 197, 199.   [90] *Straton* v. *Rastall* (1788) 2 T.R. 366, 370.

the transaction. What was unconscionable was not the conduct of the defendant *then*, but the attempt *now* to enforce a transaction that the court had
judged to be unfair. It was the transaction or its enforcement that was unconscionable, not the conduct of the defendant. In *Cavendish Square*, the U.K.
Supreme Court used the word in its traditional equitable sense, as the
equivalent of exorbitant, extravagant and disproportionate, but some modern
courts have used the word unconscionable to imply some kind of wrongdoing
on the part of the party profiting by the transaction. Unconscionability has
been given a narrow interpretation in many American and in some English,
Australian and Canadian cases, partly due to its modern meaning in common
usage of 'disgraceful'. The attempt to define unconscionability, for example, as
requiring proof of wrongdoing on the part of the party who profits by the
transaction, or proof of inequality of bargaining power, is unhistorical and has
been unduly restrictive. It was not in the tradition of equity to limit its
jurisdiction by laying down rigid prerequisites to its exercise. Not all cases of
unfairness involve misconduct, nor do all cases of unfairness involve inequality of bargaining power.

The old cases on mortgages and penalties did not require proof of wrongdoing, or of inequality of bargaining power. Relief was granted because strict
enforcement of contractual provisions would sometimes result in awards that
were perceived as disproportionate and extravagant, given that the claimant's
real interest was the enforcement of security for the debt (in the case of a
mortgage) or for the performance of the main contractual obligation (in the
case of a penalty). Relief was independent of any question of inequality of
bargaining power. The unjust enrichment perspective was prominent: it was
unjust to confer an extravagant windfall on one party at the expense of the
other, when the claimant's legitimate expectation could be satisfied by a more
moderate award. The *Çukurova* case,[91] discussed earlier, is a modern instance
of relief from forfeiture where there was no question of inequality of
bargaining power.

The concept of conscience, though it has a long history in this context, is
not very agreeable to the framework of modern thought. The word has
religious overtones, and it suggests a matter that is for the private guidance
only of the person whose conscience is said to be affected. Civilian legal
systems, not having a separate system of equity, have exercised a power to
control contracts through the concepts of good faith and abuse of rights.
Professor Martijn Hesselink has made the comparison:

---

[91] *Çukurova Finance International Ltd* v. *Alfa Telecom Turkey Ltd (Nos 3 to 5)* [2016] A.C. 923.

[T]he concept of good faith in itself should not keep common law and civil law lawyers divided. ... Good faith does not differ much from what the English lawyers have experienced with equity. ... It does not make any more sense for a common law lawyer to fight the concept of good faith than it would have been to fight the whole of equity.[92]

The Supreme Court of Canada has accepted the idea of good faith in contract law, but without making it clear whether the test is subjective (dishonesty) or objective (reasonableness).[93] In referring to Quebec law, the court said that the concept of good faith includes the concept of abuse of rights.[94] If the civilian concept of good faith is to be embraced as equivalent to equity it is essential to note, as Hesselink also explained, that the concept is widely understood in civilian systems in an objective sense.

CONCLUSION

The fusion/fission debate cannot be resolved in its own terms, but it can be transcended. It is desirable that there should be an integrated framework of thought to deal with cases of mistake (including frustration) and unfairness in contracts, but this can only be achieved by openly including within that framework a residual power in the court to depart from legal rules where necessary to avoid extreme injustice. As a matter of history, such a power would be known to have been largely, though not exclusively, derived from equity and it could be regarded as, in a sense, a vindication of the spirit of equity, but it should not be necessary always to refer directly to equity in determining modern cases. Concepts of unjust enrichment, good faith and abuse of rights are also capable of supporting a residual power. In the present context, this suggestion entails open recognition that the proposition that contracts should be enforced, though a valid and necessary principle, is nevertheless subject to a residual power in the court to modify contractual obligations in order to avoid severe injustice.

[92] M. W. Hesselink, 'The Concept of Good Faith', in A. S. Hartkamp, M. Hesselink, E. Hondius, C. Mak and E. du Perron (eds), *Towards a European Civil Code*, 4th edn (Alphen aan den Rijn: Kluwer, 2011), 648; and see C. von Bar and E. Clive (eds), *Principles Definitions and Model Rules of European Private Law: Draft Common Frame of Reference (DCFR)* (Oxford University Press, 2010), vol. 1, 677, where an objective standard seems to be contemplated ('community standards of decency and fairness'). The comparison between good faith and equity is also made by M. Chen-Wishart, 'The Nature of Vitiating Factors in Contract Law', in G. Klass, G. Letsas and P. Saprai (eds), *Philosophical Foundations of Contract Law* (Oxford University Press, 2014), 313.

[93] *Bhasin v. Hrynew* [2014] 3 S.C.R. 494; 2014 SCC 71. See at [83] referring to Quebec law.

[94] Ibid., [83].

11

Lex Sequitur Equitatem

Fusion and the Penalty Doctrine

P. G. TURNER*

INTRODUCTION

Since an early article of Professor Simpson's,[1] historians and lawyers have held that the penalty doctrine which disallows the enforcement of penal stipulations in voluntary transactions derives from a fusion of law and equity. Specifically, they have accepted that the doctrine derives from fusion by convergence:[2] the independent development by separate law and equity courts of similar rules concerning relief from penalties. The doctrine has become a model of the fusion of law and equity dating to the birth of modern equity during the life of its 'father', Lord Nottingham.[3] After transacting parties began using them in the fourteenth century,[4] English law condoned the use of penalties in voluntary transactions for upwards of one century. Gradually, the Court of Chancery found situations in which it would be inequitable to condone the penalty: initially because of special circumstances, later simply because the penalty was a penalty. The common law soon followed, inverting the maxim *equitas sequitur legem*. By the late seventeenth century, common

---

* The author is grateful for the assistance of Sir John Baker in translating and deciphering the roll of *Vanbergh v. Sterne*, and for the comments of Professor Michael Lobban, Professor Richard Nolan, Dr Tim Rogan and Dr Ian Williams. Quotations of manuscripts are given in modern orthography.

[1] Simpson, 'Penal Bond' (incorporated into Simpson, *History of Contract*, ch. 2). Earlier, see D. E. C. Yale, 'Introduction', in D. E. C. Yale (ed.), *Lord Nottingham's Chancery Cases Volume II* (London: Selden Society, 1961) (79 S.S.), 28–29.

[2] *Andrews v. Australia and New Zealand Banking Group Ltd* (2012) 247 C.L.R. 205, [55]; [2012] HCA 30.

[3] L.K. 1673–75; L.C. 1675–82.

[4] R. C. Palmer, *English Law in the Age of the Black Death 1348-1381* (London: University of North Carolina Press, 1993), 82–87; J. Biancalana, 'Contractual Penalties in the King's Court 1260-1360' [2005] C.L.J. 212, 215 ('by 1348').

law courts routinely relieved against penalties and by the nineteenth century had taken over the bulk of such litigation. The penalty doctrine became a common law doctrine solely or nearly so.[5]

The prevailing account suggests a daringness hidden in stories of common law judges as slaves of their own intricate rules of procedure and pleading. It suggests the early arrival of modern liberal attitudes following revolutions, where revolutions occurred,[6] and may show a glimpse of how a wholly fused system of common law could be. However, reconsideration of that account in light of previously unexamined evidence supports quite different conclusions. The penalty doctrine applied in common law courts in the modern period did follow the doctrines and practises of the Court of Chancery. But it depended wholly upon parliamentary legislation. Statutes of 1697 and 1705 empowered and required common law judges to relieve from penalties by applying equitable principles initially developed in the Court of Chancery. Those statutes remained on the statute book in England until after the Second World War, meaning there was no need or opportunity to develop a judge-made doctrine of relief from penalties in separate common law courts. In late modern courts of concurrent equitable and common law jurisdiction, relief from penalties derives wholly from equitable principles – including equitable principles once elaborated by judges in common law courts invested with equitable powers.

The understanding of the penalty doctrine in accounts of fusion, and vice versa, needs revision. To give as complete account as the available space admits, this chapter concentrates on the doctrine in England.

---

[5] Maintaining one or more of these points are: P. S. Atiyah, *An Introduction to the Law of Contract*, 5th edn (Oxford: Clarendon, 1995), 298; J. Getzler, 'Patterns of Fusion', in P. Birks (ed.), *The Classification of Obligations* (Oxford: Clarendon, 1997), 185; A. Lyall, 'Introduction', in A. Lyall (ed.), *Irish Exchequer Reports* (London: Selden Society, 2009) (125 S.S.), cxxx; M. Macnair, 'Imitations of Equitable Relief', 125; J. Oldham, *The Mansfield Manuscripts* (London: University of North Carolina Press, 1992), 352 n. 2; Parliament of New South Wales, *Report of the Law Reform Commission on the Application of Imperial Acts*, L.R.C. 4 (Sydney: Government Printer, 1967), 50–51; A.M.E.V.-U.D.C. *Finance Ltd* v. *Austin* (1986) 162 C.L.R. 170, 189, 191, 195, 197, 201–03, 212; *Andrews* v. *Australia and New Zealand Banking Group Ltd* (2012) 247 C.L.R. 205, [53], [55]–[63]; *Paciocco* v. *Australia and New Zealand Banking Group Ltd* (2016) 258 C.L.R. 525, [115], [122]–[126], [248]; [2016] HCA 28; *Cavendish Square Holding B.V.* v. *Makdessi* [2016] A.C. 1172, [4]–[10], [15], [17], [32], [41], [42], [87]; [2015] UKSC 67.

[6] See A. Laussat, *An Essay on Equity in Pennsylvania* (Philadelphia, PA: Desilver, 1826), 92 and *passim* (fusion attributed to American Revolution); *Andrews* v. *Australia and New Zealand Banking Group Ltd*, ibid., [55] (fusion attributed to Glorious Revolution).

THE EARLY MODERN LAW

Penal Bonds

The penalty doctrine of today developed from Chancery doctrines first adopted in respect of penal bonds, the preferred instrument of contract from medieval to Victorian times. Bonds were instruments under seal which became channelled into common forms. 'Simple' or 'single' bonds founded a definite liability to pay a money sum on a day certain. Penal bonds – which were often called 'obligations' or, less often, conditional bonds – had two aspects: a definite liability to pay – the 'penalty' – which was normally twice the sum or value of the desired performance, and a condition by the fulfilment of which the obligor could avoid paying the penalty. Strict performance was essential to avoid forfeiting the penalty.[7] Forfeiture was possible because bonds were dispositive.[8] '[T]he instrument *was* the obligation'.[9]

Regular relief from the common law's strict attitude towards forfeiture of penalty bonds is first seen in the late fourteenth-century Chancery,[10] and became common under Elizabeth I.[11] Early cases put relief on no fixed ground. They were miscellaneous cases of 'accident, extremity or trifling default'[12] linked perhaps by a wide notion of fraud.[13] The penalty alone supposedly became sufficient to attract relief in the Restoration. The equitable jurisdiction to relieve then acquired a modern form founded on a principle of compensation.[14] An obligor seeking equitable relief from the penalty of a money bond must pay the principal, interest and the obligee's just costs.[15]

Advent of Common Law Relief

That penalties were unconscionable 'seems to have been a familiar notion long before relief came to be routinely granted'.[16] The common lawyers shared this notion. Indeed, they perhaps felt it firmly: three times before

---

[7] D. Ibbetson, 'Absolute Liability in Contract: The Antecedents of *Paradine* v. *Jayne*', in F. D. Rose (ed.), *Consensus ad Idem* (London: Sweet & Maxwell, 1996), 10–11, 13–15.
[8] *Loveday* v. *Ormesby* (1310) Y.B. 3 Edw. II; 20 S.S. 191.
[9] Simpson, 'Penal Bond', 399 (italics original).
[10] *De Brampton* v. *Seymour* (1386) 10 S.S. 2; *Bodenham* v. *Halle* (1456) 10 S.S. 137.
[11] W. J. Jones, *The Elizabethan Court of Chancery* (Oxford: Clarendon Press, 1967), ch. 12; O.H.L.E., vol. VI, 823.
[12] Simpson, 'Penal Bond', 417.   [13] Jones, *The Elizabethan Court of Chancery*, 422–27.
[14] Yale, 'Introduction', 15–16, 20.   [15] E.g., *Hall* v. *Higham* (1663) 3 Ch. Rep. 3.
[16] O.H.L.E., vol. VI, 825. See Plucknett and Barton, *Doctor and Student*, 76–79, 189–90.

1700, the known materials show the common law courts willing to relieve from penalties informally. But legally speaking, the strength of feeling lacked strong practical effect. Relief first appears in 1308/9, in a case of debt on bond in the Common Pleas.[17] The obligor failed to deliver a writing to the obligee at a day certain, but afterwards tendered the writing in court. Though the obligor had defaulted, the obligee had suffered no loss. Bereford J. said it were well that the obligee receive the writing, and that 'this is not, properly speaking, a debt; it is a penalty; and with what equity (look you!) can you demand this penalty?'[18] The judges declined to enter judgment. The next instance appears in 1596/7, when a 'foolish fellow' had granted two simple (not penal) bonds in succession for the one debt without obtaining surrender of the first bond when he entered the second.[19] Walmsley J. said it lay outside the Common Pleas' authority to redress such folly. Regarding penalty bonds, however, the reporter adds:

> Their course here is for the most part that if the defendant will at the first appearance confess the debt or the greater part and tender the rest with costs and forbearance according to 10 in the 100, the Justices will moderate the matter. But if he denies the debt, or does not come until after judgment or verdict, then they will rarely meddle with it, but let the law run.[20]

Perhaps Horwitz had this in mind when he remarked that the Common Pleas 'especially' relieved from penal bonds 'at least a generation before' the legislation of 1697 and 1705,[21] although no evidence of this practice lasting into the seventeenth century has been found. Indeed, in King's Bench in 1669 Keyling C.J. described the 'course of the court' – its practice, rather than common law – thus: 'You know the old character of the three courts in Westminster Hall, viz. Common Pleas is all law and no equity; the Chancery, all equity and no law; and this court both law and equity.'[22] If the Common Pleas earlier had such 'equitable' authority informally to relieve penalties outside the common law, it evidently disappeared by the Restoration period.

Simpson's account rests on a third emergence of informal relief. Writing in the mid-1670s, Lord Nottingham said:

---

[17] *Umfraville* v. *Lonstede* (1308/9) 19 S.S. 58.   [18] Ibid., 59.
[19] *Anon.* (1596/7) B.L. MS Add. 25199 f. 2.
[20] Ibid., trans. by C. Gray, 'The Boundaries of the Equitable Function' (1976) 20 A.J.L.H. 192, 214–15 n. 61. Compare *Tatnall* v. *Gomersall* (1598) 12 S.S. xxxviii.
[21] H. Horwitz, *A Guide to Chancery Equity Records and Proceedings 1600-1800* (Kew: Public Record Office, 1998 imprint), 38.
[22] [*Vanbergh* v. *Sterne*] (1669) M.T. MS 2C 301, 302.

[I]n all suits on bonds it's now become the course of the Court,[23] that, if the defendant will pay the principal and interest and charges, the plaintiff shall be obliged to accept it till plea pleaded, else the defendant shall have a perpetual imparlance, and all this to prevent a suit in Chancery, which otherwise would give the same relief.[24]

Nottingham's account has been accepted with slight corroboration[25] as showing that the common law adopted equitable doctrines on penalties by the mid-1670s[26] or late in the century[27] or well before the statutes of 1697 and 1705.[28] However, it now appears from unnoticed manuscript and printed materials that Nottingham recorded no such development. He recorded a practice of accepting motions to pay money into court, which Raymond C.J. said began 'in Keylinge's time[29] to avoid the hazard and difficulty of pleading a tender'.[30] Payment in was already allowed in Chancery.

The foremost case on the adoption of this Chancery practice at common law is *Vanbergh v. Sterne*, during Kelyng's chief justiceship.[31] A linen merchant, James Vanbergh, sued his customer, Thomas Sterne, in debt on a penal bond of £600 conditioned for payment of £438 10s.[32] by an initial payment of £8 10s. then half-yearly instalments of £10. Believing he had three months' grace after each payment day, Sterne pleaded tender of the initial sum within three months of the appointed day and Vanbergh's refusal of tender, and averred that he was always and remained willing to pay. Vanbergh demurred. The condition required payment on the appointed day, no later. In court Vanbergh again refused to accept payment.

Thus the parties joined issue on tender. When the case was discussed on Saturday 6 November 1669, Sterne abandoned his plea and averment, confessing his indebtedness of £600. Sterne now said his tender of £8 10s. in court should be accepted in discharge of the arrears. Whether his new stance was that a late payment to the creditor should effect a discharge or that the court should accept payment under a new practice of payment in is unclear from

---

[23] *Semble* the Court of King's Bench.   [24] Finch, *'Manual'* and *'Prolegomena'*, 203.
[25] Simpson, 'Penal Bond', 418–19. See below, n. 55.   [26] Ibid., 419.
[27] *Cavendish Square Holding B.V. v. Makdessi* [2016] A.C. 1172, [6], [291].
[28] *Andrews v. Australia and New Zealand Banking Group Ltd* (2012) 247 C.L.R. 205, [53].
[29] Sir John Kelyng, J.K.B. 1663–65; C.J.K.B. 1665–71.
[30] *White v. Woodhouse* (1727) 2 Str. 787; 1 Barn. K.B. 25. See W. Tidd, *The Practice of the Court of King's Bench in Personal Actions* (London: Whieldon, 1790), 408.
[31] Chancery (H. 1667) C.6/179/52 (bill and answer), C.33/230 ff. 333–34 (injunction); (M. 1669) K.B.27/1912/1 m. 336; 2 Keb. 553 pl. 39; 2 Keb. 555 pl. 46 (*sub. nom. Stern v. Vanburgh*); 1 Vent. 42 (*sub. nom. Anon.*); L.I. Misc. 500 55 (*sub. nom. Vanberge v. Sterne*); B.L. MS Lansdowne 1064, 170 (s.n.); M.T. MS 2C 301 (s.n.).
[32] Except the penalty, Keble's figures are inaccurate.

off#

the plea roll and the sole printed report[33] of the day's proceedings. But other signs point towards payment in. Vanbergh opposed, arguing that a discharge would bar the obligee from suing the obligor for default in any later payment. The court disagreed, 'for until judgment that a record is made of the bond it may be sued again on any later breach, and the defendant cannot plead any breach before'.[34] That is consistent with the practice of payment in as afterwards elaborated.[35] The obligor could be discharged without judgment if the court allowed the obligor to pay the sum owed into court and the creditor accepted that payment, requiring the creditor to strike the sum from the declaration. No claim on the bond surviving, there could be no judgment to merge the bond in the record. The obligee could sue again on the bond and the obligor could not plead an earlier breach to escape liability later.

When the case was discussed again the next Monday, Sterne's final stance was that his tender of payment into court, not to Vanbergh, should discharge him. And the court stated a principle by which any discharge would follow payment into court rather than payment direct to the obligee: the court was participant rather than spectator. But the court was told new information. Sterne had preferred a bill and obtained a common injunction in Chancery 'where . . . the case had depended for two years' through Sterne's delay.[36] The court said:

> If the defendant comes before plea pleaded, and makes such a proffer [of principal, interest and costs], they are ex debito justitiae to allow it: but now he having delayed the plaintiff in Chancery two years, it was in their discretion.[37]

A manuscript report indicates the court's role:

> In debt upon a bond if the obligor come before pleading and tender the money sc. principal,[38] *the Court is bound to take it and to discharge the bond*, because here is no delay to the plaintiff. Aliter if such tender be made after plea pleaded, per Curiam.

[33] 2 Keb. 553 pl. 39.
[34] 2 Keb. The common law rule that the *plaintiff* in debt could assign only one breach was distinct: *Painter* v. *Manser* (1584) 2 Co. Rep. 3a, 4a.
[35] See J. Impey, *The New Instructor Clericalis*, 2nd edn (Dublin: Lynch, 1785), 178.
[36] 1 Vent. 42. Vanbergh was in breach of the injunction of 1667 ordered by consent: n. 31. The injunction permitted Vanbergh to declare in King's Bench on the bail already put in, otherwise staying those proceedings until the hearing of the cause in Chancery (which never occurred).
[37] 1 Vent. 42. The 'dissent' of Kelyng C.J. mentioned by Ventris is not mentioned in other reports.
[38] The two references to principal in this quotation are simplifications. Interest and charges were also required: see 2 Keb. 553; 1 Vent. 42; and K.B.27/1912/1 m. 336.

In debt upon a bond [if] the defendant stops proceedings and goes into
Chancery and thereupon 2 years are spent in the controversy and after[wards]
the defendant comes into the Court [of King's Bench] and tender the
principal, though this was before any plea pleaded, *yet the Court would not
take the principal*, per Curiam.[39]

The principle is consistent with Nottingham's recollection and recurs in later
authorities on payment in.[40] Why the case attracted such attention is unclear.
Payment into court *after* judgment in a court of law was discussed in Chancery in 1663,[41] and in one report of *Vanbergh* Twisden J. recalls: 'When I once
moved this matter before Justice Bacon,[42] I was answered, that it was the
course o'the court; and Hoddesdon[43] said it had been so ever since he
remembred.'[44] That dates a practice of payment in at the pleading stage to
the 1640s. Perhaps *Vanbergh* drew attention because it dispelled doubts from a
neglected yet useful practice after a period of instability, including legal
instability, throughout the realm.

The perpetual imparlances mentioned by Nottingham alongside relief from
penalties may simply have been stays. Like a stay, a perpetual imparlance
would have stopped the plaintiff suing to judgment on the penalty. Ordinary
imparlances were used daily in common law pleading until their abolition.[45]
The theory of common law pleading required each party to respond immediately to the adversary's last plea. Leave to imparl was to 'allow [the unready
party] a farther day [to respond]; which was accordingly granted by the Court
to any day that, in their discretion, they might award, either in the same or the
next succeeding term'.[46] The imparlance was to allow parties to '*talk together,
and amicably settle their controversy*'.[47] A perpetual imparlance must have

---

[39] B.L. MS Lansdowne 1064, 170 (italics added). Treby's report is similar. Only Keble says the
court retained that discretion until joinder of issue: 2 Keb. 555 pl. 46.
[40] E.g., *Anon.* (1732) 2 Barnes 279; *Griffiths* v. *Williams* (1787) 1 T.R. 711.
[41] *Crispe* v. *Blake* (1663) 1 Cas. Chan. 23.   [42] Sir Francis Bacon, J.K.B. 1642–49.
[43] Christopher Hoddesdon (of Hornchurch, Essex, and Inner Temple), recorded as Secondary of
the King's Bench as early as 1638 (*Anon.* (1638) Croke Car. 513) and of the Upper Bench as late
as 1650 (d. not later than 1660: see inventory of estate created 28 October 1660, Essex Record
Office, D/DYw 17 and *Roch* v. *Cotterell* (1663) 1 Keb. 776). The dates of Hoddesdon's tenure as
Secondary may never be known: the Secondaries' Remembrance Rolls after 1598 have not
survived.
[44] M.T. MS 2C 301.
[45] Uniformity of Process Act 1832 (U.K.), 2 Wm IV c. 39, s. 11 and the Hilary Term Rules 1834, r. 2,
made under s. 14 of that Act.
[46] H. J. Stephen, *A Treatise on the Principles of Pleading in Civil Actions*, 1st edn (London:
Butterworth and Son, 1824), 90–91 (citations omitted).
[47] Ibid., 90 (citations omitted).

supposed the obligor and obligee on a penal bond should discuss settlement perpetually.[48] Perpetual imparlances may have been given against plaintiffs who accepted the defendant's money in court, and discharged once the plaintiff's declaration was amended.[49] A perpetual imparlance may also have been proper where amending a plaintiff's declaration would have been futile because nothing else was claimed.[50] But while perpetual imparlances may have been essential to the purpose of accepting payment into court – 'to prevent vexation, and make an end of the cause'[51] to recover a liquidated claim – no evidence that they were so used has been found. Indeed, in a puzzling statement the King's Bench said in an action for false imprisonment in 1704 that they 'knew no such thing as a *perpetual imparlance*, though they had known *perpetual injunctions*'.[52] Nothing appears of perpetual imparlances in later sources on penalties. This mystery may be irrelevant if Nottingham was writing about permanent stays. Certainly, *Vanbergh v. Sterne* was discussed as a motion for a stay.[53] By 1704 the supposed uses of perpetual imparlances were served by stays: stays to assist a process intended to shorten actions for liquidated sums generally, not only for penalties. The worry was not that enforcing penalties was unconscionable, but that once a defendant admitted a liquidated liability[54] and paid into court all that was owing, justice required that the claim immediately end.

Five aspects of the known instances of informal relief from penalties in common law courts before 1700 are notable. First, the relief granted at each date was distinct. Secondly, none of the forms of relief applied generally. The Common Pleas customs seem especially narrow. Thirdly, each form of relief

[48] See diary of John Pym, Northants Record Office, FH/N/C/0050, f. 23r. (9 March 1624). Pym recalled John Glanville's speech in the House of Commons on the Bill of Monopolies. Glanville noted a clause limiting parties aggrieved by false monopolies to one imparlance 'to avoid delay by perpetual imparlance'. The clause became section 4 of the Statute of Monopolies 1623 (Eng.), 21 Jac. I c. 3.

[49] See *Suister v. Coel* (1668) 1 Sid. 386 (perpetual imparlance discharged once the plaintiff in assumpsit, who declared without making *profert* of the writing, struck 'per scriptum' from his declaration); *Anon.* (1686) Comb. 20 (indebitatus count struck from the declaration upon payment in).

[50] See *Coke v. Heathcot* (1706) 12 Mod. 598: 'Note: The Court will never give leave to bring principal and interest into Court, and stay proceedings upon a bond when the suit is upon a counter-bond, or when there is any pretence of a collateral agreement.'

[51] Impey, *The New Instructor Clericalis*, 179. See *Anon.* (1702) 7 Mod. 141; *Gregg's Case* (1706) 2 Salk. 596.

[52] *Grant v. Southers* (1704) 6 Mod. 183. The marginal note to the case in the Modern Reports (5th edn, 1794) – 'The Court may grant imparlances perpetually, for the ends of justice' – seems erroneous: see e.g., *Calliland v. Vaughan* (1798) 1 B. & P. 210 (C.P.).

[53] M.T. MS 2C 301; L.I. Misc. 500 f. 55.

[54] Payment into court with a denial of liability first became possible in 1883: R.S.C. Ord. 22, r. 1.

arose spontaneously. A Whiggish development towards 'common law relief
from penalties' is not apparent. Fourthly, whereas the Common Pleas customs
were directed specifically against penalties, payment into court had a wider
target. Fifthly, each practice except that in the 1308/9 case places the source of
relief *outside* the common law in a sort of equity. In common law, the penalty
was an enforceable debt.

Simpson's evidence of the larger change now dominating legal-historical
understanding was limited[55] to *King* v. *Atkyns*,[56] in King's Bench in 1670.
Counsel argued that in an action in debt for the penalty of an indemnity bond,
the action will be 'waived' and an issue of *quantum damnificatus* be directed
where the breach of condition was little and the penalty great.[57] Simpson
thought this confirmed Nottingham's account. However, it now appears that
counsel's argument in *King* v. *Atkyns* was rejected: the court said the obligor
'had best consent to go to issue upon *quantum damnificatus*, and save a
chancery suit'.[58] (King and Atkyns were already in litigation in Chancery.[59])
And Nottingham referred to the renewed 'equitable' practice of payment into
court, not to relief from penalties as such.[60] Evidence of the large change
supposed by Simpson has not been found.

Admission to Law?

To become common law, the opinion that penalties are unconscionable had
to be strong among common lawyers and admitted by the judges into pleading
rules or doctrine. Some think this occurred generally. Enactments of 1697 and
1705 allowing relief from penalties in common law courts, it is said, regulated[61] or sanctioned[62] a position already reached in common law.[63] As seen
previously, there is no evidence of such a general change. In particular,

---

55 Simpson, 'Penal Bond', 418–19, mentioning 'R. v. *Atkyns*', scil. *King* v. *Atkyns*. The plaintiff was
    a Thomas King, surety for Thomas Atkyns on a penal bond granted to the officers of excise to
    the use of the sovereign.
56 (1670) K.B.27/1906 m. 1372; 1 Sid. 442; M.T. MS 2C 366; also 2 Keb. 529 pl. 33, 597 pl. 22, 609
    pl. 43, 642 pl. 72, 739 pl. 39, 746 pl. 58; 1 Vent. 35, 78; M.T. MS 2C 411.
57 1 Sid. 442. For a specimen of such a direction, see *Rolfe* v. *Peterson* (1772) 2 Bro. P.C. 436, 441.
58 M.T. MS 2C 366.
59 (T. 1668) C.10/127/3; subsequent proceedings (M. 1671–H. 1672) C.8/219/21. No decree or order
    has been found.
60 Contrast Simpson, 'Penal Bond', 418–20.
61 See n. 5, esp. A.M.E.V.-U.D.C. *Finance Ltd* v. *Austin* (1986) 162 C.L.R. 170, 189, 202; see at 212
    ('regularise').
62 Horwitz, A *Guide to Chancery Equity Records and Proceedings 1600–1800*, 38.
63 They do not mention the Crown Debts Act, 33 Hen. VIII c. 39 (1541), s. 55, which empowered
    common law courts to accept equitable pleas to actions on bonds enforceable by the king.

Nottingham's account of Restoration-era practice on bonds at common law provides no such evidence.

Other evidence contradicts the supposed reformation of common law. A view that penalties were unconscionable became an attitude of common lawyers that judges then adopted as common law in only two situations. In bail, common law eventually limited plaintiffs to bail for the sum due and unpaid, for '[a] defendant cannot be held to bail for a penalty, but only for the sum secured by the penalty'.[64] In executorship, where a testator while alive paid all sums that fell due on a bond, the common law confined the executor's right of retainer to such of the testator's assets as would cover the sum justly due. The testator could not retain assets up to the penalty.[65] These two rules were not aspects of a general common law doctrine against penalties. Both rules were narrow. Cases on bail considered the penalty 'the debt in law'[66] in all other respects. Decisions on executors held that an executor might retain assets up to the penalty where the testator forfeited the penalty while alive.[67] The narrow rules against penalties in bail and executorship admitted an attitude against penalties to thwart two specific injustices: unjust incarceration and fraud upon a penalty.

Otherwise the substantive common law remained unchanged by lawyers' opinions and informal judicial practice. *Brightman* v. *Parker*[68] came before the King's Bench on a writ of error on a judgment of the Norwich Court. In debt on a bond conditioned for the payment of a lesser amount, the defendant had confessed the penalty and prayed a writ of enquiry under a custom of the City of Norwich. As in the Cities of London[69] and Bristol,[70] the custom in Norwich was to award a writ of enquiry to have a jury try the debt and interest

---

[64] *Hatfeild* v. *Linguard* (1795) 6 T.R. 217. See *Stinton* v. *Hughes* (1794) 6 T.R. 13. Bail for the penalty could still be required in the 1680s–90s: *Eld* v. *Bootle* (M. 1686) E.126/15 f. 46r.; W. Style, *Practical Register*, 3rd edn (London: Dring and Lee, 1694), 115. Mr Serjeant Williams thought an obligor might also sue for malicious arrest for arrest on a sum greater than that justly due on a penal bond: *Gainsford* v. *Griffith* (1667) 1 Wms Saund. 58*d* n. (f).

[65] *Bank of England* v. *Morice* (1735) 2 Str. 1028, 1035–36.

[66] *Judd* v. *Evans* (1795) 6 T.R. 399, 399.

[67] *Bank of England* v. *Morice* (1735) 2 Str. 1028, 1035–36. The law of executors presented another difficulty. Did an executor who accepts payment of the principal and interest due by the condition of a bond to the deceased and who executed a release of the penalty thereby commit a devastavit? Differing opinions were expressed in *Kniveton* v. *Latham* (or *Katham*) (1637) Cro. Car. 437; W. Jones 400. Thus a third potential exception to the doctrine that the penalty is a debt at law faltered.

[68] *Brightman* v. *Parker* (1673) 1 Mod. 96; 3 Keb. 212 pl. 17.

[69] W. Scott, *Somers's Tracts*, 2nd edn (London: Cadell, Davies et al., 1812), vol. 8, 389.

[70] *Brightman* v. *Parker* (1673) 1 Mod. 96 (Wilde J.).

truly due.[71] The alleged error was that the parties could not join issue on this customary 'equitable' plea; this was no plea at common law. Conforming to old authority,[72] the King's Bench affirmed the judgment. The custom was good. Hale C.J. said, 'this course prevents a suit in chancery' and 'it were well if it were established by act of parliament as the common law'.[73] In a near identical case one year later, the court decided the point the same way.[74] Around this time, Sir Francis North[75] wrote in his commonplace book: 'Where the *Chancery* is regular in its remedy, why is not that law?' He listed relief against penalties as an illustration.[76] Throughout this period equitable relief was regularly granted on the Court of Exchequer's equity side from actions on penalties leading to verdicts,[77] judgments[78] or execution[79] in common law courts – including actions in the Exchequer of Pleas directed by the Exchequer in equity.[80] The common law had no general doctrine against penalties. It remained common law that *solvit post diem* (payment after the day) was no plea in actions of debt on bond conditioned for payment at a day certain.[81] The rules of tender, payment and enforceability of penalties were unchanged. The 'well known' and 'major development[] in substantive contract rules'[82] by which Simpson thought the common law set its face against penalties is a scholarly invention.[83]

When the law altered, it altered considerably. The 1705 Act[84] applied only to common money bonds, in which the penalty secured the payment of a lesser sum at a day certain.[85] Before the Act, the judicial practice of accepting payment into court often failed obligors who wished to avoid verdicts,

---

[71] J. Bridall, *Speculum Juris Anglicani* (London: Streater, Flether and Twyford, 1673), 90; C. Viner, *A General Abridgment of the Law and Equity*, 2nd edn (London: Robinson et al., 1791), vol. 7, 192.

[72] *Grice v. Chambers* (1602) Cro. Eliz. 894 pl. 12.   [73] 1 Mod. 96.

[74] *Rogerson v. Jacob* (1674) 3 Keb. 251, 302; 1 Freem. K.B. 281; 1 Vent. 256 (*sub. nom. Anon.*); B.L. MS Add. 32527 f. 43.

[75] C.J.C.P. 1675–82, L.K. (Lord Guilford) 1682–85 (d. 1685).

[76] Quoted in Macnair, 'Imitations of Equitable Relief', 119.

[77] *Stinton v. Deynes* (E. 1683) E.126/14 f. 53r.-d.   [78] *Snowe v. Wayne* (E. 1688) E.126/15 f. 181r.

[79] *Blackthorne v. Banister* (M. 1684) E.126/14 f. 221r.-d.; *Tobias v. Barthrop* (T. 1685) E.126/14 f. 276r.-d.; *Buggin v. Grace* (H. 1690) E.126/15 f. 305r.-d.

[80] *Barton v. Hanckes* (H. 1679) E.126/13 ff. 114d.–115r.; *Emes v. Wicke* (T. 1689) E.126/15 f. 265d.–266r.; (E. 1690) E.126/15 f. 46r.-d.; *Cowling v. Ewbank* (E. 1692) E.126/16 f. 3d.; (H. 1693) E.126/16 f. 88d.

[81] *Nesson v. Finch* (1696) 1 Ld Raym. 382; *Bonafous v. Rybot* (1763) 3 Burr. 1370, 1373–74.

[82] Macnair, 'Imitations of Equitable Relief', 125.

[83] It can no longer be supposed that the fall in cases of relief from penalties in Chancery 1627 and 1685 'clearly reflects' the development of an anti-penalty common law doctrine: contrast Horwitz, *A Guide to Chancery Equity Records and Proceedings 1600–1800*, 38.

[84] 4 & 5 Anne c. 3.

[85] Contrast *Anon.* (1702) 7 Mod. 141 (same distinction under pre-1705 practice).

judgments and execution upon penalties, for payment in was not specifically concerned with penalties. Timing was critical. Motions to pay in before bail was in were too early: until then the parties were not in court.[86] Lateness was fatal: motions for stays could succeed not later than joinder of issue.[87] The relief after judgment available in Chancery[88] and Exchequer in equity[89] could only be imagined at common law:[90] the common law insisted on 'do[ing] injustice, as of course'.[91] Under section 13 of the Act, however, payment into court was explicitly used to relieve from penalties. Whereas the full satisfaction and discharge of a bond at common law required payment and a deed of acquittance,[92] section 13 deemed the bond to be satisfied and discharged by payment in of the principal, interest and costs while action was pending. By section 12, the common law rule that caused such penalties to be forfeited was altered. 'A new plea'[93] of *solvit post diem* was founded.[94] It was 'as effectual a bar, as if the money had been paid at the day and place according to the condition or defeazance, and had been so pleaded' (s. 12). Provided that the debtor or the debtor's heirs, executors and administrators paid the principal and interest before action was brought, the plea applied regardless of time, even to debt or *scire facias* on a judgment.

The alterations under the 1697 Act[95] were major. Before the Act commenced, payment in was unavailable on performance bonds to protect obligors against the force of penalties at common law.[96] Payment in only applied to liquidated claims.[97] (Nottingham said the new practice at common law was 'in all suits on bonds',[98] but the requirement to pay principal, interest and costs was apt only for money bonds.) The Act said all sorts of instruments were

---

[86] *Anon.* (1703) 6 Mod. 11.

[87] See nn. 37, 39. See also *Kettleby* v. *Hales* (1683) 3 Lev. 119 ('payment is no plea in debt upon a bill *obligatory* . . . *a fortiori* not in *debt* upon a judgment of record').

[88] See n. 115.   [89] See nn. 77–80.

[90] *Le Sage* v. *Pere* (1702) 7 Mod. 114 pl. 150; *Burridge* v. *Fortescue* (1703) 6 Mod. 60 pl. 73. See n. 41.

[91] *Bonafous* v. *Rybot* (1763) 3 Burr. 1370, 1373–74.

[92] See R. Atkyns, *An Enquiry into the Jurisdiction of the Chancery in Causes of Equity* (London: [s.n.] 1695), 36–37 (p. 37 is misnumbered '33').

[93] *Ex p. Winchester* (1744) 1 Atk. 116, 118.

[94] *Fowell* v. *Forrest* (1668) 2 Wms Saund. 47, 48 n.(h); *Giddings* v. *Giddings* (1756) 1 Keny. 335, 337.
       [95] 8 & 9 Wm III c. 11 s. 8.

[96] *Smith* v. *Broomhead* (1797) 7 T.R. 300, 304–05; H. J. Stephen, *New Commentaries on the Laws of England* (London: Butterworth, 1842), vol. 2, 159.

[97] Payment in first became possible for unliquidated sums generally by the Common Law Procedure Act 1852, s. 70.

[98] Finch, 'Manual' and 'Prolegomena', 203.

objects of relief: bonds, indentures, deeds 'or writing' (s. 8). It empowered courts to relieve from penalties for not performing 'any covenants or agreements', to direct juries to ascertain the losses plaintiffs sustained by defendants' breaches, to enter judgment for the penalty to stand as security for any subsequent breaches, and so on.

The Acts' words show how much change they made. Both assumed that the common law upheld penalties. The 1705 Act assumed that, apart from its provisions, forfeited penalties in money bonds were valid and enforceable. The courts held that assumption true.[99] The 1697 Act spoke explicitly of strict common law. In an action on a penalty, it said 'the like judgment shall be entered ... as heretofore hath been usually done in such like actions', namely a judgment for the penalty plus 'damages' for the detention of the debt. The validity and force of the penalty at common law were notorious. Lord Mansfield said that under the 1697 Act '[t]he judgment is [still] to be for the whole penalty, and is to remain as further security' but, unlike before, to be enforced only to the extent of that security.'[100] Those responsible for preparing each Act – Lord Somers, a past Lord Chancellor,[101] and Simon Harcourt, a future Lord Chancellor[102] – must have known the practice and law they were reforming. If they did not, others in those fractious Parliaments could not have failed to notice such ignorance.[103]

The suggestion that the Acts 'regulate[d]'[104] or 'confirmed'[105] a position already reached at common law is incorrect – and was rarely thought correct until quite recently. The Common Pleas once said the Act of 1705 'conform[ed] to the common law before' that a common money bond 'is to be considered as only a security for the principal money due, together with interest and costs'.[106] Sometimes, counsel spoke and writers wrote similarly.[107] Blackstone was nearer the mark, while wide of it. He said Chancery relief from common money bonds 'had before these statutes in some degree obtained a footing' in courts of law.[108] But all these are misunderstandings. The 1697 and

---

[99] *Moreland v. Bennett* (1725) 1 Str. 652; *Bonafous v. Rybot* (1763) 3 Burr. 1370, 1373–74.
[100] *Collins v. Collins* (1759) 2 Burr. 820, 824. See *Howell v. Hanforth* (1775) 2 W.Bl. 1016.
[101] L.K. 1693–97; L.C. 1697–1700. See n. 69.   [102] L.K. 1710–13; L.C. 1713–14.
[103] Macnair, 'Imitations of Equitable Relief', 122–23 (on the 1705 bill). Harcourt's bill: H.C. Jour., vol. 15, 624, 689, 719. Somers's bill: H.L. Jour., vol. 18, 69–70, 78, 145–47, 161; H.C. Jour., vol. 15, 150–51, 191–93, 194, 196–99, 199.
[104] *A.M.E.V.-U.D.C. Finance Ltd v. Austin* (1986) 162 C.L.R. 170, 189, 202.
[105] Getzler, 'Patterns of Fusion', 185.   [106] *Amery v. Smalridge* (1771) 2 W.Bl. 760, 760.
[107] E.g., *Brangwin v. Perrot* (1777) 2 W.Bl. 1190; Stephen, *New Commentaries on the Laws of England*, vol. 2, 159.
[108] W. Blackstone, *Commentaries on the Laws of England*, book III ed. by T. P. Gallanis (Oxford University Press, 2016), 286, 354.

1705 Acts neither regulated nor confirmed existing common law practice or common law rules that penalties should not be enforced. What they provided was new.[109]

Over the following century, the common law courts became regular venues of relief from penalties. Did a new general attitude against penalties arise, with new judge-made law tailored to fit?

A PERENNIAL ATTITUDE

Long after payment into court was re-established and the 1697 and 1705 enactments were made, the common law – outside statute – recognised, tolerated and enforced penalties in penal bonds and other instruments. A general 'refusal of the common law courts to enforce penalties'[110] never took place. Outside statute the perennial attitude of the common law has been toleration towards penalties.[111]

Wide though the Acts of William and Anne were, the judge-made law was often applied. Except in the special rules of bail and executorship, the common law was as strict as ever.

Examples abound. In its first century, the 1697 Act was construed as enabling legislation.[112] It was not compulsory. '[T]here [were] now two methods [of enforcement] at the election of the plaintiff, either at common law or on the statute.'[113] Plaintiffs often elected to proceed at common law. Where that occurred, the plaintiff was entitled to a verdict, judgment and execution for the penalty. Plaintiffs could adopt some parts of section 8 (assigning breaches) and otherwise proceed at law (recovering the penalty, because the loss thereby suffered need not be determined).[114] Defendants wanting relief after judgment[115] or after a

---

[109] Ibbetson, *Historical Introduction*, 150, 214, 255. Contrast Simpson, *History of Contract*, 122; A.M.E.V.-U.D.C. *Finance Ltd v. Austin* (1986) 162 C.L.R. 170, 189, 202, 212; *Cavendish Square Holding B.V. v. Makdessi* [2016] A.C. 1172, [6].

[110] A.M.E.V.-U.D.C. *Finance Ltd v. Austin* (1989) 162 C.L.R. 170, 189.

[111] See P. S. Atiyah, *The Rise and Fall of Freedom of Contract* (Oxford: Clarendon, 1979), 414–16.

[112] *Cavendish Square Holdings B.V. v. Makdessi* [2016] A.C. 1172, [6].

[113] *Baron v. Hagger* (1719) 130 S.S. 184, 184 (C.P.). Similarly, *Martin v. Hardy* (1781) 1 Mansf. MSS 352.

[114] *Walker v. Priestly* (1723) 1 Com. 376, 377.

[115] *Gardner v. Pullen* (M. 1700) C.33/295 f. 51d.; (M. 1700–H. 1701) C.22/295 ff. 63r., 149d., 299d., 341r.; 2 Vern. 394; *Humphreys v. Humphreys* (M. 1735) C.33/365 f. 1r.; 3 P. Wms 395; *Roy v. Beaufort* (1741) 2 Atk. 190; *Hardy v. Martin* (E. 1783) C.33/457 f. 41d., C.33/459 ff.

verdict[116] for the penalty, or because proceedings to recover the penalty were threatened,[117] had to approach equity courts. Common law also applied to common money bonds within the scope of the 1705 Act where the Act was not pleaded,[118] or tender was not followed by payment.[119]

Penalties were recognised and enforced in diverse cases. Where an obligor did not perform the conditions of a penal bond, Jekyll M.R. said the obligee's 'plain, proper and natural remedy ... was to sue the bond [at law], whereon the penalty would be recovered'.[120] Elsewhere, the Common Pleas[121] and the King's Bench[122] followed the opinion of Lord Hardwicke L.C.[123] that the penalty on an annuity bond was the debt at common law even after the sum justly due was paid. Again, when an obligor failed to pay the first of three annual payments to be made on a penal bond, the Common Pleas held the bond to be absolute.[124] Again, where the Chancery relieved from the penalty in a charterparty upon the defendant's offering to pay principal, interest and costs, it nevertheless held the plaintiff had properly sued for the penalty in King's Bench.[125] Each party was as right in his claim in each court as the other party was in the other court: the plaintiff obtained costs at law, the defendant costs in Chancery.[126] And where the question was whether a penalty is a debt in equity, not whether Chancery would relieve from the penalty as a debt, Grant M.R. held it 'clear ... that both at Law and in Equity the penalty is the debt'.[127]

Arguments for the incorporation of equitable doctrines against penalties into the judge-made common law would have been wasted air had fusion already happened. Such arguments were in fact made, unsuccessfully. The common law had scarcely changed and the judges were unwilling to change it. John Strange[128] argued in *Bank of England* v. *Morice*[129] that an executor's right of retainer should be confined to the sum justly due on bonds the

478r. –479d.; 1 Cox 26; 1 Bro. C.C. 419 n. (2) (tried at nisi prius by Lord Mansfield, *Martin* v. *Hardy* (1781) 1 Mansf. MSS 352, in breach of the plaintiff's injunction).

[116] *Sloman* v. *Walter* (1783) 1 Bro. C.C. 418; (M. 1784) C.33/364 f. 14r. (injunction) (no final decree found).

[117] *Le Sage* v. *Pare* (E. 1702) C.9/461/134, C.6/331/2 (bill and answer); (T. 1705) C.33/304 f. 364r. (dismissal for want of proceeding); *Forward* v. *Duffield* (H. 1742) C.33/379 f. 229d.; (E. 1744) C.33/281 f. 347r. –348d.; (T. 1746) C.33/389 f. 594; (H. 1748) C.33/389 ff. 170d., 175d., 241d.; 3 Atk. 555; *Errington* v. *Aynesly* (H. 1789) C.33/471 ff. 229d. –231d.; (T. 1789) f. 430d.; 2 Bro. C.C. 341. The situation may have been similar in the equity side of Exchequer.

[118] *Moreland* v. *Bennett* (1725) 1 Str. 652, 652.

[119] *Underhill* v. *Matthews* (1715) 130 S.S. 20 (C.P.).   [120] *Hall* v. *Hardy* (1733) 3 P. Wms 187, 188.

[121] *Perkins* v. *Kempland* (1776) 2 W.Bl. 1106.   [122] *Wyllie* v. *Wilkes* (1780) 2 Doug. 519, 523.

[123] *Ex p. Winchester* (1744) 1 Atk. 116.   [124] *Coates* v. *Hewit* (1744) 1 Wils. K.B. 80.

[125] *Forward* v. *Duffield* (1747) 3 Atk. 555.   [126] Ibid., 555.

[127] *Clarke* v. *Seton* (1801) 6 Ves. Jun. 411, 415.   [128] M.R. 1750–54.   [129] (1735) 2 Str. 1028.

penalties of which were forfeited while the testator lived. He commended 'the laudable endeavours of Courts of Law, to let in as much of equity as they can' to the King's Bench, yet was disappointed.[130] Confining the right of retainer to the sum justly due was acceptable where the testator performed the conditions of the bond while alive. But that rule could not extend to bonds forfeited during the testator's lifetime. After 'great deliberation', Hardwicke C.J. said: 'how much soever the law of executors wants alteration', regarding the penalty's force 'it may be dangerous for us to blend the rules of law and equity together'.[131] Similarly, in *Bevan v. Jones*[132] the Common Pleas denied jurisdiction 'at common law, or by statute' to order a prothonotary to determine the sum truly due, and interest and costs, on a penal bond after execution executed, and to order restitution of the overplus. The defendant must sue in an equity court.[133]

Had the common law reconstructed its rules on penalties as nineteenth-century contracting parties turned from bonds to unsealed writing to record their agreements, its strict attitude might then have ended. But the past was not closed off. As late as 1936 and 1938, the House of Lords said the procedures of the 1697 Act were 'well established'[134]: the obligee 'recovers judgment on the whole amount of the bond, but can only issue execution for the amount of the damages proved'[135] to 'flow from' the assigned breach.[136] Penalties in unsealed instruments received much the same treatment, since the Act applied to penalties in 'bonds, or ... in any indenture, deed, or writing'. The basic features of penalties in bonds and unsealed instruments were the same. In a neglected case of 1849, the House of Lords held that a forfeited penalty arising from a contract in unsealed writing was the debt at law. That debt vested in the creditor's assignees in bankruptcy 'subject to the provisions of the [1697] statute so far as they may be applicable'.[137] The Act apart, a plaintiff at law in debt for a penalty in articles could obtain a verdict, judgment

[130] *Bank of England v. Morice* (1735) 2 Str. 1028, 1014 (order varied on another ground (1737) 2 Bro. P.C. 456).
[131] Ibid., 1034–35.   [132] (1739) Barnes 203.   [133] Ibid.
[134] *Workington Harbour and Dock Board v. Trade Indemnity Co. Ltd (No. 2)* [1938] 2 All E.R. 101, 105.
[135] Ibid.
[136] *Workington Harbour and Dock Board v. Trade Indemnity Co. Ltd (No. 1)* [1937] A.C. 1, 23.
[137] *Beckham v. Drake* (1849) 2 H.L.C. 579, 618–19 (Wightman J.); also at 598 (Williams J.), 615 (Cresswell J.), 622 (Maule J., elliptically), 629–30 (Parke B.), 631 (Wilde C.J.). Similarly, *Brooke v. Crowther* (argued 1795) 128 S.S. 243, 247 (an undelivered opinion).

and execution for the whole debt.[138] The perennial view of the common law from the mid-fourteenth century[139] until into the twentieth was that a forfeited penalty is the debt in law.

Forging a new common law that was intolerant of penalties became legally impossible in actions of debt.[140] All writings that imposed penalties on obligors to secure their performance of promises were within the 1697 Act. It eventually dawned on the judges that unless that Act should be compulsory on plaintiffs in debt, injustice would routinely be done to those liable to penalties. The Common Pleas held the Act compulsory on plaintiffs in 1768.[141] However, the King's Bench only settled the matter twenty-six years later,[142] holding that the Act must be compulsory[143] because its purpose was to protect defendants from the cost and inconvenience of proceeding in Chancery after suffering the application of the unmodified common law.[144] As all cases on penalties securing the performance of promises or covenants were within the Act, and the Act was compulsory in actions of debt, cases in which a new common law doctrine by which penalties in unsealed writings were not valid enforceable debts in law could not be.[145]

The perennial attitude of the common law is, in law, its attitude today. 'The penalty is in legal contemplation the debt', subject to equitable and statutory relief.[146] The penalty is still a debt which the creditor is entitled to have paid.[147] *Obiter dicta* in which penalties have been said to be void[148] are mistaken and made in apparent ignorance of binding House of Lords'

---

[138] *Drage* v. *Brand* (1768) 2 Wils. K.B. 377 (*sub. nom. Dry* v. *Bond* (1768) Bull. N.P. 164); *Beckham* v. *Drake* (1849) 2 H.L.C. 579, 598, 615, 618, 629, 631, 645. See also *Turnor* v. *Goodwin* (1713) Fort. 145 discussing the common law apart from the 1705 Act.

[139] *Baker and Milsom*, 281–82.

[140] Contrast *Cavendish Square Holdings B.V.* v. *Makdessi* [2016] A.C. 1172, [6]–[8].

[141] *Drage* v. *Brand* (1768) 2 Wils. K.B. 377.

[142] *Hardy* v. *Bern* (1794) 5 T.R. 636; *Roles* v. *Rosewell* (1794) 5 T.R. 538. In the interim, see e.g., *Howell* v. *Hanforth* (1775) W.Bl. 1016; *Martin* v. *Hardy* (1781) 1 Mansf. MSS 352 (the defendant was forced into Chancery: *Hardy* v. *Martin* (1783) 1 Cox 26; 1 Bro. C.C. 419 n.(2)).

[143] Excepting the Crown: *R.* v. *Peto* (1826) 1 Y. & J. 171.

[144] *Hardy* v. *Bern* (1794) 5 T.R. 636, 637.   [145] *Roles* v. *Rosewell* (1794) 5 T.R. 538, 542.

[146] *Beckham* v. *Drake* (1849) 2 H.L.C. 579, 618–19. Similarly, see 598 (Williams J.), 615 (Cresswell J.), 622 (Maule J.), 629–30 (Parke B.), 631 (Wilde C.J.); 645 (Lord Campbell), 644–45 (Lord Brougham, relying on Parke B.'s judgment: (1841) 9 M. & W. 79).

[147] Contrast *Andrews* v. *Australia and New Zealand Banking Group Ltd* (2012) 247 C.L.R. 205, [54] (legislation equivalent to the 1697 Act seemingly applicable but not applied).

[148] *Cavendish Square Holding B.V.* v. *Makdessi* [2016] A.C. 1172, [9], [42], [87]–[88], [226], [255]. The lead was, again, given by Simpson, 'Penal Bond', 415.

decisions holding otherwise. However, while the penalty is the debt in law, statute today requires English courts to limit creditors' enforcement to what is necessary to compensate them for the debtor's default.[149]

How can the common law have kept this attitude while common law courts gained the bulk of cases on relief from penalties from the eighteenth century until separate courts of law and equity were abolished by the Judicature Acts in 1875?

'EQUITY' FLOWERS AT COMMON LAW

Between the eighteenth century and the Judicature reforms, 'equity' flowered at common law in the soil of penal transactions. This happened in two ways.

First, the judges construed the statutes that empowered them to relieve from penalties in accordance with the purpose of the statutes – which they called an Act's 'equity'.[150] Situations outside the letter were thus brought within each statute, and the scope of each Act was otherwise delineated.[151]

More importantly, however, the new enactments were intended to function in imitation of Chancery equity.[152] The devices they spoke of – actions on penal sums and penal bonds, pleas, assignments of breaches, stays and so on – operated at common law in tolerance and furtherance of penalties. How could those same devices be turned to bring relief?[153] Since the new powers were intended to make it unnecessary for debtors to seek relief in Chancery (and the Exchequer in equity?), the answer was that the common law courts must apply equitable principles. Hence, they deliberately, faithfully and extensively imitated equitable principles and equitable relief from 1697 to 1705 until the courts fused in 1875.

Thus, in delivering the reasons of the House of Lords, Lord Eldon L.C. explained that Parliament had pursued its purpose of making it unnecessary for debtors to seek relief from penalties in Chancery 'by giving the Courts of Law an equitable jurisdiction' to grant such relief under the 1697 Act.[154] Chambre J. had earlier said that the Acts were 'to take away the necessity of applying for relief to a court of equity' by equipping the common law courts with equitable

---

[149] See text between nn. 218–21.
[150] S. E. Thorne, 'Introduction', in Anon., *A Discourse upon the Exposicion and Understandinge of Statutes*, ed. by S. E. Thorne (San Marino, CA: Huntington Library, [c. 1557–67] 1942), 45–92.
[151] E.g., *Bonafous v. Rybot* (1763) 3 Burr. 1370, 1373; *Wyllie v. Wilkes* (1780) 2 Doug. 519, 522–23.
[152] See Macnair, 'Imitations of Equitable Relief, 120–27.
[153] 'That there was regular relief against the enforcement of penalties says nothing about what constituted a penalty': Ibbetson, *Historical Introduction*, 214.
[154] *Johnes v. Johnes* (1814) 3 Dow. 1, 19.

powers to extend 'the same benefit to Defendants in actions at law' as the Chancery.[155] Such observations were commonplace,[156] and began early. In 1703, the King's Bench described a motion under the 1697 Act for a stay of action in debt on bond as 'an equitable motion to be relieved against the penalty'.[157] The new common law powers conferred by statutes were modelled on equity courts' powers, and depended on substantive Chancery equity.

A judicial counterpoint to this explanation enables the relationship of law and equity under the Acts to be shown simply. An influential Australian case supposed that 'over more than two centuries before the introduction of the Judicature system' in 1875, the doctrines of relief from penalties at law and in equity were independent and dissimilar.[158] While the Chancery exercised a discretionary and 'dynamic jurisdiction which seems to have applied constantly changing criteria' to relief from penalties, the common law laid down stable rules resistant to equitable whims of change.[159]

The facts show these contrasts to be false. The supposed 'common law' after 1697 and 1705 until 1875 comprised statute and decisions thereon; in those decisions the central common law courts applied the Chancellor's principles to decide whether a stipulation was a penalty (as the Acts required). Thus, the Chancery declined to relieve where interest was reserved at, say, 5 per cent p.a. with a condition to accept interest at 4 per cent p.a. if punctually paid but was willing to relieve where interest was reserved at, say, 4 per cent p.a. on condition that the rate rise to 5 per cent p.a. if not punctually paid.[160] Under the 1705 Act, the common law judges followed that distinction.[161] Secondly, the Chancery distinguished between penalties and liquidated damages for default,[162] which distinction was also followed in cases at law.[163] Thirdly, the Chancery distinguished[164] between common penalties and stipulations for a sum which the obligor might choose to pay as the price of diverging from what an instrument primarily required. That distinction also was followed in cases at law.[165] Fourthly, the common law cases followed the Chancery's willingness to consider whether a stipulation alleged to liquidate a promisor's liability for default was truly a penalty – sometimes complaining, but nevertheless doing so.[166] Fifthly, the judges copied Chancery practice on procedural points

[155] *Astley* v. *Weldon* (1801) 2 B. & P. 346, 354.
[156] E.g., *Collins* v. *Collins* (1759) 2 Burr. 820, 824; *Bonafous* v. *Rybot* (1763) 3 Burr. 1370, 1373.
[157] *Burridge* v. *Fortescue* (1703) 6 Mod. 60 pl. 73.
[158] A.M.E.V.-U.D.C. *Finance Ltd* v. *Austin* (1986) 162 C.L.R. 170, 183.   [159] Ibid.
[160] E.g., *Sewell* v. *Musson* (1683) 1 Vern. 210.   [161] *Bonafous* v. *Rybot* (1763) 3 Burr. 1370, 1375.
[162] E.g., *Roy* v. *Beaufort* (1741) 2 Atk. 190, 194.   [163] *Lowe* v. *Peers* (1768) 4 Burr. 2225, 2227.
[164] *Rolfe* v. *Peterson* (1772) 6 Bro. P.C. 470.   [165] *Bird* v. *Randall* (1762) 1 W.Bl. 373.
[166] *Astley* v. *Weldon* (1801) 2 B. & P. 346; *Kemble* v. *Farren* (1829) 6 Bing. 141.

as to the entry of judgment[167] and award of costs[168] under the 1697 Act, and payment in under the 1705 Act.[169] The principles applied under the Acts changed as frequently as the principles in Chancery: not often.

A late judicial statement in England also supposes independent penalty doctrines at law and in equity after 1697 and 1705. Following those enactments, it is said, 'the equitable jurisdiction was rarely invoked, and the further development of the penalty rule was entirely the work of the courts of common law'.[170] But reasoning from the assumed rarity of equitable relief is problematic. The pressure that persuaded the common law judges that the 1697 Act must be mandatory came from the routine injustice that required defendants to seek relief in equity courts from verdicts, judgments or executions upon penalties in common law courts.[171] However, the critical facts concern the equitable *jurisdiction* to relieve from penalties. Parliament did not remove that jurisdiction.[172] Legislation was founded upon it. Had the Acts not empowered the common law judges to apply equitable principles to identify the penalties they ought to relieve, the Acts could not have functioned as Parliament intended.[173]

One of equity's less ardent lovers, Bramwell B., repeatedly insisted that the Acts could only operate by reference to Chancery equity. Where a party to a written agreement claimed relief from an alleged penalty in a court of law, he said, the question was 'whether the agreement is within the 8 & 9 Wm 3, c. 11, s. 8', which in turn required the courts to consider whether courts of equity would relieve.[174] Soon before the Judicature Act system was introduced,[175] he held that true of the 1697 and the 1705 Act and Channell and Pigott BB. agreed. Bramwell repeated those views once the Judicature system commenced.[176]

THE JUDICATURE SYSTEM

The Judicature Acts abolished and replaced the various superior courts, including of law and equity, with a new Supreme Court of Judicature of concurrent legal and equitable jurisdiction. The sources of relief from

---

[167] *Goodwin v. Crowle* (1775) 1 Cowp. 357, 359.
[168] *Burridge v. Fortescue* (1703) 6 Mod. 60 pl. 73.   [169] *R. v. Clark* (1714) Gilb. Cas. 291, 294.
[170] *Cavendish Square Holding B.V. v. Makdessi* [2016] A.C. 1172, [7].
[171] See G. Price, *A Treatise of the Law of the Exchequer* (London: Saunders and Benning, 1830), 673.
[172] *Codd v. Wooden* (1790) 3 Bro. C.C. 415.
[173] *Beckham v. Drake* (1849) 2 H.L.C. 579, 598, 615, 618, 629, 631, 645.
[174] *Betts v. Burch* (1859) 4 H. & N. 506, 511.   [175] *Preston v. Dania* (1872) L.R. 8 Ex. 19, 20–21.
[176] *Re Newman, Ex p. Capper* (1876) 4 Ch.D. 724, 733–34.

penalties were immediately unchanged. The Acts of 1697 and 1705 stayed in force.[177] In important appeals soon after the new system commenced, the House of Lords and the Privy Council said little of the origins and development of relief from penalties in English law. To interpret those as noiseless signals that the source of English legal doctrine had suddenly changed would be a mistake. The appeals were from mixed jurisdictions without a distinct system of equity: the Cape of Good Hope,[178] Ceylon[179] and Scotland.[180] It was proper to say little of the source of the English doctrine. And, constitutionally, those decisions could not alter the grounding jurisdiction of the English doctrine. Indeed, statements in these cases affirm equity as the source of relief in English cases. In one Scottish appeal, Lords FitzGerald and Halsbury approved the views of (the now) Lord Bramwell on the basis of statutory relief from penalties in English law.[181] In another Scottish appeal, Lord Halsbury L.C. said the Act of 1697 was 'that upon which English lawyers rely when this question of occurs' because of 'the mode of administering in this country to the two branches of jurisprudence which we call law and equity'.[182] The proposition that equity is the source of relief from penalties in the unwritten law formed part of the *rationes decidendi* of the House of Lords in cases of 1917[183] and 1962,[184] and cases of the Privy Council in 1935 and 1941:[185] authorities since quite overlooked.[186]

As the 'common law' penalty doctrine before and after 1875 consisted of case law construing and applying statutes whose operation depended on

---

[177] Both later received short titles: Statute Law Revision Act 1948, s. 5 and Sch. 2. See nn. 193 and 198.

[178] *Commissioner of Public Works* v. *Hills* [1906] A.C. 368.

[179] *Webster* v. *Bosanquet* [1912] A.C. 394.

[180] *Lord Elphinstone* v. *Monkland Iron and Coal Co.* (1886) 11 App. Cas. 332; *Clydebank Engineering and Shipbuilding Co.* v. *Don Jose Ramos Yzquierdo y Castaneda* [1905] A.C. 6; *Dunlop Pneumatic Tyre Co. Ltd* v. *New Garage and Motor Co. Ltd* [1915] A.C. 79.

[181] *Lord Elphinstone* v. *Monkland Iron and Coal Co.*, ibid., 346, 348, referring to *Betts* v. *Burch* and *Re Newman, Ex p. Capper* (1876) 4 Ch.D. 724, 734.

[182] *Clydebank Engineering and Shipbuilding Co.* v. *Don Jose Ramos Yzquierdo y Castaneda* [1905] A.C. 6, 10. The statement that 'the law of penalties has been held to be the same in England and Scotland' (*Cavendish Square Holdings B.V.* v. *Makdessi* [2016] A.C. 1172, [42]) is too wide.

[183] *Watts, Watts & Co. Ltd* v. *Mitsui and Co. Ltd* [1917] A.C. 227, 235 (Lord Finlay L.C., Lord Parker of Waddington concurring), 246 (Lord Sumner).

[184] *Bridge* v. *Campbell Discount Co. Ltd* [1962] A.C. 600, 616 (Lord Morton), 624 (Lord Radcliffe), 629–32 (Lord Denning), 632 (Lord Devlin); and arguably also *Tool Metal Manufacturing Co. Ltd* v. *Tungsten Electric Co. Ltd* [1955] 1 W.L.R. 761, 767.

[185] *Faruqi* v. *Aiyub* (1935) L.R. 2 Pal. 390, 394; *Ayoub* v. *Farouqi* [1941] A.C. 274, 281–82.

[186] *A.M.E.V.-U.D.C. Finance Ltd* v. *Austin* (1986) 162 C.L.R. 170, 191; *Cavendish Square Holdings B.V.* v. *Makdessi* [2016] A.C. 1172, [42].

equity, it would be meaningless to ask how the common law on penalties developed in the fused system. That would assume a distinct common law doctrine which has never existed. More informative is to ask what, after 1875, became of the statutory powers and procedures of common law courts before 1875 to relieve from penalties.

The powers and procedures that the common law courts wielded under the Act of 1705 were superseded in 1875.

Section 13 of the 1705 Act (payment into court in actions on common money bonds) alluded to 'that which had always been the doctrine of equity',[187] viz. that the penalty on a common money bond was mere security for payment of the sum justly due. Section 13 had been superseded by the Hilary Term Rules of 1834,[188] which on this point were themselves superseded by general provisions in the Common Law Procedure Acts,[189] the Judicature Rules[190] and the 1883 Rules of the Supreme Court.[191] In courts equipped with those powers and full equitable jurisdiction, and which owed a duty to recognise such equitable defences and grant such equitable relief against legal claims as the Court of Chancery would have given before Judicature,[192] section 13 served no distinct purpose. It was repealed in 1948.[193]

Section 12 more nearly expressed the rule of equity that, though *solvit post diem* was no plea in debt at common law, an obligor could be relieved from a penalty upon paying principal, interest and costs. The legal rule and the equitable rule conflicted: outside section 12, 'the Court of Chancery alone had jurisdiction' to grant relief by accepting late payment[194] or a plea of accord and satisfaction[195] or variation by an unsealed writing.[196] In the new courts, which were required to recognise such equitable defences and grant such equitable relief against legal claims as the Court of Chancery would previously have given – and in which conflicts and variances between legal and equitable

---

[187] *Re Dixon* [1900] 2 Ch. 561, 582. Strictly, the statement is true only from sometime in the seventeenth century.
[188] Hilary Term Rules 1834, r. 17.
[189] Common Law Procedure Act 1852 (U.K.), 15 & 16 Vict. c. 76, s. 70 (payment in generally); Common Law Procedure Act 1860 (U.K.), 23 & 24 Vict. c. 126, s. 25 (payment into court pleadable in actions on common money bonds regardless of when paid in).
[190] Judicature Rules 1875, O. 30, r. 1. See *Goutard* v. *Carr* (1883) 13 Q.B.D. 598n.
[191] Order 22, r. 1 (rules made under the Judicature Act 1875 (U.K.), s. 17).
[192] See esp. Judicature Act 1873 (U.K.), ss. 24(1) –(2), 25(11).
[193] Statute Law Revision Act 1948 (U.K.), s. 1 and Sch. 1.
[194] *Re Dixon* [1900] 2 Ch. 561, 579. The equitable jurisdiction of the Court of Exchequer until its abolition in 1841 also empowered that court to grant such relief.
[195] *Steeds* v. *Steeds* (1889) 22 Q.B.D. 537, 539–40.
[196] *Berry* v. *Berry* [1929] 2 K.B. 316. See *Davey* v. *Prendergrass* (1821) 5 B. & A. 187 (parol variation).

rules were to be resolved by applying the equitable rule[197] – section 12 served no distinct purpose. It was repealed in 1948.[198]

The senescence of the 1697 Act took longer. Section 8 was expressly amended to allow trial from 1833 of writs of inquiry by jury before a sheriff instead of a judge;[199] the amended provision was preserved in 1852.[200] Implied amendments followed, making trial of issues of fact by jury[201] – and, eventually, jury trial in most civil cases – unnecessary.[202] Otherwise section 8 stayed in force.[203] The House of Lords could say in 1938 that the 'special procedure' for penalty bonds under section 8 was 'well established'[204] because it was preserved from the liberal new procedures of the Judicature system.[205] Since relief from penalties was otherwise available only in equity, as Lord Halsbury L.C. observed in 1904,[206] the statute still depended on equitable jurisdiction. Far from there being 'no need to invoke the equitable jurisdiction' before or after Judicature,[207] the need was constant. The opinions of Lord Bramwell were approved in dicta of Lord FitzGerald and Lord Halsbury in 1886.[208] In 1917 the House of Lords[209] approved an analysis of Bailhache J.[210] to the same effect, as a matter of decision. In a judgment which Lord Dunedin and Lord Sumner praised as 'admirable',[211] Bailhache J. had followed three decisions:

---

[197] Successively: Judicature Act 1873 (U.K.), s. 25(11); Supreme Court of Judicature (Consolidation) Act 1925 (U.K.), s. 44; Senior Courts Act 1981 (U.K.), s. 49. See Steeds v. Steeds (1889) 22 Q.B.D. 537, 540; Berry v. Berry [1929] 2 K.B. 316, 320.

[198] Statute Law Revision Act 1948 (U.K.), s. 1 and Sch. 1. Under the Supreme Court of Judicature (Consolidation) Act 1925 (U.K.), s. 99(1)(f), (g), Sch. 1, sections 12 and 13 of the 1705 Act had been repealable by rules of court but were not so repealed.

[199] Civil Procedure Act 1833 (U.K.), 3 & 4 Wm IV c. 42, s. 16; see also s. 18.

[200] Common Law Procedure Act 1852 (U.K.), s. 96.

[201] Common Law Procedure Act 1854 (U.K.), 17 & 18 Vict. c. 125, s. 1.

[202] E.g., Rules of the Supreme Court 1883 (U.K.), O. 36, rr. 2–7; Juries Act 1918 (U.K.), ss. 1–2; Administration of Justice Act 1920 (U.K.), s. 2; Administration of Justice (Miscellaneous Provisions) Act 1933 (U.K.), s. 6.

[203] Re Newman, Ex p. Capper (1876) 4 Ch.D. 724, 733–34.

[204] Workington Harbour and Dock Board v. Trade Indemnity Co. Ltd (No. 2) [1938] 2 All E.R. 101, 105.

[205] Tuther v. Caralampi (1888) 21 Q.B.D. 414, 416; also Strickland v. Williams [1899] 1 Q.B. 382.

[206] Clydebank Engineering and Shipbuilding Co. v. Don Jose Ramos Yzquierdo y Castaneda [1905] A.C. 6, 10. See Dendy v. Evans [1910] 1 K.B. 263, 270.

[207] A.M.E.V.-U.D.C. Finance Ltd v. Austin (1986) 162 C.L.R. 170, 191; also at 195.

[208] Lord Elphinstone v. Monkland Iron and Coal Co. (1886) 11 App. Cas. 332, 346, 348.

[209] Watts, Watts & Co. Ltd v. Mitsui and Co. Ltd [1917] A.C. 227, 235 (Lord Finlay L.C., in whose judgment Lord Parker of Waddington concurred), 245 (Lord Dunedin), 246 (Lord Sumner).

[210] Wall v. Rederiaktiebolaget Luggude [1915] 3 K.B. 66.

[211] Watts, Watts & Co. Ltd v. Mitsui and Co. Ltd [1917] A.C. 227, 245, 246.

all[212] expressly stating that relief at law depended on the 1697 Act, two[213] recognising that that Act required the common law judges to apply Chancery equity.

A significant fact concerning section 8 has been forgotten. Except the Crown, every plaintiff who sued for a penalty on 'bonds, or … in any indenture, deed, or writing' was subject to its compulsory provisions from 1794 until 1957.[214] Until its repeal in 1957, section 8 required plaintiffs seeking to enforce penalties to assign breaches. The House of Lords held as much with respect to a penal bond in 1936,[215] but the requirement applied generally. This helps to explain the alleged rule in England that relief from penalties requires a breach of contract.[216] By limiting claims on written penalties to the recovery of damages proved to result from breaches assigned by claimants, the alleged rule ensured that plaintiffs complied with the 1697 Act.

The powers of common law courts under the 1697 Act were at length determined in 1957. 'Common law' relief from penalties came to an end too. For the first time in 260 years, only equitable principles remained. As to bonds, legislation said that '[t]he procedure prescribed by section 8 of the [1697 Act] … in the case of actions on bonds shall no longer be followed'[217] and:

> In an action on a bond, the indorsement of the writ and the statement of claim shall be framed so as to claim the amount which the plaintiff is entitled to recover, regard being had to the rules of equity relating to penalties, and not the penalty provided for by the bond, and these Rules shall apply to any such action as they apply to any other action.[218]

The legislation was silent on penalties in all other writings. However, Parliament had already provided a means of mollifying the common law's traditional attitude, that a penalty is in law the debt, in the absence of the 1697 Act. The rule that the penalty is the debt in law was to be unchanged. Creditors who claimed on penalties were still entitled, in law, to the penalty but they could no longer recover it fully. As courts in Judicature Act systems owe a duty to recognise such equitable defences and grant such equitable relief against legal claims as the Court of Chancery would have given,[219] they must enforce the

---

[212] *Lowe v. Peers, Hardy v. Bern* and *Harrison v. Wright* (1811) 13 East 343.
[213] *Lowe v. Peers* and *Hardy v. Bern.*   [214] See also n. 142.
[215] *Workington Harbour and Dock Board v. Trade Indemnity Co. Ltd (No. 1)* [1937] A.C. 1, 33.
[216] See *Meagher, Gummow and Lehane*, 5th edn, [18-040]–[18-050].
[217] R.S.C. O. 53G, r. 1(1), inserted by S.I. 1957/1178 r. 7.
[218] R.S.C. O. 53G, r. 1(2), inserted by S.I. 1957/1178, r. 7.   [219] Nn. 192–97.

legal claim no further than will compensate the creditor for the debtor's default.[220]

When Lord Radcliffe spoke in *Bridge* v. *Campbell Discount Co. Ltd*[221] of the 1697 and 1705 Acts as still applying in England, their provisions for relief from penalties had been repealed for five and fourteen years, respectively. In the courts of mid-twentieth century England, the special procedures of the 1697 and 1705 Acts were no longer needed. Each repeal made authorities on the construction of each Act otiose. To the extent that it rephrased the proposition that the 1697 Act was mandatory on plaintiffs, any breach requirement of the English penalty doctrine also became otiose in 1957, when the statute it related to was repealed. Other decisions on the old Acts kept their authority: they were decisions on equitable principles as applied under each Act. The common law judges had followed equity cases in construing and applying the Act. Their decisions on general principles in turn elaborated equitable principles on relief from penalties.

> The present position is therefore that there is no longer any statutory relief against a penalty in a bond, but the equitable rule as to penalties has effect and prevails over the common law (see the Senior Courts Act 1981 s. 49) and will be applied without the need for the defendant to bring separate proceedings for relief.[222]

The same is true with respect to penalties in other writings.

FUSION

The evidence surveyed here requires conclusions that diverge from recent understanding. Relief from penalties was informally available at moments in the history of the common law before 1700. The relief differs each time it appears in the historical record, the most important form being payment into court as a common law practice imitating Chancery practice. If the judges were daring in establishing this practice, then their daring was concentrated on practice related to all payments, not penalties as such. They left the common law distinctly tolerant of penalties.

---

[220] Contrast A.M.E.V.-U.D.C. *Finance Ltd* v. *Austin* (1986) 162 C.L.R. 170, 192–93; *Cavendish Square Holding B.V.* v. *Makdessi* [2016] A.C. 1172, [83]–[87], [283].

[221] *Bridge* v. *Campbell Discount Co. Ltd* [1962] A.C. 600, 622.

[222] *Halsbury's Laws of England*, 5th edn (London: LexisNexis, 2012), vol. 32, § 326 n. 2. Contrast *Financings Ltd* v. *Baldock* [1963] 2 Q.B. 104, 120; *Bridge* v. *Campbell Discount Co. Ltd* [1962] A.C. 600, 632.

A fused English penalty doctrine and a fused system of law and equity cannot be seen in the relevant materials. No discernible fusion of the substance of legal and equitable rules on penalties occurred. Equity did not disappear: it was the source of jurisdiction to relieve from penalties in courts of law and courts of equity between 1697 and 1957 in the case of penalties to secure performance, and between 1705 and 1948 in the case of simple money bonds. Equity is still the source of such relief. No common law of relief from penalties appeared, either concurrent with[223] or exclusive of[224] equitable jurisdiction. The 'common law' of penalties before Judicature was merely decisions on the construction of statutes empowering and requiring common law judges to apply equitable principles. When the Judicature Acts commenced in 1875, the judges of the new court acquired a new duty to apply the equitable rules as to penalties where equity and the rules of common law conflicted or varied.[225]

English law stubbornly holds a view that penalties in transactional documents are valid debts. Penalties are valid in law because all liabilities voluntarily assumed in contracts without illegality are, in general, valid. Enforcement is different from validity, yet equitable and statutory principles allowing relief from the enforcement of such valid debts likewise treat the penalty as a valid debt in law. A penalty doctrine which fused the rules reflected in those positions would be unappealing. It would weaken or discharge the equitable view that penalties are mere securities, and make penalties valid *and* fully enforceable in general. It is difficult to accept that such a return to the law of the Tudor and early Stuart periods would be appreciated today.

Substantive fusion is simply unlikely. Judicial attempts to make such changes would be vulnerable to criticism as being *per incuriam*. The Supreme Court and its subordinates are bound by decisions that the 1697 Act depended on equitable doctrines, and not judge-made common law. By statute, a conflict or variance between the relevant rules of common law and equity must be resolved in favour of the equitable rule. Legislation has further directed that applications for relief from penal bonds from 1957 onwards be framed within equitable principles. None of this should worry judges and lawyers. There are developed, stable equitable principles of relief from penalties which Judicature Act courts apply to relieve deserving claimants from the effects of the common law theory of penalties, as has occurred throughout the modern era.

---

[223] Contrast *Andrews* v. *Australia and New Zealand Banking Group Ltd* (2012) 247 C.L.R. 205, [63].

[224] Contrast *A.M.E.V.-U.D.C. Finance Ltd* v. *Austin* (1986) 162 C.L.R. 170, 192–93.

[225] *Jobson* v. *Johnson* [1989] 1 W.L.R. 1026, 1039; and n. 197.

12

Rediscovering the Equitable Origins of Discovery

The 'Blending' of Law and Equity Prior to Fusion

PATRICIA I. MCMAHON

INTRODUCTION

Powers and procedures once exclusive to equity now dominate modern civil procedure. Few think twice about adding or subtracting parties to an action, amending pleadings or seeking specific performance or injunctive relief. Documentary discovery is a right, albeit an expensive, time-consuming one. Each originated in equity, available only to parties in Chancery. So entrenched are these elements in modern civil litigation that we lose sight of their origins.

As England embarked on an era of civil justice reform in the mid-nineteenth century, reformers called discovery – the ability to inspect documents and to ask questions of an opposing party – 'indispensable to the due administration of justice'.[1] They called it 'a settled principle that a party, before proceeding to the trial of an action at Law, has a right to a discovery of all matters material to sustain the action'.[2] In fact, the principle was not settled.

Originally, discovery was available to English litigants, whether at law or in equity, exclusively through the Court of Chancery. The desire to make this tool more readily available to parties at common law was a reason why reformers sought to blend the jurisdiction of law and equity with statutory reforms prior to the enactment of the Judicature Acts 1873–75.[3] The courts of common law acquired the power to order discovery in 1854.[4] In keeping with its equitable origins, discovery was paper-based. Questions, asked and answered, were in writing. Oral examination was available only if the written

---

[1] *First Report Chancery Commissioners*, 23. [2] Ibid.
[3] Judicature Act 1873 (U.K.); Judicature Act 1875 (U.K.).
[4] Common Law Procedure Act 1854 (U.K.), 17 & 18 Vict. c. 125.

responses were insufficient. None of this was by right; judges ordered discovery as an exercise of their discretion.

The extent to which the Judicature Acts of 1873–75 brought about the substantive fusion of law and equity may be a matter of debate,[5] but there can be no dispute that the legislation abolished procedural barriers between the two. That was the clear purpose of fusion. Yet, amid the disagreements about the need for or benefits of substantive fusion, it is easy to forget the procedural accomplishments of 1875. The statutes marked the culmination of a series of choices about the manner in which the system of English civil justice was to be reformed. As Laycock states, 'The war between law and equity is over. Equity won.'[6]

Discovery may have been the jewel of nineteenth-century Chancery procedure, but few are so laudatory today. Stephen Subrin has complained about equity's triumph over common law in civil procedure. In his account, the current problems, particularly the 'fishing expeditions' associated with discovery, illustrate the shortcomings of equity run amok.[7] John Beisner, referring to the origins of the American Federal Rules of Procedure of 1938, writes:

> [P]retrial discovery has been one of the most divisive and nettlesome issues in civil litigation in the United States. Discovery was designed to prevent trials by ambush and to ensure just adjudications. But it has fallen well short of these laudable goals. Instead, the pretrial discovery process is broadly viewed as dysfunctional, with litigants utilizing discovery excessively and abusively.[8]

This chapter examines the equitable origins of discovery and its use in English common law courts over the course of approximately thirty years, beginning in 1850. It traces how the principles underlying the procedure remained constant during that period. When Chancery controlled bills of discovery, discovery was supposed to allow one party to examine documents within the possession of the other with the goal of helping the applicant's case. Early common law decisions required the same. Discovery allowed an applicant to secure documentary evidence from and to ask questions of an opposing party to make his

---

[5] P. M. Perell, *Fusion of Law and Equity* (Toronto: Butterworths, 1990), 19; Burrows, 'We do This at Common Law', 4; Polden, 'Mingling the Waters', 575–76, 613; Mason, 'Fusion', in S. Degeling and J. Edelman (eds), *Equity in Commercial Law* (Sydney: Lawbook Co., 2005), 11–18; *Meagher, Gummow and Lehane*, 5th edn, [2-130]–[2-320].

[6] Laycock, 'Triumph of Equity', 53.

[7] Subrin, 'How Equity Conquered Common Law', 911–14; S. N. Subrin, 'Fishing Expeditions Allowed: The Historical Background of the 1938 Federal Discovery Rules' (1988) 39 B.C.L. Rev. 691.

[8] J. H. Beisner, 'Discovering a Better Way: The Need for Effective Civil Litigation Reform' (2010) 60 Duke L.J. 547, 549.

or her case at trial. It did not allow a party to explore the details of the responding party's case nor was it supposed to be a dry run of the trial. The contemporary discovery process is, in many respects, the opposite of what it once was. Now, discovery is a right that includes access to a mountain of documents and an emphasis on oral examination. Parties engage in the discovery process as much to test their opponent's case as to build their own.

Understanding the equitable origins and the historical purpose of discovery offers useful insights into the current problems associated with discovery and how we might resolve them. Concerns about the time and expense of discoveries are not new. Although the power to order discovery was regarded as the best of Chancery procedure, even reformers worried about the potential for abuse.[9] Subrin complains that there is too much equity in modern procedure – particularly discovery – but perhaps modern litigation asks more of discovery than it was designed to bear. This chapter suggests that common law procedure, with its emphasis on oral examination and cross-examination, has overtaken discovery and done so to its detriment.

THE EQUITABLE ORIGINS OF DISCOVERY

Prior to the fusion of law and equity under the Judicature Acts, law and equity dealt differently with the collection and the assessment of evidence. Parties at law relied on *viva voce* evidence from witnesses who were subject to oral examination and cross-examination. Typically, common law parties adduced evidence orally, from witnesses, in open court, before a judge at trial. Those who wanted access to documentary discovery had to turn to Chancery to obtain a bill of discovery.[10]

Documents dominated the evidentiary process in equity, and Chancery evidence took several forms. Affidavits allowed a witness to provide his or her evidence in the form of a written statement. Interrogatories, which were questions that lawyers wrote and examiners or masters administered to the opposing party, did something similar.[11] Questions were designed to elicit facts pertaining to the suit in issue, but there was no opportunity to ask follow-up

---

9   Discovery was 'too often made an engine of mere oppression and vexation, involving the parties in litigation on points wholly beside the merits of the case': *First Report Chancery Commissioners*, 23.

10 T. Chitty, *Archbold's Practice of the Court of Queen's Bench in Personal Actions and Ejectment*, 8th edn (London: Sweet, 1848), 298–336; T. H. Ayckbourn and H. Ayckbourn, *The New Chancery Practice*, 3rd edn (London: Butterworth, 1849), 263–66.

11 Ayckbourn and Ayckbourn, *The New Chancery Practice*, 150, 158–59 (and see 158–62, 451–52, on interrogatories); the Evidence on Commission Act 1831 (U.K.), 1 Wm IV c. 22, s. 10.

questions in response to the information provided because interrogatories were administered in private by an examiner, a commissioner or a master. The party who drafted the questions did not ask them. Without the opportunity to probe witness responses or to ask additional questions, interrogatories had to cover every potential question related to a suit. Cross-interrogation was possible but not practical because evidence was secret until all examinations were complete, and cross-interrogation was based on the notice of the original interrogation.[12] Masters could also take oral evidence, but did so only in limited circumstances.[13]

Unlike pleadings at common law, pleadings in Chancery – the sworn bill and answer – contained evidence. Unlike a modern statement of defence, an answer also contained responses to interrogatories and to discoveries. The defendant did not merely respond positively or negatively to the allegations contained in the plaintiff's bill, but was required 'to answer as to the general truth of the matter'.[14] Chancery's power to secure the defendant's response under oath was unique; common law rules rendered incompetent anyone with an interest in the outcome of the proceeding. Discovery thus afforded litigants in Chancery an enormous procedural advantage over parties at common law. So significant was the tool that common law parties often turned to Chancery to secure a bill of discovery for use in their common law proceedings.[15]

EARLY ENGLISH REFORMS

Legislative changes in the 1850s brought discovery to common law, and were a key part of the reforms that led to full fusion in the 1870s. Reconciling the manner in which each court handled evidence was a significant part of the conflicts that fusion resolved.

In 1851 Parliament enacted the Evidence Act (U.K.),[16] which empowered common law judges to order inspection of documents without recourse to Chancery, and eliminated the prohibition against a party serving as a

---

[12] See Ayckbourn and Ayckbourn, *The New Chancery Practice*, 158–62 (a witness attended an examination alone, with neither the party nor counsel present) and 164–66 (on cross-examination by interrogatory).
[13] Ibid., 184.
[14] J. H. Langbein, R. L. Lerner and B. P. Smith, *History of the Common Law: The Development of Anglo-American Legal Institutions* (New York, NY: Aspen Publishers, 2009), 290.
[15] Ayckbourn and Ayckbourn, *The New Chancery Practice*, 263.   [16] 14 & 15 Vict. c. 99.

competent, compellable witness in most civil proceedings.[17] However, the legislation did nothing to authorise interrogatories or examinations on those documents.

In the following year, Parliament enacted the first components of fusion with the Common Law Procedure Act[18] and the Court of Chancery Procedure Act.[19] The Chancery legislation broadened the availability and the timing of documentary discovery,[20] allowed each party to seek discovery of documents before the close of pleadings[21] and gave the court discretion to manage the resulting document production.[22] The statute introduced oral examination to Chancery,[23] and gave parties considerable choice between presenting evidence in writing or in person.[24] Consistent with practice in common law proceedings, Chancery parties and their counsel could now attend the examination, cross-examination and re-examination of witnesses,[25] although examiners remained in use.[26] Parliament was mindful of the potential for abuse and allowed judges to intervene to limit or prohibit an examination in which the witness lacked 'sufficient interest in the Matters in question'.[27]

Despite these improvements, problems remained with the discovery process. Questions, drafted by counsel and administered by examiners, continued to be prolix.[28] Examiners had almost no power to control the process. An examiner could express his opinion about the merits of an objection to the attending parties and lawyers, but he could not determine the materiality or relevance of a particular question.[29] Although the legislation simplified the

---

[17] Ibid., s. 6. The legislation did not render a husband or a wife competent and compellable against the other, and protected individuals from self-incrimination in criminal matters: ss. 2–4. In Chancery, an interested party gave evidence via the bill and the answer, which were sworn documents. The defendant's responses to interrogatories were contained in the answer.

[18] Common Law Procedure Act 1852 (U.K.), 15 & 16 Vict. c. 76. The legislation was based on the recommendations of two separate commissions tasked with investigating issues related to practice and procedure in law and equity. The Common Law Commission was appointed in May 1850. The Chancery Commission was appointed six months later. They shared a basic mandate to improve judicial process by making it more practical and more efficient: *First Report Common Law Commissioners*, iii–iv and *First Report Chancery Commissioners*, iii–iv.

[19] Court of Chancery Procedure Act 1852 (U.K.), 15 & 16 Vict. c. 86.

[20] Ibid., s. 18. The commissioners had dealt extensively with the practice surrounding discoveries.

[21] Ibid., ss. 18, 20.   [22] Ibid., s. 18.

[23] Court of Chancery Procedure Act 1852 (U.K.), ss. 29–31.

[24] Ibid., esp. s. 29. Judges had discretion to permit the examination of witnesses upon written interrogatories according to the prior practice, although it was rarely used. See E. R. Daniell, *Pleading and Practice of the High Court of Chancery*, 3rd. Am. edn by J. C. Perkins (Boston, MA: Little, Brown and Co., 1865), 908–09.

[25] Court of Chancery Procedure Act 1852 (U.K.), s. 31.   [26] Ibid., ss. 32, 38.   [27] Ibid., s. 30.

[28] W. S. Holdsworth, *A History of English Law* (London: Methuen, 1926), vol. 9, 353–58.

[29] Ibid.; Court of Chancery Procedure Act 1852 (U.K.), s. 32.

manner in which Chancery judges ordered discovery for use in common law proceedings, it did so only in relation to documents in the possession of the opposing party. The power to order discovery remained exclusive to Chancery.[30]

The commissioners of inquiry into the reform of common law procedure finally addressed discovery in the spring of 1853. In their second report, the commissioners said it was 'altogether wrong' that common law parties had to turn to Chancery to obtain full rights of discovery.[31] It was 'an indisputable proposition' that every court should have the necessary authority to administer 'complete justice within the scope of its jurisdiction'.[32] They complained that the existing approach caused expense and delay, and offered an easy solution: permit discovery in 'the court in which the suit is already pending'.[33]

The commissioners did not just want discovery at common law but also wanted to expand it beyond access to documents to include 'all matters relating to the questions in dispute'.[34] Expanding pre-trial investigation in this way would 'make more clearly manifest the matters which are alone in contest between the parties'.[35] Such access to discovery might eliminate the need for a trial by exposing 'groundless actions' and 'unfounded defences' introduced only for the purposes of delay.[36]

Parliament agreed, but only to a point. Incorporating many of the commission's recommendations, the Common Law Procedure Act 1854 allowed common law judges to order and to control discoveries in their own proceedings.[37] Based on an affidavit, a party could seek an order for discovery of documents known to the other 'relating to the Matters in dispute'.[38] The legislation[39] also permitted the use of written interrogatories in conjunction with discovery, which allowed either party to seek leave from the court on an affidavit to ask written questions of the opposite party relating to 'any Matter as to which Discovery may be sought'.[40] The Act also empowered common law judges to order the oral examination of witnesses and to compel their production of any necessary documents.[41]

---

[30] Court of Chancery Procedure Act 1852 (U.K.), s. 18. The Common Law Procedure Act 1854 (U.K.) abolished forms of action but did not change how common law parties dealt with discovery.
[31] *Second Report Common Law Commissioners*, 35.   [32] Ibid.   [33] Ibid.   [34] Ibid., 36.
[35] Ibid.   [36] Ibid.   [37] Common Law Procedure Act 1854 (U.K.), s. 50.   [38] Ibid., s. 50.
[39] Ibid., ss. 51 and 52.   [40] Ibid., s. 51.   [41] Ibid., s. 53.

DISCOVERY IN COURTS OF EQUITY

As Ayckbourn explained in 1849, a bill of discovery was filed for the purpose of obtaining 'a discovery of facts resting in the knowledge of the defendant, or of deeds or writings or other things in his custody or power'.[42] Before examining how the common law dealt with discovery, it is useful to review the approach in Chancery.

Some cases will illustrate the point. In 1844, a dispute arose over which of the Crown or the City of London owned various property rights to the Thames River.[43] At common law, a party claiming an estate in freehold was required to recover on the strength of his or her title and was not entitled to discovery of the opposing party. In equity, however, the plaintiff was entitled to discovery from the defendant to help establish title.[44] Lord Cottenham L.C. directed the defendant to respond specifically to the plaintiff's interrogatories relating to deeds and charters. A defendant, he explained, could not defeat a request for inspection merely by claiming that the requested documents did not contain evidence on the point in issue. However, there were limits to the discovery. Lord Cottenham L.C. refused to permit discovery of evidence that the defendant intended to use to support its case,[45] rejecting four proposed interrogatories that sought just that.[46]

Pollock C.B. offered a similar view of discovery from the Court of Exchequer in *Hunt v. Hewitt*.[47] Mr Hunt, an architect, sued Mr Hewitt for payment of services related to the construction of Hewitt's estate. Hewitt defended by claiming that the amount in issue was excessive and the work was incomplete. Relying on the new Evidence Act, Hewitt sought to inspect Hunt's daybook for records about business with Hewitt, and to inspect any plans that related to the estate. The chambers judge ordered production of the plans, but denied the request to inspect the daybook because there was no evidence that it would help Hewitt prove his case. Clarifying the new powers available under the legislation, Pollock C.B. pointed out that discovery in Chancery was limited, and that section 6 of the Evidence Act was even more restricted with its focus on the inspection of documents.[48] A bill of discovery was 'confined to the questions in the cause' and 'such material documents as relate to his, the plaintiff's, case on the trial'; it did 'not extend to the discovery of the manner in which the defendant's case is to be established, or to evidence which relates exclusively to his case'.[49] Although this new provision

---

[42] Ayckbourn and Ayckbourn, *The New Chancery Practice*, 263.
[43] A.-G. v. *Corp. of London* (1850) 2 Mac. & G. 247.   [44] Ibid., 255–63.   [45] Ibid., 256–58.
[46] Ibid., 253–54.   [47] (1852) 7 Ex. 236.   [48] Ibid., 242.   [49] Ibid., 244.

was more limited than what was available in Chancery, Pollock C.B. was convinced it would be nearly as effective.[50]

COMMON LAW DISCOVERY

Over the next decade, the common law courts grappled with questions related to the timing of interrogatories and the scope of document production. Several themes appear from the reported cases. At the outset, it should be noted that judges dealt with most applications in chambers, not in open court, and these decisions were rarely reported. A recurring concern was the extent to which discovery at law would differ from that which was available in equity. Most common law judges said they were adhering to Chancery's approach to discovery, and they routinely affirmed that the power to order inspection of documents or to allow interrogatories was discretionary. Although oral examination was available under statute, case law suggests it was ordered rarely, and only when the responses to written interrogatories were insufficient.

One of the first cases to deal with discovery at common law affirmed the court's discretion to refuse an application. *Martin* v. *Hemming*[51] involved a bill of exchange. Mr Martin filed a suit to collect on the bill. Mr Hemming responded that he had already settled the bill with a bank pursuant to a deed of arrangement in bankruptcy drawn by Martin. The complication was Hemming's allegation that Martin had acted as an agent or as a trustee for his father, who had participated in settling the bill. Hemming wanted Martin to answer a number of preliminary questions, including several about the relationship with a person whom Hemming alleged was Martin's father. The court's decision turned on the timing of the application. Hemming had not yet delivered his declaration or his plea, but sought interrogatories anyway. The court refused to order interrogatories prior to the close of pleadings absent an 'urgent necessity' to do so.[52]

The grounds upon which one could object to interrogatories or refuse to answer them were narrow, limited almost exclusively to privilege. *Osborn* v. *The London Dock Co.*[53] involved a dispute about the delivery of approximately 2,500 gallons of red wine. Osborn claimed the wine had gone missing; the London Dock Company argued that wine belonging to third parties had been substituted for Osborn's, and that Osborn himself was party to the fraud. Osborn sought to avoid responding to any of the proposed interrogatories (almost 160 of them) on the ground that his answers might be incriminating.

---

[50] Ibid., 244–45.   [51] (1854) 10 Ex. 478.   [52] Ibid., 478.   [53] (1855) 10 Ex. 698.

The court held that Osborn could object to a particular interrogatory on the ground that the answer might incriminate him, but could not avoid responding to interrogatories altogether. Invoking the rule in equity, the court required the witness to be under oath when he refused to answer on the grounds of incrimination. 'The rule must be absolute. The mere affidavit of his attorney is not sufficient,' explained Parke B.[54] A similar approach was taken in cases where forfeiture was possible.[55]

Common law judges stated repeatedly that discovery rights at law were the same as those available in equity, yet counsel still tried to expand the scope of discovery. Discovery allowed a party to make his or her own case, but a party could also obtain evidence about his or her opponent's case, provided that that was not the exclusive purpose of the interrogatories. Fishing expeditions – interrogatories to determine the opponent's case at trial and nothing more – were impermissible. Over time, however, counsel and some judges urged the common law courts to take a broader approach, analogising between pre-trial discovery and the examination of a witness at trial.

In *Martin v. Hemming*, counsel suggested that discovery provided an opportunity to review and to assess the case in its entirety before trial. Counsel said that purpose of discovery:

> is to give a party the opportunity of obtaining information as to the real facts of the case, so as to enable him to frame his case properly, and to give him the means of judging whether he has any chance of success, so that he may either proceed with or abandon the cause of action or the defence, in cases where he is respectively plaintiff or defendant.[56]

The court disagreed in reasons echoing Parke B.'s objections during argument. In particular, Parke B. cited the need for court approval to proceed with discoveries. Absent that requirement, 'interrogatories would be added in all cases, and would be delivered with every declaration and every plea'.[57] 'We must', Parke B. noted, 'see in each case that the interrogatories are necessary'.[58]

The Exchequer Court took a similar approach in *Osborn v. London Dock Co.*[59] Parke B. affirmed that interrogatories were limited to circumstances that would have given rise to a bill of discovery in Chancery, despite provision that permitted interrogatories to be independent of the documents produced.[60]

---

[54] Ibid., 703.   [55] E.g., *Chester v. Wortley and Cole* (1856) 17 C.B. 410, 417.
[56] *Martin v. Hemming* (1854) 10 Ex. 478, 484 (Mr Quain).   [57] Ibid., 484.
[58] Ibid., 484. See *McCay v. Magill* (1854) 3 Ir.C.L.R. 83.   [59] (1855) 10 Ex. 698.
[60] Ibid., 702.

Reflecting the sentiments of counsel in *Martin* v. *Hemming*,[61] Alderson B. said the administration of interrogatories was 'analogous to that of the examination of a witness at the trial'.[62]

Similar arguments were grappled with in *Whateley* v. *Crowter*,[63] but with different results. *Whateley* was a negligence claim against a land surveyor who had appraised an estate for a mortgage the plaintiff intended to hold. The proposed interrogatories focused on issues relating to the diligence of the land surveyor in valuing the property. In refusing the application, Lord Campbell C.J. emphasised that common law discovery was supposed to make judicial proceedings more efficient. 'The object of the enactment was to obviate what was a scandal to the law, namely the necessity of commencing a fresh suit in a [c]ourt of equity for the purpose of obtaining discovery in aid of an action at law.'[64] He expressly rejected Alderson B.'s approach, explaining:

> I think it is too wide an interpretation to say, as seems to have been said by Alderson B. in the case cited in the Exchequer, that every question may be asked on interrogatories which might be asked if the party were a witness at the trial. I think the interrogatories must be confined to matters which might be discovered by a bill of discovery in equity.[65]

Instead the Chief Justice took a traditional approach, adopting the extra-judicial view of Sir James Wigram:

> The right of a plaintiff in equity to the benefit of the defendant's oath, is limited to a discovery of such material facts as relate to the *plaintiff's case* – and does not extend to a discovery of the manner in which the *defendant's case* is to be established, or to evidence which relates exclusively to his case.[66]

As Lord Campbell explained:

> You may inquire into all that is material to your own case, though it should be in common with that of your adversary; but you may not inquire into what is exclusively his case. . . . We have a discretion in these cases: but it is to be exercised for the purpose only of seeing that the process of the Court is not abused; where the discovery is legitimate it should not be refused.[67]

---

[61] Quain, who made the suggestion as counsel in *Martin* v. *Hemming*, was appointed to the Judicature Commission in 1867 and to the Queen's Bench in 1871: J. A. Hamilton, 'Quain, Sir John Richard (1816–1876)', rev. by P. Polden, in *O.D.N.B.*, available: www.oxforddnb.com/view/article/22938.

[62] *Osborn* v. *London Dock Co.* (1855) 10 Ex. 698, 702.   [63] (1855) 5 El. & Bl. 708.

[64] Ibid., 712.   [65] Ibid., 712.

[66] J. Wigram, *Points in the Law of Discovery*, 2nd edn (London: Maxwell, 1840), 261 (emphasis original), quoted ibid., 712.

[67] *Whateley* v. *Crowter* (1855) 5 El. & Bl. 708, 712–13.

A similar situation arose in *Edwards* v. *Wakefield*,[68] an action in trover for bills of exchange and policies of insurance. The defendant, Wakefield, was a London merchant, who had been trading between England and Australia. Wakefield posed a series of interrogatories to inquire into the relationship between Houghton and a group of Australians. In 1852, Wakefield had made consignments to Houghton and others in Australia to whom Houghton was indebted. Houghton went to Australia in 1854 at the request of his principal creditors to realise the Australian property and to make consignments and remittances to the defendants. The action involved the proceeds. When Houghton returned to England in 1855, he declared bankruptcy. The defendants did not know whether Houghton relied on acts of bankruptcy committed in England prior to the trip, because of the trip or of fraudulent preferences.[69]

The interrogatories dealt with the plaintiff's case at trial. Wakefield asked specifically about the plaintiff's case at trial to allow recovery; the grounds for claiming the bill of exchange, policies of assurance and other documents set out in the particulars; the grounds on which the plaintiffs claimed particular sums and whether the defendants received any of those sums after notice of bankruptcy; and the particular acts of bankruptcy relied upon. The court rejected these proposed interrogatories as a fishing expedition. Lord Campbell C.J. rejected an expansive approach to discovery that would have previewed the case at trial.[70]

The court took a similar approach in *Moor* v. *Roberts*.[71] A mortgage had been taken out on certain properties, the sale of which left a shortfall. The plaintiff claimed the defendant had pledged to cover the deficiency, and the proposed interrogatories sought to illicit evidence about the parties and the underlying sale.[72] The court refused the application, holding that the defendant was trying to discover the shape of the plaintiff's case without furthering any part of his own.[73] Cockburn C.J. reminded the parties of the rationale for interrogatories at common law.

> [T]he obvious intention ... was to supersede the necessity of recourse being had in all cases to a court of equity for the purpose of aiding by discovery the proceedings in an action at common law, and to give the courts of common law power to afford the same sort of assistance to suitors there.[74]

---

[68] (1856) 6 El. & Bl. 462.   [69] Ibid., 463–64.
[70] *Edwards* v. *Wakefield* (1856) 6 El. & Bl. 462, 469.   [71] (1857) 2 C.B. (N.S.) 671.
[72] Ibid., 674–75.
[73] Ibid., 679–80. The court also refused interrogatories for the purpose of contradicting the contents of a written document.
[74] Ibid., 679.

The purpose of discovery was more general:

> where either party has a case, but the materials for proving it are not in his own possession or under his own control, but in the possession of his adversary, he should be enabled to interrogate his adversary in order to establish his own case.[75]

The legislation was not intended to allow one party to discover how the other 'intends to shape his own case, and to see whether there are any defects in it which he may avail himself of'.[76] Williams J. agreed, saying it 'would . . . make the statute an instrument of oppression to the suitor' if the defendant were permitted 'by indirect means to obtain a knowledge of what the plaintiff intends to rely on in support of his case'.[77]

The common law courts insisted that requests to inspect be specific. *Thompson* v. *Robson*[78] involved a chartered ship and its condition upon delivery. Mr Thompson sought an order directing Mr Robson to provide an affidavit listing all the documents in his possession that related to the dispute, including letters and documents Robson had written and sent to third parties about the ship's condition. Thompson argued that section 50 of the Common Law Procedure Act allowed him to secure a list of documents from the defendant, and then decide which documents to inspect. The court disagreed. Pollock C.B. explained:

> We cannot grant a rule calling on the defendants to give a list of documents, which is a mere attempt to fish out evidence to make a case. A proper foundation must be laid for the application; the Court must see that inspection is required for the purposes of justice.[79]

Bramwell B. said the search for these types of documents was 'troublesome and expensive'.[80] He explained: 'It would be strange if a man could say, "I do not know whether there are any documents, but if so I am entitled to a discovery of them".'[81] Watson B. warned against allowing applications for discovery that create 'embarrassment and expense',[82] the implication being that this was an example of each.

Despite these repeated statements of principle, courts sometimes allowed discovery on broader terms. *Price* v. *Harrison*[83] is a case in point. The 1860 case involved the demise and lease of property in Gloucester. There was no formal

---

[75] Ibid.   [76] Ibid.   [77] Ibid., 680.   [78] (1857) 2 H. & N. 411.   [79] Ibid., 414.
[80] Ibid.   [81] Ibid.
[82] Ibid., 415. The court took a similar approach in *Houghton* v. *London and County Assurance Co. Ltd* (1864) 17 C.B. (N.S.) 79.
[83] (1860) 8 C.B. (N.S.) 617.

written agreement, but a series of letters outlined the terms and conditions of the transaction, including who had agreed to give up what to whom in exchange for something else. Mr Harrison had not kept copies of the letters, and wanted to look at the copies Mr Price had retained. The court permitted the inspection of the letters. Erle C.J. remarked that the process promoted 'the interest of truth and justice by the discovery of documents in the possession or under the control of the one party which are essential to support the claim or the defence of the other'.[84]

Erle C.J. reiterated this sentiment in *Bartlett* v. *Lewis*,[85] a case involving an action to recover an alleged debt in which the defendant pleaded discharge under the Bankruptcy Act. At issue was the validity of the discharge. Rejecting earlier case law, the Chief Justice said that common law discovery was broader than what was available in Chancery, and was supposed to secure 'truth and justice'.[86] He tried to promote a similarly broad approach in *Zychlinski* v. *Maltby*,[87] an action involving allegations that the plaintiff had obtained money from the defendant for the benefit of the latter's family under false and fraudulent pretences. Mr Maltby wanted to ask Mr Zychlinski about his relationship with the family and the nature of the payments. Erle C.J. allowed the interrogatories. The questions were relevant to the matter in issue, and counsel had argued that they were similar to what a party would be bound to answer as a witness at trial.[88]

Grappling with the parameters of common law discovery involved assessments of privilege. The results were inconsistent. *Chartered Bank of India, Australia and China* v. *Rich*[89] involved a bank that carried on business in several locations, including Bombay, where the defendant, Mr Rich, served as the bank's agent. There were allegations of breach of agreement between the bank and Rich. The requested documents, a series of letters between the bank's home office in London and officers of the bank branch in Bombay, had been prepared after Rich had left the bank and after the alleged breaches occurred. Part of the correspondence included information needed to allow the bank to determine how it should respond to Rich. Some documents were prepared directly at the request of counsel. Others contained evidence from the branch in Bombay to help the bank prove the alleged breaches of contract, and had nothing to do with how Rich would establish his case.

---

[84] Ibid., 632. He wrote about the inherent power of the court to order document inspection in certain circumstances, e.g., where there was a single copy of an agreement. See *Shadwell* v. *Shadwell* (1858) 6 C.B. (N.S.) 679; *Bluck* v. *Gompertz* (1851) 7 Ex. 67.
[85] (1863) 12 C.B. (N.S.) 249.   [86] Ibid., 260.   [87] (1861) 10 C.B. (N.S.) 838.
[88] See also *Bartlett* v. *Lewis* (1862) 12 C.B. (N.S.) 249, discussed earlier.
[89] (1863) 4 B. & S. 73.

The court decided that all the documents were confidential (but not necessarily privileged), and rejected the application for discovery. Cockburn C.J. adopted Pollock C.B.'s approach in *Hunt* v. *Hewitt*,[90] and treated the application as a fishing expedition in which the documents did not relate to the defendant's case.[91] Whether at law or in equity, Cockburn C.J. said it was insufficient to request documents on the basis that they 'relate to the matters in dispute'.[92] Blackburn J. took a more expansive approach, focusing on the differences between the rules governing discovery at law and those in equity. He pointed to the discretionary language in section 50 (i.e., that the court or the judge 'may make such further order thereon as shall be just'). He claimed that Parliament had not intended to bind the courts of common law to the rules in Chancery. Instead, the court was supposed to assess what was 'just as between the parties':

> We have to see whether the documents are such as would tend to elucidate the facts material to the case of the party in the cause applying for inspection: in a [c]ourt of equity the test would be, whether they were material to the case of the plaintiff on the bill of discovery, who can shape his bill in various ways. It is not necessary that the documents should be legal evidence; though it may be material to discuss whether they would be so.[93]

He continued:

> The practice of the Court and of the Judges at Chambers has been to inquire what, from the nature of things and of the facts in the particular case, would tend to further the ends of justice, and, looking at all the circumstances and exercising a sound and rational discretion, to order the inspection of those documents which appear to be material to the case of the party applying.[94]

Although the debate about whether there were differences between discovery at law and in equity remained alive into the mid-1860s, the courts tended to abide by the approach in Chancery. For example, in *Pye* v. *Butterfield*,[95] a case of ejectment in which the application for interrogatories was rejected because responses might lead to forfeiture, Cockburn C.J. reiterated that discovery at law was intended to save parties the time and the expense of having to turn to Chancery to benefit from the procedure.[96] Nevertheless, he explained, 'whether we are fettered or left free to exercise our judicial discretion, we ought to abide by the principle on which this branch of jurisprudence has for centuries been administered in [c]ourts of equity'.[97]

[90] (1852) 7 Ex. 236.
[91] *Chartered Bank of India, Australia and China* v. *Rich* (1863) 4 B. & S. 73, 81.   [92] Ibid., 80.
[93] Ibid., 83.   [94] Ibid.   [95] (1864) 5 B. & S. 827.   [96] Ibid., 837.   [97] Ibid.

THE JUDICATURE ACTS

In the autumn of 1867, Lord Derby's government appointed the Judicature Commission to examine the reorganisation of the courts. The commission had a broad mandate to assess the operations of all the major courts in England and Wales, and the commissioners reviewed everything from the number of judges on each court to the court calendar. They also inquired into whether to unite or consolidate any courts, or change their jurisdiction. The objective was 'to provide for the more speedy, economical, and satisfactory dispatch of the judicial business now transacted by the same Courts'.[98] Justices Erle, Bramwell and Blackburn all joined the commission, as did Richard Quain and William Bovill, lawyers who had argued for an expansive approach to discovery at common law.

The commission's first report in March 1869 endorsed full procedural fusion.[99] The commission recommended using one system of procedure in a new consolidated court, noting that a uniform system of procedure for taking evidence would 'be attended with the greatest advantages'.[100] Despite the various reforms implemented since 1852, nothing short of full procedural fusion would resolve continuing problems of expense and delay.[101]

Lord Hatherley tried to combine the courts of law and equity into a single court of general jurisdiction in the spring of 1870,[102] but many criticised the legislation.[103] The bills empowered the Judicial Committee of the Privy Council to make the new rules of procedure, and some worried whether the committee could 'be trusted with so great a power and discretion'.[104]

Sir Alexander Cockburn, the Lord Chief Justice of the Queen's Bench, was especially vocal in his criticism. He complained that the proposed new rules lacked sufficient detail, particularly with respect to resolving conflicts between

[98] *First Report Judicature Commissioners*, 4.   [99] Ibid., 9.   [100] Ibid., 10–11.
[101] Ibid., 5–6.
[102] The High Court of Justice Bill unified the courts and the Appellate Jurisdiction Bill unified appeals. They were first read in the House of Lords on 11 March 1870: H.L. Deb., 11 March 1870, vol. 199, col. 1733.
[103] Critics called the legislation 'hasty' and 'ill-considered': Anon., 'The Lord Chancellor's Judicature Bills' (1870) 29 Law Mag. 152, 152. Many reformers supported the legislation in principle, but worried about the preparation of the rules. Depending on their drafting, the new rules could 'revolutionize our whole system of trial' or they might 'leave matters exactly as they were at present': Anon., 'Events of the Quarter' (1870) 29 Law Mag. 373, 380.
[104] Anon., 'Events of the Quarter', 380.

law and equity.[105] He wanted the court to have rule-making authority to resolve difficulties arising from the lack of direction in the text.[106] Arguing in favour of preserving judicial independence,[107] Cockburn was vehemently opposed to allowing the Chancellor to serve as the 'presiding and directing power' of the new high court. With the prospect of the Privy Council setting the new rules,[108] Cockburn lamented the relegation of the common law judges to 'subordinate divisions of a general Court' under the authority of the Chancellor where '[t]he controuling [sic] power of the Chancellor is every where, even to the most minute particulars'.[109] Instead, Cockburn wanted the High Court judges to make the rules relating to all aspects of the new court.[110] Unsurprisingly, the legislation stalled.

It took a new Lord Chancellor to enact civil justice reform. Lord Selborne L.C. introduced the Judicature bill in the House of Lords in February 1873,[111] just months after he became Chancellor. It was based largely on the recommendations contained in the commission's first report and Hatherley's failed bills, but deviated from earlier efforts by abolishing the appellate jurisdiction of the House of Lords for English proceedings.[112] Intended to come into force November 1874,[113] the Act also made provision for a committee of judges thereafter to develop the necessary Rules of Court.[114]

The Rules under the act itself dealt with discovery in three sections, reducing from four the provisions contained in the Common Law Procedure Act of 1854. Under that Act, an applicant could seek documents for inspection, request written interrogatories about the applicant's case and follow-up with oral examination if necessary. Each required court approval. The Judicature Acts framed discovery differently. Now, a party was entitled to exhibit interrogatories and to obtain discovery from any opposing party. The responding party could object to any interrogatory on the ground of irrelevance, subject to

---

[105] *Law Magazine* reprinted the letter and concerns, ibid., 376–80, and the recommendations were published in a detailed 64-page pamphlet; A. Cockburn, *Our Judicial System* (London: Ridgway, 1870), 28–30.

[106] Anon., 'Events of the Quarter', 377. Cockburn urged Hatherley to direct those preparing the new rules to resolve conflicts between law and equity, and to consider 'how the two systems might best be made to coalesce and blend into one': Cockburn, *Our Judicial System*, 61.

[107] The preservation of judicial independence was not one of the six recommendations discussed in the *Law Magazine*.

[108] Cockburn, *Our Judicial System*, 38–39.   [109] Ibid., 46.

[110] Anon., 'Events of the Quarter', 378; Cockburn, *Our Judicial System*, 38–42.

[111] H.L. Deb., 13 February 1873, vol. 214, col. 331.

[112] Judicature Act 1873 (U.K.), s. 53. See R. Stevens, 'The Final Appeal: Reform of the House of Lords and Privy Council 1867–1876' (1964) 80 L.Q.R. 343, 351–52.

[113] Judicature Act 1873 (U.K.), s. 2.   [114] Ibid., ss. 68, 74–75.

approval by the court or a judge. Interrogatories found to be unreasonable, vexatious or improper in length were subject to a costs award.[115] Any party was entitled to inspect and to obtain a copy of any document referred to in the pleadings of the opposing party, and the court could order production of any document relating to the matter in question.[116] Failure to produce such document would exclude the document from evidence unless the court was satisfied that the document related exclusively to the title of the referring party or there was some other 'sufficient cause for not complying with such notice'.[117] Separately, the Judicature Act authorised the court or a judge to order the examination of any witness or person 'where it shall appear necessary for the purposes of justice'.[118]

After Parliament passed the Judicature Act, there was a fourteen-month period to re-assess the rules of procedure. Enacted in 1875, the next version of the Judicature Act included expanded rules of discovery. Now, there were twenty-three provisions dealing with every aspect of discovery, inspection and interrogatories. The new rules included more detail and not always to the benefit of clarity. The provisions expanded powers previously available, and provided greater specificity with respect to the procedures available to litigants and to the court. Although discretion remained, the new provisions were more rigid in their requirements.

Written questioning, not oral examination, continued to dominate. Under the Judicature Act 1875, a party was entitled to deliver written interrogatories for examination of the opposite party.[119] As under the Act of 1873, the court could award costs to counter interrogatories that were unreasonable, vexatious or an improper length.[120] The Act of 1875 provided more guidance for a party seeking to avoid interrogatories. Now, a party could apply in chambers to strike out specific interrogatories 'on the ground that it is scandalous or irrelevant, or is not put bonâ fide for the purposes of the action, or that the matter inquired after is not sufficiently material at that stage of the action, or on any other ground'.[121] The new legislation specified the manner (sworn affidavit) and time within which interrogatories were to be answered.[122] As with the previous legislation, the court or a judge could determine the sufficiency of such affidavit[123] and order the affiant to respond (or provide additional responses) by affidavit or through oral examination.[124]

---

[115] Judicature Act 1873, Sch. 1 (Rules), r. 25.   [116] Ibid., r. 27.   [117] Ibid., r. 26.
[118] Ibid., r. 45.   [119] Judicature Act 1875 (U.K.), Sch. 1 (Rules of Court), O. 31, r. 1.
[120] Ibid., O. 2, r. 2 (previously part of r. 25).   [121] Ibid., O. 31, r. 5 (previously part of r. 25).
[122] Ibid., O. 31, r. 6.   [123] Ibid., O. 31, r. 9 (previously part of r. 25).
[124] Ibid., O. 31, r. 10 (previously part of r. 25).

The Judicature Act 1875 continued to allow the court or a judge to order any party to produce any documents in his or her possession or power 'relating to any matter in question in such action or proceeding, as the Court or Judge shall think right'.[125] Any party was subject to discovery on documents,[126] with objections to production set out in an affidavit.[127] As under the prior legislation, a party was entitled to inspect and to copy documents referred to in the pleading, failing which the document could be excluded from use.[128] To be clear, the Judicature Act 1875 did not create a general entitlement to inspect documents. Rather, a party still had to apply to a judge, relying on an affidavit to show why he or she was entitled to inspect specific documents beyond those referred to in the pleading.[129]

The legislation also permitted determination of an issue or a question in dispute to deal with an objection to discovery or inspection. The provision allowed a party to object to an application for discovery as being premature,[130] something that was already part of the court's practice.[131] The Act also gave the court greater discretion to deal with a party who failed to comply with discovery requirements: a plaintiff could have his or her action dismissed, and a defendant could have his or her defence struck for failing to do so.[132]

JUDICIAL INTERPRETATION OF THE JUDICATURE ACT

The new Supreme Court pledged to continue to interpret the rules of discovery in a manner that was true to their equitable origin. In the years immediately following the introduction of fusion, the court tended to limit the documents withheld from discoveries to those that were privileged. Over time, the court began to suggest that parties could withhold otherwise relevant documents where it would be oppressive to produce them. The court also started to consider what was 'just' in claims for privilege.

Anderson v. Bank of British Columbia[133] was among the first cases to interpret the new discovery provisions. Mr Anderson alleged that the bank had improperly transferred a sum of money from an account in London to another bank branch in Oregon. He filed a bill to compel the bank to replace the money. Before the bill was filed, but after the litigation was anticipated,

---

[125] Ibid., O. 31, r. 11 (previously part of r. 27).
[126] Ibid., O. 31, r. 12 (probably part of former r. 27).   [127] Ibid., O. 31, r. 13.
[128] Ibid., O. 31, r. 14 (previously r. 26). The new rules included the use of a Form: r. 15 (App. B, Form No. 10).
[129] Ibid., O. 31, r. 18.   [130] Ibid., O. 31, r. 19.
[131] See *Martin* v. *Hemming* (1854) 10 Ex. 478, 484.   [132] Judicature Rules O. 31, r. 20.
[133] (1876) 2 Ch.D. 644.

the manager in London asked the manager in Oregon to send him the details of the transaction. The bank claimed privilege to defeat the application for discovery. Jessel M.R., a member of the Judicature Commission who had also been instrumental in shepherding the new Judicature legislation through Parliament,[134] refused. In holding that the letters, which had been handled by an agent and not a solicitor, were subject to discovery, the Master of the Rolls invoked Chancery's approach to privilege.[135] Relying on section 25(11) of the Judicature Act, which requires equity to prevail over common law where the two conflict, Jessel M.R. rejected common law precedents that had withheld confidential documents from production. In doing so, he overruled the argument that discovery at law and in equity were somehow informed by different principles.[136] The Judicature Act, he explained, 'conclusively settled ... that where there is any conflict between the rules of law and the rules of equity, the rules of equity are to prevail'.[137]

The bank and the managers found no relief in the Court of Appeal. Mellish L.J. explained that a letter written by an agent seeking evidence to be used at trial would be privileged, 'but this is not like that'.[138] Here, discovery was 'not to obtain evidence, but to learn what the facts were, in order to know whether the claim should be resisted. It seems to be an extension of the rules as to privileged communications to apply it to such a case'.[139] James L.J. agreed, calling it 'one of the clearest and plainest cases that have ever come before the Court; and according to all the cases decided ever since I have known the Court, and everything I have ever read about the practice of the Court, I think that this is a document which ought to be produced'.[140] He stated succinctly the approach:

> The old rule was that every document in the possession of a party must be produced if it was material or relevant to the cause, unless it was covered by some established privilege. It was established that communications that had passed directly or indirectly between a man and his solicitor were privileged, and the privilege extended no further.[141]

---

[134] Jessel M.R. considered himself to be among the top three equity judges (third behind Lords Hardwicke and Cairns): G.H. Jones, 'Jessel, Sir George (1824–1883)', in *O.D.N.B.*, available: www.oxforddnb.com/view/article/14803.

[135] *Anderson v. Bank of British Columbia* (1876) 2 Ch.D. 644, 648–49. Jessel M.R. relied on the rule set out in *Greenough v. Gaskell* (1833) 1 My. & K. 98 and explained in *Reid v. Langlois* (1849) 1 Mac. & G. 627, 638–39.

[136] *Anderson v. Bank of British Columbia* (1876) 2 Ch.D. 644, 654. See *Chartered Bank of India, Australia and China v. Rich* (1863) 4 B. & S. 73, 82–83.

[137] *Anderson v. Bank of British Columbia* (1876) 2 Ch.D. 644.   [138] Ibid., 654.   [139] Ibid., 655.
[140] Ibid., 655–56.   [141] Ibid., 656.

James L.J. rejected the applicability of the Chancery case *Ross* v. *Gibbs*,[142] which he described as a departure 'from the whole tradition and course of this Court with respect to the production of documents', and contrary to the treatises on discovery.[143] He was more sympathetic to the existing common law jurisprudence, based on 'an intelligible principle, that ... you have no right to see your adversary's brief, [and] you have no right to see that which comes into existence merely as the materials for the brief'.[144] *Anderson* was different. The rule did not apply 'to a communication between a principal and his agent in the matter of the agency, giving information of the facts and circumstances of the very transaction which is the subject-matter of the litigation. Such a communication is, above all others, the very thing which ought to be produced'.[145] He described the activities thus:

> The agent has sent to the principal the account, or we must assume that what the agent has sent in answer to the telegram is a statement of what took place between him and the other party. The other party says, 'You have got that statement of facts, produce it; it shews what the facts are within your own knowledge, and is the best evidence of what you know as to what took place'.[146]

Supporting discovery of the document in issue, Mellish L.J. dismissed attempts to distinguish discovery practice at law and in equity. The rule under the Judicature Act 'differs very little from a similar provision in the Common Law Procedure Act'.[147] Such past practice, however, was irrelevant. The Act included a 'general rule that the principles of equity are to prevail, [so] there can be no doubt that the rules previously existing respecting discovery in the Court of Chancery are binding now upon all the [c]ourts'.[148] The bank's communication was precisely the sort to be subject to discovery because it would hasten the collection of evidence.[149] 'It appears to me as a matter of principle, looking at what is right and just, and for the purpose of saving expense, and enabling the truth to be discovered, it is in the highest degree desirable that such a discovery should be afforded.'[150] Production would be 'just, right and expedient'.[151]

The court continued to deal with privilege and the exercise of discretion in *Bustros* v. *White*,[152] an action for damage to a cargo of cotton seed. The plaintiffs were the consignees, and the defendant's ship carried the cotton seed. The issue was whether bad stowage or some inherent shortcoming with

---

[142] (1869) L.R. 8 Eq. 522.   [143] *Anderson* v. *Bank of British Columbia* (1876) 2 Ch.D. 644, 656.
[144] Ibid., 656.   [145] Ibid., 657.   [146] Ibid.   [147] Ibid., 658.   [148] Ibid.   [149] Ibid., 659.
[150] Ibid., 661.   [151] Ibid.   [152] (1876) 1 Q.B.D. 423.

the seed led to the damage. The plaintiff claimed privilege over certain documents, arguing that they were correspondence between law firms relating to the condition of the cargo and the plaintiff's claim against the defendants, and thus related only to plaintiff's case. Included among the documents were letters to and from the plaintiff's mercantile agent, and letters to and from the plaintiff's law firm.

The case dealt with the court's discretion to refuse discovery (in this case, the inspection of documents) for a reason other than privilege. Speaking for the Court of Appeal,[153] Jessel M.R. (again) rejected attempts to distinguish between the practice at law and in equity. Once more, he invoked the former practice in Chancery, and its incorporation into the Judicature Act.[154] He reasoned that the new legislation could not confer discretion on the court when the former had not,[155] particularly when the Judicature Act expressly provided for equity to prevail over common law in the event of a conflict. '[E]ven were our opinion different from what it is as to the construction of the rule standing alone, we should not be at liberty to put any other construction upon it than that which had been so long adopted.'[156] Documents were subject to production unless privileged, and here they were not. Jessel M.R. explained, 'if it is a matter of right . . . it is no ground for extending the rule as to privilege to say that the production of the document might be injurious to the party producing it if made use of before a jury'.[157]

Consistency of approach seems to have been difficult to achieve. Two years later, the court reached a different result in a case that dealt with a similar issue. In *Southwark and Vauxhall Water Co.* v. *Quick*,[158] the company brought an action against its former engineer to recover sums of money that were said to be wrongly debited from already settled accounts. Relying on *Anderson* and *Bustros*, the defendant applied to inspect documents prepared at the request of the plaintiff in contemplation of litigation. Cockburn C.J. denied the request, holding that the documents were privileged because they contained information to be used for the purposes of legal consultation.[159] A Court of Appeal division comprising Bramwell, Brett and Cotton L.JJ. agreed.[160]

---

[153] *Coram* Jessel M.R., Kelly C.B., James and Mellish L.JJ., Baggallay J.A., Lush and Denman JJ., and Pollock B.
[154] Rules of Court, O. 31, r. 11 was based on the Court of Chancery Procedure Act 1852 (U.K.), s. 18.
[155] *Bustros* v. *White* (1876) 1 Q.B.D. 423, 426.   [156] Ibid.   [157] Ibid., 427.
[158] (1878) 3 Q.B.D. 315.
[159] *Southwark and Vauxhall Water Co.* v. *Quick* (1878) 3 Q.B.D. 315, 317–18.   [160] Ibid., 319–23.

By the early 1880s, however, courts were starting to exercise discretion to limit discovery for reasons other than privilege. *Parker* v. *Wells*[161] in 1881 is one such example. Mr Parker claimed that the defendant Mr George Wells had sold Australian gold dust in 1854. George paid most of the money to the defendant Mr Edward Wells, and Edward agreed to hold the money in trust for his mother, Mrs Susannah Wells for her life, and after Susannah's death for his sister, Miss Ann Maybee Wells, for her life. After Ann died, the principal was supposed to be divided between her sister, Mrs Susan Kirkwood, and Parker. Parker claimed that Edward had paid interest on the funds to Susannah and Ann during their lifetimes. However, after the women died Edward refused to pay anything to Parker. Parker sought to have Edward declared a trustee of the sum for Parker and Susan Kirkwood.[162] In his defence, Edward claimed that George had sold the gold dust and disposed of most of the proceeds around that time. He said that George had given him the money to look after so that George could draw upon the funds, and claimed that George had already received most of the money, which meant there was no trust and no payments.

Parker delivered a series of interrogatories to Edward. Questions related to the dates and particulars of payments; an account of profits from the proceeds; and whether Edward had paid interest to Susannah and Ann. Originally, the court directed Edward to answer interrogatories relating to the first and third types of questions. On appeal, the court decided that Edward did not have to answer the first set because the responses could not help Parker establish the existence of a trust. At most, they might discredit Edward's evidence if there were mistakes about the particulars of payments. In reaching its decision, the court held that it would be oppressive to require Edward to review years of records to find information about payments and profits.

Jessel M.R. suggested that the interrogatories were premature, but he relied on the fact that they would be oppressive in denying the application.[163] Brett L.J. took a different approach. After delving into the changes of practice under the Judicature Acts, he concluded that the old Chancery practice was no longer applicable and the Judicature Acts introduced 'a new intermediate practice'.[164] In this case, '[t]he answers to the interrogatories ... could not determine any issue in the action, and if they have to be given at all they ought not to be required to be given till after the issues have been decided'.[165] Cotton L.J. expressed similar sentiments: 'the Court has a discretion as to whether it will order it be given before the decree, and where the discovery sought is so

---

[161] (1881) 18 Ch.D. 477.   [162] Ibid., 478–79.   [163] Ibid., 482–84.   [164] Ibid., 485.
[165] Ibid., 485–86.

oppressive as an answer to [an] interrogatory ... it is the duty of the Court to exercise that discretion by refusing the discovery'.[166] Here, Cotton L.J. was concerned about the breadth of the proposed interrogatories.

> [T]o require a full answer to the interrogatory as it stands would be oppressive, and, whatever the old practice in Chancery may have been, I think that if a question has been substantially answered, a further answer ought not to be compelled.[167]

The Court of Appeal continued to reflect upon the purpose and scope of discoveries within the meaning of the Judicature Act in *A.-G. v. Gaskill*.[168] The plaintiffs, the Attorney General and a local board, tried to stop Mr Gaskill from erecting a building across from a local footpath. The claim alleged that Gaskill had signed an agreement to settle the action on terms which the plaintiffs sought to enforce. In the alternative, the plaintiffs wanted to prevent interference with the footpath by virtue of the original title. Now, Gaskill denied the existence of the right of way, and said he signed the agreement under pressure and without a full explanation. The plaintiffs delivered interrogatories about the existence of a public right of way, what occurred at a board meeting and a conversation between Gaskill and the plaintiffs' solicitor before that meeting. In his defence, Gaskill denied the existence of the right of way, and thus refused to answer interrogatories on the subject. He also wanted to postpone responding to interrogatories about his conversation with the plaintiffs' solicitor until after their own examination and cross-examination.

On the application, Bacon V.-C. agreed with Gaskill. He held that the old rules remained in force[169] and the plaintiffs' right to discovery was always limited where (as it was said in *Saull v. Browne*[170]) 'the discovery is sought vexatiously or oppressively – or is discovery which it will be burdensome or injurious to the [d]efendant to give, and which probably may never be used at all'.[171] Bacon V.-C. concluded that the existence of the footpath was an issue of law, not a matter of fact. Gaskill had provided 'a perfectly good pleading, and being a matter of pleading, no discovery can be asked for as to that'.[172] The Vice-Chancellor explained that the Judicature Act had changed the court's *practice*, but not the underlying principles or powers.[173] Limits on discovery

---

[166] Ibid., 486–87.   [167] Ibid., 487.   [168] (1881) 20 Ch.D. 519.   [169] Ibid., 524.
[170] (1874) L.R. 9 Ch. App. 364.
[171] Ibid., 367–8, quoted *arguendo* in *A.-G. v. Gaskill* (1881) 20 Ch.D. 519, 522.
[172] *A.-G. v. Gaskill* (1881) 20 Ch.D. 519, 524.   [173] Ibid., 524–25.

had existed under the Common Law Procedure Act and continued under the Judicature Act. The court was supposed to determine:

> whether the interrogatories ... are necessary to the ends of justice, and in accordance with the rights of the interrogating party, or are merely a harassing attempt, by reviving an obsolete practice, to impede and obstruct the hearing of the cause, and the decision of the real question between the parties.[174]

On appeal, Gaskill relied on the rules, and argued that a party was entitled to object to unreasonable interrogatories. He complained that the plaintiff could not use discovery to obtain evidence for trial, and had no right to discovery on known matters between the parties when he had the burden of proof.[175] To compel answers to interrogatories in this case would 'sanction a revival of the old practice of interrogating all through a bill'.[176]

The Court of Appeal disagreed, and ordered Gaskill to respond. The court said that interrogatories were meant to help one party obtain admissions from the other, thus negating the need to adduce that evidence at trial.[177] Jessel M.R. agreed that the old Chancery rules remained applicable,[178] but unlike Bacon V.-C., he allowed interrogatories on the right of way precisely because the plaintiffs had the burden of proof. Jessel M.R. explained:

> [O]ne of the great objects of interrogatories when properly administered has always been to save evidence, that is to diminish the burden of proof which was otherwise on the [p]laintiff. Their object is not merely to discover facts which will inform the [p]laintiff as to evidence to be obtained, but also to save the expense of proving a part of the case.[179]

He noted that there was a good deal of effort required to prove the facts of this case. 'It involves the calling of a great number of old people to prove the use of this footpath as a public footpath for many years past. It causes great expense and trouble.'[180]

Cotton L.J. agreed and affirmed the existing Chancery-influenced approach to discoveries. He rejected the idea 'that everything which related to discovery existing in the practice of the Court of Chancery before the Judicature Act must be thrown aside as a matter of the past having no application to the present state of things'.[181] Although the legislation allowed every party to interrogate the opposing party as of right, Cotton L.J. noted the court's power to award costs as a 'check' for interrogatories that were 'exhibited

[174] Ibid., 524–25.   [175] Ibid., 526.   [176] Ibid., 525.   [177] Ibid., 519–20.   [178] Ibid., 526–27.
[179] Ibid., 528.   [180] Ibid., 527.   [181] Ibid., 528.

unreasonably, vexatiously, or at improper length'.[182] He said, 'the right to discovery remains the same, that is to say, a party has a right to interrogate with a view to obtaining an admission from his opponent of everything which is material and relevant to the issue raised on the pleadings'.[183] Cotton L.J. affirmed the efficiencies derived from discoveries, saying that it was 'not limited to giving the [p]laintiff a knowledge of that which he does not already know, but includes getting an admission of anything which he has to prove on any issue which is raised between him and the [d]efendant'.[184] Pleadings set out the issues, but interrogatories allowed a party to 'obtain an admission from his opponent which will make the burden of proof easier than it otherwise would have been'.[185]

CONCLUSION

Written interrogatories and documentary inspection – the two separate components of nineteenth-century discovery now combined into one in modern practice – originated in equity. When the Judicature Acts came into force in 1875, litigants had already benefited from a form of fusion with respect to discovery at common law for more than twenty years. Both before and after the enactment of the Judicature Acts, the courts affirmed repeatedly that discovery rules were grounded in equity and past Chancery practice.

Much of the reported case law dealt with in this chapter highlights the court's willingness to exercise its discretion to permit interrogatories to proceed in a particular action. In this regard, common law judges do not appear to have been reluctant to facilitate discoveries in their own courts, although they were generally determined to maintain the practice as it was in Chancery. Even when the Judicature Act made discovery a right, discretion remained; the court retained the ability to refuse interrogatories that were unreasonable, vexatious or otherwise oppressive to the party under interrogation. Throughout, privilege could defeat an application for discovery, but only with respect to specific documents or interrogatories.

Although the common law courts consistently affirmed Chancery practice with respect to discovery, over time the approach changed. In the years immediately following the enactment of the Common Law Procedure Act in 1854, the common law courts focused on limiting interrogatories and inspection of documents to situations in which the party seeking the interrogatories intended to use discovery to build his or her own case.

---

[182] Rules of Court, O. 31, r. 2.   [183] A.-G. v. Gaskill (1881) 20 Ch.D. 519, 528.
[184] Ibid., 528–29.   [185] Ibid. Lindley L.J. agreed at 530–31.

Interrogatories were also permitted even if the applicant obtained evidence from the opposing party about the latter's case provided that was not their primary focus. Fishing expeditions were clearly impermissible. Gradually, however, the common law courts began to permit discovery to unearth the 'truth' about a dispute in the name of 'justice'. In this spirit, the courts began to applaud the use of discovery as a way to save time and money at trial.

What to take from the equitable origins of discovery? Although discovery was born of equity, many of the hallmarks of common law procedure now overwhelm the process in modern civil litigation. Rigidity has replaced judicial discretion; oral examination has come to dominate in North America, supplanting the use of written interrogatories. Recent reforms, which give courts more power to limit discovery, are a welcome reflection of earlier equitable principles, including focus on the need for proportionality and increased judicial oversight of the process. These changes, which are more consistent with the equitable origins of discovery, may offer respite from the oppression that many nineteenth-century reformers feared would accompany universal access.

PART III

Functional, Analytical and Theoretical Views

13

Wrongful Fusion

Equity and Tort

JOHN C. P. GOLDBERG AND HENRY E. SMITH

INTRODUCTION

Historically, equity and tort seem to have had little to do with one another. True, injunctions have long been available to certain tort plaintiffs, as have actions for contribution to certain tort defendants. Beyond this, the two bodies of law appear to have operated largely in separate spheres.

Despite the lack of contact, much less friction, between these domains, the fusion of law and equity, combined with the rise to dominance in the US legal academy of Legal Realism, has raised a puzzle about their relationship: what distinguishes the two? According to standard Realist accounts, equity and tort arguably fit the same description. Each is understood as an all-purpose legal tool: an unstructured grant of authority to judges to issue rulings that promote some good or rectify some ill.

Equity's reputation for open-endedness long precedes Realism. In the Coke–Ellesmere conflict, and the jurisdictional tussles it epitomised, common lawyers, formalists and the more 'parliamentary' or 'puritan' side of political clashes famously critiqued equity as too discretionary, too civilian, too royal and thus threatening to common law.[1] Selden's famous quip about the Chancellor's foot was in part an expression of the worry about judges operating under a roving commission to do equity. After equity won the jurisdictional battle, a degree of peace was achieved through its self-imposed limits, most notably the doctrine that equity would stay its hand when the law affords an adequate remedy. Whether these limits were robust or sufficient has been controversial. But in the heyday of Realism (roughly 1930–75) – in which there was great enthusiasm for context-sensitive, adventurous judging and little patience for 'arid' conceptual distinctions between equity and law – equity was

---

[1] Baker, *I.E.L.H.*, 4th edn, 109–11.

once again cast (albeit now more favourably) as a broad, unstructured mandate for judges to achieve fairness.

As typically characterised by academic commentators in the United States, tort law has many of these same features. Following Holmes's lead, post-fusion scholars such as Leon Green and William Prosser argued that older notions of tort as a structured, moralistic law of rights and wrongs had given way to the idea of tort law as regulation through liability in the name of public welfare.[2] This picture of tort law was hardly a prescription for restraint. Indeed, in the Realist era tort law expanded not only internally but externally. For example, when Grant Gilmore declared contract dead, he did not claim that it had simply disappeared. Rather he concluded that it had been folded into tort.[3] Interestingly, Gilmore saw as one of the main vehicles for this transformation the doctrine of promissory estoppel, which traces back to equity.

With both tort and equity described in terms that arguably permit either to swallow up much of private law, there seems little ground to distinguish them. Indeed, in their most expansive and gaseous phase, tort and equity (on the foregoing descriptions) are indistinguishable: each fills up all the space there is. The only question is whether to refer to the general grant of judicial authority to achieve good outcomes as 'equity' or 'tort'. This question, it is supposed, was answered at a terminological level when equity was fused into law. Although equity and tort – on the Realist understanding – refer equally to the idea of judges using their powers to achieve socially valuable ends, the label 'equity' was discarded, leaving us with 'tort'.

This chapter aims to rethink the tort–equity interface. It argues against hyper-fusion and the Realist reduction of equity to tort and tort to equity. To achieve this goal, it will be necessary to give an account of how equity operates at the boundaries of tort law. This in turn presupposes an account of tort as a body of law that actually has some boundaries.

The key distinction between tort and equity is not jurisdictional but conceptual and functional. Tort law is for the most part 'first-order' law. It specifies, in relatively general terms, legal duties that we owe to one another and legal rights that we have against one another. The tort of trespass to land, for example, imposes (roughly) a duty not to enter another's land and a right against such entry. Negligence, meanwhile, specifies a broad duty not to injure others through actions that are careless towards them and a right not to be so injured.

---

[2]   See, for example, L. Green, 'Tort Law Public Law in Disguise' (1959) 38 Tex. L. Rev. 1.
[3]   G. Gilmore, *The Death of Contract* (Columbus, OH: Ohio State University Press, 1974).

In the process of articulating duties to refrain from wrongfully injuring others and rights against being wrongfully injured, tort law operates by identifying paradigmatic forms of mistreatment, defined at a general or abstract level. Tort law is in this respect relatively formal in that it is relatively invariant to context.[4] For example, trespass to land issues a focused and powerful legal directive that subsumes many situations under a general directive (that amounts to 'Keep out!'), thereby marking off as wrongful and injurious one person's entering or remaining on another's land.[5]

Equity is not conduct-guiding in this way, nor is it general. Rather, it is a gap-filling, second-order regime. In the famous formulation of Aristotle, equity corrects 'law in so far as it is deficient because of its universality'.[6] The most expansive renditions of Aristotle's notion treat equity as an all-purpose, *ex post* fix-it for whenever a new problem arises or conditions change.[7]

In this chapter, we entertain the hypothesis that equity is a second-order intervention to address certain inherent deficiencies in any body of doctrine, such as tort law, that operates largely as first-order law.[8] From a functional

---

4   F. Heylighen, 'Advantages and Limitations of Formal Expression' (1999) 4 Found. Sci. 25, 26–27, 49–53 (defining formalism); H. E. Smith, 'The Language of Property: Form, Context, and Audience' (2003) 55 Stan. L. Rev. 1105, 1112–13, 1135–36 (discussing 'differential formalism').

5   Where this formalism comes from and how it is grounded is another story. For example, Kantians see the formality of torts like trespass as grounded in the nature of the interpersonal relationship involved in the interaction at issue: A. Ripstein, 'Possession and Use', in J. Penner and H. E. Smith (eds), *Philosophical Foundations of Property Law* (Oxford University Press, 2013), 161–78; see also E. J. Weinrib, *The Idea of Private Law*, revised 1st edn (Oxford University Press, 2012), 22–55.

6   Aristotle, *Nicomachean Ethics*, trans. by C. D. C. Reeve (Indianapolis, IN: Hackett Publishing, 2014), ¶ 1137b25; see e.g., *Riggs v. Palmer*, 22 N.E. 188, 189 (N.Y. 1889) (quoting Aristotle); E. G. Zahnd, 'The Application of Universal Laws to Particular Cases: A Defense of Equity in Aristotelianism and Anglo-American Law' (Winter, 1996) 59 Law & Contemp. Probs. 263, 270–75(documenting influence of Aristotelian equity on Anglo-American law); but see D. Shanske, 'Four Theses: Preliminary to an Appeal to Equity, Note' (2005) 57 Stan. L. Rev. 2053, 2066–68 (arguing that Aristotle's equity was not primarily legal).

7   Zechariah Chafee, Jr, expressed a moderately expansionist view of equity when he opined that '[e]quity is a way of looking at the administration of justice; it is a set of effective and flexible remedies admirably adapted to the needs of a complex society; it is a body of substantive rules': 'Foreword', in E. D. Re (ed.), *Selected Essays on Equity* (New York, NY: Oceana, 1955), iii; see also Z. Chafee, Jr, *Some Problems of Equity: Five Lectures Delivered at the University of Michigan &c.* (Ann Arbor, MI: University of Michigan Law School, 1950).

8   See H. E. Smith, 'Equity as Second-Order Law: The Problem of Opportunism', working paper (15 January 2015), available: https://papers.ssrn.com/sol3/papers.cfm?abstract_id=2617413; Smith, 'Fusing the Equitable Function'. For other recent treatments of equity as a system, see S. L. Bray, 'The System of Equitable Remedies' (2016) 63 UCLA L. Rev. 530; I. Samet, 'What Conscience Can Do for Equity' (2012) 3 Jurisprudence 13; P. G. Turner, 'Equity and Administration', in *Equity and Administration*, ch. 1.

John C. P. Goldberg and Henry E. Smith

standpoint, we view equity as a cluster of second-order legal rules or principles that sometimes modifies or suspends first-order law. Think here of the classic injunction against suit, but also doctrines of unclean hands and unconscionability. There is a characteristic set of problems that are suited for second-order treatment – a set that includes multipolar conflict, conflicting rights and opportunism. One of us has defined opportunism as follows:

> behavior that is undesirable but that cannot be cost-effectively captured – defined, detected, and deterred – by explicit ex ante rulemaking ... It often consists of behavior that is technically legal but is done with a view to securing unintended benefits from the system, and these benefits are usually smaller than the costs they impose on others.[9]

Such problems were traditionally labelled constructive fraud in the equity jurisprudence, with Justice Story providing this (partly dated) near-definition:

> In this class [of constructive or legal, as opposed to actual intentional, fraud] ... may properly be included all cases of unconscientious advantages in bargains, obtained by imposition, circumvention, surprise, and undue influence over persons in general; and in an especial manner, all unconscientious advantages, or bargains obtained over persons, disabled by weakness, infirmity, age, lunacy, idiocy, drunkenness, coverture, or other incapacity, from taking due care of, or protecting their own rights and interests.[10]

Problems of opportunism or constructive fraud are difficult to anticipate in advance in a way that does not invite further adjustments by opportunists. There is a corresponding tendency for such problems to elicit second-order *ex post* solutions, at least in part. In this sense, opportunism provides an occasion for Aristotelian equity: the law's generality makes it a sitting duck for the unscrupulous. Equity's defence is to build on law – it is second order.

While equity in this way makes reference to first-order law, the reverse is not true. In the words of Maitland (a sceptic of a unitary equitable function), if equity had been abolished, 'in some respects our law would have been barbarous, unjust, absurd, but still the great elementary rights, the right to immunity from violence, the right to one's good name, the rights of ownership and of possession would have been decently protected and contract would have been enforced'.[11] By contrast, abolishing common law would have meant

---

[9] Smith, 'Equity as Second-Order Law', 14–15.
[10] J. Story, *Commentaries on Equity Jurisprudence, as Administered in England and America* (Boston, MA: Hilliard, Gray & Co., 1836), vol. 1, § 221.
[11] Maitland, *Equity*, 19.

'anarchy', because '[a]t every point equity presupposed the existence of common law'.[12] In his memorable summation, '[e]quity without common law would have been a castle in the air, an impossibility'.[13]

As elsewhere in equity but perhaps to an even greater degree, the proxies triggering second-order intervention carry a heavy burden. In this part of the chapter we will emphasise constructive fraud, with side glances to multipolar problems. Accordingly, the proxies we need to focus on are those correlating with opportunism. These proxies are based on custom, commercial morality and professional norms. The point of equity is not to enforce custom or commercial morality directly. As in contract law, in which a violation of custom can be treated as prima facie evidence of – and trigger a presumption of – bad faith,[14] so too in the area of equitable wrongs, the violation of custom or an egregious violation of commercial morality can create a presumption favouring closer scrutiny.

Because our topic is the tort-equity interface, we will focus on correcting for the particular problem of law's misuse and mistakes giving rise to potential advantage taking. As we will see, there is a special set of equitable triggers when it comes to situations governed in the first instance by tort law, or at the edges of tort law. Within the domain of targeted intervention, the second-order safety valve of equity is cabined precisely because it does not apply all the time. Conversely, with equity as a backstop, tort law (and other law) can afford to be more general.[15] So understood, equity is in some respects the opposite of tort law. It does not aspire to set rules of interpersonal interaction, or if it does, it does so at a very high level of abstraction so as to provide little by way of specific conduct guidance. (Think here of equity's maxims, such as the maxim that no person should profit from his or her own wrong.) Its domain is circumscribed, derivative and, to a degree, retroactive, whereas tort law's domain is general, primary and conduct-guiding. Though tort law's directives often take the form of standards of conduct rather than strict rules – the most obvious example being negligence law's reasonably prudent person standard – tort law is more formal and equity is more context-sensitive.[16] The kinds of

[12] Ibid., 19.   [13] Ibid.
[14] Compare E. Kadens, 'The Myth of the Customary Law Merchant' (2012) 90 Tex. L. Rev. 1153, 1193–94 (discussing how medieval litigants would establish good faith by showing adherence to custom).
[15] See Smith, 'Equity as Second-Order Law', 61. Anti-fusionists sometimes made an argument along these lines: e.g., Letter from Lord Hardwicke to Lord Kames.
[16] As to which, see the citations and text to n. 8.

moral considerations that each body of legal rules invokes may be different as well.[17] Equity incorporates moral standards in a way that is more particularised, appropriate to a targeted view of a situation. By contrast, the morality of tort law is local, robust and generalisable.

In keeping with our functional rather than jurisdictional or historical approach, we begin under the heading of 'Equity and tort' by identifying doctrines *within* tort law that are equitable, as we use that term, including a particular application of the 'coming to the nuisance' doctrine, qualifications to privileges that deem them lost when abused and certain grounds for awarding punitive damages. Each of these doctrines operates as a way of blocking opportunistic invocations of primary tort rules or related procedural law. This part of the chapter also discusses how equitable reasoning – reasoning that focuses on the need to shape tort doctrine to limit the ability of actors to game it – has figured in the development of important doctrines.

The next part, 'Constructive fraud as equitable wrong', discusses cases in which courts have issued equitable remedies, particularly injunctions and constructive trusts, in response to actors who take unfair advantage of certain kinds of legally conferred powers or opportunities, but whose conduct does not amount to the commission of a recognised tort. Included here are decisions in which courts enjoin unfair competition. In this class of cases, equity operates to fill gaps that inevitably emerge because tort law – in order to guide conduct and comply with rule-of-law principles – operates by identifying a limited menu of wrongs, each of which has a limited reach, and which, taken together, leave uncovered various forms of wrongful conduct.

The next part briefly considers 'dynamic' aspects of the relation of tort to equity. It discusses how equitable interventions to limit opportunism can give rise to the recognition of new tort claims for damages. Developments such as these are often salutary, we argue, but also have potential costs. In particular, there is the risk that, out of a desire to retain the flexibility of equity, particular torts and tort law more generally can be defined in ways that render it too unstructured to perform its conduct-guiding role. We conclude with some thoughts on how to implement the equitable function in torts against a background of the fusion of law and equity.

---

[17] A. S. Gold and H. E. Smith, 'Sizing Up Private Law', unpublished paper (9 August 2016), 24–5, available: https://ssrn.com/abstract=2821354.

EQUITY IN TORT

On our understanding of equity as second order, nothing requires it to carry a separate label, or to be administered by special courts. Indeed, a moderate version of fusion – the fusing of courts and jurisdictions while maintaining separate substance – requires as much. It is no surprise, then, to find that the second-order equitable function sometimes finds a home within tort law.

Equity through the Application of Tort Doctrine

Within tort law the equitable function is not distributed randomly. Instead it tends to appear where problems of variability involving complexity and uncertainty call for second-order solutions. Among these are certain aspects of nuisance law and qualified privileges.

Among torts, private nuisance is functionally and historically closely entwined with equity. In a functional sense, nuisance involves conflicting rights and much of nuisance law (sometimes under the banner of *sic utere tuo ut alienum non laedas*, 'use what is yours in way that does not harm that of others') can be regarded as a second-order adjustment of the conflicting rights of neighbouring landowners.[18] In a historical (and also often functional) connection to equity, nuisance suits and claims for injunctive relief have gone hand in hand. As Zygmunt Plater noted some time ago, courts of equity presiding over claims for injunctive relief required nuisance claimants to clear various hurdles, including the irreparable injury requirement, as well as defences such as laches and unclean hands. In addition, he observed, claims could also be defeated by affirmative defences 'grounded in principles of equitable estoppel', including the doctrine of 'coming to the nuisance'.[19]

Some commentators today insist that it is erroneous to use the phrase 'coming to the nuisance' to refer to a discrete doctrine within nuisance law.[20] They do not deny that if, at the time of purchasing (or putting to new use) his or her land, the plaintiff was aware that the defendant's activities were interfering or might interfere with his or her use of the land, such awareness is relevant to liability. Instead they maintain that awareness of this sort should

---

[18] Smith, 'Fusing the Equitable Function', 190–91.
[19] Z. J. B. Plater, 'Statutory Violations and Equitable Discretion' (1982) 70 Cal. L. Rev. 524, 537.
[20] J. J. Murphy, *The Law of Nuisance* (Oxford University Press, 2010), 106 ('It is no defence that the claimant came to the nuisance by moving into occupation of land adjacent to that of the defendant. For the purposes of nuisance law, it makes no difference "whether the man went to the nuisance or the nuisance went to the man".') (citations omitted).

figure as one factor among many in the assessment of whether the defendant's activity *unreasonably* interferes with the plaintiff's use and enjoyment.[21] On this view, there is no defence that goes under the name 'coming to the nuisance'. Rather, that phrase refers to one of a host of factors that figure in the determination of whether plaintiff has made out a prima facie case.

In gauging the extent to which the coming-to-the-nuisance idea figures in modern nuisance law, one must take care not to be misled by mere verbal disputes. For example, some who deny that it stands as a distinct defence are still prepared to recognise doctrines, such as assumption of risk and contributory negligence, which resemble the doctrine that shall not be named.[22] For those who would allow such defences – e.g., by deeming certain nuisance plaintiffs to have been contributorily negligent in creating the interference – the refusal to recognise 'coming to the nuisance', as such, is probably best understood as expressing a worry that coming-to-the-nuisance language invites courts to find against plaintiffs more often than they should.[23]

Seeing modern hostility towards the coming-to-the-nuisance doctrine as grounded in this concern about its anti-plaintiff tendency may help explain the relatively narrow articulation of the doctrine that is offered in section 840D of the *Restatement (Second) Torts*, which treats coming to the nuisance as an affirmative defence.[24] The Restatement is careful to limit the scope of the defence: first, by making it applicable only to cases where the plaintiff purchases or improves land in the face of an existing nuisance; second, by deeming this fact to be relevant to, but not sufficient for, the establishment of the defence:

§ 840D. Coming to the Nuisance

The fact that the plaintiff has acquired or improved his land after a nuisance interfering with it has come into existence is not in itself sufficient to bar his action, but it is a factor to be considered in determining whether the nuisance is actionable.

---

[21] Ibid.   [22] Ibid., 107.

[23] In this respect, the call to eliminate 'coming to the nuisance' is akin to the call of some commentators to eliminate the 'assumption of risk' defence from negligence law on the ground that judges tend to overuse it, and that its proper application can be handled through the related defence of comparative fault.

[24] *Restatement (Second) Torts* § 840D (1979). Section 840D is located in the portion of the Restatement discussing 'defenses' to nuisance actions, which is why the word 'nuisance' appears in its concluding clause. The question to be addressed under the heading of 'coming to the nuisance', according to the Restatement, is not whether the defendant has engaged in conduct amounting to a nuisance – he or she has. It is whether conduct that has already been deemed a nuisance is 'actionable' by the plaintiff.

The black-letter of section 840D is admittedly a little odd. It purports to identify 'Coming to the Nuisance' as a distinct defence, but then fails to indicate what will suffice to establish the defence. Suppose a court were to find that a plaintiff acquired his or her land after a nuisance interfering with its use had already come into existence. Section 840D advises the court that it should not rule for the defendant based on this finding alone. Instead, the court must determine whether other considerations, when combined with this finding, defeat the plaintiff's claim.[25] Yet the *Restatement* does not enumerate these 'other factors'.[26]

Whatever its quirks, section 840D in the end does a decent job of gesturing towards the coming-to-the-nuisance doctrine, and, in certain applications, instantiates the idea of equity that we articulated above. Consider the following *Restatement* illustration:

> 2. A operates a copper smelter near the land of B. Smoke, fumes and gases from the smelter create a private nuisance interfering with the use and enjoyment of the land of B. For the sole purpose of bringing a lawsuit and forcing A to buy him out a high price, C buys the land from B and moves in upon it. In his action for the private nuisance, the fact that C has acquired the land with the nuisance in existence, together with his purpose, will prevent his recovery.[27]

As this example suggests, even though the doctrine may have other applications (and section 840D's other illustrations suggest that it does), it is in part meant to serve the equitable function of preventing actors from exploiting the rules of nuisance law. In particular, it empowers courts to prevent strategic plaintiffs from using the law of nuisance to 'hold up' their neighbours.[28]

Section 840D points to the need for – and is itself consistent with – a second-order solution. A flat rule always defeating liability when an activity or condition operated for a time without interfering with another's use and

---

[25] Ibid., § 840D, cmt c: 'Although it is not conclusive in itself, the fact that the plaintiff has "come to the nuisance" is still a factor of importance to be considered in cases where other factors are involved.'

[26] Nor does it explain why a defence that turns on the presence of multiple factors, only one of which is the plaintiff's having come to the nuisance, should be styled as the defence of 'Coming to the Nuisance'. By comparison, imagine if, in defining the consent defence to claims for battery, the *Restatement* stated that a plaintiff's consent to contact by the defendant is insufficient to render that contact non-actionable, but is to be considered in determining whether the contact is actionable.

[27] *Restatement (Second) Torts* § 840D, cmt c, illustration 2 (1979). The illustration is based on *Edwards* v. *Allouez Mining Co.*, 38 Mich. 46 (1878), which we discuss at nn. 45 and 63.

[28] See D. B. Kelly, 'Strategic Spillovers' (2011) 111 Colum. L. Rev. 1641, 1660–67.

enjoyment of his or her land would invite a wasteful and unfair race to be the first to generate noises, odours or the like in a particular location. Likewise, a flat rule that coming to the nuisance is never a defence itself invites the strategic behaviour of potential plaintiffs deliberately setting up conflicts where otherwise none would exist. An indication of how difficult it is to come up with a 'first order' solution to the problem are the complicated and controversial models in the law and economics literature that attempt exactly that.[29] The defence assesses both parties' behaviour and how they interact – a classic situation for second-order intervention. As is often true of equity, there is potential for opportunism on both sides, reinforcing the difficulty of a one-level solution.

While applications of coming-to-the nuisance doctrine illustrate the equitable function of a particular doctrine within a part of tort law that historically has had close ties to equity, examples from other parts of tort law can also be found. As we discuss in more detail later, the notion of 'abuse of right', elusive though it may be, looms large in equity, even if courts have not always recognised it by that name. Some have even suggested that the prevention and rectification of abuses of right is the very essence of equity.[30] One need not go that far, however, to see manifestations within tort doctrine of a concern to prevent right-holders from abusing their rights.

Most relevant, perhaps, is the recognition of qualified privileges, exemplified by certain privileges recognised in the law of libel and slander. It is tortious to publish a false and defamatory statement about another. Yet liability for such statements can be avoided by invoking a privilege, such as the so-called 'common interest' privilege. Among other things, this privilege protects from liability a person who, in good faith, mistakenly defames another person in the course of providing an evaluation of her to a third party. For example, if A's former employer, based on confusion or even carelessness, submits a reference letter to a prospective employer containing a false and defamatory statement about A, the statement will be privileged so long as made in good faith.

Unlike the privilege to defame in the course of court proceedings, which is absolute, the common interest privilege is qualified: it can be lost or forfeited if a court deems the defendant to have abused it. While abuse of privilege can

---

[29] R. Innes, 'Coming to the Nuisance: Revisiting *Spur* in a Model of Location Choice' (2009) 25 J. L. Econ. & Org. 286; D. Wittman, 'First Come, First Served: An Economic Analysis of "Coming to the Nuisance"' (1980) 9 J. Legal Stud. 557.

[30] D. Klimchuk, 'Equity and the Rule of Law', in L. M. Austin and D. Klimchuk (eds), *Private Law and the Rule of Law* (Oxford University Press, 2014), 268.

take various forms, it clearly covers cases in which a defendant publishes the defamatory statement for reasons other than those that the privilege is intended to further. Thus, an employer who provides a false and defamatory evaluation out of spite for the person being evaluated, or as part of a plan to advance its bottom line by preventing would-be competitors from hiring that person, will be denied the ability to invoke the privilege.[31]

The framework deployed by courts when analysing claims of qualified privilege have the same layered quality we saw in discussing the coming-to-the-nuisance doctrine. Tort rules first set out, in general terms, a kind of interaction that is forbidden – defaming another, or interfering with another's use and enjoyment of his or her property. Equitable doctrines in turn provide a kind of safety valve by blocking persons subject to those rules from exploiting their generality.

Equitable Reasoning in Tort Cases

Among the landmarks of modern tort law is Judge Cardozo's opinion for the New York Court of Appeals in *MacPherson v. Buick Motor Co.*[32] *MacPherson* is still taught for its rejection of the infamous 'privity rule' adopted by the Court of Exchequer in *Winterbottom v. Wright*,[33] and its powerful insistence that manufacturers owe a duty to take care that their products do not injure consumers. Cardozo's famous opinion, we would suggest, also includes equitable reasoning.

Relying on *Winterbottom*, Buick argued that it owed no duty of care to MacPherson because he had not purchased his car directly from Buick but rather through an independent dealer. In addition to rejection of Buick's characterisation of New York precedents, Judge Cardozo observed that Buick's argument, if accepted, would have an odd consequence:

> The dealer was indeed the one person of whom it might be said with some approach to certainty that by him the car would not be used. Yet the defendant would have us say that he was the one person whom it was under a legal duty to protect. The law does not lead us to so inconsequent a conclusion.[34]

---

[31] See, for example, *Swengler v. I.T.T. Corp. Electro-Optical Products Division*, 993 F.2d 1063 (4th Cir. 1993) (applying Virginia law) (defendant's allegations that former employer committed fraud amounted to an abuse of the common interest privilege because made with malice towards former employer); *Hines v. Shumaker*, 97 Miss. 669 (1910) (even if defendant enjoyed a privilege to publish defamatory remarks in response to plaintiff's criticisms, the response exceeded the scope of the privilege); *Restatement (Second) Torts* § 605, cmt a (1979).

[32] 111 N.E. 1050 (N.Y. 1916).   [33] (1842) 10 M. & W. 109.

[34] *MacPherson v. Buick Motor Co.*, 111 N.E. 1050, 1053 (N.Y. 1916).

While a lot can be said about Judge Cardozo's reasoning here, we will focus on an overlooked equitable aspect of it. Under the privity rule, manufacturers had an easy way of evading their duties – namely, by adopting distribution networks that call for sales through intermediaries. While one can imagine situations in which such a situation was tolerable, this was not one of them, and for good reason.

First, it is not clear that dealers who sell cars purchased from reputable manufacturers such as Buick could be deemed negligent, at least with respect to their failure to detect defects not readily discoverable through the sort of inspection that, at the time, they were equipped to undertake. Second, the point of imposing a duty of care is not merely to ensure that there is some deep pocket available to cover certain injury-related losses, but to have relevant actors actually take steps to reduce the risks of injury to others generated by their activities. The privity rule essentially invited sophisticated actors – product manufacturers – to evade negligence law's directives. *MacPherson*'s rejection of privity prevented that.[35]

Our point is not that judges, in the name of equity, must ensure that actors have no leeway to organise their activities to reduce or avoid potential tort liability. The law, after all, empowers actors to use the corporate form precisely to limit owners' liabilities. But it is one thing to allow investors to limit their personal liability for managerial actions over which they have relatively little control, quite another to impose a duty of care but then allow those subject to the duty to use their legal powers to ensure that *nobody* – not the corporation, its managers, or shareholders – faces liability for breaches of that duty.[36]

In a similar fashion, equitable intervention often limits the ability of tort defendants to invoke a recognised tort defence in a strategic effort to avoid tort liability. This is true of 'public policy' limitations on 'express assumption of risk', according to which an otherwise valid negligence claim against a defendant is dismissed on the ground that the plaintiff agreed in advance to

<hr/>

[35] S. H. Clarke, 'Unmanageable Risks: *MacPherson* v. *Buick* and the Emergence of a Mass Consumer Market' (2005) 23 L.H.R. 1, 22–28 (suggesting that, by about 1908, car manufacturers were aware of the legal implications of adopting different methods of distribution, though also suggesting that liability for personal injury was not foremost among their concerns).

[36] Again, a full evaluation requires knowing what the alternatives are in various sets of circumstances. In the corporate law context, there is a theoretical case that limited liability should not extend to those with tort claims against the corporation: H. Hansmann and R. Kraakman, 'Toward Unlimited Shareholder Liability for Corporate Torts' (1991) 100 Yale L.J. 1879. This is why in some high-risk contexts, like the operation of taxis, regulations require insurance. Knowing use of the corporate form as part of an illicit scheme to evade or limit liability for wrongdoing would be a reason to pierce the corporate veil – itself an equitable doctrine.

waive liability for such negligence.[37] Likewise, in policing waivers obtained by physicians against malpractice liability, courts have claimed the authority to refuse to enforce tort waivers in situations where the defendant's activity is one 'affected with a public interest'.[38] Instead of a paternalistic protection of short-sightedness of potential plaintiffs, this type of intervention can be seen as unenforceability as a matter of tort law, for (functionally) equitable reasons – to control strategic behaviour by sophisticated actors who are subject to tort duties.

CONSTRUCTIVE FRAUD AS EQUITABLE WRONG: ABUSE OF RIGHT AND UNFAIR COMPETITION

Equity not only pops up within tort doctrine; it is also available to respond to what might be called equitable wrongs. Equitable wrongs are not torts, because they come about differently. Tort law specifies duties *ex ante* even if some of the content is filled in *ex post* and in a contextual fashion. Aside perhaps from an area such as fiduciary law,[39] equity typically operates more in an *ex post* manner.

The availability of equity to provide relief for wrongs is a touchy subject, because it edges equity closer to matters like criminal law, from which it was historically cabined off. Thus, the idea of allowing Chancellors to use their personal sense of morality in a sort of 'roving commission to do good' has always been looked upon with suspicion.[40]

Nevertheless, when it comes to second-order functions like reconciling conflicting rights, solving multipolar conflict or countering opportunism, there is, as we have seen, a limit on how much can be specified *ex ante*. What is set out in advance are the triggers for the second-order intervention:

---

[37] *Tunkl v. Regents of University of California*, 383 P.2d 441 (Cal. 1963).

[38] Ibid., 444. Jennifer Arlen has made the related point that competent medical care is a good that will not be secured through contracting because of collective action problems: J. Arlen, 'Contracting Over Liability: Medical Malpractice and the Cost of Choice' (2010) 158 U. Pa. L. Rev. 957, 992–97.

[39] On the role of *ex ante* and *ex post* in an account of fiduciary law that emphasises its equitable aspect, see H. E. Smith, 'Why Fiduciary Law Is Equitable', in A. S. Gold and P. B. Miller (eds), *Philosophical Foundations of Fiduciary Law* (Oxford University Press, 2014), ch. 13. Even if it is debatable whether to call broad *ex ante* rules in fiduciary law (no self-dealing, no conflicts of interest) functionally equitable, they do respond to an extreme danger of opportunism.

[40] Like the 'Chancellor's Foot', this phrase encapsulates a sceptical attitude to expansive equity: D. Laycock, *Modern American Remedies: Cases and Materials*, 4th edn (New York, NY: Aspen, 2010), 307; Laycock, 'Triumph of Equity', 73.

what it takes to get a claimant into the domain of equity. In the area of equitable wrongs, these triggers are violations of custom and commercial morality, as well as professional norms.

Equity and custom have maintained a close association. Although the common law courts enforced custom, they did so differently. Roughly speaking, they would decline to enforce a custom unless it possessed attributes – stability, reasonableness, generality and so on – that make it more like law.[41] Equity invoked custom in a more second-order fashion. Sometimes custom would involve a group, leading to a complex procedural problem. And equity devised the precursors to the class action (and interpleader) in order to make possible the enforcement of customary rights of intermediate-sized groups, such as common pool resource users and parishioners.[42]

On the substantive side, custom's association with natural law and 'natural equity' served as the historical way for equity courts to draw on custom.[43] This intervention can be narrower than it sounds. Thus, equity courts would take a blatant violation of custom as evidence of bad faith or unclean hands, with the result of non-enforcement of transactions. In the realm of equitable wrongs, violation of custom could be the trigger for constructive fraud (perhaps through bad faith or disproportionate hardship).

Equity's intervention in response to unfair competition is a second-order analogue to tort law. Competition is a complex process that is governed by an interlocking system of private law: contract, tort, property and restitution. These bodies of law can sometimes misfire, inviting courts to override their effects. Even actions and transactions that result from individuals and firms acting within their legal rights will sometimes generate serious inequities. As we noted earlier, rights can be abused. Much of equity's attention to competition is concerned with what in civil law would be called abuse of right.[44]

One way in which equity intervenes in response to an abuse of right is to refrain from enforcing an otherwise valid claim of right. In *Edwards* v. *Allouez Mining Co.*,[45] the defendant's mill deposited sand on plaintiff's downstream

---

[41] See, for example, W. Blackstone, *Commentaries on the Laws of England* (Oxford: Clarendon, 1765), vol. 1, 76–78.

[42] S. C. Yeazell, 'Group Litigation and Social Context: Toward a History of the Class Action' (1977) 77 Colum. L. Rev. 866, 868 (citing Chafee, *Some Problems of Equity*, 149, 200–1).

[43] See H. E. Smith, 'Custom in American Property Law: A Vanishing Act' (2013) 48 Tex. Int'l L.J. 507, 518–31.

[44] See, for example, A. di Robilant, 'Abuse of Rights: The Continental Drug and the Common Law' (2010) 61 Hastings L.J. 687; L. Katz, 'Spite and Extortion: A Jurisdictional Principle of Abuse of Property Right' (2013) 122 Yale L.J. 1444; J. M. Perillo, 'Abuse of Rights: A Pervasive Legal Concept' (1995) 27 Pac. L.J. 37.

[45] 38 Mich. 46 (1878).

land. The plaintiff had bought the land solely in order to sue for an injunction; the court denied equitable relief on those grounds. As we will see, post-fusion commentary has made much of the anti-holdout flavour of the case without equal attention to the style of analysis. The court did not hold that buying in the face of a trespass or nuisance would always lead to a denial of an injunction. For one thing, if the original owner could have sued, one could argue that the right to sue should pass to the new owner along with the other rights in the land. We could also imagine an owner who lacked the wherewithal to sue selling to one who could more easily bring suit. In *Edwards*, though, the court apparently concluded that the suit was solely or overwhelmingly motivated by its potential to harass through holdup power. One can argue whether a court's permitting itself such latitude is more destabilising than is worthwhile. In any event, the court was performing a targeted intervention: when the law confers the holdup power on owners, its purpose is not to permit the type of manufactured suit in *Edwards*. Courts will employ equitable notions of disproportionate hardship, laches, estoppel and the like to deny injunctions in these 'manufactured suit' cases.[46] Without the possibility of such equitable intervention, the law might have to be much more complex (and unstable) to prevent them. Or, as in other contexts, the law might announce in advance that such behaviour is the price we pay for a simple system; those who disagree with the result in *Edwards*, starting with the dissent in that case, would argue that such per se legitimacy should apply here. Seeing the intervention of equity as second order allows us to sharpen the true stakes.

In the second-order analysis, a purpose on the part of one party to target the other can be important to withholding an injunction. Sometimes purpose can play a role in furnishing grounds for granting such relief, as in unfair competition.

Traditionally, judges looked upon competition as beneficial but reined it in through various doctrines. Initially, this intervention occurred through the courts of equity drawing on custom and commercial morality and through a version of the law of nuisance. Both of these avenues were often second order and equitable in our terms. Although an analysis of unfair competition is beyond the scope of this chapter, we emphasise a few points. First is that doctrines against unfair competition are quite different from anti-trust analysis. Consistent with judicial knowledge and competence, the information to be used must be quite local, rather than needing to be developed by

---

[46] See also *Bassett v. Salisbury Manufacturing Co.*, 47 N.H. 426 (1867).

comprehensive economic studies of the relevant market. Second, the role played by custom and commercial morality helps avoid the need for a more global intervention and is consistent with a safety-valve approach. Unfair competition itself has its origins in equity, and in drawing on custom to prevent opportunistic behaviour between identified competitors, it is equitable in our sense. As one of us has argued,[47] the famous 'hot news' opinion in *International News Service* v. *Associated Press*[48] is best read as an equitable intervention (as the court announced it was) rather than a fount of new intellectual property rights.

Finally, some of the focus on malice in unfair competition cases evinces the second-order approach characteristic of equity. In what we would call a functional sense of equity, some kinds of malice involve an opportunistic type of targeting. In their reconstruction of torts that identify the causation of economic loss as wrongful, Simon Deakin and John Randall point to features that we would call second order (and equitable). Thus, if an activity is targeted to cause harm to a particular competitor, this makes liability more likely.[49] Again, targeting is not per se a problem, but may indicate a conscious misuse of a structure not built to withstand that kind of pressure. Perhaps the controversy over the chestnut case of *Tuttle* v. *Buck*[50] can be explained by the weight that targeting had to bear in that case. It was alleged that the defendant had hired a barber in competition with his personal enemy, the plaintiff, solely to drive him out of business. Judge Elliott, the author of the opinion, averred that if it had been up to him, he would have required evidence of running at a loss or an intention of leaving the business when the plaintiff was ruined, but in the end he joined his colleagues in concluding that the plaintiff's allegation of the defendant's targeted 'malicious' motive was enough.[51] Minnesota never had separate equity courts, and the opinion can be read as an attempt to translate into common law tort terms an aggressive use of the second-order equitable function.

THE DYNAMICS OF TORT AND EQUITY

Although we have drawn a relatively bright-line distinction between tort and equity, we have also emphasised the ways in which the two interact and

---

[47] H. E. Smith, 'Equitable Intellectual Property: What's Wrong With Misappropriation?', in S. Balganesh (ed.), *Intellectual Property and the Common Law* (Cambridge University Press, 2013), ch. 2.
[48] 248 U.S. 215 (1918).
[49] S. Deakin and J. Randall, 'Rethinking the Economic Torts' (2009) 72 M.L.R. 519.
[50] 119 N.W. 946 (Minn. 1909).   [51] Ibid., 948.

intermingle. There are equitable doctrines within tort law, and equity often steps in to plug holes and gaps left open by tort law. In this part of the chapter we briefly consider a different dimension of the equity–tort relationship, one very much tied up with the phenomenon of fusion. With equity now fused into law, courts have become more prone to take what once were targeted or self-contained equitable doctrines and convert them into new tort causes of action, or treat them as aspects of multi-factor inquiries into whether a given tort has been committed.

What we explore here is part of a larger dynamic of equity as a source of legal innovation. That equity can play this role is not news.[52] More striking is that a second-order equitable function of the kind we have explored at the tort–equity interface serves as an important source of tort law. We will argue that this is to be welcomed, as long as the equitable function is well understood. Conversely, in exaggerated forms of fusion not sensitive to this second-order function, things can go quite wrong.

Among the problems that call for a second-order equitable function are those that are uncertain and difficult to foresee. Once such problems have arisen and equity has dealt with them, we face a different problem. If, say, the opportunism in question is likely to arise again, we can fashion a legal rule for the future to deal with it. The problem is no longer one of opportunism.[53]

Equity is thus a moving frontier. The process by which equitable intervention becomes a regular part of the common law can be termed 'sedimentation'.[54] The equitable function applies to new material, and the set of problems to which it applies is constantly shifting.

Post fusion, what were once relatively self-contained equitable interventions have in some instances become torts unto themselves. While there is certainly nothing wrong with recognising new torts, because tort law provides general, conduct-guiding directives, the transition from equity to tort can generate torts that are relatively ill-defined and open-ended.

---

[52] E.g., *Spect* v. *Spect*, 26 P. 203, 205 (Cal. 1891) (Harrison J., misattributing a statement to Lord Redesdale). The quoted statement comes from J. Millar, *An Historical View of the English Government*, 4th edn (London: Mawman, 1818), vol. II, 354.

[53] The process of a standard becoming a rule is similar, but the literature on that process does not emphasise the second-order aspect.

[54] The term is meant to contrast this phenomenon with the oscillation between 'crystals' and 'mud' identified by C. M. Rose in 'Crystals and Mud in Property Law' (1988) 40 Stan. L. Rev. 577, 588; H. E. Smith, 'Rose's Human Nature of Property' (2011) 19 Wm & Mary Bill Rts 1047. In making this suggestion, we do not mean to commit ourselves to the stronger proposition, sometimes associated with Lord Kames, that equity is a vehicle through which the law achieves moral progress. See Carr, Chapter 8.

At the outset, although the Realist impulse may have been to contextualise and thereby expand the scope for something that looks like equity, the Realists had little, if any, appreciation of the distinction between first- and second-order law. They actively sought to break it down. Realists were not against discretion, balancing or fairness and yet when the torts scholars Page Keeton and Clarence Morris analysed how courts 'balanced the equities' in determining whether to grant injunctions in nuisance cases, they recast familiar equitable doctrines through a first-order tort lens.[55] Equity's proxies and presumptions became in their hands policy-infused liability factors.[56] Injunctions were analogised to punishment. And undue hardship analysis was cast as an exercise in quasi-legislation, with abundant invocations of 'social value' and the 'common weal' as opposed to the narrow interests of the parties.[57]

In case law, the hyper-fusion mentality evinced by Keeton and Morris is most closely associated with the New York Court of Appeals' decision in *Boomer v. Atlantic Cement Co.*[58] It denied an injunction to residents whose properties were regularly invaded by dust from the defendant's cement plant because the damage to the residents was far exceeded by the investment in the plant – an investment that would be lost if the plant were forced to shut down. The relegation of the plaintiffs to damages is famously associated with Calabresi and Melamed's notion of a liability rule, which allows an entitlement to be taken at an officially determined fair price.[59] The injunction, by contrast, would have implemented what they call a property rule, which is aimed at forcing a potential taker to obtain the holder's consent or forbear from taking. The fear that motivated the court and commentators in the law and

---

[55] W. P. Keeton and C. Morris, 'Notes on "Balancing the Equities"' (1940) 18 Tex. L. Rev. 412.
[56] In the hands of American Legal Realists, equitable doctrines and defences were often replaced with multi-factor balancing tests: Smith, 'Fusing the Equitable Function', 188–91. In other jurisdictions, separate equity tended to give way to standards and finely tuned complex doctrine. See J. Getzler, 'Patterns of Fusion', in P. Birks (ed.), *The Classification of Obligations* (Oxford: Clarendon, 1997), 191–92. This too can be seen as a first-order substitute for a second-order equitable function.
[57] Keeton and Morris, 'Notes on "Balancing the Equities"', 423–25. ('But the interests of the parties are not the only interests to be taken into account in arriving at just results. If the defendant is conducting an enterprise of social value exceeding the social value of the plaintiff's interests, the common weal may be best served by permitting the defendant's plant to remain undisturbed, requiring him to compensate the plaintiff for his financial losses, and punishing him sufficiently for mis-locating his plant to discourage similar future wrongdoing.').
[58] 257 N.E.2d 870 (N.Y. 1970).
[59] G. Calabresi and A. D. Melamed, 'Property Rules, Liability Rules, and Inalienability: One View of the Cathedral' (1972) 85 Harv. L. Rev. 1089, 1092.

economics literature is the holdout power and the coordination costs of the residents.[60] As Douglas Laycock has shown, the court and the commentators misunderstood the traditional equitable defence of undue hardship and so wound up reinventing the wheel, yet managed to produce an inferior one.[61] To this we could add that the newer incarnations of the undue hardship defence tend, like Keeton's and Morris's analysis, to involve very rough policy guesses at the primary level of tort. Gone are the proxies and presumptions and the integration into a second-order analysis of the entire bilateral interaction.[62]

The same flattening can be seen in academic commentary on abuse of rights cases. Returning to *Edwards* v. *Allouez Mining Co.*,[63] Ian Ayres and Kristen Madison make it a centrepiece in their account of litigants inefficiently insisting on injunctions (and specific performance).[64] Although the problem they identify is real, the traditional equitable solution is second-order intervention based on proxies and presumptions that kick in selectively and then, once invoked, operate more holistically – at a second level. Again, policy-infused first-order rules and standards are the modern substitute. They necessarily give up whatever advantage systems theory would indicate can be obtained by second-level analysis. The modern approach also loses the connection to everyday morality that equitable analysis more transparently reflects.

In modern times, the fusion of equity and tort has often taken the form of a relocation and recharacterisation of law from equity to tort. This can be beneficial but it has also at times been taken in more extreme and undesirable directions.

One example of a relatively successful evolution from equity to tort involves the emergence, in the early twentieth century, of the tort of appropriation of likeness – a tort later identified by William Prosser as one of four privacy torts.[65] While equity courts had long made available equitable relief for

---

[60] Ibid., 1106–10.
[61] D. Laycock, 'The Neglected Defense of Undue Hardship (and the Doctrinal Train Wreck in *Boomer* v. *Atlantic Cement*)' (2011) 4 J.T.L. Iss. 3, Art. 3. Laycock is well known for his scepticism about any special equitable function, and his point is that *Boomer* and the modern approach are not faithful to the law and are inferior to the previously accepted law in this area.
[62] See M. P. Gergen, J. M. Golden and H. E. Smith, 'The Supreme Court's Accidental Revolution? The Test for Permanent Injunctions' (2012) 112 Colum. L. Rev. 203, 226–30; H. Smith, 'Exclusion and Property Rules in the Law of Nuisance' (2004) 90 Va. L. Rev. 965, 1037–45.
[63] 38 Mich. 46 (1878). See the citation and text at n. 45.
[64] I. Ayres and K. Madison, 'Threatening Inefficient Performance of Injunctions and Contracts' (1999) 148 U. Pa. L. Rev. 45, 50–1.
[65] W. L. Prosser, 'Privacy' (1960) 48 Cal. L. Rev. 383, 401–07.

breaches of confidence, courts started treating such situations as giving rise to
a claim for redress in the form of compensatory damages. Thus, in one of the
first court decisions to recognise the appropriation-of-likeness tort, *Pavesich*
v. *New England Life Insurance Co.*,[66] the Georgia Supreme Court allowed a
new claim for damages for the defendant's use of a photograph of the plaintiff
in a newspaper advertisement for its life insurance policies, with a fabricated
quotation stating that the plaintiff was thankful to have purchased one of its
policies. The court has moved from a second-order intervention to prevent
misuse of rules or violation of custom to setting out rules of conduct protecting
the plaintiff's right to 'be let alone',[67] i.e., his right to determine, within limits,
when and how he would 'exhibit his person in [a] public place'.[68] In place of
equity we now have a tort in which the primary duty is to refrain from publicly
displaying another's image in aid of one's commercial venture.

A century later, misappropriation of likeness is the name of a well-
established tort. And for the most part it is one that functions reasonably well.
As defined by the courts, it gives actors relatively clear notice as to the sort of
conduct from which they are required to refrain. And it presents relatively
manageable questions for judges and juries to adjudicate when claims are
litigated.

Other instances of equity giving rise to torts are somewhat more troubling.
We noted in the 'Equity and Tort' section that some commentators today
advocate eliminating references within tort law to 'coming to the nuisance' as
a defence to liability. A standard rationale is that the relevance of the plaintiff's
conduct can be treated as one among a laundry-list of factors relevant to the
determination of whether the defendant's actions have unreasonably interfered with the plaintiff's use and enjoyment of his or her land. Here we see the
same problematic instinct towards hyper-fusion evinced in Keeton's and
Morris's treatment of equitable relief for nuisances. Prosser's famous quip –
'[t]here is perhaps no more impenetrable jungle in the entire law than that
which surrounds the word "nuisance"'[69] – takes on an air of irony when one
recognises that it is to a substantial degree a jungle of his and his fellow
Realists' own creation. Rather than take the law out of tort law in the name of
equity, it would be better to allow equitable adjustments to tort law by, for
example, denying relief to plaintiffs who opportunistically come to the nuisance or denying injunctions in genuine cases of disproportionate and extreme
hardship.

---

[66] 50 S.E. 68 (Ga. 1905).   [67] Ibid., 71.   [68] Ibid., 70.
[69] W. L. Prosser, *Handbook of the Law of Torts*, 1st edn (St. Paul, MN: West, 1941), 549.

Equity's unfair competition jurisprudence, meanwhile, gave birth to the tort that now goes under indicatively ungainly names such as 'improper interference with prospective contract', 'improper interference with non-contractual expectancy' and 'improper interference with inheritance or gift'. Here, the transition from targeted intervention to correct or enjoin opportunism to a generally defined injurious wrong has arguably gone less well.

One problem is that a great deal of intentional interference – most notably, market competition in which one competitor aims to defeat another – is permissible. There is thus a tension in marking off, at a general level, interference with expectancies as wrongful. True, these torts are limited to instances of 'improper' interference. Even so, there is something awkward, in our economy, about the idea of treating interference with non-contractual expectancies as candidates for torts. Contrast battery or trespass. While these, too, only apply to 'improper' contacts with another's person or land, their respective base-level directives – 'Don't touch!' and 'Keep off!' – are decent approximations of the behaviour the law demands. 'Don't interfere with another's expectancies!' seems less so.

Relatedly, liability for the interference torts turns on an unstable mixture of factors. Retained is the traditional equitable focus on cases of malice. Liability, as noted, attaches only for 'improper' interferences, with impropriety determined by giving consideration to a list of factors, including (in the Second *Restatement of Torts*' formulation of the interference-with-prospective-contract tort):

(a) the nature of the actor's conduct, (b) the actor's motive, (c) the interests of the other with which the actor's conduct interferes, (d) the interests sought to be advanced by the actor, (e) the social interests in protecting the freedom of action of the actor and the contractual interests of the other, (f) the proximity or remoteness of the actor's conduct to the interference and (g) the relations between the parties.[70]

One need not be a formalist (in the pejorative sense) to worry about the stability and clarity of an inquiry into impropriety conducted on these terms.

Ironically, the interference torts are also, in certain instances, defined very elastically so that they can reach the very scenarios in which equity once comfortably intervened and, in doing so, gave rise to these new tort claims. For example, as noted earlier, many courts today recognise interference with inheritance as a tort, even though the standard case of interference – involving the exercise of undue influence on the donor to the detriment of a beneficiary

---

[70] *Restatement (Second) Torts* § 767 (1977).

who has no right to the assets he or she is hoping to inherit – recognises as tortious conduct that is not regarded as tortious in any other setting, and recognises as injuries the loss of legally fragile expectancies. No wonder then, that in drafting the interference-with-inheritance provision of the Second Torts Restatement, Dean Wade suggested that this cause of action could be understood as recognising an 'equitable tort'.[71]

CONCLUSION

Our legal systems have seen a fusion of law and equity. But of course the idea of fusion admits of different interpretations. Somewhat ironically (given their focus on observables and empirics), Realists tend to understand fusion as an instance of transubstantiation. The moment at which equity disappeared into law, they reason, is the moment at which law lost its formalism and became equitable, flexible and result-oriented – whatever it needs to be for it to do what we want it to do. We have sketched and argued for a different understanding of fusion. Equity and law are no longer separated by jurisdiction. But, however they are labelled, they remain distinct aspects of our legal system and continue to play distinct roles within it.

Tort is not equity and equity is not tort. Tort law specifies through a complex scheme of rules and standards those interpersonal interactions that are wrongfully injurious. These interactions are not to be done, and if they are done, generate in the victim a right to invoke the court system to obtain redress from the wrongful injurer. Meanwhile, from a functional standpoint, equity, whether it traces back to equity jurisdiction or not, operates in a second-order fashion on tort law to limit the ability of actors to take advantage of the rights and powers that first-order tort law confers. It further stands ready to fill gaps or holes at the edges of tort law by undoing or modifying the legal consequences of equitable wrongs.

---

[71] J. C. P. Goldberg and R. H. Sitkoff, 'Torts and Estates: Remedying Wrongful Interference with Inheritance' (2013) 65 Stan. L. Rev. 335, 393–94 (quoting a comment of Dean Wade made during a meeting of the American Law Institute).

14

Avoiding Anarchy?

Common Law *v*. Equity *and* Maitland *v*. Hohfeld

BEN MCFARLANE[*]

INTRODUCTION

This chapter aims to explain and resolve aspects of two apparent conflicts. The first is between common law and equity. Maitland famously argued that, for two centuries before 1875, 'the two systems had been working together harmoniously'.[1] He used the trust as an example of an apparent conflict which dissolved on closer inspection. This chapter aims to shed light not only on the operation of the trust but also on the wider relationship of common law and equity in a modern legal system. It therefore discusses not only the trust but also some other forms of equitable intervention, such as the recognition of equitable assignment. Employing a Hohfeldian analysis, the chapter identifies three important general features of equitable intervention in each of those areas: those features are summarised in the conclusion. Each of those features is consistent with Maitland's analysis of the relationship between common law and equity; and each demonstrates the importance of paying close attention not only to the outcomes arising from the application of equity but also to the *means* by which equity achieves those results. It is thus argued that a Hohfeldian analysis can be used to support Maitland's central point: the conflict between the two writers as to the relations between common law and equity, like the conflict between the two systems of law itself, may therefore be more apparent than real.

The chapter also explores a third conflict: between form and substance. It is often said, or assumed, that one distinctive feature of equity is its preference for the latter.[2] It is true that, in assessing the parties' objective intentions, a

[*] I am grateful for the support of a British Academy/Leverhulme Trust Small Research Grant and for comments received at the 'Equity and Law: Fusion and Fission' seminar.

[1] Maitland, *Equity*, 17.   [2] E.g., *Parkin v. Thorold* (1852) 16 Beav. 59, 66–67.

court may in some cases look beyond the formal expression of the parties' transaction.[3] Yet this desire to discover the reality of the parties' dealings is certainly not confined to equity;[4] equally, in equity as at common law, a court cannot simply disregard the legal form chosen by the parties.[5] The broader point made in this chapter is that, to understand apparent conflicts between common law and equity, it is crucial to consider precisely the relevant legal relations. For example, it might be said that by acknowledging the rights of a beneficiary of a trust of land or of an equitable assignee, equity undermines the common law rules as to when a party can acquire an estate in land or as to when a chose in action can be transferred. This is because the beneficiary or assignee may be seen as, in *substance*, enjoying the same benefits as conferred by a legal estate or by a chose in action, even though the beneficiary has not satisfied the common law rules as to when and how such rights can be acquired. The key rejoinder, explored in this chapter, is that the rights of the beneficiary differ in their *form* from that of an unencumbered holder of a legal estate and the rights of the equitable assignee similarly differ in their form from that of an unencumbered holder of a chose in action. At this formal level (which can be usefully understood by a Hohfeldian analysis) there is no conflict between common law and equity, as the content of the rights afforded to the beneficiary or equitable assignee differ subtly but significantly from those held by an unencumbered holder of a legal estate or a chose in action.

Crucially, this is not a purely technical point. As will be explored in this chapter, important practical consequences, particularly for third parties, depend on the fact that the rights of the beneficiary or equitable assignee are formally different from those of an unencumbered holder of a legal estate or of a chose in action. It is not the case that the equitable rights are different only trivially: rather, the differences ensure that concerns as to, for example, notice and information costs for third parties can be met. An awareness of the formal differences between common law rights and their supposed equitable 'equivalents'[6] is therefore necessary, not only to resolve apparent conflicts

---

[3] E.g., when determining whether a right is a security interest or absolute: G. & C. *Kreglinger* v. *New Patagonia Meat and Cold Storage Co. Ltd* [1914] A.C. 25, 47.

[4] E.g., *Orion Finance Ltd* v. *Crown Financial Management Ltd (No. 1)* [1996] B.C.C. 621 (whether statutory assignment absolute or by way of security); *A.G. Securities* v. *Vaughan* [1990] 1 A.C. 417 (whether an agreement created a licence or a tenancy).

[5] For example, parties may structure a transaction to escape any equitable penalties doctrine, by making clear that a party's duty to pay is a primary and not a collateral obligation: *Astley* v. *Weldon* (1801) 2 B. & P. 346, 353.

[6] E.g., *R.* v. *Tower Hamlets London Borough Council, Ex p. von Goetz* [1999] Q.B. 1019, 1023 (Mummery L.J.), citing with approval the analysis of Carnwath J. at first instance that an equitable lease is 'for all practical purposes, and interest as good as a legal interest'.

between the two systems but also to understand how equity responds to the same practical concerns that set the limits of common law rights.

EQUITY, OWNERSHIP AND THE TRUST

Maitland and Hohfeld

Competing Views

To support his contention that common law and equity worked together harmoniously, Maitland gave the example of the trust. A university examiner might be told that: 'whereas the common law said that the trustee was the owner of the land, equity said that the *cestui que trust* was the owner', but such a statement was crude and dangerously misleading: it would mean 'civil war and utter anarchy' if two courts of co-ordinate jurisdiction varied on such an essential question.[7] Where A holds on trust for B, the better view according to Maitland is that equity does not challenge the common law position that A is the owner: it simply 'add[s] that [A is] bound to hold the land for the benefit of [B]'.[8] The apparent conflict is resolved.

Hohfeld took a different view. In 'The Relations between Equity and Law',[9] he argued that there is in fact:

> a very marked and constantly recurring conflict between equitable and legal rules relating to various jural relations ... Though [the legal rule] may represent an important *stage of thought* in the solution of a given problem, and may also connote very important possibilities as to certain other, closely associated (and valid) jural relations, yet as regards the very relation in which it suffers direct competition with a rule of equity, such a conflicting rule of law is, *pro tanto*, of no greater force than an unconstitutional statute.[10]

To choose a simple example from the extensive list provided by Hohfeld, if A holds a fee simple on trust for B then in equity A has a duty to B not to cut down ornamental trees on the land, whereas at common law A has a privilege against B to do so.[11] The jural relation consisting of A's duty to B is thus not one also recognised at common law and so is, in Hohfeld's terms, 'exclusively equitable';[12] and in 'every such case there is a conflict, *pro tanto*, between

---

[7]   Maitland, *Equity*, 17.   [8]   Ibid.

[9]   W. N. Hohfeld, 'The Relations between Equity and Law' (1913) 11 Mich. L. Rev. 537.

[10]   Ibid., 544 (emphasis original).   [11]   Ibid., 555.

[12]   Some care must be taken with this term. Hohfeld did not refer only to exercises of equity's exclusive jurisdiction. He intended to refer to a jural relation recognised only in equity, and not

some valid and paramount equitable rule and some invalid and apparent legal rule'.[13] In such case, the 'jural relation is finally determined by the equitable rule rather than by the legal',[14] so the *genuine* jural relation between A and B is that A *is* under a duty to B not to cut down the trees.

Reconciling the Competing Views

It is very hard to argue against Hohfeld's logic;[15] it is also reasonable to allow some margin for exaggeration in material intended by Maitland for oral presentation to students.[16] It is also worth noting that Maitland conceded, when considering the role of section 25(11) of the Judicature Act 1873, that '[p]erhaps' there was a conflict between common law and equity as to so-called equitable waste: in the example of A's cutting down ornamental trees, Maitland admitted that 'we might here say that equity did consider that [A] must pay for his act, while law held that he need not'.[17] As Hohfeld notes,[18] it is hard to understand Maitland's hesitation, as the conflict is clear. At the level of genuine jural relations between A and B, either A is under a duty to B not to act in a particular way or A is not under such a duty. One of two answers must be given, and the answer reached once equity supplements the common law's rules differs from that which would be given at common law alone. That should be no surprise: if there were no jural relations recognised by equity but not by common law, there would be no point in the equitable jurisdiction.

This does not mean, however, that Maitland's general analysis must be dismissed. There are two key points to be borne in mind. The first relates specifically to the example of the trust. It will be argued here that there is a great deal to be said for Maitland's observation that the trust does not operate by way of equity's establishing in the beneficiary an independent property right that conflicts with that of the trustee. Indeed, Maitland was right to warn that it is dangerous to adopt the competing property rights model of the trust: such a model can lead a court to err. Maitland himself admitted that:

also at common law: e.g., the power, historically existing only in equity, of a litigant to obtain discovery can be seen as part of the auxiliary jurisdiction of equity (in the sense that it may aid a litigant in enforcing a common law right), but was in Hohfeld's terms an exclusively equitable power, as it did not exist at common law.

[13] Hohfeld, 'The Relations between Equity and Law', 555.   [14] Ibid., 557.

[15] For discussion of one objection, see G. Peller, 'Privilege' (2016) 104 Geo. L.J. 883.

[16] Indeed, Hohfeld, 'The Relations between Equity and Law', 541, refers to Maitland's 'entertaining' series of lectures. Even the most ardent admirer of his work would hesitate to apply that adjective to Hohfeld's writing.

[17] Maitland, *Equity*, 157.   [18] Hohfeld, 'The Relations between Equity and Law', 570 n. 36.

for the ordinary thought of Englishmen 'equitable ownership' is just ownership pure and simple, though it is subject to a peculiar, technical and not
very intelligible rule in favour of *bona fide* purchasers ... let the Herr
Professor say what he likes, so many persons are bound to respect [B's rights]
that practically they are almost as valuable as if they were *dominium*
(ownership).[19]

Indeed, part of the attraction of the trust, for legislatures[20] as well as individual
settlors, is that the interest of the beneficiary (B) can often be regarded '[as] for
all practical purposes, an interest as good as a legal interest'.[21] The holder of a
registered company charge, for example, has little in practice to fear from the
fact that its right, as an equitable interest, is subject to a bona fide purchase
defence.[22] The benefits of B's position should not, however, be allowed to
obscure the important structural differences between the nature of B's rights
and those of an unencumbered holder of a legal title. The key point, made
clear by a Hohfeldian analysis, is that when comparing the impact of B's rights
on third parties with the impact of ownership on such parties, the differences
extend beyond an inability to assert a right against a bona fide purchaser for
value without notice. Two such differences, each of importance in practice,
will be examined here: first, the rights of B against a stranger interfering with
the trust property; second, the rights of B against an innocent donee of that
property. In each case, it will be seen that B generally has no claim against the
defendant, even though that defendant is not a bona fide purchaser.

The second key point extends beyond the trust and relates to the wider idea
of what it means for law and equity to conflict. The model applied in this
chapter to the trust can be applied to other important equitable doctrines
which might seem to involve a conflict between law and equity. In relation to
equitable assignment, for example, it might be thought that equity permits

---

[19] F. W. Maitland, 'Trust and Corporation', in D. Runciman and M. Ryan (eds), *F. W. Maitland:
State, Trust and Corporation* (Cambridge University Press, 2003), 94, citing J. W. Salmond, *The
First Principles of Jurisprudence* (London: Stevens and Haynes, 1893), 278, where B is referred
to as the 'real owner', with the trustee's ownership described as 'nominal' and 'fictitious'.

[20] E.g., the scheme of the Law of Property Act 1925 (U.K.), under which estates in land that, by
virtue of section 1, are no longer permitted at law (such as a life estate) may instead operate as
equitable interests behind a trust.

[21] R. v. *Tower Hamlets London Borough Council, Ex p. von Goetz* [1999] Q.B. 1019, 1023.

[22] The phrase 'bona fide purchaser defence' is used here as convenient shorthand for the
circumstances (see, for example, *Pilcher* v. *Rawlins* (1872) L.R. 7 Ch. App. 259) in which, as
a result of acquiring a right in good faith, for value, and without notice of B's prior equitable
interest, a third party has an immunity to later coming under a duty to hold that right subject to
the same core duty as A, the party initially subject to the equitable interest.

something to occur that is not allowed at common law. It will be argued, however, that whilst the very fact of equitable intervention means there is a conflict at the level of jural relations between two parties (A and B), a Hohfeldian analysis can in fact show that there is no inconsistency between common law and equity at the broader level of principle. So, as will be argued later, equitable assignment does *not* provide a means for A and B to achieve a result prohibited at common law (i.e., the transfer of a chose in action from A to B). Whilst such an assignment may be seen to operate in substance as a form of transfer, at the level of jural relations it does not as the duty of the debtor is still owed to A rather than to B. It is equity's focus on form rather than substance that allows conflict at the level of deeper principle to be avoided: the common law rule is not, at a formal level, undermined. There is, of course, a conflict of the kind Hohfeld identified in relation to the duty of A to B, but there is no such conflict at the more significant level of principle. Anarchy is avoided.

Interference with Trust Property

Example 1: A holds a legal estate in land on trust for B. X, who is unaware of the trust, carelessly damages the land.

No bona fide purchaser defence is available in such a case, but the orthodox position is that B's position as beneficiary does not in itself[23] give B any claim against X.[24] Certainly, the power to bring a claim against X in negligence or trespass is held by A. As that power derives from A's legal title to the property, the power is itself trust property and, should A in breach of trust refuse to exercise the power for B's benefit, it will be possible for B to seek an order requiring A to do so. By taking advantage of the *Vandepitte* procedure,[25] B, by joining A and X, can combine that (equitable) claim against A with A's (legal) claim against X in one set of proceedings, but this is simply a 'procedural short-cut'[26] and two distinct claims are involved.[27] This has important substantive consequences. First, if A has authorised X's conduct, so that A has no tort

[23] If B was in fact in possession of the trust property at the relevant time, the fact of that possession may give B a legal title permitting B to sue X (*Healey* v. *Healey* [1915] 1 K.B. 938); but then B's claim is based on that legal title, not on B's position as beneficiary.
[24] E.g., *Lord Compton's Case* (1587) 3 Leo. 196; *Leigh and Sillavan Ltd* v. *Aliakman Shipping Co. Ltd* [1986] A.C. 785; *Restatement (Third) of Trusts* §§ 107–8 (2003).
[25] Named for *Vandepitte* v. *Preferred Accident Insurance Corp. of New York* [1933] A.C. 70.
[26] *Don King Productions Inc.* v. *Warren* [2000] Ch. 291, 321.
[27] E.g., *Barbados Trust Co. Ltd* v. *Bank of Zambia* [2007] 1 Lloyd's Rep. 495, [29], [45]; [2007] EWCA Civ 148.

claim against X, then B's only protection comes from a claim against A under the trust. Second, when calculating the extent of X's liability, the relevant claim for those purposes is A's claim as holder of the legal title to the property against X: consequential losses suffered by B as a result of the damage to the property are not in themselves recoverable from X.

B's lack of a direct claim against X in example 1 is not, it is submitted, simply an accident of history or of jurisdictional divides. Maitland, tongue no doubt somewhat in cheek, characterised the trust beneficiary as 'the spoilt child of English jurisprudence',[28] indulged as equity extended B's rights so as to bind not only A but also parties acquiring the trust property from A with notice of the trust or as donees. He also stated, however, that there was a limit to the generosity of the Chancellor, as he could not give 'true ownership, a truly *dingliches Recht*' to B, as such a step would undo rather than supplement the work of the common law courts.[29] The line would be crossed were B to have a direct claim against a stranger interfering with trust property. This can be seen by contrasting the rules as to the acquisition of legal title with those that need to be satisfied before B can become a beneficiary of a trust. The former rules generally require certain steps to be taken (in relation to land, for example, registration may be necessary)[30] that may make it easier for a stranger, X, to establish who has legal title to particular property.[31] This gives X, at least in theory, a greater chance of knowing whom to approach for consent should X wish to make use of the property, and also of discovering for whose consequential losses X might be liable were X tortiously to damage the property. The *numerus clausus* principle similarly limits the inquiries that X may have to undertake.[32] In contrast, even in relation to land, a trust can be established without any formality[33] or any change in possession, and there is

[28] Maitland, *State, Trust and Corporation*, 95.
[29] Ibid., 90. See too C. Langdell, 'A Brief Survey of Equity Jurisdiction' (1887) 1 Harv. L. Rev. 55, 60: 'Upon the whole, it may be said that equity could not create rights *in rem* if it would, and that it would not if it could.'
[30] E.g., Land Registration Act 2002 (U.K.), ss. 4, 27.
[31] The prominent role played by possession in the acquisition of title to tangible personal property can be explained partly by the salience it confers: H. E. Smith, 'The Elements of Possession', in Y. C. Chang (ed.), *Law and Economics of Possession* (Cambridge University Press, 2015), ch. 3.
[32] T. W. Merrill and H. E. Smith, 'Optimal Standardization in the Law of Property: The *Numerus Clausus* Principle' (2000) 110 Yale L.J. 1, 9.
[33] Under section 53(1)(b) of the Law of Property Act 1925 (U.K.), writing is required for the proof of a declaration of trust relating to land, but not for its establishment, as such writing can come into existence even after the declaration: *Gardner* v. *Rowe* (1825) 2 Sim. & St. 346; aff'd (1828) 5 Russ. 258.

no limit other than the rule against perpetuities on the content of the rights of a beneficiary of a trust. As a result, it would impose an undue burden on X if careless interference with a thing would lead to X's being directly liable not only to those with legal property rights in that thing, but also to any beneficiaries of a trust related to it.

Hohfeld's distinction between a duty and a liability is useful in demonstrating the differences, as far as the position of X is concerned, between two cases: first, where A, a holder of a legal estate in land, creates a lesser legal interest, such as an easement; second, where A instead declares that his or her legal estate is held on trust for B. In each case, the general duty of non-interference with the land is still owed by X to A. Where a legal easement is granted, there is no transfer of a particular proprietary stick from A to B; both before and after A's grant, X, along with the rest of the world, is under a prima facie duty to A not to physically interfere, deliberately or carelessly, with A's land. As a result of the grant, X does come under a new duty: a duty to B. X's strict duty to A is 'cloned'[34] in the sense that X now owes a similarly strict but more limited duty to B: a duty not to physically interfere, deliberately or carelessly, with A's land in such a way as to prevent X's exercise of the liberty (e.g., to use a path on A's land) involved in the easement. Where a trust is declared there is, again, no unbundling or fragmentation of A's rights and liberties against third parties,[35] as A continues to enjoy those rights; although, as noted by Hohfeld, A does of course lose liberties of use as against B. In contrast to the grant of a legal easement, however, where a trust is declared there is no such cloning in B's favour of any strict duty owed by X to A. As with any creation of a fiduciary duty, X does come under a new duty not to dishonestly assist in breaching A's fiduciary duty to B but liability in such a case is not strict.[36] The significance of the equitable interest acquired by B is rather that if X acquires the trust property or its traceable proceeds in circumstances where the bona fide purchaser defence does not apply, and whilst still holding that property or its traceable proceeds X then acquires knowledge of the trust, X may come under

---

[34] The term used by B. Rudden, 'Economic Theory v. Property Law: The *Numerus Clausus* Problem', in J. Eekelaar and J. Bell (eds), *Oxford Essays In Jurisprudence* (Oxford: Clarendon, 1987), 251–52.

[35] See P. Matthews, 'The Compatibility of the Trust with the Civil Law Notion of Property', in L. Smith (ed.), *The Worlds of the Trust* (Cambridge University Press, 2013), 320.

[36] See, for example, *Twinsectra Ltd v. Yardley* [2002] 2 A.C. 164, [26]; [2002] UKHL 12; *Novoship (U.K.) Ltd v. Mikhaylyuk* [2013] Q.B. 49; [2014] EWCA Civ 908.

the same core[37] duty as A, the initial trustee: a duty not to use that property for X's own benefit.

There are thus two linked differences between the effect on X of a legal interest on the one hand and B's interest under a trust on the other. The former imposes a general duty on the rest of the world, and the duty is a strict one. The latter instead consists of the immediate duties of A, the initial trustee, and the core duty of A can be extended to a third party, but only if such a party acquires the trust property or its traceable proceeds – and even then the duty is not strict as it depends on the conscience of the third party's being affected. To the extent that the existence of a general, strict duty of non-interference (often summarised by focusing on the *in rem* 'right to exclude' to which it correlates) is characteristic of ownership,[38] a Hohfeldian analysis supports Maitland's claim that it is inaccurate to think of a beneficiary as an owner of the trust property. That does not mean that it is necessarily appropriate to think of the trustee, A, as holding all the usual incidents of ownership. The 'self-seeking-ness'[39] permitted by an owner's general liberty against all others to use the property as he or she pleases is absent, but only because of A's duties as trustee to B and thus only in relation to B: A has a liberty to use the property for A's own ends as against everyone other than B. On the assumption, then, that questions of ownership and proprietary rights are best judged by considering the general effect of a party's rights on strangers, it is a mistake to confuse B's ability in practice to enjoy the benefits of trust property with genuine owner-ship of that property.

A useful practical example of the danger of regarding B as an owner of the trust property is provided by the decision of the Court of Appeal in *Shell U.K. Ltd* v. *Total U.K. Ltd.*[40] The carelessness of the defendant, X, caused

---

37 This does not mean that X is then subject to all the trustee duties of A. For the differences between the duty that may arise on a third party recipient and the duties of A, see e.g., R. C. Nolan, 'Equitable Property' (2006) 122 L.Q.R. 232.

38 E.g., A. M. Honoré, 'Ownership', in A. G. Guest (ed.), *Oxford Essays in Jurisprudence: First Series* (Oxford: Clarendon, 1961), ch. 5; T. Merrill, 'Property and the Right to Exclude' (1998) 77 Neb. L. Rev. 730.

39 This aspect of ownership is only incidentally addressed by Honoré in 'Ownership', but is discussed by J. W. Harris, *Property and Justice* (Oxford University Press, 1996), 5–6 and later by A. M. Honoré, 'Property and Ownership: Marginal Comments', in T. Endicott, J. Getzler and E. Peel (eds), *Properties of Law: Essays in Honour of Jim Harris* (Oxford University Press, 2006), ch. 7.

40 [2011] Q.B. 86, further discussed from a Hohfeldian perspective in B. McFarlane, 'The Essential Nature of Trusts and Other Equitable Interests: Two and a Half Cheers for Hohfeld', in S. Balganesh, T. Sichelman and H. E. Smith (eds), *The Legacy of Wesley Hohfeld: Edited Major Works, Select Personal Papers, and Original Commentaries* (Cambridge University Press, forthcoming).

significant damage to fuel storage and pipeline facilities used by B. As a result, B suffered serious economic loss through its inability to supply fuel to its customers. B did not, however, have legal title to the land or facilities: that title was instead held by A (in fact, two service companies) on trust for four companies, of which B was one. Such was the legal form chosen by the companies when co-operating to establish the terminal. It was held at first instance that, as B had no legal ownership or possessory title to the property, the loss it had suffered as a result of the damage was purely economic loss, and so the general 'exclusionary rule' applied meaning that X was not liable for having carelessly caused such loss.[41]

The Court of Appeal, in contrast, allowed B's claim for substantial damages. Particular weight was placed on the ability of B to describe itself as an 'equitable owner' of the damaged property, with the court holding that: 'it is legalistic to deny [B] a right to recovery by reference to the exclusionary rule. It is, after all, [B] who is (along with [the other three beneficiaries]) the "real" owner, the "legal" owner being little more than a bare trustee of the pipe-lines'.[42] The court then went on to find that the exclusionary rule was justified by the need to prevent the 'unacceptable indeterminacy' that would result if a general liability for carelessly causing pure economic loss were admitted, and that recovery of such loss could be permitted only if some special relationship of proximity can be established between claimant and defendant, which 'goes beyond mere contractual or non-contractual dependence on the . . . property'.[43] It held that:

> Beneficial ownership of the damaged property goes well beyond contractual or non-contractual dependence on the damaged property and does indeed constitute a special relationship of the kind required.[44]

The reasoning of the Court of Appeal in *Shell U.K.* has been subject to widespread criticism,[45] chiefly as a result of its departure from the settled precedent[46] establishing that the existence of a trust does not impose

---

[41] *Colour Quest Ltd v. Total Downstream Ltd* [2009] 2 Lloyd's Rep. 1; [2009] EWHC 540 (Comm).
[42] *Shell U.K. Ltd v. Total U.K. Ltd* [2011] Q.B. 86, [132].
[43] Ibid., [133], citing A. M. Jones and M. A. Douglas (eds), *Clerk & Lindsell on Torts*, 19th edn (London: Sweet and Maxwell, 2006), [8.116].
[44] *Shell U.K. Ltd v. Total U.K. Ltd* [2011] Q.B. 86, [134].
[45] E.g., K. F. K. Low, 'Equitable Title and Economic Loss' (2010) 126 L.Q.R. 507; P. G. Turner, 'Consequential Economic Loss and the Trust Beneficiary' [2010] C.L.J. 445; J. Edelman, 'Two Fundamental Questions for the Law of Trusts' (2013) 129 L.Q.R. 66.
[46] See the text to n. 23.

additional direct duties of non-interference on strangers to the trust.[47] Even on its own terms the decision is hopelessly confused. First, whilst emphasis is placed on B's equitable ownership, the exclusionary rule is seen as prima facie applicable. This means that the analysis is in fact consistent with the orthodox view that X is not in the same position as a party with a legal property right in the damaged thing: in other words, B's loss is purely economic as it does not flow from interference with B's property. So, whilst the rhetoric of the judgment is inconsistent with Maitland's analysis and with the traditional analysis of the effect of B's right on strangers, a critical step in the reasoning in fact supports Maitland's view. Second, the court regards the case as falling within an exception to the exclusionary rule, as B's beneficial interest provided the required relationship of proximity. This must be wrong, as the exception depends on the existence of a special relationship of proximity between claimant and *defendant*, not between the claimant and a different party, such as the trustee. It is surprising to find an appellate court making such an error, but the chances of such sloppiness of thought are increased when B's beneficial interest is conceived of as ownership.

Receipt of Trust Property by an Innocent Donee

Example 2: A holds property on trust for B. Acting in breach of trust, and without authority from B, A makes a gift of that property to C. C receives the property as a gift and has no knowledge or notice of the trust. C sells the property, spending the proceeds on groceries, which C consumes. Only then does C acquire knowledge of the trust.

The orthodox position is that, although C is not a bona fide purchaser, B has no claim against C. If C acquires notice of the trust[48] whilst still holding the trust property or its traceable proceeds, C will come under a direct equitable duty to B. If, however, C acquires notice only at a point when C no longer has the trust property or its proceeds, then B has no claim against C. In English[49] and Australian[50] law at least, that is the case even if, as in example 2, C retains a benefit from the receipt of the trust property.

---

47 The Supreme Court gave permission to appeal, but the appeal was settled. Even if the defendant had succeeded on the point as to the negligence claim, A was also pursuing a claim against X based on public nuisance.

48 Whether from B or otherwise: see *Lloyd* v. *Banks* (1868) L.R. 3 Ch. App. 488.

49 *Bank of Credit and Commerce International (Overseas) Ltd* v. *Akindele* [2001] Ch. 437, 450–58.

50 *Farah Constructions Pty. Ltd* v. *Say-Dee Pty. Ltd* (2007) 230 C.L.R. 89, [112], [123]–[129], [134], [140]–[158]; [2007] HCA 22.

A thorough understanding of this example is important as, whilst the traditional position is clear, there is some current controversy in each of English, Australian and American law as to whether that position is justifiable. The argument made here is that the orthodox position has much to recommend it and is consistent not only with Maitland's view of the nature of B's rights but also with a Hohfeldian analysis of the particular effects of B's rights on third parties. The orthodox position has, however, been subject to some academic and judicial objections, one strand of which involves arguing that the strict restitutionary liability imposed on a recipient at common law (e.g., in a case of mistaken payment)[51] should also be available in equity.[52] The difficulty with such an argument is that it mistakenly equates the beneficiary's position with that of an owner,[53] and wrongly assumes that B has an *abstract* entitlement to the value of the trust property. A parallel to the decision in *Shell U.K. Ltd v. Total U.K. Ltd*, showing the dangers of equating B's position with that of a holder of unencumbered legal title, is that of the Court of Appeal of New South Wales,[54] later reversed by the High Court of Australia in *Farah Constructions Pty Ltd v. Say-Dee Pty Ltd*.[55] One of the errors identified by the High Court concerned the nature of the liability owed to B by C, the recipient of property transferred in breach of trust. The Court of Appeal had taken the view that, even if C has no knowledge of the trust, C may be subject to a constructive trust in favour of B arising to reverse C's unjust enrichment at B's expense. That view was described by the High Court as a 'grave error'[56] and rested on the fallacy that 'equity should now follow the law'[57] by extending to B the protection afforded by the law of restitution to a holder of a common law right. The difference in the levels of protection is not, however, 'irrational',[58] nor a mere result of a history and jurisdictional accident. It is rather a result of the particular means by which equity provides B with protection against third

---

[51] E.g., *Kelly* v. *Solari* (1841) 9 M. & W. 54; *Restatement (Third) Restitution and Unjust Enrichment*, § 6, cmt f, illustration 22 (2011).

[52] E.g., Lord Nicholls, 'Knowing Receipt: The Need for a New Landmark', in W. R. Cornish, R. Nolan, J. O'Sullivan and G. Virgo (eds), *Restitution: Past, Present and Future: Essays in Honour of Gareth Jones* (Oxford: Hart, 1998), 236–39; P. Birks, 'Receipt', in P. Birks and A. Pretto (eds), *Breach of Trust* (Oxford: Hart, 2002), ch. 7.

[53] As noted by L. Smith, 'Unjust Enrichment, Property and the Structure of Trusts' (2000) 116 L.Q.R. 412, 431. See McFarlane, 'The Essential Nature of Trusts and Other Equitable Interests'.

[54] *Say-Dee Pty Ltd* v. *Farah Constructions Pty Ltd* [2005] NSWCA 309.

[55] (2007) 230 C.L.R. 89.   [56] Ibid., [131].

[57] *Say-Dee Pty. Ltd* v. *Farah Constructions Pty Ltd* [2005] NSWCA 309, [221]–[222], citing from Nicholls, 'Knowing Receipt', 238–39.

[58] The view of K. Mason, 'Where Has Australian Restitution Law Got to and Where is it Going?' (2003) 77 A.L.J. 358, 368, quoted and disagreed with in *Farah Constructions Pty. Ltd* v. *Say-Dee Pty. Ltd* (2007) 230 C.L.R. 89, [148].

parties: by finding that C's conscience is affected in such a way as to justify extending the duty characteristic of a trustee from A to C.

In example 2, the enrichment initially received by C takes the form of a right[59] (the trust property) initially vested in A. The effect of the transfer from A to C is that A gains, and C acquires, that right. C's enrichment is at the expense of A rather than of B, and so it is no surprise that neither common law nor equity recognises a strict liability restitutionary claim of B against C. The key point is the same as made already: if A initially holds a right, then the impact on third parties of A's then declaring a trust in favour of B is limited. It is now possible that such a third party, if holding the trust property or its proceeds with knowledge of the trust, may come under a duty to B in relation to that property but, as emphasised by Maitland,[60] such a liability (like that arising where a third party dishonestly assists in a breach of trust) arises only where C's conscience is affected. Indeed, it is significant that whether it is based on dishonest assistance or on knowing holding of trust property, such liability is said to involve C's being a constructive trustee:[61] it is not the case that when the trust arises, third parties come under an immediate general, strict liability to B; rather, C may be liable if but only if C's particular actions justify regarding C as being subject to the same core duty of A, the initial trustee.[62] The trust gives B a right *against A (and future trustees)* that such parties do not use the property for their own benefit, but rather use it for the benefit of B.

The American Position and Ames's Analysis
In the United States the position of C, the innocent donee in example 2, is less clear: the *Restatement (Third) of Restitution* follows the first and second *Restatements of Trusts* in assuming, without citation of authority, that B does have a claim against C. On C's receipt of the trust property, it is said, a prima facie liability arises[63] and if C retains the benefit of such property[64] then the

---

[59] For the importance of distinguishing between enrichments taking the form of rights and other forms of value, see R. Chambers, 'Two Kinds of Enrichment', in R. Chambers, C. Mitchell and J. Penner (eds), *Philosophical Foundations of the Law of Unjust Enrichment* (Oxford University Press, 2009), ch. 9.

[60] E.g., Maitland, *State, Trust and Corporation*, 91: 'The concept with which the Chancellor commences his operations is that of a guilty conscience.'

[61] *Barnes v. Addy* (1874) L.R. 9 Ch. App. 244.

[62] See *Westdeutsche Landesbank Girozentrale v. Islington London Borough Council* [1996] A.C. 669, 705.

[63] *Restatement (Third) Restitution and Unjust Enrichment*, § 17, cmt c, illustration 9 (2011).

[64] As is the case where, as in example 2, C spends the proceeds of the property on costs C would have incurred even in the absence of any receipt of the property.

fact that he or she no longer holds either the property or its traceable proceeds does not displace B's personal restitutionary claim.[65] One explanation for this stance is its consistency with Austin Scott's view,[66] opposed to Maitland's, that B's interest is proprietary in nature: it may rest on the idea challenged earlier that B has a general right to the value inherent in the trust property, rather than simply a right that A (or future trustees) must use that property consistently with the terms of the trust.

A different explanation for the stance taken in the *Restatement* focuses instead on the nature of a restitutionary claim. James Barr Ames, for example, argued that B's ability to assert a right against an innocent donee still holding trust assets rested on the same general foundation as a claimant's ability to seek restitution after making a mistaken payment to the defendant: '[a] court of equity will compel the surrender of an advantage by a defendant whenever, but only whenever, upon grounds of obvious justice, it is unconscientious for him to retain it at another's expense'.[67] On this view, C may be liable in example 2 if he or she retains a *benefit* when acquiring notice of the trust, whether or not C at that point retains a *right* that can be identified as either the trust property or its traceable proceeds. C's liability depends on a broader view of the basis of restitutionary liability rather than on a characterisation of B's initial right as proprietary: indeed, Ames himself agreed with Maitland that it is 'clearly inaccurate' to regard B as an 'equitable owner'.[68]

The most important point for present purposes, is that, even if Ames's analysis were accepted, there would still be a clear difference – when considering claims against an innocent donee of property – between the position of B and the position of a party with an unencumbered legal title to property. Where the claimant has legal title, a prima facie duty of non-interference with the property is imposed on the rest of the world and a stranger can be liable for such interference even if unaware that the property is not his or her own. The conscience of the defendant is therefore irrelevant, as is the fact that the defendant was never enriched or is no longer enriched as a result of the interference with the property.[69] Where B instead has only an equitable

---

[65] C's retention of an abstract enrichment prevents C's relying on the change of position defence set out in the American Law Institute's *Restatement (Third) Restitution and Unjust Enrichment*, § 65 (2011).

[66] A. W. Scott, 'The Nature of the Rights of the Cestui Que Trust' (1917) 17 Colum. L. Rev. 269. Scott was the Reporter for the *Restatement of Trusts*, and, with Warren Seavey, the Reporter for the *Restatement of Restitution*.

[67] J. B. Ames, 'Purchaser for Value Without Notice' (1887) 1 Harv. L. Rev. 1, 3.   [68] Ibid., 9.

[69] Conversion may 'cause hardship for innocent persons': *Kuwait Airways Corp. v. Iraqi Airways Co (Nos 4 and 5)* [2002] 2 A.C. 883, [103]; [2002] UKHL 19.

interest under a trust then, on each of the orthodox position and Ames's analysis, B's claim depends instead on the conscience of C's being affected and therefore on C's acquiring knowledge of B's rights in relation to the trust property. The difference between the traditional position and Ames's analysis is that, on the former, such knowledge must arise when C still has *either the trust property or its traceable proceeds*, whereas on the latter it suffices if C acquires such knowledge at a point when C retains an *abstract benefit* derived from his or her initial receipt of the trust property.

This leads to a second point. It is possible to argue that in example 2, it seems arbitrary, or even overly formal, to deny B a claim given that B has in substance lost out and C has, in substance, gained from the unauthorised use of the trust fund. Ames argued that in such a case, whilst the right itself is acquired by C, the *value* of that right is not and remains throughout with B. A Hohfeldian analysis, however, shows the difficulties with this argument and reveals something significant about the operation of a trust. As a party's claim-rights are rights against another party that such a party act or not act in a particular way,[70] it makes little sense to talk of a transfer of value or indeed of a right to value. In the case of a trust, as noted earlier, B has no abstract entitlement to value but rather has a claim-right against A that A use the property for B's benefit as according to the terms of the trust. As against parties other than B, indeed, A has the same general privilege as an unencumbered owner to use the trust property for his or her own benefit, and to that extent it is A who has a right to the value of the trust property. This aspect of the trust is closely linked to the point discussed earlier: it is the trustee (A) who may hold rights against third parties, and B's protection against a third party is either indirect (depending on A's rights) or depends on B's providing a good reason why a third party can be said, like A, to have come under a duty to B in relation to a specific right held by that third party. This is the formal means by which equity ensures that third parties are spared the notice and information costs that would arise were an equitable interest to bind such parties in the same way as a legal interest.

BEYOND TRUSTS

Equitable Assignment

A wider point, applying beyond the context of trusts, arises from the discussion above: it is as to the importance of distinguishing between the *practical outcome* of a particular equitable intervention and the *technical means* by

[70] J. Finnis, 'Some Professorial Fallacies About Rights' (1972) 4 Adel. L. Rev. 377, 377.

which that result is achieved. The fact, for example, that an equitable interest may be 'for all practical purposes, an interest as good as a legal interest'[71] does not mean that it is identical to a legal interest in its operation. The technical differences, seen clearly by adopting a Hohfeldian analysis, are essential to supporting Maitland's point that apparent conflicts between common law and equity disappear on closer inspection. Indeed, there is something of an irony: the very success of equity in allowing parties to achieve certain desired practical results without breaking common law rules may lead to the mistaken conclusion that equity is operating inconsistently with such rules.

The operation of equitable assignment provides a good example of this broader point. The clear common law rule is that other than in limited, exceptional cases[72] if D owes a duty to A, for example to pay A a fixed sum, it is not possible for A to transfer A's claim-right to B. In a case where D's duty arises from a contract between A and D, this reflects the simple point that it would be inconsistent with D's freedom to choose his or her contracting partner if a variation in D's duty could be unilaterally effected by A.[73] In such a case, however, there is no difficulty in A's declaring a trust in favour of B of A's claim-right against D: D's duty would continue to be owed to A, even if, were A to refuse in breach of trust to B to enforce that duty, B would then be able to invoke the *Vandepitte* procedure[74] to initiate proceedings against A and D. Such a trust might be seen in practice to give B many of the same benefits as would come from having a direct right against D but, crucially, it does not conflict with the common law rule preventing such transfers, or with the underlying principle that A should not be free unilaterally to alter D's duty.

It might be thought that, given the possibility of equitable assignment, such a trust is unnecessary. Traditionally, however, equitable assignment has been understood to operate by way of trust.[75] This is consistent, for example, with the general requirement that, after such an assignment, A must be joined in any action by B to enforce D's duty.[76] That understanding has become less

---

[71] R. v. *Tower Hamlets London Borough Council, Ex p. von Goetz* [1999] Q.B. 1019, 1023.
[72] Such as debts owed to or by the Crown.
[73] See C. H. Tham, 'The Nature of Equitable Assignment and Anti-Assignment Clauses', in J. W. Neyers, S. G. A. Pitel and R. Bronaugh (eds), *Exploring Contract Law* (Portland: Hart, 2009), 291.
[74] Discussed *Barbados Trust Co. Ltd* v. *Bank of Zambia* [2007] 1 Lloyd's Rep. 495, [30]–[47], [74]–[76], [98]–[119], [129]–[141].
[75] W. Blackstone, *Commentaries on the Laws of England* (Oxford: Clarendon, 1766), vol. 2, ch. 30; *Gorringe* v. *Irwell India Rubber & Gutta Percha Works* (1886) 34 Ch.D. 128. See too J. Edelman and S. Elliott, 'Two Conceptions of Equitable Assignment' (2015) 131 L.Q.R. 228.
[76] *Roberts* v. *Gill & Co.* [2011] 1 A.C. 240, [71]; [2010] UKSC 22.

prominent, and equitable assignment has come to be seen, particularly in the United States, as involving a transfer to B of A's claim-right against D.[77] This raises the awkward question of the basis on which equity may permit a result clearly barred by the common law. The apparent conflict, however, arises only if the practical result of equitable assignment is confused with the technical means by which it is achieved. It has been argued,[78] for example, that an equitable assignment consists of a trust for B of A's chose in action against D, plus a special form of irrevocable agency, recognised in equity, by which A permits B to exercise certain of A's powers (including the power to release D's duty to A if D makes payment to B) in B's own interest. On that view, in a case involving a legal chose in action the requirement for joinder of the assignor is no mere technicality, but rather demonstrates that the claim-right being enforced against D is held, as it was prior to the equitable assignment, by A. This may have a practical impact: in one case,[79] the question was whether an insurer, B, with a right of equitable subrogation to A's claim against D could pursue that claim directly where A was a company that had ceased to exist. Drawing on the rules applying to equitable assignment, the Court of Appeal held that no claim could be made unless and until A was reinstated on the companies register:

> [t]o contend, as counsel for the insurers suggested, that the problem is only one of form and not substance, is as untenable in the present state of the law as it would be in relation to the different consequences of an equitable, as opposed to legal, assignment.[80]

Unjust Enrichment

The analogy drawn by Ames between the claim of B in example 2, and the personal restitutionary claim available to Y where Y mistakenly transfers a right to Z, was considered earlier. The premise of that analogy was rejected as it depends on the idea, exposed as dubious by a Hohfeldian analysis, that each of B and Y holds an abstract and independent right to value. That point is not, however, fatal to Ames's broader contention that there may be an underlying

---

[77] See, too, G. Tolhurst, *The Assignment of Contractual Rights*, 2nd edn (Oxford: Hart, 2016), [1.01]; M. Bridge, *Personal Property Law*, 4th edn (Oxford University Press, 2015), 231.
[78] C. H. Tham, 'The Mechanics of Assignments: Functions and Form' (D.Phil. dissertation, University of Oxford, 2016), 74–80.
[79] *M.H. Smith (Plant Hire) Ltd* v. *D.L. Mainwaring (t/a Inshore)* [1986] 2 Lloyd's Rep. 244.
[80] Ibid., 246 (Kerr L.J.).

equitable basis to the core personal restitutionary claim. As well as having some support in precedent,[81] that contention now seems remarkably prescient: it is closely reflected in the language currently used (but adopted only relatively recently) by courts in England when considering liability in knowing receipt[82] and by courts in Australia when considering restitutionary liability.[83] The use of such language in the case of knowing receipt reflects a conscious judicial decision to emphasise the equitable basis of the liability and to reject arguments that, on the basis of fusion between law and equity, a common law strict liability model should be extended. So, whilst the weight of academic opinion at one point favoured the recognition of prima facie strict liability on a recipient of trust property, so as to remove a supposed inconsistency between common law and equity, there is now a judicial trend that not only re-asserts the traditional equitable position as regards recipients of trust property but also emphasises the equitable nature of restitutionary liability itself.

Indeed, it can be argued that whatever its precise jurisdictional origin, a personal restitutionary claim has a distinctly equitable function as it works to mitigate the effects on a particular claimant of a primary set of rules (as to the validity of a transfer of rights) which, whilst justified by wider concerns, may in certain cases create the prospect of unconscionable conduct by the defendant recipient as against the claimant transferor. To adopt the language used by Henry Smith,[84] such a defendant might be seen as taking opportunistic advantage of the generally phrased primary rules as to transfers of rights. In a case where Y's transfer of a right to Z is made as a result of a subjective mistake, the need to provide third parties with clarity as to the location of rights[85] may justify the validity of the transfer, so that Z does indeed acquire the right. That does not mean that the effect of such rules on Y's position *as regards* Z is necessarily justified. In a case where Z remains factually better off, at least by the time that he or she is aware of the mistake, there is a prima facie

[81] E.g., *Moses* v. *Macferlan* (1760) 2 Burr. 1005, 1010–11.

[82] *Bank of Credit and Commerce International (Overseas) Ltd* v. *Akindele* [2001] Ch. 437, 455: 'The recipient's state of knowledge should be such as to make it unconscionable for him to retain the benefit of the receipt.'

[83] *Roxborough* v. *Rothmans of Pall Mall Australia Ltd* (2001) 208 C.L.R. 516, [24], [71], [91]; [2001] HCA 68; *Australian Financial Services Ltd* v. *Hills Industries Ltd* (2014) 253 C.L.R. 560, [65]–[76]; [2014] HCA 14.

[84] H. E. Smith, 'Property, Equity, and the Rule of Law', in L. M. Austin and D. Klimchuk (eds), *Private Law and the Rule of Law* (Oxford University Press, 2014), ch. 10.

[85] In *Cressman* v. *Coys of Kensington (Sales) Ltd* [2004] 1 W.L.R. 2775; [2004] EWCA Civ 47, for example, the transfer of the privilege to use a specific car registration number was valid as the defendant was registered as holding that privilege.

case for the defendant paying the value of that benefit to the claimant. As recently confirmed by the High Court of Australia,[86] however, the case is only a prima facie one and events occurring after Z's receipt, even if not resulting in a clearly measurable reduction of the enrichment, can make it no longer unconscionable for Z, even with knowledge of Y's mistake, to retain the enrichment.

It can thus be argued that there is no conflict between, on the one hand, a primary legal rule that, notwithstanding Y's subjective mistake, Y's right has been transferred to Z; and, on the other hand, the possibility of Z's nonetheless being under a liability[87] to pay the value of that right to Y. Indeed, in justifying the effect of the primary legal rule on Y, the possibility of a restitutionary claim may play a vital role. Far from undermining the primary rules as to the transfer of rights, the personal restitutionary claim can instead be seen as an important part of the justification for those rules.[88] Indeed, this seems to be an example of the broader argument that equitable doctrines, whilst leaving some room for discretion in the interpretation of core concepts such as unconscionable retention, may nonetheless support the rule of law by mitigating the potentially harsh effect of primary legal rules and 'contributing to conditions under which citizens are likely to form and maintain a disposition to engage with law'.[89] In unjust enrichment, as is the case when considering each of the effect of a beneficiary's rights on third parties, and equitable assignment, equity can thus add to the common law by offering important substantive protection to a claimant. The form in which that protection is provided ensures that at the level of principle equity does not conflict with the common law rules it supplements.

---

[86] *Australian Financial Services Ltd* v. *Hills Industries Ltd* (2014) 253 C.L.R. 560. See too Lord Goff in *Lipkin Gorman* v. *Karpnale* [1991] 2 A.C. 548, 580, on the scope of the change of position defence.

[87] As noted by S. A. Smith, 'A Duty to Make Restitution' (2013) 26 Can. J. L. & Juris. 157, 173–76, it is difficult to think of Z as being under an immediate duty to make restitution as soon as Z acquires the right: after all, Z may at that point be entirely unaware of the transfer. The language used in the *Restatement (Third) Restitution and Unjust Enrichment* (2011) §§ 1, 2, 5, 13–17 may therefore be more accurate: Z is *liable* to make restitution: see S. Smith, 'The Restatement of Liabilities in Restitution', in C. Mitchell and W. Swadling (eds), *The Restatement Third: Restitution and Unjust Enrichment—Critical and Comparative Essays* (Oxford: Hart, 2013), ch. 10.

[88] See B. McFarlane, 'Unjust Enrichment, Rights and Value', in D. Nolan and A. Robertson (eds), *Rights and Private Law* (Oxford: Hart, 2012), ch. 20; Smith, 'A Duty to Make Restitution'.

[89] M. Harding, 'Equity and the Rule of Law' (2016) 132 L.Q.R. 278, 302.

CONCLUSION

Hohfeld was clearly correct in observing that as there are exclusively equitable principles, those principles when applied will alter the jural relations recognised at common law that would otherwise exist. To that extent, there may be conflict between common law and equity. Maitland, however, was correct in observing that many apparent conflicts between common law and equity are illusory. A Hohfeldian analysis will often bear out the truth of Maitland's view: the apparent conflict is dispelled by shifting from the level of general impression and practical benefits (e.g., the position of a beneficiary is as good as that of a holder of unencumbered legal title; an equitable assignment, in effect, involves a transfer of a right) to a more detailed examination of the parties' rights. It is often said, when considering the operation of particular principles, that equity focuses on substance rather than form; at a more abstract level it might instead be said that the opposite is true: it is the employment of particular technical, formal means that permits equity to give a party certain practical benefits unavailable at common law whilst at the same time respecting the operation of primary common law rules.

The examination of the trust and of other forms of equitable intervention in this chapter has led to three broader points about the operation of equity in a modern legal system. The first concerns the need for the conscience of the specific defendant to be affected. In looking at the trust, and the question of ownership, the crucial Hohfeldian distinction is the simple one between, on the one hand, the position of A (the trustee) who is under an immediate duty to B (the beneficiary) and, on the other hand, the position of third parties, who are not under that same, immediate duty. After all, the core duty of A is a duty not to use a particular right or rights (the trust property) inconsistently with the terms of the trust – and third parties, such as X, not holding that right cannot be under that same duty. A condition of X's coming under the same duty is therefore the receipt by X of a particular type of right: a right that is, or is part of, the initial trust property or its traceable proceeds.

This leads to the second point: equitable principles often have a 'backwards-looking' aspect, as they are based not on recognising and enforcing pre-existing duties of a defendant, but instead on asking if, given what has occurred in relation to the claimant, it would now be unconscionable for the defendant to act in a particular way.[90] Such principles can play an

---

[90] The reference to 'backwards-looking' aspect of equitable intervention derives from Hoffmann L.J.'s analysis of equitable estoppel in *Walton* v. *Walton* (unreported, Court of Appeal (Civ. Div.), 14 April 1994).

important practical role in mitigating the effects of primary, common law rules; the operation of the principles, by imposing liabilities rather than duties, can nonetheless be consistent with those primary rules. Those primary rules are often related to the acquisition or exercise of particular rights by the defendant,[91] and this leads to the third distinctive feature of equity: its principles can regulate and respond to a party's holding of a particular right. Indeed, Maitland's view as to the support often provided by equity to the common law[92] is reflected in the argument that equitable liabilities of a holder of a right may play a vital role in justifying the common law rules that have permitted the acquisition of that right, or the continued enjoyment of a privilege associated with the right. Structurally speaking, equity can thus take advantage of its secondary position to supplement, but also support, primary common law rules. Similarly, Hohfeld's reference to certain common law rules as a 'stage of thought'[93] suggests that there may be a potentially fruitful interaction between common law and equity, and that the initial common law position has some significance even if displaced by a contrary equitable result.

Two final points can be made. First, an emphasis on technical differences between the formal operation of particular common law and equitable rules does not mean that no useful analogies can be drawn between such rules. For example, this chapter has emphasised the differences between the position of a beneficiary of a trust and that of an unencumbered holder of a legal property right. Nonetheless, the focus of trusts on the rights held by the trustee means that a valid but limited analogy may be drawn between those two cases. In each, there is an element of depersonalisation. It is not the identity of A, the initial trustee, that is crucial to the operation of the trust; it is rather the identity of the right initially held by that trustee. Just as the scope of the protection of a party with a legal interest depends on the fate of the thing to which that interest relates, and so is not tied to a specific individual, so does the scope of B's protection depend on the fate of the right or rights initially held on trust. The crucial point made by this chapter, however, is that the ability to draw an analogy between two things does not mean that those things are the same.

Second, it would of course be a mistake to regard common law rules as an immoveable structure around which equitable principles grow and develop.

---

[91] E.g., *Australian Financial Services Ltd* v. *Hills Industries Ltd* (2014) 253 C.L.R. 560, [86] (analogy between equitable estoppel and the change of position defence to a restitutionary claim).

[92] Maitland, *Equity*, 17: 'Equity had come not to destroy the law, but to fulfil it.'

[93] Hohfeld, 'The Relations between Equity and Law', 544. See the text to n. 10.

Where equitable doctrines allow parties to achieve some practical benefits not permitted by common law, even if those doctrines initially operate in a way consistent with the common law rules, it may be that over time the practical success and importance of the equitable doctrines leads to a reconsideration of the common law rules. In the United States, for example, it would probably be difficult now to argue that assignment operates as anything other than a transfer of a chose in action. In England, the Law Commission has proposed that types of right which would currently, as restrictive covenants in land, take the form of an equitable interest should be capable in the future of operating as legal interests:[94] experience with such rights, it seems, has led to the view that there is no need for an 'extension in equity of the doctrine of negative easements'[95] as statute can ensure that such an extension occurs directly at common law. Far from undermining common law, equity may thus assist not only in the justification of existing common law rules but also in the development of new ones.

[94] Law Commission, *Making Land Work: Easements, Covenants and Profits à Prendre*, Report No. 327 (2011), [5.4]–[5.11], [5.69]–[5.75].
[95] *London & South West Railway Co.* v. *Gomm* (1882) 20 Ch.D. 562, 583 (Jessel M.R.).

15

Equity and the Modern Mind

EMILY SHERWIN*

Mostly by chance, our legal system developed as a dual system of law and equity. The law side was comparatively rule-bound. The equity side took on in a limited, secondary and often obscure way the role of Aristotelian equity, correcting injustice when general rules produced unsatisfactory outcomes.[1] This division of labour largely survived the procedural merger of law and equity. It came to an end, or at least was much diminished, in the course of the twentieth century as courts and legal scholars embraced the core principles of American Legal Realism.

I begin with an overview of the benefits and drawbacks of rules and the historical role of equity in softening the impact of rules. Towards the end of the essay, I turn to the Realist movement in the United States. Realism brought equity into the light and gave it open precedence over the system of rules. The results are widely credited as a victory for candour over obfuscation. Without drawing any overall conclusions about modern equity, I will argue that some important benefits were also lost as equity gained prominence over law.[2]

* Thanks for excellent comments from Kevin Clermont, John Goldberg, Peter Martin, Henry Smith, Peter Turner and participants in workshops at St Catharine's College, Cambridge, and Cornell Law School.

[1] Aristotle, *Nicomachean Ethics*, trans. by C. D. C. Reeve (Indianapolis, IN: Hackett Publishing, 2014), ¶ 1137b25 ('And this is the nature of what is decent – a rectification of law in so far as it is deficient because of its universality').

[2] My interest is primarily with the formal role of equity in law. For an excellent discussion of the procedural ascendancy of equity in modern law, see Subrin, 'How Equity Conquered Common Law'.

THE ROLE OF RULES IN A LEGAL SYSTEM

The Problem of Rules

To explain my argument, I begin with some basic observations about the operation of rules in a legal system.[3] The first is that, under certain conditions, a legal system obtains significant benefits from rules. To provide these benefits the rule must be reasonably determinate, so that a person subject to the rule can follow it without engaging in an extensive exercise of judgment about its meaning.[4] It also must be authoritative in the sense that it implicitly requires compliance with its terms in all cases it covers. In other words, the rule must be more than a rule of thumb; it must constrain decision-making.

The third condition for beneficial rules is that they must be good rules. A good rule is one that, if always followed, will produce a better set of outcomes than would occur if all actors and judges followed their own best judgment case by case. Of course, not all rules meet this criterion. Some rules are poorly designed, and in some areas of conduct no determinate rule will outperform individual judgment in the run of cases. Whether a given rule qualifies as a good rule is fundamentally an empirical question. It seems likely, however, that at least some rules are good rules.[5] In any event, my arguments apply only to the extent that there are good rules in place.

If this third condition is met, general, determinate and authoritative rules will not only improve outcomes but will also enable people to coordinate their own conduct with the conduct of others. In transactional settings, a rule can resolve prisoners' dilemmas by reassuring each party that if certain preconditions are met, the legal system will require reciprocal action by the other party. In other settings the existence of a rule of conduct, together with the

---

[3] At greater length, see L. Alexander and E. Sherwin, *The Rule of Rules: Morality, Rules, and the Dilemmas of Law* (Durham, NC: Duke University Press, 2001), 11–36; J. Raz, *The Morality of Freedom* (Oxford: Clarendon, 1986), 48–50; F. Schauer, *Playing By the Rules: A Philosophical Examination of Rule-Based Decision-Making in Law and Life* (Oxford: Clarendon, 1991), 1–121, 149–55; G. J. Postema, 'Coordination and Convention at the Foundations of Law' (1982) 11 J. Legal Stud. 165, 172–86.

[4] I assume that rules have a core of determinate meaning, even if their meaning is uncertain in some contexts. See K. Greenawalt, *Law and Objectivity* (New York, NY: Oxford University Press, 1992), 34–89; H. L. A. Hart, *The Concept of Law* (Oxford: Clarendon, 1961), 122–38; Schauer, *Playing By the Rules*, 53–68; J. L. Coleman and B. Leiter, 'Determinacy, Objectivity, and Authority' (1992) 142 U. Pa. L. Rev. 549; L. B. Solum, 'On the Indeterminacy Crisis: Critiquing Critical Dogma' (1987) 54 U. Chi. L. Rev. 462.

[5] A simple example is the rule 'Drive on the Right'. To the extent this rule is widely followed, it will produce coordination benefits that exceed the costs it might impose on a few oddly situated actors.

knowledge that most people follow the rules, allows actors to predict what others will do and to organise their own actions accordingly.

At the same time, general rules are imperfect in application. Because they are fixed in advance for categories of cases, they will cover unpredicted sets of particular facts not all of which fall within the objectives of the rule. Because their terms are blunt, they will also cover some cases, predicted or not, in which another outcome may be best. Imperfect rules can nevertheless be good rules when assessed over the long run, but not all the outcomes they require will be good outcomes.

The errors that arise in the application of rules cannot be eliminated by a general corrective principle such as 'follow the rule except when it calls for the wrong outcome', or 'follow the rule unless the result is inconsistent with the purposes of the rule' because those who apply the corrective principle may not judge accurately which results are wrong. Human reasoners are not omniscient and the inferences they draw are not always accurate. This holds true even when the reasoner evaluates the facts before him or her in a 'rule-sensitive' way, taking into account the value of the rule and the collateral consequences of a rule violation, such as the bad example a well-reasoned violation provides to inferior reasoners.[6] To some extent, miscalculation by individual actors may be counterbalanced by the threat that rules will be enforced, because the possibility of legal penalties creates an additional reason to follow the rule. Yet the officials who enforce the rule may also miscalculate, or may calculate correctly but be reluctant to enforce rules against actors who have concluded in good faith that the rule should not apply.

A further difficulty is that human reasoners are subject to common forms of cognitive bias. In particular, the immediate facts that make application of a rule appear mistaken are likely to be more salient in the actor's mind than background consequences such as loss of coordination that might follow from the example of a rule violation.[7] As a result, mis-judgment about when the outcome prescribed by a rule is incorrect will tend systematically to favour rule violations. Judges as well as individual actors are subject to this type of bias: their attention is focused on the particular cases that come before them and

---

6 Frederick Schauer coined the useful term 'rule-sensitive particularism': Schauer, *Playing By the Rules*, 97–100; F. Schauer, 'Rules and the Rule of Law' (1991) 14 Harv. J. L. & Pub. Pol'y 645, 676, n. 66.

7 See generally A. Tversky and D. Kahneman, 'Availability: A Heuristic for Judging Frequency and Probability', in D. Kahneman, P. Slovic and A. Tversky (eds), *Judgment under Uncertainty: Heuristics and Biases* (Cambridge University Press, 1982), ch. 11; D. Kahneman, D. Griffith and T. Gilovich (eds), *Heuristics and Biases: The Psychology of Intuitive Judgment* (Cambridge University Press, 2002).

they may hesitate to impose sanctions on actors who have made reasonable errors of judgment in close cases.

The problem of general rules and their application to particular cases results in an asymmetry or 'gap' between the point of view of a rule-making authority and the point of view of an individual actor considering what to do in a particular case governed by the rule.[8] The rule-maker, observing the operation of the rule in advance, rationally prefers full compliance with the rule because full compliance by all actors will lead to a better sum of outcomes. For an actor facing a particular case in which he or she believes the outcome of the rule is wrong, the rational course is to disobey the rule.

This chapter is about equity, meaning both the doctrines, remedies and procedures traceable to pre-merger equity courts and the function of rule-correction traditionally associated with the equity side of law. Equity in both senses is difficult to codify and therefore has been developed and applied primarily by judges.[9] Accordingly, the focus of the essay will be on judges as decision-makers.

Judges share the rulemaker's point of view when they take office and when they announce rules of common law. When asked to apply rules to a particular case, they see the case from the particularised point of view of the individuals involved and will be tempted to make equitable exceptions to the rules. Judges may understand the potential value of good rules and the impact that exceptions will have on actor's perceptions of the rules' reliability. Like individual actors, however, they will tend systematically to undervalue the long-term effects of equity in comparison to the rules' immediate impact.[10] Therefore, if judicial decisions are fully public, equitable correction will tend to diminish the value of determinate rules over time.

The asymmetry between the point of view of a rule-maker and the point of view of an individual actor or a judge called on to apply a rule affects any legal system that is governed in part by general, determinate rules rather than particularised edicts. It is unavoidable as long as human reasoning is

---

[8]   Frederick Schauer has used the term 'asymmetry of authority' to describe this difference in perspective: Schauer, *Playing By the Rules*, 128–34. Larry Alexander has referred to this problem as 'The Gap': L. Alexander, 'The Gap' (1991) 14 Harv. J. L. & Public Pol'y 695, 695.

[9]   One interesting example of legislated equity can be found in the laws and regulations governing Social Security benefits, where restitution of overpayments can cause hardship: hence United States Code, 42 U.S.C. § 404(b), amplified by the Code of Federal Regulation, 20 CFR § 404.508. Thanks to my colleague Peter Martin for this example.

[10] See J. J. Rachlinski, 'Bottom-Up versus Top-Down Lawmaking' (2006) 73 U. Chi. L. Rev. 933, 942–43 (discussing the effects of affect and availability biases in the context of judicial decision-making); F. Schauer, 'Do Cases Make Bad Law?' (2006) 73 U. Chi. L. Rev. 883, 895 (observing that judges, as rule makers, are subject to the availability bias).

imperfect. A general equitable exception to rules cannot reconcile equity and rules because a general equitable exception, imperfectly applied, will undermine the capacity of rules to control error and coordinate conduct. Sensitivity to the value of rules does not solve this problem because mistaken judgments will diminish the value of rules over time. Similarly, a presumption in favour of rules over equity does not solve the problem because the presumption will also be imperfectly applied, diminishing the value of the rules and therefore, progressively, the weight of the presumption.[11] This is not to say that the value of good rules is inherently superior to the value of equitable relief from good rules, but only that some trade-off between these values is unavoidable.

The Example of Contract

The coordination benefits of rules are particularly significant in the law of contract. Rules governing the creation, enforcement and excuse of contractual obligations serve a variety of purposes, such as ensuring that parties create reliable records of their intentions, deterring misconduct, encouraging disclosure of information and promoting efficient behaviour. The overarching objective of contract law, however, is to support the social institution of contractual exchange by assuring parties that if they follow certain steps and avoid certain missteps, their agreements will be enforced by the courts. In this way, the law resolves the impasse that might result from sequential obligations.

To support private exchange, the rules of contract law must be determinate enough to guide conduct and to eliminate most doubts about the enforceability of agreements that conform to their requirements. At the same time, determinate rules provide openings for opportunists who see a chance to profit from technical missteps in contract formation, mistaken calculation by the other party or any form of misconduct that falls outside the policing rules of contract law. An opportunistic buyer may suspect that the seller intended a higher price than what is stated in the document they both sign.[12] A sophisticated party may offer an unsophisticated party a complex transaction

---

[11] Schauer has proposed a form of presumptive rule enforcement: Schauer, *Playing By the Rules*, 203–6; Schauer, 'Rules and the Rule of Law', 674–79. For criticism, see Alexander and Sherwin, *The Rule of Rules*, 68–73; G. J. Postema, 'Positivism, I Presume?; . . . Comments on Schauer's "Rules and the Rule of Law"' (1991) 14 Harv. J.L. & Publ. Pol'y 797, 809–22.

[12] See *Panco v. Rogers*, 87 A.2d 770 (N.J. Ch. Div. 1952) (plaintiff signed an agreement for sale of his home for a low price, in circumstances suggesting the buyer was aware of the seller's mistake).

that amounts to a very bad deal.[13] Even in the absence of opportunism, determinate rules may lead to significant hardship for parties who are unwise or unlucky. A seller may willingly agree to sell his or her home for a particular price, then encounter an extended string of bad luck that makes it very difficult to transfer possession.[14] Determinate rules may also appear to misfire in adhesion situations when a buyer signs a form contract that assigns a certain risk to the buyer in fine print and the risk later comes to pass.[15]

At least traditionally, standard rules of contract law did not recognise an excuse for the unlucky party in the situations just described. Yet, in each of cases from which these examples are drawn, the court rightly or wrongly made an equitable exception to the rules and allowed a defence. Each such decision marginally impairs the reliability of rules that are widely relied upon to define the practice of contractual exchange. A decision in the other direction, however, would be likely to leave the judges with a sense that they had denied justice to deserving parties.

Equity

Equity and Rules

Equity, meaning the part of our law that originated in the English Chancery court, is often associated with equity in the sense of correction of harsh results that follow from strict application of rules. In the early days of English equity, Chancellors typically were ecclesiastics whose role in the system of law was to give special relief to individuals who were unable to obtain justice in the king's courts. There is no lack of systematic records of early Chancery decisions suggesting that the Chancellors of the time did not pay strict attention to precedent and relied instead on broad principles of decision or their own sense of fairness to resolve disputes.[16]

---

[13] See *Ryan* v. *Weiner*, 610 A.2d 1377 (Del. Ch. 1992) (alcoholic plaintiff facing foreclosure signed an agreement transferring title to his house in exchange for a lease-back and discharge of overdue mortgage payments).

[14] See *Patel* v. *Ali* [1984] Ch. 283 (after signing a purchase and sale agreement, seller encountered substantial personal obstacles that made it very hard for her to convey).

[15] See *C. & J. Fertilizer Inc.* v. *Allied Mutual Ins. Co.*, 227 N.W.2d 169 (Iowa 1975) (buyer of burglary insurance was burgled by outsiders but form contract excluded coverage in the absence of exterior marks of forcible entry). Arthur Leff made the point that in adhesion situations, the problem does not lie with the form itself, but with the unexpected bad outcome that later occurs: A. A. Leff, 'Unconscionability and the Code: The Emperor's New Clause' (1967) 115 U. Pa. L. Rev. 485, 504–7.

[16] See generally Maitland, *Equity*, 2–11.

Commentators have differed about the extent to which pre-merger equity, in its more mature form, operated to correct determinate rules of law. In the introduction to his treatise on equity, published in 1760, Lord Kames made this comment:

> A court of equity, by long and various practice, finding its own strength and utility, and impelled by the principle of justice, boldly undertakes a matter still more arduous; and that is, to correct or mitigate the rigour, and what even in a proper sense may be termed the *injustice* of common law. It is not in human foresight to establish any general rule, that, however salutary in the main, may not be oppressive and unjust in its application to some singular cases.[17]

Blackstone, in contrast, denied that Chancery decisions conflicted with the rules of common law. The role of equity, in his view, was merely supplemental rather than corrective.[18] Frederic Maitland also took the view that there was no special association between English equity courts and Aristotelian equity. In Maitland's view, the only accurate way to define the equitable component of the legal system was as 'that body of rules administered by our English courts of justice which, were it not for the operation of the Judicature Acts, would be administered only by those courts which would be known as Courts of Equity'.[19] In the United States, Joseph Story was more equivocal. He endorsed Blackstone's comments but also recognised that equity courts might intervene to 'give such relief and aid, as the exigency of the particular case may require' when legal remedies were incomplete.[20]

Procedural merger of law and equity in the United States took place through a long process that began in the mid-nineteenth century with the Field Code and was mostly complete when the Federal Rules of Civil

[17] Lord Kames (H. Home), *Principles of Equity*, 3rd edn by M. Lobban (Indianapolis, IN: Liberty Fund, [1778] 2014), 24–25 (original emphasis).

[18] W. Blackstone, *Commentaries on the Laws of England* (Oxford: Clarendon, 1768), vol. 3, 430–31. Blackstone also rejected the claim that law was more rule-like than equity: at 434.

[19] Maitland, *Equity*, 1. Although Maitland argued that equity was not formed around or defined by principles of equity, he did view it as a supplement or 'gloss' on the common law, which softened the operation of common law rules: at 18–19.

[20] J. Story, *Commentaries on Equity Jurisprudence, as Administered in England and America*, 4th edn (Boston, MA: Little and Brown, 1846), vol. I, § 33; see also §§ 8, 12, 13, 33. This is a posthumous edition prepared by Story. Story's reservations about corrective equity appear to have been based on the dangers of uncontrolled judicial discretion (at § 19). Yet he also wrote favourably about the equity doctrine of 'constructive fraud': e.g., at § 262 (referring to 'the innumerable instances, in which the persuasive morality of Courts of Equity has subdued the narrow, cold, and semi-barbarous dogmas of the Common Law').

Procedure were promulgated in 1938.[21] Equity, of course, did not disappear with the merger.[22] Certain substantive fields of law that were first developed by the Chancellors, such as the law of fiduciary relations, were still viewed as equitable. Courts also continued to grant historically equitable remedies such as injunctions and constructive trusts, to refer to these remedies as equitable and to recognise special equitable defences to injunctive relief.

The association between equity and correction of unjust or overbroad outcomes of legal rules also survived the merger. Equity was no longer a separate form of adjudication, but the connection between the equitable components of law and equity in the Aristotelian sense continued to play a conscious role in judicial decision-making.[23] For example, Judge Cardozo, discussing a problem of mortgage foreclosure, stated that:

> Equity follows the law, but not slavishly nor always... However fixed the general rule and the policy of preserving it, there may be extraordinary conditions in which the enforcement of such a clause according to the letter of the covenant will be disloyalty to the basic principles for which equity exists.[24]

Cardozo was not a thorough-going rule sceptic: in the same opinion, he acknowledged the importance of the general rule that contractual provisions for acceleration of mortgage debts are enforceable.[25] Instead he appeared to view equity as a special, supplemental component of law that enabled judges to adjust the outcomes of a valid rule.

---

[21] For background, see generally Subrin, 'How Equity Conquered Common Law', 931–74.

[22] Constitutional rights to a civil jury in proceedings at law (but not in equity) have helped to preserve the distinction between law and equity, but the history and vocabulary of equity is also useful in explaining remedial categories that date to the time of separate courts.

[23] If anything, the connection became stronger following the merger. The evolution of Story's treatise on equity provides an example. The editor of the 14th edition, published in 1918, retained Story's original arguments but added a number of statements such as this explanation of the doctrine of unclean hands:

> Equity imperatively demands of suitors in courts fair dealing and righteous conduct with reference to the matters concerning which they seek relief. He who has acted in bad faith, resorted to trickery and deception, or been guilty of fraud, injustice, or unfairness will appeal in vain to a court of conscience, even though in his wrongdoing he may have kept himself strictly 'within the law'. Misconduct which will bar relief in a court of equity need not necessarily be of such a nature as to ... constitute the basis of a legal action.

> J. Story, Commentaries on Equity Jurisprudence as Administered in England and America, 14th edn by W. H. Lyon (Boston, MA: Little, Brown and Co., 1918), vol. I, § 99.

[24] Graf v. Hope Building Corp., 254 N.Y. 1, 9, 11 (1930) (Cardozo C.J., with whom Lehman and Kellogg JJ. concurred, dissenting).

[25] Ibid., 10 ('There is neither purpose nor desire to impair the stability of the rule').

Example: Equitable Defences

The corrective function of equity is particularly evident in the area of equitable defences. In pre-merger history, the Chancellors' primary method of correcting the harsh results of determinate legal rules was to enjoin the defendant in equity from suing at law on a rule-based claim, or from enforcing a rule-based judgment. The Chancellor's injunctions were *in personam* orders: they proposed a course of action to the defendant but did not purport to alter either party's legal rights or the outcome of any proceeding at law. As a result of the Chancellor's very effective contempt power, however, the defendant almost always obeyed.[26]

Many of the defences initially recognised by the Chancellor, such as fraud, were adopted early on by the law courts as defences to legal claims. A number of defences continued to apply only in equity courts. Following merger these became equitable defences in the sense that they applied only to equitable remedies. At least in theory, equitable defences do not affect the traditional legal remedy of money damages.[27]

In cases involving equitable defences, judges often self-consciously invoke the corrective function associated with the equity side of law. For example, in *Panco v. Rogers*,[28] Panco agreed to sell his house to Rogers. The agreement, prepared by Rogers after conversations with Panco's wife, named a price of $5,500. Panco intended to ask $12,500 and the court found the house was worth at least $10,000. Panco was an uneducated carpenter who built the house himself and at the time of the transaction was elderly and deaf. The court found no evidence that Rogers had engaged in fraud, concealment or undue influence, and stated that rescission was not available as a remedy for one party's mistake. It nevertheless denied Rogers's claim for specific performance, saying:

[A]n application for [specific performance] is addressed to the sound discretion of a court of equity. . . [T]he court must be satisfied that the claim is fair,

---

[26] An example, in which the defendant chose to remain in Fleet Prison rather than obey, is *J.R. v. M.P.* (1459) Y.B. 37 Hen. VI, f. 13, pl. 3, printed in E. Sherwin, T. Eisenberg and J. R. Re, *Remedies: Cases and Materials* (New York, NY: Foundation Press, 2012), 257–59. See generally, Maitland, *Equity*, 9–10 (describing common injunctions).

[27] See *Restatement (Second) Contracts* § 364 (1979). Edward Yorio discussed equitable defences at length in his 1989 book on specific performance: E. Yorio, *Contract Enforcement: Specific Performance and Injunctions* (Boston, MA: Little, Brown and Co., 1989), 73–126. Yorio defended the modern retention of equitable defences to specific performance on the ground that these defences often had the practical effect of producing a compromise when the facts supported neither full enforcement nor none: at 96–99.

[28] 87 A.2d 770, 773 (N.J. Ch. Div. 1952).

reasonable and just, and in judging of its fairness, the court will look not only at the terms of the contract itself, but at all of the surrounding circumstances, including the relations the parties … Where the enforcement of a contract for the sale of land would be harsh, oppressive or manifestly unjust to one of the parties thereto, its specific performance will not be decreed, but the parties will be left to their remedy at law.[29]

Another example is *Patel* v. *Ali*.[30] Mrs Ali agreed to sell her house for a stated price to the Patels. The closing was delayed for four years due to a missing co-owner and an adverse claim by Mr Ali's bankruptcy trustee. During this time, Mrs Ali had two new babies, was diagnosed with bone cancer and lost a leg. Her husband also went to prison, leaving her heavily dependent on help from neighbours and nearby relatives. The court began by stating that hardship arising after a contract is signed normally does not support relief. It added, however, that 'the principle so stated cannot be erected into a fixed limitation of the court's equitable jurisdiction'.[31] Given the unusual delay, '[e]quitable relief may, in my view, be refused because of an unforeseen change of circumstances not amounting to legal frustration'.[32]

In *McKinnon* v. *Benedict*,[33] the Benedicts purchased a lakeside summer resort. The McKinnons, who owned surrounding land, lent the Benedicts $5,000, interest-free, to meet their down payment. In exchange for this loan and some vague promises by the McKinnons to help promote the resort, the Benedicts entered into a contract with the McKinnons in which they agreed not to construct new improvements on the lakeshore part of their property for twenty-five years. The Benedicts repaid the loan after seven months. Five years later, the resort was not doing well and the Benedicts began clearing a part of their land for a trailer park and tent camp. The McKinnons sued for specific performance of the contract. The court first noted that '[w]e are … not confronted with the question of damages … and confine ourselves solely to the right of the plaintiffs to invoke the equitable remedy of specific perform-ance'.[34] It then found that 'the inadequacy of consideration is so gross as to be unconscionable and a bar to the plaintiffs' invocation of the extraordinary equitable powers of the court'.[35] The court concluded that:

> Considering all the factors – the inadequacy of the consideration, the small benefit that would be accorded the McKinnons, and the oppressive condi-tions imposed upon the Benedicts – … this contract failed to meet the test of

---

[29] Ibid., 773.   [30] [1984] Ch. 283.   [31] Ibid., 287.   [32] Ibid., 288.   [33] 157 N.W.2d 665.
[34] Ibid., 669.   [35] Ibid., 671.

reasonableness that is the *sine qua non* of the enforcement of rights in an action in equity.[36]

Equitable defences are not limited to contract cases. In *Carmen v. Fox Film Corp.*,[37] Carmen, an actress, entered an employment contract with Fox. At the time of the contract, she was a minor; accordingly, the contract was voidable at her option. She then entered a more favourable contract with Keeney, another film-maker. Two days after reaching the age of majority, Carmen repudiated the Fox contracts. Fox responded by applying pressure to Keeney to break its contract with Carmen. Carmen sued Fox, seeking an injunction based on the tort of interference with contractual relations. The court concluded that although Carmen was legally free to repudiate her contracts with Fox, she was old enough to be morally obliged to perform them. Accordingly, it denied the injunction, saying:

> A court of equity acts only when and as conscience commands, and if the conduct of the plaintiff be offensive to the dictates of natural justice, then, whatever may be the rights [she] possesses and whatever use [she] may make of them in a court of law, [she] will be held remediless in a court of equity.[38]

Over time, treatises and *Restatements* have given names to various equitable defences, which carry a suggestion of greater determinacy. *Panco v. Rogers* might be labelled a case of unilateral mistake and unconscionability. *Patel v. Ali* might be called a case of extraordinary subsequent hardship. *McKinnon v. Benedict* might be called a case of inadequate consideration. *Carmen v. Fox Film* might be categorised as a case of unclean hands. The courts' opinions, however, rely on a combination of particularised contributing factors that is hard to capture in a rule.

The idea of an equitable defence in a merged court, where one judge grants all remedies, may seem illogical. If the dictates of natural justice apply to one remedy, they should apply equally to another remedy for the same wrong. In the cases just cited, however, courts distinguished explicitly between legal and equitable defences. Their comments also show that in granting equitable defences they saw themselves as correcting harsh results of legal rules.

---

[36] Ibid., 672. It may not have helped that Mr McKinnon was a prominent lawyer.

[37] 269 F. 928 (1920).

[38] Ibid., 932 quoting *Deweese v. Reinhard*, 165 U.S. 386, 390 (1897). *Carmen* was a federal equity decision, prior to the full merger of law and equity in the federal courts. After the decision described here, Carmen recovered $43,500 damages in a state court: *Carmen v. Fox Film Corp.*, 198 N.Y.S. 766 (N.Y. App. Div. 1923).

One sensible explanation for the persistence of equitable defences in merged courts is that they often result in rough compromise where neither full enforcement nor complete denial of judicial remedies is a satisfying result. Technically, an equitable defence leaves the legal damage remedy intact. In practice, however, the damage remedy may be unsatisfactory. Damages may be difficult to measure or may be subject to limiting rules, or may fail to capture subjective values. Further, damage calculation is often left to juries, which apply their own principles of equity. In the following sections, however, I will suggest that in addition to providing a compromise between full enforcement and no enforcement, equitable defences and similar legal phenomena have at least at some points in the development of our legal system provided a partial solution to the problem of rules described at the beginning of this essay.

Example: Duty of Loyalty

Equity is not always corrective in nature. In some fields of law, the primary standards of conduct trace their origins to equity. A prominent example is the law governing fiduciaries. Fiduciary law originated when the English Chancellors began to enforce uses[39] and continued as an exclusively equitable field of law after the Statute of Uses was read as not applying to active uses, uses upon uses or trusts. In addition to this series of historical accidents, Chancery procedure, in which the Chancellor was the sole fact-finder and had power to interrogate the fiduciary, was particularly well-suited to investigating allegations of breach of fiduciary duty. *In personam* equitable remedies such as injunctions and constructive trusts, enforced through the equitable power of contempt, were also useful for policing fiduciary relationships.

In the area of fiduciary law, basic standards of conduct are highly indeterminate. In another well-known opinion, Judge Cardozo defined the standard governing fiduciary loyalty as requiring '[n]ot honesty alone, but the punctilio of an honor the most sensitive'.[40] This is a very vague standard of behaviour, but in context its vagueness makes it effective. One problem in this area is that fiduciaries exercise control over other people's assets without direct supervision and thus are in a position to cheat in multiple ways that are difficult to enumerate in a rule. Indeterminacy also serves the deterrent objectives of

---

[39] On which, see generally Maitland, *Equity*, 7–8.
[40] *Meinhard v. Salmon*, 249 N.Y. 458, 464 (1928). Meinhard involved a joint venturer rather than a trustee, but is widely cited in trust cases.

fiduciary law.[41] A relatively indeterminate standard of behaviour backed by strong sanctions encourages trustees to protect themselves by avoiding all behaviour that a court might later interpret as disloyal.

Determinate rules have a role in the equitable field of trustee disloyalty but their role is secondary, to buttress the primary standards of conduct. Courts traditionally hold that trustees must never transact business with the trust: any transaction in which one party is the trustee and the other is the beneficiary is strictly forbidden.[42] Nor have the courts taken a lenient attitude in administering this rule. Instead, the rule against self-dealing is enforced without regard to mistake or hardship on the part of the trustee.[43] Thus, the self-dealing rule is both determinate and unbending. This rule, however, is not the main source of conduct regulation for trustees; instead it serves to supplement the highly indeterminate standard of 'honor the most sensitive'.

This example suggests that one function equity may serve in a merged system is to mark off areas that are *not* well-suited to primary governance by determinate rules. Areas of law that were best suited to the Chancellor's fact-specific procedures and tailored remedies also tend to be areas in which determinate rules do not function well. The role of equity here is not to correct unfair outcomes of legal rules, but to set the presumptive mode of regulation.

THE ROLE OF EQUITY IN MODERN LAW

Equity as a Means of Policing Opportunism

In a series of articles, Henry Smith has proposed that equity can play a useful role in modern law if it is understood and employed as a means for detecting

---

[41] Opinions differ on whether over-deterrence of disloyalty is a significant consideration. John Langbein has argued for greater leniency towards trustees who engage in conflicts of interest: J. H. Langbein, 'Questioning the Trust Law Duty of Loyalty: Sole Interest or Best Interest?' (2005) 114 Yale L.J. 929. Others consider that the difficulty of monitoring fiduciaries for breach of loyalty makes strong deterrence necessary: M. B. Leslie, 'In Defense of the No Further Inquiry Rule: A Response to Professor John Langbein' (2005) 47 Wm & Mary L. Rev. 541; R. H. Sitkoff, 'Trust Law, Corporate Law, and Capital Market Efficiency' (2003) 28 J. Corp. L. 565, 572–73.

[42] See *In the Matter of the Last Will & Testament of Mary Gleeson (dec'd)*, 124 N.E.2d 624 (Ill. App. 1955); *Restatement (Third) Trusts* § 78(2) and cmt c (2007); A. W. Scott, W. F. Fratcher and M. L. Ascher, *Scott and Ascher on Trusts*, 5th edn (New York, NY: Aspen, 2007) § 17.2.

[43] *In the Matter of the Last Will & Testament of Mary Gleeson (dec'd)*, 124 N.E.2d 624, 627 (Ill. App. 1955) ('[t]he good faith and honesty of the petitioner or the fact that the trust sustained no loss on account of his dealings therewith are all matters which can avail petitioner nothing').

and penalising opportunism. One of the difficulties posed by determinate legal rules is that unscrupulous parties can take advantage of the loopholes that occur when conduct is regulated in blunt terms. Conduct that offends the purposes of the rules in unforeseen ways may be technically permissible, allowing clever parties to obtain unwarranted results. In cases of this type, the standards and defences developed in equity permit courts to review transactions after the fact and impose penalties on parties who have taken unfair advantage of the openings left by the rules.[44]

What Smith has in mind is not simply a system of law that incorporates both determinate rules and equity and allows judges to strike an appropriate balance. For reasons associated with the 'gap' described earlier, this type of balancing is likely to cause too much damage to coordination and other benefits associated with rules. Accordingly, Smith suggests instead that equity should play a 'second order' role in the system of law.[45] In Smith's proposed system, the primary means of governance are rules of conduct stated in relatively determinate form and presumed to be authoritative. Equity consists of standards that are broad enough to capture unpredictable forms of advantage-taking, but operate *ex post* and *in personam* within a limited domain marked off by indicia of opportunism. Opportunism means conduct designed to extract gains from the inability of determinate rules to capture all future situations of the type at which they are aimed. In other words, opportunism means, roughly, deliberate gaming of the 'gap'.

This is an attractive conception of how a fairly traditional body of equity doctrines, procedures and remedies might function in a merged system of law. Equity, in Smith's picture, addresses the need for fairness but is also limited in ways that avoid too much damage to rules. Equitable exceptions to rules are made after the fact and are directed specifically at parties who have not relied legitimately on the rules.[46] The hope is that honest parties, not seeking to

---

[44] E.g., H. E. Smith, 'Why Fiduciary Law Is Equitable', in A. S. Gold and P. B. Miller (eds), *Philosophical Foundations of Fiduciary Law* (Oxford University Press, 2014), ch. 13; Feldman and Smith, 'Behavioral Equity'; H. E. Smith, 'Equity as Second-Order Law: The Problem of Opportunism', working paper (15 January 2015), available: http://papers.ssrn.com/sol3/papers .cfm?abstract_id=2617413.

[45] See Smith, 'Equity as Second-Order Law', 19–64.

[46] Feldman and Smith also suggest that equity aimed at opportunism results in an acoustic separation of messages sent to good and bad actors within the legal system. Good actors are likely to treat equitable standards as standards of conduct, following rules only when an accidental lapse into self-interest requires them to do so. Bad actors – opportunists – will treat the rules as their primary standards of conduct, but will understand that, if they wish to rely on the rules, they must also conform to the equitable standard in the interstices of the rules. See Feldman and Smith, 'Behavioral Equity', 40.

profit from defects in the rules, can still depend on the courts to enforce the rules on which their agreements are based.

I am not persuaded, however, that this understanding of equity solves the problem of rules. One difficulty is that the scope of equity depends on how opportunism is defined. If opportunism means that at the time two parties interact one of them intends at the time to take advantage of the formal limitations of a legal rule, then a model of equity based on reduction of opportunism will not provide correction in the full range of situations traditionally associated with the equity side of law. In particular, it will miss a significant number of cases in which courts have applied principles of charity to give relief based on unilateral error or disproportionate hardship.[47] Accordingly, it does not fully address the moral and cognitive difficulties associated with faithful enforcement of rules. Alternatively, opportunism can be understood more broadly, to include one party's willingness after the fact to take advantage of an unexpectedly unequal result.[48] If so, then the doctrinal picture is accurate and judges will be more comfortable with the outcomes of their decisions, but there is no significant limitation on the domain of equity.

A related problem is that, assuming equity is limited in principle to the domain of premeditated opportunism, it is likely to exceed that domain in practice. One reason for this is simply that judges may not respect the domain. As long as equity does not reach the full range of cases in which the outcome of a rule conflicts with the rule's apparent purposes or with common notions of fairness, judges will be disposed to engage in some form of correction.

Another reason why equity may exceed its assigned domain is that judges may not identify opportunism accurately. By definition, opportunism is conduct that cannot be captured in determinate rules. Without the benefit of a rule-like definition, judges will sometimes mistake luck for opportunism. If so, the message sent to parties acting under rules is not that the rules are reliable if you avoid opportunism but that the rules are reliable unless you are later accused of opportunism. The second message casts a significantly greater shadow over the rules of conduct.

Assigning equity a second-order function in the system of law does not eliminate these difficulties, as long as the second-order functions remain visible. If equity is fully accessible to the public, the fact that judges apply

---

[47] *Patel v. Ali* [1984] Ch. 283; see *Restatement (Second) Contracts* § 153 (1979) (supporting relief for unilateral mistake).

[48] E.g., Smith, 'Equity as Second-Order Law', 49–50 (discussing forfeiture), 66–67 (discussing 'ex ante and ex post opportunism').

equitable principles *ex post* does not shield those principles from view *ex ante*. Nor does the *in personam* character of equitable remedies and equitable defences soften the impact of equity on rules. A potential opportunist can easily generalise from an *in personam* order against a previous opportunist to the possibility of an *in personam* order against himself or herself; in fact, an anti-opportunism theory of equity depends on the visibility of *ex post, in personam* rules to achieve deterrence.

Equity as Acoustically Separate from Law

This leads to a further observation about equity, which may explain why at least historically corrective equity did not completely undermine the relatively determinate rules of common law: traditional equity operated covertly. The comparative obscurity of equity is easiest to see in the case of equitable defences which for much of our legal history were a primary vehicle for equitable correction of law. As described earlier, Chancery courts often used common injunctions to prevent parties from pursuing otherwise viable legal claims. Post-merger courts continued to recognise a variety of relatively open-ended defences, such as unclean hands, disproportionate hardship and unconscionability that applied only to equitable remedies.[49] In theory, the legal damage remedy remained available for violation of whatever substantive rule was in play, but a damage remedy may be of little use.

Judicial assessment of the potential impact of an equitable exception on a determinate legal rule is no more reliable in the context of an equitable defence than in any other setting. Yet, because equitable defences operate in a narrow and little-known corner of the law, their effect on public perceptions of the reliability of legal rules may be limited. The law of remedies is itself relatively obscure, in comparison to the rules that govern primary conduct. Within the field of remedies, equitable remedies are less accessible to many actors than ordinary damage remedies. Equitable remedies traditionally are viewed as a special and secondary set of remedies, available only when legal remedies are not adequate.[50] Moreover, at least in the United States,

---

[49] A classic case of equitable unconscionability is *Campbell Soup Co. v. Wentz*, 172 F.2d 80 (3rd Cir. 1948), discussed in V. Goldberg, *Framing Contract Law: An Economic Perspective* (Cambridge, MA: Harvard University Press, 2006), 213–14.

[50] See *Restatement (Second) Contracts* § 359(1) (1979) (specific performance and injunction). Contrast D. Laycock, *The Death of the Irreparable Injury Rule* (Oxford University Press, 1991), 3–23 (arguing that although courts continue to cite the rule that equitable relief is not available if the plaintiff has an adequate legal remedy, they do not in practice withhold equitable relief unless there are functional reasons to do so).

lawsuits are popularly associated with transfers of cash rather than specific relief.

Finally, it is difficult to grasp the potential importance of equitable defences without first understanding both the reasons why an equitable remedy is important in a given context and the various defects in what appears to be a simple and effective damages remedy. Damage remedies are subject to a variety of restrictions that affect proof and computation of damages; they also typically are calculated by juries with significant practical discretion to take the 'equities' of a case into account. For all these reasons, the possibility that courts will use special defences to equitable belief to correct unjust outcomes of rules is not likely to be widely perceived.

The obscurity of equity is not limited to equitable defences: a number of equitable remedies and the limits courts place on them are similarly difficult to disentangle. Constructive trusts, for example, apply principles of restitution by recognising a fictitious trust between parties who never intended to create a trust and may never have interacted at all, then add more layers of fiction to determine what property is held in the fictitious trust. Equitable liens reach somewhat different results through the mechanism of an imaginary lien. Either of these remedies is likely to confuse any actor not closely familiar with the law of remedies.

Another way to put this point is that the relatively obscure legal devices associated with equity create a condition of 'acoustic separation'[51] in which conduct rules addressed to the public are coupled with a layer of decision rules addressed primarily to courts and not well-understood by individual actors. The result is to allow the legal system as a whole to maintain fairly reliable general rules of conduct that facilitate coordination and also to allow judges to follow their intuition that the rules have misfired in particular cases. Aristotelian equity is preserved, but it stays mainly out of the public eye.

This is by no means an ideal state of affairs. Assuming that equity works as described, the capacity of the legal system to maintain both determinate rules and particularised edicts depends on a form of deception. There is no master-mind involved: judges do not intentionally deceive legal actors, and judicial decisions continue to be publicly accessible. Nevertheless, the system lacks the virtues of clarity and candour. Another difficulty with a system that protects the value of rules by obscuring the operation of equity is that hidden equity will not effectively deter opportunism. Some opportunists will be caught and prevented from achieving success, but only legally sophisticated opportunists

---

[51] This term comes from M. Dan-Cohen, 'Decision Rules and Conduct Rules: On Acoustic Separation in Criminal Law' (1984) 97 Harv. L. Rev. 625.

will receive a message of general deterrence. Spur-of-the-moment opportunists, such as Mr Rogers in *Panco* v. *Rogers*, may never be aware that in a litigated case they might lose the fruits of their manoeuvres. To some extent, however, the combination of easily accessible rules of conduct and relatively obscure equitable rules of decision provides a partial solution to the problem of the 'gap'.

EQUITY AND THE MODERN MIND

Whatever conclusions one may draw about the merits of the mixed but acoustically separate system just described, its capacity to narrow the gap between determinate rules and fair results is much diminished in modern law. The explanation for this lies in the change in attitudes towards law that began with the emergence of American Legal Realism in the 1920s. For better or worse, Realism altered the dynamic of law and equity, not by eliminating equity but by bringing Aristotelian equity into the light and encouraging liberal use of it by judges.[52]

Setting aside the more peculiar strands of Realism, the Realists made a number of claims that have greatly changed how American lawyers think about the nature of law and the role of judges. Realism began with the proposition that law is not a set of pre-existing rules that govern legal decision-making, but consists instead of the decisions courts reach in response to particular facts. 'Law is what has happened or what will happen in concrete cases.'[53]

A related theme was scepticism about the capacity of rules to guide judicial decisions.[54] The argument was not that language lacks objective meaning, but that most or all legal rules are either matched by contradictory rules or subject to conflicting interpretations, leaving judges to choose an outcome based on fairness or instrumental ends.[55] Some Realists suggested that the primary force

---

[52] For a similar argument in the realm of procedure, see Subrin, 'How Equity Conquered Common Law'.

[53] J. Frank, *Law and the Modern Mind* (New York, NY: Anchor Books, [1930] 1963), 297. See K. N. Llewellyn, *The Bramble Bush: Some Lectures on the Law and Its Study* (New York, NY: Oceana, 1930), 4 ('to my mind the main thing is seeing what officials do ... and seeing that there is a certain regularity in their doing - a regularity which makes possible prediction').

[54] See K. N. Llewellyn, 'A Realistic Jurisprudence – The Next Step' (1930) 30 Colum. L. Rev. 431, 447–48 (discussing 'paper' rules and 'real' rules).

[55] See Llewellyn, *The Bramble Bush*, 64–69, especially at 69: 'every single precedent, according to what may be the attitude of future judges, is ambiguous, is wide or narrow at will'; B. Leiter, 'American Legal Realism', in D. Patterson (ed.), *A Companion to Philosophy of Law and Legal Theory*, 2nd edn (Oxford: Wiley-Blackwell, 2010), 253–54 (discussing 'rational' indeterminacy).

behind judicial decision-making is the personal and political biases of judges, or simply their intuitive 'hunches' about proper outcomes.[56]

Given the inability of legal rules to control judicial decision-making, Realists argued that judicial decisions respond primarily to facts, including facts that are not stated as preconditions for application of any legal rule.[57] On a Realist view, judges rightly are moved by their impressions of what result is fair, all things considered, in the particular circumstances of a case. They are also guided, and should be guided, by their notions of sound social and economic policy and how these play out in the situations before them.

Several prescriptions followed from these basic claims. Rules should be reformulated in fact-specific ways or, alternatively, should be stated in broad terms that invite judges to take particular facts into account.[58] Legal theory should take the form of empirical investigation of the decision-making process and legal reforms should accept and build on the relationship of decision-making to facts.[59] Most importantly, law-makers, judges and legal theorists should be candid about legal decision-making. Whatever the real grounds for legal decisions may be, these should be exposed, studied and made clear to

---

[56] E.g., J. C. Hutcheson, 'The Judgment Intuitive: The Function of the "Hunch" in Judicial Decision' (1929) 14 Cornell L.Q. 274, 278 ('I, after canvassing all the available material ... wait for the feeling, the hunch - that intuitive flash of understanding which makes the jump-spark connection between question and decision'); Frank, *Law and the Modern Mind*, 119 ('The peculiar traits, dispositions, biases and habits of the particular judge will, then, often determine what he decides to be the law'); see also Leiter, 'American Legal Realism', in Patterson (ed.), *A Companion to Philosophy of Law and Legal Theory*, 2nd edn, 255–56 (discussing causal indeterminacy).

[57] E.g., Frank, *Law and the Modern Mind*, 112 ('whatever produces the judge's hunches makes the law'); Llewellyn, *The Bramble Bush*, 69 (advocates must build an inductive case for their desired result); H. Oliphant, 'Stare Decisis – Continued' (1928) 14 A.B.A. J. 159, 159 ('we see that courts are dominantly coerced not by the essays of their predecessors but by a surer thing, – by an intuition of fitness of solution to problem, – and a renewed confidence in judicial government is engendered.'); Leiter, 'American Legal Realism', 257 ('the Core Claim of realism' is that 'judges respond primarily to the stimulus of the underlying facts of the case').

[58] See Llewellyn, 'A Realistic Jurisprudence', 452 (law-makers 'must so shape [the rule] as to induce its application') (emphasis omitted); Oliphant, 'Stare Decisis – Continued', 160 (proposing 'reclassification of most of law in terms of the human relations affected by it'); B. Leiter, 'American Legal Realism', in W. Edmundson and M. P. Golding (eds), *The Blackwell Guide to Philosophy of Law and Legal Theory* (Oxford: Blackwell, 2003), 53.

[59] See Llewellyn, 'A Realistic Jurisprudence', 442–43 (the focal point of legal thought should be 'the area of contact between judicial (or official) behavior and the behavior of laymen') (emphasis omitted); W. W. Cook, 'The Logical and Legal Bases of the Conflict of Laws' (1924) 33 Yale L.J. 457, 460 (proposing to 'observe concrete phenomena first and form generalizations afterwards').

individual actors. In Llewellyn's words, 'Covert tools are never reliable tools'.[60]
Realism had a quick and lasting effect on the American legal system. The
Realist program was exemplified and substantially advanced by Llewellyn's
Uniform Commercial Code, which relied heavily both on facts about commercial custom and on broad standards such as unconscionability and good
faith.[61] Influential Realist-inspired *Restatements* incorporated similar standards
and invited judicial assessment of particular facts.[62]

Realism combined strong scepticism about the value of determinate legal
rules with confidence in the ability of judges to reach fair and socially responsible outcomes if given the prerogative and procedural tools to investigate
particular factual contexts. It also aimed to eliminate artifice and make the
process of legal decision-making as clear as possible. All of this amounts to a
recipe for elimination of a secondary, shadowy form of equity with limited
impact on rules. Instead, the particularised methods of equity – close attention
to facts, reliance on broad standards of decision, trust in the situational sense of
judges – were brought directly and unreservedly to the fore. Mechanisms that
separate law and equity, such as equitable defences, continue to exist[63] but
they compete with even broader legal defences such as unconscionability,
lack of good faith and unilateral mistake. The functional approach of modern
Realism also tends to enlarge the domain in which traditional equitable
remedies operate and thus to bring these remedies and their defences under
greater scrutiny.[64]

To most people educated in law in the United States in the last eighty years,
the Realist expansion of the principles of equity across all of law seems obvious
and sensible. The conceptual fog is lifted. Grounds of decision are forthright
and therefore open to judicial reflection, public criticism and statutory reform.
Individual actors can better understand how the legal system operates.

---

[60] K. N. Llewellyn, *The Common Law Tradition: Deciding Appeals* (Boston, MA: Little, Brown
and Co., 1960), 365 quoting K. N. Llewellyn, 'Book Review' (1939) 52 Harv. L. Rev. 700, 703.
See Oliphant, 'Stare Decisis – Continued', 159 ('With eyes cleared of the old and broad
abstractions which curtain our vision, we come to recognize more and more the eminent good
sense in what courts are wont to do about disputes before them').

[61] See U.C.C. § 1-201(b)(3) (defining 'agreement' as 'the bargain of the parties in fact, as found in
their language or inferred from other circumstances, including course of performance, course
of dealing, or usage of trade'); § 1-304 (good faith in performance and enforcement), § 2-302
(unconscionability). For strong criticism of the unconscionability provision of the UCC, see
Leff, 'Unconscionability and the Code'.

[62] E.g., *Restatement (Second) Contracts* §§ 153 (unilateral mistake), 205 (good faith and fair
dealing) (1979).

[63] See Yorio, *Contract Enforcement*, 27, Cumulative Supplement 45–75 (2010) (updating decisions).

[64] See Laycock, *The Death of the Irreparable Injury Rule*.

Questions of social and economic policy affected by legal decisions are examined rather than submerged.

All this improvement, however, comes at some cost. The value of rules, understood as relatively determinate prescriptions for conduct that are taken as authoritative, is either forgotten or dismissed as improbable. There is a tendency to overestimate the ability of judges to assess current reasons for decision. Meanwhile, we have lost the compromise between the value of rules and the importance of equitable correction of rules that once was provided inadvertently by traditional, limited and covert equity.

In any event, there is no going back.[65] The type of obscurity that initially surrounded the doctrines and practices governing equitable remedies in the merged legal system cannot be engineered. It can only happen by accident and Realism put an end to the accident.

---

[65] Grant Gilmore had this to say about American Legal Realism in 1951:

> Legal Realism was a destructive movement. We stand amid the wreck and ruin of a jurisprudence which cannot be rebuilt. But the Realists gave us nothing to put in place of what they destroyed. Their confident optimism that the thing to do was to 'integrate law with the social sciences' has proved ill-founded. Some of those who chased the will-of-the-wisp through what used to be called 'related disciplines' may have been more learned; no one became any wiser.
> At twenty years distance we may with the prescience of hindsight pass judgment. Llewellyn and his co-conspirators were right in everything they said about the law. They skillfully led us into the swamp. Their mistake was in being sure that they knew the way out of the swamp: they did not, and at least we are still there.
> (G. Gilmore, 'Book Review: The Bramble Bush' (1951) 60 Yale L.J. 1251, 1252.)

16

An Argument for Limited Fission

MATTHEW HARDING[*]

INTRODUCTION

In this chapter, I set out an argument in support of limited fission. The argument is for 'fission' in that it is committed to the proposition that in some ways and for some purposes equity should retain a certain separateness in the legal system. The argument is for 'limited' fission in that it claims value for equity's separateness only in certain legal settings and not in others. My starting point is not the doctrines or remedies of equity, although I will have something to say about both; nor is it the debates about jurisdiction that have been the preoccupation of many equity scholars writing on questions of fusion and fission. Instead, following Henry Smith, I begin with an interest in equity's functions. As Smith suggests, analysis of equity's functions promises to expose, even to the equity sceptic, reasons to value equity's distinctive offering of doctrines, remedies, perspectives and commitments and perhaps therefore reasons to value fission as well.[1] In contrast, traditional defences of maintaining the separateness of equity rooted in claims about the implications of the nineteenth-century judicature reforms tend to leave the equity sceptic unmoved.[2]

First, I set out an argument for fission. There, using the example of trustees' liability following the taking of a common account, I argue that equity brings distinctive normative perspectives to bear on the problems with which it deals. I then argue that these distinctive normative perspectives help to constitute institutions and practices that support personal autonomy in important ways.

[*] My sincere thanks to Professor Paul Miller and Dr Peter Turner for engaging conversations and insightful comments on the topic of this chapter.

[1] Smith, 'Fusing the Equitable Function'.
[2] E.g., M. J. Tilbury, *Civil Remedies: Volume One, Principles of Civil Remedies* (Sydney: Butterworths, 1990), [1018]–[1019].

To the extent that such a function is enhanced by a legal culture in which equity is seen as a separate component of the legal system as a whole, a case for fission can be made. I then point out that my argument for fission has limits because in some legal settings a function of constituting the autonomy-enhancing institutions and practices that, historically, equity has constituted does not depend on a sense of equity's separateness. In these settings, fission is unnecessary and possibly counterproductive. I illustrate this point using as an example the law of charity.

AN ARGUMENT FOR FISSION

In presenting an argument for fission, I want to concentrate on an area of equity that has been the subject of much controversy in recent times: the liability of trustees to monetary remedies following the taking of an account.[3] Such liability may follow the taking of three types of account: the account in common form; the account on the basis of wilful default; and the account of profits. The account in common form is typically sought and taken to expose unauthorised disbursements of trust assets: where such an unauthorised disbursement is identified upon the taking of a common account, the beneficiary may falsify the disbursement in question,[4] and the trustee is then personally liable to an order requiring that the assets be restored to the extent of the unauthorised disbursement. The account on the basis of wilful default typically exposes the extent to which a trustee has, in breach of duty, failed to benefit a trust fund: where an account on the basis of wilful default reveals such a failing the beneficiary may surcharge the account, and again the trustee is then personally liable to an order to pay money into the fund to compensate for the lost benefit. The account of profits is suited to revealing unauthorised profits obtained by a trustee within the scope of his or her fiduciary office; following the taking of this sort of account the trustee is liable to an order to disgorge the profits, subject to any allowance that the court makes in its discretion in his or her favour.

---

3 Here I draw on the formulation in *Agricultural Land Management Ltd* v. *Jackson (No. 2)* (2014) 48 W.A.R. 1, [334]; [2014] WASC 102 (Edelman J.), clearly distinguishing the process of taking the account from the relief to which that process may lead. My understanding of the different types of account has been greatly influenced by Edelman J.'s judgment and that of Lord Millett N.P.J. in *Libertarian Investments Ltd* v. *Hall* (2013) 16 H.K.C.F.A.R. 61.

4 The beneficiary may also adopt the unauthorised disbursement, for example, where the disbursement may be traced into a valuable asset: *Libertarian Investments Ltd* v. *Hall* (2013) 16 H.K.C.F.A.R. 61, [169].

In relation to the account in common form, equity's traditional view is that the liability of a trustee who has made an unauthorised disbursement is a type of primary liability, analogous to liability for a debt or to an order for specific performance.[5] Thus, when a trustee is liable on the taking of a common account, inquiries into whether an unauthorised disbursement caused any loss to the beneficiary are irrelevant; questions of causation do not arise when primary liability is imposed. The liability is simply to restore to the fund the unauthorised disbursement. In contrast, when an account is taken on the basis of wilful default, questions of causation are relevant because, in order for a trust fund to be placed in the position it would have been in had the trustee not acted in breach of duty, an inquiry must be undertaken to discern the current value of the investment that would have been made absent that breach.[6] As Edelman J. observed in *Agricultural Land Management Ltd v. Jackson (No. 2)*, the irrelevance of causation in cases where a common account is taken shows that these cases are 'fundamentally different' from cases of wilful default.[7] The situation in relation to accounts of profits is complex, and there are divergent views as to whether trustee liability on the taking of that sort of account is primary liability, as when a common account is taken, or demands that attention be paid to questions of causation, as when an account is taken on the basis of wilful default.[8]

For present purposes I want to focus on the common account. Why, it might be asked, does equity impose primary liability on a trustee in cases where such an account reveals an unauthorised disbursement? Why, in such cases, is equity not interested in questions of causation, to the point where a trustee will be liable for an unauthorised disbursement even though that unauthorised disbursement has caused no loss to the beneficiary? At this point in the inquiry, one of equity's distinctive normative perspectives comes into view. This perspective entails two elements. First, in its treatment of trustee liability on the taking of a common account, equity demonstrates a commitment to a certain norm associated with trusteeship, viz. a norm demanding that a trustee, when dealing with the assets of the trust, act only according to

[5] *Ex p. Adamson* (1878) 8 Ch.D. 807, 819 (James and Bagallay L.JJ.); *Agricultural Land Management Ltd v. Jackson (No. 2)* (2014) 48 W.A.R. 1, [336].
[6] *Libertarian Investments Ltd v. Hall* (2013) 16 H.K.C.F.A.R. 61, [170] (Lord Millett N.P.J.); L. Ho, 'An Account of Accounts' (2016) 28 S.Ac.L.J. 849, 856.
[7] (2014) 48 W.A.R. 1, [348].
[8] Contrast L. Smith, 'Fiduciary Relationships: Ensuring the Loyal Exercise of Judgement on Behalf of Another' (2014) 130 L.Q.R. 608 and G. Virgo, *The Principles of Equity and Trusts*, 3rd edn (Oxford University Press, 2016), 525–33.

the mandate delivered by the terms of his or her trust.[9] From a perspective informed by this norm, the fact that a disbursement is not mandated is in itself sufficient reason for equity to intervene and impose liability on a trustee, irrespective of any other facts about the case; the failure to adhere to the mandate is the only salient fact, and facts about consequences that might or might not have been caused by the disbursement are irrelevant. Secondly, in cases where a common account is taken, equity expresses its commitment to a norm demanding only mandated performance by guaranteeing conformity with that norm. As Lusina Ho has pointed out, equity's strategy here is to respond to breaches of the norm demanding only mandated performance by ordering the trustee to act so that the beneficiary's position is as if the mandated performance had occurred at the time when the unauthorised disbursement was made.[10] This guarantee of mandated performance is the signature of equity's distinctive normative perspective in cases where a common account is taken.

In recent years, courts in parts of the Commonwealth have begun to depart from equity's guarantee of mandated performance in common account cases.[11] In her influential judgment in *Canson Enterprises Ltd v. Boughton & Co.*,[12] McLachlin J. of the Supreme Court of Canada considered that where a defaulting fiduciary has caused loss to his or her beneficiary, equity should apply rules different from the rules that apply in the law of torts or the law of contracts.[13] But while McLachlin J.'s judgment seemed to accept that equity ought to adopt a distinctive approach when dealing with defaulting fiduciaries, that judgment also assumed that all monetary orders against a defaulting trustee are orders to compensate for loss caused by breach of duty, an assumption that is difficult to reconcile with equity's guarantee of mandated performance in cases where a defaulting fiduciary is subject to a

---

[9] This norm is part of the package that Charles Mitchell calls 'stewardship': C. Mitchell, 'Stewardship of Property and Liability to Account' [2014] Conv. 215, 215–16.

[10] Ho, 'An Account of Accounts', [13]. See also J. Getzler, '"As if": Accountability and Counter-factual Trust' (2011) 91 B.U.L. Rev. 973.

[11] How best to understand doctrinally these recent developments remains debatable: contrast M. Conaglen, 'Equitable Compensation for Breach of Trust: Off *Target*' (2016) 40 M.U.L.R. 126 and P. G. Turner, 'Want of Causation as a Defence to Liability for Misapplication of Trust Assets', in P. Davies, S. Douglas and J. Goudkamp (eds), *Defences in Equity* (Oxford: Hart, 2018), ch. 9. All evidently agree that the recent developments depart from equity's traditional view.

[12] [1991] 3 S.C.R. 534.   [13] Ibid., 556.

common account.[14] Moreover, in the English case of *Target Holdings Ltd v. Redferns*,[15] where there was an unauthorised disbursement of trust assets, Lord Browne-Wilkinson framed the question for decision as follows:

> Is the trustee liable to compensate the beneficiary not only for losses caused by the breach but also for losses which the beneficiary would, in any event, have suffered even if there had been no breach?[16]

This framing of the question for decision, invoking the conceptual architecture of breach of duty, causation and loss, cannot be reconciled with equity's traditional readiness in cases where a common account is taken to order a trustee to perform his or her mandate irrespective of questions of causation. From the perspective of equity's guarantee of mandated performance, an exercise of comparing the consequences of the trustee's actions with consequences that would have been generated in a counterfactual world in which the trustee acted differently is a distraction.

The departure from equity's guarantee of mandated performance is also clear in the recent decision of the United Kingdom Supreme Court in *A.I.B. Group (U.K.) Plc v. Mark Redler & Co. Solicitors*,[17] another case in which there was an unauthorised disbursement of trust assets and a disagreement about the extent to which the beneficiary's loss was caused by that action. Lord Reed J.S.C.'s judgment demonstrated some degree of sensitivity to the fact that equity takes a distinctive approach to cases where defaulting trustees have caused loss to their beneficiaries. However, Lord Reed J.S.C. did not endorse equity's traditional view that questions of causation are altogether irrelevant in cases where a common account is taken; rather, in asserting that 'the loss must be caused by the breach of trust',[18] he confirmed his view that questions of causation are relevant in cases of falsification, even if they require the application of distinctive principles shaped in light of equity's purposes when imposing liability on defaulting trustees.[19] Lord Toulson J.S.C. also expressed the view that questions of causation are relevant:

> It is one thing to speak of an 'equitable debt or liability in the nature of a debt' in a case where a breach of trust has caused a loss; it is another thing for equity to impose or recognise an equitable debt in circumstances where the

[14] L. Smith, 'The Measurement of Compensation Claims against Trustees and Fiduciaries', in E. Bant and M. Harding (eds), *Exploring Private Law* (Cambridge University Press, 2010), 369–73.
[15] [1996] A.C. 421.   [16] Ibid., 428.   [17] [2015] A.C. 1503; [2014] UKSC 58.
[18] Ibid., [136].   [19] Ibid., [136]–[138], and see also [92]–[93].

financial position of the beneficiaries, actual or potential, would have been the same if the trustee had properly performed its duties.

. . .

[A] monetary award which reflected neither loss caused nor profit gained by the wrongdoer would be penal.[20]

These statements represent an unequivocal departure from equity's guarantee of mandated performance.

What are we to make of these developments? From one point of view they are to be welcomed as bringing greater order to the law. In his seminal essay on fusion, Andrew Burrows identifies trustees' liability on the taking of a common account as within an area of private law in which 'common law and equity do not co-exist coherently'.[21] For Burrows, in this area of private law, the common law and equity should be brought into alignment – fused – so that the law will be coherent and like cases treated alike.[22] However, once we have a sense of equity's distinctive normative perspective in cases where a common account is taken, Burrows's appeals to coherence and procedural justice seem difficult to sustain. Equity's perspective, as reflected in its guarantee of mandated performance, identifies certain facts as salient, whereas common law perspectives, with their interest in questions of breach of duty, causation and loss, identify certain other facts as salient. In these circumstances, for equity to treat a case differently than the common law is not incoherent; it is a reflection of equity's different underpinning normative concerns, just as differential treatment of a set of facts by the law of torts and the law of contracts is entirely coherent given the different normative concerns of those two bodies of law.[23] Moreover, in these circumstances any constraint that like cases be treated alike seems not to be activated; rather, to the extent that the common law constitutes a case for decision in one way and equity constitutes a case for decision in another, different, way, the two cases are not alike. After all, facts are not out there in the world with their own, inbuilt,

[20] Ibid., [61], [64].
[21] Burrows, 'We do This at Common Law', 6. The discussion of common account cases is at 10–12.
[22] See ibid., 4 ('There are numerous instances of inconsistencies between common law and equity; and to support fusion seems self-evident, resting, as it does, on not being slaves to history and on recognizing the importance of coherence in the law and of "like cases being treated alike"').
[23] See J. Raz, 'The Relevance of Coherence', in his *Ethics in the Public Domain: Essays in the Morality of Law and Politics* (Oxford: Clarendon, 1994), 277, arguing that the most that can be expected from a legal system is 'local' rather than global coherence.

salience. It is only once they are interpreted that they come to have any meaning at all.

So there seems no reason to accept Burrows's view that the departure from equity's guarantee of mandated performance in recent cases is a welcome development in light of the value of coherence or a principle of procedural justice. However, in trying to work out whether those developments are desirable or a matter for regret it also seems insufficient simply to point to the fact that, in common account cases, equity has operated via a guarantee of mandated performance and is to that extent uninterested in questions of causation. After all, it might be argued that this perspective needlessly renders the legal system obscure,[24] or is based on a misunderstanding of the values and goals in play in cases of unauthorised disbursements of trust funds, or is inconsistent with a sound account of private law adjudication.[25] In order to meet challenges like these it is necessary to do more than demonstrate the weakness of Burrows's arguments. It is necessary to argue that equity's distinctive normative perspective in cases where a common account is taken is a good or useful perspective to be maintained and deployed in those cases. I believe that such an argument is available in light of the important political ideal of personal autonomy.

If people are to enjoy autonomy, certain conditions must obtain.[26] Among those conditions are that people should have an adequate range of options to choose from in fashioning a self-determining path through life.[27] The constitution and maintenance of such options depends on a range of social, economic and cultural factors. Many, indeed most, of those factors lie beyond the legal system, but crucially for present purposes some of them lie within it. For example, the civil peace and order of a community under law is a key condition for the constitution and maintenance of the full range of options

---

[24] The charge is prominent in Peter Birks's writings on equity: e.g., P. Birks, 'Equity in the Modern Law: An Exercise in Taxonomy' (1996) 26 U.W.A.L. Rev. 1. Note also *Glazier Holdings Pty Ltd* v. *Australian Men's Health Pty Ltd* (No. 2) [2001] NSWSC 6, [38] (language of falsification and surcharging 'arcane').

[25] According to certain accounts of private law adjudication, the fact that equity seems not to operate by corrective justice in common account cases would be cause for concern: see, for example, E. J. Weinrib, *The Idea of Private Law*, 2nd edn (Oxford University Press, 2012); A. Beever, *Forgotten Justice* (Oxford University Press, 2013). For an explanation of the proposition that equity eschews corrective justice in common account cases: M. Harding, 'Constructive Trusts and Distributive Justice', in E. Bant and M. Bryan (eds), *Principles of Proprietary Remedies* (Pyrmont: Thomson Reuters, 2013), 22–23.

[26] The vision of political morality that underpins the argument of this part of the chapter is set out in J. Raz, *The Morality of Freedom* (Oxford: Clarendon, 1986), chs 14 and 15.

[27] Ibid., 372.

that the members of that community might access and with which they might engage. To take another example, the law of contracts is one of the central resources on which people may draw in order to generate new normative frameworks for choice and action;[28] by entering into contracts supported by law, people may create normative opportunities for themselves and others – including opportunities to be bound to specific obligations – that would not otherwise be possible.[29] Providing a law of contracts to people within a jurisdiction thus seems a significant way in which a legal system may contribute to the overall conditions of autonomy.

Just like the law of contracts, the part of equity that is the law of trusts may be viewed as a source of normative opportunity.[30] One of the key insights of law and economics scholarship on trusts law is that trusts are packages of norms which people may use in a modular way in ordering their affairs.[31] For economists, such packages are appealing because they enable people to put in place legally binding arrangements that will redound to their welfare without incurring certain transaction, monitoring and enforcement costs.[32] But one need not adopt a law and economics perspective to grasp the value in

---

[28] Of course, it is not the only one, and indeed part of the distinctive value of contracts may lie in the opportunity that they offer to generate normative frameworks for action on terms different from those available through other social practices. See further, in relation to the distinction between promises and contracts: D. Kimel, *From Promise to Contract: Towards a Liberal Theory of Contract* (Oxford: Hart, 2003).

[29] For reflections on the outworking of this basic insight for the design of contract law: H. Dagan, 'Autonomy, Pluralism and Contract Law Theory' (2013) 76(2) Law & Contemp. Probs. 19; H. Dagan and M. Heller, *The Choice Theory of Contracts* (Cambridge University Press, 2017).

[30] This is a reminder that, contrary to some leading accounts of equity, equity is not purely remedial in character: see further P. B. Miller, 'Equity as Supplemental Law', in D. Klimchuk, I. Samet and H. E. Smith (eds), *Philosophical Foundations of the Law of Equity* (Oxford University Press, forthcoming).

[31] Two qualifications are in order here. First, in talking about trusts as packages of norms, I refer only to express trusts. Whether resulting and constructive trusts are to be understood in a similar way is a large and much-debated question: see, for example, W. Swadling, 'The Fiction of the Constructive Trust' [2011] C.L.P. 399. Secondly, while express trusts are always packages of norms, the composition of the package varies depending on the type of express trust in view. Indeed, there is much work to be done thinking creatively about the taxonomy of express trusts in light of their propensity to constitute valuable options that may be the subject of autonomous choice. In this regard, inspiration may be drawn from the important work in relation to contracts of Dagan and Heller, *The Choice Theory of Contracts*.

[32] See, for example, J. H. Langbein, 'The Secret Life of the Trust: The Trust as an Instrument of Commerce' (1997) 107 Yale L.J. 165, 182–83. Langbein's focus is on the fiduciary characterisation of trusts; the focus is therefore only on some trusts, because certain (express) trusts (such as bare custodial trusts) are not fiduciary in character. That said, Langbein's emphasis on the packaging of norms is one that is appropriate to all trusts.

packaging norms in trusts. One may understand that value in light of the political ideal of autonomy and the conditions on which it depends. Constituting trusts as packages of norms and then enabling people to organise their affairs on the basis of those packages enables people to tap into options in relation to a range of transactional, asset management and wealth distribution goals that would not otherwise be available to them. Specifically, people are thus enabled to put in place arrangements by which their assets are held, controlled and distributed by others with the assurance that the others will be subject to the 'irreducible core of obligations' of trusteeship of which Millett L.J. spoke in *Armitage* v. *Nurse*,[33] including in the usual case 'the duty ... to perform the trusts honestly and in good faith for the benefit of the beneficiaries'.[34] The appeal of such options is manifest; trusts have been and continue to be widely used in a variety of social and economic settings, so much so that the development of the trust as a legal institution with its own distinctive identity is sometimes spoken of as one of the most significant achievements of English law.[35]

None of this is to suggest that autonomy necessarily depends on a law of trusts and the associated opportunity to subject others to norms of trusteeship. It is perfectly possible to imagine a legal system that fully supports autonomy and yet does not recognise trusts at all.[36] But in thinking about the value of the options that the law of trusts makes available in light of the political ideal of autonomy, the proper backdrop is not a tabula rasa on which a legal system is being drawn in a way that best stands to promote autonomy all things considered. The proper backdrop is the complex of social, economic and cultural conditions in which we find ourselves today. Given this picture, and the indisputable and enormous role that the trust plays in it, it seems scarcely credible to deny that trusts are inextricably connected with a range of important options that may be the subject of self-determining choice and therefore contribute to the conditions of autonomy. A moment's reflection on the importance of trusts to the pursuit of a range of important projects and goals,

---

[33] [1998] Ch. 241.
[34] Ibid. I should add that the options extend to people subjecting themselves to norms of trusteeship in cases where trusts are declared. For simplicity, in the text I refer to cases where trusts are established by imposing trusteeship on others.
[35] This, of course, was Maitland's view: Maitland, *Equity*, 23; F. W. Maitland, 'The Unincorporate Body', in H. A. L. Fisher (ed.), *The Collected Papers of Frederick William Maitland* (Cambridge University Press, 1911), vol. 3, 272.
[36] On the extent to which trusts are in fact recognised by the legal systems of the world, see generally L. Smith (ed.), *The Worlds of the Trust* (Cambridge University Press, 2013).

including saving for retirement, passing on wealth upon death, promoting public benefit and pooling wealth to maximise financial returns, supports this claim.

Where does equity's guarantee of mandated performance fit into this overall picture of the value of the law of trusts as a source of autonomy-supporting options? I want to suggest that the guarantee of mandated performance has particular value because of the signal it sends to those who would set up trusts, and to trustees as well, about the seriousness with which equity takes the norm demanding that trustees act only within their mandate when dealing with trust assets. This signal is apt to serve two related functions. First, it gives assurance to those who would set up trusts that they may have a high degree of confidence in achieving the goals they wish to achieve through their chosen structure. There are reasons to think that such assurance is especially valuable to those who are contemplating giving title and control of their assets to others so as to benefit certain persons or purposes. And secondly, the signal makes clear to trustees precisely what is expected of them in carrying out the terms of the trust, and precisely what consequences will follow should they fail to do this. As a result, trustees are more likely to proceed cautiously when dealing with trust assets, aiming to ensure that they act only in ways mandated by the terms of the trust. To the extent that trustees exhibit this sort of caution, the assurance given to those who would set up trusts that they will be able to achieve their goals through their chosen structure is augmented. In these ways, equity's guarantee of mandated performance in cases where a common account is taken may be viewed as one aspect of a larger project of promoting the integrity of valuable social and economic institutions and frameworks for action.[37]

To my mind, this argument about the signalling function of equity's guarantee of mandated performance in common account cases supplies reasons to be cautious about Lord Browne-Wilkinson's suggestion in *Target Holdings* that, in settings where trusts are deployed to facilitate transactions, equity should take a different approach to norms governing trustees' dealings with trust assets from the approach it takes in cases of more traditional enduring trusts. Lord Browne-Wilkinson identified the guarantee of mandated performance as an example of a rule well-suited to traditional trusts but

---

[37] Paul Finn identifies this aim with fiduciary law as well: '[The fiduciary principle] originates, self-evidently, in public policy: in a view of desired social behaviour for the end this achieves. To maintain the integrity and the utility of those relationships in which the (or a) role of one party is perceived to be the service of the interests of the other, it insists upon a fine loyalty in that service': P. D. Finn, 'The Fiduciary Principle', in T. G. Youdan (ed.), *Equity, Fiduciaries and Trusts* (Toronto: Carswell, 1989), 54.

inappropriate to trusts in transactional settings; he also said that, as a transactional trust does not survive the transaction which it helps to facilitate, there is
no justification for requiring the trustee of such a trust to restore the trust fund
once the transaction is complete and that compensation is sufficient to satisfy
the beneficiary's claim at that moment in time.[38] But a focus on what will
satisfy the beneficiary's claim *ex post* risks neglecting the important signalling
function of equity's guarantee of mandated performance *ex ante*. This signalling function seems just as valuable in relation to transactional trusts as it is in
relation to traditional trusts. Indeed, given that transactional trusts often arise
and are administered in complex and fast-changing settings, in circumstances
where opportunities for monitoring trustees are limited, and against the
backdrop of a commercial culture in which attitudes to risk are not always
characterised by caution, it seems arguable that the signalling function of
equity's guarantee of mandated performance is even more valuable in relation
to transactional trusts than in relation to traditional trusts.[39] At the very least,
the signalling function of equity's guarantee of mandated performance should
be brought into view before Lord Browne-Wilkinson's suggestion from *Target
Holdings* is endorsed in relation to transactional trusts.

To what extent does a function of constituting autonomy-enhancing institutions like the trust depend on fission; in other words, to what extent does it
depend on a sense that equity is somehow a separate component within the
legal system as a whole? This question admits of no easy answer, as the case of
equity's guarantee of mandated performance in common account cases demonstrates. After all, an interest in mandated performance is not unique to
equity; indeed, it is arguably the central normative concern of the law of
contracts. Neither is the technique of the guarantee a uniquely equitable
phenomenon;[40] it has been pointed out that the common law action in debt,
to which trustees' liability on the taking of a common account is often likened,

---

[38] [1996] A.C. 421, 434–36. Note also the discussion in *Youyang Pty Ltd* v. *Minter Ellison Morris
Fletcher* (2003) 212 C.L.R. 484, [37], [49]; [2003] HCA 15 (Gleeson C.J., McHugh, Gummow,
Kirby and Hayne JJ.); *A.I.B. Group (U.K.) Plc* v. *Mark Redler & Co. Solicitors* [2014] A.C. 1503,
[70] (Lord Toulson J.S.C.).

[39] In traditional trusts some assurance may be available through knowledge that trustees are likely
to adhere to extra-legal norms demanding diligence, prudence and so forth. For a discussion of
such norms as they applied and developed during the nineteenth century: C. Stebbings, *The
Private Trustee in Victorian England* (Cambridge University Press, 2002).

[40] Although it is arguably more prominent in equity than at common law. For example, equity
operates by a guarantee in cases where the no profit rule is invoked against a fiduciary: see
further M. Harding, 'Disgorgement of Profit and Fiduciary Loyalty', in S. Degeling and
J. N. E. Varuhas (eds), *Equitable Compensation and Disgorgement of Profit* (Oxford: Hart,
2017), ch. 2.

also operates by way of a guarantee of mandated performance.[41] Indeed, the guarantee of mandated performance in common account cases itself appears to have had common law origins.[42] So the guarantee of mandated performance is not uniquely equitable, nor does it depend in any absolute sense on the existence of a separate equity. But an argument for fission need not go so far. Rather, it seems sufficient to establish that, given prevailing conditions, the distinctive normative perspective entailed in equity's guarantee of mandated performance is promoted or supported by a legal culture in which equity is viewed as separate, at least in some ways and for some purposes. Such a legal culture might view equity as a separate legal tradition, along the lines suggested by Lionel Smith in an insightful essay.[43] In a legal culture in which equity is viewed this way, legal actors are likely to look for the value in perspectives associated with equity, even where those perspectives are not also found in common law or statutory doctrines and remedies that seem to perform similar functions within the legal system.

To my mind, recent debates about equity's guarantee of mandated performance in common account cases underscore the importance of a legal culture in which equity is viewed as a separate legal tradition to maintaining the distinctive normative perspectives associated with equity. It seems undeniable that efforts to introduce a causation inquiry into common account cases have at times been connected with efforts to bring about the fusion of common law and equity. For example, as we saw earlier, Burrows begins his approach to such cases by assuming a general case for fusion in light of coherence and procedural justice; in light of that assumption he then moves to a consideration of equity's guarantee of mandated performance, unsurprisingly finding it unjustified to the extent that it does not entail the interest in causation that is found in the common law.[44] From a starting point that does not view equity as a separate legal tradition, then, Burrows argues for the removal from the legal system of a normative perspective that has value when seen in light of an important political ideal. In contrast, if one starts to think about equity's

<hr/>

[41] Smith, 'The Measurement of Compensation Claims against Trustees and Fiduciaries', 370–71.
[42] See Ho, 'An Account of Accounts', 851–54.
[43] 'A legal tradition is a way of understanding and solving legal problems. The same legal problem may be approached in different ways by different legal traditions, even if ultimately they arrive at the same solution. They may use different terminology, and they may employ different legal abstractions as tools in the reasoning process. The result is that discourse that is intelligible within one tradition may not be intelligible within another': L. Smith, 'Fusion and Tradition', in S. Degeling and J. Edelman (eds), *Equity in Commercial Law* (Sydney: Lawbook Co., 2005), 19.
[44] Burrows, 'We do This at Common Law', 4, 10–12.

guarantee of mandated performance with a sense of equity as a separate legal tradition, one will not be disposed, as Burrows is, to evaluate that guarantee by looking sideways to what appear to be cognate doctrines of the common law (or, for that matter, cognate statutory provisions). One will instead seek to make direct connections between the doctrinal substance of the guarantee and the values, goals and purposes that underpin it; in approaching the guarantee in this way, one will be well placed to develop justifications for it that serve to bolster and promote it.

THE LIMITS OF THE ARGUMENT

The argument for fission that I have presented depends on three broad propositions: first, that equity brings distinctive normative perspectives to bear on the problems with which it deals; secondly, that these perspectives help to constitute autonomy-enhancing institutions and practices; and finally, that to some degree these perspectives are promoted or supported by a legal culture in which equity is viewed in certain ways and for certain purposes as a separate component of the legal system as a whole. In this part of the chapter, I want to point out that this argument for fission has limits. Specifically, I want to introduce a qualification to the third proposition set out earlier, viz. that to some degree the distinctive normative perspectives associated with equity are promoted or supported by a sense of equity's separateness in the legal system. The qualification is that this third proposition is only true in certain legal settings, and not in others. In other words, there are legal settings in which normative perspectives associated with equity serve to constitute autonomy-enhancing institutions and practices, but the maintenance of those institutions and practices is unlikely to be aided by a prevailing sense that equity is separate within the legal system as a whole. Indeed, in some legal settings, such a sense might even confuse and thwart the maintenance of the institutions and practices in question. Thus, my overall argument in this chapter recognises that fission is desirable only under certain conditions.

To illustrate, consider the law of charity. As is well known, this body of law was developed in Chancery over centuries and, to that extent, has been and continues to be part of equity. Charity law, as developed in equity, has three central organising ideas. The first is that purposes that are sufficiently analogous to the purposes described in the preamble of the Statute of Charitable Uses 1601[45] are marked out and identified as 'charitable' in

---

[45] 43 Eliz. I c. 4.

law.[46] In the famous case of *Commissioners for Special Purposes of Income Tax* v. *Pemsel*,[47] Lord Macnaghten interpreted this idea to mean that charitable purposes must fall within one of four 'heads': the relief of poverty, the advancement of education, the advancement of religion and other purposes beneficial to the community that are analogous to the purposes in the preamble of the Statute of Charitable Uses.[48] This interpretation has helped to constitute the bedrock of charity law ever since. The second organising idea of charity law, as developed in equity, is that in order for charitable purposes to be recognised in law they must stand to benefit the public if carried out.[49] In the case of purposes within the fourth head as set out in *Pemsel*, this may mean an inquiry into any benefits and detriments associated with carrying out the purpose in question.[50] In the case of all purposes except for those within the first head from *Pemsel*, charity law's public benefit requirement means an inquiry into whether the class that stands to benefit from the purpose being carried out constitutes the public or a sufficient section of the public.[51] The third organising idea underpinning equitable charity law is that the pursuit of charitable purposes for the public benefit is to be enabled and encouraged by the legal system. Equity makes available to those who carry out charitable purposes for the public benefit legal facilities that are usually not otherwise available, such as the facility of setting up a purpose trust in perpetuity.[52]

In short, then, through charity law equity sets out a vision of what count legally as charitable purposes for the public benefit and enables the pursuit of those purposes through the provision of certain legal facilities. The normative perspective informing this project is highly distinctive. Take the first and the third organising ideas of equitable charity law to which I have just referred. Equitable charity law highlights certain types of purpose as bearing special

[46] The key case is *Morice* v. *Bishop of Durham* (1804) 9 Ves. Jun. 399, 405; (1805) 10 Ves. Jun. 522, 541.

[47] [1891] A.C. 531.   [48] Ibid., 583.

[49] The historical development of this requirement is surveyed in M. Mills, 'The Development of the Public Benefit Requirement for Charitable Trusts in the Nineteenth Century' (2016) 37 J.L.H. 269.

[50] See *National Anti-Vivisection Society* v. *Inland Revenue Commissioners* [1948] A.C. 31, 41–49 (Lord Wright). Purposes within the first three heads are typically assumed to be beneficial as opposed to detrimental: see *R. (Independent Schools Council)* v. *Charity Commission for England and Wales* [2012] Ch. 214, [54]–[71]; [2011] UKUT 421.

[51] *Oppenheim* v. *Tobacco Securities Trust Co. Ltd* [1951] A.C. 297, 306 (Lord Simonds). The requirement in relation to purposes within the first head is described in the judgment of Lord Cross in *Dingle* v. *Turner* [1972] A.C. 601, 616–23.

[52] It is worth noting that at times this facilitative stance has been overridden by the legislature: see the discussion of the Mortmain Act 1736 (U.K.), 9 Geo. II c. 36, in G. Jones, *History of the Law of Charity 1532–1827* (Cambridge University Press, 1969), 109–19, 128–33.

legal meaning as 'charitable', and then extends legal facilities only to those who pursue those types of purpose and not to those who pursue other types of purpose. In these ways, equitable charity law reveals a commitment to normative underpinnings that are absent from contract law and property law; in those latter bodies of law, people are typically enabled to pursue whatever types of purpose they choose (within the limits of lawfulness and public policy).[53] Thus, an association may be formed for the purpose of promoting the breeding and racing of homing pigeons, but a testamentary trust for that purpose will be invalid because the purpose is not analogous to anything in preamble to the Statute of Charitable Uses and therefore is not charitable in law.[54] Moreover, equitable charity law shows itself to be at odds with the normative underpinnings of much public law, according to which state institutions should not be in the business of articulating and promoting conceptions of the good, at least where reasonable people disagree about such matters.[55]

The normative underpinnings of equitable charity law's second organising idea – its public benefit requirement – are also distinctive. This is because the public benefit requirement helps to support a particular mode of social interaction: altruism. Altruism may be contrasted with self-interest on the one hand, and loyalty on the other. The altruist does good for others not in order to receive any return or reward[56] nor because of special ties or affection;[57] the altruist is moved by the thought of doing good for others per se. Through its insistence that the class that stands to benefit from the pursuit of a charitable purpose must be the public or a sufficient section of the public, equitable charity law enables and encourages altruism understood in the way

---

[53] This is a simplistic view of the normative underpinnings of contract law and property law, but it will suffice for the purpose of drawing the contrast I wish to draw here.

[54] The example is drawn from *Royal National and Agricultural and Industrial Association v. Chester* (1974) 48 A.L.J.R. 304.

[55] See generally J. Rawls, *Political Liberalism*, rev. edn (New York, NY: Columbia University Press, 2005).

[56] See R. A. Epstein, *Principles for a Free Society: Reconciling Individual Liberty with the Common Good* (Reading, MA: Perseus, 1998), ch. 5, esp. at, 135–38. It is a presupposition of classical economic theory that human interactions are always to be understood as exchanges; this has led some economists to insist that altruism entails a welfare gain for the altruist in the form of a 'warm inner glow': see J. Andreoni, 'Giving with Impure Altruism: Applications to Charity and Ricardian Equivalence' (1989) 97 J. Pol. Econ. 1447. However, in the absence of argument there seems no reason to accept a presupposition that human interactions are always to be understood as exchanges, and therefore no reason to assume that altruism must entail any welfare gain for the altruist: see further A. K. Sen, 'Rational Fools: A Critique of the Behavioural Foundations of Economic Theory' (1977) 6 Phil. and Pub. Aff. 317.

[57] See J. Gardner, 'The Virtue of Charity and Its Foils', in C. Mitchell and S. R. Moody (eds), *Foundations of Charity* (Oxford: Hart, 2000), 20–24.

I have just described. For example, a purpose of generating private profit via the production of beneficial outcomes for others fails to satisfy the public benefit requirement and cannot be recognised as a charitable purpose as a result.[58] In this way, equitable charity law refuses to facilitate the production of beneficial outcomes in self-interested ways. Similarly, the public benefit requirement demands that charitable purposes stand to benefit the public or a section of the public as opposed to some private class with a shared employment, family or associational tie;[59] in this way, albeit imperfectly, equitable charity law tries to ensure that charitable purposes are not pursued out of a sense of loyalty to the employer, family or association in question.[60]

Elsewhere I have argued at length that the distinctive normative perspective of equitable charity law – and the associated project of facilitating and encouraging the altruistic pursuit of purposes bearing a particular legal meaning as 'charitable' – has considerable value when seen in light of the political ideal of autonomy.[61] Through charity law, equity helps to constitute a range of options associated with the identification of certain types of purpose as charitable in law. It enables trustees of charitable trusts to generate social meaning for their activities; it also enables donors to such trusts, and others, to tap into this social meaning when making choices and interpreting action. For example, many donors will give only to charities; without the legal structure that constitutes certain types of purpose as charitable in law, the distinction on which such a donor choice depends cannot be drawn. Moreover, and perhaps more significantly, through charity law equity helps to sustain and promote altruism as a mode of social interaction. Earlier, I pointed out that one of the conditions of autonomy is that people have an adequate range of options to choose from in living a self-determined life. Such an adequate range includes diversity not only in goals and end states, but also in ways of achieving those goals and end states.[62] A society in which people were able to deal with each other only on the basis of one set of norms and understandings would be of considerable concern in light of the political ideal of autonomy, all else being

---

[58] *Incorporated Council of Law Reporting of the State of Queensland* v. *Federal Commissioner of Taxation* (1971) 125 C.L.R. 659, 669–70 (Barwick C.J.); *Incorporated Council of Law Reporting for England and Wales* v. *A.-G.* [1972] Ch. 73, 86 (Russell L.J.).
[59] *Oppenheim* v. *Tobacco Securities Trust Co. Ltd* [1951] A.C. 297, 306 (Lord Simonds).
[60] See further M. Harding, *Charity Law and the Liberal State* (Cambridge University Press, 2014), 94–97.
[61] Ibid.
[62] See H. Dagan, 'Pluralism and Perfectionism in Private Law' (2012) 112 Colum. L. Rev. 1409, 1424 ('law should facilitate (within limits) the coexistence of various social spheres embodying different modes of valuation').

equal. Thus, equity's contribution to the maintenance of diversity in modes of social interaction, via its support for and promotion of altruism in charity law, may be viewed as autonomy-enhancing and valuable to that extent.[63]

Earlier I said that my argument for fission depends on three broad propositions: first, that equity brings distinctive normative perspectives to bear on the problems with which it deals; secondly, that these perspectives help to constitute autonomy-enhancing institutions and practices; and, finally, that these perspectives are promoted or supported by a legal culture in which equity is viewed in some ways and for some purposes as separate. I hope to have said enough to suggest that in the case of equitable charity law, the first two of these propositions hold true. The third proposition, on the other hand, is more problematic; given the way in which charity law has developed, it does not seem clear that the distinctive project of equitable charity law is enhanced by fission. As is well known, equitable charity law has since the nineteenth century been adopted in the interpretation of tax statutes.[64] It has been so adopted in order to extend favourable tax treatment to those who pursue charitable purposes for the public benefit.[65] To this extent, equity's project of promoting the altruistic pursuit of purposes identified as charitable in law has been taken up and embedded in tax law and has thereby migrated from equity into statute law. More recently, across the Commonwealth, statutes have been enacted setting out heads of charity and public benefit requirements that to a large extent reflect and build on equitable charity law.[66] Once again, such statutes are designed to promote the altruistic pursuit of charitable purposes, and to this extent it may be said that normative underpinnings of equitable charity law are now also associated with statutory charity law.

In today's legal setting, in which equitable and statutory charity law are deeply interconnected, it seems unlikely that the distinctive normative

---

[63] Indeed, given the dominance of norms and understandings associated with the market as a mode of a social interaction in public life and discourse, it is arguable that charity law's emphasis on altruism is an especially important contribution to the conditions of autonomy in society. For further discussion of the dominance of market norms and understandings: R. M. Titmuss, *The Gift Relationship: From Human Blood to Social Policy* (London: Allen & Unwin, 1970); P. Singer, 'Altruism and Commerce: A Defence of Titmuss against Arrow' (1973) 2 Phil. & Pub. Aff. 312; M. J. Sandel, *What Money Can't Buy: The Moral Limits of Markets* (London: Penguin, 2013).

[64] See, for example, *Commissioners for Special Purposes of Income Tax v. Pemsel* [1891] A.C. 531; *Chesterman v. Federal Commissioner of Taxation* [1926] A.C. 128.

[65] For example, charities have been exempt from income tax from the time it was first raised: M. Gousmett, 'A Short History of the Charitable Purposes Exemption from Income Tax of 1799', in J. Tiley (ed.), *Studies in the History of Tax Law: Volume 5* (Oxford: Hart, 2012), 125.

[66] See, for example, Charities Act 2005 (N.Z.); Charities Act 2011 (U.K.); Charities Act 2013 (Cth).

perspective associated with equitable charity law is promoted or supported by a continuing sense that equity is separate within the legal system.[67] In the case of trustees' liability on the taking of a common account, recent developments have represented a threat to the perspective traditionally brought to bear in equity; in these circumstances, where it is necessary to argue for the maintenance of that perspective, fission may perform useful work. In contrast, in the case of charity law, recent developments have either augmented the scope of or reinforced equitable charity law's project of promoting the altruistic pursuit of charitable purposes. There is no work for fission to do in defence of that project, precisely because the project is not under any threat.

That said, a note of caution is in order because equitable and statutory charity law need not be aligned forever around the one normative perspective, and circumstances may obtain in which it is desirable for equitable charity law and statutory charity law each to develop differently in response to different normative considerations. For example, given that equitable charity law is embedded in the law of trusts, it may be appropriate for that body of law to develop a more accommodating approach to the recognition of charitable purposes for the public benefit, so as to respond more fully to the value of settlors' autonomy in choosing the terms on which their assets are to be held and used. At the same time, given that statutory charity law applies in tax settings, it may be appropriate for that body of law to develop a more restrictive approach, so as to ensure that the revenue is protected to some sufficient degree.[68] Indeed, it is possible to grasp the value in a legal system in which equitable and statutory charity law diverge to such an extent that charity law ceases to exist altogether, say because the law of trusts recognises as valid purpose trusts of all types,[69] while tax concessions are extended only to those who pursue a range of purposes much narrower than the range of purposes that are presently identified in law as charitable.[70]

---

[67] This statement should be qualified. Equitable charity law is embedded in trusts law and, as I argued earlier, trusts law and its autonomy-enhancing potential depend in key ways on fission. Thus, when I say that the distinctive normative perspective of equitable charity law does not depend on fission, I mean this only insofar as equitable charity law is charity law and not insofar as it is trusts law.

[68] In *Central Bayside General Practice Association Ltd v. Commissioner of State Revenue* (2006) 228 C.L.R. 168, [76]–[120]; [2006] HCA 43, Kirby J. expressed some sympathy for such a development in the interpretation of tax statutes.

[69] See further G. Dal Pont, 'Why Define "Charity"? Is the Search for Meaning Worth the Effort?' (2002) 8 Third Sector Rev. 5.

[70] See further M. Chesterman, 'Foundations of Charity Law in the New Welfare State' (1999) 62 M.L.R. 333. As Chesterman points out, in Australia, this development has already occurred in relation to tax deductions for charitable gifts; such deductions are available only where the gifts

The possibility of divergence in the normative perspectives of equitable and statutory charity law seems a relatively remote one in current legal settings. However, in my home country of Australia, the possibility may become less remote in the years to come. In Australia, the Commonwealth Parliament enacted a new Charities Act in 2013; this statute sets out heads of charity and a public benefit requirement that apply for the purposes of Commonwealth law. As I mentioned earlier, the Charities Act 2013 is designed to build on extant equity jurisprudence, but in some key respects its terms differ substantially from that jurisprudence. The charity law in the Charities Act 2013 applies when the question arises whether an organisation is charitable for the purposes of Commonwealth law, most notably Commonwealth tax law. At the same time, in the states and territories of Australia tax statutes that refer to charitable purposes or some cognate term typically refer to equitable charity law. And equitable charity law continues to apply, unaffected by statutory developments, when a state or territory court has to consider the validity of a purpose trust. However, state and territory legislatures have increasingly sought to depart from equitable charity law when giving meaning to the term charity and its cognates in tax statutes.[71] And there is a move afoot to harmonise charity law for tax purposes across the federation, so that tax statutes, whether at Commonwealth, state or territory level, pick up the understanding of charity set out in the Charities Act 2013.[72] If this harmonisation is successful, or the trend of departing from equitable charity law when drafting and interpreting state and territory tax statutes continues, then the likelihood will increase that the normative underpinnings of equitable charity law might diverge from those of statutory charity law.[73]

If such divergence were to occur, then a case for fission might emerge in relation to charity law, even though such a case seems not to be made out under current conditions. Divergence would mean that the autonomy-enhancing options currently made available by charity law would change. In equitable charity law, those options might be augmented; in statutory

---

are to 'deductible gift recipients', a category that in some respects is much narrower than the category of organisations pursuing 'charitable' purposes. See further Income Tax Assessment Act 1997 (Cth), Div. 30.

[71] See further I. Murray, 'The Taming of the Charitable Shrew: State Roll Back of Charity Tax Concessions' (2016) 27 Public L. Rev. 54.

[72] See Australian Charities and Not-for-Profits Commission, 'A Common Charity Definition?' conference paper (26 July 2016), available: www.acnc.gov.au.

[73] Although this would depend on the extent to which state and territory courts would seek to reason by analogy with the Charities Act 2013 when developing equitable charity law: I deal more fully with this point in M. Harding, 'Equity and Statute in Charity Law' (2015) 9 J. Eq. 167, 182–87.

charity law they might be diminished or their meaning changed in some way. There would be work to do articulating the distinctive normative perspective associated with the law of purpose trusts, and illuminating that perspective in contrast to the different normative perspective associated with the tax treatment of charities. This work would ensure that the autonomy-enhancing options associated with charitable trusts, and for that matter with the tax treatment of charities, continue to be sustained and promoted. Given that the law of purpose trusts is part of equity, the work might be assisted by a sense of equity's separateness within the legal system as a whole and, to the extent that this is the case, fission might be desirable. Of course, there is no reason to think that fission would be necessary to the work of elucidating and promoting distinctive normative perspectives associated with equitable charity law and statutory charity law in a world where divergence in the perspectives of those two bodies of law had occurred. Such work might be supported in other ways, through the deployment of other mediating concepts and ideas. But, as I pointed out earlier, an argument for fission need not establish that fission is a necessary condition of desirable developments in the legal system; that fission might aid such developments seems enough.

CONCLUSION

Much ink has been spilt over questions of fusion and fission; a great deal of this writing has focused on the judicature reforms of the late nineteenth century, or on the demands of coherence and procedural justice in the legal system, or on both. One conclusion that I hope may be drawn out of this chapter is that we may think productively about fusion and fission by putting questions of jurisdiction, coherence and procedural justice to one side and focusing instead on equity's functions in the contemporary legal system. Another, perhaps related, conclusion is that arguments for fission need not be in the nature of sweeping defences of equity taken as a whole; rather, such arguments can be modest, local and conditional. Nonetheless, such arguments do exist, as I hope to have demonstrated here. Finally, I think my chapter suggests that, in a post-Judicature Act world questions of fusion and fission are helpfully conceived as questions about legal culture, i.e., questions about the sort of disposition and discourse we might expect to see from legal actors in a society where the legal system is kept up to its underpinning normative commitments, sensitive to the possibility of change in those commitments and oriented to the service of overarching political ideals like personal autonomy. Fission has value in such a legal culture, even if only sometimes.

17

'Single Nature's Double Name'

The Unity of Law and Equity?

DENNIS KLINCK

In a case from 1464 – over 400 years before the Judicature Acts – counsel for the defendant made a pitch for the fusion of common law and equity, foreshadowing a debate that, as the contents of this volume attest, continues today. In an action of trespass in the Court of Common Pleas, the defendant pleaded that he conveyed the land to the plaintiff to his own use. Justice Moyle objected this was 'good ground of defence in Chancery' but not in a common law court. Catesby, for the defendant, responded that '[t]he law of Chancery is the common law of the land' and that the defence available there should be available 'here'.[1] Justice Moyle insisted upon the fission of law and equity: 'That cannot be so here in this court ... for the common law of the land is different from the law of Chancery on this point'.[2]

This exchange prefigures the broad issue of fusion *versus* fission, and hints at particular dimensions of the controversy. One is the obvious jurisdictional fact that there were separate courts applying different, if not incompatible, rules. There was also a suggestion of important procedural differences that limited the common law court's capabilities. The plaintiff's counsel, Jenney, maintained that a person's 'sufferance and will cannot be tried, for the intent of a man is uncertain, and a man should plead such matter as is or may be known to the jury'.[3] That is, the issue was not amenable to the way facts were ascertained in common law courts. The more inquisitorial or even confessional procedure of the early Chancery was better suited to getting at these matters that a jury could not 'know'. And there was the substantive point that the subject matters Chancery would concern itself with were qualitatively unlike those that common law courts would entertain. As Moyle J. observed, 'in the Chancery a man shall have remedy according to conscience upon the

---

[1] *Anon.* (1464) Y.B. 4 Ed. IV, f. 8 pl. 9, printed *Baker and Milsom*, 106.   [2] Ibid.   [3] Ibid.

intent of such a feoffment'.[4] The Chancery was concerned with internal psychological dispositions, and accounted for them in articulating and applying its rules.

Of these three distinctions, one would have expected the unification of the courts to have obviated the first two. All rules were to be applied in the same court; the 'different courts, different rules' rationale was gone. And with the harmonisation of procedures in the two courts, the second was significantly attenuated. So any consideration of the continuing separation of law and equity must primarily address the substantive issue: is equity qualitatively – or, to use Daniel Carr's term, 'intellectually'[5] – distinct from common law (including statute law)?

Before pursuing that inquiry, we must first consider what sorts of things we might mean by the terms 'equity' and 'fusion' (and by implication, its converse, 'fission'). The contributions to this volume illustrate that these concepts are ambiguous, and any analysis of the issue in play requires clarity in this regard. The matter is complicated by the fact that ingrained attitudes towards and assumptions about equity vary between jurisdictions within the common law world.[6] Communication issues may be deeper than mere questions of definition. For example, when Emily Sherwin considers 'Equity and the modern mind', we should remember that 'the modern mind', even in this context, is no unitary phenomenon.[7]

The variety in meanings of equity is evinced by the qualifiers associated with it: Aristotelian equity, moral equity, technical equity, natural equity, Chancery equity, *epieikeia*, equity in an 'ethical and somewhat nebulous sense',[8] the equity of the statute and so on. For our purposes, equity imports two different concepts.[9] First, there is Aristotelian equity: the invocation of notions of justice to make the general law more attentive to the particulars of cases, and to render outcomes satisfying our sense of what is right. This

---

4 Ibid. 5 Carr, Chapter 8.
6 For example, while Samuel Bray tells us that '[e]quity has not been offered as a course in most American law schools ["the nurseries of the profession"] since the 1960s' (Chapter 2, text before n. 34), Mark Leeming observes that New South Wales provides a 'legal environment' 'where the teaching and practice of equity flourishes' in the twenty-first century (Chapter 6, text after n. 141).
7 Sherwin, Chapter 15. Compare Turner, Chapter 1, text after n. 2, referring to the 'intellectual inheritance' that 'shapes the modern lawyer's mind'.
8 Kremer, Chapter 9, text at n. 19 (quoting H. G. Hanbury).
9 For a more nuanced discussion of the semantic range of 'equity' in this context, see D. R. Klinck, '"Nous sumus a arguer la consciens icy et nemy la ley": Equity in the Supreme Court of Canada', in J. E. C. Brierley et al. (eds), *Mélanges offerts par ses collègues de McGill à Paul-André Crépeau* (Cowansville: Yvon Blais, 1997), ch. 16.

concept probably characterised early English equity, as reflected in Christopher St German's description in the sixteenth-century *Doctor and Student*:

Equytye is a [rightwysenes[10]] that consideryth all the pertyculer cyrcumstaunces of the dede the whiche also is temperyd with the swetnes of mercye. And [such an equytye] must always be obseruyd in euery lawe of man and in euery generall rewle therof . . . And it is called also by some men epicaia. The whiche is no other thynge but an excepcyon of the lawe of god or of the lawe of reason from the generall rewles of the lawe of man: when they by reason of theyr generalytye wolde in any partyculer case Iuge agaynste the lawe of god or the lawe of reason the which excepcion is secretely vnderstande in euery generall rewle of euery posytyve lawe.[11]

On this view, equity, secretly understood in every general rule of every positive law, potentially operates whenever a positive law is applied; it is sensitive to circumstances which might make the strict or literal application of the rule inconsistent with the law itself. The criteria of its application involve something more fundamental than the decreed human law: 'the Law of God, or . . . the Law of Reason'.

Many authors in this collection take account of equity in something like this sense.[12] Carr cites Lord Stair's seventeenth-century *Institutions of the Law of Scotland* as regarding equity as 'suffusing the whole law',[13] and observes that still today '[d]iscretion, fairness and a general equitable "spirit" are undoubtedly important component of equity as understood in Scotland'.[14] Scotland is a mixed – that is civil law and common law – jurisdiction, so that the relationship of equity to law there will not exactly reflect the position in the Anglo-common law.[15] John Goldberg and Henry Smith, explicitly invoking Aristotle's definition, state that equity on their approach 'is a second-order intervention to address certain inherent deficiencies in any

---

[10] Righteousness.   [11] Plucknett and Barton, *Doctor and Student*, 95, 97.
[12] I use the expression 'something like' to indicate the presence of some broad concept of right or justice, not necessarily involving the natural law assumptions underlying, say, St German's statement.
[13] Carr, Chapter 8, text after n. 15.   [14] Ibid., text after n. 80.
[15] A classic statement of the place of equity in the civil law is that of Portalis in his discourse preliminary to the presentation of the French Civil Code: 'Equity is the return to the natural law in case of the silence, the opposition, or the obscurity of positive law' (my translation): 'Discours préliminaire prononcé lors de la présentation du projet de la commission du gouvernement', in P.-A. Fenet (ed.), *Receuil complet des travaux préparatoires du Code civil* (Paris: [s.n.], 1827), vol. I, p. 463. R. A. Newman remarks that '[i]n most civil law systems the fundamental principles of equity are applied as a matter of course in all situations in which they are relevant': 'The Hidden Equity: An Analysis of the Moral Content of the Principles of Equity' (1967) 19 Hastings L.J. 147, 147.

body of doctrine',[16] although they would appear not to accept that it suffuses the law as St German and Lord Stair might suggest. But their analysis of the fusion issue is inseparable from their conception of equity. Similarly, Sherwin critically assesses the impact of American Legal Realism, which she sees as having 'altered the dynamic of law and equity, not by eliminating equity but by bringing Aristotelian equity into the light and encouraging liberal use of it by judges'[17] – indeed, expanding 'the principles of equity across all of law'.[18]

The other main depiction of equity is Maitland's: 'that body of rules administered by our English courts of justice which, were it not for the operation of the Judicature Acts, would be administered only by courts that would be known as Courts of Equity'.[19] On this account, there would not necessarily be anything qualitatively distinctive about equity: it would consist only of a system of rules developed in a forum other than the common law courts. Thus, Sherwin observes that, for Maitland, 'there was no special association between English equity courts and Aristotelian equity'[20] whatever might have been the case in earlier times. So, for example, the project of 'regularising' equity into a system of more or less predictable rules predates Lord Nottingham, who deliberately promoted it,[21] and Lord Eldon's denial that equity involved a broad discretionary jurisdiction, rather than determinate binding rules, is notorious.[22] Kellen Funk quotes Blackstone's view that '[the systems of jurisprudence, in our courts both of law and equity], are now equally *artificial systems*, founded on the same principles of justice and positive law'.[23] Many of the contributors to this volume appear to be thinking of equity in this way.[24]

These differing ideas of what equity is will impact significantly on the way that fusion (or fission) is conceived. Reconciling equity as broad principles of justice that must somehow be integrated into positive law involves different

---

[16] Goldberg and Smith, Chapter 13, text after n. 6.   [17] Sherwin, Chapter 15, text to n. 52.
[18] Ibid., text after n. 64. She seems, with some reservations, to approve this development.
[19] Maitland, *Equity*, 1.   [20] Sherwin, Chapter 15, text after n. 18.
[21] See D. R. Klinck, 'Lord Nottingham's "Certain Measures"' (2010) 28 L.H.R. 711.
[22] E.g., *Davis* v. *Duke of Marlborough* (1819) 2 Swans. 108, 163: 'It is not the duty of Judge in equity to vary rules, or to say that rules are not to be considered as fully settled here as in a court of law.' See D. R. Klinck, 'Lord Eldon on "Equity"' (1999) 20 J.L.H. 51, which examines the stereotype and attempts to give a nuanced account of it.
[23] Funk, Chapter 3, n. 49, citing W. Blackstone, *Commentaries on the Laws of England* (Oxford: Clarendon, 1759), vol. 3, 434 (my emphasis).
[24] Perhaps Paul Perell's *The Fusion of Law and Equity* (Toronto: Butterworths, 1990) exemplifies this approach; that is, an examination of the interaction and degree of integration of equitable and common law doctrines in various particular areas of law, although he does consider ostensible general qualitative differences as well.

Dennis Klinck

considerations from joining together two bodies of positive law that might apply in factually distinguishable situations.[25]

The other basic concept whose protean significance must be addressed at this stage is fusion itself. Unless we have an appreciation of the sense in which the word is being deployed, we may find ourselves at cross purposes.

I begin this part of the analysis by considering *Canson Enterprises Ltd v. Boughton & Co.*,[26] a Supreme Court of Canada case in which the issue of fusion was explicitly explored and several different characterisations of it (and fission) were presented. The issue was, where there has been a breach of fiduciary obligation – an equitable wrong – whether it is appropriate to measure the remedy, compensation, only according to equitable principles or to the arguably more developed criteria for the award of tort damages. May a common law remedy be married to an equitable cause of action?

For the majority, La Forest J. cited Lord Diplock in *United Scientific Holdings Ltd v. Burnley Borough Council*,[27] who had repudiated Ashburner's notorious characterisation of the effect of the fusion of courts: 'the two streams of jurisdiction', that is, law and equity, 'though they run in the same channel, run side by side and do not mingle their waters'.[28] That is the fairly conventional view that the Judicature Acts effected an amalgamation of the separate institutional containers, without affecting the substantive distinction between the two bodies of law. Lord Diplock opined that this 'fluvial metaphor' – while it might at one time have had some cogency – had by 1977 become 'both mischievous and deceptive',[29] and that 'the waters of the confluent streams of law and equity have surely mingled now' like those of the Rhône and Saône after their confluence at Lyon.[30] This suggests that substantive mingling is the natural result of institutional fusion, and that conjoining of legal and equitable concepts is appropriate and perhaps inevitable.

La Forest J. apparently agreed with Lord Diplock's approach,[31] but qualified his position in a way that involves a retreat from a full-fledged intermingling. He envisaged a 'selective fusion': fusion in some areas, while fission continues in others, and varying degrees of fusion. 'There might', he said, 'be room for concern if one were indiscriminately attempting to meld the whole of the two systems. Equitable concepts like trusts, equitable estates, and consequent

---

[25] E.g., Carr, Chapter 8, text before n. 82, observes that 'Scotland's law contains a number of different understandings ... of equity, some of which are more theoretically attuned to fusion or fission respectively'.
[26] [1991] 3 S.C.R. 534.   [27] [1978] A.C. 904, 924–25.
[28] W. Ashburner, *Principles of Equity* (London: Butterworth, 1902), 23.
[29] *United Scientific Holdings Ltd v. Burnley Borough Council* [1978] A.C. 904, 925.   [30] Ibid.
[31] *Canson Enterprises Ltd v. Boughton & Co.* [1991] 3 S.C.R. 534, 585.

equitable remedies must continue to exist apart, if not in isolation from, common law rules.'[32] This suggests a tripartite division between distinctively equitable concepts, distinctively common law concepts and doctrines that can be mixed or combined. On this analysis, fusion and the degree of fusion would depend upon the compatibility of specific concepts from the two jurisdictions. Fusion would not work in the case of trusts, but would work in at least some fiduciary situations. His criterion for the mixing category is whether the common law doctrine and the corresponding equitable doctrine have different policy objectives;[33] where they do not, combining of common law redress with equitable wrongs is acceptable. He goes so far with this selective fusion as to fracture fiduciary wrongs themselves: while the common law method of measuring damages is appropriate where a fiduciary performing a *task* causes a *loss* to his principal, equitable principles must still apply where the fiduciary makes an improper gain or where the fiduciary controls the principal's property. The picture is a complex one, involving modular fusion which varies according to the doctrines in play.

McLachlin J. agreed with La Forest J. in the result, but reached that result using what she would characterise as equitable reasoning, endorsing Ashburner's position. She insisted on underlying theoretical distinctions between equity and common law – or, at least, between fiduciary obligation and tort or contract – that require their separation. She referred to 'the unique foundation and goals of equity';[34] while contract and tort contemplate essentially self-interested actors, the fiduciary concept is defined by loyalty or selflessness. The two are based on radically different assumptions about relationships. Simultaneously, she allowed that 'we may take wisdom where we find it',[35] suggesting the possibility of interchange between law and equity. However, she did not envisage mixing, but the borrowing by one system of concepts from the other, without changing the essential nature of the receiving stream. Language provides an analogy: we might assimilate a term like *raison d'être* into English but that does not make the language a hybrid of English and French. *Equitas sequitur legem*, but that does not mean equity and common law become a mixed system or that equity becomes common law.

So, we have several possible views of what fusion might entail: two separate bodies of substantive law administered in the same courts; indiscriminate mixing of the doctrines of law and equity; selective mixing of specific doctrines, depending upon particular compatibilities; one system's borrowing

---

[32] Ibid., 587.   [33] Ibid., 588.   [34] Ibid., 543.   [35] Ibid., 545.

from or imitating the other. Other possibilities are fusion by colonisation[36] (more extreme borrowing which implies a taking over of the other system) and fusion by convergence[37] (in which independent evolution results in congruent doctrines in the two systems).

A third judge in *Canson*, Stevenson J., while in 'substantial agreement' with La Forest J., seemingly applied '[equitable] principles of fairness'[38] to the fiduciary's obligation to compensate the principal for the consequences of a breach. Tellingly, Stevenson J. said that he did 'not think that the so-called fusion of law and equity has anything to do with deciding this case', and that, if it did, 'the rules of equity would prevail'.[39] This supposes the continuing substantive separateness of law and equity. Then Stevenson J. added cryptically: 'the *Judicature Acts* were not a new *Statute of Uses*'.[40]

This suggests another kind of fusion. The Statute of Uses converted equitable interests into their legal equivalents – what Sir Francis Bacon, quoting Kingsmill J., described as the 'transsubstantiation' of uses into possessions.[41] Such fusion involves not just a combining of legal and equitable doctrines, nor a straightforward legislative importation of equity, but an explicit transformation of one into the other. What Stevenson J. presumably meant was that the Judicature Acts did not have a similar effect – that is, converting equitable rules into legal rules or *vice versa*. At one level, one can readily assent to this. The Acts contemplate that there will continue to be equitable rules and legal rules. At another level, this is the very question this volume is addressing: did the legislation implicitly compromise the distinction between law and equity?

The range of meanings that fusion might have is displayed in Michael Lobban's exploration of the debates leading up to the Judicature Acts.[42] That debate went well beyond what the Acts themselves were understood to effect. Lord Hatherley's understanding of Lord Selborne's bill was that it 'did not mean any abolition of the distinction between law and equity' but had the more 'modest' aim of 'allowing one court to have charge of any case brought before it from start to end'.[43] This is similar to Ashburner's view. Lord Selborne himself apparently envisaged that the 'union of courts and

---

[36] See Kremer, Chapter 9, text after n. 178.
[37] Turner, Chapter 11, text to n. 2, notes that this is a conventional account of the development of the penalty at law and in equity. He critiques this account.
[38] *Canson Enterprises Ltd* v. *Boughton & Co.* [1991] 3 S.C.R. 534, 590.   [39] Ibid.
[40] Ibid., 591.
[41] F. Bacon, *The Learned Reading of Sir Francis Bacon ... upon the Statute of Uses* (London: Walbancke and Chapman, 1642), 26.
[42] Lobban, Chapter 4.   [43] Ibid., text after n. 112.

procedures' would be followed by 'a natural convergence of law and equity',[44] and Lord Cairns and Sir George Jessel hoped there might be 'an unproblematic fusion following naturally from the union of the present judicatures'.[45] This is what Lord Diplock, a century later, thought had occurred. Others – not speaking directly to the effect of the Judicature Acts – argued for a fusion like the transubstantiation under the Statute of Uses. Thus, in his address to the Law Amendment Society in 1851, Francis Trower argued that the legislature should declare 'that henceforth all equitable doctrines shall be Common Law doctrines likewise',[46] and Cockburn C.J. 'wished to see the distinction between law and equity removed "for-ever – even to the very name of Equity – by Equity being converted into Law"'.[47] The latter's reference to the 'very name of Equity' suggests a further dimension to the fusion/fission conundrum: the possibility that the distinction between law and equity is in some measure rhetorical. I shall return to this point later.

The ambiguity of fusion is attested by historical circumstances involving courts not immediately affected by the Judicature Acts. Several contributors describe courts that were originally unitary, in which fission of jurisdiction nevertheless occurred. Where there were not separate courts, the duality of pre-Judicature Act English courts developed. For example, Philip Girard, noting that in British North America there were several fusions, describes variants involving both unitary and non-unitary jurisdictions.[48] James McComish observes that, although there was never a separate court of equity in the Australian colony of Victoria,[49] there was fission of law and equity: 'the institutional structure of the courts was less important than the substantive content of the law they administered, in which the distinction between law and equity was preserved'.[50] Similarly, Mark Leeming traces the 'process of fission, creating separate common law and equity jurisdictions within the same court' in New South Wales,[51] although 'there was never a need to abolish existing courts and to create a single new court of common law and equity; that existed from the beginning'.[52] This phenomenon is readily accounted for by the English pedigree of the law in these places, but it reinforces the idea that institutional fusion can co-exist with substantive fission.

---

[44] Ibid., text after n. 116.   [45] Ibid., text after n. 137.
[46] C. F. Trower, 'On the Union of Law and Equity' (1851) 15 L. Rev. & Q.J. Brit. & Foreign Juris. 107, 119. Trower's position is rather ambiguous, since in the next sentence he says, 'Swallow up Law in Equity'.
[47] Selborne MSS 1865, f. 215 (7 February 1873).   [48] Girard, Chapter 5.
[49] McComish, Chapter 7.   [50] Ibid., text after n. 61.
[51] Leeming, Chapter 6, text after n. 26.   [52] Ibid., text after n. 35.

402   *Dennis Klinck*

Carr describes an analogous situation in Scotland, although equity for him means something different from what it means to Girard, McComish and Leeming. '[U]nlike in England where the dichotomy endured, there was no institutional separation of forums in which to vindicate positive rights or claim equitable assistance', in Scotland nevertheless 'an intellectual distinction was drawn between law and equity'.[53] What this means is a little unclear: Carr explains that 'the Court of Session was, and still is, commonly described as a court of law and equity'.[54] Attaching the two labels does not mean that they reflect an actual state of affairs. Earlier, Carr quotes Lord President Clyde who apparently took a different position: 'the law of Scotland has never known either distinction or conflict between common law and the principles of equity'.[55] If that is accurate, we are in the presence not so much of the fusion of two previously distinct things as of the suffusion or infusion of equity in the law.

One further version of fusion is statutory integration. We have noticed, for example, the legislative transmutation of equitable to legal property interests by the Statute of Uses, which thereafter had to be recognised by the common law courts. Aspects of this incorporation of equitable doctrine into 'the law' by legislative fiat appear elsewhere. Lobban identifies one category of pre-Judicature commentators who advocated comprehensive integration of law and equity by codification.[56] On this view, fusion would be complete, but it could not occur by spontaneous or natural development – only by deliberate enactment.

More modestly, particular equitable doctrines have been assimilated to the law by statute. For example, Turner – rejecting the convergence theory – argues that an independent common law doctrine of relief from penalties was at best inchoate, and that integration occurred via statutory adoption of equitable doctrine.[57] From one perspective, there was no fusion of common law (that is, judge-made law) and equity in this area. From another, there was ˘ incorporation of equitable principle into the law to be administered by common law courts. This could be understood as the borrowing to which McLachlin J. referred. It suggests that there is nothing essential about equity that makes it inimical to becoming law – although it leaves unspecified the relationship of legal and equitable doctrines where legislative incorporation has not occurred.

---

[53] Carr, Chapter 8, text before n. 44.   [54] Ibid.   [55] Ibid., n. 27.
[56] Lobban, Chapter 4, text to n. 50.
[57] Turner, Chapter 11. Patricia McMahon (Chapter 12) analyses the common law courts' treatment of the statutory adoption of discovery – originally a Chancery doctrine.

I introduce these different conceptualisations of fusion not to exhaust the possibilities, but to indicate the semantic variability of the term. Saying that the two systems are fused can mean something modest[58] or something thoroughgoing.

This brings us back to the question with which we began: what is it about equity that might justify our keeping it separate from law generally? What, if anything, renders it resistant or amenable to fusion or integration with law? What are the characteristic features of equity that might keep it, at least conceptually, apart from law? The contributors to this volume canvass a range of possibilities.

One is that equity addresses distinctive areas of human conduct; that is, distinctive kinds of issues. Lobban cites the report of the Chancery Commission (1852) that the 'distinct subject matter' addressed by equity would continue to require 'a distinct procedure, even if there were to be a single court'.[59] This suggests that what distinguishes equity is that its concerns differ from those of the common law.

But this does not necessarily point to a fundamental qualitative difference – only that, traditionally and today, equity and law deal with different topics. One could say that the rules of fiduciary law and contract are essentially coordinate (literally, of the same order) rules, but applicable in different situations, and distinct in that way. The same might be said of contract and tort. They deal with distinct bundles of rights and duties, and therefore are separate doctrines, but presumably are not to be categorised as different *orders* of law, laws different from each other as law, apart from dealing with different kinds of social interaction. Another way of putting this is to ask: 'Is there any reason – other than provenance or "historical accident" – to maintain the intermediate level of generality, "equity", between "law" and the particular area, "fiduciary doctrine"?' But if by 'subject-matter' is meant just the relationships that equity (rather than law) addressed, then its invocation to maintain any very significant distinction between equity and law is not particularly persuasive.[60]

Even with respect to trusts, which some see as the equitable doctrine most resistant to assimilation to law,[61] one could say that they are simply subject to a set of rules co-ordinate with common law rules. We will recall the anonymous

---

[58] Matthew Harding (Chapter 16) exemplifies this approach explicitly in arguing for 'limited fission', 'in some ways and for some purposes'.

[59] Lobban, Chapter 4, text to n. 23.

[60] Apart from identifying provenance for applying the Judicature Act's provision for conflicts.

[61] Recall La Forest J. in *Canson*, n. 32. See also Lobban, Chapter 5, text after n. 76.

case from 1464 where it was argued that uses should be understood as part of the common law of England. Arguably, uses merely modified the law in response to additional factual circumstances. So, where A enfeoffed Blackacre to B, simply, those circumstances gave rise to a set of rights in B. But where there was a further circumstance – that the feoffment was to the use of A – that reconfigured B's rights and obligations. Regarding the argument that we require separate notions of legal and equitable rights and obligations to explain the result, the answer may lie in the concept of property as a bundle of rights – with the implication that different persons may have different sticks in the bundle.[62] In the case of trusts, it may not be necessary to label these rights as 'common law' versus 'equitable'. B has rights against the whole world where B has unqualified property. But where the property is qualified, B's absolute rights are limited by certain rights that A retains against B, in relation to the thing. And, since B's rights are so modified, so will be the rights of some persons acquiring the thing from B – again depending on further factual variations.

Aspects of this issue are explored with sophistication by Ben McFarlane who, particularly referring to trusts, asks what it means for law and equity to conflict.[63] This is crucial: if law and equity conflict, then fission is unavoidable unless one or the other is simply obviated. If they do not conflict, the obstacles to integration are less daunting. McFarlane argues that they do not conflict; the rights of the trustee and the rights of the beneficiary can co-exist without any contradiction. Of course, the fact that law and equity do not conflict does not mean that they are indistinguishable. Indeed, McFarlane makes an anti-fusion argument, based not on conflict but on the fact that equity *operates* differently from the common law,[64] and that underlying equitable rationales, notably conscience,[65] differ sometimes, at least.

This takes us to our next point. Equitable rules may not be coordinate with legal rules in the way I have suggested, but may be different at some deeper – intellectual, conceptual,[66] structural[67] or operational – level. Some have suggested that the mentality or the spirit of equity is different from that of the common law.[68] Arguably, only such deeper systemic differences can

---

[62] See, e.g., Worthington, *Equity*, 2nd edn, 57 ff.   [63] McFarlane, Chapter 14.
[64] Ibid., text before n. 2, emphasising the '*means* by which equity achieves [its] results'.
[65] Ibid., text before n. 90.
[66] L. Rotman, 'The "Fusion" of Law and Equity?: A Canadian Perspective on the Substantive, Jurisdictional, or Non-Fusion of Legal and Equitable Matters' (2016) 2 C.J.C.C.L. 499, 504.
[67] McFarlane, Chapter 14, text after n. 22.
[68] So, Lobban observes that, around the time of *Judicature Acts*, some maintained that 'the very mentality of equity was distinct': Chapter 4, text after n. 8. See also W. S. Holdsworth,

justify any ongoing robust distinction between law and equity. If the norms of the two systems are just rules, having the common characteristics of all rules, one might question the utility of persisting in the broad dichotomy.

Perhaps the most radical claims for such deeper difference come from those who suggest that law and equity are essentially – that is, at a fundamental ontological level – distinct. Lobban notes that some pre-Judicature Acts commentators saw 'law and equity [as] distinct in their very nature',[69] and Leonard Rotman quotes Lord Selborne as saying that the 'distinction, within certain limits, is real and natural'.[70] This 'natural' difference may be ambiguous, but Sir John Coleridge apparently thought it essential and unable to be modified by positive law: 'Law and equity were two things inherently distinct, and the distinction was not capable of being destroyed by Act of Parliament.'[71] Carr suggests that, at least historically, theoretical dualism might be partly accounted for by the intimate association of equity with natural law.[72] So far as that is true, the essential distinction – at least at once – was perhaps that common law was positive law and that equity was natural law.

This position is, however, unsustainable. For one thing, positive common law, as reflecting justice, would historically have been seen as manifesting natural law, at least in part. For another, where equity was understood to involve the law of God or the law of reason – as it was for St German – that law inhered in the positive law: it was tacitly understood as an element in every rule of positive law. Even if there was an intimate association of equity with natural law, that changed with time. I have alluded to Lord Nottingham's project of positivising equity and to Blackstone's observation that common law and equity had both become artificial systems. Lord Kames points out that the boundaries between law and equity 'are not ascertained by any natural rule': not only does the boundary between the two vary from country to country,[73] but in at least some jurisdictions – notably Scotland – the boundary keeps shifting as equitable developments are assimilated to the common law by virtue of having become 'fully established in practice'.[74] And Lord Mansfield,

'Blackstone's Treatment of Equity' (1929) 43 Harv. L. Rev. 1, 28 ('separate intellectual cast') and Lord Millett, 'The Common Lawyer and the Equity Practitioner' (2016) 6 U.K. Supreme Court Yearbook 193, 193 ('Equity is not a set of rules but a state of mind').
[69] Lobban, Chapter 4, text after n. 8.   [70] Rotman, 'The "Fusion" of Law and Equity?', 527.
[71] Lobban, Chapter 4, n. 138. Funk, Chapter 3, text to n. 92, quotes a similar observation from an 1860 US case.
[72] Carr, Chapter 8, text after n. 12.
[73] Lord Kames (H. Home), *Principles of Equity*, ed. by M. Lobban (Indianapolis, IN: Liberty Fund, 2014 [repr. of 3rd edn, Edinburgh, 1778], 20.
[74] Ibid., 30.

in a letter to Lord Kames, opined that any supposition that law and equity could be separated into two sciences on the basis of a 'natural division' would 'only lead to mistakes'.[75]

If we are to seek a deeper distinction between law and equity, we probably cannot go so far as to say that they are different in the very nature of things. To identify the ostensible deeper difference, we should consider more modest non- (or less) essentialist possibilities. One way of organising our thinking about this is to invoke the dichotomy of substance and form. Substance here means the content of the norms of equity – the qualities that rules share which make them distinctively equitable, rather than their content. Form here refers to characteristics of the norms themselves, apart from their content.

Among substantive features we might include equity's reputed regard for the particular (as opposed to the general), its ostensibly distinctive objectives, and its alleged resort to moral criteria for its doctrines. While I am provisionally categorising these features as substantive, they partake of the formal as well. Basing rules, or decisions, on particular circumstances tells us something about the *content* of those rules, but the approach also involves a method or process which is more a matter of form. So, in some measure, my invoking the substance/form dubiety should be regarded as for presentational convenience only. Substance and form are as mutually dependent or fused as some would say law and equity should be.

Regarding equity's focus on the particular circumstance, Rotman suggests that an important way in which equity 'maintains a conceptual separation from law' lies in its being 'a process by which positive law is brought closer to the human condition'.[76] He explains that equity 'provides law with a sense of humanity and context which makes law more just'.[77] This is reminiscent of Aristotle: the subject-matter of positive law is the standard or typical case, while that of equity is the particular circumstance. Is that actually true? The tendency of traditional English equity has been to develop into quite rigid generally applicable rules, for the sake of consistency and predictability. At the same time, one could say that much of the development and modification of common law rules has arisen from the incremental distinguishing of the facts in different cases, as is implied in Lord Halsbury's classic statement in *Quinn v. Leathem*:[78]

---

[75] Ibid., xxiv.
[76] Rotman, 'The "Fusion" of Law and Equity?', 531–32. 'Process' again possibly suggests that this might be as much a formal as a substantive characteristic.
[77] Ibid.　　[78] [1901] A.C. 495.

[E]very judgment must be read as applicable to the particular facts proved . . .
since the generality of expressions which may be found there are not
intended as expositions of the whole law, but govern and are qualified by
the particular facts of the case in which such expressions are to be found.[79]

In some sense, a common law rule is what is decided on the facts of the
particular case. In a significantly different context, Emily Sherwin observes
that an effect of American Legal Realism was to construe law (not just equity)
not as 'a set of pre-existing rules' but as 'the decisions courts reach in response
to particular facts',[80] a point echoed by Goldberg and Smith when noting that
in the 'heyday of Realism' 'there was great enthusiasm for context-sensitive,
adventurous judging'.[81] My point is that one need not go to the extremes of
Legal Realism, or the radical rule-scepticism of the Critical Legal Studies
school, to find in the common law a careful responsiveness to particular facts.
Again, it is disputable whether pre-Judicature Act equity was greatly different
from the common law.

Other commentators have suggested that a fundamental distinction
between law and equity is that they are based on different, or even incompatible, policies or social objectives. The doctrines of each are rooted in very
different aims. Perhaps Turner is getting at this when he speaks of the many
doctrines of equity having objectives 'similar enough that they cluster
together'.[82] The broad difference may be suggested by Lord Kames's observation that 'the moral sense' teaches a distinction between duty and benevolence, and his association of the latter particularly with equity.[83] In Lobban's
words, according to Kames, '[o]nly matters which could be reduced to rules
could be regarded as duties which could be enforced as a matter of justice',
while the obligation of benevolence 'could not usually be reduced to a rule'
except in the case of 'certain peculiar connections among individuals', in
which case benevolence would be 'enforced by rules passing commonly
under the name of the law of equity'.[84] This suggests that equity might be
more inclined to promote positive, selfless conduct as opposed to imposing
negative restraints. We have seen already that, in arguing for a continuing
distinction between fiduciary obligations, on the one hand, and contract and
tort on the other, and internal exclusivity within each, McLachlin J. in
Canson insisted that the former was grounded in a concept of selflessness,
while the latter treated the parties as self-interested actors.[85] It is not clear

---

[79] Ibid., 506.   [80] Sherwin, Chapter 15, text before n. 53.
[81] Goldberg and Smith, Chapter 13, text after n. 1.   [82] Turner, Chapter 1, text after n. 91.
[83] Home, *Principles of Equity*, xii.   [84] Ibid., at xiv.
[85] *Canson Enterprises Ltd* v. *Boughton & Co.* [1991] 3 S.C.R. 534, 543.

whether this observation applies only to the equitable doctrine of fiduciary obligation or to equity generally.

In the present volume, Harding appeals to 'equity's distinctive normative perspectives'[86] in arguing for 'modest fission' in relation to the taking of an account in common form pursuant to a trustee's unauthorised disbursement of trust assets. However, his articulation of the distinctive normative perspective in issue does not convincingly support the conceptual disjunction he endorses. The presence of different normative perspectives *per se* does not necessarily lead to the law/equity dichotomy. As Harding acknowledges, while equity's approach to the taking of a common account 'reflects equity's different underpinning normative concerns', so the 'differential treatment of a set of facts by the law of torts and contract is entirely coherent given the different normative concerns of those two bodies of law'.[87] Fiduciary obligation and contract might be understood as distinct doctrines, but designating one as equitable and the other as legal may not be necessary to the distinction.

As for the specific perspective of equity, Harding suggests that equity is here providing 'a guarantee of mandated performance'.[88] However, he again acknowledges that 'an interest in mandated performance ... is arguably the central normative concern of the law of contracts'.[89] More broadly, he suggests that equity's perspective can be related to 'the important political ideal of personal autonomy',[90] but says that a law of contracts also 'seems a significant way in which a legal system may contribute to the overall conditions of autonomy'.[91] Indeed, if those who emphasise the relinquishment of self-interest characteristic of some equitable doctrines are correct, one might ask how such constrained altruism is compatible with enhanced autonomy, at least from the point of view of the fiduciary. What is substantively distinctive about equity's normative perspective remains unclear. Addressing this objection, Harding speaks of 'the importance of a legal culture in which equity is viewed as a separate legal tradition to the maintenance of distinctive normative perspectives associated with equity'.[92] What this rather circular statement seems to emphasise is the psychological force of having a different tradition which reinforces the normative perspectives he is considering in some, non-exclusive, circumstances.

Another feature commonly associated with equity is its supposedly moral quality. Bray observes that 'in an exceptional case, equity offers a moral

---

[86] Harding, Chapter 16, text after n. 8 and *passim*.   [87] Ibid., text to n. 23.
[88] Ibid., and *passim*.   [89] Ibid., text before n. 40.   [90] Ibid., text before n. 26.
[91] Ibid., text after n. 29.   [92] Ibid., text after n. 43.

reading of the law',[93] and Goldberg and Smith state that an equitable approach 'more transparently' reflects a 'connection to everyday morality'.[94]

Closely involved with this moral dimension is what is often said to be a defining element in the equitable jurisdiction: conscience.[95] In this volume, Girard refers to conscience as 'the central idea of equitable doctrine',[96] and McFarlane suggests that what distinguishes legal from equitable doctrines of restitution of property from third parties is that equitable liability should arise only where the recipient's conscience is affected.[97] Equity regards what is objectively right and the moral disposition of actors.

I treat conscience as a substantive concept here, as providing the moral criteria for the *content* of equitable principles and rules. Conscience tells us what is right and what is wrong. However, historically, conscience had additional procedural and evidentiary limitations.[98] As our 1464 case intimates, one distinctive thing about Chancery – the court of conscience – was that its inquisitorial procedure permitted the Chancellor to probe the mind of a defendant, to access internal dispositions that were resistant to the common law's greater concern with, or limitation to, objectively observable facts. Lord Kames thought it a 'a feature of equity' to '[look] more closely at the intentions and motivations of parties, so that it could root out injustices to which the common law was blind'.[99] In doing so, equity was not identifying or discovering moral criteria upon which to base rules, but trying to get at facts involving the parties to determine whether recognised moral criteria had been transgressed. Conscience in one sense (perhaps in the expression 'the conscience of the King' or 'the conscience of the Chancellor'[100]) identified those criteria. But in another sense, it referred to a procedure whereby the facts that might satisfy those criteria might be discerned. With procedural fusion – increasingly common forms of fact-finding – conscience in this sense is no longer very significant. We do not speak of courts in dealing with matters of equity searching the consciences of the parties – although cross-examination of witnesses in all manner of legal proceedings may serve a similar function.

---

[93] Bray, Chapter 2, text after n. 1.   [94] Goldberg and Smith, Chapter 13, text after n. 64.

[95] Much has been written on this subject: e.g., I. Samet, 'What Conscience Can Do for Equity' (2012) 3 Jurisprudence 35, and A. Hudson, 'Conscience as the Organising Concept of Equity' (2016) 2 C.J.C.C.L. 261. Some concept of conscience in relation to equity is not a feature unique to the common law tradition: H. J. Berman, 'Conscience and Law: The Lutheran Reformation and the Western Legal Tradition' (1987) 5 J. Law & Relig. 177.

[96] Girard, Chapter 5, text to n. 29.   [97] McFarlane, Chapter 14, n. 82.

[98] M. Macnair, 'Equity and Conscience' (2007) 27 O.J.L.S. 659.

[99] Home, *Principles of Equity*, xxii.

[100] Although even this could refer to the need for the Chancellor to be satisfied, in conscience, of the facts upon which he was deciding.

Dennis Klinck

The same diminished significance is also true, I think, of conscience in the substantive sense, that is, as criterial of what the norms should be. Again, no doubt, historically, the Chancellors developed norms on the basis of moral considerations that were not acknowledged in the common law courts (for example, 'it would be against conscience for a person to whom an estate in land was transferred subject the confidence that he or she was to hold it for the transferor's benefit to set up his or her legal title in defiance of that confidence'). But those norms over time became objective rules, manifesting different aspects of what was regarded as just. This approach was enunciated explicitly by Lord Nottingham in his *Prolegomena of Chancery and Equity*: 'there is a twofold conscience, *viz. conscientia politica et civilis, et conscientia naturalis et interna*; [m]any things are against inward and natural conscience, which cannot be reformed by the regular and political administration of equity'.[101] He drew the same distinction in the case of *Cook v. Fountain*,[102] adding that the conscience by which he must proceed is 'tied to certain measures'.[103] I take 'certain measures' to mean fixed rules.[104] That is, to the extent that morality, defined by conscience, informed the norms generated in the court of equity, those norms have necessarily, to become law, become settled. Similarly, Lord Kames observed:

> a clear idea [must] be formed of the difference between a court of law and a court of equity. The former we know follows precise rules: but does the latter act by conscience solely without any rule? This would be unsafe while men are the judges.[105]

I am here moving from substantive features of equity to more formal ones – the extent to which equitable norms take the form of rules, as opposed to vaguer moral notions. But my point is that, regardless of the provenance of equitable norms in moral considerations (and I doubt that it can be said that many common law doctrines were not similarly motivated[106]), juridical equity can hardly be understood in any sense as morality at large.

---

[101] Finch, '*Manual*' and '*Prolegomena*', 194. See Klinck, 'Certain Measures', 125. This kind of observation pre-dated Nottingham. For example, John Cook, in *The Vindication of the Law* (London: Walbancke 1652), argued that with the advent of common lawyers as Chancellors about the time of Henry VIII, 'Equitie began to be spun with such a fine thred that none but the eye of a Chancellor could discerne it, as Bacon ... was wont to say, Conscionable equitie being converted into politique equity' (at 27).

[102] (1676) 2 Swans. 585.   [103] Ibid., 600.   [104] Klinck, 'Certain Measures'.

[105] Kames, *Principles of Equity*, 17.

[106] One might as easily say that for someone to deny a promise made to another, at least when that other gave value in return for the promise, was against conscience, and that is a way of explaining contractual obligation. Conscience has been an element in the common law as

This brings us more directly to the question whether there are distinctive formal features of equitable norms and their application that give equity a separate identity. This issue is connected to the question of the strict application of clear rules: are equitable processes inherent in the application of rules generally, or because of their 'extraordinary' character, should they be kept separate from and supplementary or subordinate to the legal rules themselves? There is the further question whether, even if such processes are often an element in the application of rules, there is anything to be gained by describing them as equity?

The language used to describe what might broadly be called equitable process is varied, but it all tends to point in the same direction: that equity, in contrast to law, is flexible.[107] Among commonly recognised dimensions of this flexibility are what Turner calls equity's 'discretionariness', 'open texture' and *post hoc* application.[108] The association of equity with discretion is a commonplace: in this volume, Bray describes equitable discretion as involving 'broad range of choice across a distribution of cases'.[109] 'Open texture' refers to the ostensible tendency of equitable norms to take the form of principles or standards, as contrasted with the more determinate or fixed rules said to characterise common law. Leeming, for example, quotes Allsop C.J. of the Federal Court of Australia as saying that 'equity [is] a reflection of underlying norms or values', 'often expressed thus rather than by rules that are precisely linguistically expressed'.[110] Several authors besides Turner remark that, in contrast to law's *ex ante* operation, equity tends to operate *ex post* – that is, rather than dictating in advance what shall be done, equity responds at a later stage to prevent injustice. Goldberg and Smith say this;[111] and Sherwin implies as much in seeing equity as moderating harsh *outcomes* resulting from the strict application of legal rules.[112] That is, equity is said less to involve prescriptive rules than to respond, in terms of the discretionary deployment of broad

well as in equity: e.g., L. A. Knafla, 'Conscience in the English Common Law Tradition' (1976) 26 U.T.L.J. 1; J. D. Davies, 'The Re-awakening of Equity's Conscience: Achievements and Problems', in S. Goldstein (ed.), *Equity and Contemporary Legal Developments* (Hebrew University of Jerusalem, 1992), 71.

[107] For example, Dickson J. in the Supreme Court of Canada describes 'the great advantage of ancient principles of equity' as their 'flexibility'; they are 'malleable principles': *Pettkus v. Becker* [1980] 2 S.C.R. 834, 847.

[108] Turner, Chapter 1, text after n. 94.   [109] Bray, Chapter 2, text before n. 20.

[110] M. Leeming, 'The Comparative Distinctiveness of Equity' (2016) 2 C.J.C.C.L. 403, 419, citing *Paciocco v. Australia and New Zealand Banking Group Ltd* (2015) 236 F.C.R. 199, [271]; [2015] FCAFC 50.

[111] E.g., Goldberg and Smith, Chapter 13, text after n. 40.

[112] Sherwin, Chapter 15, text to n. 44.

principles of fairness or justice, to inequities arising from the strict application of the rules.

However, this picture requires qualification. For one thing, not all equitable norms are articulated at the 'high level of abstraction'[113] typical of principles. Much of equity is technical and precise: as Lobban notes, trust law is highly artificial and complicated.[114] We are all familiar with *rigor æquitatis*. On the other hand, one finds principles as a feature of non-equity law.[115] Goldberg and Smith acknowledge that, for example, 'tort law directives often take the form of standards of conduct rather than strict rules', although they maintain that 'tort law is more formal and equity is more context-sensitive'.[116] In the law of evidence (which I teach), courts increasingly invoke principles as opposed to pigeon-hole rules. Thus, to assess the admission of hearsay, the Supreme Court of Canada relies less on categorical exceptions than on broad standards of necessity and reliability, assessed on the particular facts and involving judicial appreciation or discretion.[117] I realise that this is different sphere of law from that where equity traditionally operates. All I mean to suggest is that what is said to be distinctive of equity appears elsewhere in the law as an approach to norm articulation. Even so detailed and precise law as the Income Tax Act seems to need an equity-like default provision. Thus, section 245 provides that even a tax benefit strictly authorised by the act – a legal right – may be restrained on the broad, context-specific basis of what is reasonable in the circumstances.[118] As for equity's traditional role of softening the 'hard, coarse doctrines of the Law',[119] one can point to instances of *equity's* rigidity being mitigated by other kinds of law, notably legislation. Dickson J., in the Supreme Court of Canada, remarked that legislation relieving a trustee for breach of trust where that person acted

---

[113] Goldberg and Smith, Chapter 13, text after n. 15.   [114] Lobban, Chapter 4, text to n. 131.

[115] Even historically, broad principles – or 'maxims' – were part of the discourse of the common law. As is well known, Sir Francis Bacon (*Maxims of the Law* (1st edn 1630) printed in J. Spedding, R. L. Ellis and D. D. Heath (eds), *The Works of Francis Bacon* (London: Longmans, 1872), vol. 7) attempted to reduce the law to maxims, 'to sound into the true conceit of law by depth of reason' so as not only to give the reason of the law 'wherein the authorities do square' but also to provide for new cases 'wherein there is no direct authority' (at 319). Sir John Dodderidge (*The English Lawyer* (London: Assigns of J. More, 1631)) and Sir Henry Finch (*Law or a Discourse Thereof* (London: Society of Stationers, 1627)) give lists of maxims applicable to the law. Dodderidge explained that the grounds, or maxims, or axioms of the law of England, '[a]ll which, being either Conclusions of naturall Reason, or drawne and derived from the same ... serve as directions and Principles of the Law' (at 156).

[116] Goldberg and Smith, Chapter 13, text to n. 16.

[117] Perhaps this is an instance of what Goldberg and Smith describe as a current tendency to articulate 'policy-infused first-order rules and standards': ibid., text after n. 64.

[118] R.S.C. 1985 c.1 (5th Supp.).   [119] See Lobban, Chapter 4, text to n. 111.

'honestly and reasonably and ought fairly to be excused'[120] mitigates the 'unduly harsh and inflexible' judge-made equitable doctrine.[121] Respecting the supposed *ex post* operation of equity, Harding, for example, suggests that this is inconsistent with the 'important signalling function of equity's guarantee of mandated performance *ex ante*'.[122] My point is that the rather conventional attribution of these features to equity must yield to a more complex picture of the relationship between determinate rules and flexible standards.

It must be said as well that, in describing the operation of equity in these ways, the authors tend to be speaking about equity in a broad sense – something like Aristotelian equity – rather than equity as a system of rules worked out in the Court of Chancery.[123] It may be that, in their inception, those rules arose from the broad considerations that I have mentioned, but once they became rules, they became as non-discretionary, specific, formal and prescriptive as legal rules. So, when authors invoke these broad equitable notions, they are often speaking about equity in one of its senses – that of a kind of remedial justice. Kremer argues that the equity that Lord Mansfield (controversially) imported into his common law decisions was not technical equity but 'equitable substance': he employed 'quintessentially equitable reasoning', infusing aspects of the common law with broad principles based on the same concerns, *ex æquo et bono*, said to lie behind early Chancery equity.[124] Goldberg and Smith specifically invoke Aristotle's concept of equity,[125] and distinguish it from equity as 'a body of substantive rules'.[126] So, when we are confronting the fusion issue in this light, we are dealing not with the reconciliation of parallel bodies of specific doctrines, but with general principles respecting the fair application of rules.

This is the approach that Sherwin addresses: what is the role of equity in the application of rules? She begins with the observation that, though determinate rules are desirable,[127] they will sometimes be 'imperfect', in the sense that 'not all the outcomes they require will be good outcomes'.[128] This gives rise to the need for a complementary regime, to address those cases in which the outcomes required by the rules are not good, presumably meaning right or just. What are required are the 'relatively indeterminate standard[s]' we have

---

[120] See, for example, Trustee Act, R.S.O. 1990, c. T.23, s. 35(1).
[121] *Fales* v. *Canada Permanent Trust Co.* [1977] 2 S.C.R. 302, 324.
[122] Harding, Chapter 16, text after n. 38.
[123] Turner is an exception: he explicitly attributes these features to 'technical equity': Chapter 1, text after n. 92.
[124] Kremer, Chapter 9.   [125] Goldberg and Smith, Chapter 13, text before n. 6.
[126] Ibid., n. 7.   [127] Sherwin, Chapter 15, text to n. 5.   [128] Ibid., text after n. 4.

already seen and 'correction of unjust or overbroad outcomes of legal rules'.[129] She proceeds to consider the comprehensive kind of fusion fostered by American Legal Realism. Aristotelian equity, which she sees as having previously operated rather 'covertly', but in a confined way that preserved the determinacy of legal rules, was brought 'into the light' by Realism,[130] whose exponents' 'scepticism about the value of determinate legal rules' rendered the equitable nature of judicial decision-making explicit:

> All of this amounts to a recipe for elimination of a secondary, shadowy form of equity[[131]] with limited impact on rules. Instead, the particularised methods of equity – close attention to facts, reliance on broad standards of decision, trust in the situational sense of judges – were brought directly and unreservedly to the fore.[132]

Sherwin opines that this 'expansion of the principles of equity across all of law seems obvious and sensible',[133] at least to most American lawyers, although its comprehensiveness carries the significant cost of compromising the certainty of all legal rules.

Goldberg and Smith similarly acknowledge the impact of Legal Realism on the role of equity *vis-à-vis* law as determinate rules and, like Sherwin, they are chary of the unrestrained nature of that impact.[134] They see the need for an element in the application of legal rules having the characteristics of Aristotelian equity, but they would formally limit the ambit of that element. They argue against what they call 'hyperfusion' – that is, the view that all law is to be applied according to the processes of equity. Indeed, they use a word we have encountered before – transubstantiation[135] – to describe the phenomenon they decry: the loss by law of its formalism and its becoming generally 'equitable, flexible and result-orientated'.[136] At the same time, they recognise the importance of this equitable element in the legal system, but in a carefully circumscribed form.[137]

---

[129] Ibid., text after nn. 22, 41.   [130] Ibid., text to nn. 49, 52.

[131] By 'covert' and 'obscure' equity, Sherwin presumably means broad equity as imported into the application of common law rules, since the application of distinct 'Chancery equity' would have been quite apparent.

[132] Sherwin, Chapter 15, text after n. 62.   [133] Ibid., text after n. 62.

[134] Although similarly concerned, Sherwin expresses reservations about the efficacy of their approach.

[135] Goldberg and Smith, Chapter 13, text after n. 71.   [136] Ibid.

[137] Bacon gave this rationale for the continued separation of courts of law and equity. Confining discretion to the latter would prevent it from 'in the end supersed[ing] the law': 'Example of a Treatise on Universal Justice or the Fountains of Equity, by Aphorisms', appended to Book 8 of *De Augmentis* (1623) in Spedding, Ellis and Heath (eds), *The Works of Francis Bacon* (1861), vol. 5, 96.

In taking this position, they manifest an attitude insisting on a clear line of demarcation between law and equity. Moreover, they see equity as being in a hierarchical relationship with law: law is first-order, 'conduct-guiding' normativity; equity, on the other hand, is 'a gap-filling, second-order regime'.[138] Like others, they suggest that this equity consists significantly of principles and that it operates *ex post*. Their position is that Aristotelian equity is an essential dimension of legal systems, but that it is not inherent in all the rules, or at least in the application of the rules. Rather, it is to be consciously and deliberately deployed only after the application of the rules exposes some defect in their efficacy. Presumably, they would accept this second-order equitable function even in relation to first-order rules whose provenance is traditional Chancery equity. The origin of the rules would not be critical, but their characteristics as determinate, *ex ante*, etc., would. Theirs is a fission position, but only in a special sense: that is, not between different systems of rules, but between different kinds of norms.

Waddams similarly identifies two elements in the application of legal rules: the ('generally sound') prescribed rules themselves, plus 'a supplementary power in the court to depart [from them] where extraordinary circumstances [such as 'mistake or unfairness'] make such a departure necessary'.[139] Although he describes this power – traditionally associated with equity – as supplementary, he is perhaps less insistent on its rigorous conceptual distinction from the rules themselves. He cites Maitland's observation that equity had come not to destroy the law but to fulfil it:[140] this suggests that, far from being antithetical to strict law, equity assists in achieving its underlying purpose, broadly, justice. Similarly, he says that the fusion/fission 'dichotomy can and should ... be transcended',[141] perhaps in so far as the two elements are distinguishable, but mutual.

Another dimension of this close relationship between legal rules and their equitable qualification might be described as diachronic. In the preceding paragraphs, I have outlined the synchronic amelioration of strict law by equity: that is, at a particular point in time, application of a legal rule has been (or is) softened by the invocation of equity, or some equivalent principle. But a related phenomenon is that, over time, the equitable qualification itself becomes a new legal rule. Lord Kames saw equity as a source of dynamic

---

[138] Goldberg and Smith, Chapter 13, text after n. 5.   [139] Waddams, Chapter 10, text after n. 2.
[140] Ibid. Compare R. Evershed, 'Reflections on the Fusion of Law and Equity after 75 Years' (1954) 70 L.Q.R. 326, 328: 'The function of equity [historically] was ... not so much to correct [the common law] as to perfect it.'
[141] Waddams, Chapter 10, text after n. 2.

legal development, as Lobban explains: 'Once a rule in equity had become fully established in practice, it became part of the fixed rules of common law.'[142] A concomitant of this was that 'the borderline between common law and equity was flexible'.[143] That is, equitable principles evolve into common law rules, and, as they do the line between the two kinds of law moves. The fact that equity mutates into law in this way again suggests another kind of fusion. Goldberg and Smith similarly remark this process: 'Equity is thus a moving frontier. The process by which equitable intervention becomes a regular part of the common law can be termed "sedimentation".'[144] Once this transformation occurs, the equitable function will then apply to the new first-order law thus generated.

Again, Lord Kames's observations occur within the Scots setting, where law and equity were (and are) administered in the same court. In pre-Judicature Act England, the process would have been rather different. Presumably, apart from common law courts' borrowing or imitating equitable doctrines, equitable development of the law of equity would have been incorporated into the rules of equity: as an equitable advance became established in practice, it would have become part of Chancery law. Almost certainly, a similar process would have occurred in common law courts – to the extent that the common law permitted modification of the law in response to previously unanticipated circumstances. With the merger of the courts, the process of the equitable modification of prescriptive rules, as adumbrated, for example, by Goldberg and Smith, would result in new legal rules.

Thus, arguably, the case for continuing fission is tenuous. If we are considering equity as essentially a parallel system of positive law, the issue of fusion might be limited to reconciling specific doctrines, and perhaps giving precedence to those whose provenance is equity in the rare instances of conflict (as opposed to complementation). If we think of equity in the Aristotelian sense, there is a strong case to be made that it is a complementary element in the application of rules generally, although to preclude unfettered indeterminacy we might want, with Goldberg and Smith, to mark off the boundary between the two processes of strict application of prescriptive rules and discretionary deviation from those rules in hard cases.

Another consideration germane to the question of maintaining the distinction is that of the word 'equity' itself. This matter has at least two aspects: whether 'equity' refers to anything at all and, if it does, whether retaining that

---

[142] Kames, *Principles of Equity*, xv.   [143] Ibid.
[144] Goldberg and Smith, Chapter 13, text to n. 54. Compare Rotman, who uses the metaphor of equity 'bleeding' into the common law: Rotman, 'The "Fusion" of Law and Equity?', 534.

epithet for what is meant is necessary or desirable, especially considering the ambiguities it involves.

As regards the first aspect, we have noticed already Cockburn C.J.'s plea for eliminating the distinction, 'even to the very name of Equity'.[145] This could imply that, in this context, the name has no meaningful referent. Funk points out that others made this point more explicitly, David Dudley Field, for example, stating that names like equity are not real existences[146] and Arphaxad Loomis saying that the difference between law and equity 'was more in words than reality'.[147] Funk calls this attitude nominalism.[148] In a sense, such claims are easily answered: historically, equity did refer to something real, if not in the nature of things, at least in respect of human institutions: the doctrines of the Court of Chancery. But this leads to the very question this volume addresses: does the name denote anything very significant now?

Another possibility is that equity can meaningfully refer to Goldberg and Smith's 'second-order equitable function', which in turn brings us to a second aspect of the issue of the name: is there any continuing need for the label 'equity' for this phenomenon? Goldberg and Smith acknowledge that, on their view of equity as second-order, 'nothing requires it to carry a separate label',[149] although they do continue to use the designation. Waddams suggests that the supplementary power need not be conceived of as or called equity; what is important is to recognise the distinction 'between rules of general application and the concept of an open-ended power to depart from those rules for sufficient reason'.[150] He suggests that the traditional function of equity might today be equally effected under such concepts as unjust enrichment, good faith and abuse of rights – all of which, without any mention of equity, are 'capable of supporting a residual power' to depart from legal rules.[151] Similarly, Carr points to the case of *Smith* v. *Bank of Scotland*,[152] where, he says, the House of Lords, in 'introducing a novel rule which was designed to ameliorate recognised hardship flowing from a strict application of an existing rule, chose not to invoke "equity" or any form of "equitable reasoning"'.[153] Given that this ameliorating function exists, is equity an indispensable or optimal best name for it?

Carr offers a partial answer. Admitting that the continuing law/equity duality may be 'mere labelling', he argues:

---

[145] N. 47 of this chapter.   [146] Funk, Chapter 3, text to n. 43.   [147] Ibid., text to n. 45.
[148] Ibid., text after n. 43.   [149] Goldberg and Smith, Chapter 13, text before n. 18.
[150] Waddams, Chapter 10, text after n. 2.   [151] Ibid., text after n. 94.   [152] 1997 S.C. (H.L.) 111.
[153] Carr, Chapter 8, text after n. 77.

 *Dennis Klinck*

but that is what a huge amount of law is about. While other terms might be used with greater precision,[154] the term 'equity' has a counter-advantage of greater potential content insofar as the term carries so many discrete connotations.[155]

That is, it is not so much that equity denotes a separate concept from law as that it is laden with connotations which make its continued invocation important – at least as regards 'the evolution ... of structured rules and discretion'.[156] But this cuts both ways. That the word 'equity' is so variously and perhaps richly connotative carries with it the danger (as this volume attests) that it will be confusing. Concomitant with this danger is the possibility that it will be relied on just or mainly for its emotive – or even 'talismanic'[157] – power. And, as Bray's observation that, in the United States, '[t]he basic terminology and conceptual content of equity are unfamiliar to generations of students' suggests,[158] the psychological space created by the word and psychological force of the word may be quite different from one jurisdiction to another – while similarities in the substance of the law may exist.

In the end, I find it challenging to discern what is really, fundamentally distinctive about equity today. Without question, historically, legal rules and equitable norms emanated from different courts. Historically as well, the latter were probably more open-textured and discretionary in application – although part of the difference was that equity took cognisance of factors that common law courts did not recognise, so that a wider array of circumstances came to be included in what was legally significant. Taking account of such factors meant that a different outcome, in the same case, was reached in equity from that at common law. But, over time the quality of rules in equity seems to have become similar to that of common law rules: fixed, technical, prescriptive, albeit addressing different subject matters. With the amalgamation of the courts, arguably this wider array of rules became available in every case, as long as the factual circumstances warranting their application were present. The provenance of the rules became significant only in the rare cases where there was a real incompatibility – that is, apart from the presence of additional facts.

Even if we think of equity not as a set of specific doctrines, but as an approach to rule-making and the application of rules that is more flexible or liberal than strict law, the distinction is problematic. One can point to

---

[154] That is, with greater substantive analytical validity.   [155] Carr, Chapter 8, text after n. 82.
[156] Ibid. Rotman perhaps makes a similar point when he refers to the role of equity 'in the shaping of modern legal *discourse*': Rotman, 'The "Fusion" of Law and Equity?', 530 (emphasis added).
[157] See Funk, Chapter 3, text after n. 44.   [158] Bray, Chapter 2, text to n. 34.

examples of current common law doctrines that do not involve strict law but invoke a principled approach that involves broad standards, inviting the exercise of judicial discretion in relation to the particular facts of cases. In adopting this approach, courts may have made no mention of equity or evinced any awareness that what they were adopting was equitable reasoning. So it appears that, just as specific *ex ante* rules are not exclusive to common law, neither are broad principles exclusive to equity.

In the eighteenth century, in a letter to Lord Kames, Lord Hardwicke L.C., responding to the former's argument that the application of equity to the law generated new norms which then became law themselves, insisted on the need for fission between 'stated law' and equity on the basis, first, that a separate jurisdiction where corrective discretion *could* be exercised was required, but, second, that the separation was required to confine that discretion. Without such separation, doctrines developed in the discretionary jurisdiction would tend to become like the norms of the other jurisdiction, that is, non-discretionary norms. Lord Hardwicke opined that the result of this development would be the need for a 'superfœtation of courts of equity', for a new level of equity,[159] because fixed rules can never anticipate all circumstances, and a discretion, whether called equity or something else, to address legally unforeseen consequences must always be a concomitant of rules. In this way, equitable reasoning is arguably distinct from strict legal reasoning, but, at the same time, it is an inherent element in it.

From one perspective, this might seem like the monism which concerns Turner,[160] for example: it implies legal norms and equitable norms are essentially similar. But it is not simple monism, because it identifies another distinct element: a principle of adaptive application of the norms. Nor is it straightforward dualism, however, because the other distinct element is so intimately complementary to the basic norms: perhaps more intimately complementary than traditional equity in a separate jurisdiction was to the common law.

---

[159] P. C. Yorke, *The Life and Correspondence of Philip Yorke, Earl of Hardwicke* (Cambridge University Press, 1913), vol. 2, 554.
[160] Turner, Chapter 1, text to n. 96 and after n. 109.

Index